PHILOSOPHICAL EXPLANATIONS

Robert Nozick

PHILOSOPHICAL
EXPLANATIONS

The Belknap Press of
Harvard University Press
Cambridge, Massachusetts

10   9   8   7   6

Library of Congress Cataloging in Publication Data

Nozick, Robert.
Philosophical explanations.

Includes index.
1. Philosophy.   2.   Knowledge, Theory of.
3.   Values.   I.   Title.
B53.N7   191   81-1369
ISBN 0-674-66448-5 (cloth)   AACR2
ISBN 0-674-66479-5 (paper)

For Emily and David

ACKNOWLEDGMENTS

This book was written over a four-year period, and sustained during that time by much help. During the academic year 1976–77, I spent a sabbatical leave in Jerusalem, paid for by Harvard University. The Van Leer Jerusalem Foundation provided an office and secretarial help, as well as a very pleasant working environment; there the first draft of this work (except for Chapter 5) was written. Some preliminary work on Chapter 4 was done during the summer of 1976 and the first draft of Chapter 5 was written during the summer of 1978; the work of both these summers was supported by the (Ford Foundation) Program in Basic Research at Harvard Law School. The manuscript was expanded, rewritten thoroughly, and completed during another year off from teaching in 1979–80, supported in part by a Rockefeller Foundation Humanities Fellowship, and by the very generous research support of the John Olin Foundation.

Portions of the book were delivered as lectures at various universities and institutions: at Hebrew University, the University of Tel Aviv, the University of Haifa, Ben-Gurion University in Beersheva, and the Van Leer Jerusalem Foundation during 1976–77; afterwards in three lectures at Princeton University, two Howison lectures at

ACKNOWLEDGMENTS

the University of California at Berkeley, three Thalheimer lectures at
Johns Hopkins University, an invited address to the Western Division of the American Philosophical Association, and talks at the University of Washington, Linfield College, the University of Massachusetts at Amherst, and the Society for Ethical and Legal Philosophy.
Bill Puka and Hilary Putnam each read the whole manuscript and
wrote out extensive comments on it. Others commented on portions
of the book: Sissela Bok, Dale Gottlieb, Dieter Henrich, Steven Luper,
Eric Mack, Jay Neugeboren, Larry Thomas, Judith Thomson, and
Eddy Zemach. I am very grateful to these people, and others, as well
as to the various institutions mentioned, for their help and encouragement.

During the past ten years of teaching, my colleagues in the Harvard
Philosophy Department uncomplainingly have watched me wend my
way across a range of courses without repeating any. That freedom to
pursue diverse intellectual interests, sometimes offbeat ones, has
been quite important to me.

I would like to thank my parents, but now can only thank my father,
for their love and encouragement, their tolerance of their son's meander-
ing academic way (which included failing five courses as an under-
graduate, three of them in philosophy), and their ready acceptance of
the very early decision not to become a doctor.

For many extended stretches of time during the past four years, I
have been intensely preoccupied with thinking and writing about
philosophical matters. This cannot have been easy for my family, for
my children Emily and David or for my wife Barbara, yet throughout
they have been remarkably tolerant and uncomplaining—providing
an anchor during the most extensive flights of philosophical fancy.

That I take such flights sometimes strikes me as absurd, anyway.
Isn't it ludicrous for someone just one generation from the *shtetl*, a
pisher from Brownsville and East Flatbush in Brooklyn, even to touch
on the topics of the monumental thinkers? Of course it is. Yet it was
ludicrous for them too. We are all just a few years past something or
other, if only childhood. Even the monuments themselves, so serenely
in command of culture and intellect, must have been children once
and adolescents—so they too are immigrants to the realm of thought.
It wouldn't hurt for an acknowledgment of this occasionally through
their magisterial prose to peep.

CONTENTS

CONTENTS

EPISTEMOLOGY

VALUE

CONTENTS

PHILOSOPHICAL EXPLANATIONS

INTRODUCTION

I, too, seek an unreadable book: urgent thoughts to grapple with in agitation and excitement, revelations to be transformed by or to transform, a book incapable of being read straight through, a book, even, to bring reading to *stop*. I have not found that book, or attempted it. Still, I wrote and thought in awareness of it, in the hope this book would bask in its light. That hope would be arrogant if it weren't self-fulfilling—to face toward the light, even from a great distance, is to be warmed. (Is it sufficient, though, when light is absent, to face in the direction it would emanate from?)

Familiar questions impel this essay: Does life have meaning? Are there objective ethical truths? Do we have free will? What is the nature of our identity as selves? Must our knowledge and understanding stay within fixed limits? These questions moved me, and others, to enter the study of philosophy. I care what their answers are. While such other philosophical intricacies as whether sets or numbers exist can be fun for a time, they do not make us tremble.

Our various questions stem from one: how are we valuable and precious? Consider the issue of free will, for example. Often, philosophers treat this as a question about punishment and responsibility: how can we punish someone for an action, or hold him responsible, if it was causally determined, eventually by factors going back to

1

before his birth, hence outside his control?* My concern with free will, however, is not rooted in a desire to punish people or hold them responsible, or even to be held responsible myself. Without free will we seem diminished, merely the playthings of external causes. Our value seems undercut. The various questions arise from, are shaped and made vivid by, a concern with our value, significance, importance, stature, and preciousness. If our lives cannot have meaning, if we are no more than puppets of causes, if our attempts at knowledge are foredoomed to failure, if we have no worth that the actions of others ought to respect, then we are devoid of value.

My concern is not only intense but directed. I want (to be able) to conclude that we *are* worthwhile and precious. But this bias does not mean I refuse to follow philosophical reason where it leads. Fortunately, two factors help me avoid conclusions of valuelessness. No philosophical argument forces us to accept its (unpleasant) conclusion; instead, we always can pursue the philosophical task of uncovering the argument's defects. This is the way Berkeley's arguments, and skeptical arguments generally, have been treated. Or we can try to find a route (believing it exists although it has not yet been found) to something almost as good as what the argument seemed to eliminate; such has been the response to Hume on induction. The second factor is an optional stop rule. I do not stop the philosophical reasoning until it leads me where I want to go; then I stop.

This description oversimplifies. In the course of the philosophical quest, the destination gets modified somewhat. Nevertheless, a value criterion is at work. The goal is getting to a place worth being, even though the investigation may change and deepen the idea of worth.

Are other philosophers more dispassionate about the important questions? A philosopher's concerns are exhibited within his work on a topic as well as in selecting that topic. When a philosopher sees that premises he accepts logically imply a conclusion he has rejected until now, he faces a choice: he may accept this conclusion, or reject one of the previously accepted premises, or even postpone the decision about which to do. His choice will depend upon which is greater, the degree of his commitment to the various premises or

---

* I do not know of a way to write that is truly neutral about pronoun gender yet does not constantly distract attention—at least the contemporary reader's —from the sentence's central content. I am still looking for a satisfactory solution.

the degree of his commitment to denying the conclusion. It is implausible that these are independent of how strongly he wants certain things to be true. The various means of control over conclusions explain why so few philosophers publish ones that (continue to) upset them. I do not recall any philosopher reporting in distress that on some fundamental question he is forced to conclude that the truth is awful, worse even than the third best way he would want it. (Did not even Schopenhauer come to relish his conclusions?)

We may wonder whether a philosophy with a foregone conclusion can have any value at all. That a philosophy aims at a conclusion, though, does not guarantee it will reach it. We learn something of value in discovering that our goal can be reached. Since also the general aim will not determine the precise character of the conclusion reached, and since the very process of reaching may be worthwhile itself, we need not devalue a philosophical inquiry that is teleologically directed.

No philosophical inquiry can restrict itself to the central questions; in pursuing these, we are led to others as well. Common themes unite our consideration of the diverse questions but, rather than begin with these as first principles, I prefer to let linkages emerge. Philosophers often seek to deduce their total view from a few basic principles, showing how all follows from their intuitively based axioms. The rest of the philosophy then strikes readers as depending upon these principles. One brick is piled upon another to produce a tall philosophical tower, one brick wide. When the bottom brick crumbles or is removed, all topples, burying even those insights that were independent of the starting point.

Instead of the tottering tower, I suggest that our model be the Parthenon. First we emplace our separate philosophical insights, column by column; afterwards, we unite and unify them under an overarching roof of general principles or themes. When the philosophical structure crumbles somewhat, as we should expect on inductive grounds, something of interest and beauty remains standing. Still preserved are some insights, the separate columns, some balanced relations, and the wistful look of a grander unity eroded by misfortunes or natural processes. We need not go so far as to hope that the philosophical ruin, like some others, will be even more beautiful than the original. Yet, unlike the philosophical tower, this structure will remain as more than a heap of stones.

Coercive Philosophy

It was not arbitrary of philosophers to start with apparently necessary first principles, given their desire to prove their views. If the tower-like structure is abandoned, we must forsake its purpose as well. But can philosophy have an aim other than proof? Philosophical training molds arguers: it trains people to produce arguments and (this is part of the arguing) to criticize and evaluate them. A philosopher's seriousness is judged by the quality of his arguments.[1]

Children think an argument involves raised voices, anger, negative emotion. To argue with someone is to attempt to push him around verbally. But a philosophical argument isn't like that—is it?

The terminology of philosophical art is coercive: arguments are *powerful* and best when they are *knockdown*, arguments *force* you to a conclusion, if you believe the premises you *have to* or *must* believe the conclusion, some arguments do not carry much *punch*, and so forth. A philosophical argument is an attempt to get someone to believe something, whether he wants to believe it or not. A successful philosophical argument, a strong argument, *forces* someone to a belief.

Though philosophy is carried on as a coercive activity, the penalty philosophers wield is, after all, rather weak. If the other person is willing to bear the label of "irrational" or "having the worse arguments", he can skip away happily maintaining his previous belief. He will be trailed, of course, by the philosopher furiously hurling philosophical imprecations: "What do you mean, you're willing to be irrational? You shouldn't be irrational because . . ." And although the philosopher is embarrassed by his inability to complete this sentence in a noncircular fashion—he can only produce reasons for accepting reasons—still, he is unwilling to let his adversary go.

Wouldn't it be better if philosophical arguments left the person no possible answer at all, reducing him to impotent silence? Even then, he might sit there silently, smiling, Buddhalike. Perhaps philosophers need arguments so powerful they set up reverberations in the brain: if the person refuses to accept the conclusion, he *dies*. How's that for a powerful argument? Yet, as with other physical threats ("your money or your life"), he can choose defiance. A "perfect" philosophical argument would leave no choice.

What useful purpose do philosophical arguments serve? Do we, trained in finding flaws in history's great arguers, really believe argu-

4

ments a promising route to the truth? Does either the likelihood of arriving at a true view (as opposed to a consistent and coherent one) or a view's closeness to the truth vary directly with the strength of the philosophical arguments? Philosophical arguments can serve to elaborate a view, to delineate its content. Considering objections, hypothetical situations, and so on, does help to sharpen a view. But need all this be done in an attempt to prove, or in arguing?

Why are philosophers intent on forcing others to believe things? Is that a nice way to behave toward someone? I think we cannot improve people that way—the means frustrate the end. Just as dependence is not eliminated by treating a person dependently, and someone cannot be forced to be free, a person is not most improved by being forced to believe something against his will, whether he wants to or not.[2] The valuable person cannot be fashioned by committing philosophy upon him.

So don't look here for a knockdown argument that there is something wrong with knockdown arguments, for the knockdown argument to end all knockdown arguing. It will not do to argue you into the conclusion, even in order to reduce the total amount of presentation of argument. Nor may I hint that I possess the knockdown argument yet will not present it.

Mightn't there be a legitimate use of argument, in self-defense against argumentative bludgeoning by others? Could one wield arguments to attack the other person's position, but only after he has attacked your own—intellectual karate in response to his initiating argument? Alternatively, arguments might be used solely to disarm an attacker. Deftly, the force of the assault could be diverted or even turned against the attacker—intellectual judo or aikido. Perhaps others could thus be defended from the onslaught of third parties, though it would be difficult to bring our argumentative defense to their attention without thereby subjecting them to coercion from *our* arguments. For one's own protection it should not be necessary to argue at all, merely to note publicly what bludgeoning the others are attempting—intellectual satyagraha, to use Gandhi's term for nonviolent resistance.*

---

* Is this the explanation of why philosophy department audiences try especially to refute or poke holes in lectures? The lecturer is trying to ram an opinion into their minds, so quite appropriately the audience resists, because even if it is something they want to believe anyway, they don't want to allow themselves to be *forced* to believe it.

Since a successful proof or argument must utilize premises the listener accepts, in what way does it proceed against the person's will? In arguing for a conclusion, are you not just showing him what he already implicitly accepts? While autonomy is not violated by argument as it would be by (involuntary) brain surgery that instilled belief, still, to argue for a conclusion is not merely to point out the consequences of statements which it turns out the person believes; it is to search and cast about for suitable premises, for statements the person does accept that will lead him to the desired conclusion. Recognizing the deductive connection, the person may either accept the conclusion or reject one of the statements he previously accepted, now that he sees where it leads. So the arguer will seek premises the person will not abandon. His goal is not simply to point out connections among statements but to compel belief in a particular one.*

I find I usually read works of philosophy with all defenses up, with a view to finding out where the author has gone wrong. Occasionally, after a short amount of reading, I find myself switched to a different mode; I become open to what the author has to teach. No doubt the voice of the author plays a role, perhaps also his not being coercive. An additional factor affects my stance. Sometimes a writer will begin with a thought similar to one I have had and been pleased with, except that his is more profound or subtle. Or after reading the first few sentences I may have thoughts or objections which the author then will go on to state or meet more acutely. Here, clearly, is someone from whom I can learn.

I am willing to accept thoughts I read when I have had similar ones myself; I am more willing to accept my own thoughts than those I read. Yet, having a new thought is not an action intended in advance; we don't set ourselves to have that specific new thought. If our own thoughts just "come to us" unbidden, why should we be less receptive to ones that come through reading? Perhaps because we spontaneously have only those thoughts to which we are already receptive. This may lead me to miss out on learning from those who can teach me most, those who think in a way completely different from mine. Unfortunately, however, my trust in them cannot grow in

---

* "If a person is wondering whether or not to believe p, can't we offer him reasons to believe it as *help?*" Yes, if your help is neutral. But do you also offer reasons for not believing p? Do you pursue with further reasons for p if the first fail to convince?

the way described, so I continue to read them from an adversary stance.

Philosophy without arguments, in one mode, would guide someone to a view. The first chapter presents thoughts the reader has had (or is ready to have), only more deeply. Reading this chapter stimulates new thoughts which, pleased with, he tentatively adopts as his own. The second chapter deepens and extends these very thoughts; the reader willingly accepts them in this form. They are almost exactly what he was thinking already; he does not have to be argued into them. This second chapter also stimulates further new thoughts, which please the reader, and he tentatively adopts these thoughts as his own; in the third chapter, he finds these thoughts deepened and extended, and so on.

At no point is the person forced to accept anything. He moves along gently, exploring his own and the author's thoughts. He explores together with the author, moving only where he is ready to; then he stops. Perhaps, at a later time mulling it over or in a second reading, he will move further.

With this manner of writing, an author might circle back more than once to the same topic. Not everything can be said at once or twice; a reader may not be ready yet to think it all himself.[3] Within the structure of each chapter, the thought might go further out as it goes along, reaching finally ideas so speculative that even the author is not willing (yet?) to assert them, barely willing even to entertain them.

Such a book could not convince everybody of what it says—it wouldn't try. (Should it then be judged by goals not its own?) I have said such a book would guide without forcing, but won't it be manipulating its readers? Not every way a teacher can help someone to see something himself, more deeply, counts as manipulation, especially when the activity is acknowledged mutually.

This is not my prelude to an announcement, even though I would like to present a philosophical view in this way, author and reader traveling together, each continually spurting in front of the other. Not only do I lack the art to do this, I do not yet have a philosophical view that flows so deeply and naturally. Perhaps a philosophy should be tested by whether it can be presented so.

Even this least dominating mode of writing maintains a hierarchy wherein the reader is to be attentive to the writer's thoughts but not conversely. (Though the writer must attend to the unknown readers' possible responses, this does not alter the asymmetry.) Do some contemporary French critics propose to deconstruct texts in order to destroy that hierarchy, held to be undesirable, to destroy the very distinction between writer and reader? It would be ironic if a writer's desire not so to dominate his readers were to lead him to withhold thoughts. (How can thoughts or worries about the writer–reader or speaker–listener asymmetry be conveyed without invoking that very asymmetry?) It is only the writer's thoughts, though, that can be rejected and dismissed—is it because asymmetrical attentiveness is matched by asymmetrical vulnerability that anything (voluntarily) gets written and read?

I place no extreme obligation of attentiveness on my readers; I hope instead for those who read as I do, seeking what they can learn from, make use of, transform for their own purposes. Much as they wanted to be understood accurately, the philosophers of the past would have preferred this response, I think, to having their views meticulously and sympathetically stated in all parts and relations. The respect *they* paid their predecessors was philosophy, not scholarship. Rather than our listening to them, wouldn't they prefer we spoke to them? (We have to listen closely enough, though, to speak to *them*.)

Philosophical Explanations

There is a second mode of philosophy, not directed to arguments and proofs: it seeks explanations. Various philosophical things need to be explained; a philosophical theory is introduced to explain them, to render them coherent and better understood.

Many philosophical problems are ones of understanding how something is or can be possible. How is it possible for us to have free will, supposing that all actions are causally determined? Randomness, also, seems no more congenial; so, how is free will (even) possible? How is it possible that we know anything, given the facts the skeptic enumerates, for example, that it is logically possible we are dreaming or floating in a tank with our brain being stimulated to give us exactly our current experiences and even all our past ones? How is it possible that motion occurs, given Zeno's arguments? How is it possible for something to be the same thing from one time to another, through change? How is it possible for subjective experiences to fit into an objective physical world? How can there be stable meanings (Plato asked), given that everything in the world is changing? How is it possible for us to have synthetic necessary knowledge? (This last question, Kant's, shows, if none did earlier, that the question's presupposition that the item *is* possible may be controversial or even false, in which case the question would be withdrawn.) The theological problem of evil also takes this form: how is evil possible, supposing the existence of an omnipotent omniscient good God? One central question of twentieth century philosophy has been: how is language possible? And let us not omit from our list: how is philosophy possible?

The form of these questions is: how is one thing possible, given (or supposing) certain other things? Some statements $r_1, \ldots, r_n$ are assumed or accepted or taken for granted, and there is a tension between these statements and another statement p; they appear to exclude p's holding true. Let us term the r_i *apparent excluders* (of p). Since the statement p also is accepted, we face the question of how p is possible, given its apparent excluders.* Note that the question is not: given p, how are the apparent excluders possible? Tension and incompatibility are symmetrical relations among statements, yet typically philosophical problems focus on the possibility only of some statements on one side of the relation. It is an interesting issue, what determines in which direction the question is salient.

The strongest mode of exclusion would be logical incompatibility: the apparent excluders, in conjunction, logically (appear to) imply that p is false; they imply the negation of p, which we may write as not-p.

Philosophical arguments show or draw upon (apparent) incompatibilities or other tensions between statements; these can have an im-

---

* A physical analogue of a philosophical problem is the familiar puzzle of the pencil or rod with a nondetachable closed loop of string attached to one end of it, a loop too small to reach also around the other end. Placed in a buttonhole in the appropriate way, attached to it, it quickly comes to seem impossible to remove, *provably* impossible—the loop is shorter than the length of the rod. Yet you don't doubt that it can be removed, since another person has done it again and again; the question is how this is possible. (The solution also provides an illuminating analogue to one way of solving a philosophical problem, of explaining how something is possible.)

portant role in setting-up philosophical problems without being designed to force belief.

Given the (apparent) incompatibility between the apparent excluders and p, there are two ways to continue to maintain (the possibility of) p. First, one of the apparent excluders can be denied, or there can be a denial of their conjunction all together. To save the possibility of p, it is not necessary to prove these denials, only to show we need not accept one of the apparent excluders or their conjunction. Second, each of the apparent excluders can continue to be maintained, while their apparent incompatibility with p is removed, either by close scrutiny showing the reasoning from them to not-p to be defective, or by embedding them in a wider context or theory that specifies how p holds in the face of these apparent excluders.

To rebut an argument for not-p from specific apparent excluders removes a reason for thinking p cannot hold, and so counts as a kind of explanation of how p can be possible. This task is unending, for as knowledge advances, or seems to, new apparent excluders come to the fore, and hence new questions arise about the possibility of p. "If we know that whenever a new apparent excluder comes along, we will try to show that p remains standing, wouldn't it be more economical simply to prove p once and for all?" This proposal misconstrues the need. A proof of p will give us the conviction that p is true, but it need not give us understanding of how p *can* be true (given the apparent excluder). Even when the argument from an apparent excluder does not lead us to deny p or to doubt its truth, it still may leave us puzzled as to how p can be true. Typically, the arguments of the epistemological skeptic do not lead us to conclude we don't have knowledge; but they do leave us wondering how we can know what we do. A proof that p is true, however, need not show how p is compatible with the apparent excluders, or show which apparent excluder is false—it need not mention them at all. So the task of showing how p is possible cannot be done once and for all by a proof that p. What a proof can do—show us that p is true—is not what we need, for we already believe this. Why isn't it enough to know that p is true, why do we also need to understand how it can be true? To see how p can be true (given these apparent excluders) is to see how things fit together. This philosophical understanding, finding harmony in apparent tension and incompatibility, is, I think, intrinsically valuable. Yet I would not try to bludgeon anyone into needing or wanting it.

The task of explaining how p is possible is not exhausted by the rearguard action of meeting arguments from its apparent excluders. There remains the question of what facts or principles might give rise to p. Here the philosopher searches for deeper explanatory principles, preferably with some independent plausibility, not excluded by current knowledge. To show that these principles, if true, would explain p involves deducing p from them—at least so holds the deductive-nomological view according to which each explanation deduces the fact to be explained from general laws and initial conditions.[4] Yet still, this is no attempt to prove p; and the explanatory hypotheses used in the explanation need not be known to be true, or be believed on grounds independent of p itself.

To produce this possible explanation of p is, by seeing one way p is given rise to, to see how p can be true. "How is it possible that p? This way: such and such facts are possible and they constitute an explanatory route to p." The more true-like these explanatory hypotheses, the more we understand how p can be true. The (possible) explanation of p from them is put forward tentatively, subject to withdrawal in the face of difficulties or alternative, better explanations, perhaps using deeper principles that also would explain other things.[5]

Status of the Hypotheses

Which hypotheses may be introduced in a philosophical explanation? May the hypothesis be known to be false? I believe increased understanding can be produced even by an explanation known to be false; seeing what in principle could give rise to a phenomenon illuminates some of its aspects by the way it latches onto these. Richard Feynman notes[6] that the inverse square character of gravitation would follow if particles flew equally in all directions but were partially blocked by bodies, so fewer reached the earth sunward than from the other side (and fewer hit the sun earthward than from the other side), so that each body was propelled toward the other by the hitting particles. Yet this potential explanation is known to be false; no effect is observed of the moving earth's being slowed down by the larger number of particles hitting it from the front. Still, even though false, this explanation produces some illumination and increased understanding.

I am tempted to say that explanation locates something in actuality, showing its actual connections with other actual things, while *understanding* locates it in a network of possibility, showing the connections it would have to other nonactual things or processes. (Explanation increases understanding too, since the actual connections it exhibits are also possible.) Recall how illuminating it can be to place something, something actual even, in a typology or a two-by-two matrix, how salient is the insight gained through locating it in that network of alternative possibilities. No less understanding is provided by an explanatory hypothesis which might coexist with the phenomenon and generate it. When this book explores hypotheses depicting eccentric possibilities, as it sometimes does, even a reader who is convinced the hypothesis fails, who will not take the possibility seriously, even a reader who does not enjoy (as I do) the playful exploration of possibilities for its own sake, may see benefit in the increased understanding gained.

However much it may increase understanding, a hypothesis known to be false will not explain how something *is* possible. (If we can find no other explanation, though, we may reconsider whether we know the hypothesis is false.) In addition to not being known to be false, must the hypothesis also be plausible? I do not think so, even leaving aside how fragile and parochial are judgments of plausibility. The question of how *p* is possible may cut so deeply that the only answers which suffice are implausible, at least as one judges before investigating how *p* is possible. Moreover, insisting the hypothesis be plausible antecedently would guarantee that philosophy could not lead us to radically new and surprising truths or insights. One should not rule out even rejecting the *p* begun with, if intensive effort fails to show how it is possible while showing how something similar is.[7]

Does the philosopher who explains how *p* is possible, by putting forth potential explanations of *p*, differ from the scientist who puts forth and tests potential explanations of *p* in order to explain why *p* is true? I would not want to claim that philosophical explanation must be discontinuous with scientific activity. Yet typically, the philosopher's hypothesis is not testable or disconfirmable, because he puts forth only an existentially quantified statement; he says there is something or other, some process or other, that satisfies certain general structural conditions and so yields *p*. That there is or might be a

12

process of that sort shows how p is possible. To specify the particular details of a process of that sort would be to engage in empirical science: differing scientific specifications each would fit the philosopher's existential statement, which holds merely that there is some or another true specification.[8]

The epistemologist may need for his purposes only the fact that our perceptions somehow respond to presented facts so as to satisfy certain general conditions of responsiveness; to show how knowledge is possible he need only speculate on a linkage of that sort existing. To explain why our perceptions thus respond to the facts, however, is a task for the perceptual and physiological psychologists, who must specify the details of the particular mechanism whereby responsiveness is achieved, and for the evolutionary psychologist who must explain how that mechanism arose and was selected for. Still, although the philosophical and scientific activities typically differ, the philosopher's existential hypothesis may suggest detailed investigations to the scientist; conceivably the philosopher might specify the sort so completely that its existence is immediately open to empirical test.[9]

Explanation versus Proof

Philosophical argument, trying to get someone to believe something whether he wants to believe it or not, is not, I have held, a nice way to behave toward someone; also, it does not fit the original motivation for studying or entering philosophy. That motivation is puzzlement, curiosity, a desire to understand, not a desire to produce uniformity of belief. Most people do not want to become thought-police. The philosophical goal of explanation rather than proof not only is morally better, it is more in accord with one's philosophical motivation. Also it changes how one proceeds philosophically; at the macro-level (as we already have noted), it leads away from constructing the philosophical tower; at the micro-level, it alters which philosophical "moves" are legitimate at various points.

Even if (deductive) proof and (deductive) explanation have the same abstract structure, wherein p is deduced from the statements q, the pragmatics of the two activities differ. In the case of explanation, the thing (p) to be explained, to be deduced, must be known or at least believed to be true. If you are asked to explain why you are not reading this book now, you reject the request. Since you *are* reading it now, there is no fact that you are not, to be explained. You do not set out to explain what you don't believe to be true. However, you may set out to prove what you don't (yet) believe to be true; establishing it as true will induce the belief. In order to set about proving something, you need not actually (yet) believe the conclusion *p* to be deduced.

In order to prove *p*, however, you must start from premisses *q* which you, or those to whom you are proving *p*, know or believe. Suppose I set out to prove to you that God exists by beginning with the statement "everything Maimonides believed is true"; I then cannot waive aside your objection that you do not believe that, saying I am going to proceed to prove God's existence nonetheless. A proof transmits conviction from its premisses down to its conclusion, so it must start with premisses (*q*) for which there already is conviction; otherwise, there will be nothing to transmit.[10] An explanation, on the other hand, may introduce explanatory hypotheses (*q*) which are not already believed, from which to deduce *p* in explanatory fashion. Success in this explanatory deduction itself may lend support and induce belief, previously absent, in the hypothesis.

The activity of explaining how something is possible is hardly new to philosophy, but we here diverge from previous views of its nature; for example, Kant required philosophy to be apodictic, using only principles that were certain and necessarily true.

Philosophical explanations, however, can be offered tentatively, the hypotheses or theories presented might be believed only tentatively or even not believed initially at all; they can be held subject to revision, or introduced for the purpose of seeing in principle how *p* could be explained. To propose that explanation replace proof as the goal of philosophy is not to suggest a completely new activity that rejects all previous philosophical work. That would be absurd. Many important arguments philosophers offered can be viewed as raising explanatory questions by the incompatibilities they appear to establish—hence philosophers have a continuing interest in paradoxes—while others can be recast into explanatory form so as to present possible explanations rather than purported proofs. Indeed, much of the practice of philosophers, especially recently, as opposed to their metaphilosophical talk, easily fits the explanatory mold; making the explanatory goal explicit has the virtue of legitimating the introduction of explanatory hypotheses that are uncertain.* The shift from the interpersonal goal of proof has the further micro-effect of altering which statements may be introduced when. Consider the philosophical problem of skepticism; this has been presented and pursued as the problem of *refuting* the skeptic,[11] of proving to him that he does know what he doubts he knows, or of proving to him that you do know what he denies you know. My concern with skepticism is different, fitting within philosophy as an explanatory activity.[12]

My purpose is not to refute the skeptic, to prove he is wrong, to convince him, to marshal arguments and reasons which must convince him (if he is rational). In being unconcerned to convince the skeptic, I may seem not to be taking what he says seriously, but in a way I am taking what he says more seriously than someone does who merely sets out to convince him. If I attempt to convince the skeptic of something *p*, that is a task of the foreign relations department of my belief system. I have to find something *q* which the skeptic accepts (it does not matter whether I also accept it) from which he will conclude that *p*. In a discussion of skepticism, if *q* is said, someone can appropriately object that the skeptic will not or need not or should not accept *q*, if the purpose of the discussion is to convince the skeptic or to discover what will or must convince him. In trying

---

* Philosophers sometimes have offered arguments or proofs, namely transcendental arguments, in which explanatory considerations were intermixed. Philosophical explanations and transcendental arguments both start from a *p* which is accepted, and seek explanatory hypotheses *q* which play a role in giving rise to *p*. However, a transcendental argument seeks a *q* which is a precondition of *p*, something without which *p* could not be true. Thereby, and that is its purpose, it argues for the truth of *q*; *q* must be true, for *p* is true and *p* could not be true unless *q* were. A transcendental argument begins with the question "how is *p* possible?", but since its goal is to *prove* something it must find a *q* which not only explains *p*'s possibility (as part of a set of sufficient conditions for *p*) but also is a necessary condition of it. If we were concerned only to explain how *p* is possible, a sufficient condition would do. For the philosophical questions we shall be concerned with, it is difficult enough to conjure up sufficient conditions, without also searching for necessary ones and trying to prove they are necessary. There is a difference between explaining *p* via *q*, and proving *q* is the correct explanation of *p*. A transcendental argument attempts to prove *q* by proving it is part of any correct explanation of *p*, by proving it a precondition of *p*'s possibility.

to convince the skeptic, what is relevant is how *his* beliefs fit to-gether—that is why it is foreign relations.

But the attempt to explain how knowledge is or can be possible, given what the skeptic says, is a task for my belief system's bureau of internal affairs. Some of the things the skeptic says or points out (for example, that certain situations are logically possible) I accept; these are or become part of my own belief system. My problem is that I don't see (or no longer see, after the skeptic has spoken) how these things go along with yet other things in my belief system, namely, numerous beliefs that I and others know certain things. My task here is to remove the conflict, to put my own beliefs in alignment, to show how those of the things the skeptic says which I accept can be fit in with other things I accept. In this way, I take very seriously what the skeptic says, for I acknowledge that what he says creates a problem for *me* and my beliefs. In thus trying to explain to myself how knowl-edge is possible, what is relevant is what I accept; the explanation is no less acceptable to me because the skeptic rejects part of it. The goal of explanation makes it legitimate for the philosopher to intro-duce statements as hypotheses (acceptable to him) that the goal of proof would exclude as begging the question (of proving to the skep-tic that he knows). Although my goal is not interpersonal, I assume that I am not idiosyncratic in how what the skeptic says presents a problem to me; others also will not see how knowledge is possible given what the skeptic says. If the explanation I offer draws only on things these other people also (can) accept, it will be acceptable to them as well, whether or not the skeptic accepts it, even though my goal is not to explain it to them.*

I might describe the situation as follows. I take the skeptic less seriously than someone does who sets out to convince him, whose concern is what the skeptic thinks or continues to think; but I take what the skeptic says more seriously than someone does who merely sets out to convince him, for I view what the skeptic says as a prob-lem for me, for my beliefs. My problem does not disappear if the

---

* If, however, the skeptic's words convince you, or lead you no longer to believe you know, then you do not face the task of explaining how it is possi-ble for you to know, and no hypothesis will gain support (in your eyes) by performing this task. Isn't it rash, though, to be convinced by the skeptic's arguments, to have more confidence that the apparent incompatibility he in-vokes is a real one than that you know various things?

skeptic does, or if the skeptic says he was only joking, that he really does believe he know things. If I succeed in my task, I (and others like me) learn from the skeptic, my beliefs change and are reorganized, while the skeptic need not learn anything. Whereas if the convincer succeeds, the skeptic will learn something, though the convincer himself need not. I do not take the skeptic seriously enough to want to teach him; I do take what he says seriously enough to want to learn from it. It should be emphasized that, though internal to my (nonidiosyncratic) belief system, this task is not one of self-development; the goal is to explain, to understand (in this case) how knowledge is possible.

This distinction between the foreign and domestic relations of my system of beliefs illuminates another puzzle. In discussions of ethics one sometimes thinks, "how could one convince some particular evil figure, say Stalin, Hitler, or Mao, that he is wrong; if there is no argument guaranteed to convince him, doesn't that show that ethics really is subjective, merely a matter of preference or opinion?" The puzzle is why we take this possibility of irresolvable disagreement to threaten the objectivity of ethics, while, for example, an irresolvable disagreement about whether someone in a mental institution is Napoleon or Jesus does not, we think, threaten the objectivity of such factual matters, even though there is no way we can convince the deluded person that he is wrong. I suggest the distinction lies here: the mental patient presents us with a problem of foreign relations, but what he says does not cause difficulties about how our beliefs fit together within our own belief system. Therefore, it need not concern us if some parts of our explanation of why he is not and cannot be Napoleon or Jesus are rejected by him. We have a general conception of past history, how we come to know some facts about it, why (even were a "return" possible) not everyone who claims to be Napoleon or Jesus can be right, why some people form self-important delusions, and so forth. Our general picture of the world of objective historical truths and of our connection to it leads us to think we know why the (deluded) person's claims must be wrong; we have some conception of how we can and do know he is wrong. The disagreements that worry us are those that fix upon tensions or anomalies or unclarities in our own belief system. It is because we do not see how an objective ethics is *possible* that we worry about irresolvable moral disagreements. For this reason, we do not need actually to find such disagreement—if it doesn't exist, we will invent it. For it is the possibility of such disagreement that worries us; it worries us because we do not see clearly how there can be an objective ethics. If we did see how an objective ethics was possible, we would not attribute theoretical importance to someone who could not be brought to agree.

Thus, what is philosophically interesting, what demarcates the philosophically important disagreements from the others, is the domestic problem presented for our own beliefs. Because this is what creates the philosophical interest, it is on this explanatory issue we shall concentrate, rather than on the philosophically pointless task of attempting to convince the other person.[13]

Philosophical Pluralism

Can a philosophy begin by seeking philosophical explanation? Doesn't the desire for explanation rather than something else already presuppose philosophical views about what is intellectually desirable? And, even given the goal of explanation, won't philosophies differ in their conception of an acceptable or adequate explanation, in the conditions that they hold an explanation must meet? One view will hold that explanation must be deductive while another will not, one that the principles used in explanation must be necessary or self-evident, or that explanation must utilize general laws, or that explanations must be causal, or mechanical, or teleological, or contain a picturable model, or not refer to unobservable entities, or be poetic, or be testable by observation, or comport with revealed religious doctrines, while other views will differ. Since each philosophy will have its own ideas about explanation and when it is suitable, how can we begin philosophy by seeking explanations? Must we not already have answered many important philosophical questions or presupposed answers to them in order to fix what it is we are seeking? Similar questions to these about explanation can be asked also about the notions of 'incompatibility' and 'tension' which set up the need for certain explanations, and about the statements themselves which are held to be in tension.

These questions are not unique to the goal of explanation. To seek for proofs also has its presuppositions, and philosophies can differ in the conditions they impose on adequate proofs. (Are they deductive, formalizable, formalizable in first-order logic, finitistic, may they proceed by reductio ad absurdum? In addition, there are the many conditions that can be imposed on the axioms or propositions from which proofs begin.) It is clear that any goal put forth for philosophy will be philosophically controversial in that some philosophies will reject that goal in favor of another, while yet other philosophies which accept it will specify it differently. How, then, is it possible for philosophy to get started?

I do not see how to satisfy the desire to start philosophy in a neutral way, making no philosophical assumptions, remaining neutral among all possible philosophical views. We cannot reasonably hope to settle on one philosophical view by showing it uniquely satisfies all of the apparently neutral desirable general conditions on a philosophy; many different philosophies will equally well satisfy those. Anyway, why think the goal of neutrality itself is neutral? Would every philosophy accept *it*? And when neutrality ends eventually, as we want, what selective factor will point to one philosophy rather than others, and what status—neutral or not—will *this* factor have? If a neutral beginning is chimerical, the alternative of starting just where we are seems parochial and dogmatic, especially if there are some theoretical places we can't get to from here.

We can build modes of change into a view, hoping parochialism is avoided when any theory can be reached, in principle, given suitable input. Nevertheless, some places will not be reached with specified inputs, starting from here; philosophical views will differ in what gets reached when. A metaphilosophy will be part of a total philosophical view rather than a separate neutral theory above the battle.

The treatment for philosophical parochialism, as for parochialism of other sorts, is to come to know alternatives. We can keep track of the different philosophical views that have been put forth and elaborated; we can pay attention to foreign traditions and their diverse viewpoints, to the special slant of these traditions on our questions, both the different ways they pose their most nearly equivalent question, and the different answers they offer.[14] There even may be ways of catapulting oneself, at least temporarily, into different philosophical perspectives. Various drugs seem to have given the experience of how the world looks and feels from one or another of the diverse Eastern perspectives to Westerners, including some people previously unfamiliar with the conceptual framework into which they were catapulted.*

Not all philosophical cosmopolitans, keeping track of alternative positions, will end up the same, for they start differently. I stand on my position keeping track of the others, while you stand on yours. The position I occupy is modified somewhat by my broader knowledge, but I do not imagine that all the different positions so modified by knowledge of the others will converge. After all, we do not even have agreement among philosophies within the same tradition. Nor do I recommend withdrawing assent from every particular position and merely contemplating the panoply of alternatives; I do not, that is, recommend "rootless cosmopolitanism".** Assent will, though, be more tentative, perhaps more transient. (This tentative attachment to one view, while carrying along the rest, would not jibe with the goal of convincing others or proving conclusions.)

This fits my experience in studying philosophy: I confess I have found (and not only in sequence) many different philosophies alluring and appealing, cogent and impressive, tempting and wonderful. I think this says something about the subject, not about me—I am not noticeably wishy-washier than most. Treating philosophy as a black box, we might view its "output" not as a single theory, not even as one set of theories, but as a set of questions, each with its own set of associated theories as possible answers. Should we view the highest products of philosophy as the philosophical questions themselves, the theories and systems being commentary to exhibit the value of the questions? On this view, philosophy's wonders are the ones in which it begins; as important as new answers are its new questions.

I feel discomfort, though, with the aesthetic view of philosophy, the uncommitted praise of the diverse philosophical "visions". The goal is finding out the truth, after all. (Yet is that goal, or its specification, neutral among philosophies?) Recall the distinction made ear-

---

* The explanation of why some years ago books on Eastern thought started to appear in profusion in philosophy sections of paperback bookstores, previously almost purely Western, surely was the onset of widespread experimentation with drugs. People were turning to these books as fitting and explaining what they suddenly were experiencing unpreparedly.

** Applied to Jews throughout the world before the establishment of the state of Israel, this term confused lack of roots with lack of the land to nourish them.

lier between explaining and understanding. Embedding the world in the network of alternative philosophical theories and visions, seeing how each of these different philosophical possibilities gets a grip on the world, does produce understanding. The major philosophical theories of continuing interest are readings of possible worlds accessible from here, that is, possible readings of the actual world. We understand the world by seeing it in its matrix of possibilities, in its possibility neighborhood.

Still, this book does not aim at understanding; by and large, it aims more narrowly—at explanation, at truth. In any case, I would not think it a good strategy to aim at illuminating possibility; we are all too likely to fail in our aim. Aiming for the true explanation might well yield understanding, while striving for understanding probably will not produce even that, only inaccessible possibilities. (Such intellectual playfulness has its own value, though, and is not excluded from this book.) Moreover, my desire is to explain how knowledge is possible, how free will is possible, how there can be ethical truths, how life can have meaning. That is what I want to know. Other philosophical views are scanned and searched for help.

Yet, it seems to me I value truth less than do other philosophers I know. (Do I love truth less or love understanding more?) How could I so admire the writings of history's great philosophers if falsity were a fatal or debilitating flaw?

I see the situation as follows. There are various philosophical views, mutually incompatible, which cannot be dismissed or simply rejected. Philosophy's output is the basketful of these admissible views, all together. One delimiting strategy would be to modify and shave these views, capturing what is true in each, to make them compatible parts of one new view. While I know of no reason in principle why this cannot be done, neither has anyone yet done it satisfactorily. Perhaps, as knowing a subject (such as logic or physics) involves seeing the different ways it can be organized and viewed, the different ways around it, so too (only this time the views are incompatible so the analogy is imperfect) knowing the world involves seeing the different ways it can be viewed.

Are we reduced to relativism then, the doctrine that all views are equally good? No, some views can be rejected, and the admissible ones remaining will differ in merits and adequacy, though none is completely lacking. Even when one view is clearly best, though, we do not keep only this first ranked view, rejecting all the others. Our total view is the basket of philosophical views, containing all the admissible views.[15] This total view notices which component is best, and perhaps will order the others. Yet the first ranked view is not completely adequate all by itself; what it omits or distorts or puts out of focus cannot be added compatibly, but must be brought out and highlighted by another incompatible view, itself (even more) inadequate alone.

The position is not relativism, for the views are ranked, but neither is just one view settled upon.[16] True, philosophers will differ in what they hold inadmissible, and in how they rank the views that remain. I am not proposing a neutral way to do this, simply describing how things look from within the view I rank first (which includes a meta-component). Is there at least this agreement: even if there are different perspectives on the world, isn't it true on all perspectives that the world looks a particular way from a particular perspective? These relational facts are about a perspective but hold independently of a perspective. Can't we use them to figure out what the world is like, what character of world would give rise to these relational facts?[17] However, with philosophical views, there is no way to identify the point from which the world looks a certain way, other than by how it looks—the world looks as if it fits Plato's theory from the position of standing on Plato's theory. It is misleading to call the different views "perspectives", in the absence of any independent way of identifying positions.

Still, we can ask what the world and our cognitive relation to it are like so as to give rise to this situation: a basketful of admissible (partially) ranked philosophical views. We shall return to this question at the close of the book. Meanwhile, we have explored the metasituation sufficiently to get on with offering specific philosophical explanations.

I would not want, however, to leave the impression that explanation is the sole legitimate goal of philosophy. Even within the realm of truth and actuality, there are linkages, connections, and contrasts other than explanatory ones mediated by general laws; these ways of setting something in (actual) context produce understanding too. Furthermore, the broader end of understanding something in its (possible) context is valuable. Other philosophical activities also have independent legitimacy, not merely as subordinate within the explanatory framework; the skeptic's arguing that certain things are *not* possible is an example. My pluralism extends to ways of carrying on philosophy; though I elaborate one, I keep track of and appreciate others. Even argument, despite its coerciveness and distortion of philosophical direction, has its own virtues: it is responsive to a person's rationality (if not his autonomy), and perhaps in caring what he believes it evidences some caring about the person. But though philosophical arguing is somewhat responsive to and respectful of the person, it is not responsive and respectful enough.

The view of philosophy as philosophical explanation is put forth here as a tentative hypothesis, designed to encompass much of the actual historical activity of philosophers while demarcating a legitimate and important task. Moreover, the view applies to and fits itself. In explaining how philosophy is possible, given the formidable obstacles to it as a useful mode of knowledge, the view itself is an instance of what it says philosophy should be: the explanation of how something is possible. In contrast, the view that philosophy is the theory of self-evident fundamental principles and their consequences, for example, seems neither to be self-evident nor derivable from such. No doubt, not everything in this book (and certainly not everything of value in the history of philosophy) fits the mold sketched here. Still, this view has the virtue of delineating one important direction philosophy can pursue, a direction whose nature is reasonably well understood and which does not appear beyond our capacity.

Many philosophers have dreamed of setting philosophy upon the sure path of a science. As this book's closing makes evident, this dream is not mine. Even the path of science, though, does not involve the proof of theories. It is a commonplace of the philosophy of science that evidence is incomplete, that alternative hypotheses and possibilities can be imagined, that theories are held tentatively until a better one is produced, and so on. Philosophy has aspired to more than this, as did explanatory science itself once, but surely we long ago reached the point when philosophy should cease striving for so much more while accomplishing so much less.

The explanations to follow are put forward not as the sole correct view on their topics, but as members among others of admissible classes, with the hope that they will be ranked first, or at least highly. On the view presented here, philosophical work aspires to produce a highest ranked view, at least an illuminating one, without attempting to knock all other theories out as inadmissible. (Even this general view of the basketful with rankings need aspire only to being first ranked in its basket.)

This view of philosophy is in harmony with our earlier substitution of explanation for proof as the goal of philosophy. Yet, though proof and convincing fit best with admissible sets of only one member, they are not excluded even by the view of the full basket. Why not try, then, to convince the reader or prove to him that the explanations offered are admissible and should be highly ranked? I don't say there could *not* be occasions when it was possible and appropriate to convince someone of this, or of the fact that he was enjoying tennis, or to prove to someone that he is in love—but should we build an activity and methodology around those occasions? It is (hard) enough to offer an explanation which the reader will find illuminating. There is no need also to prove it is. (Would one prove it by presenting something the reader simply accepts as proof, or would one also have to prove that proves it?)

This book puts forward its explanations in a very tentative spirit; not only do I not ask you to believe they are correct, I do not think it important for me to believe them correct, either. Still, I do believe, and hope you will find it so, that these proposed explanations are illuminating and worth considering, that they are worth surpassing; also, that the process of seeking and elaborating explanations, being open to new possibilities, the new wonderings and wanderings, the free exploration, is itself a delight. Can any pleasure compare to that of a new idea, a new question?

There is sexual experience, of course, not dissimilar, with its own playfulness and possibilities, its focused freedom, its depth, its sharp pleasures and its gentle ones, its ecstacies. What is the mind's excitement and sensuality? What its orgasm? Whatever, it unfortunately will frighten and offend the puritans of the mind (do the two puritanisms share a common root?) even as it expands others and brings them joy.

METAPHYSICS

Chapter
One

THE
IDENTITY
OF THE
SELF

What am I? What kind of entity, what kind of being? To what exactly does the term "I" refer? The dictum from Greece, "know thyself", courses through Western philosophy; it echoes in calls from gnosticism, Vedanta, and Samkhya yoga to uncover our own true nature. The wide range of theories is somewhat surprising: soul, material object, Turing machine realization, Atman as Brahman, and so on. Since one of the self's distinctive properties, surely, is its capacity for self-consciousness, you would think that if it knew anything, it would know its own nature. Yet the self is a problem and puzzle to itself. A theory should explain both the self's special awareness and its continuing mystery, even to itself.

Our desire to know our natures is not solely theoretical. This knowledge by itself will not settle the question of how we ought to live, but in fixing the range and limits of the possibilities open to us, it determines what alternatives we choose among when we choose how to live and be.

We each want to understand not only the kind of being we are, but also what constitutes our individual identity as a particular being of that kind. If what we are is persons, to use a relatively neutral term, we want to know what differentiates or individuates one person from another. Even things as basic as how to count persons can be baffling. If an exact physical replica is made of you, with the same exact psychology and (apparent) memories, are there two persons or one? When "multiple personalities" are exhibited in alternation by one human body, how many persons are there? If the corpus callosum between the right and left cerebral hemispheres is severed, how many persons are there? We also want a view of when events constitute a change in the same person, as opposed to his destruction followed by the substitution or creation of another person. It is this topic, the identity of a person through time, that the philosophical literature refers to under the rubric: personal identity. A view of the kind of entity a person is, of what differentiates one person from another and in what his identity over time consists, is a view from the outside, so to speak. Viewing ourselves from the inside, we also each want to understand what makes ourself a particular one of those persons.

The very puzzling questions that arise, quickly, in trying to understand the nature of the self, together add up to the question: how is the self possible? (Presumably, this is a question we can investigate without being tempted to wonder whether the thing is, after all, possible.) I shall not be able in this chapter to consider all these questions, not even all the most important ones.

I. PERSONAL IDENTITY THROUGH TIME

So many puzzling examples have been put forth in recent discussions of personal identity that it is difficult to formulate, much less defend, any consistent view of identity and nonidentity. One is driven to describe and judge some cases in ways apparently incompatible with how one judges and describes others.[1] Not all of the difficulties, however, uncover something special about personal identity; some concern the general notion of identity through time, and stem, I think, from a natural but mistaken principle about identity. These issues, interesting and puzzling in their own right, raise the metaphysical question: how, given changes, *can* there be identity of something from one time to another, and in what does this identity consist?

The Closest Continuer Theory

A recent essay by Bernard Williams provides convenient entry to these issues.[2] Williams tells two stories, each individually coherent, which are designed to puzzle us together. He first presents a case, aseptically, which we are prone to describe as involving a person coming to occupy a new body, indeed as involving two people switching bodies. Two persons, A and B, enter some machine; upon leaving, the A-body person, the person (whoever that now is) now connected with that A-body, has all of (the previous person) B's memories, knowledge, values, modes of behavior, and so on. (When compatible with the constraints of the A-body, this B-material is produced exactly; otherwise, what is present in the A-body is the vector result of this previous B-material plus the limits of the A-body.) Similarly the B-body person emerges with A's memories, knowledge, modes of behavior, character traits, values, and so on. When enough details are filled in (though not details of the mechanism by which the transfer is effected), we are prone to say or conclude that the people have switched bodies. If these events were to be described beforehand, aseptically, and A was to decide solely on selfish grounds to which body something very painful was to be done afterwards, then A would designate the A-body, for he would believe that *he* would be occupying the B-body at that later time. Moreover, supposing this actually were carried out, at that later time the occupant of the B-body, with A's memories and character, would say "I'm glad I decided then that the painful thing was to be done to the A-body so that I am not feeling it now." We, readers of philosophy, are not so tied to our bodies that we find it impossible to imagine coming to inhabit another. We do not conceive of ourselves as (merely) our particular bodies, as inextricably tied to them.

We can wonder, nevertheless, what constitutes a transfer. What difference is there between your moving from one body to another, and the other body's just acquiring memories and character identical to yours, but without your moving to that body? Williams presses this question with his second story. Suppose you are told you will undergo terrible suffering. This prospect is frightening. You next receive the information that before this suffering comes, you will have changed enormously in psychological traits, perhaps so greatly as to possess exactly the character, memories, values, and knowledge of someone else who now is alive. This would frighten you even more, perhaps. You do not want to lose your character, memories, values, modes of behavior, knowledge, and loves—to lose your identity, as we might say—and afterwards to undergo enormous suffering. Yet how does this differ, asks Williams, from what happened in the first story, which we took to depict a transfer from body to body? In that story, too, the A-body loses its old memories and acquires new ones (which are those of another person); it loses its knowledge, values, and modes of behavior, acquiring new ones. When hearing the first story beforehand, why didn't the A-person have exactly the fear he would have upon learning the second story foretells his future? He reacts differently to the first story because he thinks *he* will occupy the B-body. Yet if terrible things happen to him in the second story, why do they not happen to him in the first one, also? Don't the two stories describe exactly the same events happening to the A-body? What then makes the first story one about the transfer of a person to another body, and not about something terrible happening to a person who stays where he is?

How can the difference be, asks Williams, that in one situation, the first, in addition to everything happening to the A-body, also A's

	Body A	Body B
First situation	acquires the memories and character which person B had one hour earlier.	acquires the memories and character which person A had one hour earlier.
Second situation	acquires the memories and character which person B had one hour earlier, or perhaps no previous person had.	stays with the continuation of the memories and character which it had one hour earlier.

memories and psychological traits end up or arise in body B? Surely, whatever happens elsewhere cannot affect whether or not A continues to inhabit the A-body. When it happens to just one body it is a psychological disintegration and acquisition of a new psychology. How, then, can two psychological disintegrations and acquisitions of new memories and values make or add up to an exchange of bodies?

Let us formulate the general principle that underlies Williams' discussion and leads to these perplexing questions.

> If x at time t_1 is the same individual as y at later time t_2, that can depend only upon facts about x, y, and the relationships between them. No fact about any other existing thing is relevant to (deciding) whether x at t_1 is (part of the same continuing individual as) y at t_2.

How could the existence (or nonexistence) of something else be relevant to whether x at t_1 is (part of the same continuing individual as) y at t_2? There is a related principle, also plausible:

> If y at time t_2 is (part of the same continuing individual as) x at t_1 in virtue of standing in some relationship R to x at t_1, then there *could not* be another additional thing at t_2 also standing (along with y) in R to x at t_1. If there also were this additional thing z at t_2, then neither it nor y would be identical to x. If that z could exist, even if it actually does not, then y at t_2 is not identical with x at t_1—at least, it is not in virtue of standing in the relationship R.

Williams assumed this principle in earlier articles,[3] in order to argue

31

that bodily continuity is a necessary condition of personal identity. We are prone, otherwise, to think that a person could enter a machine, disappear there, and appear in another machine ten feet to the left, without ever having occupied any intervening space. Williams asks us to imagine that there also had been an additional machine ten feet to the right, and at this one too had appeared simultaneously another (qualitatively) identical being. Neither of the two then would be that original person who entered the machine in the middle. Furthermore, if in that situation of double materialization, the person on the left is not the original person, then neither is he in the different situation where only one person appears on the left. The mere possibility of someone also emerging (discontinuously) on the right is enough, according to Williams, to show that anyone who emerges (discontinuously) on the left, even if all alone, is not the original person.[4]

The first principle says that identity cannot depend upon whether there is or isn't another thing of a certain sort; the second says that if there could be another thing so that then there would not be identity, then there isn't identity, even if that other thing does not actually exist. (If there were identity only when that other thing happened not to exist, the first principle would be violated; the second principle follows from the first.) Both of these principles are false.

First, consider a case that does not involve any question of a person's identity. The Vienna Circle was driven from Austria and Germany by the Nazis; one member, Hans Reichenbach, landed in Istanbul. (Later he left and went to the United States.) Suppose there were twenty members of the Circle, of whom three ended up in Istanbul. These three keep meeting through the war years, discussing philosophy. In 1943, they hear that all of the others are dead. *They* now are the Vienna Circle, meeting in Istanbul. Carrying on its discussions, they proclaim that the Vienna Circle lives on in exile. In 1945, however, they learn that nine members of the Circle had gotten to America, where they continued to meet, discuss philosophy, adhere to the same philosophical program, and so on. That group in the United States is the Vienna Circle in exile; the group in Istanbul turns out not to be the Vienna Circle but its Istanbul offshoot.

How can this be? Either the group in Istanbul is the Vienna Circle or it isn't; how can whether or not it is be affected by whether other members survived and continued to meet in another place? (Isn't it clear, though, that if these nine others had gone underground and continued to meet in Vienna, this would show that the Istanbul group was not the Vienna Circle?) It is not plausible to apply the first principle to this case; it is not plausible to say that if the group of those three persons meeting in Istanbul is the same continuing entity as the earlier Vienna Circle, then this can depend only upon relationships between the two, and not on whether anything else of a certain sort exists.

Rather, the group in Istanbul is the Vienna Circle when it is the *closest continuer* of the Vienna Circle. If no other group exists, the Istanbul group is the closest continuer; but if the group in the United States exists, *it* is the continuer (supposing no closer continuer exists) of the Vienna Circle. Whether or not a particular group constitutes the Vienna Circle depends on what other groups there actually are.[5]

To be something later is to be its closest continuer. Let us apply this view to one traditional puzzle about identity over time: the puzzle of the ship of Theseus. The planks of a ship are removed one by one over intervals of time, and as each plank is removed it is replaced by a new plank. The removal of one plank and its replacement by another does not make the ship a different ship than before; it is the same ship with one plank different. Over time, each and every plank might be removed and replaced, but if this occurs gradually, the ship still will be the same ship. It is an interesting result, but upon reflection not so very surprising, that the identity of something over time does not require it to keep all the very same parts. The story continues, however. (We can imagine this as a continuation of the previous story, or as a new one which begins like the first.) It turns out that the planks removed had not been destroyed but were stored carefully; now they are brought together again into their original shiplike configuration. Two ships float on the waters, side by side. Which one, wondered the Greeks, is the original?

The closest continuer view helps to sort out and structure the issues; it does not, by itself, answer the question. For it does not, by itself, tell which dimension or weighted sum of dimensions determines closeness; rather, it is a schema into which such details can be filled. In the case of the ships, there are two relevant properties: spatiotemporal continuity with continuity of parts, and being composed of the very same parts (in the same configuration). If these have equal weight, there is a tie in closeness of continuation. Neither, then, is the closest continuer, so neither is the original ship. However, even when the two properties receive equal weight, if there actually had been one ship existing without the other, then it, as the closest continuer, would be the original ship. Perhaps the situation is not one of a clear tie, but one of an unclear weighting. Our concepts may not be sharp enough to order all possible combinations of properties according to closeness of continuation. For complicated cases, we may feel that which is closest is a matter to decide, that we must sharpen our concept to settle which is (identical with) the original entity. It is different, though, with persons, and especially with ourselves; we are not willing to think that whether something is *us* can be a matter of (somewhat arbitrary) decision or stipulation.

Although it does not answer the question about which ship, if any, is the same as the original one, the closest continuer schema does fit and explain our response to this puzzle. When we hear the first story of the ship gradually altered, plank by plank, we are not puzzled or led to deny it really is the same ship. Only when we learn also of the reconstituted ship are we thrown into puzzlement, not only about its status but about the earlier product of gradual rebuilding, too. It is only when we learn of another candidate for closest (or equally close) continuer that we come to doubt whether that gradually altered ship is the same ship as the original one. If our notion of closeness is unsharp, we will not be able to say that either, or neither, is the original; whether one is closest will remain unclear. The nature and contours of people's responses to the puzzle of the ship fits the closest continuer schema and supports it, if not as a metaphysical truth then at least as a component of a psychological explanation of these responses.

The closest continuer view presents a necessary condition for identity; something at t_2 is not the same entity as x at t_1 if it is not x's closest continuer. And "closest" means closer than all others; if two things at t_2 tie in closeness to x at t_1, then neither is the same entity as x. However, something may be the closest continuer of x without being close enough to it to be x. How close something must be to x to be x, it appears, depends on the kind of entity x is, as do the dimensions along which closeness is measured.[6]

If the closest continuer view is correct, our judgments of identity reflect (implicit) weightings of dimensions; therefore, we might use these judgments themselves to discover those dimensions, the ordering and weighting among them. Notice that on the closest continuer view, a property may be a factor in identity without being a necessary condition for it. If persons conceivably can transfer from one body to another, still, bodily continuity can be an important component of identity, even (in some cases) its sole determinant. The dimension of bodily continuity can receive significant weight in the overall measure of closeness for persons.

To say that something is a continuer of x is not merely to say its properties are qualitatively the same as x's, or resemble them. Rather it is to say they grow out of x's properties, are causally produced by them, are to be explained by x's earlier having had its properties, and so forth. (See also our later discussion of tracking.) Indeed, even the notion of spatiotemporal continuity is not to be explained merely as something that when photographed would produce continuous film footage with no gaps; for we can imagine a substitution of one thing for another that would not break film continuity.[7] The later temporal stages also must be causally dependent (in an appropriate way) on the earlier ones. The condition that something is a continuer incorporates such causal dependence.* The closest continuer view is not committed to the thesis that identity through time depends only upon the qualitative properties of temporal stages to the exclusion of causal relations and dependencies between (aspects of) stages.

This causal dependence, however, need not involve temporal continuity. Imagine that each and every thing flickers in and out of existence every other instant, its history replete with temporal gaps. (Compare how messages are transmitted on telephone wires.) According to concepts developed later in this chapter, if every thing leads this mode of existence, then it is the best kind of continuity there actually is, so all such will count as continuing objects. However, if some have continuity without any temporal gaps, then the others that flicker, though otherwise similar, are not the best realization of continuity; so perhaps their stages do not closely enough continue each other to count as constituting objects that continue through time. How much temporal continuity is necessary for there

---

* If this causal component indeed is needed, it raises problems for theological views that hold God maintains everything in continued existence, where this includes all causal connections. How does He distinguish continuing an old thing from producing a new one, qualitatively identical, without any filmstrip "break"?

to be a continuing object depends on how closely things continue temporally elsewhere.

If it governs our judgments about identity over time, it seems plausible that the closest continuer schema also should fit our *perception* of things continuing through time; it should fit what we see as (a later stage of) what. In parallel to Piaget's famous experiments with objects disappearing behind a screen, we should be able to devise experiments to uncover the closest continuer schema and reveal aspects of the metric of closeness. Show a film of an object x going behind a screen followed by something y coming out at a different angle (Figure 1.1); with color and shape held constant and velocity suitably maintained, a person should see this as the same object emerging, deflected by a collision with something behind the screen. Similarly, with a suitably chosen delay followed by emergence with increased velocity, it should be seen as the same object popping out after being somewhat stuck. Yet if along with y an even closer continuer z also is presented, for example, something emerging straight out at the same velocity, that thing z, rather than y, would be seen as the earlier x emerging, even though in z's absence, y would be seen so, since it then would be x's closest continuer (Figure 1.2). Following this plausible hunch that such psychological experiments could exhibit the closest continuer schema, I inquired of psychologist friends whether experiments like these had ever been done. Though the research seemed plausible, no one I spoke to knew of any, until I met an Israeli psychologist, Shimon Ullman, who had just completed his doctoral dissertation where he had done these experiments.[8] His results fit the closest continuer schema; also he included more detailed experiments in which the color, shape, and velocity of the figures were varied in order to uncover (in my terminology) the details of the metric. (Unfortunately no experiments were done that sharply focus on how people perceive the hard situations that will puzzle us below: tie cases and overlap cases.)

The closest continuer view holds that y at t_2 is the same person as x

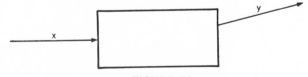

FIGURE 1.1

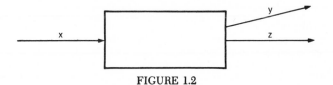

FIGURE 1.2

at t_1 only if, first, y's properties at t_2 stem from, grow out of, are causally dependent on x's properties at t_1 and, second, there is no other z at t_2 that stands in a closer (or as close) relationship to x at t_1 than y at t_2 does.

Closeness, here, represents not merely the degree of causal connection, but also the qualitative closeness of what is connected, as this is judged by some weighting of dimensions and features in a similarity metric. Moreover, it seems plausible that closeness is measured only among those features that are causally connected (instead of a threshold being passed when there is a causal connection, while then closeness is measured among all features of x and y, including those features of y that are causally unconnected with x, even any that pop up spontaneously and at random).

The Theory Applied

Let us now investigate how the closest continuer theory handles particular cases.

> Case 1. After precise measurements of you are taken, your body, including the brain, is precisely duplicated. In all physical properties this other body is the same as yours; it also acts as you do, has the same goals, "remembers" what you do, and so on.

Intuitively, we want to say that you (continue to) exist in this case, and also that a duplicate has been made of you, but this duplicate is not you. According to the closest continuer theory, too, that other entity is not you, since it is not your closest continuer. Although it exhibits both bodily and psychological similarity (to the earlier you), and though its psychological traits stem from yours via the intermediaries who made it, it does not show bodily continuity. That duplicated body does causally depend, in some way, on the state of your body; it is no accident that it duplicates your properties. Your own body's continuance, though, does not require a duplicator to make a choice in the causal process. The duplicate's causal connection to your earlier body is not this close, so it loses out (as being you) to the continuing you.

Case 2. You are dying after a heart attack, and your healthy brain is transplanted into another body, perhaps one cloned from yours and so very similar though healthier. After the operation, the "old body" expires and the new body-person continues on with all your previous plans, activities, and personal relationships.

Intuitively we want to say, or at least I do, that you have continued to exist in another body. (We can imagine this becoming a standard medical technique to prolong life.) The closest continuer theory can yield this result. The new body-person certainly is your closest continuer. With psychological continuity and some bodily continuity (the brain is the same), is it a close enough continuer to still be you? I would say it is.

My intention is to show how the closest continuer schema fits my judgments. Perhaps you make different judgments; you thereby differ in judging comparative closeness, but you still are using that same schema. Then is there any content to the claim that the closest continuer schema fits our judgments? When y and z are stages occurring after x, cannot dimensions be given weights so as to yield either one as closer to x, whichever judgment a person makes? It appears that the closest continuer schema excludes nothing. However, though any judgments about one case or situation can be fit to the closest continuer schema by a suitable choice of dimensions and weights, by a suitable choice of metric, it does not follow that any and every group of judgments can be made to fit. Only some (range of) weightings can fit particular judgments J_1 and J_2; these weights, once fixed, give determinate content to the schema. Some judgments J_3 about other cases are excluded, since any weights that would yield J_3 fall outside the range of weights already fixed by judgments J_1 and J_2. The closest continuer schema is compatible with any single judgment about identity or nonidentity, but it is not compatible with each and every set of judgments. Add the assumption that the same dimensions and weights function, when applicable, in various judgments; the closest continuer schema now does exclude some (combinations of) things, and so does have determinate empirical content. The situation is similar with utility theory. Given any one preference in a pair of alternatives, utility always can be assigned to give the preferred alternative a higher utility; however, some combinations of pairwise preferences among various alternatives cannot be fit to a utility function. To gain empirical content, the assumption must be added that the underlying preferences remain constant during the sequence of pairwise judgments, that it is one utility function which accounts for all the pairwise preferences—just as it is one metric space determining closeness, which must account for the person's various judgments of identity and nonidentity. To say that some straight line or other fits the data, has no restrictive content if there is only one data point, or two; a third point, however, might fail to fall on the straight line fixed by the other two.

Reassured that the closest continuer schema has determinate content, let us return to cases.

Case 3. As you are dying, your brain patterns are transferred to another (blank) brain in another body, perhaps one cloned from yours. The patterns in the new brain are produced by some analogue process that simultaneously removes these patterns from the old one. (There is a greater continuity—or impression of it— with an analogue process as compared to the transmission of digitally coded data.) Upon the completion of the transfer, the old body expires.

Here, there need be no physical continuity at the time of transfer (though there may have been a previous cloning). Still, I believe, this can be you; I believe this is a way a person can continue on. When I contemplate this happening to myself, I believe this continuation would be close enough to count as me continuing.

Notice that the duplicate being in the first case may be exactly like the new you in this case. However, in that case it was not a new you, for the old you still was around—an even closer continuer existed.

Case 4. Suppose medical technology permitted only half a brain to be transplanted in another body, but this brought along full psychological similarity.

If your old half-brain and body ceased to function during such a transplant, the new body-person would be you. This case is like case 2, except that here half a brain is transplanted instead of a full one; we are imagining the half-brain to carry with it the full psychology of the person.

Case 5. Suppose that after an accident damages a portion of your brain, half of it is surgically removed and ceases to function apart from the body. The remaining half continues to function in the body, maintaining full psychological continuity.

Although half of your brain has been removed, you remain alive and remain you.

Case 6. Let us now suppose the fourth and fifth cases are combined: half of a person's brain is removed, and while the remaining half-brain plus body function on with no noticeable difference, the removed half is transplanted into another body to yield full psychological continuity there. The old body plus half-brain is exactly like the continuing person of case 5, the new body plus transplanted half-brain is exactly like the continuing person of case 4. But now both are around. Are both the original person, or neither, or is one of them but not the other?

It appears that the closer continuer in case 6 is (the person of) the original body plus remaining half-brain. Both resultant persons have full psychological continuity with the original one, both also have some bodily continuity, though in one case only half a brain's worth. One appears to have closer continuity, however—not more kinds of continuity (both have psychological and physical continuity with the original) but more of one of the kinds. One has greater physical overlap with the original person.

If this one is closer, as appears, then he is the original person and the other is not. True, it feels to the other as if *he* is the original person, but so did it for the duplicate in the very first case. Still, I am hesitant about this result. Perhaps we should hold that despite appearances there is a tie for closeness, so neither is the original person; or that though one is closer to the original person, close enough to him to constitute him when there is no competitor (as shown by case 5), that closer one is not enough closer than the competitor to constitute the original person. On this last view, a continuer must be not only closest and close enough, but also enough closer than any other continuer; it must decisively beat out the competition.

Case 7. As you die, a very improbable random event occurs elsewhere in the universe: molecules come together precisely in the configuration of your brain and a very similar (but healthier) body, exhibiting complete psychological similarity to you.

This is not you; though it resembles you, by hypothesis, it does not arise out of you. It is not any continuer of you. In the earlier cases, by *psychological continuity* I meant "stemming from" and "similar to". Of course, we can have the first without the second, as when drastic changes in psychology are brought on by physical injury or emotional trauma; case 7 shows the second without the first.[9]

Consider the mode of long distance travel described in science fiction stories, wherein a person is "beamed" from one place to another. However, the person's body does not occupy intermediate places. Either the molecules of the decomposed body are beamed or (truer to the intent of the stories) a fully informative description of the body is beamed to another place, where the body then is reconstituted (from numerically distinct molecules) according to the received information. Yet the readers of such stories, and the many viewers of such television programs, calmly accept this as a mode of travel. They do not view it as a killing of one person with the production of another very similar person elsewhere. (We may suppose that those few who do view it that way, and refuse so to "travel", despite the fact that it is faster, cheaper, and avoids the intervening asteroid belts, are laughed at by the others.) The taking and transmission of the informative description might not involve the dematerialization of the person here, who remains also. In that case, the newly constituted person there presumably would be viewed as a similar duplicate.

Do we need to stipulate that the process of transporting by beaming, by its nature, must involve the dematerialization of the original here? In the case of people, at least, a merely accidental ending of the person here may seem inadequate for continuation there; consider the case where as the information is beamed to create what is intended to be only a duplicate, the original person is shot, so that (to speak neutrally) the life in that body ends. Yet, imagine a beamer which can work either way—dematerializing here or not—depending upon which way a switch is thrown. If the process with dematerialization is far more expensive, might not those who wished to travel there choose the less expensive method combined with an alternative ending (accidental with respect to the transporting process) of their existence here? I shall leave these issues unresolved now.

In addition to the closest continuer, we also must focus on the closest predecessor, for similar reasons. Something y may be the closest continuer of another thing x even though x is not y's closest predecessor. Though nothing at t_2 more closely continues x than y does, still, y more closely continues z at t_1 than it does x at t_1. For a later stage y to be part of the same continuing object as an earlier stage x, not only must y be the closest continuer of x, also x must be the closest predecessor of y. Let us say that two things or stages so related are mono-related. This mono-relation need not be transitive, since neither closest continuer nor closest predecessor need be transitive.[10]

How shall a view of identity over time cope with these nontransitivities of mono-related, closest continuer, and closest predecessor? Let X refer to the entity over time that continues x at t_1. I see the following four possibilities.

1. Entity X follows the path of closest continuation. We can state this most easily if we suppose each moment of time has an immediate predecessor. The component stage at t_2 of X is just that entity, if any, which is the closest continuer of x at t_1, and which continues it closely enough to be (identical with) X at t_1. The component at t_{n+1} of X is just that entity, if any, which is the closest continuer of the component at t_n of X, and which continues it closely enough to be (identical with) the component at t_n of X. Entity X is constituted from moment to moment by the closest (and close enough) continuer of the immediately preceding component of X. When there is no closest continuer because of a tie, or because nothing continues it at all or closely enough, then X ends.

2. Entity X follows the path of closest continuation, unless it is a short path. If a t_{n+1} is reached when there is no continuer of the component at t_n of X, then backtracking occurs to the nearest component C of X for which there exists at t_{n+1} something z which continues C closely enough to be (identical with) it. The component at t_{n+1} of X is then z, and X continues from z on the path of closest continuation. At t_{n+1}, there is a "jump" to the segment of the path that z begins.

3. This alternative is like the preceding one, except that between the time of C and t_{n+1}, the components constituting X are some continuation path of C that leads to z, without jumps. (Each succeeding

step from C will be to a continuer, but not all will be to an adjacent *closest* continuer.)

4. Entity X originates with x at t_1 and each later component of X is the closest continuer existing at that time of the original x at t_1. Since everything harks back to x at t_1, there may be considerable hopping, either around or back and forth.[11]

Overlap

With these four possibilities in mind, let us consider the following most difficult case.

Case 8. Half of an ill person's brain is removed and transplanted into another body, but the original body plus half-brain does not expire when this is being done; it lingers on for one hour, or two days, or two weeks. Had this died immediately, the original person would survive in the new body, via the transplanted half-brain which carries with it psychological similarity and continuity. However, in the intervening hour or days or weeks, the old body lives on, perhaps unconscious or perhaps in full consciousness, alongside the newly emplanted body.

Does the person then die along with it (as in option 1 above)? Can its lingering on during the smallest overlapping time interval, when the lingerer is the closest continuer, mean the end of the person, while if there was no such lingerer, no temporal overlap, the person would live on? It seems so unfair for a person to be doomed by an echo of his former self. Or, does the person move to the new body upon the expiration of the old one (as in option 2 above)? But then, who was it in the new body for the hour or two days or two weeks preceding his arrival there, and what happened to that person? Perhaps during that initial time interval, it was a duplicate of the person in that new body (with old half-brain), a duplicate which becomes the person upon the expiration of the old body. It seems strange that at a certain time, without any (physical) change taking place in it, the new body could become the person when the old body expires. However, once we have become used to the idea that whether y at t_2 is (identical with) x at t_1 does not depend only upon the properties and relations of x and y, but depends also upon whether there exists a z of a certain sort (which more closely continues x), then perhaps we can swallow this consequence as well.[12] Still, there is a difficulty. If the old body plus half-brain linger on for long enough, three years say, then surely that is the person, and the person dies when that body expires—the duplicate does not suddenly become the person after three years. A one-minute period of lingering is compatible with the new body-person being the original person, a three-year period is not. But the interval can be varied gradually; it seems absurd that there should be some sharp temporal line which makes the difference to whether or not the person continues to live in the other body. ("Doctor, there's only one minute left! Hurry to end life in the old body so the person can live on in the new one." And out of which body would these words come?)[13]

Or, does the person move to the new body immediately upon the transplantation of the half-brain into it (as in option 3 above)? Are we opportunists who leave a sinking body before it is sunk? And what if, despite predictions, it has not sunk but makes it to port—where are we then? Does whether we move at one time depend upon how things turn out later, so there is identity ex post facto? If the person moves over at the time of the transplant, who is it that dies (in the old body) two days later?

None of these positions seems satisfactory. Even if our intuitions did fit one of them completely, we would have to explain why it was such an important notion. Perhaps we are willing to plunk for one of these options as compared to its close variants when the overlap involves ships, tables, countries, or universities. We do not so arbitrarily want to apply a concept or theory of identity to ourselves; we need to be shown a difference between it and its apparently close variants, deep enough to make the difference between our being there and not.

Let us examine more closely the structure of the problematic overlap situation. In Figure 1.3, the closest successor of A is B, and the closest successor of A + B is D. However, the closest predecessor of D is C, and the closest predecessor of C + D is A. Neither A + B + D nor A + C + D is a mono-related entity. Taking a longer view, though, A and D are mono-related: D is the closest successor of A plus A's closest successor; also A is the closest predecessor of D plus D's closest predecessor.

When B and C are small in comparison, the mono-relation of A and

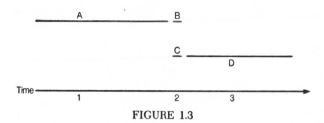

FIGURE 1.3

D would seem to constitute them as part of the same entity. Thereby, is marked off an extensive entity.[14] Are we mono-related entities that need not be temporally continuous? On this view, there could be a person with temporal parts A and D during times 1 and 3, yet that person does not exist during the intervening time 2. Something related does exist then, so this discontinuous person does depend upon some continuities during time 2, but these are not continuities through which he continues to exist then. (A watch repairer takes a watch completely apart and puts it together again; the customer later picks up his watch, the same one he had brought in, though there was an intervening time when it did not exist.)

This view encounters difficulties, however. C might think to himself, "Since it is unjust for someone to be punished for a crime he did not do, D may not be punished for a crime planned and executed during time 2, when D does not exist. No one will be apprehended until time 3, so it is safe for me to commit the crime without fear of punishment." Surely we may punish D for what C does. Is it B or C we punish for the acts of A? Or do we wait until time 3 and punish D? (Yet, if D certainly will escape punishment if we wait, do we punish B or C?) It would appear that D may not be punished for acts of B (unless C does not exist). However, B might assassinate a rival political candidate to bring about the election of D. If this continued a calculated plan put into effect by A, then D may be punished; but suppose B first thinks of this act during time 2, or that A planned it thinking his life would end with B, in order to ensure that the later person D who claimed to be A—falsely on A's view—would be punished for usurping A's identity. It is clear that a morass of difficulties faces the position that one continuing entity includes A and D as parts but not the overlapping segments B and C.

The problem of temporal overlap is not unique to people, we have seen. It arises in the Greek ship case if the original planks are recon-

45

figured into a ship one day before the ship consisting of replacement planks catches fire and burns. Is the reconfigured ship the original ship, or not?

This quandary about temporal overlap is intrinsic, I believe, to any notion of identity applicable to more than atomic-point-instants. Any such notion trades off depth to gain breadth; in order to encompass larger entities, it sacrifices some similarity among what it groups together. Maximum similarity within the groupings would limit them to atomic-point-instants. The purpose of the identity notion is wider breadth, but a grouping that included everything would not convey specific information. The closest continuer theory is the best Parmenides can do in an almost Heraclitean world.

The notion of identity itself compromises between breadth and (exact) similarity (which similarity can include being part of the same causal process). Since spatial and temporal distances involve some dissimilarity, any temporal or spatial breadth involves some sacrifice of (exact) similarity. For our cases, width and breadth are measured along spatiotemporal dimensions, closeness or similarity along other dimensions. The informativeness of a classification varies positively with the extent of its subclasses, and with the degree of similarity exhibited within each subclass; similar norms apply to the clumping of entities from the flux.[15]

Usually, the closest continuer schema—or more generally (when the temporal relation is not the most salient), the closest relation schema—serves to achieve the right measure of breadth. It extends entities X to the maximum feasible extent: further extended, something would be included that is not close enough to link with X rather than something else, or X would no longer be sharp enough to be an informative category. When there is temporal overlap, however, the immediate closest continuer view, holding that A's existence continues through B and then stops, does not give the maximum feasible extension. Yet the wider view of the entity as continuing on from A to D brings the difficulties of the overlapping segments.

For the structure of overlap in Figure 1.3, the norm of breadth would place A and D together, as would the norm of similarity. The similarity relation also would place together A and B, and C and D. Yet the disconnected spatial positions, along with the different activities occurring there simultaneously, fall under the dissimilarity relation; this relation, which places things separately in classification, separates B and C. There is no way to bring A and D, A and B, and C and D together into one entity or subclassification, while keeping B and C separate. Still, how can an entity's continuation (from A to C + D) be blocked by the merest continuing tentacle or echo (B) of its previous stage?

The quandary over the overlap situation, I have said, is intrinsic to the notion of identity over time, and stems from its uneasy compromise between the outward and the inward urges. Overlap falls at precisely the point of tension between two different modes of structuring a concept: the closest relation mode and the global mode. We are familiar with the closest continuer or closest relation mode. The global mode looks further. It holds that Y is (a later stage of the same entity as) X if Y is the closest continuer of X, and if there is no even longer extending thing Z that more closely continues X than any equally large thing of which Y is part. Since these distinct structures, local and global, are not peculiar to the one concept of identity, let us pause to notice how various philosophical concepts can each be structured in different modes.

Thereby, we will see the overlap quandary not as peculiar to the closest continuer theory but as a symptom of a wider and inescapable intellectual torque. When a writer treats an apparent refutation of his theory as a genuine antinomy, we are entitled to be very suspicious. Nevertheless, when I contemplate my entering a situation of temporal overlap, my notion of self begins to dissolve. Is temporal overlap a koan for philosophers?

Structuring Philosophical Concepts

The closest continuer theory illustrates one stage of a progression for structuring philosophical concepts. In listing the first three of the five stages, the concept of personal identity will provide a convenient example.

    I. *Intrinsic Abstract Structural.* A concept C's holding at a time is analyzed in terms of an abstract structural description involving only monadic predicates holding at that time. The personal identity of something is an intrinsic feature of

47

it, most usefully discussed without considering any entities other than it or any of its features at any other time. (For example, the identity resides in the soul.)

II. *Relational.* X falls under concept C if X stands in a certain relationship R to another, sometimes earlier, thing of a specified sort. For example, X is the same thing as the earlier Y if X is spatiotemporally continuous, or psychologically continuous, with Y.

III. *Closest Relative.* To the relational view is added the condition that nothing else is as closely related under R to that other (previous) thing. The closest continuer theory of personal identity is of this sort.

Let me illustrate these first three modes of structuring with some other concepts. (The first was personal identity.)

2. *Reference.* What a term refers to, one intrinsic theory holds, is determined (solely) by features of, or associated with, the term. One relational theory holds that the reference of a particular use of a term depends upon what earlier thing stands in a causal relation to that use. The closest relative version adds that if that earlier thing is to be referred to by the use of the term, then no other contemporaneous thing also stands in as close a causal relationship (of the same type) to that use.

3. *Justice.* An intrinsic theory holds that the justice of a distribution is determined by intrinsic features of the distribution, by how closely its (current) profile exemplifies some ideal pattern. One relational theory holds that a distribution is just, whatever its pattern, if it grows out of an earlier (just) distribution in specified ways. (In *Anarchy, State, and Utopia* I termed such theories historical; the entitlement theory presented there is of this form.) One closest relative version of this theory adds that the current distribution also must not be as closely related (under the specified historical relation) to previous unjust distributions.[16]

4. *Attribution of Action.* Whether an action is your doing or not is an intrinsic feature of the action; or, an action is a person's own if it stands in a certain specified relationship to his intentions and motives; or, an action is a person's own if it stands in that relationship to his own motives and intentions, and does not stand in as close a relationship to someone else's motives and intentions.

Writers on coercion have puzzled over why it is important whether another person intentionally directs your behavior in a certain direction. What is the difference, they wonder, between being kept inside a house by a lightning storm or by another person's playing with electricity outside your house, or by another person's threat to electrocute you if you leave the house. When the probabilities of electric shock are equal in the three situations, isn't one equally coerced in all three? Whether an act is yours, though, depends upon whose will is operating. In the lightning situation, your will keeps you indoors —no other's motives and intentions are as closely connected to your act. Whereas in the threat situation, it is another person's will that is operative. In the intermediate situation where another person acts but without intending to influence you to do act A, it is your intentions that are operating in your doing A. Those writers who focus only upon what your incentives and intentions are, denying it can make a difference whether and how another person's intentions are operative in the situation, presuppose either an intrinsic or relational view of coercion, not the closest relative view.

5. *Knowledge.* An intrinsic view holds that whether a state is a state of knowledge depends upon features internal to that current state; knowledge is being in a cognitive state. A relational view holds that whether something, usually a belief, is knowledge depends upon its relationship to something else: to evidence, or (in the case of our theory in Chapter 3 below) to the truth. A closest relative version of this last theory, as we shall see, holds that a person knows, via method M, that p, if his belief, via M, that p tracks the fact that p, and if there is no other method M' outweighing M but not tracking the truth, via which also he believes that p.

6. *Projectability.* Whether or not a predicate is projectable is an intrinsic syntactic or semantic feature of the predicate; or, a predicate is projectable if it (fits the evidence and is) entrenched by successful past projections; or a predicate is projectable if it is entrenched and there is no other contrary and equally well entrenched predicate that fits the evidence.

7. *Confirmation.* Whether or not evidence E confirms a hypothesis H is an intrinsic feature of the pair E, H. (This is the view popular lore attributes to Carnap in *Logical Foundations of Probability*, even though there, as some objected, confirmation also depends on what other predicates are in the language.) A relational view described in

49

Chapter 3 holds that E confirms H if H stands in a certain specified subjunctive relationship to E; while its closest-relative version adds that not-H does not also stand in that same subjunctive relationship to E.

8. *Acceptability of Theory.* Whether or not a theory is acceptable is an intrinsic feature of the theory; or, a theory is acceptable if it has certain desirable intrinsic features and it fits the evidence; or a theory is acceptable if it has certain intrinsic features and fits the evidence better than any contrary theory.

I do not claim that for any concept, a theory of higher type always is truer or more likely to be true than one of lower type; that one of type II is more likely to be true than one of type I, one of type III than one of type II. Nor does this typology[17] fit or illuminate every interesting difference of theory. One further example should be mentioned which, though somewhat different from the rest, suggested to me the fourth mode of conceptual structuring.

9. *Rightness of Action.* Some views have held that the rightness of actions is intrinsic. W. D. Ross held it to be relational; an act is right when its right-making characteristics outweigh its wrong-making ones. In Chapter 5 below, I present a closest relative version of Ross's relational view: an act A is right if its right-making characteristics outweigh its wrong-making characteristics, and there is no alternative action B available, less weighty in wrong-making characteristics, such that the extra wrongness of A over B outweighs the extra rightness of A over B. Such an alternative action would undercut A. A further condition, a global condition, then is formulated: an act A can be right, even when its wrong-making characteristics outweigh its right-making ones, if it is (a necessary) part of a larger course of action D whose right-making characteristics outweigh its wrong-making ones, provided this act D itself is not undercut by some other course of action that does not include A.[18]

For some topics, a global condition and structure is a natural successor to the closest relative one. It widens horizons, holding that something satisfies concept C only if it stands closest in R to a specified y, and also is a (necessary) part of any wider thing that stands closer in R to y than do other comparably wide things. Thus, one might hold that an acceptable theory not only must fit the evidence as well as any alternative theory of the same phenomena, but also must be part of any wider theory of more inclusive phenomena that fits the evidence more closely than any other theory alternative to it. The quandary with temporal overlap stems from the tension between closest relative and global structures. The expansive purpose of an identity notion—otherwise, atomic-point-instants would be good enough—pushes toward the global view; but even more than with other notions, its being an identity notion restrains the outward move. Indeed, this inward feature of identity has led others to presume a relational view must be true, and so to ignore the possibility of even a closest relative view, though that fits their judgments better.

The global view, seen more accurately, is a form of a closest continuer view, not an alternative to it; the global view also explicitly excludes there being other equally close alternatives to what it selects. The local closest continuer structure and the global one each exhibit the same closest continuer structure but differ in the span or extent covered. The problem of temporal overlap concerns which form of closest continuer theory to adopt, local or global.

The typology of structuring presents a progression of modes of increasing logical power and complexity: from a monadic predicate to a relation to an existentially quantified relation statement to one that requires quantification over wider entities (perhaps even sets, when the full details are given) to one (as we shall see below) that quantifies over relations themselves. Yet the correct view on each topic need not be of highest type.[19] While it is not worthwhile to dispute over which mode a particular philosophical view exemplifies, or to devote much energy to pigeonholing views, nevertheless, I do find the grouping in the accompanying table illuminating.

When we presented the closest continuer theory of personal identity, we did not specify a particular relation R; we spoke, at times, of the closest continuer *schema*. This generality of approach masked the fact that the relation itself might shift. The fifth mode of structuring focuses upon this. (The fourth was the *global* mode.)

V. *Closest Instantiated Relation R'*. Previously, the conditions for application of the concept C were that X stand in some specified relationship R to *a*—the relational condition; that there was no contemporary as close to *a* as x is (or as close to x as *a* is)—the closest relative condition; that no wider thing without x is as close (under R) to *a* as what includes x—the

	Identity	Reference	Justice	Attribution of Action	Knowledge
Intrinsic Abstract Structural Description	Soul	What best satisfies cluster of predicates	Pattern conceptions	Action itself bears stamp of doer	Intrinsically specified cognitive state
Relational	Continuity theory	Causal theory	Historical theory, entitlement theory	Actions yours if stands in certain relation to your intentions	Belief that p tracks truth that p
Closest Relative R	Closest continuer theory	Causal theory + no other entity as closely related to use of term	Arises from previous just distribution and not equally closely from an unjust one	Action yours if stands in certain relation to your intentions and not as closely to someone else's intentions	Belief that p via M tracks truth that p and there is no M' outweighing M, via which one believes p, that does not track the truth that p
Global			Wider distribution of which it is a part also is closest relative under R to earlier just distribution	Action yours if closest to your intentions; wider pattern of action of which it is part does not stand more closely to someone else's intentions than to yours	

	Projectability	e Confirms h	Acceptability of Theory	Meaning of Sentence	Rightness of Action A
Intrinsic Abstract Structural Description	Depends on intrinsic syntactic or semantic features of predicate	Depends on syntactic and semantic properties of e and h		Structure of senses (Frege)	Intrinsic feature of A
Relational	Predicate projectable if it is entrenched	e stands in specified subjunctive relation R to h	fits the evidence	Connection to stimuli and behavior (Skinner)	Rightness of A outweighs wrongness of A
Closest Relative Under R	Predicate entrenched and no other predicate, which fits the evidence, is as well entrenched	e stands in R to h, but not to not-h	fits the evidence and no other contrary theory fits the evidence as well	Connection to stimuli and behavior and not more closely connected to other stimuli and behavior	Rightness of A outweighs wrongness of A and there is no B, less wrong than A, where extra wrongness of A over B outweighs extra rightness of A over B
Global	Predicate entrenched and better so than any other predicate that fits the evidence, and part of family of predicates which is better entrenched than any other family of predicates that fits the wider evidence	e stands in R to h, but not to not-h, and there is no wider h', which excludes h, to which e stands in R		(Quine)	Rightness outweighs wrongness or part of larger course of action, not undercut, whose rightness outweighs its wrongness

global condition. The fifth mode of structuring adds that there is no other instantiated relation R' which comes closer to the concept C than R does, no other which is as good as or better than R as a realization of C.

How are we to understand closeness to C among relations? Certain features are associated with C, and R' realizes these features more fully (it realizes more of them, or the same ones to a greater extent) than R does. Perhaps, according to the relation R itself, there are better and worse cases of C, in virtue of differences along some dimensions D. Further along or at the limit of these dimensions, at the better end, we leave the realm of the relation R and enter R'. Something that stands to something else in the relation R' scores better and more fully on the dimensions D than do things in the field of R. In this way, the discriminations R itself makes distinguish R' as an even better realizer of the concept C. Alternatively, there might be metaconditions for C which R' satisfies better than R does. Other theorists might say that R' more closely resembles the Platonic Form of C than R does.

The relation R' competes with R only if R' is instantiated. (Is *one* instantiation enough or must it be regularly instantiated?) Over time, new relations come to be instantiated; if these do better as C they can displace the old relation R which was the previous (best) bearer of C. Consider the example of knowledge. The more closely a belief varies with the truth of what is believed, the better it is as knowledge. The concept delineated in Chapter 3 below marks it as varying subjunctively; but we can imagine beings whose beliefs vary with the truth of what is believed over a far wider range of situations, a wider range of possible worlds than merely those close worlds necessary to establish the requisite subjunctives. At the extreme is a being whose belief varies with the truth of what he believes in all possible worlds. What we have when our beliefs vary subjunctively with the truth *is* knowledge, but if there were beings whose beliefs varied more closely and extensively with the truth of what they believed, beings whose beliefs did more than track, in that case our beliefs which are knowledge would not be knowledge. For our beliefs then would not stand in the best instantiated relationship R' for knowledge. The superior relation R' would displace contemporaneous instances of R as instances of C, but how would it affect previous instances of R, in their time the best instantiated cases? Would future human beings with developed powers of telepathy say that we know (now) what another person is thinking or feeling? Can what was once knowledge no longer be so retrospectively—is a sixth mode of structuring concepts needed to incorporate Hegelian laws of motion of conceptual society?

On the closest instantiated relation view, something can be knowledge in this actual world while in another possible world the very same thing would not be knowledge because it doesn't measure up to the superior form of knowledge existing in that world. What knowledge is in the actual world does not fix it in all possible worlds. Some philosophical worries about things being C in virtue of standing in the relation R, may stem from the ease of imagining an R' which would displace R as the bearer of C.

The best instantiated relation view of whether a relation constitutes concept C, the reader will have noticed, parallels the closest continuer theory of identity over time. According to that theory, whether Y is the same as X or not depends on whether there is an even better candidate around, on whether there exists a Z even closer to X than Y is. Similarly, whether R is the relation embodied in C depends on whether there is an even better candidate, on whether there exists (that is, is instantiated) another relation R' that is even closer to C than R is. The type of consideration introduced by the closest relation structure is repeated by the best instantiated relation mode, one level up.

Some years ago, Arthur Eddington and L. Susan Stebbing engaged in controversy over whether tables composed of darting particles with mostly empty space in between were solid.[20] Though tables are a paradigm example of solid things, just the sort of things via which we learn the term "solid", this does not show that tables are solid. For perhaps we (and our teachers) had the belief that those objects contained no internal spaces anywhere, and it was in virtue of this belief that we applied the term solid. Even so, solidity is not divorced from macro-properties such as resisting other objects. Moreover, tables are further along the relevant dimensions of solidity than are other things: liquids and gases. Unlike the counterexamples of their critics ("she is a paradigm case of a witch"), the proponents of paradigm cases (of solidity, free action, rational inference) did produce examples which were further along the relevant dimensions than were some other actual contrasting cases; and no other actual cases were further yet along those dimensions. Still, it is not surprising that most hesitated to accept any of these instances of the so-called paradigm case argument, for it was very easy to see that the cases produced as paradigms did not fall at the extreme end of the relevant dimensions: no spaces, nothing at all getting you to do it, no steps that could not be justified. Even if the cases described are actually cases of C, are cases of C in the actual world, there are other possible worlds where they are not because other things realize C better there. It is not my purpose to decide here, for any particular concept C, whether the best instantiated realizations are good enough to be C, given their distance from the ends of the relevant dimensions. The general point holds: the best actual case is C if it is C enough and it beats out the other actual competition. Still, that it is the best C around may be faint praise indeed.

This suggests yet another way a concept C can embody a relation or property: as an ideal limit. The best instantiated relation view sees C as constituted by that instantiated relation which best realizes it. The ideal limit view removes the requirement that the relation actually be instantiated. The relevant relation R' is the limit of the relations, instantiated or not, which (do or would) better and better realize the concept C. If anything else can be imagined to be a better realization of C then, under this mode of structuring, nothing actual exhibits C. Perhaps Stebbing and Eddington should be understood to disagree over modes of structuring the concept of solidity: a best instantiated relation mode and an ideal limit one. Under this latter mode of structuring, subjunctive variation of a belief with the fact would not count as constituting knowledge, even if nothing actually bests it, since a wider variation of belief with fact is conceivable. Isn't it possible, though, to *overshoot* the concept C; cannot continuing to the limit on the path of better realizations get one to the other side of the concept, so that after a while, although going in the same direction, the realizations start to get worse?

Consider a notion of identity through time which specifies not only that there *is* no other closer continuer (or predecessor) but also that there couldn't be one. There could not be anything else (at the relevant time) that more closely continued x than y does, or that more closely preceded y than x does. Those who hold identity cannot be contingent upon what other entities actually exist, opposing the closest continuer theory, might have this notion in mind instead. It falls under the closest instantiated relation mode, if some things exhibit it, while if none do then under the ideal limit mode.

One further way a relation R' might come to replace another is by being part of a more informative and fruitful classification than the other is. How informative a particular classification is depends upon what exists to be classified. Tversky reports that the addition or deletion of some objects can alter how other objects are classified. This is surprising until we realize that "clusters are typically selected so as to maximize the similarity of objects within a cluster, and the dissimilarity of objects from different clusters."[21] Whether we classify a natural face with frowning or with smiling ones may depend upon the preponderant numbers of each; these numbers will fix the dichotomy as smiling–nonsmiling or as frowning–nonfrowning. To Tversky's illuminating discussion, we can add some remarks about change of concepts over time. As there is change in the cases to be classified, some other classification may score better on a measure of informativeness. Still, we would expect some inertia in changing concepts; we will not change concepts every time a switch in the numbers of the objects we face makes a new classification superior in distinguishing power. Yet when we move deep into the inertial realm, the old concepts will show more strain until there is a discontinuous shift in classification. Tversky's discussion also provides a historical theory of concept formation. Two otherwise identical people who are now classifying the same objects may classify them differently if, even though previously presented with the same *types* of objects to classify, they had been given them in different relative proportions.

We should not expect the motion of philosophical concepts to halt. A new relation R' cast forth by the fifth mode of structuring may itself be a timeless abstract structural pattern of mode I or provide a relation of mode II, and so present a new basis for moving along the modes. Nor is there a way to arrive at a final philosophy by looking ahead to discern the limit of this process. For we have seen various ways the relevance of a relation depends upon what the world actually is and will be like; it depends upon what relations are instantiated more than rarely, upon the relative proportions of things, and so forth. In this sense, all philosophy is like philosophy of language or of art, in being philosophy *of* something; namely, the philosophy of this and similar worlds.

The concept of philosophy itself can be structured along the different modes—by an abstract structural description in terms of questions or problems and methods of approach, by a historical closest continuer view that starts with the Greeks and sees each stage as a continuer of an earlier stage, by a global structuring that does not require the earlier stage necessarily to be the immediately preceding stage. We can even imagine a different activity being introduced, discontinuous with previous ones, which better gave us what we wanted from philosophy (Wittgenstein thought this true of his later writings); on a best-instantiated relation view, would that be (or become) philosophy?

I do not mean to exclude the metaphilosophical reflections here from their own purview. We have given an abstract structural description of five possible philosophical structures. This classification itself would appear to be a view of mode I. However, since we also have described how philosophical structures are linked to general facts about their world, the metaphilosophical view presented here is a relational one, of mode II. I assume this view too can be pushed to the other levels, closest relative and global, and also that if the linkage relation R were formulated precisely, then the world (including our theories) might push us to a new and better (meta)philosophical relation R'.

Problem Cases

Temporal overlap presents an issue within a closest continuer view: should it be a local closest continuer view or a global one? Overlap exacerbates the tension between these two modes of structuring a concept, each with its own attractions and force, but the issue raises no special objection to a closest relation or closest continuer analysis.*

---

* In the two film versions of *Invasion of the Body Snatchers*, pods are grown into new bodies which exactly duplicate the bodies of already existing people. The psychology of the new body resembles that of the old body it matches, except it lacks all emotion and affect. In a synchronized replacement, this body replaces the old one (which shrivels and is disposed of) in its social setting, aiding in the plan of replacing other bodies by the pod-produced ones. The characters in the film flee this fate and struggle against it. They do not see the situation as one in which they are murdered and die, and

How shall we view this issue over the appropriate mode of structuring? We might view ourselves possibly as applying different conceptual structurings to external objects, tables or ships or stars, or even to other people. Can we view our own identity through time as open to determination by this type of conceptual structuring, though; could we view it even as a matter of choice how our own identity is configured, whether locally or globally?

---

someone else replaces them. Rather they see it, and so does the audience, as one where *they* are altered for the worse—made zombielike or perhaps taken over while still being them—by alien affectless beings.

When years ago I saw the first version of the film, I thought the plot was incoherent, presenting (what everyone responded to as) alterations or takeovers by a mechanism—the pods—that really could produce only murders and substitution. By the time I saw the second film version (1978), I fortunately was armed with the closest continuer theory, and so could understand and explain the responses of the characters and the audience. A pod nonaccidentally duplicates someone's body close-by, and its psychology is explained by and duplicates the one already existing except for the difference in affect. Since the old body shrivels (with the mechanism of replacement apparently allowing no overlapping time when both bodies are functioning—the second film makes this especially clear), becoming inert and without a psychology, the new body and (altered) psychology is the closest continuer at that time of the old person. It continues the person, nothing else continues the person as closely, and it continues the person closely enough to be the person; it is the person. Although the change in psychology is great enough and distressing enough to make the characters struggle and even risk their lives to avoid it, the resulting person is a close enough continuer of them to be them. Pod products tell their old friends, the old friends of the body-persons they continue, that it is better to be the new way, it is an improvement to lose the capacity for disturbing emotions. This claim is vehemently contested by their audience, within the film and within the theater, who, it should be noted, do not reply that it cannot be better because the earlier person is murdered and replaced.

If, however, the plot were different, the audience response also would differ. If the pods came to life while the person they were patterned after continued to live, and those persons were pursued by the pod people who tried to kill them and take over their social roles, with significant time of overlap, then it definitely would be not a story of alteration or takeover, but one of replacement by a duplicate. It might be horrible to be killed and replaced by someone so like yourself, but the struggle would not be to prevent your own zombielike existence later.

The closest continuer theory is able to account for and explain the character's response in the film, and the audience's response to it, and also the response both would have if the film were altered as imagined, so that the pod person no longer was the closest continuer. Since it is difficult to see how any other theory could do this, this supports the closest continuer theory.

It is a remarkable fact that for many of the cases or examples about personal identity, we can say with reasonable confidence which if any of the resultant beings is us. We can say this without being told of the movement of a soul-pellet or any similar item. How are we able to say which will be us? Are we so familiar with the laws of motion of soul-pellets that we know where they will go? Or do we, as the soul-pellet, decide where to go; in saying which would be us, are we stating where we would choose to move? Might the soul-pellet change its decision; or end up in the wrong place by accident, because it was not paying sufficient attention? Surely, none of these possibilities holds.

We answer the question about which person, if any, we would be, by applying a general schema of identity, the closest continuer schema, to our own case. That general schema is called forth by general features of the world which press us to classify and identify, even in the face of complexities and flux.

We need to predict how something will behave or affect us, provided the world shows some patterns in that not every two properties are equally correlated. When no unchanging atoms are known to us, the closest continuer schema will serve best. This schema leaves room for specifying closeness by selecting and weighting dimensions, and so leaves room to learn from experience. Any organism whose learned appropriate responses were restricted to things exactly identical to something it already had encountered would not fare well. Sometimes, it will be useful merely to classify types of things, a job done by generalization gradients. Sometimes there will be a point to reidentifying the very same individual, distinguishing it even from others of its type; here, the closest continuer schema comes into its own. There would be no point to reidentifying some particular thing if things never behaved similarly over time, and never behaved differently from others of their kind.[22]

One philosophical approach to a tangled area of complicated relationships of varying degree, rather than trying to force these into somewhat arbitrary pigeonholes, rests content with recognizing and delineating the underlying complicated relations. Concerning personal identity, it might say that future selves will have varying degrees of closeness to us-now in virtue of diverse underlying relations and events, such as bodily continuity, psychological similarity, splitting or fusion; and that the real and whole truth to be told is of the existence and contours of these underlying phenomena.[23] Why impose any categorization—the closest continuer schema being one— over this complexity?

The underlying level itself, however, also will raise similar problems. For example, in what way is something the same body when all its cells other than neurons, as well as the particular molecules composing the neurons, are replaced over time? Should we speak again only of the complicated relations that underlie *this* level? We cannot avoid the closest continuer schema, or some other categorization, by restricting ourselves to the full complexity of the underlying relations; in the absence of changeless enduring atoms, any underlying level will present the same type of difficulties. Eventually we are pushed to a closest continuer schema or something similar at some level or other. (Even if we are able to reach unchanging particles, our subatomic theory may hold it makes no sense to reidentify particular ones of them.) The alternative to a closest continuer schema is Heraclitean flux, down through all levels. If it becomes legitimate, because necessary, to use the schema at some level, then why not simply begin with it?

Still, it is not satisfactory to say merely that we apply the same identity schema used to organize other flux to the flux underlying ourselves. About ourselves, the schema has limited predictive usefulness. True, contexts can be imagined where it has some use: am I that previous person; should I keep his promises and worry about his tendency to overeat or to behave erratically? But most of the purpose of reidentifying some particular thing, to orient our behavior toward it, is lacking when that thing is ourself. There might remain the sort of choices Bernard Williams described: in choosing which future being will suffer, we want to know which one will be us. Here, though, I do not use the schema to identify something as an aid to my goals; I use it to identify whose goals are mine.

Anyway, something appears cockeyed about the view that we apply the closest continuer schema to ourselves. We can bring out the strangeness of this view by asking: who is it that applies the schema to itself? We who use the schema to organize the external flux seem already to be unfluxed. Does the I who applies the closest continuer schema exist apart from application of the schema? Or is it a schematized I? Then who or what applied the schema in order to delineate the I? Apparently, only when there already is an I can the schema come into play; when the identity of the self is at issue, the schema does not appear able to get a grip. We shall reconsider these issues in the second part of this chapter. Notice, for now, that these issues apply only to a view of the closest continuer schema as arising from and embodied in conceptualizing and categorizing activity, not to a view of it as an independent metaphysical truth.

Ties and Caring

Our theory of identity is one of the closest continuer, rather than of the continuer than which none other is closer. This aspect of having decisively to surpass the competition is tested most severely in the case of an exact tie: Y at t_2 and Z at t_2 continue X at t_1 equally closely, closely enough so that either, in the absence of the other, would be (part of the same continuing entity as) X at t_1. There are the following possibilities.

(1) Neither is the continuation of X at t_1. Since there is no closest continuer, X's existence ends.

But if you imagine yourself as X at t_1, looking ahead, it certainly will not seem as if death is awaiting you. If you do not continue to exist, still they do, each of them who would be you if it alone existed; and they might, without getting in each other's way, fulfill different parts of your incompatible aspirations. (Might this seem even a pleasant prospect?)

(2) Both are the same entity as X at t_1, both are you.

Since they so clearly are not the same as each other, as their future divergence shows, there will be problems apart from the breakdown of the transitivity of identity. If one of them is killed, has anyone been killed who is not still alive? If one kills the other, has anyone been killed? And so forth.

(3) There are two different people later; but unnoticed, there always were two different people there, though this became evident only after the appearance of the tied continuers.[24]

(4) One of Y and Z, and only one, is the continuation of the individual of which X at t_1 was a part. There is no further fact in virtue of which it is, just the luck of the draw.

This does not seem possible, however, provided no other asymmetry is smuggled in, unless it is a way of asserting there is some other feature that cannot be duplicated or doubly exhibited, in virtue of which someone is you. But what is that further feature? A soul? A spiritual pellet? Do we know that *such* things cannot split into two tied, equally close continuers?

I find the first of these positions most plausible. I am neither Y nor Z, and I no longer exist. This is not so very distressing in this case, for what I care about is that there remains something that continues me closely enough to be me if it were my sole continuer; and if there are two such, I care especially about the fate of the closest continuer. This requires some explaining.

Let cl(x,y) be a measure of the degree of closeness of y to an earlier stage x. This measure (within a metric space of weighted dimensions) depends only on the features of x and y and the relations between them; unlike identity through time, it does not depend on whether any other thing z exists. Degree of closeness does satisfy the two principles we listed at the beginning of the chapter, the ones Williams implicitly assumed held true for identity.

Let care(x,y) be a measure of the degree of care that x has for (the fate and circumstances of) the later stage y.[25] It might seem plausible that care(x,y) is proportional to cl(x,y), that you care about a future stage directly in proportion to its degree of closeness to you. I do not think this is correct uniformly.

True, I care equally about the tied continuers. But where there is a closest continuer, I care especially about it in a way that is not captured merely by—in proportion to—its extra degree of closeness. Recall cases 1 and 3 that we examined earlier when applying the closest continuer theory: within each a comparable duplicate is made, equal in closeness, but the mere duplicate of case 1 is the closest continuer of case 3. Looking ahead in the case 1 situation, I care somewhat for the duplicate, but not as much as I care about the continuing me; while looking ahead in the case 3 situation, I care as much about the fate of the person in the duplicated body who is (or will be) me as I do about my own future fate in any situation, including the situation of case 1. So degree of care is not directly proportional to degree of closeness.[26]

Let c(x,z) be the amount of care that x has for z when z is x's closest continuer, the care which is especially for the closest continuer qua closest continuer. When z is not x's closest continuer, then c(x,z) = 0.

We might think that this special care for one's closest continuer simply gets added on to an existing care proportional to the degree of closeness, so that

care(x,y) = cl(x,y) + c(x,y).

(I suppress here and below a factor of proportionality multiplied by cl(x,y) which transforms it into a measure of proportional caring.) However, this is incorrect. In different situations, we care equally about our closest continuer, whatever its degree of closeness. (See step 3 in note 26.)

The degree of care for our closest continuer, c(x,y), is equal across situations for each closest continuer equidistant in time (though perhaps we care more for ones closer in time than for more temporally distant ones); and it is greater than any degree of caring for a (temporally equidistant) continuer that is not closest.

We can summarize our preceding discussion as follows. We care equally about our closest continuers, whatever their degree of closeness, and about nonclosest ones we care proportionally to their degree of closeness.

Care(x,y) = Max[c(x,y), cl(x,y)].

Notice that this formula embodies mathematical discontinuity. Varying closeness slightly can produce a large change in care by altering which is the closest continuer or by creating or breaking a tie.*

We care especially about our closest continuer, when it exists, but do we care especially that there *be* a closest continuer; when there are multiple continuers which singly would be close enough to be us, do we care especially that there not be a tie for closest? I think we do not, or at any rate, I do not. (I feel very unsure of this, though.) Provided they do not get in each other's way (who will live in the house?)—they need not go separate and noninteracting ways—I think I would not especially want to avoid ties. I would not now pay a lot of money to eliminate all but one of the future continuers,

---

* It may be that the formula needs altering for cases where there are more than two (singly) close enough continuers. Perhaps then the closest is cared for in accordance with c(x,y), while the others share out a fixed amount of care in accordance with the ratios of their degrees of closeness. If an enormous number of (singly) close enough continuers is created, will c(x,y) be an upper limit to the sum of the carings for all the nonclosest continuers?

thereby to avoid ties. I do care especially that there be a continuer that continues me closely enough to be me when it is my single continuation, but, given this, I do not care that there be a closest continuer.

It may appear incoherent to care especially about the closest continuer qua closest continuer, but not care especially that there be a continuer that is closest. Focusing on the gap between the closest continuer and the next closest, it is as if I care a lot about this gap when it exists, but do not care at all whether there is this gap. If the gap is important enough to care about when it exists, how can its existing not be important?

A similar pattern is shown, however, by our attitudes toward infanticide and nonconception. Is infanticide bad or wrong for the reason that the infant's existing is better than its not existing, and infanticide yields the latter? Yet consider the choice of whether or not to fertilize an egg cell, the choice between uncontraceptived sexual relations during a time of ovulation, and abstention from that. Abstention too yields the nonexistence of an infant, yet abstention (unlike infanticide) is not wrong or worse. The infant, once it exists, has a certain moral status and exerts certain moral claims, yet we are not similarly required to bring something with this status into existence. The infant is something which when it exists has a special importance, yet it is not especially important that it exist (be brought into existence). Thus, the structure of our carings about the gap, caring especially when it exists but not caring especially that it exist, is not an incoherent or absurd structure. Yet although we reasonably find this structure elsewhere, which shows that it is not incoherent as a structure, there is a puzzle why it is exhibited here with personal identity.

There are three levels of question about our carings about our future selves. (1) Why do we care especially about our closest continuer, and not merely in proportion to its degree of closeness? (2) Why do we care especially about continuers, and not equally about qualitatively similar entities that are not causally continuers? (3) Why do we care about those particular properties and dimensions that constitute the metric of closeness, and not equally about some other properties and dimensions?

This first question is the appropriate version within our theory of the question of what matters in identity over time, discussed by Parfit, Lewis, and Perry. For us to understand why identity matters, we must understand why the closest continuer, when it exists, gets special caring. They note that we cannot answer any such question by saying "I care about that because it is I", "I care especially about my future closest continuer because that is what I will be." For then the question becomes "why, given that my identity through time consists in closest continuity, do I especially care about myself in the future; why do I especially care about my future self if it is simply (merely?) my current self's closest continuer?" And that question is just the one about why we especially care, not merely in proportion to its degree of closeness, about our closest continuer.

We care about continuation rather than merely that some qualitatively similar entity will exist. Will the reason why, which the second question asks for, make it evident why we care especially about the closest continuer? A later continuer, unlike a mere qualitative resembler, has its aspects connected, causally or subjunctively or however, to the characteristics of the earlier self; it would not be like it is (through that route) if the earlier self had not been its way. Part of the profile of the later self may stand to the characteristics of the earlier self in the very same relation a belief stands in to the fact when it constitutes knowledge. It is as if your later self knows you now, and so (except in special cases) views you as its closest predecessor. Connecting with that later continuer is a way of not sinking into oblivion. Why it is important to your current self to connect tightly with something outside it, to transcend its limits, we shall consider in Chapter 6. Yet, although these considerations may show why continuation matters to us, even why a close enough continuation matters, they do not show or explain why we care especially about our closest continuer.

Recall the special contours required for an explanation of why we especially care about our closest continuer. It must explain why we do so care when a closest continuer exists, yet not be so powerful, I have said, as to have the consequence that we care that a closest one exists, even when tied close-enough ones do. It is difficult to see how anything could do that explanatory job. Even the answer already dismissed as unhelpful, "I care about my closest continuer because that is who I will be," addresses only half the task, at best. If the closest continuer is what will be you, then why don't you especially care that there be one? Don't you care that you continue to be?

I suggest we reconsider our quick rejection of "I care because it will be *me*." Perhaps we care about identity, about our continued identity over time; we each care especially about the future person who is ourselves. The closest continuer relation is the best instantiated realization of the relation of identity (recall the fifth mode of structuring a philosophical concept), and we care about it as identity. We care about our closest continuer because we care about our continued identity, and that is what our continued identity comes to.

One might now ask: if the closest continuer relation is the best instantiated realization of identity over time, then why care especially about identity? Let us distinguish two ways caring about something might function. The first we might call the Platonic mode: you care about C and this care spills over (or you transfer it) to C's best instantiated realization. The second mode looks first at C's best instantiated realization in order to decide how much to care about C, how much C is worth caring about.

With the first mode, we see the world in its aspect of realizing what is beyond it, we see and can respond to glimmerings of something finer which shine through; but correspondingly there is an unrealistic overestimate of actuality, a seeing it through Platonic glasses. The second mode gives a more realistic assessment of things, seeing them as they are in themselves apart from whatever they might best (and closely enough) realize; but this mode makes one a prisoner or a victim of the actual world, limited by the ways it falls short, by how it happens to be or must be. The first mode sees the world from the top down, the second from the bottom up.

It is not my purpose to persuade those with the second view to adopt the first. No doubt many of us alternate in the modes, depending on the topic or time. If our caring about identity takes the form of caring about its best realization in our case (it is our own identity we care about), then we will care especially about our closest continuer when there is one, for that then will stand in the best realized relation of continuing us; while also when there is a tie among continuers close enough to be us singly, we will care especially about these, disproportionate to their closeness, since they then best realize our continued identity. If I care equally for the best realization of my continued identity, without regard to exactly how good a realization it is, then I will care especially for my existing closest continuer but I will not care especially that there be one. Just as on the simpler closest continuer view I will care equally about my closest continuer, whatever its degree of closeness happens to be (provided it is close enough), so also on the best realization view we are now presenting, I care equally about whatever future self is most close to me under that relation (which holds) which is the best realization (and a good enough one) of identity, whatever that relation's degree of realization of identity. Find the relation to some future self which best realizes identity, and I care equally about that future self to degree c(x,y), no matter which of those realizing relations it is. Thus, the substitution of the more complex best instantiated relation view for the closest continuer view, the substitution of the fifth mode of structuring for the third, explains why, given that we care about our identity, we care especially about our closest continuer when it exists, yet do not care especially that we have a closest continuer, provided we have close enough continuers.

How is the tie case to be described on this view? I do not view a tie as like death; I am no longer there, yet it is a good enough realization of identity to capture my care which attaches to identity. (So apparently we can have a good enough realization of a concept without that concept strictly applying.)

If however, we care somewhat about how good a realization of identity there is, about how well the relation that obtains realizes identity, then we will care to some extent that there be a closest continuer. (For the closest continuer relation better realizes identity than does the relation: tie with close enough continuers.) Thus, if your position is close to but short of the neutral best instantiated realization view (which is neutral between all realizations past the threshold of good enough), you will prefer mildly that you have a closest continuer, preferring it enough to do something to bring it about, but not enough to engage in life and death struggle over it.

An explanation has been offered of quite convoluted carings, given the fact that we each care about our own continued identity through time. But what is our self that we should be mindful of it? What explains why we each care especially about our own continued identity through time? ("If not me, who?") The fact that we each care especially about our current selves. ("If not now, when?")[27] But what explains why we each care especially about our current selves in comparison to how we care about other people's selves? The question has now moved somewhat far from personal identity through time, but it is a good one nonetheless.[28] A theory of value, perhaps, might have the consequence that such self-caring is especially valuable; even so, surely we do not especially care about ourselves out of a disinterested concern for maximizing value. We will be in a better position to understand the self's special concern for itself later in this chapter.

There remains the last of the three questions we asked above. Which particular properties, features, and dimensions constitute the measure of closeness, and with what relative weights? The closest continuer theory is merely a schema; what then are its particular contents? What precisely is the metric, why that one, and why is it precisely that which we care about? Does psychological continuity come lexically first; is there no tradeoff between the slightest loss in psychological continuity and the greatest gain in bodily continuity; is bodily continuity (to a certain degree) a necessary component of identity through time; how are psychological similarity and bodily similarity to be weighed (for noncontinuers when some other continuer is present); what are the relevant subcomponents of psychological continuity or similarity (for example, plans, ambitions, hobbies, preferences in flavors of ice cream, moral principles) and what relative weights are these to be given in measuring closeness? And so forth.

I make no attempt here to fill in the details; and not merely because (though it is true that) I have nothing especially illuminating to say about these details. I do not believe that there are fixed details to be filled in; I do not believe there is some one metric space in which to measure closeness for each of our identities. The content of the measure of closeness, and so the content of a person's identity through time, can vary (somewhat) from person to person. What is special about people, about selves, is that what constitutes their identity through time is partially determined by their own conception of themselves, a conception which may vary, perhaps appropriately does vary, from person to person. We shall be in a better position later to say more about this. Note that if the measure of closeness is partly up to the person himself, there is a simple answer to the question of why his caring is proportional, at least, to degree of closeness: he fixes the measure of closeness in accordance with how much he cares.

If the details of personal identity have not yet been specified (though some have been mentioned in passing), in what way has the topic, until now, been personal identity, rather than simply the general notion of identity through time? This general notion fits the closest continuer schema, but how does that help us with the problems special to personal identity? It gives us a framework in which to embed those problems, and perhaps that will help some. Still, it must be granted that it does not focus especially upon personal identity. It does help us, however, with very many of the problems discussed in the literature under the rubric "personal identity", for these problems, though phrased about persons, to a surprising extent turn out to be general problems that apply to any kind of thing's identity through time. Not only our discussion thus far but also, I claim, the existing literature usually hasn't been concerned with the problems special to personal identity. To distinguish and clear away the more general issues that infest the area is a necessary first step. The special problems cannot be attacked without being isolated first; I doubt they can be attacked fruitfully in isolation from the correct general framework for identity, certainly not if an incorrect one is presupposed. In any case, the next part of this chapter is designed to illuminate the special nature of the self.

II. REFLEXIVITY

What is a self? How is a self possible? A self stands in a peculiarly intimate relationship to itself, being aware or conscious of itself, of itself as itself—or, at least, it has the capacity for this. How is such knowledge possible, is the capacity for it part of the essence of selves, an essential feature of what is a self?

The self's special knowledge of and relationship to itself is expressed at the linguistic level in the use of such terms as "I", "me", "my", in contrast to proper names and definite descriptions. To become clearer about the self's knowledge of itself, we shall have to look especially closely at this linguistic phenomenon. For it seems plausible that in knowing itself, a self utilizes such linguistic items or their analogues, or at least that this structure of a person's referring to himself is the self's knowledge of itself writ large—writ public anyway. If these hunches should turn out not to be the case, we will be led to a sharper and deeper and harder question about the self.

Reflexive Self-Reference

To what does the term "I" refer? It is plausible to think that "I" refers to whatever it is that produced the token utterance containing "I".[29] When a phonograph and record produce the token utterance, though, the "I" does not refer to them; nor does it refer to the vocal cords, tongue, and mouth cavity that produced the sound. Should we say then that "I" refers to the human being who utters it? If chimpanzees can learn to speak or otherwise produce linguistic tokens, are they debarred from saying "I" (this is indirect quotation) because it refers only to human beings? The extension to organisms will not solve this difficulty; "I" is perfectly at home in fairy stories or science fiction or theological contexts when what it issues from is not an organism.

Let us ignore the complications of someone translating, quoting, acting in a play, referring to the ninth letter of the English alphabet, and so on. Let us say, as a first approximation, that "I" refers to that being (entity, x) with the capacity of referring to itself which (who) produces that very token "I". Although the combination of vocal cords, tongue, and mouth cavity produce the token "I", this combination does not have the capacity to refer to itself and so the produced token "I" does not refer to it. Does this beg the question? For if we were willing to attribute self-referring to the combination of vocal cords, tongue, and mouth cavity, we also would be willing to attribute to it the capacity for self-referring. I cannot say this combination lacks the structure needed to have the capacity of self-referring, since I have no idea what structure, if any, is necessary. I want to say that I know that when I say "I", I (and also the word token I produce) do not refer to my tongue. (Can't we imagine distinct centers of consciousness and self-consciousness, though? If each of the parts of my body, including neurons, that cooperated in producing the word token had its own center of consciousness and each was referring to itself, as it did its share, then there would not be any one entity, capable of self-referring, which produced the token.)

How do I know what thing I am? Do I know myself as the possessor of some property? Is there any such property P so my knowing that the individual who has P also has Q guarantees that I know that Q applies to me? Not the property "being the producer of this spoken token", for I might produce the token intoned very convincingly and upon hearing it believe it of its speaker, without knowing that I myself produced it, having become convinced my vocal cords were incapable of sound-production. Not the property "being the thinker of these words" for I might think someone else is thinking these words which I am telepathically overhearing or receiving as a message from another communicator. Not the property "being the person who has this awareness", for similarly I might believe there is not only one such being, that two beings have it, or that God also is aware of everything of which I am aware.[30]

Much recent literature has focused upon the peculiarities of self-knowledge as it utilizes terms like "I", "me", "my".[31] For a person X to reflexively self-refer is not merely for X to use a term that actually refers to X; this omits as internal to the act of referring that it is *himself* to which he refers. When Oedipus sets out to find "the person whose acts have brought trouble to Thebes," he is referring to Oedipus but he is not referring to himself in the requisite reflexive way. He does not know that he himself is the culprit. To do that, he would have to think or know some suitable first-person statement using "I", "me", "my".

Imagine that you and two other persons have been in an accident and are lying completely bandaged on three beds in a hospital, all suffering from amnesia. The doctor comes in and tells what has happened, that examinations have been made, and that (where the three persons boringly are named X, Y, and Z) person X will live, Y will die, and Z has a 50/50 chance. Since you are suffering from amnesia you do not remember your own name, so there is something important you don't know yet, namely, what is going to happen to *you*. The situation is not helped if the doctor gives the full life histories of each of the three. Nor are you helped if she says the person closest to the window will live, to the door will die, for, being completely bandaged, you still do not know which of these people you are. The three people can be given complete (physicalistic) descriptions of the past, present, and future of the world, yet still each will not know what is going to happen to him. It will not help if the doctor points you out and says "here is what is going to happen to you;" for you won't know she pointed to you.

How can the doctor tell me? She can wheel the patients into three separate rooms, enter mine and say, "Here is what is going to happen to the only patient who can hear my voice, who is Mr. X." Now I know she is referring to me since I know I hear her voice. I can deduce that I am Mr. X from the statement that the only patient who hears her voice is Mr. X, since I already know I am a patient and I know I hear her voice. It seems that to deduce a statement (essentially) containing "I", "me", "my", one of these terms must appear among the premises. If we cannot get started without already knowing one such statement, how then do we first come to know it? And how do such terms function?

When a sentence contains the word "I", whom it refers to depends upon who said or wrote or thought the sentence. It is a particular utterance, instance, token of the sentence wherein the word "I" refers, and its reference depends upon who produced the token. The reference of some other terms varies with something about the context of utterance too, for example, the terms "here", "two hours ago", "this"; these are 'indexical' or 'token reflexive' terms. Let us now consider two theses:

(1) No indexical statement is derivable from only nonindexical ones;

and where an 'I-statement' is one containing "I", "me", "my", "mine",

(2) No I-statement is derivable from only non-I-statements.

Some indexical terms have a reference that not only varies with the context of their utterance, but also depends essentially on the very utterance in which they appear; for example, "this very phrase" refers to that phrase itself, and "I . . ." refers to the producer of that token itself. Let us call such linguistic devices *reflexively self-referring*. There are two further theses to consider:

(3) No reflexive self-referring statement is derivable from only nonreflexively self-referring ones.

(4) No I-statement is derivable only from nonreflexively self-referring statements.

Note that thesis 4 permits an I-statement to be derivable from reflexively self-referring statements which however are not I-statements. Theses 1, 3, and 4 seem plausible. However, 2 seems false, for "I" seems understandable in terms of the more general reflexive self-referring phrase "this very": "the producer of this very token".

How can we demarcate more precisely the notion of reflexive self-reference? The phrase "the only phrase on the blackboard of Emerson Hall, Room 315, on November 16, 1977" actually refers to itself, since that is the phrase written there then, but it does not reflexively self-refer. If another phrase had been written there, then the phrase beginning "the only phrase on" would refer to that other phrase, not to itself. This suggests that a phrase reflexively self-refers when it not only actually self-refers but refers to itself in all possible situations and worlds. This suggestion is not fully adequate. Let "Elbert" be a proper name which refers to the proper name written on the blackboard of Emerson Hall 315, on November 17, 1977. As it happens, what is written there then is "Elbert", and so it refers to itself. Assuming with Kripke that proper names are rigid designators, this proper name refers to itself in all possible worlds, yet still it is not reflexive. (Note that it is an accident that "Elbert"self-refers, even though it refers to Elbert in all possible worlds.) The term "Elbert" does not refer in virtue of its meaning or sense. Though "the phrase on the blackboard there" does refer to itself (let us suppose) in virtue of its meaning or sense, it does not refer to itself in all possible worlds. There are two components to referring to itself in all possible worlds: (a) rigidly referring to itself, in that as used in the actual world, it refers in any possible world to that same thing it actually refers to in the actual world; and (b) in any possible world, when used with the sense it has in the actual world, it refers to itself (in that possible world). For the second to hold, it will have to follow from the sense that the term is self-referring (in any world where it is used). Therefore, contingent facts need not be introduced to establish that the reference, given that there is some reference utilizing the sense, is self-reference.[32]

That a phrase rigidly refers and (given its sense) necessarily self-refers is not enough to yield reflexive self-reference. Consider self-reference via Gödel numbering (where the sense is fixed by the particular convention of numbering), or "the result of substituting ———for . . . in   " where the blanks are filled in so that the result is that quoted phrase itself.[33] These devices yield reference which is rigid and necessarily self-referring, it follows from the sense of the expression that it refers to itself; yet still they are not reflexive —they do not refer to themselves *from the inside*. If following from the sense that it is self-referring and rigid is not enough to constitute reference from the inside, then what is?

The outside references (whether contingent or necessary) pick out their referent in virtue of some property or feature it independently has, a feature it has independently of being referred to then. Whereas, reference from the inside refers to something as having a feature that is bestowed in that very act of reference; the reference is peculiarly internal to the act of referring since that act refers in virtue of a feature created by or produced in that very act itself. (Compare how some sentences are made true in their tokening, as in "some people drone on and on and on" or "SOME PEOPLE SPEAK VERY LOUDLY," and so are true from the inside.) It follows from its sense that the term "I" refers to the producer of that very token (of its type), and that the person is referred to in virtue of the property he acquires in the very act of referring or producing the token, the property of being the producer of that token. It is part of the sense of the term "I" that it so refers "from the inside".

When referring is in virtue of a feature that the very token act of referring bestows or creates, must the referent otherwise lack that feature? The act of referring is sufficient to bestow it, but may the referent also have it independently, apart from the act of referring? We need not decide this now.*

With reflexive self-reference, it follows from—is part of—the sense that the term necessarily self-refers in virtue of a feature bestowed in the token act of referring.[34] We now seem to have an explanation of why reflexively self-referring phrases always contain indexical terms. A nonreflexive Gödel self-reference without indexicals is necessarily self-referring, while "the yellow token on the blackboard" may self-refer in virtue of a feature of the tokening. However, to accomplish having these two features together, so that it follows from the sense that there is self-reference in virtue of a feature of the tokening, does seem to require the use of indexicals. Note that reference to something having a property is not from the "inside" merely when that property is bestowed by the act of reference. If I now say "the molecules whose velocity is changed by human speech occurring in Pusey Library, Room 216, on July 7, 1980, at 12:20 P.M.," then that act of spoken referring to molecules bestows upon them the property via which they are referred to, but it is not reference from the inside. It does not follow from the sense of the expression that it is self-referring or refers in virtue of a bestowed property.

Let us now turn to the second thesis above; are I-statements derivable from reflexives that are not I-statements? Given the general reflexive term "this very", it seems promising to see the sense of 'I' as "the producer of this very token" or "this very producer of this very token". However, these second two phrases will have different tokenings than "I" does; the proposal that they have the same sense as "I" must therefore maintain that they can be substituted for "I" in

* Fichte refers to the "I" as positing itself, which includes at least the reflexive phenomenon we are isolating, referring to itself in virtue of a property bestowed or constituted in the act of referring; and when Fichte speaks of the "I" as positing itself as positing, perhaps we should understand him as denying that the property also applies independently of the act of referring (and holding that this denial, too, is part of the sense of the term "I").

any tokening (as subject of sentence) so that necessarily the reference is unchanged.

The basic reflexive operator is "this very" followed by a noun phrase: "this very P", where P includes or is appropriately related to the words "this very P", for example, this very phrase, this very sentence is short, this very book is uneven, this very token is seven words long. (Can we also say "this very person" or only "the person who utters this very token"?) There are ways to fill in P so that its holding is not bestowed (solely) by the tokening. Consider 'this very tokening in a universe of radius r'; if it refers, it follows from the sense (of the first part) that it self-refers in virtue of the tokening, but other facts (about the radius of the universe) are needed to establish that it refers at all. If you later write "this very phrase once written by Robert Nozick" then it self-refers if it refers, and your tokening's referring is parasitic upon my earlier one's doing so. Furthermore, if you mistakenly believe that you are Robert Nozick, then when you write the preceding phrase which successfully reflexively self-refers, you will be mistaken about the mechanism by which it does so.

Puzzles arise even for the apparently straightforward "this very producer of this very token." If I dictate a letter to a secretary, the "I" refers to me, not to the person who types it. Should we understand "this very token" as referring to my vocal one, rather than the typed one? Surely I would not send a letter to people with a demonstrative term where they cannot perceive what is demonstrated. So "this token" refers to the typed one they receive; but "the producer" is to be understood as referring to the agent responsible in the appropriate way—not to the typewriter, or secretary, or person who suggested I write the letter. Yet if there is a typographical error in someone's autobiography, then the typesetter or proofreader may be the one responsible for (that aspect of) the token. Leaving aside the question of the precise relation to the token, a more interesting question is whether we should understand "I" as (a) the producer of this very token, (b) the self-referring producer of this very token, (c) the reflexively self-referring producer of this very token. Do we get driven all the way to c; to explain how "I" refers, must we use the notion of reflexive self-reference, speaking of someone producing a token with the intention of reflexively self-referring? A child who thinks his name is "I" will produce that token with the intention to self-refer, but not to reflexively do so. So it seems we should understand 'I' as 'this very reflexive self-referrer', as 'the producer of this very token with this intention of invoking a device of necessary self-reference in virtue of a property exhibited in the tokening'.

Essence as a Self

To be an I, a self, is to have the capacity for reflexive self-reference. Something X which could refer, even to X, but not reflexively, is not an I, not a self. Though a self does have this (developable) capacity, is that something important about it and crucial to it?

Let me tell you an imaginary story in which you are one of the participants. A princess comes to a pond and sits down on a rock. Looking out at the pond, she sees on a lily pad a frog. She talks to it; it hops off, and swims over to the shore. She kisses it and it turns into a prince. Now, how is this story about you? "Am I the princess?" you ask. No. "Am I the frog who turns into a prince?" No. "Then who?" You are the stone the princess sits on; or, you are the lily pad.

Now we can imagine this, perhaps; just as the prince was put under a spell by the witch and turned into a frog, so perhaps, too, the stone has been bewitched, and sits there thinking, "How I long to be transformed again; if only the princess would kiss *me!*" But no, in this story I told, you are not an enchanted stone; in that story, in that possible world, you are just an ordinary dumb stone, or you are a lily pad without self-consciousness or a sense of your own plight—not Woody Allen as a lily pad. Now, is this possible, can you imagine yourself as this, and if not, is it simply a limitation of your imagination? I want to say that it is part of the essence of selves that they are selves or have the capacity to be selves, to reflexively self-refer, though this capacity may have been blocked temporarily or not yet have been developed. Anything that never has this capacity *could not* be you. Furthermore, any change in me that destroys the capacity permanently, ends the selfhood; *I* am no longer there. Thus, dead bodies are not selves, neither are certain severely brain-damaged ones.

Of course, something that lacks the capacity of reflexive self-reference couldn't so refer to itself and so could not then be "an I", could not be something reflexively present to itself. It does not follow from this, however, that it is not I—such an argument would have the flavor of Berkeley's that nothing can exist unconceived of. Though it could not refer to itself as "I", couldn't it be I; can't I now, possessing the capacity of reflexive self-reference, imagine that it is I, even though it will not be able to imagine this? From the fact that I have this property of being a self, it does not follow that the property is essential to my nature. Moreover, even though the capacity for reflexive self-reference is essential to being a self, and even though reflexive self-referring provides the access of a self to itself, it does not follow that it is of my essence (though I actually am a self) to be a self. (It does not follow that "I am a self" expresses a *de re* necessity. All the linguistic facts about how "I" refers only will give *de dicto* necessities, not necessity *de re*.)

Though it does not follow from considerations about how the term "I" refers, it nonetheless is true, I think, that selves are essentially selves, that anything which is a self could not have existed yet been otherwise. I am an I—necessarily I am an I. Is this an ur-fact, or is it somehow engendered? An adequate theory of the self, I think, should explain why selves are, as part of their essence, selves. Toward this end, let us examine reflexive self-referring more closely.

How Is Reflexive Self-Knowledge Possible?

When I reflexively self-refer, I know I am referring to myself—unlike Oedipus. When I reflexively self-refer, I intentionally produce a token with the knowledge that its sense is such that in any possible world, any producer X of it refers to X in virtue of a property (being the producer) bestowed upon him in the producing of the token "I".

How do I know I am referring to myself? We might have the following picture. I produce a sentence token, for example, "I am in Cambridge", with the intention of invoking its standard sense. So I know that the "I" in the token refers to its producer. I know, then, that the producer referred to himself; but in what does my reflexive knowledge that I produced it consist, what is the nature of my knowing I was that producer? Perhaps I produce another token expressing that knowledge, namely, "I produced the token 'I am in Cambridge.'" Once again, I know the producer of that larger token referred to himself, and perhaps I know that Robert Nozick produced that larger token, but in what does my knowledge consist that the first token of "I" in the larger token refers to me? For me to have reflexive self-knowledge is not merely for me to know that some token sentence containing "I" is true of whoever produced it, even when that token is one I produced. I must also know reflexively that I produced the token. This further knowledge cannot consist merely in knowing that some other token containing "I" is true, for once again I would have to know that this other token is produced by me. The truth conditions for an I-statement make crucial reference to a token. In

S is true ≡ _____

not only is a term referring to a token part of what is substituted for S, but the right-hand side of the equivalence must refer to the token and who produced it. If to know a statement is true is to know the right-hand side of the truth-equivalence, then to know an I-statement is true is to know something about a token, and hence to know a metalinguistic statement. The problem, though, is that the person also needs to know that he himself produced the token. So his knowledge of the right-hand side of the equivalence can constitute reflexive self-knowledge only if that side itself contains an occurrence of "I" which is not in quotation marks, and he knows that right-hand side to be true. So the question, in what such knowledge consists, remains unanswered.

A person with reflexive self-knowledge does not merely know of a token "I" (which he produced) what the linguist would say about it, namely, that it refers to whoever produced it, and so forth. Any explanation of what he knows must keep a reflexively self-referring term in the content of what he knows, not merely in quotation marks within that content.

Is my knowledge, "I am in Cambridge", captured by my knowing "the producer of this very token is in Cambridge"? Or is it more like my knowing "this very producer of this very token is in Cambridge"? Yet this knowledge cannot consist simply in my knowing that the producer of the first part of that token referred to himself, for that involves the same problem of no guarantee that I (reflexively) know that I produced it.

Reflexive self-knowledge is not merely a person's knowing that the semantics of reflexive self-reference holds of some (thought or sentence) token. We need to add the very phenomenon to be understood: his knowing that he himself produced the token. Thus, an apparently promising route toward understanding reflexive self-knowledge is blocked. How then is any reflexive self-knowledge possible? There are two tasks we would like a theory of the self to accomplish: to explain how reflexive self-reference is possible, and in so doing to provide the materials for showing that and why selves essentially are selves.

If I always knew something of myself via a term or referring token, there would be needed the additional (unexplained) fact of my knowing the term referred to me, of my knowing I was its producer. Therefore, it seems we each must have a kind of access to ourselves which is not via a term or referring expression, not via knowing that a term holds true (of something or other). What is the nature of this access not mediated by a reflexive term? (The access may be mirrored by such a term, though, at the linguistic level.) We might imagine there is some way of observing ourselves which cannot be used to observe anything else. On this view, I know it is I who is in pain, for example, by observing in that particular way that someone is in pain. (And concluding that it must be I?) This does not easily fit knowing nonpsychological statements that are reflexively self-referring (as my knowing I was born in Brooklyn, New York). Moreover, my knowing that someone or other observes himself in pain in this way still does not constitute my knowing that I am the one who so observed himself.[35] Reflexive access to ourselves, then, cannot be a special mode of relating to ourselves as objects. Since knowledge of something as the referent of referring expressions is a kind of knowledge by description, we might think reflexive self-knowledge must be knowledge by acquaintance. Yet if an I is directly acquainted with itself as itself, this cannot be by a mode of acquaintance that is like being acquainted with an object.

We might try to avoid these problems by treating reflexive beliefs or desires as dispositions to behave. On this view, the difference between my believing reflexively that I am in danger from something coming from the left, and my believing that someone else is, is that the first belief is fed into an action-execute system in a particular way and the second is not, yielding the action of fleeing rather than calling out a warning. Reflexive beliefs and desires differ from others in being different dispositions to behave and execute actions.[36] However, this attempt to avoid the reflexiveness problem still needs to explain why I acquire a particular disposition, for example, to run to the right or to take a defensive stance toward the left; it would seem the explanation is that I have acquired the reflexive belief that I am in danger from the left, for example, after hearing the called warning "Robert Nozick, danger from the left." To think of the reflexive belief or desire as constituted by the disposition, or by special feeding into the action-execute mechanism, leads to trouble in explaining why this takes place— the explanation, it seems, must reintroduce self-reflexive beliefs and desires.

The possibilities I can see about the nature of reflexive self-knowledge are the following. First, that reflexive self-knowledge is a basic phenomenon, not understandable in terms of anything else which constitutes or gives rise to it. While some things might parallel it, for example, linguistic reflexive self-reference, they do so only because reflexive self-knowledge underlies these other linguistic phenomena. The linguistic phenomenon then would be the reflection of reflexive self-awareness rather than its explanation. Uniquely, selves know themselves in virtue of being identical with themselves, and this basic property of selves cannot be further explained. (I take eastern theories of "non-dual consciousness" to fit this category.) The question, "What is it about selves in virtue of which they have reflexive knowledge merely in virtue of the self-identity in which everything stands to itself?" would be a question without any answer. The phenomenon would be a basic phenomenon; it would be a brute fact that some things have it and others do not. (Would we have to hold that others do not, or would panpsychism be an alternative?)

Second, we might imagine that the self places itself into its reflexive self-referrings. I think "Zvi is tired", "Yitzchak is tired", "Rami is tired", substituting different names, terms, referring expressions into the mental linguistic-like framework "_____ is tired". When I think that I am tired, rather than similarly substituting a term or referring expression, perhaps I put myself forward to fill the blank; with a little "mental-english" I twist myself into the blank place.

It is not necessary, is it, that a vehicle for referring always be a term or linguistic-like item? True, a referring item always has to be available when needed, and terms are easily produceable; but other things also might fit the bill. In a land where the sun never set, could not that be the item, always available, which referred to some kind of tree or happening or whatever. At certain times during people's speech, they would gesture toward the sun, introducing it into a sentence by pointing or a glance; thus introduced, the sun would refer. "But wouldn't it be the pointing or gesturing to the sun that did the referring, rather than the sun itself?" Pointing to the sun is like uttering a word; the sun would function like the word, the gesturing like the uttering. Also, if the sun was a referring item, must it refer to something else; could it not be an item that the people use to refer to the sun?

That we use linguistic bits and sounds to refer is a technological fact; these items are easily produceable, even in the absence of the referent, without great exertion, starting at an early age. Organisms anything like us would not use double back-flips as a standard referring item, or any sound that so contorted and ached the mouth and larynx that it could be produced only once a month.

If a nonlinguistic item can be used to refer, then, why cannot the self place itself into the blank, and in so doing refer to itself? The word "I" might be the marker for the blank, holding space in which the self can appear. The self would thus be part of a reflexively self-referring thought; it, not another mental item, refers to the self. However, when I think "Emily, David, Barbara, and I went to the movies", no felt difference corresponds to substituting myself for the term; nor, when I try to think Fregean unsaturated concepts, is it I especially who appears in the gap or closes it.

Is the problem of how reflexive self-reference is possible solved if the self inserts itself in the blank? By putting itself into the blank, mentally stepping forward into the space (as in the dance where "you put your whole self in") the self, we are imagining, succeeds in referring to itself. Still, how does it know it is referring to itself, in what does this knowledge consist? How does the self, placed inside the sentence or thought-frame, know that it itself is what is there? (By looking out from the inside?) The self's placing itself in the blank will serve here, only if the self is reflexively self-aware that it is itself that it places in the blank. Thus, the problem of the nature of reflexive self-awareness arises again; it will not help to explain the reflexive awareness of filling this blank in terms of filling yet another blank. There seems to be no way to escape this circle; any placing into a blank that can do the trick seems to presuppose reflexive self-awareness. Even the view—the extreme view—that the self places itself into a sentence-blank cannot explain the nature of reflexive self-knowledge. How then is reflexive self-awareness possible?

Classification and Entification

It will be helpful, before treating this question, to have at our disposal an abstract model of a procedure of classification. An array of things (events, acts, physical objects) is to be grouped together in a classification; these things stand in various distances from each other, according to some assumed or presupposed metric. We may represent the things by different dots (Figure 1.4), and the degree of similarity or difference between any two things by their distance from each other in an n-dimensional space (where n is the number of dimensions which underlie salient similarities and differences). One procedure of classification would be to classify each and every entity as separate from every other, drawing a circle (which represents entityhood) around each dot (Figure 1.5). This classification gives the maximally specific information about the nature of each thing without including anything about the differing degrees of similarity. A second procedure would be to classify all of the dots together (Figure 1.6). This is a most uninformative classification; putting everything in the same class tells us nothing about the differences between the component points.

An informative classification will classify somewhere in between, drawing circles to include more than one point while yet not including every point. An informative classification will group the points so as to minimize the distance between the points in the same subclass while maximizing the distance between points in different subclasses. Ideally, the circles should be drawn so that the distance between any two points within a circle is less than the distance between any two points from different circles. Not every array of points will permit of this; for example:

$$\dot{1}\ \dot{2}\ \dot{3}\ \dot{4}\ \dot{5}\ \dot{6}\ \dot{7}\ \dot{8} \qquad \dot{9}\ \dot{10}\ \dot{11}$$

Here it is natural to draw one circle around the first 8 points, another around the last three, even though points 8 and 9 (from different circles) are closer together than are points 1 and 8 (from the same circle).

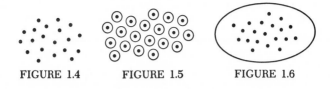

FIGURE 1.4   FIGURE 1.5   FIGURE 1.6

Here, two things are part of the same class (circle) when they are close enough and there is no third thing not in the class which is closer to one of them than each and every other thing in the class is. Notice that the way this principle of classification uses a negative existential quantifier ("and there is no third thing not in the class"), puts it in accord with a closest relation schema. Even under the closest relation schema, though, not every array of points will give rise to an illuminating classification; for instance, points arranged along a line with each equidistant from its neighbor yet the first and last too distant to be classed together illuminatingly. No boundaries can be drawn to delimit different classes when the two points adjacent to a boundary will be as closely related as any two points within the boundary.

We might have the following picture of classification. First, entities are built up at one time, time-slices of entities, in accordance with the maximally informative classification in that time-slice space; next comes the question of identity over time, where again a closest relation schema, the closest continuer schema, is applied to classify stages as stages of the same entity. Thus it is one schema, a closest relation schema, which first unifies an entity at a time, and then unifies one object over time.

I see no compelling reason, however, why entification must be conceived of in these stages, first entity at a time (transverse identity) followed by entity over time (longitudinal identity). Indeed, if causal interconnections among parts are part of closeness in the transverse metric space then, via causal connection, time already enters into transverse identity and so is not restricted only to longitudinal considerations. We can imagine the abstract metric space to include time as one of its dimensions; entification, the classifying which produces entities, takes place in one fell swoop, rather than in the stages of transverse followed by longitudinal. On this view, the distinction between transverse and longitudinal identity is derivative, abstracted from a clumping together in a larger space. (Compare the treatment of "spacelike" and "timelike" within relativity theory.) We can understand, however, why it was natural to think of entification as taking place in stages, for we are not given the whole space-time picture at once; our entifications are done at a time or in a small time interval, not from outside of time looking at the whole time-spread. (For some situations, perhaps, the separate abstracting of transverse and longitudinal might not go so smoothly. Is the overlap problem an instance of this?)

The principle of clustering things together in a classification maximizes within-class similarity while also maximizing between-class dissimilarity. An informative classification brings together a diversity that it unifies (more than one point in a circle) while not bringing together such a great diversity that it doesn't get significantly unified (not all the points in the same circle). Unity in diversity has been called organic unity; in establishing these different unities in diversities, the different circles, the classification maximizes the sum of the degrees of organic unity.[37]

My remarks about classification intentionally have been so general as to encompass different more precise principles of classification found in the literature.[38] Since I have written no specific formula for the process of classifying, forming, and delineating entities within the abstract metric space, there remains the question of why a particular entification takes place in accordance with one particular formula, not another plausible formula that would yield a different result. It would be premature to attempt to answer such questions here.

Another point needs emphasizing. Classification and entification takes place within an assumed or already given abstract space wherein points differ in closeness: X is closer to Y than Z is to W. If the dimensions were changed by which closeness was judged, if different dimensions were salient, a different classificational grouping would result. The classification is relative to the assumed structure of the space, just as the closest continuer schema needs to have fed into it information about closeness and distance. Thus, one will not have a full explanation of a classification without an explanation of why it is within *that* abstract space that it takes place, why those dimensions and why that particular metric or set of comparative similarity judgments, rather than others.

Self-Synthesis

I have been able to think of only one view of the self that would account for its reflexive self-awareness. I put forward the possibility with great hesitation, driven to entertain it (but not quite to endorsing it yet) by the problem, otherwise apparently quite intractable.

Let us begin with the act of reflexive self-referring. Make it nothing but: this very act of reflexive self-reference. Beginning with this act, this dot, this point of reflexive self-reference, we can ask what its extent is, what its boundaries are. One way to draw boundaries around the act is to search for a preexisting entity, the doer of the act, and include it in the boundaries drawn. This already embodies a particular theory, namely, that every act has a doer. Recall Lichtenberg's criticism that all Descartes was entitled to assert was that thinking was going on, not that he or anyone was doing the thinking. On the agent-view, we should treat the reflexive "I" as equivalent to "this very act's doer"; I am tired = this very act's doer is tired. In what does my knowledge that I am this very act's doer (my previous knowledge that I was that very act's doer) consist? If we start with a separate preexisting I, and a reflexive reference to 'this very act's doer', there will be the problem, familiar by now, of the nature of my knowledge that I = this very act's doer. I know it by doing the act, but how do I know that the preexisting I is the doer of that reflexive act?

Let us suppose, then, there is no preexisting I; rather the I is delineated, is synthesized around that act of reflexive self-referring. An entity is synthesized around the reflexive act and it is the "I" of that act. There are two ways we can imagine the delineation of this entity. First, that an agent as doer of the reflexively self-referring act A is postulated or hypothesized and then the boundaries of this agent, its extent in space and time, are delineated (Figure 1.7). Second, we can imagine that some entity is delineated and synthesized around the act A of reflexive self-referring and then that the I is that entity, or something that is taken to correspond to it (Figure 1.8).

What principle governs how this synthesizing takes place? What makes something get grouped with the originally pointlike reflexive act A, and so synthesized within A's boundaries? The act A of reflexive self-referring has its own aspects: it is an intentional action, embodied (perhaps) in some physical production of sound or mark,

FIGURE 1.7

located somewhere, and so on. Around these dimensions and components of the act, in the space of all the things spread out from the act, a delineation of an entity takes place—an entity coagulates.

Some dimensions and features are made salient for the grouping of things as similar or relevantly close to the reflexive act A by components and dimensions of that act itself. To refer to anything is to perform an action, with a certain intention. The token "I" refers to the entity (capable of self-referring) which produces the token; the token "this very reflexive self-referring act" refers to that act of producing the token. Thus, within the reflexive self-referring act are components of action, intention, causal production. It seems reasonable that these should provide the lineaments, the dimensions and metric, to the abstract space wherein the "I" is synthesized. Or perhaps, human bodies congeal in a classification similarly to other physical objects, while the components of self-referring fix the demarcated body as especially connected with the act A, as causally relevant to producing it, variations in whose position and orientation produce variations in aspects of the act.[39]

What is it that is doing the synthesizing? Is the principle of classification applied by me, by a me who exists apart from the classifying and its result? Or is it a synthesized I? Who then, or what, is doing the synthesizing?

Let us imagine, initially, acts without a doer, with no agent behind them. Better, imagine acts so as to leave open the question of whether or not an agent is behind them. Acts $A_1, \ldots, A_n$ take place; these include (but are not restricted to) acts of applying the closest relation schema, unifying and synthesizing entities in classification, bringing together things to constitute demarcated entities.

FIGURE 1.8

Consider now another act A_0 of unification and synthesis which brings together $A_1, \ldots, A_n$ and A_0 itself. A_0 is (partially) a reflexively self-referring act: the act of synthesizing $A_1, \ldots, A_n$ and this very act itself. A_0 unites these acts together as parts or components or things arising from the same entity E. Though there will be ways of unifying acts without attributing them to a doer, let us now concentrate on the agent mode of unifying acts. Entity E, thus synthesized, is the doer of the acts, including A_0.

Now this is easy to understand if E preexists independently, and A_0 is merely a demarcation, a drawing of a boundary, around the preexisting entity E which was there all the time and, among other things, performed the act of outlining itself. But let us take the term "synthesis" more seriously, and see the entity as coming to exist in the act A_0 of synthesis. Can we say (afterwards) that what did A_0 was the entity E which A_0 itself synthesized? Can the rabbit be pulled out of the rabbit? It is some such theory as this that Fichte presents; he speaks of the self as positing itself, also of the self as positing itself as positing itself. (Is there a limit to how many levels up this qua must go?) A_0 seems to be an act of positing the self which, since it reflexively refers to that very act as included within the entity E, posits itself as positing itself, synthesizes itself as synthesizing itself. This theory of the self arising in an act of self-synthesis seems bizarre if not incoherent. Is there really no preexisting self independent of the act A_0 of reflexive synthesis? Can the self really be a Fichtetious object?

A current synthesis does not determine the precise character of a later synthesis, even when it looks ahead to it, but it can affect what happens later as a precedent. This precedent is not binding. However, the same type of synthesis, around the same dimensions and weighting, will happen repeatedly in the absence of reason to deviate and override the precedents; thereby syntheses at different times can mesh into a larger continuing entity. A fresh creative act is not necessary with each act of reflexive self-reference. Usually, the self habitually follows the earlier precedents, aligning itself with those precedents that can cover it most closely. Sometimes self-reference will occur more self-consciously, a self will step back from habit to consider its nature; on some occasions the self-reference may occur self-consciously, as a self-synthesis. Not every reflexive self-reference need involve an explicit delineation of boundaries; one can presuppose earlier delineations, or assume whatever delineation would best include that very act of self-reference, without marking that delineation explicitly or completely. Sometimes a reflexive self-reference might mark the boundaries not at all, leaving completely open the nature and extent of what best includes it—the act of reference leaves a place for a synthesizing but does not carry it out fully then. Since the delineation follows principles of classification and entification as well as earlier precedents, it is not arbitrary. This might give rise to the illusion that the reference is to an independently preexisting and bounded entity.[40]

What Synthesis Explains

The problem of reflexive self-awareness has been to understand in what reflexive knowledge consists. Shoemaker speaks of being "immune to error through misidentification"; whatever mistakes one makes in a first-person I statement, it cannot be that of misidentifying whom one is talking about. With a preexisting I, however, there always is room for a mistake; also there remains the question of what constitutes the knowledge, when that preexisting thing is referred to, that what is referred to is oneself.

However, if the self is synthesized around the reflexive act, there is no room for the act to refer to something other than it. The self is synthesized as the object referred to in the reflexive tokening of "I". I know that when I say "I", the reference is to myself, because myself is synthesized as the thing which that act refers to, as the tightest and greatest organic unity including the act, and referred to by the act because including it. The reflexive act refers to the thing of greatest organic unity (judged by the principle of classificatory grouping) which includes it; and that thing is synthesized for the purpose of being referred to, by the very act of referring to it. Thus, there cannot be any error due to misidentification.[41] Only an object synthesized by the act of referring is guaranteed to be hit by that act. Only a theory of such a synthesized self can explain why, when we reflexively self-refer, we know it is *ourselves* to which we refer.

Recall our claim earlier that selves are essentially selves, so that no thing in any possible world which always lacked the capacity for reflexive self-reference (for example, the stone or the lily pad) could be me. Or you. We can understand why this is so if the self is synthesized

—is synthesized by an act of reflexive self-referring, and is synthesized around an act of reflexive self-referring. A self could not always (in some world) lack that capacity of reflexive self-reference, since it is synthesized by that capacity and around it qua something having it.[42] Thus, the theory of the self as reflexively synthesized can explain (while it is difficult to see how else to explain) how reflexive self-awareness is possible, and why a self is essentially a self. If we think that these things yielded in explanation do hold true, as I do, then these are significant virtues of the theory. We now see that the features of the use of "I" cut very deep. Unlike the Gödelian self-descriptions which self-refer in all possible worlds, reflexive self-reference is self-reference from the inside, which we understood as reference in virtue of a characteristic (or to an entity) created in the very act of referring. This linguistic feature of reflexive self-reference, we now see, reflects the underlying reality. The self which is reflexively referred to is synthesized in that very act of reflexive self-reference. Reflexive reference from the inside corresponds to and reflects the reflexive synthesizing of the self (as synthesizing itself). "If the self synthesizes itself at a time, isn't it only a momentarily existing self? How then can we have identity over time?" The self synthesizes itself not only transversely, among things existing only at that time, but also longitudinally so as to include past entities, including past selves which were synthesized. My currently synthesized self includes past self-stages in accordance with a closest continuer and closest predecessor schema. Will the self continually rewrite its history, like a Soviet historian disowning and rewriting a currently undesired past? There are limits on this; when some past self-stage is incorporated in a synthesis, brought in also is its conception of its past, as incorporated in its own self-synthesis. And while one might attribute a mistake to one's past self about its past self, this will not be done casually—the mistake would have to be explained. Thus, generally, my past self's past self will be carried into the current synthesizing as my own, too.

Could some preexisting entity be identical with the self that is synthesized, posited in the reflexive act of its self-positing; or rather, could a preexisting entity have as parts all the parts of the newly synthesized entity E except for the latest act A_0 of reflexive self-synthesis? If so, wouldn't it turn out that this preexisting thing was what was synthesized, that is, newly delineated though already existing independently? As Kant's theory does not exclude the happenstance of there

91

being things in themselves which correspond exactly to the synthesized phenomena, having exactly the same features, so mightn't there be a preexisting self corresponding to the synthesizing one, and wouldn't it be that, then, which was reflexively self-referring?

To introduce this entity preexisting apart from any acts of self-synthesis would leave unexplained once again in what its reflexive knowledge consisted, as well as again opening the question of whether the self in its essence is a self. We are saved from this, since the picture of the preexisting entity containing all the same things as the synthesized entity E except for the new reflexive act A_0 is inadequate. E also contains previous acts of reflexive self-referring, understood as self-synthesis, in its past. If all these are to be excluded also along with A_0 as incompatible with the entity's status as existing independently, then the entity will have no reflexively self-referring acts in its past; and that preexisting thing, surely, is not I. The act of self-synthesis does not presuppose that nothing is preexisting, for it acts on and incorporates earlier existing things, including an earlier self previously synthesized reflexively. Certainly, I can think I existed before this moment, and that it is a later stage of my earlier self who now refers to himself. Yet all this holds true in virtue of the current act A_0 of self-synthesis, not independently of it.

The theory we have presented of a self-synthesizing self, while it explains the self, does not explain all reflexive self-reference, for it is built upon what clusters around a reflexively self-referring act. Someone might think that this reflexive act of reference is possible only when done by selves who model it on their own ur-reflexive consciousness. On this view, the reflexive "this very" cannot be used to explain the self, since it presupposes the self's own reflexive self-consciousness. To show our theory constitutes progress in understanding reflexive self-knowledge, it seems we must explain how reflexive self-referring in general is possible. Clearly, if it merely is a reflection of an underlying reflexive self-knowledge, then no progress has been made; and if the nature of the reflexive "this very" is taken as a basic phenomenon, not susceptible to further explanation, then why not simply take the self's reflexive self-consciousness as basic, and leave it at that? (Might it be emergent from other phenomena but not reducible to them?)

Starting with the notion of an act of referring, A refers to x, we can build up to the notions of A happening to refer to A, and then to the

Gödelian self-reference whereby A refers to A in virtue of some abiding structurally defining feature of A and so, referring to A in all possible worlds, is necessarily self-referring. The next step is to a device whose sense is to be necessarily self-referring (as is the Gödel reference), but not in virtue of some abiding feature, rather in virtue of a feature created in the act of referring. Created in an act of referring or created in that very act of referring? If the latter is its sense, are we not utilizing reflexive self-reference in order to explain it? But "that very" is not reflexively self-referring; it merely harks back to an earlier constant or bound variable. The step was to a device whose sense holds that a utilization A of the device is necessarily self-referring, not in virtue of some abiding feature but in virtue of a feature created or bestowed on the referent by A. A device can refer to something else in virtue of a feature it bestows on it; these are indexical devices that are not reflexive. There is no special problem about something A that refers to itself in virtue of a property it bestows on itself. The thing A is sure to be there to receive the bestowed property, since it is doing the bestowing, and though the property was not previously enduring, it is bestowed by A as needed, and bestowed only on what is itself. (We describe this from the outside, with a nonreflexive "that very".) Thus, there is no special problem in understanding how reflexive self-referring is possible, how it is possible for there to be necessary self-referring in virtue of a feature bestowed in the act of referring. "How are we to understand these acts? Mustn't there be a previously and independently existing doer of them?" These are not special questions about reflexivity, but rather about the intelligibility of speaking of acts, even nonreflexive ones, without presupposing independently existing agents. I do not deny these difficulties, but we must not forget how willing we are to put them aside as we hold that Descartes can only reach "thinking is going on" and not "I think," at least not with an independently existing I (even if its nature is only to think).

We have explained how reflexive self-knowledge or awareness is possible, in terms of a self synthesized around an act of reflexive self-reference, while reflexive self-referring has been treated as a combination of simpler intelligible components, not as an irreducibly mysterious phenomenon.

Granting that the nature of reflexive self-referring can be explained, will we have to explain why these acts occur, by reference to a preexisting self who performs them? Our explanations will see them as done by the person who existed before, but this, as we have seen, need not involve existing independently of the act of synthesis. However, there is no denying the intuitive and compelling quality of the view that the self exists independently of all acts of self-referring, underlying them as doer instead of being synthesized by them. (Is it so intuitive and compelling when put that way?) The self-synthesizing view at some point needs to explain why this is so, and to explain it away.

Does the self-synthesizing view conflict with grander aspirations and theories, for example, those that view the underlying self as identical with the underlying substance of the universe, as in the Vedanta theories that Atman is Brahman? Nothing we have said thus far limits what the self-synthesizing self can synthesize itself as, what it can include within its boundaries or retrospectively say did the synthesizing. It does conflict with the view that this self exists independently of any act of synthesis, a contention massively and inconclusively debated between Vedantists and Buddhists. Given the perplexing questions about the self-synthesizing view, there is no need at this point to worry about its implications for such grander issues.

Unities and Wholes

Doesn't the self-synthesizing view give the self the status of a collection or bundle (to use Hume's term), rather than a true unity? Yet don't we otherwise think the self is a unity, a whole rather than simply a collection or sum of parts? If the act A_0 of reflexive self-synthesis is to induce a unity in other things, must it not have a unity of its own? In what, though, can this unity consist other than in the whole act being done by the same agent? Are we returned, once again, to an independently existing agent, and the attendant problems for understanding reflexive self-knowledge? Or is the problem one about unity in general, rather than especially about the self?

Consider the standard example from the Kant literature (due to William James, I think), this time with the sentence "I wonder how things can be unified." First imagine that each of these seven words is thought by a different person, but that the order is such that the first person's thinking "I" is immediately followed in time by the second person's thinking "wonder" and so on until the sixth person's thinking "be" is immediately followed by the seventh person's thinking "unified" (and by an eighth person's thinking "period"?). In contrast consider one person's thinking all of the seven words in sequence. The second, it is said, is a unified thought whereas the first is not. What unifies the thought in the second case, according to the literature, is that it takes place in one mind. Whereas in the first case each word is thought in a different mind.

What makes one mind one, rather than a composite of different entities?* And why aren't the separately thought words also united in the temporal entity that consists of the first person's mind at the time the first word was thought and the second person's mind at the time the second word was thought . . . and the seventh person's mind at the time the seventh word was thought? Why isn't this a unified entity, uniting those words into one thought? Thus, the problem is thrown back to the unity of what does the unifying. (How can a purported unifier, which is not itself unified, produce unity?)

Can the words be unified in one mind by the "I think" which accompanies or can accompany each of them? Are thoughts unified by the ubiquitous "I think"? But those two words in order, "I" and "think", can accompany your thoughts and also his thoughts and her thoughts. (Different readers nod in agreement when they read Kant on the "I think" which can accompany all of their thoughts.) So whose "I think" is it that does or can accompany each of my thoughts? Mine. If the thoughts are to be unified as mine by the "I think's" accompanying them, each of these "I think's" also must be mine. In the first case above, no unity is produced merely by each of the seven persons accompanying that word he thinks by an "I think",

---

* And if one mind, what makes the thinking of the words one unified thought, rather than separate ones or merely the thinking of a list of words? If the fact that they are thought by one act of thinking, what makes that one unified act? Robert P. Wolff finds the unity of thoughts within one mind constituted by their content being attributed to the same object. (*Kant's Theory of Mental Activity*, Harvard University Press, Cambridge, 1963, pp. 100–169.) Why cannot different acts, even ones in different minds, attribute (the same or different) content to the same object? That you and I both attribute properties to this book I now am writing and you now are reading (note how the two tokens of the token-reflexive "now" shift reference in the very same token-sentence) does not mean that both thoughts are in the same mind (even if we are of one mind about the book).

each by his own "I think". Different "I think's" provide unity only if they themselves are unified, for example, if each is thought by the same I.

Perhaps it is not different "I think's", "I think x, I think y, I think z", that are supposed to unify x and y and z; perhaps there is just one "I think" unifying them, namely, "I think xyz" or "I think x and y and z." Are my thoughts unified because there is one "I think" that can accompany all of them together? Over a lifetime, though, it will have to include the past tense: "I thought x and y and z and w". This must differ from: I thought x and he thought y and she thought z. Perhaps the point is that when that "I think" or "I thought" is thought, at least then the thoughts are unified by all being included in its scope. What makes that one "I think" a one thing that can include all of them in its scope? Why weren't the seven persons' words included in the scope of the (composite) "I think", the first one seventh of which consists of the first one seventh of the first person's "I think", and whose i[th] seventh consists of the ith seventh of the ith person's "I think"?

Once the problem of unity presses upon us—the problem of the one and the many—it seems we shall never be rid of it unless some things are intrinsically unified. For it appears that a unification can be effected by something, an entity or act, only if it itself is unified. It appears that unless something has a unity not effected by, or due to, something else, unification can never get started.

Thus might a search be launched for some simple, atomic, intrinsically unified acts, about whose unity no question can possibly or legitimately arise; if some of these unified acts also are acts of unification, they will yield the unity of other things.[43] Or some might look to a Platonic Form or universal to stop questions about unity, and to specify which relations and dimensions can enter in a closest continuer or relation schema.[44] But how can Forms or universals solve problems about unity, when they do not even handle the problem of applying general terms? For all we know, different color universals, different bluenesses, inhere in blue things in different continents or places, the universals shifting when the object moves from place to place. Similarly, identical universals might alternate in some thing over time. It might be suggested that the principle of the identity of indiscernibles applies to universals, but what do we really know about such things? Will the fact that two otherwise identical universals inhere in different entities be enough to discern them? And perhaps the North American Blueness Universal differs from the South American one in some feature other than color, along some dimension that is not even exhibited in our world or universe. If universals really are entities, we surely do not know all of their properties. So we don't know whether the same one stays in an object from one day to the next, or is in two objects.

Unity seems to fare no better. Perhaps some entity we mark off as most natural and entity-like is not unified by a universal—there just isn't a universal of it. (Is the realm of universals full, so that every possible one exists?) Or perhaps though the universal does exist, it happens not to inhere in this thing which otherwise is like others in which it does inhere. Or perhaps in something E we think of as a unity, there is not one universal E but rather three, each universal for parts or aspects of E that happen to have come together; so as far as universals are concerned, there is no unity to E at all. If I find a purpose in attaching a desk chair to a desk, and begin to build them together as one entity, making many such, does this show there always was a universal of desk-chair console (dair? chesk?) which now has been brought at long last to inhere in something? Or is this an entity without a true unity? (But what of pencils with eraser tips; or typewriters with more than one letter, or more than one typing element?) Finally, which predicates correspond to universals and which do not? Are "grue", "bleen", and other even more unnatural predicates so because there is no corresponding universal, or do we say there is no corresponding universal because they strike us as gimmicky? We will not have a powerful or secure explanation of the unity of entities E if we have to appeal to specific factors in whose existence we have no reason to believe apart from our belief that E has unity.[45]

We seem unable to solve the general problem of unity. Does the reflexive nature of the I help to make the problem of unity any easier? Must not whatever so refers to itself possess the requisite unity? It seems that if the relation "refers to" itself lacks the requisite unity, then it cannot confer it within its field, though for other reasons what is in its field already may have unity. (So must we also solve the problem of distinguishing natural unified relations from artificial ones?) The self-synthesizing view does not presuppose an independently existing unified I, but doesn't it presuppose that the act of referring is one unified act, that the tokens used in referring are unified entities, and so forth? How can relations and acts induce unity if they are not themselves already unified?

If the token is a sound then wherein lies the unity of that external physical thing? It was intentionally made by me, but wherein lies the unity of that intentional act? If the token is a thought-token, we are back with Kant wondering wherein its unity lies. Wherein lies the unity of the reflexive act A_0?

When I pursue such questions I feel everything dissolving under me. The problem is not that without answers we are open to being confounded by an articulate skeptic. For if nothing can be taken as possessing unity then there is nothing the skeptic can be articulate about, there is no (unified) thought the skeptic can articulate, there is nothing with which the skeptic can be articulate (nothing with sufficient unity to be a word, predicate, or concept), and there is no articulator to be frustrated by all this. Even if the skeptic is reduced to silence—and he's not allowed any meaningful looks either—even if a transcendental argument were constructed to show some unity is a condition of possibility of all sorts of things (including arguments), this would constitute only an argument for unity, a proof that there is unity. I do not need any convincing that there is unity; what I need is to understand how unity is possible. If I need a transcendental argument, it is not one that starts with other things and reaches unity as a condition of their possibility; it is one that starts with unity and delves to the conditions of *its* possibility.

Won't at least one of the preconditions of the possibility of unity have to be unified, for how else will unity arise? And of this precondition can we not ask how its unity is possible? If unity is not somewhere in what does the explaining (of the possibility of unity), then the possibility of unity will not be explained; yet if unity is in what does the explaining, then some possibility of unity will be presupposed, so not all of the phenomenon of unity will be explained. It is difficult to see how anything possibly could serve to answer these questions about unity, so deeply do they cut.*

The assumption that unity can emerge only if (a part of) what it

* In this, the perplexity about unity resembles the famous question "why is there something rather than nothing?", where it seems that anything one might appeal to in order to answer this question is a something about which the question also asks. This question is taken up in the next chapter.

emerges from is unified seems so natural and evident yet leads us into a quandary and impasse. When there seems to be no conceivable alternative, yet the one view leads us to a philosophical impasse, suspect entrapment by a particular picture or model of how things must be.[46] Merely to say this, of course, is cold comfort. In addition, we need to find another way of viewing things.

Various writers have put forth the slogan that the whole is greater than the sum of its parts; others have complained that these writers never give meaning to "the sum of the parts" clear enough to fix what it (in contrast to the whole) is, and so to determine if there is a difference between it and the whole.[47] For our purposes, we shall consider the sum to be the sum as conceived within the calculus of individuals.[48] At a given time, the sum individual of parts is the possibly disconnected entity containing exactly those constituent parts; any two things with exactly the same parts constitute the same sum individual.

We can use the closest continuer theory of identity over time to specify how a whole may differ from the sum of its parts. The closest continuer of a sum is the sum of the closest continuers of the parts. (Otherwise, the entity is not being treated merely as a sum.) The closest continuer of the sum of various parts x_i is (identical with) the sum of each of the closest continuers of each part x_i. Thus, the closest continuer of the sum $X + Y + Z$ is the closest continuer of X plus the closest continuer of Y plus the closest continuer of Z. (Note that this holds even if the x_i are time slices of parts.)

The closest continuer of a whole, however, is not the sum of the closest continuers of the parts of the whole. Consider the sum of the cells of your body plus the other noncellular material of the body. Cells are continually being sloughed off, while new ones are made; also there sometimes are more drastic happenings, for example, removal of an organ or dismemberment. The closest continuer of this sum of cells plus stuff is the sum of the closest continuers of the parts, including the closest continuers of your sloughed off cells and your removed appendix, but not including the newly made cells. The closest continuer of the whole body, on the other hand, does not include as parts the continuers of the sloughed off cells, removed appendix, and lost eye, while it does include new cells, newly generated tissue, and perhaps an artificial heart valve. There is no division of the body into parts so that the body's identity over time is simply the sum of those parts' identities over time. Since the body and the sum of its parts differ in their properties—one is the same as some later entity but the other is not—they are not the same. Thus, we have reached the result that some things are different from the sum of their parts; we may call those things wholes. (Note that we have given a sense to the difference between wholes and a sum of parts only for things which continue over time.) Whether or not wholes, in addition to being different, also are greater than the sum of their parts is a question we may leave aside for now.

A whole need not involve any significant organic unity. The standard example of something without such unity is a heap of sand. Whether or not that heap is a whole depends upon its identity conditions over time. Is it the same heap even though some few grains have blown away and others have been added? If so, then the heap's integrity is maintained even through a small change of parts. I used the passive voice in the previous sentence, to contrast with the biological situation, when something maintains its own integrity even through some change of its parts.[49] An organic unity does something to maintaining the integrity and continuance of the whole, unlike a heap which just lies there like a lump. Further talk of interrelations would bring in the type of consideration spoken of by systems theorists.[50]

Unity can be an emergent property, based upon parts without unity of their own. The unity of X consists of X's integrity at its own level. It has this integrity provided its identity is not reducible to that of its parts; there are not parts of X such that X's identity over time is equivalent to the sum of the identities over time of these parts. This formulation does not assume that the parts themselves have unity or that there are any proper parts. Something is a unity, whether by its metaphysical nature or as carved out, if its identity over time is not equivalent to the sum of the identities over time of proper parts it may have. No underlying unity is presupposed. Unity sometimes does arise from an underlying unity; but the picture that unity can arise only out of unity no longer grips us.[51]

Our criterion for something's not being identical with the sum of its parts applies only to entities that endure through time. The identity of a whole through time is not specified by the identity through time of its parts. I say "is not specified", rather than that the whole actually is distinct from this entity which is the sum of its parts, for it could happen that over some stretch of time the whole actually keeps all of its parts and gains no new ones. The point then needs to be formulated modally: a whole need not be the sum of its parts. Something X at time t_1 with parts $p_1, \ldots, p_n$ is a whole if it is possible that there is a later time t_2 such that X at t_2 does not contain as its exact parts p_1 at t_2, p_2 at t_2, $\ldots$, p_n at t_2; or if it is possible that something Y at t_3 contains as its parts exactly p_1 at t_3, p_2 at t_3, $\ldots$, p_n at t_3 while yet Y at $t_3 \neq$ X at t_3. A whole is different from the sum of its parts in that it is possible that these diverge over time.

Can we extend this notion to entities that do not endure through time, terming them wholes if they could possibly have had different constituent parts while being the same whole, or if exactly those parts could have existed without that whole's existing? Temporal development provides the clearest case of divergence of a whole from the sum of its parts, but we need not preclude atemporal analogues, atemporal wholes, modally understood.

We need to sharpen the criterion for a whole somewhat. (Our discussion here can be viewed as a metaphysical account of a whole, or a conceptualist account of when a concept is a whole-concept.) We have said that W is a whole relative to parts $p_1, \ldots, p_n$ when the closest continuer of W need not be the sum of the closest continuers of the parts p_i, when (a) it is possible that the closest continuer of W exists yet does not contain as a part some existing closest continuer of one of the p_i's; or (b) it is possible that the closest continuer of W exists and contains some part q that is not a closest continuer of any of the p_i (nor a sum or other odd carving up of these); or (c) it is possible that at some later time no continuer of W is close enough to be it, even though each of the p_i then has a continuer close enough to be it—the parts exist at the later time but the whole does not.

Yet consider the composite: one-half table plus one-half person's body. This would count as a whole relative to the parts: molecules of the table, cells. For different molecules can come and go while it remains the same half-table. Similarly, their meanderings will not destroy what is clearly a conglomerate, the sum-entity table plus person.

How are we to exclude this? It would be fruitless to hold that no physically discontinuous object can be a whole, or that no whole can consist of parts of other wholes, slicing across them. In the elementary school I attended, children sat in fixed rows with the furniture bolted to the floor. The separate physical objects are shown in Figure 1.9, viewed from the side (with the front of the class to the right). However, this was not an object which we separately discriminated, delineated, or had a name for. A pupil's place consisted of the top of the object in front as his desk, plus the front vertical piece and horizontal pivoting flap of the object behind as his seat. Actually the dotted delineation of a pupil's place in Figure 1.10 should pass directly through the two vertical lines, if only to represent the frequent fights over boundaries. It is a remarkable fact, when I think of it, that we children had a concept which applied to a discontinuous physical object (ah, but was the continuing floor part of the entity?) composed of proper parts of other continuous physical objects for which we had no names and which had no saliency for us.

A better diagnosis of the problem with the conglomerate table plus person is that this conglomerate contains parts, the table and the person, which are wholes relative to their parts; because we have gone down to those parts, the table plus person was counted as a whole by the criterion as an artifact of the wholeness of the table and of the person. Therefore, the criterion must be formulated so as to block reaching down through parts which themselves are wholes to their parts. We might think to add: and there are no wholes w_1, w_2, such that each of the $p_1, \ldots, p_n$ are proper parts of one or another of these wholes W_i which each are proper parts of W. This will not do, however, in the face of the worry that there is no distinction to be drawn, that every conglomerate is a whole. For then there always will be intermediate wholes (since there always are intermediate conglomerates) through which we must reach to get to the parts.

Instead we will have to build up wholes from parts in sequential order. Starting at the bottom with parts, which either are not wholes themselves or into whose own parts we will not inquire or reach, wholes W_i will be built up that satisfy the criterion; then in assessing

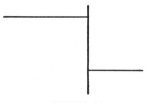

FIGURE 1.9

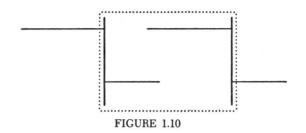

FIGURE 1.10

by the criterion whether W with parts W_1 is a whole itself, we will not reach through to the parts of W_1. For the purposes of the criterion, the parts of W are the W_1 along with any nonwhole parts that are not parts themselves of intermediate built-up wholes. Thus far, I have spoken of something's being a whole relative to a specification into parts $p_1, \ldots, p_n$. It seems we can eliminate this relativization by saying that W is a whole if it is a whole relative to each and every partitioning into proper parts, if no partitioning into proper parts renders it a conglomerate.[52]

Two notions have been intertwined in our discussion: first, that the identity of something can be maintained over time even though the parts change; second, that the mere continued existence of all the parts is not enough to maintain the existence of the whole, presumably because these parts haven't remained (or entered) in certain relations to each other. Let us call the first a whole, and the second a unity; something is a whole if its parts can be replaced, something is a unity if its parts must stay in certain relations for the entity to continue to exist. The tighter the relations, the greater the unity; while the more whole the whole is, the looser the limits are on which new parts might substitute in—for example, they need not be of the same material if they can serve the same function in the whole. A sentence is not a whole, in that to change any part is to change the sentence, but it is a unity in that it is the parts in a certain relation which constitute the sentence, not merely the parts existing. (Even if we make the relation-in-intension a part, the sentence is not merely the other parts and that relation—it is those parts in that relation.) We may conjecture that it is the tightness of the unity relations which allows the looseness of the restriction on what may replace parts within a whole. Though there are unities that are not wholes, we should not expect to find (many?) wholes that are not unities. A

103

unity/whole unifies a diversity, the diversity of what, over time, constitutes the parts of the whole; and it can unify the even wider diversity of what could constitute the parts.

Consider now the much maligned heap. If that heap must have precisely those grains of sand, if to change a single grain is to make a different heap, then it is not a whole. It is a unity, however, in that its parts must be in a certain spatial proximity—scattered grains do not a heap make. If, furthermore, its criterion of identity over time does permit replacement of grains provided most stay present from one time interval to the next, then it will be a whole also. Not a very exciting one, to be sure, not one with a very interesting unifying relation or any internally generated tendency to maintain its identity or restore its identified equilibrium in the face of minor disturbances, but a unity and a whole nonetheless, and not merely sport for the calculus of sum individuals.

The heap does not have high intrinsic value, its intrinsic value is not significantly different from the sum of the intrinsic value of its parts. Unified wholes, we shall see in Chapter 5, often differ in value from the sum of the value of the parts, and differing thus in intrinsic value seems to be a sufficient condition for something's being a unified whole. The theory of value, formulated below, will give sense to the notion that a whole not only is different from the sum of its parts, but is greater than that sum—greater in intrinsic value.

Let us return now to the self, to what is synthesized in the self-reflexive act A_0. It is not crucial to the unity of this that it be imposed by some other already unified entity. What matters is whether, as synthesized, its conditions of identity delineate a whole rather than a conglomerate. If the "I" is to be a whole at one time, its later identity must possibly diverge from the sum of its parts later; or it must be possible for that same I to have contained different parts.

Is the self-synthesizing self a unity or a conglomerate and mere collection? We need not worry especially whether if the reflexive act A_0 of synthesis of $A_1, \ldots, A_n$ along with A_0 had synthesized one other thing instead, say A_{n+1} instead of A_n, that would have made it a different act. For the I synthesizes itself as a unifed whole—it does not specify its identity over future time as "whatever is the sum of the continuers of my current constituents." It construes itself as able to lose bodily parts, perhaps even a body, to lose memories, perhaps even memory. The I synthesizes itself as having the identity through time of a unified whole.[53]

The Self-Conception of the Self

In synthesizing itself the I does not merely include certain items; it also conceives itself as (under certain circumstances) incorporating specified future items or stages. The I's self-synthesis includes a self-conception which projects itself into the future. We might view that self-conception partially as a hypothesis about what ties together the items A_0, A_1, . . . , A_n; in virtue of what precisely were those other things A_1, . . . , A_n included by the act A_0 of synthesis? This hypothesis, which A_1, . . . , A_n fit, need not be limited to them; other items will fall under its general characterization as well. The self will have a conception of its future self, of what under various possibilities will be part of itself, but this self-conception need not be sharp enough to resolve all imaginable puzzle cases. The very fact that the self is a whole, neither a conglomerate nor a simple, should lead us to expect difficult puzzle cases; for no one enduring part (soul or whatever) specifies the self's identity by its presence. The self's conception of itself will be, in the terms of the closest continuer theory, a listing and weighting of dimensions. This provides, implicitly, a measure of closeness whereby the self judges various problem cases, deciding which of various future entities will be its closest continuer, will be itself. This judgment will be in accordance with the self's own weighting of the dimensions in its conception of itself.

The closest continuer schema, as we presented it, gave the framework within which to discuss identity and closeness, but did not provide the metric whereby closeness is determined. The question of which dimensions are included with what weight remained open, as did questions about the general structure of what underlies closeness: are there tradeoffs among dimensions, are some ranked lexically before others, and so on. When people disagree about some of the problem cases of personal identity, for example, transfer of self from one body to another, this may stem from their different views of which dimensions, with what relative weights, constitute the metric of closeness. What is the correct measure of distance for persons, then, and upon what does its being the correct one depend?

Persons have conceptions of themselves, of what is important about their being themselves. It seems plausible to suppose they judge problem cases in accordance with the dimensions and weighting embodied in their own view of themselves. They imagine themselves in the described (problem) situation, one that begins with what is assumed to be an unproblematic case of identity, and they think: if the things in that story happened to me, which if any of the resulting persons or beings would I be? We answer a question about another's identity by asking the question about ourselves, thereupon projecting our own dimensional weightings onto his or her case.

I suggest that there is not simply one correct measure of closeness for persons. Each person's own selection and weighting of dimensions enter into determining his own actual identity, not merely into his view of it. Because of our differing notions of closeness, for the same structural description of a problem case we can give different answers about which resulting person would be us, each answer correct. If the story were about me, then Z would be X and Y would not, whereas if it were about you, Y would be X and Z would not. Which continuer is closest to a person depends (partially) on that person's own notion of closeness. Only with selves, reflexively self-referring beings with conceptions of themselves, is the closeness relation fixed in this way. Since their images of what constitutes their identity (partially) fixes which their closest continuer is, such beings partially choose themselves. I have a special authority in fixing who I am—it is my view of closeness that (partially) specifies my identity. In its self-synthesis, the self incorporates a (partial) metric of closeness; does bodily continuity have greater weight for basketball players than it does for philosophers?*

Not only do I (partially) determine the closeness metric for myself, I also can realize you do this for yourself too. Instead of applying my own metric imperialistically to you, then, I can leave room in my conception of you for your own self-conception. I can leave a space, a place-holder, in my general conception of what constitutes a person, to be filled in, for each person, by his own weighted sum of dimensions which fixes what will be his own closest continuer. My conception of him is as someone whose identity is partially fixed by his own self-conception. This may not be as much leeway as he would like; it

---

* I have not discussed the limits upon self-synthesis, upon what may be incorporated as past stages or items, or in the dimensions and weights to judge comparative closeness about future stages or items. One would hope to find some limits specified by features of the act of reflexive self-synthesis; but those may tell us only that certain things cannot be given zero weight, and not that some other farfetched dimensions or items must be given zero weight.

leaves him only some choice within my (largely filled in) general conception of a person. Still, to the extent we share this general conception, we can grant each other special authority over each's own identity.*

That different notions of identity through time apply to people who specify themselves differently, that selves are special among entities in having their identity over time be (partially) self-determined, seems to me to confer a special, and desirable, dignity on each of us. We should recall this virtue of the self-synthesizing view, when it faces the considerable complexities of a person through his own self-conception partially fixing the correct closeness relation for himself. I will list only three. First, suppose that according to X's weighting of dimensions, the future Y will be him and Z will not, but according to Y's weighting of dimensions, X is not a close enough predecessor to be Y. For good measure, suppose also that according to Z's weighting of dimensions, X is his closest predecessor and he (Z) is X's closest continuer, so Z holds that he is X. Second, if there also are changes in the weighting of the dimensions over time, which participant's weighting of dimensions has special authority in answering the question of who's who? The answer that continuity of weighting is necessary for sameness of identity merely appears to express one particular weighting, the one that gives great weight to sameness or continuity of weighting. Third, two different beings might view the same being as their predecessor. My weighting makes X a continuation of me and not you, while yours makes him a continuation of you and not me. Perhaps X himself is or would be confused, or perhaps he would plunk for one of us because the nature of his connection to that one brings him also to apply that one's weighting. It cannot be said that we are both right. (Don't say: that's right too.) Similar problems of overlap can arise at one time, given the different possibilities of carving up the world. If you can clump yourself along any (artificial) relations around reflexive self-referring, can your demarcation of yourself include my arms, or my whole body? Or even my capacity to reflexively self-refer? Some uniformity of delimitation is achieved in a social matrix. Rewards and punish-

* Hugh Kenner describes James Joyce's narrative technique wherein a character or his actions would be described in the terms he would use, even though the character is not then talking. (*Joyce's Voices*, University of California Press, Berkeley, 1978, ch. 2.)

ments will lead to a boundary in a particular location along given innate salient features or dimensions. Recalcitrant individuals who act on their deviant classifications wherein part of their own body includes someone else's arms, will be punished, institutionalized, or killed. Usually, the mutual compatibility of self-definitions occurs with less hardship.[54]

If I synthesize myself by specifying, for me, dimensions and metric within a closest continuer schema, and also view myself as filling in a place-holder and reflexively specifying my own identity over time by specifying the metric in the dimensional space, then this invites the most iterated Fichtean terminology: the self synthesizes itself as a self synthesizing itself as a self. (Should we stop when the breath runs out? Or just trail off with dots?) Further, the self might have as part of its self-conception not only that it has a self-conception (that is, fills in the place-holder), but that it has that particular self-conception (fills in the place-holder in that particular way). If its dimensional weighting gives having this particular self-conception great weight, then a self-conception which can be seen as naturally growing out of this one (as its closest continuer) will be seen as an important component of a future self—of this self's future self. If, however, having this particular self-conception is not ranked lexically first, there is the possibility of the following interesting divergence: Y might be closer to an earlier X than Z is according to the weighted dimensions specified in X's self-conception C, while, since Y itself does not have that self-conception C though Z does, Z would be ranked closer by the dimension "having the same self-conception".

Reflexive Caring

At the close of Part I of this chapter, we considered why we care especially about our closest continuers, and answered that we care about the best instantiated realization for us of identity through time. Through a series of questions, this led finally to the question of why the self cares especially about itself, about its own current self. The view of the self as self-synthesizing helps provide an answer to this question. Note, first, that the special caring of the self for itself is a self-reflexive caring. It is not that the self cares especially for itself as a bearer of some non-self-reflexive property, as an especially sterling example of some general property P that it happens to have. The self cares especially for itself as itself; I care especially for myself as me. In contrast, self-hatred, I conjecture, always is based on the self's possession of some denigrated property that is non-self-reflexive (which the self knows reflexively that it has); in self-hatred, the self does not hate itself as itself, but as a possessor of some undesirable (nonreflexive) trait.

The I synthesizes itself around the self-reflexive act A_0, as a self-synthesizing I. Whatever else is included in its boundaries and nature is not (fully) fixed externally, but determined in the act of synthesis. Is it, then, an artifact of self-synthesis that the I cares especially about itself; does the I simply synthesize itself so as to include within its boundaries and concept of identity what it cares about? It draws the boundary line around what it especially cares about, and so it especially cares about what is within the boundary.

This view faces the difficulty that the I might care equally about some things outside the boundaries, things that could be included within only by stretching the classification too far and so diminishing its integral organic unity. The view appears to explain why the I cares about itself—it includes some things it cares about—but not why it cares especially about itself. However, we should remember that the I's measure of closeness (the metric in the space in which clustering around A_0 takes place) is not completely fixed externally, either. How the I measures closeness may depend on what measure will allow it to include within its boundary things about which it cares (especially?). Why does the I care about anything at all, including the act A_0 of reflexive self-synthesis? Should we say that if it didn't care it wouldn't do it?

The view of the I as synthesizing within itself what it cares (especially?) about, gives us the I's caring about itself, even about what may be essential to it, but it does not yet give us the I's reflexively caring about itself as itself, merely the I's caring about itself as including (nonaccidentally) those cared about things. What gives rise to the I's reflexive caring?

To care reflexively is to care in virtue of a feature bestowed in the very act of caring. It is difficult to see why the self's caring about itself must go along with any other activity. However, the self's reflexive caring is not a separate activity, which must be brought along with or transcendentally presupposed by some other activity which it does (or must do). To preserve something or create it for no ulterior purpose is to care for it; the reflexive self-synthesis of the self is itself an act of caring. And the self is cared for in virtue of a feature bestowed upon it by the very act of synthesizing-caring, the feature of being the synthesized self, the self synthesized in that self-reflexive act A_0.

We have seen earlier that the self reflexively synthesizes itself as a self, as a self synthesizing itself—it synthesizes itself as itself. Since the intentional creation and maintenance for no external or ulterior purpose also constitutes a caring, the self cares for itself as itself, it cares for itself as caring for itself—it cares for itself reflexively.

The self's care for itself is special in being reflexive, care for itself as itself rather than as a bearer of some nonreflexive property. This care need not be greater than its care for all other things. The theory of the self does not entail egoism. The self's care about itself is special, not in its unique magnitude but in its distinctive reflexiveness; each of us can say "I care about myself simply for being me." We care specially about our current and our future selves because they are us; we care about identity because we care about ourselves. Such caring is rather like the pride of craftsmanship, except that it is more like the act of craftsmanship, but with no external object: a reflexive act of craftsmanship. Thus we have an explanation of the specialness of the self's care about itself. A further explanation would be needed for why the self (usually? appropriately?) cares so greatly about itself. Here a beginning is provided by some points already mentioned: the act A_0 includes in the synthesis what is cared greatly about; the act of synthesis would not take place unless the components were significantly valued; a theory of value may hold some strong reflexive caring is significantly valuable.

An Ontologically Solid Self?

Some readers may find the self-synthesizing view objectionable in that it does not locate the self as an entity (apart from the self's own self-synthesis), as an ontological item, part of "the furniture of the universe". There is one way I should mention of understanding the self's status, a way I do not find attractive or enticing despite the fact that it fits or explains certain persistent puzzles about the self. We might understand the self as a property—in Frege's terminology, as an unsaturated entity—rather than as an object. (Will Marxists view this as the bourgeois theory of the self: the self as property?)

This would illuminate some well-known perplexities confronting any theory of the self, perplexities I will just list here.

1. We cannot find the self. As Hume wrote in a well-known passage: "For my part, when I enter most intimately into what I call *myself*, I always stumble on some particular perception or other, of heat or cold, light or shade, love or hatred, pain or pleasure. I never catch *myself* at any time without a perception, and never can observe anything but the perception" (*Treatise of Human Nature*, Book I, Part IV, Section IV). The literature of eastern meditative techniques is full of advice about how to still the mind and quiet the thoughts and impressions so that the self will shine through. Perhaps Hume just went about looking for the self in the wrong way. He didn't do anything special to find the self, did he? Perhaps only special techniques can succeed in removing what covers over the self, in removing exactly what Hume found. We shall have occasion later to examine the question of what these meditative and yoga techniques show; for now we need only say that it is not an object which shows through. If the self were a property, we would expect Hume's quest to have had its result, for the self could not then be found as an object of introspective search.

2. It is difficult to imagine the self apart from any embodiment or realization. There need not be a physical realization, but it is difficult to imagine the self floating free, without any tie to any kind of stuff at all. (Even the literature on experiences out of the body speaks of subtle bodies.)

On an Aristotelian view of a property as existing in the entities that possess it, and not floating free as a separate entity or object, we would understand why the self must be instantiated in some stuff, however wispy.*

3. Yet it is difficult to see how the self can be identical with any particular stuff, or even to see how the self is connected with that

---

* Moreover, if we took a Fregean view that concepts cannot be referred to (as concepts), we would get the consequence that the self is, in Ryle's terminology, systematically elusive.

stuff, whether it be matter or wispier material (for example, ethereal "bodies").

Again, this would be expected on an Aristotelian view of properties, and certainly on a Platonic one. Also, for the earlier difficult tie cases, the view would see the property as multiply realized, as had by two distinct persons.

A property is not identical to any object in which it is. The relationship of the self to the body is the relationship of a property to an object in which it is. The reason we find it difficult to specify the relationship of self to human body is that we are unable to specify the relationship of property to object. This is indeed a difficulty, but it is not a special problem about the self and the body.[55] (And perhaps we are helped in understanding the general problem by thinking of the particular case of the self. We can try to illuminate one relation by the other, depending upon which we find more obscure.)

Thus, the first three perplexities about the self are illuminated by viewing the self as a property. There are two ways, at least, that one might identify a person with a property: first with a nonindexical and nonreflexive property, for example, "being Robert Nozick"; second, with one whose statement utilizes a first person reflexive pronoun, for example, "being I". The second has the virtue of putting reflexivity directly into the nature of the self; but in placing a reflexive term in the statement of a property, it has a defect of obscurity. If the theory holds that the particular concept or property I am is being I, then it will place reflexivity into the essence of the self, and also explain why all public or physicalistic descriptions of the world seem to leave me out, lacking as they do reflexive terms.

The view of the self as a property also may illuminate talk in some traditions about the self's merging with the One,* wherein the self does not stay separate from the One, yet does not disappear either. Being I becomes a property of the One, so I do not disappear but neither am I distinct from it.

A word more about the reflexivity of the property: being I. Let P be the property: being reflexively self-referring. People have P and tables do not. In virtue of having the property P, I also have the property of being I. You also have the property P, and in virtue of

---

* Let me tell you a very short story entitled "On Merging with the One". "Merging with another to form a higher unity is all very well, but where precisely does that leave *me*?" asked the sperm cell.

that property have the property of being you, which you would state as "being I". We each have a being-I property but, being indexical, these properties differ. They arise however from our having the same nonindexical property P: being reflexively self-referring.

The property of being I came into being somewhere around the time when I did, when there came to be some locatable distinct thing with (or which would have) the capacity for reflexive self-referring, the thing whose closest continuer eventually did reflexively self-refer to me, that is, to some closest predecessor of the entity to which I just reflexively self-referred. Though philosophers tend to speak of properties as unchanging and existing eternally, the view of properties as coming into existence is a quite natural one. Was there the property of being the President of the United States before the United States was even a gleam in anybody's eye? That property came into existence before George Washington became the first President, it certainly existed by the time the Constitution was ratified. Exactly when it came into existence, I would not try to say.

The property of being I came into existence at a certain time in virtue of the property P becoming instantiated in what arose from the fertilization of Sophie Cohen Nozick's ovum by Max Nozick's sperm, a fact for which I am very grateful. And doesn't the property of being I also change? Isn't it a different property from what it was thirty-five years ago? Alternatively, perhaps viewing the property as eternal and unchanging will satisfy the desire of some for immortality, or at least for a self which is nonmortal.

A property has a durable ontological status. Yet, if the property of "being I" is specified by the closest continuer theory, if that property is, for example, the property of being the closest continuer (and predecessor) of the doer of this very self-reflexive act, then although it has the ontological status of a property, it will seem too sinuous, too serpentine in its windings, to supply the desired permanent, underlying, abiding, valuable self. But am I not more limited by such an abiding entity than by the range of freedom the closest continuer theory gives? So which is better, a self with less intrinsic unity, or with fewer limits? Might there even be a kind of unity which a whole has more of than does something with a fixed and unchanging part or component? (Note that these remarks in defense of a closest continuer conception do not apply merely against a simple property view of the self.)

The view that we are like properties likens us to monadic properties. Our survey of philosophical structures above showed this to be the simplest of possibilities, so the line of approach might be pursued into other structural modes and forms. Leaving aside these extensions, this view of us as Fregean concepts or properties is different enough to put old and perhaps stale issues in a fresh perspective, and so is valuable even if it is too crazy to endorse or believe. True, sometimes an appearance of craziness can stem from a view's novelty rather than its content. And perhaps sometimes the craziness of a philosophical view is not such a serious drawback. Is it unreasonable to think, for those philosophical problems that have withstood centuries of determined attempts to solve or dissolve them, that all the sensible alternatives have been tried and explored, and therefore that only a crazy approach has any hope of succeeding?

Yet, in this instance I do not find the view of the self as a property sufficiently illuminating, clarifying, and fruitful in its consequences to put it forth, except as a curiosity, despite its explaining why certain puzzles about the self have arisen, and despite its providing some enduring entity for the self to be. The view seems too much like a bit of philosophical chicanery, too much froth and too little substance. Still, it is worth having raised these metaphilosophical considerations about sensibleness right now, before turning to the next question.

Chapter

Two

WHY IS THERE SOMETHING RATHER THAN NOTHING?

The question appears impossible to answer.* Any factor introduced to explain why there is something will itself be part of the something to be explained, so it (or anything utilizing it) could not explain all of the something—it could not explain why there is *anything* at all. Explanation proceeds by explaining some things in terms of others, but this question seems to preclude introducing anything else, any explanatory factors. Some writers conclude from this that the question is ill-formed and meaningless. But why do they cheerfully reject the question rather than despairingly observe that it demarcates a limit of what we can hope to understand? So daunting is the question that even a recent urger of it, Heidegger, who terms it "the fundamental question of metaphysics", proposes no answer and does nothing toward showing how it might be answered.[1]

* That it is perhaps dangerous as well appears to be indicated in Hagigah 2:1 of the *Mishnah:* "Whosoever reflects on four things, it were better for him if he had not come into the world—what is above; what is beneath; what is before; and what is after." See also *Midrash Rabbah* (Soncino Press, London, 1939), 1:10, 8:2.

For Leibniz's discussion, see "On the Radical Origination of Things" in L. Loemaker, ed., *Leibniz Philosophical Papers and Letters* (2nd ed., Reidel, Dodrecht, 1969), pp. 486–491.

This chapter considers several possible answers to the question. My aim is not to assert one of these answers as correct (if I had great confidence in any one, I wouldn't feel the special need to devise and present several); the aim, rather, is to loosen our feeling of being trapped by a question with no possible answer—one impossible to answer yet inescapable. (So that one feels the only thing to do is gesture at a Mark Rothko painting.) The question cuts so deep, however, that any approach that stands a chance of yielding an answer will look extremely weird. Someone who proposes a non-strange answer shows he didn't understand this question. Since the question is not to be rejected, though, we must be prepared to accept strangeness or apparent craziness in a theory that answers it.

Still, I do not endorse here any one of the discussed possible answers as correct. It is too early for that. Yet it is late enough in the question's history to stop merely asking it insistently, and to begin proposing possible answers. Thereby, we at least show how it is possible to explain why there is something rather than nothing, how it is possible for the question to have an answer.

Explaining Everything

The question "why is there something rather than nothing?" quickly raises issues about the limits of our understanding. Is it possible for everything to be explained? It often is said that at any given time the most general laws and theories we know (or believe) are unexplained, but nothing is unexplainable in principle. At a later time we can formulate a deeper theory to explain the previous deepest one. This previous theory wasn't unexplainable, and though the new deepest theory is unexplained, at least for the time being, it too is not unexplainable.

The question about whether everything is explainable is a different one. Let the relation E be the relation *correctly explains*, or *is the (or a) correct explanation of*. One partial analysis of E is the Hempelian analysis of deductive nomological and statistical explanation, which we may view as providing necessary but not sufficient conditions for two types of explanation.[2] The explanatory relation E is irreflexive, asymmetrical, and transitive. Nothing explains itself; there is no X and Y such that X explains Y and Y explains X; and for all X, Y, Z, if X explains Y and Y explains Z then X explains Z.[3] Thus, E establishes a strict partial ordering among all truths, or (alternatively) within the set of true sentences of English plus contemporary mathematics whose length is no more than 20,000,000 words. (I assume that anything of scientific interest can be expressed in such sentences, and shall treat their number as *in effect* infinite.) Notice that we are not talking only of what explanations are known to us, but rather of what explanatory relations actually hold within the set of truths.

How is the set of truths structured by the explanatory relation E? There appear to be only two possibilities. Either (1) there is some truth that no further truth stands in E to, or (2) there are infinite explanatory chains, and each truth has something else that stands in E to it. Either there are no foundations to science, no most fundamental or deep explanatory principles (the second possibility) or there are some truths without any explanation (the first possibility); these actually will be unexplainable in that *no* truths (known or not) explain them. About such truths *p* lacking further explanation, there also appear to be two possibilities. First, that such truths are necessarily true, and could not have been otherwise. (Aristotle, as standardly interpreted, maintained this.) But it is difficult to see how this would be true. It is not enough merely for it to be of the essence of the things which exist (and so necessarily true of them) that *p*. There would remain the question of why those and only those sorts of things (subject to *p*) exist; only if *p* must be true of everything possible would this question be avoided.

The second possibility is that *p* is a brute fact. It just happens that things are that way. There is no explanation (or reason) why they are that way rather than another way, no (hint of) necessity to remove this arbitrariness.

One way to remove some arbitrariness from the end of the explanatory chain is illustrated by the program of deriving moral content from the form of morality, a persistent attempt since Kant. Part of the motivation, no doubt, is the goal of convincing others of particular moral content: "If you accept any morality at all (the form), then you must accept this content." Apart from this interpersonal task, there is the desire to understand the structure of the realm of moral truths and, if that realm is autonomous and so underivable from nonmoral truths, to determine whether the fundamental moral truths or principles are arbitrary brute facts. If moral content could be gotten from moral form, that content would not be merely a brute fact; it would be the only possible moral content, holding true if any truths at all fit the form of morality. Particular moral content, thus, would be shown to be conditionally necessary: necessary given that there are any moral truths (of that form). To be sure, though that particular content would be rendered less arbitrary, the question would remain of why there were any truths exhibiting that form.

Within the factual realm, the parallel endeavor would derive particular empirical content from the form of facts, or more narrowly from the form of scientific laws or theories. This would show that if there are ultimate scientific laws, so nothing else does or can stand in the explanatory relation E to them, then these must have particular content. Such a project might formulate various symmetry and invariance conditions as holding of fundamental scientific laws,[4] showing that only particular content satisfied all these conditions about form. This would render the particular content less arbitrary, but the question would remain of why there were any ultimate scientific laws, any truths of that specified form. In any case, there will be the question of why there are any laws at all. This question is narrower than our title question but raises similar problems. If all explanation utilizes laws, then in the explanation of why there are any laws, some law will appear. Will not the question of why it holds, and hence of why any law holds, thereby go unanswered?*

Is there any way at all to remove these last unexplained bits? Since a fact that nothing explains is left dangling, while a fact explained by something else leaves the problem of explaining that something else, only one thing could leave nothing at all unexplained: a fact that explains itself. However, if anything has appeared obvious about explanation, it has been that the explanatory relation E is irreflexive. Explanations of the form "p because p" are inadequate and unsatisfactory. We want an explanation of p to provide a deeper reason why p is true; this is not provided by p itself. To answer "why is the sky blue?" by saying "because the sky is blue" would be taken as rejecting the question rather than answering it. A small literature exists that attempts to formulate precise conditions whereby circular expla-

---

* Could one try to show that if there are any truths at all, there must be ultimate scientific laws (of that form)?

nations are excluded.[5] Viewing the explanatory relation E as deductive but irreflexive, it must distinguish the legitimate ways a fact to be explained may "be contained in the (explanatory) premisses" from objectionable self-explanation.

The objectionable examples of explanatory self-deduction (total or partial) involve deductions that proceed via the propositional calculus. Would the explanation of a law be illegitimate automatically if instead the law was deduced from itself via quantification theory, as an instance of itself? If explanation is subsumption under a law, why may not a law be subsumed under itself?

Suppose a principle P presented sufficient conditions for a fundamental law's holding true; any lawlike statement that satisfies these conditions, such as invariance and symmetry, will hold true. P says: any lawlike statement having characteristics C is true. Let us imagine this is our deepest law; we explain why other fundamental laws hold true in accordance with the deep principle P, by their having the characteristic C. Those laws are true because they have C.

Next we face the question of why P holds true, and we notice that P itself also has characteristics C. This yields the following deduction.

P: any lawlike statement having characteristic C is true.
P is a lawlike statement with characteristic C.
Therefore P is true.

This is not presented to justify P or as a reason for believing P. Rather, granting that P *is* true, the question is whether what explains its being true, is its having characteristics C (since everything with C is true). A general statement is not proven true simply by being susceptible to an inference of this form. Many false statements also are derivable from themselves in this way, for example

S: Every sentence of exactly eight words is true.
S has exactly eight words.
Therefore S is true.

Although derivable as an instance of itself, S is false, nevertheless. Our question is not whether such self-subsumption as an instance of itself can constitute a proof, but whether it can constitute an explanation; *if* the statement is true, can the reason why be the very content it itself states?

Is self-subsuming explanation thwarted by the fact that explanations must be deeper than what they (purport to) explain? Within Tarski's framework, P would have to be assigned a fixed metalinguistic level of depth, and so could not be used to deduce itself as above; however, there could be a hierarchy of metalanguages, each one enabling a deduction of the next most superficial law of the family of similar P laws. Another theory recently has been presented by Saul Kripke, in which statements are not assigned fixed levels but each seeks its own appropriate level—the most superficial one wherein the statement applies to its referent(s).[6] Hence, P when used in a deduction will be one level deeper than what instances it. In this spirit, a theory statement deduced as an instance of itself via quantification theory is deeper as subsuming than as subsumed. In contrast, when p is deduced from itself via the propositional calculus, both premiss and conclusion will have the same depth. A truth can go so deep that it holds in virtue of being subsumed under that very deep truth itself.[7]

Explanatory self-subsumption, I admit, appears quite weird—a feat of legerdemain. When we reach the ultimate and most fundamental explanatory laws, however, there are few possibilities. Either there is an infinite chain of different laws and theories, each explaining the next, or there is a finite chain. If a finite chain, either the endmost laws are unexplainable facts or necessary truths or the only laws there can be if there are laws of a certain sort at all (the fact that there are laws of that sort is classified under one of the other possibilities)—or the endmost laws are self-subsuming.

We face two questions about such self-subsumption: does it reduce the arbitrariness and brute-fact quality of the endpoint at all? If so, does it remove that quality completely? It does reduce that quality, I believe, though I cannot quite say it removes it altogether. If a brute fact is something that cannot be explained by anything, then a self-subsumable principle isn't a brute fact; but if a brute fact is something that cannot be explained by anything *else*, such a principle counts as a brute fact. We normally have no need to distinguish these two senses of 'brute fact', and perhaps usually presume the second. However, we should not be too impressed by the literature's unanimity that explanation is irreflexive. Those writers were not considering explanatory self-subsumption, via quantification theory, of the most fundamental laws and principles. With these ultimate facts, explanatory self-subsumption seems illuminating and legitimate. What, after all, is the alternative?

Inegalitarian Theories

There is one common form many theories share: they hold that one situation or a small number of states N are natural or privileged and in need of no explanation, while all other states are to be explained as deviations from N, resulting from the action of forces F that cause movement away from the natural state. For Newton, rest or uniform rectilinear motion is the natural state requiring no explanation, while all other motions are to be explained by unbalanced forces acting upon bodies. For Aristotle, rest was the natural state, deviations from which were produced by the continual action of impressed forces. This pattern is not, however, restricted to theories of motion.[8]

Let us call a theory of this sort an inegalitarian theory. An inegalitarian theory partitions states into two classes: those requiring explanation, and those neither needing nor admitting of explanation. Inegalitarian theories are especially well geared to answer questions of the form "why is there X rather than Y?" There is a non-N state rather than an N state because of the forces F that acted to bring the system away from N. When there is an N state, this is because there were no unbalanced forces acting to bring the system away from N.

Inegalitarian theories unavoidably leave two questions unanswered. First, why is it N that is the natural state which occurs in the absence of unbalanced external forces, rather than some other (type of) state N'? Second, given that N is a natural or privileged state, why is it forces of type F, not of some other type F', that produce deviations from N? If our fundamental theory has an inegalitarian structure, it will leave as brute and unexplained the fact that N rather than something else is a natural state, and that F rather than something else is the deviation force.

However special a state appears, to assume it is a natural state within an inegalitarian theory has significant content. We should be very suspicious of a priori arguments purporting to demonstrate that a state is a natural one, and we should search such arguments carefully for the covert assumption that the state is natural or that only certain types of forces can produce deviations from whatever the natural state happens to be.* We cannot assume any particular inegalitarian theory as our fundamental theory.

The question 'why is there something rather than nothing?' is posed against the background of an assumed inegalitarian theory. If there were nothing, then about this situation would there also be the question (though without anyone to ask it) of why there is nothing rather than something? To ask 'why is there something rather than nothing?' assumes that nothing(ness) is the natural state that does not need to be explained, while deviations or divergences from nothingness have to be explained by the introduction of special causal factors. There is, so to speak, a presumption in favor of nothingness. The problem is so intractable because any special causal factor that could explain a deviation from nothingness is itself a divergence from nothingness, and so the question seeks its explanation also.†

Is it possible to imagine nothingness being a natural state which

---

* See Ernest Nagel, *The Structure of Science* (Harcourt, Brace and World, New York, 1961), pp. 175–178. R. Harré recently has taken just such a suspicious position. He writes: "I come to the most fundamental and the most powerful of methodological principles. It is this. *Enduring is in no need of explanation.* We are not required to explain the fact that something remains the same; only if there is a change is an explanation called for." (*The Principles of Scientific Thinking*, Macmillan, 1970, p. 248.) But don't we need an explanation of why one thing counts as the same, for the purposes of the principle, while another does not? The principle is trivialized if whatever is thought to require no explanation will be said to endure relative to a set of concepts specially designed to fit.

In contrast to Harré's principle, consider the theory of the sixteenth century Kabbalist Meir ben Gabbai, according to whom only God's continuing production of the written and oral Torah maintains things in existence; "were it to be interrupted for even a moment, all creatures would sink back into their non-being." (Quoted in Gershom Scholem, *The Messianic Idea in Judaism*, Schocken Books, New York, 1971, p. 298.)

† If a fundamental inegalitarian theory holds that everything not in N is a deviation from N, also that forces of type F are not in N, then the existence of any F force will be a deviation from N. Since according to the theory, all deviations from N are explainable only by the actions of F's, the fact that there are any F's at all (which fact is a deviation from N) can be explained only by the action of F's. According to the fundamental inegalitarian theory itself, though, there cannot be any explanation of why there are any F's at all that doesn't introduce some F's as explanatory factors. That necessarily leaves us, it seems, without an understanding of why there are any F's at all.

itself contains the force whereby something is produced? One might hold that nothingness as a natural state is derivative from a very powerful force toward nothingness, one any other forces have to overcome. Imagine this force as a vacuum force, sucking things into nonexistence or keeping them there. If this force acts upon itself, it sucks nothingness into nothingness, producing something or, perhaps, everything, every possibility. If we introduced the verb "to nothing" to denote what this nothingness force does to things as it makes or keeps them nonexistent, then (we would say) the nothingness nothings itself. (See how Heideggerian the seas of language run here!) Nothingness, hoisted by its own powerful petard, produces something. In the Beatles' cartoon *The Yellow Submarine*, a being like a vacuum cleaner goes around sucking up first other objects, next the surrounding background; finally, turning upon itself, it sucks itself into nothingness, thereby producing with a pop a brightly colored variegated scene.

On this view, there is something rather than nothing because the nothingness there once was nothinged itself, thereby producing something. Perhaps it nothinged itself just a bit, though, producing something but leaving some remaining force for nothingness. Figure 2.1 graphs the amount of nothingness force it takes to nothing some part of a given nothingness force being exerted. Curve I begins above the 45° line x = y, and cuts across it at point *e*. If this curve holds true, then a certain amount of nothingness force *a*, to start with,

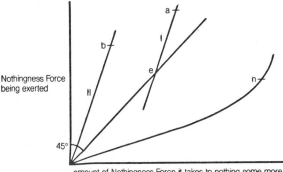

amount of Nothingness Force it takes to nothing some more of
the Nothingness Force being exerted

FIGURE 2.1

will act upon itself and nothing some of itself, thereby reducing the amount remaining and also the amount necessary to nothing some of the remaining nothingness force. The situation moves down the curve I until it crosses the line x = y. Past that point e, to nothing some more nothingness force would require more than is being exerted and hence available. If the correct curve were II, however, then a nothingness force of b, to start with, would nothing some of itself and so would move down the curve to the origin, obliterating all of the nothingness force, leaving none remaining. On the other hand, if we start at a point below the 45° line x = y, for example point n, there is not being exerted enough nothingness force to nothing any of itself, and so the situation will remain just as is; there will be no movement down the curve from n.

Even if it were true that there was an original nothingness force, the problem would remain of explaining the particular starting point and the shape of the curve that goes through it. Why was that the starting point, and in virtue of what did that curve hold? One possibility appears to leave nothing dangling: the curve is just the 45° line itself, and we start somewhere on it and move down to the origin. There will remain the problem of precisely where we start (is the only unarbitrary point infinitely far out?), but the curve itself may appear unarbitrary. The y axis measures the resistance being offered, so the curve x = y says it takes a force equal to the resistance to overcome some of it. This condition of symmetry, the 45° line, appears less arbitrary than any other. This appearance, however, is somewhat misleading. For why are we using this kind of graph paper? This 45° line would look very unsymmetrical on logarithmic graph paper, while the most symmetrical looking line there would stand for a very different phenomenon.

Thus far I have been considering the inegalitarian theory that assumes nothingness is the natural state. It is time to undermine the picture of nothingness as natural, first by imagining inegalitarian theories where it is not. We might imagine that some fullness of existence is the natural state, and that the actual situation deviates from this fullness because of special forces acting. Whether this theory allows nothingness to result eventually will depend upon whether the force producing deviations from fullness, once it has performed the rest of its task, can act upon itself thereby annihilating itself, the very last vestige of any fullness. (Or perhaps several forces operate to diverge from fullness that, after the rest of their job is done, can simultaneously annihilate each other.) The western philosophical tradition tends to hold that existence is better or more perfect than nonexistence,* so it tends to view forces that cause divergence from fullness as malignant. But one can imagine another view, wherein the movement from thick and dense matter to more ethereal and spiritual modes of energy and existence is a movement of increasing perfection. The limit of such movement toward more and more insubstantial existence will be the most perfect: nothingness itself. Since reaching such perfection might take hard work and spiritual development, the answer to the question "why is there something rather than nothing?" might be that the universe is not yet spiritually developed enough for there to be nothing. The something is not enlightened yet. Perfection is not the natural state, and there is something rather than nothing because this is not the best of all possible worlds. Against the background of some such theory, the opposite question "why is there nothing rather than something?" (as applied to the appropriate situation) would make sense, and the correct answer would specify the forces that produced the deviation from somethingness, bringing about nothingness.

Apart from any such specific background theory, we should note a general reason or argument for *something's* being the natural state. (This argument was pointed out to me by Emily Nozick, then age twelve.) If something cannot be created out of nothing, then, since there is something, it didn't come from nothing. And there never was a time when there was only nothing. If ever nothing was the natural state, which obtained, then something could never have arisen. But there is something. So nothingness is not the natural state; if there is a natural state, it is somethingness. (If nothingness were the natural state, we never could have gotten to something—we couldn't have gotten here from there.)

It is possible to think that one cannot answer any question if one cannot answer the question of why there is something rather than

---

* I am told (by Sidney Morgenbesser) that in a novel by Peter DeVries a minister is asked by a troubled parishioner whether God exists, and replies "God is so perfect he doesn't need to exist."

nothing. How can we know why something is (or should be) a certain way if we don't know why there is anything at all? Surely this is the first philosophical question that has to be answered. It doesn't seem to assume anything (other than that there is something), while the answer to any other philosophical question is liable to be overturned or undermined or transformed by the answer to this one. However, to ask this question is to presume a great deal, namely, that nothingness is a natural state requiring no explanation, while all deviations from nothingness are in need of explanation. This is a very strong assumption, so strong that we cannot merely extrapolate from more limited contexts (such as argument, where the burden of proof is on the person who makes an existence claim*) and build the assumption into our fundamental theory, one not restricted within an understood wider context.

The first thing to admit is that we do not know what the natural state is; the second is that we do not know whether there is any fundamental natural state, whether the correct fundamental theory will have an inegalitarian structure. Any theory with such a structure will leave as unexplained brute facts N being the natural state, F being the deviation-producing forces, and also the laws of operation of F. Perhaps fewer things would be left dangling as brute facts by a fundamental theory that is egalitarian.

But won't the move away from an inegalitarian theory add to our explanatory tasks? If no state is privileged or natural, then for each state we shall have to explain why it rather than some other one exists. At least an inegalitarian theory didn't have to (try to) explain every state—so it faced fewer questions. To be sure, these questions it did not ask correspond to facts it left as brute. Still, to have to explain for each and every existing state why it exists seems to make the explanatory task even more unmanageable. The shift away from an inegalitarian theory seems to add to the explanatory task because now it seems that all existing states, not just some, will be in need of explanation. However, in thinking we have to explain why all existing states exist, we once again have slipped into treating nonexis-

---

* It is not clear even how to formulate this point about the burden of proof or argument. Why is an existence claim made by someone who says there is a God, whereas one is not made by someone who says there is a God-less cosmos or universe?

tence as the natural state. An egalitarian fundamental theory will not pick out existence as especially in need of explanation.

Questions of the form 'why X rather than Y?' find their home within a presumption or assumption that Y is natural. When this presumption is dropped, there is no fact of X rather than Y. Still, isn't there the fact of X to be explained, the question 'why X?' to be answered? But this is the question 'why does X exist rather than not?', 'why does X obtain rather than not?'. If we drop inegalitarian assumptions completely, we reject the view that when X exists or obtains, it exists or obtains rather than does not or rather than something else—we eliminate the "rather than".

Egalitarianism

One way to dissolve the inegalitarian class distinction between nothing and something, treating them on a par, is to apply a version of the principle of indifference from probability theory. There are many ways $w_1, w_2, \ldots$ for there to be something, but there is only one way w_0 for there to be nothing. Assign equal probability to each alternative possibility w_i, assuming it is a completely random matter which one obtains. The chances, then, are very great that there will be something, for "there is something" holds of every possibility except w_0. On some views of statistical explanation, by (correctly) specifying a random mechanism that yields a very high probability of there being something, we thereby would have explained why there is. ("Why is there something? It is just what you would expect that random mechanism to produce.")

In regard to the use of principles of indifference within probability theory, it often has been pointed out that much rests upon the initial partitioning into (what will be treated as equiprobable) states. A state that is single in one partition can encompass many states in another partition. Even the many ways of there being something might be viewed as just one state in the two-membered partition: there is nothing, there is something. Yet while we can shrink there being something down to only one alternative, we cannot, even artificially, expand there being nothing up to more than one alternative. If there is nothing(ness), there just are no aspects of it to use to divide it into two alternatives.*

So on the worst assumptions about how the partitioning goes, yielding the two-membered partition, there initially is a one-half chance that something exists. Since all other partitions are at least three-membered, on these other partitionings the initial chance of something's existing is at least two-thirds. Can we go up one level and assign probabilities to the different partitionings themselves? If we go up levels, assigning equal probabilities to the worst case partitioning and to all others (equally), then the probability of something existing increases, and tends toward the probability in the previous equal-chance large partitioning under the principle of indifference.[9] The larger the number of alternatives partitioned, the closer the probability that something exists approaches to one.

This model of a random process with one alternative being that nothing exists (N), is illuminating. However, it does not sufficiently shake off inegalitarian assumptions. Though the model treats its possibilities on a par, it assumes a possibility will not be realized unless at random. It assumes that the natural state for a possibility is nonrealization, and that a possibility's being realized has to be explained by special factors (including, at the limit, random ones). At this deep level the presented model remains inegalitarian. What would a thoroughgoing egalitarian theory be like?

Fecundity

A thoroughgoing egalitarian theory will not treat nonexisting or nonobtaining as more natural or privileged, even for a possibility—it will treat all possibilities on a par. One way to do this is to say that all possibilities are realized.

For the most fundamental laws and initial conditions C of the universe, the answer to the question "why C rather than D?" is that

---

* Can we say nothingness includes these two alternatives: nothingness up until and including now, and nothingness after now? First, if we treat everything symmetrically, then something also will get temporally divided similarly, preserving the ratio between the number of somethingness and of nothingness alternatives. More to our point, time also is a "something", unavailable to partition nothing(ness) if there really be that.

both independently exist. We happen to find ourselves in a C universe rather than a D universe; perhaps this is no accident for a D universe might not produce or support life such as ours. There is no explanation of why C rather than D, for there is no fact of C rather than D. All the possibilities exist in independent noninteracting realms, in "parallel universes". We might call this the fecundity assumption.[10] It appears that only such an egalitarian view does not leave any question "why X rather than Y?" unanswered. No brute fact of X rather than Y is left unexplained for no such fact holds.

Will the fecundity assumption serve to avoid inegalitarianism? Doesn't it, too, specify a natural state, one where all possibilities exist, while perhaps also countenancing deviations from this induced by various forces? Let X be the situation of every possibility obtaining, and Y one of all but two possibilities obtaining. There is no fact of X rather than Y, for both of these situations are realized. Each possibility countenanced by X obtains, as do the two fewer countenanced by Y; all together, these are merely the possibilities countenanced by X.

Y was described as admitting all but two possibilities, and so was compatible with X. Can there not be a Z that admits all but two possibilities and also excludes these remaining two as obtaining? Isn't there then a fact that has to be explained, of X rather than Z? I am tempted to answer that Z is not itself merely a description of possibilities obtaining. In attempting to exclude possibilities it becomes more than a description of possibilities; just as "only world number 3 exists and the fecundity assumption is false" is not merely a description of possibilities. Those to whom this appears lame can imagine the following. X and Z both exist in independent realms R_1 and R_2. In the realm of R_1, all possibilities exist, and in the realm of R_2 all possibilities except for two exist, and these two do not. These separate realms do not interact; also within a realm the possibilities realized are independent and noninteracting. Though not all possible worlds are realized in realm R_2, all of them are in the union of the two realms, written $R_1 \cup R_2$, which contains whatever is in either. Since R_1 already contains all possibilities, $R_1 \cup R_2 = R_1$. The (negative) fact that two possibilities do not obtain holds in the realm R_2, but not in the realm $R_1 \cup R_2$. (While all the worlds in R_2 also are in $R_1 \cup R_2$, not all the facts true of R_2 also are true of $R_1 \cup R_2$; for example, the predicate "$\neq R_1 \cup R_2$" holds of R_2 but not if its union with R_1.)

Consider the question "why isn't there nothing?" There *is* nothing —that is one of the separate possibilities which is realized. If the question means to ask why there isn't *only* nothing, with no other possibility also independently realized, it makes an unwarranted, inegalitarian assumption: that nothingness is the privileged and natural state. Why is there something rather than nothing? There isn't. There's both.

When a hypothesis avoids a fact's being left simply as a brute fact, this usually is taken to provide some reason for believing the hypothesis is true. The hypothesis of multiple independent possible worlds, too, enables us to avoid leaving something as a brute fact, in this case, the fact that there is something.

How does the principle of fecundity arise? Upon what is it based? What explains the fact that all possibilities are independently realized? That only with the principle of fecundity will no fact be left dangling as a brute fact, if true, is an insufficient explanation. It would remain to be explained why the cosmos is so structured that nothing (else) is left unexplained.

The principle of fecundity follows from the thoroughgoing rejection of inegalitarian theories. If no possibility has a privileged status, including nonexistence, then all possibilities independently exist or obtain. If the reason for an egalitarian theory is that only thus is nothing left dangling as a brute fact, we are left with the (metaphysical) question of why the universe is arranged in that epistemologically fortunate way. Why does a thoroughgoing egalitarian theory hold, rather than some inegalitarian one? The answer, of course, is that both hold in their own independent realms, while in the union of the realms all possibilities hold. But if such trickiness robs us of the ability to ask "why egalitarian rather than inegalitarian?", we still want to ask "why egalitarian?". We still want to understand the ground or basis of the realization of all possibilities.

The principle of fecundity is an invariance principle. Within general relativity, scientific laws are invariant with respect to all differentiable coordinate transformations.[11] The principle of fecundity's description of the structure of possibilities is invariant across all possible worlds. There is no one specially privileged or preferred possibility, including the one we call actual. As David Lewis puts it, "actual" is an indexical expression referring to the possible world where the utterance containing it is located (*Counterfactuals*, pp. 85–86). The actual world has no specially privileged status, it merely is the world where we are. Other independently realized possibilities also are correctly referred to by their inhabitants as actual. Invariance principles previously have removed the special status of particular portions of actuality: the (absolute) position and time of an event, the orientation, a particular state of motion (distinguished from its Lorentz transformations). The principle of fecundity extends this, denying special status to actuality itself. Yet, to point out that the principle of fecundity is an invariance principle does not explain why it holds or why a deep invariance of that sort obtains. What then is the basis or ground of the realization of all possibilities?

Fecundity and Self-Subsumption

As an ultimate and very deep principle, the principle of fecundity can subsume itself within a deductive explanation. It states that all possibilities are realized, while it itself is one of those possibilities. We can state the principle of fecundity F as

All possible worlds obtain

or as

For any p, if p states that some realm of possible worlds obtains, then p is true.

But F itself states that some realm of possible worlds obtains, namely, that of all possible worlds. So the principle F is just such a p as it describes. From this fact and from F it follows, via quantification theory, that F is true. The principle of fecundity F subsumes itself because it says that all possibilities obtain, and it itself is such a possibility. If it is a very deep fact that all possibilities obtain, then that fact, being a possibility, obtains in virtue of the deep fact that all possibilities do.*

* Do all possibilities exist or obtain, including the one that not all possibilities do? If, to avoid contradiction, we restrict the principle of fecundity so that it speaks of and subsumes only first-level possibilities, those that neither entail nor exclude the existence of other possibilities, then it will not sub-

Similarly we might try to formulate the full invariance condition that the principle of fecundity satisfies as a sufficient condition for something's holding true. Using that invariance property I, we have the invariance principle P: any (general lawlike) statement with invariance feature I holds true. Now if this invariance principle P itself has the invariant property I, then it follows, via quantification theory, that P is true. If F and P are true ultimate explanatory principles, then they are subsumed under themselves. In this case, the principle of fecundity holds in virtue of being a possibility while it is a deep fact that all possibilities obtain, and the principle of invariance holds in virtue of having the property I, while it is a deep fact that every such thing holds true.

Thus, if F and P were true, they would subsume themselves and their arbitrary or brute fact quality would be (we have said) reduced or even removed. But apart from the initial difficulty that F countenances some independently existing parallel possible worlds, it makes a very strong claim, namely that all possible worlds independently exist. According to F there would obtain a world, for example, with 4,234 independent explanatory factors and laws, not to mention even more complicated possibilities. It then would be an accident that we inhabit a world with a high degree of explanatory unity. (True, any universe unified enough to contain knowers will possess a degree of explanatory unity they find striking; but ours exhibits more than the minimal amount needed to sustain knowers.) I view this consequence as highly unwelcome, even though I realize that if the full principle of fecundity were true there would be a world (among others) that realized a high degree of explanatory unity, yet whose inhabitants would find the principle of fecundity very implausible since it made the salient and striking cognitive feature of their world, explanatory unity, merely a happenstance.

This suggests that we limit or restrict the principle of fecundity to hold just that there obtain all possible worlds or realms of a certain sort S. There are two conditions we want satisfied by the sort S in the limited principle of fecundity LF: that our actual world be of sort S, and that the principle LF itself state a possibility of sort S. Moreover,

---

sume itself. Thus, as before, we interpret it to speak of all possibilities in their own noninteracting realms. This includes, in its own separate realm, the possibility that not all possibilities obtain. However, in (set-theoretical) union there is strength.

if the limitation is to meet our previous objection to the unlimited principle of fecundity then also the sort S will (among other things) specify some high degree of explanatory unity. Such a limited principle of fecundity LF would explain the existence of the actual world, as well as explaining itself via explanatory self-subsumption, all without opening the door to every possibility's obtaining.

The more limited is the sort S, the less powerful is the principle of limited fecundity (as compared to the unlimited principle) and the narrower the range of worlds said to obtain. Which is the most limited sort S that satisfies the three conditions? Perhaps there is a sort S satisfying the three conditions that fits the actual world but no other possible world. The principle LF incorporating that sort would (potentially) explain why the actual world obtains, as well as why LF itself holds (via explanatory self-subsumption), without any reification of other possible worlds.[12] Our claim is not that a (or the most) limited principle of fecundity that satisfied the three conditions must or would be true. The point, rather, is that given a true limited principle of fecundity satisfying the three conditions, there then will be an explanation of the world with nothing left dangling as an arbitrary or brute fact. Our aim is to describe how it could turn out that everything has an explanation.

One suggestion about the restrictive sort S is especially salient. Since the fundamental principle is to be self-subsuming, perhaps "self-subsuming" demarcates the sort itself. This specifies the following principle of limited fecundity:

All self-subsuming principles hold true,
All self-subsuming possibilities are realized.

There are two notions of self-subsumption to consider: a direct one wherein something subsumes itself in one step, and an indirect one where something x directly subsumes something else which directly subsumes something which . . . directly subsumes x. (Indirect subsumption is the ancestral of the direct subsumption relation.) The wider variant of this version of limited fecundity says that all indirectly self-subsuming possibilities are realized, the narrower one only that all directly self-subsuming possibilities are realized.

However, neither version limits the full principle of fecundity at all, for that full principle directly subsumes itself. (This also shows the wider version subsumes itself; it yields the full principle in one step, which yields the wider version in one or two more.) Thus the sort must be further specified: all self-subsuming possibilities of sort S are realized. Note, though, that this will raise the question of whether that principle itself is self-subsuming of sort S. Consider, for example, the narrower of the versions above of the principle of limited fecundity:

> All directly self-subsuming possibilities are realized;
> All directly self-subsuming principles hold true.

Is this principle itself directly self-subsuming? That seems undetermined by anything said thus far. If it directly subsumes itself—no contradiction follows from this supposition—then it does; while if it does not directly subsume itself—also a noncontradictory supposition—then it does not. Either supposition leads to a consistent theory.[13]

Would a similar self-subsuming explanation be possible if only nothingness had existed instead? Some principle R would have to specify a property N which only two things satisfied: the possibility of nothing's existing, and R itself.

> R: Exactly what has feature N obtains.

R would hold in virtue of having N, while nothingness would obtain in virtue of being the only other N-satisfier, there being none further. Nothingness obtaining would not be an arbitrary and brute fact only if some deep true principle R explained itself via explanatory self-subsumption and yielded nothing (else). That is what would have to be the case if there was nothingness, unarbitrarily. However, since there is something, no such principle R holds true.

Different possible self-subsuming ultimate principles can be formulated, some yielding the actual world (and more), others not. That ultimate principle which is true will, I have suggested, explain itself by subsuming itself. (There need not be only one ultimate principle; the explanatory chains can terminate in several independent ones, each self-subsuming.) Being a deep fact, deep enough to subsume and to yield itself, the principle will not be left dangling without any explanation. A question seems to remain, however: why does that particular self-subsuming principle hold true rather than one of the other ones?* Can we merely answer: it holds in virtue of having the property it ascribes? If one of the others had held instead, it would have held in virtue of having the property it ascribed. So is it not still arbitrary that the particular self-subsuming principle that holds, does hold? Perhaps it is not a brute fact that it holds—for perhaps a brute fact is one without any explanation, while this principle is explained via self-subsumption. Yet though it is not a brute fact that the principle holds, still it seems arbitrary. Why couldn't one of the others have held just as well?

The principle LF that holds true is not a brute fact because it subsumes itself. It will not be arbitrary that this principle holds if it satisfies some deep invariance principle I, specifying an invariance feature that makes its possessors, including the principle LF, nonarbitrary. A principle that varied in the way I excludes would be, to that extent, arbitrary. However, I is not an explanatory factor; it holds because LF does. Self-subsuming, LF holds because LF does, so is no brute fact. It also has the feature I, so it is not arbitrary. What more remains to be explained?

Consider all those different self-subsuming ultimate principles (of which LF is one) that also satisfy some significant invariance feature or other. Why does the one of those that holds, LF say, hold? The holding of LF is not a brute fact (because of self-subsumption), nor is it arbitrary (because of I). However, some other self-subsuming principle LF''' satisfies another invariance principle I''; and if LF''' held it would not be arbitrary either (because of I''). So isn't it arbitrary that LF (with invariance feature I) holds rather than LF''' (with invariance feature I'')? Such problems would be avoided if there were a deepest invariance principle I_0, which, among the ultimate self-subsuming principles, was satisfied uniquely by LF. In that case, LF is not a brute fact (because it subsumes itself), it is not arbitrary (because it satisfies I_0); and it is not arbitrary that LF holds rather than some

---

* Will there also remain the question of why *this* universe is one with the particular fundamental laws G (for example, general relativity and quantum electrodynamics)? Can we answer that different universes, all falling under LF, will be structured by different fundamental laws, each having those laws as part of its essence so that with different fundamental laws, it would be a different universe? Thus: Why does this universe satisfy G? It is part of its essence. Why does there exist any universe having that essence G? Because some such universe is given rise to under LF.

other self-subsuming principle LF‴, itself unarbitrary in virtue of satisfying I″, because I_0 is deeper than I″. It would be more arbitrary if LF‴ held.[14]

. We moved from the full principle of fecundity F to a more limited one LF in order to avoid the vast array of possible worlds, all obtaining, and the accompanying mere happenstance that our world has a high degree of explanatory unity. However, we seem to forgo the advantages of an egalitarian theory by restricting the possibilities that obtain to the sort S. In effect this makes of S a natural or privileged state in contrast to other possible ones, unless a deepest invariance principle can render this S-limitation unarbitrary.

If there is no such deepest invariance principle, however, merely alternates at the same level, each with its own version of nonarbitrariness, then although the particular self-subsuming principle LF which holds will not be a brute fact or completely arbitrary, still, it will hold merely in virtue of its holding, while other specifications of limited fecundity, satisfying different invariance conditions, also would have held if they had held, merely in virtue of their holding. This parity of status between different principles remains and disturbs.

Self-subsumption is a way a principle turns back on itself, yields itself, applies to itself, refers to itself. If the principle necessarily has the features it speaks of, then it necessarily will apply to itself. This mode of self-reference, whereby something refers to itself in all possible worlds where it refers, is like the Gödelian kind of the previous chapter. There we also discussed an even more restrictive mode of self-referring, reflexive self-referring. Can the fundamental explanatory principle(s) be not merely self-subsuming and necessarily self-applying, but also reflexively self-referring?

The fundamental explanatory principle will not contain an indexical term, it will not say: I am _____.* However, it can fit the general account of reflexive referring: the item refers or applies in virtue of a feature bestowed in that very token act of referring. A reflexive principle, then, will hold or self-apply in virtue of that very fact of holding or self-applying; it will hold in virtue of self-applying.

---

* Theistic theories sometimes hold that the world or universe refers to God, is a name of God. Might it be a reflexive self-reference so the universe is one of God's tokenings of "I"? (Darker yet, can something be nothing's reflexive tokening?)

WHY IS THERE SOMETHING RATHER THAN NOTHING

This puts the problems we have faced in a new guise. The specific principle of limited fecundity LF will be self-subsuming if it is, and will hold in virtue of being of the limited sort S. It will hold true as a fundamental principle *if* it holds, and in virtue of its holding. Other specifications or versions of limited fecundity also share these features. This presented the problem of explaining why one particular LF holds rather than those others, and it seemed insufficient to answer "it holds in virtue of its holding", since this also would have been true of any one of the others if it had held. Now we can see that this apparent insufficiency marks the fundamental principle as reflexive. A reflexive fundamental principle will hold merely in virtue of holding, it holds true "from the inside".*

To continue to press the question of why one self-subsuming principle LF holds rather than another assumes the ultimate self-subsuming explanatory principle will not be reflexive. But what else could it be?

Ultimacy

Philosophers push or iterate a question, usually about justification, so far that they cannot find any acceptable deeper answer. Attempting to deduce, explain, or justify the principle or position already reached, they fail, or covertly reintroduce the very result to be gotten. Whereupon a crisis for philosophy or for reason is proclaimed: a surd has been reached which cannot be justified (or explained) further Reason has been forced to halt.

What did they expect? Either the chain (of explanation or justification) goes on infinitely, or it goes in a circle, or it reaches an endpoint, either a simple point or a self-subsuming loop. What result would *not* constitute a crisis? It seems plausible that philosophy should seek to uncover the deepest truths, to find explanatory or (if that is its aim) justificatory principles so deep that nothing else yields them, yet deep enough to subsume themselves. Reaching these

---

* Is it a relevant disanalogy that in reflexive self-reference there is an act, independent of successful reference, that bestows the feature? The feature is not bestowed by successfully referring, is it? Is there a similar independent entity that bestows a feature in virtue of which a fundamental self-subsuming law holds?

should be a goal of philosophy, so when that situation occurs with some topic or area, instead of a crisis we should announce a triumph.* One of philosophy's tasks is to probe so deeply as to uncover the fundamental truths, to list and identify these, and to trace out what they yield, including themselves. To succeed in this should occasion pride, not shame.

Striving to delineate deep principles that yield others while subsuming themselves leads to change of gestalt. The goal is to get (what previously would have been called) stumped, unable to proceed further, though we do not want to reach this goal too soon. This shift in gestalt results from taking an overall view of the whole tree-like structure of explanation (or justification) so that we ask how it should eventuate, and do not merely look at the local connecting links. It is not surprising that some things that would be objectionable in the middle of the tree, such as having the same statement or principle recur, are desirable at the end.

How will we know whether we are in the middle of the explanatory (or justificatory) tree or at its end? One sign of being at the end is finding a self-subsuming principle—that is what we expect to find there. But this sign is not infallible. It is not impossible for there to be a self-subsuming principle somewhere in the middle, one which also has a further explanation (or justification). A self-subsuming statement written on a blackboard also can be subsumed by another statement, not written there, holding that all the statements on the board are true. Recall our earlier example: all sentences of exactly eight words are true. This is self-subsuming, but actually false. However, we can imagine a world where it holds true, there being some further explanation of why it holds. Not everything self-subsuming is explanatorily ultimate, without deeper explanation, even if everything ultimate turns out to be self-subsuming.

I do not know of a detectable sufficient condition for ultimacy, an infallible way to tell we have reached an ultimate explanatory (or justificatory) truth.† However, if we find a self-subsuming statement

* Some may see this suggestion, as I myself sometimes do, as like that of the senator who during the war in Vietnam proposed that the United States should announce that it had *won*, and then leave.

† One writer has claimed that the very nature of the nondual Vedantist Brahman, without distinctions, precludes further explanation. (Eliot Deutsch, *Advaita Vedanta*, East-West Center Press, Honolulu, 1969, ch. 2.) But how can one tell that it is featurelessly homogeneous throughout, including at all

that is deep enough to yield everything else in an area or realm, while repeated efforts fail to find a further truth that yields it, then it will be a reasonable conjecture, tentatively held and overturnable, that an ultimate truth has been reached. One reasonable explanation of why no deeper truth has been found is that there is not one. (Another, of course, is that we haven't been profound enough to discover it.)

If it is a fact that a principle, say LF, is ultimate, then if it is to explain and yield all truths, it also will have to yield that truth stating its own ultimacy: that there is no deeper explanatory truth that subsumes or yields LF. Otherwise, this one fact, at least, will be left dangling and unexplained. To be sure, if a principle says it is ultimate, that does not prove it is; and if a principle is otherwise true, adding the conjunct that it is ultimate might transform it into something false. But if the fundamental explanatory principle is ultimate, shouldn't it yield that fact too?

We might think that the fact of ultimacy is a negative fact ("there is no deeper . . ."), holding it unreasonable to think the explanatory principle will yield all the negative facts also. Apart from the difficulty of drawing a distinction between positive and negative facts, what then do we think does fix the negative facts? Presumably, the addition to the fundamental principle of the statement: and there are no further positive facts except those that follow from LF, all of which do. But this cannot be a positive fact, for (by hypothesis) it does not follow from LF; yet if it is a negative fact, what makes it true? Compare the issue of whether in giving the meaning of the universal quantifier by a conjunction, one must introduce or assume the additional statement that all the objects have been listed, that there are no other objects.

It is worth investigating various ways the feature of ultimacy can enter integrally into a principle, rather than merely be added as a conjunct. (Note that even the conjunction could not be LF':LF, and LF is ultimate. Rather, it would have to be LF':LF and LF' is ultimate.) Might one make the explanatory relation precise so that a statement can be constructed that yields other truths and, on the in-

---

(possible) levels beneath the one where it is experienced as such? A painted surface can look perfectly undifferentiated, until we look closer or theorize about its microstructure. Moreover, could not homogeneity be explained as resulting from a process of erosion of distinctive features?

terpretation, say of itself that it is not explainable by anything else, that is, is ultimate?

Suppose this fact of the ultimacy of LF obdurately remains unexplained, or that the reflexivity analysis of a principle's holding in virtue of a feature bestowed by its holding seems to leave unexplained why the fundamental principle is reflexive. How disturbed should we be that something is left dangling? Let us imagine a system where nothing is arbitrary, there are no brute facts, everything has an explanation. Will these features themselves be arbitrary or brute facts without explanation? Will it be a brute fact that there are no brute facts? If nothing is arbitrary will that be arbitrary? Will there be an explanation for why everything has an explanation? How complete will the rational structure be? One piece of the philosophical tradition is especially relevant to these issues: the principle of sufficient reason.[15]

The Principle of Sufficient Reason

Let us state the principle of sufficient reason as: every truth has an explanation. For every truth p there is some truth q which stands in the explanatory relation E to p.

Is this principle true, does it apply to itself, and if so what is *its* sufficient reason? Is the principle of sufficient reason, call it SR, a brute fact or does it have a sufficient reason? If we assume SR is true and apply it to itself, we can conclude that there is some truth q which explains SR. Self-applied, SR says there is something true which explains it, but does not say what that something is. In particular, SR does not provide the explanation of itself via self-subsumption.[16]

The principle SR would be explained if there was an intervening factor, an X factor, between truth and there being a sufficient reason. In that case, SR could be deduced from the premises: all truths satisfy condition X, and anything satisfying condition X is explained by some truth or other. However, I do not see any intervening factor that can do this job nontrivially. (It would be trivial to let X be the condition satisfied by p precisely when both p is true and if p is true then there is some true q which stands in the explanatory relation E to p.)

Alternatively, SR, though otherwise true, might fall outside its own scope and so be without a sufficient reason of its own.[17] In that case, would it be arbitrary that SR holds? When any other truth holds without an explanation it is an arbitrary brute fact, but when SR holds without explanation, is it an arbitrary fact? If there is no sufficient reason why everything else has a sufficient reason, is it arbitrary that everything else does? Would it not be even more arbitrary if something else *didn't* have a sufficient reason? In this manner, we might try to convince ourselves that SR can stand unarbitrarily, even without a sufficient reason of its own.

Should we expect that the principle of sufficient reason is true? It will not hold true if we can construct a statement S that says of itself that there is no explanation, and so no sufficient reason, for it. If S is true, there is no sufficient reason for it, and SR is false. On the other hand, if S is false, then there is a sufficient reason for S, but then there is a sufficient reason for a false statement. If sufficient reasons establish truth (as the tradition assumes), this is impossible. Therefore, the first possibility holds: S is true, and so SR is false.

There is, however, a problem with this line of reasoning. Would it not show that S is true and (by showing that S's falsity is impossible) also show why S is true? So doesn't it provide a sufficient reason for the truth of S? Yet S states that there is no sufficient reason for its own truth, so the line of reasoning showing that it is true had better not also provide a sufficient reason why it is. (It is this, seemingly, that is done when it shows that S's being false is impossible. Might this fail to show why S is true because it doesn't show why a sufficient reason establishes truth?)

The above line of reasoning may or may not succeed in making S a fixed point of the predicate 'is without a sufficient reason', and so make SR false. In any event it would be foolhardy indeed to place any significant weight upon the necessity or even truth of SR. This century has presented us with a well-developed physical theory, quantum mechanics, that does not satisfy SR. Moreover, theorems show that any theory that retains certain features of quantum mechanics also will not satisfy SR.[18]

There is, however, a weaker form of the principle of sufficient reason which is worth considering. It does not say that every truth has a sufficient reason or explanation. Rather, it views a truth's having a sufficient reason as a natural state, deviations from which can occur

for reasons. The first weakening of the principle would say that if p is true then there is a sufficient reason for p or there is a sufficient reason for there not being a sufficient reason for p.*
Clearly, this process of weakening can continue further. There may be a truth with no sufficient reason for it, and no sufficient reason for there being no sufficient reason, while there is a sufficient reason for that. And so forth. While the strong principle of sufficient reason SR may not hold universally, still, some weakening of it, somewhere up the multi-leveled structure, may yet hold true. I relegate the detailed delineation of this structure and its various forms and technicalities to an extensive footnote.[19]

* Almost all Jewish philosophers who discussed whether there were reasons for the commandments, the mitzvot, held that there were, though the reasons for some of them, the statutes or hukkim, might be obscure. (See the article "Commandments, Reasons for," *Encyclopedia Judaica*, Vol. 5, pp. 783 –792; an introductory survey of the reasons discussed by the commentators is presented in Abraham Chill, *The Mitzvot: The Commandments and Their Rationale*, Bloch Publishing, New York, 1974.)

In the course of presenting his own views, Maimonides (*Guide of the Perplexed*, part III, ch. 26, p. 508) mentions another view (apparently put forth in *Genesis Rabbah*, XLIV) that some commandments have as their only reason that a law be prescribed. If there is a point to a law without any further specific reason, for example, to evoke obedience to God for its own sake, then on this view, there is a reason why a law is prescribed with no specific reason for it. There is a statute without sufficient reason, but there is a sufficient reason for that.

Hegel provides another instance of a view wherein there is a sufficient reason why there is no sufficient reason for something, in his treatment of why there must be contingency.

Is not a structure inegalitarian that treats "having an explanation" as a natural state, deviations from which have explanatory reasons? Previously an egalitarian structure was motivated by the fact that an inegalitarian one leaves unexplained why the natural state is the one it is, and so on. But this cannot move us off even a weakened principle of sufficient reason to an egalitarian structure where nothing is in need of explanation. For if nothing is, then neither are the things left unexplained by the inegalitarian weak principle of sufficient reason.

Does symmetry provide a natural state in explanation, so that symmetries need not be explained whereas asymmetries must be explained as arising out of an underlying symmetrical state from the operation of an asymmetrical factor? (But unless no suitable opposing factor could exist, there will be the question of why there is this asymmetry in factors.) Given the diverse ways of categorizing the world, I believe that symmetry is a mark not of the truth of an explanation, but of our understanding a phenomenon. This requires further investigation.

How Are Laws Possible?

We have considered how the most fundamental and ultimate truths might be explained as subsuming themselves, perhaps reflexively. A puzzle was mentioned briefly about explaining the existence of any laws at all; any such explanation itself will involve a law. (Perhaps this, too, can be handled by self-subsumption.) There is one further question to mention here: how is it possible for a (fundamental) law to hold? What possible relationship could there be between a law and what conforms to it, in virtue of which such conformity occurs? This has the air of a question from F. H. Bradley—one not to be taken too seriously. Yet that would be a mistake.

Events, Hume taught us, do not stand in any logical connections. However, they can be connected, we think, by laws in accordance with which one event leads to (and produces) another. What is the relation of the events to the law, what is the ontological status of the law itself? The events instantiate the law; we might think it is the law that makes the events happen that way, or that (with a causal law) makes the second event occur given the first. The law's holding makes the second event happen. If the law's holding is another event, how does this event plus the first one reach out to make the second happen? While if the law's holding is merely a summary of all the actual pairs of events in accordance with it, then it does not make these events happen, but rather is (partly) composed of their happening. Why then do they happen that way? Moreover, lawlike statements entail subjunctives, and so do not have their content exhausted by the actual events in accordance with them. Something more than the events that actually happen must make the subjunctive hold. What and how? Again we are led to ask: what is a (fundamental) law's ontological status?

Imagine that the law is written down somewhere in or outside the universe. Even then, there would remain the question of what the connection is between the law and the events that instantiate it, that are in accordance with it. For any sentence can be interpreted differently, a lesson Wittgenstein has driven home to us. What then is it that fixes the law's being realized in precisely this way, rather than being projected differently?

In his *Philosophical Investigations*, Wittgenstein asks how language is possible, and more particularly, how correctness in the application of a term is possible.[20] A mental item (word, sentence, image) does not wear its meaning on its face. Each such item, considered as a real thing, can be applied or projected, or understood in different ways; just as any three-dimensional object can be projected onto different planes or nonplanar surfaces, pictures can be viewed as representing different situations, signpost arrows can be interpreted as directing one to go the other way, and so on. Each item, then, seems to require instructions about how it is to be applied or understood, a rule for its use, yet every such stated instruction or rule is itself merely another item which can be understood or projected in various different ways. No item applies itself or by its own very nature picks out its uniquely correct application, so no image or idea considered as a real existing thing in the world, even when occurring in the mind, can fix a word's correct application.

We do have a record of (some) past applications of the word, correct applications and incorrect ones. Does that fix how the word is to be applied in the future? Just as through any finite set of points an infinite number of curves can be drawn, so different hypotheses or rules about applying the term are compatible with all the past datapoints of application. Any batch of particular items is a subset of an infinite number of different sets, where it is joined along with different things. So how can pointing to the batch of past (correct) applications fix which is the set of all correct applications? Adding verbal instructions to the past applications does not eliminate all but one way to apply the term, for these instructions themselves need to be applied in one of the many different possible ways. Wittgenstein presses these points home with his example of continuing a mathematical series: being given the first few members of the sequence and also the formula does not by itself fix how one is to go on. These items, past applications plus written formula plus past applications in learning other formulas, are all actual past events—how then can they reach into the future to fix the character of a new application as correct or incorrect? Set this alongside Hume's lesson that there are no logical connections between events; all the past events in learning language do not logically imply any future event or its being correct. It will not help to introduce a proposition to mediate the logical implication, for the earlier events will not logically imply the proposition (if it implies the later events). We may come to wonder

144

how logical connections, not only causal ones, are possible at all, for what is the character of existing things between which there can be logical connections? In Wittgenstein's view, correctness in the application of a term is constituted by the way we actually go on to apply it. Nothing past fixes, logically determines, an application as correct, but it is just a fact about us that confronted with past teachings and applications we will go on a certain way, and we all will go on the same way. However, Wittgenstein's view cannot provide an answer to our question about how a law is connected to its conforming events (nor was it intended to), whatever be its adequacy in answering his questions about correctness in the application of a term.[21] For Wittgenstein needed to introduce the mediation of people, how they actually apply a general formula or term, to connect the terms to their instances. It cannot be people, however, that mediate the connection between a general causal law and its instances; such laws apply to people and applied before any people ever existed. Moreover, people's agreeing may well depend upon causality, and so could not underpin it.[22]

It seems that a law cannot have a separate ontological status, for then it could not reach out to events, by itself. Yet if a law simply states a pattern showing in the events, if it is merely descriptive, if the law has no bit of ontological status of its own (and how can it not if it goes beyond actual events to subjunctive facts?), then how can laws (be used to) explain? How does a higher level summary pattern's holding explain a lower one? Is every explanation merely implicit repetition? Explanatory laws need not be necessary truths, contra Aristotle, but mustn't they be *something*?

When the events that occur are lawful, what is the connection between these events and the law? Here we are asking for a real connection which makes the events conform to the law (otherwise, why do they?), for a real relationship which corresponds to and underlies "being in accord with". Yet how can any connection reach out from the law to the events? Clearly, no causal processes can fill in the gap while any logical connection, or the law it connects, itself has to be interpreted. Can some lawlike statement interpret itself, might a law give instructions for its own interpretation? But these instructions also would have to be interpreted and so, as in the earlier case of different self-subsuming laws, there would be various laws that on an interpretation also give directions or specify that they are to be interpreted that way. So the fundamental self-subsuming laws would have (on an interpretation) to fix their own interpretation through self-sustaining directions for interpretation which, on an interpretation, specify that very interpretation. Interpreted differently, the laws and directions might fix another interpretation. So a statement that fixed its own interpretation would have to embody some analogue of reflexive self-reference, applying as it does in virtue of the act of applying and being so interpreted. The means by which such a reflexively self-subsuming interpretation could occur are mysterious, another unhelpful mystery.

Treating laws as akin to statements leads to the morass of difficulties about what interprets these quasi-statements. Furthermore, Gödel's proof that there is no formal system in which all truths of number theory can be proven as theorems makes prospects dim for a picture of all facts (including necessary truths) as in accordance with statement-entities from which they can be derived. The determinist therefore is ill advised to state his thesis in terms of derivability in principle from causal laws.[23] However, there also are difficulties in the other standard way of stating the content of determinism: that if the initial state were repeated and things ran on, there would occur the same later state as happened the first time through. For it might be that if the same initial state were repeated, that could only be after the universe's gravitational collapse into a new initial stage beginning a new expansion, and in that new expansion new laws would hold, so the later state would not then follow again. Thus, the subjunctive purporting to state determinism would be false, even though the events are determined during this (expansion and contraction) cycle of the universe. Clearly, to state determinism as "if the initial state were repeated and the same laws held then . . ." leads to the same difficulties as earlier about the laws.

If a law is considered not as a quasi-statement but as a general fact (which a true lawlike statement states) then how can this general fact make true the particular ones in accord with it? It is difficult to see what this "making true" relationship would be as a real connection among facts. For it to do its job, it must be akin to causality, but then the same problems seem to arise once again. Perhaps some who spoke of laws being (in some senses) necessary meant to ascribe to laws a property whereby they constrain the facts—but this only names the problem. Yet those who saw as equally necessary the singular conditional between the facts that instantiated the law did not have in mind this constraining function for necessity. The nature of that necessity (or necessity operator) was left obscure not simply because it was undefined—it could, after all, have been a theoretical term—but because both its ontological nature and its mode of connection with other facts were unspecified. However, if the general lawlike regularity does not constrain the more specific facts, being merely a descriptive summary but ontologically unable to give rise to them, then it is unclear in what way the more specific facts are explained by the general, in what sense we come to know why the more particular holds true.

This picture of the general merely as summarizing narrower particularities, no deeper than a conjunction of them, radically undercuts the notion of a hierarchy in terms of fundamentalness. If the general facts do not actually constrain the particular ones, all facts are on a par. If anything, the ontological priority would lie with the particular facts, which mold their accurate general summary.

One might be suspicious of fundamentalness for other reasons as well: formal systems can be axiomatized in different ways, the axioms of one system being theorems in another; scientific laws can be given different but equivalent formulations and representations;[24] since not all truths can be derived within an axiomatic system, we cannot say all other truths hold because some few fundamental ones do. Philosophers have always tried to uncover more fundamental truths, to make them explicit, to justify in terms of them, sometimes to explain them or via them. Does this very notion of fundamentality, with its associated ordered structuring, need to be questioned and undercut? Has philosophy's unquestioned and unexamined presupposition been that something or other is (more) fundamental? Should we question the very notions of underlying truth, of deep truth, of explanatory ordering? This feels like a deep question, but if the presupposition is rejected, will it come to seem superficial—as superficial as everything else? And if a view uncovers and rejects this presupposition, as a presupposition, isn't the view recognizing depth even as it rejects the very idea?

Let us examine what a theory would look like that did not make any fact more fundamental than any other one. We already have con-

147

sidered egalitarian theories, in which no state is picked out as natural and so requiring no explanation while other states are explained as deviations from the natural one. All states are on a par in an egalitarian theory; all equally in need (or not) of explanation. Still, such theories order the facts in an explanatory hierarchy, with some deeper than others they (asymmetrically) explain. A view that did not make any fact more fundamental than any other one would have to be nonreductionist.[25] But could it be a theory at all, could it be an explanatory theory?

One alternative picture to fundamentality is that of an organic unity: each statement or fact coheres with all the rest, each is explained by the way it fits with the rest. However, that leaves open the questions of why things are organically unified, what the connection is between something's cohering (with what?) and its holding true, why the fact that something coheres with the rest explains why it holds. The usual analogy is to a work of art.[26] However, that does have an underlying explanation in terms of the artist's intention (sometimes unconscious?) to produce a unified work. An item within the work is explained by its cohering with the rest, through the underlying force (stemming from the artist's intention) working to produce coherence in the painting. (Further explanation would be needed of these other items, either based on the theme of the work or on tentative beginnings introduced apart from coherence with anything yet existing.) Thus, the needed explanation of why there is organic unity among the facts seems to reintroduce distinctions in fundamentalness.

Might there be a principle of (or including) organic unity, from which other facts follow, that also is self-subsuming? Since self-subsumption establishes a tight relation of something with itself, a self-subsuming principle of organic unity presumably will contribute to a high degree of organic unity of the whole, especially given its connections to the other facts, some derivable from it, others having their relationships described by it. But will not this principle of organic unity then be the deep underlying principle, having a different status from the other facts?

Recall the situation with self-subsuming principles: each, because explained by itself, is not left simply dangling; yet given the multiplicity of such principles the question remains of why one self-subsuming principle, one version of LF, holds instead of another. This question does not seem adequately answered merely by citing the ultimate principle and deriving it from itself, unless one holds this fundamental principle also is reflexive.

There might be a different sort of answer to this question with a self-subsuming principle of organic unity, for that principle might be the one that best fits in with the other facts. According to the explanation via (contributing to) high organic unity, the principle of organic unity, like everything else, would be explained by its mesh with other facts. Thus, it would not be deeper than these other facts, so the overall theory is not compelled to make distinctions in fundamentalness.

Still, won't there be many different equally coherent and unified worlds? If each is equally in accord with a principle of organic unity, why then does one hold rather than another? (This question parallels the familiar one put to coherence theories of truth.) That different worlds are (otherwise) equally coherent and so equally in accord with a principle of coherence does not show, however, that they cohere equally *with* this principle so that every combination of the principle of organic unity with each such coherent world would have the same degree of organic unity. A self-subsuming principle of organic unity, if it is to generate other facts, will embody some other characteristics as well, and each world, coherent in itself, may not cohere equally with these characteristics or with the self-subsuming nature of the principle. For example, worlds with self-reflexive beings may have a higher organic connection with a self-subsuming principle qua self-subsuming, not to mention with a reflexive principle, than a world otherwise without reflexivity. Nevertheless, I see no reason to think there is only one self-subsuming organic unity principle capable of generating other facts within a structure of high organic unity undistinguished in fundamentalness; so the question would remain of why one particular one holds, barring a reflexive account.

While such an explanatory arrangement via organic unity without distinctions in fundamentalness might conceivably be possible, I am not willing to endorse it here. Neither shall I now question whether explanation, including of how things are possible, is a favored and more fundamental route to discovering what things are really like, to the truth. There I draw the line! (At least, for now.)

Finding no happy substitute for explanation, or for laws, we are left with the nature of the real connection between general laws and the facts that instantiate them still unexplained, still in question.

Beyond

The important hymn from the Vedas, the Hymn of Creation, begins "Nonbeing then existed not nor being". This is the translation by Radhakrishnan and Moore.[27] In the Griffith translation, we find this as "Then was not nonexistent nor existent"; in the Max Muller translation, "There was then neither what is nor what is not."

How can what there was "then", that is, in the beginning or before everything else, be neither nonbeing nor being, neither nonexistent nor existent, neither is nor is not? For being and nonbeing, existent and nonexistent, is and is not, seem exhaustive. There does not seem to be any other possibility. In accordance with the law of the excluded middle, everything is either one or the other.

However, sometimes things that seem to exhaust the possibilities do not, rather they do so only within a certain realm. Consider color. Everything is either colored (singly colored or multicolored) or uncolored, that is, transparent. Either a thing is colored or it is uncolored, what other possibility is there? Yet the number 5, and Beethoven's Quartet Number 15, are neither colored nor uncolored. These are not the sort of things that can have or fail to have colors—they are not physical or spatial objects or events. (Do not confuse them with numerals or written musical scores, which can be colored.)

Let us say that this pair of terms (colored, uncolored) has a presupposition; it presupposes that the thing or subject to which the terms 'colored' or 'uncolored' are applied is a physical or spatial object or event. When the presupposition 'X is a physical or spatial object or event' is satisfied, then 'X is colored' and 'X is uncolored' exhaust the possibilities. When the presupposition is satisfied, X cannot be neither colored nor uncolored. However, when that presupposition is not satisfied, then X may be neither colored nor uncolored.[28]

Similarly, the pair of terms (loud, not loud) presupposes that X is a sound or a possible sound source, that is, a physical object or event. The number 5 is neither loud nor not-loud. The pair of terms (harmonious, unharmonious) presupposes that a thing has parts related in a certain way. An elementary particle itself is neither harmonious nor unharmonious.

Might it be that every pair of predicates that seems to exhaust the possibilities, apparently contradictory, has a presupposition beyond which neither of the terms applies? We might picture a presuppositional situation as follows (Figure 2.2). A rectangle represents all the things there are. Encircled things are the things that satisfy the presupposition. The pair of terms t_1 and t_2 divides up everything that satisfies the presupposition; each such thing is one or the other. Outside the set of things that satisfies the presupposition are all the things that are neither, things to which neither one of these terms applies. The crosshatched area contains those things that are neither t_1 nor t_2.

There are two ways we can try to avoid there being any presupposition. Where the rectangle is everything that exists, everything there is, we can simply draw a line across it, across all of it, letting t_1 apply to one resulting part and t_2 to the other (Figure 2.3). Nothing is left outside.

However, this assumes that 'exists' exhausts everything, that there is nothing that doesn't exist. This need not faze us; if there are things that do not exist, Santa Claus, golden mountains, and so on, let our large rectangle be all those things that do or could exist, and let our line then distinguish those things that exist from those that do not. Surely, there is no presupposition now.

This assumes, however, that the pair of terms (exists, doesn't exist) does not itself have a presupposition, that it does not apply just to a certain range of things with something outside. It assumes that we do not have the situation shown in Figure 2.4, with the crosshatched area being those things that neither exist nor don't exist.

There is another way we might try to eliminate any presupposition. Until now we have been specifying a domain by the rectangle, and drawing a distinction within it. (I now use a wavy line for the distinction.) But we had worries that there was something outside

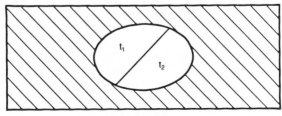

FIGURE 2.2

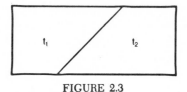

FIGURE 2.3

the domain, as in Figure 2.5. Why do we not instead just draw the distinction? In Figure 2.6 we mark t_1 off against everything else. There appears to be no further worry that there are things outside; t_1 is distinguished from whatever else there is.

However, there are reasons for thinking we encounter paradoxes and contradictions if we proceed without first specifying the domain and then drawing distinctions within it.* Also, we said "it is distinguished from whatever else there is." But why think *is* does not itself have a presupposition? We distinguish t_1 from whatever else _____. If the blank itself has a presupposition, then the structure of the situation is as represented by Figure 2.7.

I suggest we understand the beginning of the Hymn of Creation, "nonbeing then existed not nor being", as saying that the pairs being and nonbeing, existent and nonexistent, and is and isn't have presuppositions, that the terms within these pairs apply and exhaust the possibilities only within a certain domain, while outside this domain a thing may be neither. Such theories are not unknown in the West: Plato says God is "beyond being" (*Republic* VI, 509b), and Plotinus makes this central to his theory of the One; Judah Halevi (*Kuzari* II, 2) holds that neither of a pair of contrasting terms applies to God; and there are other examples.

It is plausible that whatever every existent thing comes from, their source, falls outside the categories of existence and nonexistence. Moreover, we then avoid the question: why does *that* exist? It doesn't *exist*. Strictly, that which is beyond those categories neither exists nor doesn't exist. But if you had to say one, you would mention

---

* This is the usual moral drawn from the set-theoretical paradoxes. So set theory is done without a universal set which contains everything, or with a class which does but is ontologically different from what is within it and so not subject to the same manipulations as sets. Or, most securely, set theory is done in iterative fashion, starting with the null set and iterating operations to generate new and always limited sets.

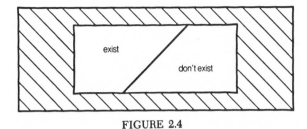

FIGURE 2.4

whichever of existence and nonexistence was closer to its status. If both were equally close or distant, if it was equidistant from both, you might say: it exists *and* it doesn't exist. We read this as: strictly speaking neither holds, and it is no more distant from one than from the other. This provides us with a possible explanation of the tendency to utter contradictions on the part of those who talk about such things.[29]

There are at least four questions to ask about a theory that holds that the pair existence and nonexistence has a presupposition that can fail to be satisfied. First, what is the presupposition, what is the condition which all things that exist and all that nonexist satisfy, yet which need not be satisfied? Second, what reason is there to believe that something does fail to satisfy the presupposition, that there is something beyond existence and nonexistence? Third, is there a biggest box, with nothing outside it? And fourth, if there is, how can one tell one has reached it, that there is not still some hidden transcendable presupposition, outside of which is another realm that fits none of the previous categories?

This chapter is not the place to deal with all of these questions. Let me say just a few words about the first. Is the presupposition statable? Well, we can coin a short word. We can say that only those

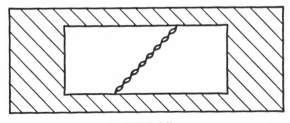

FIGURE 2.5

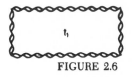

FIGURE 2.6

things which *th* exist or nonexist, that the presupposition of the pair exist and nonexist is that there be (this is a verb coming up) *thing*.* We can coin this word to denote the presupposition, but can we explain it in terms we already understand?

It seems we can only come to understand the presupposition ostensively. We can state the boundaries and understand what they are only by standing outside them. If this is so, and if experience of what is outside the boundary is necessary to get one to see what the presupposition of the boundary is and to understand what can transcend it, then such experience will be necessary to understand the position, to grasp its content. The experiences can function not only to support the position (in the next section we shall consider the intricate question of whether they do so) but also to ostensively explain it. The ostensive route to understanding the position may be the only route we have, raising the possibility that all those who understand it realize that it is true. (Shouldn't some accounts of a priori knowledge be revised, then, to exclude this realization as a priori?)

Persons who have had such experiences struggle to describe them; they say all descriptions are inadequate, that strictly the experience is ineffable. This goes beyond saying that we cannot describe it in terms already available to us, that an ostensive encounter with it is needed to know what it is like and what any term applying to it means. Perhaps such ostensive acquaintance is needed to understand what sounds or sights are, an understanding which a blind or deaf person would lack (in the absence of direct stimulation of the brain to produce the experience). Still, those of us who do have the

---

* We can continue with a verb-form theory that goes beyond merely the presuppositional view. We might view "nothing" as the present continuous of the verb 'to noth', and "something" as the present continuous of the verb 'to someth'. Clearly, an x noths or someths, it is nothing or something only if it ths. What 'to noth' and 'to someth' have in common is 'to th'. (The following sentence contains three present continuous verbs, and no nouns except insofar as the quantificational structure does duty for them.) Only thing is nothing or something.

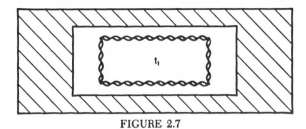

FIGURE 2.7

experience can produce a descriptive vocabulary to describe them. Sights and sounds are not ineffable. Perhaps those who call the experience of what is beyond existence and nonexistence ineffable merely mean that they cannot adequately describe it to those who have not had it. If so, their use of "ineffable" is misleading. Perhaps they mean something more, however, namely that there is a presupposition to the application of terms, that we normally live within the realm where the presupposition is satisfied and hence never consider the possibility that there is such a presupposition, and finally, that their experience has taken them beyond the realm of the presupposition to where terms, all terms, just do not apply. This raises problems of a familiar sort: what about second-level terms such as "ineffable" or "is such that first-level terms do not apply to it"? We can leave these problems aside now.

Of something that does not satisfy the presupposition of the pair exists and nonexists, and so neither exists nor nonexists, we cannot ask why it exists. But though it does not exist, it does _____. Some verb must describe its status; so let us just coin a verb, 'to aum', to fill in the blank. Auming is what that which is beyond existence and nonexistence does. It aums. Now it seems we can ask: why does it aum? Why does it aum rather than not?

If the ineffability doctrine were true and the presuppositions for the application of terms were not satisfied, then of course we could not coin a term for what it does and then ask why it does that. (But couldn't we just wonder "why?" and mentally gesture in the direction of the ineffable? Or does the term "why" fail to get à grip, along with the other terms?) To keep open the possibility of saying something further, I shall proceed on the assumption that a term can be applied so that a question can be asked. It aums, and we ask why.

Without knowing more about what is beyond existence and nonexistence, and about auming, it is difficult to see how to begin to discuss the question. There is one structural possibility worth mentioning, however. Various versions of the ontological argument (for the existence of God) founder on their treatment of 'exists'. By treating existence or necessary existence as a property or perfection, they allow us to consider the nth most perfect being (n = 1, 2, 3, . . .), and so to overpopulate our universe. What the ontological argument wanted to discuss, though, was a being whose essence included existence; it is a structural possibility similar to this, rather than the deduction of existence from the concept of a thing, that I want to take up. Can the nature of whatever is beyond existence and nonexistence include auming, so that there is no possibility that *it* does not aum? We need not suppose that we are (or aren't) speaking of God here; when it says "nonbeing then existed not, nor being" the Hymn to Creation is not speaking of God. Nor am I constructing an ontological argument from the concept of what is beyond existence and nonexistence to its auming. Perhaps auming is part of its essence without being part of the concept of it. Indeed it is difficult to suppose we have presented a determinate concept of it here at all, if the only route to knowing what is beyond existence and nonexistence and about auming is through an experience of it. My intention here is merely to raise the possibility that there is no room for the question "why does it aum?"

Consider, as an analogy, the structure of all possibilities. A particular possibility is realized or is actual or exists, and another is not realized and so nonexists. What exists and nonexists are particular possibilities. The structure of all possibilities underlies existence and nonexistence. That structure itself doesn't exist and it doesn't nonexist. A presupposition for the application of this pair of terms (exists, nonexists) is not satisfied by the structure of all possibilities. Now suppose we coin a verb for the status of the structure of all possibilities, saying that it *modes*. Is it clear that there is room for the question, why does the structure of all possibilities mode? Can *it* fail to mode?

I do not claim that the structure of all possibilities is what the Hymn of Creation begins with, or is what is found in experience. I believe that the Hymn of Creation means to speak of what underlies and gives rise to the structure of possibilities. What that might be we shall pursue in a later chapter. My purpose here is to give an example of something that does not satisfy the presupposition of the pair exists and nonexists, yet about whose status there may be no room for the question why it does that, why the structure of all possibilities modes. All this is to give one some feeling for how there might be no room for the question of why what aums does aum. Even so, there still would remain the question of how and why existence and nonexistence arise from what aums. We shall say a bit about this connection later.

Mystical Experience

Assertions of something beyond existence and nonexistence, infinite and unbounded, appear in the writings of (some) mystics, not as hypotheses to answer questions of cosmogony but to describe what they have experienced and encountered.[30]

How much credence should we give to these experiences? Undoubtedly such experiences are had and are sincerely reported, and they strike the mystic as revelatory of reality, of a deeper reality. Why deeper? What is experienced is different, but this does not show that it is deeper, rather than more superficial even than the reality we normally know. The experiences come as revelatory of something deeper. Should we believe the report of mystics that there is this reality? Should the mystics themselves believe it?

There are two major approaches to these experiences: first, to explain them away, to offer an explanation of why they occur that doesn't introduce (as an explanatory factor) anything like what the mystics claim to experience; and second, to see them as revelatory of a reality that is as it is encountered. To notice that there are special conditions under which such experiences occur, for example, after yogic practice or ingestion of certain drugs, does not settle which approach should be taken. What the first approach treats as a cause of the experience, the second will see as removing the veil from reality so that it can be perceived as it really is. Does the unusual physiochemical state of the brain produce an illusion, or does it enable us to experience reality?

We might think there is an evolutionary reason why the unusual brain states should not be trusted; our tendency to have the normal ones has been selected for in a process wherein too gross a failure to cognize reality led to extinction. However, if the underlying reality is as the mystics report, and if knowing it (as opposed to knowing the more superficial features of macro-physical objects) had no adaptive value, then we should not expect these normal brain states selected for in the evolutionary process to be ones that reveal the underlying reality as it is.

The procedure often used to induce the unusual experience, yogic or zen meditation, aims at "quieting thoughts", stopping our usual chatter of thoughts so that, as some say, we can experience the true self or at any rate a reality which the thoughts mask and cover. (And this sometimes may be an effect of other means, such as chemical ones, not consciously aimed at this result.) It is surprisingly difficult to stop thoughts from flitting about, but the difficulties of accomplishing this should not distract us from wondering what success shows. Supposing the procedure, when it succeeds in quieting the thoughts, does lead to an experience of the sort described, should we think this reveals something fitting the experience? That depends on what experience we think the procedure would produce even if there was no such unusual underlying reality to be perceived.

The following analogy may help make the point: Consider a phonograph system as an apparatus of experience. With the amplifier on, turntable turning, speakers on, a record on the turntable and the stylus moving in its grooves, sound is experienced; it (we are temporarily imagining) has the experience of sound. Now let us do the equivalent of quieting thoughts, namely, removing the record, perhaps also turning off the speakers and the turntable. When only the amplifier is on (with no ordinary "objects of experience" given it), what is the experience like? We do not know; perhaps infinite, unbounded, and so on, is what it feels like when the amplifier switch (of consciousness) is on, yet nothing is being experienced. Nothing differentiated is present to consciousness to produce a differentiated experience. It would be a mistake to think there is an unusual reality being encountered, when that merely is what it feels like when the experience-mechanism is turned on yet nothing is present to be experienced. None of the literature I know describes what experience the quieting meditative procedure would produce in the absence of any unusual reality or self, so we don't know whether the unusual experience is a revelation of an unusual reality or self, or instead an artifact of an unusual procedure of experiencing wherein most but not all functions are damped down. (Will this debunking explanation have more difficulty in explaining the surprising and often momentous changes in the people who have the experiences?)[31]

Empiricist methodology, presumably, would have us treat the mystics' experiences as on a par with all other experiences, to be fed into some procedure of theory generation and support. The question is whether the resulting theory explaining (or explaining away) the mystics' experience that p will itself incorporate p or something like it. The answer will be interesting, however, only if the procedure itself is unbiased toward the mystics' claim; for example, it must not give it an almost zero a priori probability or degree of initial credibility, or give the mystics' individual experiences lesser weight than others in fixing either what is to be accounted for or how theories are evaluated.[32]

We are far from knowing whether the mystics' p will be preserved as (roughly) true by the empiricists' account, even if we suppose it a maxim that the resulting explanatory theory incorporate (as true) as many q's as possible from the experiences that q for which it tries to account. As much as possible, the theory is to save the appearances, including the experiences that p.[33] Perhaps this is not merely a maxim but a necessary component of any (unbiased) confirmatory and explanatory procedure we can wield. That we don't yet know whether the empiricists' explanatory theory will endorse the mystics' claim does not mean it is not an important question to raise.

Does the empiricist methodology distinguish between the mystic and the nonmystic? One has the experience while the other only hears it reported, but should this make a difference to what they believe? Certainly, a higher percentage of those who have had mystical experiences that p than of those who have not believe that p is true. Some of this difference in percentages will stem from the fact that many of those without the mystical experience will not know that such experiences are had by anyone or know of the probity of those who report them; or they simply spend less time thinking about the matter because, not having had the experiences that p themselves, the question of the truth of p is less salient to them. However, I believe there will remain a difference in the percentages after we control for all such facts. A higher percentage of the mystical-experiencers will believe in the veridicality of the experience, will believe that reality is as it then was experienced.

Why should this be so? The experiences are very powerful, but the person without the experiences is told this and can weigh this in as evidence about veridicality. It is merely that the person having (had) the mystical experience cannot help believing its veridicality, or does he have reason to differ? We can imagine that a nongullible person has a powerful mystical experience, not easily dismissed, and wonders whether he should believe that reality is as it apparently has been revealed to be. What weight should he give to the fact that he himself had the experience?

Do I rationally give my experiences that q different weight than yours that r in constructing my picture of the world? My accepting that you have had the experience that r will be based on my experiences (of your reports), and so my experiences seem primary in that way. Once I have accepted the fact that you have had the experience, though, do I try to save your appearances any less than mine, your r's less than my q's?

If somehow we were telepathically connected with a creature in another galaxy or universe, having its experiences, then we must give those some credence as our access into what that world is like. Must we give more credence to them than to the experiences of other denizens of that realm (which we come to know of via our telepathic contact)? Apart from the earlier point about primacy, apparently not. And aren't we each in our own world simply in special telepathic communication with ourselves, as it were, so that it would be similarly inappropriate to give our own experiences that q special weight or credence as compared to other's experience that r?

Alternatively, imagine an amnesia victim who is being told of the experiences of different persons, including some people's mystical experiences. He comes to hold a general picture of the world which, let us suppose, rejects the mystics' claim that p. Should it make any difference to his belief if now he is told: you were one of the people who had that mystical experience. Surely not. He has already considered how much evidential weight to give the fact that such an experience was had (under certain conditions with a certain frequency), how much weight to give to the fact that *someone* had the experience; it is irrelevant further information that the someone was himself (rather than another of the same specified degree of probity, sincerity, and so on).

Yet there remains something special about the mystical experience whereby it evades this general argument. Because this mystical experience is ineffable, powerfully (if not indelibly) remembered but inadequately described, the mystic knows something the hearer of his reports does not. The hearer does know something, though, for later if he does have the experience he will know that must be what the other was reporting.* We need not hold that nothing can be transmitted by imagery, metaphor, and so on; only that something significant evades the description.

The experiencer knows what the mystical experience is like in a way and to an extent the attentive listener does not, and in a way and to an extent the amnesiac does not who is told he once had a certain sort of experience which he doesn't remember. Relevant is not simply the fact that the experiencer had the experience, for the amnesiac also had it, but the way this fact normally shows itself in the person's evidential base. There is evidence available to the experiencer (who remembers) that is not available to the hearer or the amnesiac. So there is a reason for him to reach a different conclusion than they do. We can see how he *might* reasonably believe that p (that there is an infinite underlying reality transcending existence and nonexistence) while they could not. This explanation does not show that the person with mystical experience does reasonably differ in his view that p; but it does leave room for such a difference, showing how such a reasonable difference might be possible.

What should a person without mystical experience, who realizes all that has been said thus far, believe? He knows that almost all those who have mystically experienced that p believe that p, and that something about their experience, which eludes telling and so is unknown to him, may (properly) play a role in their belief. This additional information may make it somewhat more reasonable for him to believe that p, but he still is not in the position of the experiencers. For he will face the question of whether the (unknown) character of the experience was such as to make it reasonable to believe p. Perhaps the experiencers are especially gullible, either because there is

* Though even this may be unclear. For example, Madhyamika Buddhists report experiences of emptiness, of a "vibrant void", while Vedantists report an experience of the fullest possible pure infinite existence: existence-consciousness-bliss. Are they experiencing the same thing? It would help to have someone who reported (in the suitable language) having both experiences (and that they were different), rather than all reporting only one or the other.

selective entry into the class of experiencers, the mystical experience coming only to the already especially gullible and credulous, or because the experience makes people gullible, causing them to become gullible and credulous, either generally or just about the import of this particular experience. (Should the mystics not be concerned about this, too?) Certainly mystics often appear gullible and credulous in the rest of what they accept. But is this because of a general gullibility, new or old, or rather because they reasonably have shifted their general picture of the constitution of the universe which leads to a shift in other a priori probabilities or expectations, so that some things previously excluded as impossible now will seem possible, and less evidence is needed to establish them as actual?

Lacking firsthand acquaintance with the mystical experience, and so having an ineradicably different evidence base, the nonexperiencer may reasonably reject the mystics' claim that p, while admitting the mystic may be reasonable in believing that p. The mystic may now claim one further bit of support for the truth of p, other than mystical experiences that p. If p, as a hypothesis, provides an answer to the question of why there is something rather than nothing, then performing this function provides it some support. Thus we have two independent routes to p, each reinforcing the other: the experiential route of the mystic and the explanatory route in philosophical cosmogony.

That the (purported) fact that p is the right sort of thing to explain why there is something rather than nothing does not show how it does this; it does not show what the particular connection is between the fact that p and our universe, or its contents, in detail. Here we must be careful about the mystic's claims, distinguishing those p's for which he claims or reports an experience that p from other statements that he introduces as hypotheses to connect the deep underlying reality he experiences with the superficial one he normally inhabits. These connections the mystic does not himself (even claim to) experience, and they have lesser authority than his experiences. The mystic's special knowledge of his experience does not extend to a special authority about its (and its object's) connection to ordinarily perceivable reality; for this connection does not link with, much less get revealed in, the ineffable character of the experience.

For this reason we find many theorists of the connection, even among mystics; some see our world as an illusion (to whom?), others as like a work of fiction, others as a thought, others as an emanation, others as a creation, and so on, views all based on the fundamental underlying reality described in p. The fact is, I think, that what is experienced by the mystic is so different from our ordinary world, yet is experienced as underlying that world and as more real, that the mystic gropes or leaps for some explanation, for some theory of how it underlies the world, of how the two might be connected. Similarly, the mystic who experiences himself as the infinite perfect underlay of everything, neither existing nor nonexisting, whether in the experience that Atman = Brahman or in the experience of being the void, has to explain why he did not always realize this, his own true nature. Since he didn't experience himself becoming ignorant, his explanation of his (recent) ignorance is always (only) a hypothesis. So mystics present different theories here as well. Greater credence should be given to the mystic's experiences than to his hypotheses, both by the nonmystic and by the mystic.*

---

* Though, perhaps some mystical experiences can (seem to) indicate something about the character of the connection, even if not the details.

Some of the yogic mystical experiences are of the self as being the underlying substance of the universe or an infinite purity; also, I think, of it as turned back onto itself, creating itself, the experiential analogue of self-subsuming.

The practitioner of Hatha Yoga develops extraordinary suppleness and physical capabilities, and the yoga manuals are explicitly dark and mysterious about some of the practices. In these classic manuals, the practitioner of yoga is warned to keep some things very secret and to do them only in private. For example, *Gheranda Samhita*, i, 13–44, contains five admonitions that different practices are very secret; *Siva Samhita*, iv, 41–44, says the "wise Yogi" should "practice this . . . in secret, in a retired place." See the passages quoted in Theos Bernard, *Hatha Yoga* (Columbia University Press, 1943, reprinted by Samuel Weiser, New York, 1950), pp. 34 and 69. For an indication of the suppleness of body developed, see the photographs there. Printed interpretations and explanations of what is involved leave the practice innocuous. (For example, M. Eliade, *Yoga*, Princeton University Press, 1969, ch. 6. For discussion of reading esoteric texts, see Leo Strauss, *Persecution and the Art of Writing*, Free Press, Glencoe, 1952.) They leave it wholly mysterious why secrecy is enjoined, why if that is all that is involved, the manuals do not say it straight out. It is a general principle in interpreting texts which announce they hold secrets, however, that the secret doctrine should turn out to be something the writer would go to great lengths to keep secret.

In these yoga manuals the actions and postures of the practitioner are meant to lead him to the secret. When the doctrine itself is to be conveyed by the text, though, the writer has a special problem: having announced that a secret is embedded in the work, how can he prevent its detection by the very ones from whom he wishes to keep it secret, who have been told explicitly

More than clarifying the issues somewhat, I wish I could resolve the question of whether reality is as the mystic describes it. I take the question, and the mystics' experiences, very seriously, which some will think immediately is a great mistake. (But do they think this only because they already assume a background theory that discounts the mystics' experiences; if so, what led them to that theory?) For the purposes of philosophical explaining and understanding, we need not resolve the question; it suffices to consider, elaborate, and keep track of the hypotheses. Yet there remains the question of how to act, of what path to follow.*

---

that there is some secret to be found? The writer has to bury something that can be ferreted out to satisfy the unwelcome seeker, a decoy secret. This must be something the writer plausibly would want to keep secret; otherwise it will not be a successful cover. How will one know if one has found the valuable silver or the more deeply hidden gold? If only one thing has been uncovered, being the easier to find, it is not the real secret. But has any author buried a secret doctrine underneath two covers? (Or flashed the fact of contained secrets, without announcing it, by discussing esoteric devices, I mean doctrines, rambunctiously?)

What are the yoga manuals keeping hidden, which the practitioner is expected to come to himself? What does the cutting of the fraenum linguae aid? What nectar is brought upwards and drunk? What is the mouth of the well of nectar over which the tongue is placed and what ambrosia is drunk daily? (These are the terms used in the yoga manuals. See Bernard, *Hatha Yoga*, pp. 30, 65–67.)

I conjecture that one of the acts the (male) yogis perform, during their experiences of being identical with infinitude, is auto-fellatio, wherein they have an intense and ecstatic experience of self-generation, of the universe and themselves turned back upon itself in a self-creation. (Compare the mythological theme of creation from an ouroboris, a serpent with its tail in its mouth.)

Here I have only conjecture to go on, and this conjecture may well be mistaken. But it does specify something the yogis in their altered consciousness might seek and regard as a pinnacle, yet, even with their disdain for the ordinary practices and opinions of the world, also seek to keep a secret.

What tantric yoga involves, we won't conjecture.

* However, perhaps there is less urgency to the decision than we think. Siddhartha Guatama's statement notwithstanding, is the house on fire? If the theories centering on such experiences are correct, we live a sequence of lives, and so we can hope that in a later one the matter will become clearer. While if we have only this life, then these theories are incorrect and we should not follow them. So in either case, we should not follow an arduous Eastern path now. Unless, of course, the Eastern theories are correct, and the karmic consequences of acting on this argument, having come so close to realizing the truth, push one further away from it for innumerable future lifetimes.

EPISTEMOLOGY

Chapter
Three

KNOWLEDGE AND SKEPTICISM

You think you are seeing these words, but could you not be hallucinating or dreaming or having your brain stimulated to give you the experience of seeing these marks on paper although no such thing is before you? More extremely, could you not be floating in a tank while super-psychologists stimulate your brain electrochemically to produce exactly the same experiences as you are now having, or even to produce the whole sequence of experiences you have had in your lifetime thus far? If one of these other things was happening, your experience would be exactly the same as it now is. So how can you know none of them is happening? Yet if you do not know these possibilities don't hold, how can you know you are reading this book now? If you do not know you haven't always been floating in the tank at the mercy of the psychologists, how can you know anything—what your name is, who your parents were, where you come from?

The skeptic argues that we do not know what we think we do. Even when he leaves us unconverted, he leaves us confused. Granting that we do know, how *can* we? Given these other possibilities he poses, how is knowledge possible?[1] In answering this question, we do not seek to convince the skeptic, but rather to formulate hypotheses about knowledge and our connection to facts that show how knowledge can exist even given the skeptic's possibilities. These hypotheses must reconcile our belief that we know things with our belief that the skeptical possibilities are logical possibilities.

The skeptical possibilities, and the threats they pose to our knowledge, depend upon our knowing things (if we do) mediately, through or by way of something else. Our thinking or believing that some fact p holds is connected somehow to the fact that p, but is not itself identical with that fact. Intermediate links establish the connection. This leaves room for the possibility of these intermediate stages holding and producing our belief that p, without the fact that p being at the other end. The intermediate stages arise in a completely different manner, one not involving the fact that p although giving rise to the appearance that p holds true.[2]

Are the skeptic's possibilities indeed logically possible? Imagine reading a science fiction story in which someone is raised from birth floating in a tank with psychologists stimulating his brain. The story could go on to tell of the person's reactions when he is brought out of the tank, of how the psychologists convince him of what had been happening to him, or how they fail to do so. This story is coherent, there is nothing self-contradictory or otherwise impossible about it. Nor is there anything incoherent in imagining that you are now in this situation, at a time before being taken out of the tank. To ease the transition out, to prepare the way, perhaps the psychologists will give the person in the tank thoughts of whether floating in the tank is possible, or the experience of reading a book that discusses this possibility, even one that discusses their easing his transition. (Free will presents no insuperable problem for this possibility. Perhaps the psychologists caused all your experiences of choice, including the feeling of freely choosing; or perhaps you do freely choose to act while they, cutting the effector circuit, continue the scenario from there.)

Some philosophers have attempted to demonstrate there is no such coherent possibility of this sort.* However, for any reasoning that

---

* Most recently, my colleague Hilary Putnam has used considerations from the theory of reference in an attempt toward formulating a transcendental argument that would undercut the skeptical possibility: if we can successfully describe the possibility, using constituent terms that refer, then it cannot hold true. (See his "Realism and Reason", *Proceedings and Addresses of the American Philosophical Association*, Vol. 50, No. 6, 1977, pp. 483–498; he extends the argument in a forthcoming book.) Recall another earlier attempt. The "paradigm case argument" held that since some situations were the very type of situation wherein was taught the application of a term, "free will" for example, the term must refer to that type of situation. This argument is now rightly discredited; one would expect Putnam's more sophisti-

purports to show this skeptical possibility cannot occur, we can imagine the psychologists of our science fiction story feeding *it* to their tank-subject, along with the (inaccurate) feeling that the reasoning is cogent. So how much trust can be placed in the apparent cogency of an argument to show the skeptical possibility isn't coherent? The skeptic's possibility is a logically coherent one, in tension with the existence of (almost all) knowledge; so we seek a hypothesis to explain how, even given the skeptic's possibilities, knowledge is possible. We may worry that such explanatory hypotheses are ad hoc, but this worry will lessen if they yield other facts as well, fit in with other things we believe, and so forth. Indeed, the theory of knowledge that follows was not developed in order to explain how knowledge is possible. Rather, the motivation was external to epistemology; only after the account of knowledge was developed for another purpose did I notice its consequences for skepticism, for understanding how knowledge is possible. So whatever other defects the explanation might have, it can hardly be called ad hoc.

My original aim was to make progress on the topic of free will. Early in the flurry of journal articles presenting counterexamples to increasingly complicated accounts of knowledge, stimulated by Edward Gettier's counterexample to the traditional account of knowledge as justified true belief,[3] I despaired of anyone's getting it exactly right. So messy did it all seem that I just stopped reading that literature. I was led back to the task of formulating conditions for knowledge, by the following line of reasoning.

In knowledge, a belief is linked somehow to the fact believed; without this linkage there may be true belief but there will not be knowledge. Plato first made the point that knowledge is not simply a

---

cated use of a theory of reference to fall before correspondingly more sophisticated versions of the earlier objections.

First, at best, Putnam's argument shows the terms have something they refer to, not that we are in any sort of direct contact with the referents. For all the argument shows, we could be floating in the tank using terms whose reference is parasitic on the terms of the psychologists, who are not. Second, we cannot tell from Putnam's argument which terms will have a referent that fits them; for the meaning of some can be built up out of other terms (for subatomic particles, say) which, while they do refer, are not explicitly mentioned in the skeptic's science fiction story. Third, though the "tank" is a salient device to pose the problem, the story need not assume you are materially ensconced; then the mode of influence exerted by the other consciousnesses will not be mediated materially.

belief that is true; if someone knowing nothing about the matter separately tells you and me contradictory things, getting one of us to believe *p* while the other believes not-*p*, although one of us will have a belief that happens to be true, neither of us will have knowledge. Something more is needed for a person S to know that *p*, to go alongside

(1) *p* is true
(2) S believes that *p*.

This something more, I think, is not simply an additional fact, but a way that 1 and 2 are linked. Thus, consider the traditional third condition stemming from Plato's account: S is justified in believing that *p*, or S has adequate evidence that *p*. Here, a two-part linkage connects S's belief that *p* with the fact that *p*: the link between the fact that *p* and the evidence, and the link between the evidence and the belief that *p*.

Recently it has been urged, with some plausibility, that the requisite linkage of belief to facts is a causal one, that the third condition is something like: the fact that *p* (partially) causes S to believe that *p*, that is, 2 because 1.[4] A drunk who hallucinates a pink elephant in a bar where, behind a screen, there is a pink elephant does not know there is a pink elephant there. The elephant's being there is not a cause of his believing it there. Whereas, in tracing back through the causes of your believing there now is a book before you, we eventually reach the fact that there *is* a book before you. The causal account of knowledge thus has a certain plausibility. Since, on this view, the causation (in a certain way) of our beliefs is necessary for us to have knowledge, such causation therefore is desirable. To be sure, there are difficulties with the causal account of knowledge, most noticeably with mathematical knowledge and ethical knowledge but elsewhere as well.[5] In these cases, the appropriate kind of causal connection fails to hold. Yet where it does hold, when a belief is caused appropriately by the fact, that connection appears desirable and plausibly is held to constitute knowledge.

In contrast, we strongly feel that the causal determination of action threatens responsibility and is undesirable. It is puzzling that what is desirable for belief, perhaps even necessary for knowledge, is threatening for action. Might not there be a way for action to parallel belief, to be so connected to the world, even causally, in a way that is desirable? At the least, it would be instructive to see where and why the parallel fails. If it did not fail, causality of action would be rendered harmless—determinism would be defanged.

The idea is to investigate how action is to be connected to the world, to parallel the connection of belief to fact when there is knowledge. This need not assume a causal account of knowledge. The causal linkage which appears to be a constituent in knowledge may be merely one way of realizing a more general linkage that constitutes knowledge. This would leave some room for ethical and mathematical knowledge, and perhaps even for a noncausal connection of action to the world that is not undercut by causality, just as mathematical knowledge, presumably, is not undercut by belief's being caused. To see if our actions desirably can be like knowledge, the first task is to see precisely what connection of belief to fact knowledge involves—then we shall know what it is that action must parallel.

It was this line of thought, this project of paralleling, that led me to investigate the details of the knowledge-link in the hope that it could be put to use later. What started as a means to another topic provided, along the way, an explanation of how knowledge is possible. This side result is especially fortunate in view of the free will problem's intractability.

I. KNOWLEDGE

Conditions for Knowledge

Our task is to formulate further conditions to go alongside

(1) p is true
(2) S believes that p.

We would like each condition to be necessary for knowledge, so any case that fails to satisfy it will not be an instance of knowledge. Furthermore, we would like the conditions to be jointly sufficient for knowledge, so any case that satisfies all of them will be an instance of knowledge. We first shall formulate conditions that seem to handle ordinary cases correctly, classifying as knowledge cases which are knowledge, and as nonknowledge cases which are not; then we shall check to see how these conditions handle some difficult cases discussed in the literature.[6]

The causal condition on knowledge, previously mentioned, provides an inhospitable environment for mathematical and ethical knowledge; also there are well-known difficulties in specifying the type of causal connection. If someone floating in a tank oblivious to everything around him is given (by direct electrical and chemical stimulation of the brain) the belief that he is floating in a tank with his brain being stimulated, then even though that fact is part of the cause of his belief, still he does not know that it is true.

Let us consider a different third condition:

(3) If p weren't true, S wouldn't believe that p.

Throughout this work, let us write the subjunctive 'if-then' by an arrow, and the negation of a sentence by prefacing "not-" to it. The above condition thus is rewritten as:

(3) not-$p \rightarrow$ not-(S believes that p).

This subjunctive condition is not unrelated to the causal condition.

Often when the fact that p (partially) causes someone to believe that p, the fact also will be causally necessary for his having the belief—without the cause, the effect would not occur. In that case, the subjunctive condition 3 also will be satisfied. Yet this condition is not equivalent to the causal condition. For the causal condition will be satisfied in cases of causal overdetermination, where either two sufficient causes of the effect actually operate, or a back-up cause (of the same effect) would operate if the first one didn't; whereas the subjunctive condition need not hold for these cases.[7] When the two conditions do agree, causality indicates knowledge because it acts in a manner that makes the subjunctive 3 true.

The subjunctive condition 3 serves to exclude cases of the sort first described by Edward Gettier, such as the following. Two other people are in my office and I am justified on the basis of much evidence in believing the first owns a Ford car; though he (now) does not, the second person (a stranger to me) owns one. I believe truly and justifiably that someone (or other) in my office owns a Ford car, but I do not know someone does. Concluded Gettier, knowledge is not simply justified true belief.

The following subjunctive, which specifies condition 3 for this Gettier case, is not satisfied: if no one in my office owned a Ford car, I wouldn't believe that someone did. The situation that would obtain if no one in my office owned a Ford is one where the stranger does not (or where he is not in the office); and in that situation I still would believe, as before, that someone in my office does own a Ford, namely, the first person. So the subjunctive condition 3 excludes this Gettier case as a case of knowledge.

The subjunctive condition is powerful and intuitive, not so easy to satisfy, yet not so powerful as to rule out everything as an instance of knowledge. A subjunctive conditional "if p were true, q would be true", $p \rightarrow q$, does not say that p entails q or that it is logically impossible that p yet not-q. It says that in the situation that would obtain if p were true, q also would be true. This point is brought out especially clearly in recent 'possible-worlds' accounts of subjunctives: the subjunctive is true when (roughly) in all those worlds in which p holds true that are closest to the actual world, q also is true. (Examine those worlds in which p holds true closest to the actual world, and see if q holds true in all these.) Whether or not q is true in p worlds that are still farther away from the actual world is irrelevant to the truth of the subjunctive. I do not mean to endorse any particular possible-worlds account of subjunctives, nor am I committed to this type of account.[8] I sometimes shall use it, though, when it illustrates points in an especially clear way.*

The subjunctive condition 3 also handles nicely cases that cause difficulties for the view that you know that p when you can rule out the relevant alternatives to p in the context. For, as Gail Stine writes, "what makes an alternative relevant in one context and not another? . . . if on the basis of visual appearances obtained under optimum conditions while driving through the countryside Henry identifies an object as a barn, normally we say that Henry knows that it is a barn. Let us suppose, however, that unknown to Henry, the region is full of expertly made papier-mâché facsimiles of barns. In that case, we would not say that Henry knows that the object is a barn,

---

* If the possible-worlds formalism is used to represent counterfactuals and subjunctives, the relevant worlds are not those p worlds that are closest or most similar to the actual world, unless the measure of closeness or similarity is: what would obtain if p were true. Clearly, this cannot be used to explain when subjunctives hold true, but it can be used to represent them. Compare utility theory which represents preferences but does not explain them. Still, it is not a trivial fact that preferences are so structured that they can be represented by a real-valued function, unique up to a positive linear transformation, even though the representation (by itself) does not explain these preferences. Similarly, it would be of interest to know what properties hold of distance metrics which serve to represent subjunctives, and to know how subjunctives must be structured and interrelated so that they can be given a possible worlds representation. (With the same one space serving for all subjunctives?)

One further word on this point. Imagine a library where a cataloguer assigns call numbers based on facts of sort F. Someone, perhaps the cataloguer, then places each book on the shelf by looking at its call number, and inserting it between the two books whose call numbers are most nearly adjacent to its own. The call number is derivative from facts of type F, yet it plays some explanatory role, not merely a representational one. "Why is this book located precisely there? Because of its number." Imagine next another library where the person who places books on the shelves directly considers facts of type F, using them to order the books and to interweave new ones. Someone else might notice that this ordering can be represented by an assignment of numbers, numbers from which other information can be derived as well, for example, the first letter of the last name of the principal author. But such an assigned number is no explanation of why a book in this library is located between two others (or why its author's last name begins with a certain letter). I have assumed that utility numbers stand to preferences, and closeness or similarity measures stand to subjunctives, as the call numbers do to the books, and to the facts of type F they exhibit, in the second library.

unless he has evidence against it being a papier-mâché facsimile, which is now a relevant alternative. So much is clear, but what if no such facsimiles exist in Henry's surroundings, although they once did? Are either of these circumstances sufficient to make the hypothesis (that it's a papier-mâché object) relevant? Probably not, but the situation is not so clear."[9] Let p be the statement that the object in the field is a (real) barn, and q the one that the object in the field is a papier-mâché barn. When papier-mâché barns are scattered through the area, if p were false, q would be true or might be. Since in this case (we are supposing) the person still would believe p, the subjunctive

(3) not-p → not-(S believes that p)

is not satisfied, and so he doesn't know that p. However, when papier-mâché barns are or were scattered around another country, even if p were false q wouldn't be true, and so (for all we have been told) the person may well know that p. A hypothesis q contrary to p clearly is relevant when if p weren't true, q would be true; when not-p → q. It clearly is irrelevant when if p weren't true, q also would not be true; when not-p → not-q. The remaining possibility is that neither of these opposed subjunctives holds; q might (or might not) be true if p weren't true. In this case, q also will be relevant, according to an account of knowledge incorporating condition 3 and treating subjunctives along the lines sketched above. Thus, condition 3 handles cases that befuddle the "relevant alternatives" account; though that account can adopt the above subjunctive criterion for when an alternative is relevant, it then becomes merely an alternate and longer way of stating condition 3.[10]

Despite the power and intuitive force of the condition that if p weren't true the person would not believe it, this condition does not (in conjunction with the first two conditions) rule out every problem case. There remains, for example, the case of the person in the tank who is brought to believe, by direct electrical and chemical stimulation of his brain, that he is in the tank and is being brought to believe things in this way; he does not know this is true. However, the subjunctive condition is satisfied: if he weren't floating in the tank, he wouldn't believe he was.

The person in the tank does not know he is there, because his belief is not sensitive to the truth. Although it is caused by the fact that is its content, it is not sensitive to that fact. The operators of the tank could have produced any belief, including the false belief that he wasn't in the tank; if they had, he would have believed that. Perfect sensitivity would involve beliefs and facts varying together. We already have one portion of that variation, subjunctively at least: if p were false he wouldn't believe it. This sensitivity as specified by a subjunctive does not have the belief vary with the truth or falsity of p in all possible situations, merely in the ones that would or might obtain if p were false.

The subjunctive condition

(3) not-p → not-(S believes that p)

tells us only half the story about how his belief is sensitive to the truth-value of p. It tells us how his belief state is sensitive to p's falsity, but not how it is sensitive to p's truth; it tells us what his belief state would be if p were false, but not what it would be if p were true.

To be sure, conditions 1 and 2 tell us that p is true and he does believe it, but it does not follow that his believing p is sensitive to p's being true. This additional sensitivity is given to us by a further subjunctive: if p were true, he would believe it.

(4) p → S believes that p.

Not only is p true and S believes it, but if it were true he would believe it. Compare: not only was the photon emitted and did it go to the left, but (it was then true that): if it were emitted it would go to the left. The truth of antecedent and consequent is not alone sufficient for the truth of a subjunctive; 4 says more than 1 and 2.[11] Thus, we presuppose some (or another) suitable account of subjunctives. According to the suggestion tentatively made above, 4 holds true if not only does he actually truly believe p, but in the "close" worlds where p is true, he also believes it. He believes that p for some distance out in the p neighborhood of the actual world; similarly, condition 3 speaks not of the whole not-p neighborhood of the actual world, but only of the first portion of it. (If, as is likely, these explanations do not help, please use your own intuitive understanding of the subjunctives 3 and 4.)

The person in the tank does not satisfy the subjunctive condition 4. Imagine as actual a world in which he is in the tank and is stimulated to believe he is, and consider what subjunctives are true in that world. It is not true of him there that if he were in the tank he would believe it; for in the close world (or situation) to his own where he is in the tank but they don't give him the belief that he is (much less instill the belief that he isn't) he doesn't believe he is in the tank. Of the person actually in the tank and believing it, it is not true to make the further statement that if he were in the tank he would believe it—so he does not know he is in the tank.[12]

The subjunctive condition 4 also handles a case presented by Gilbert Harman.[13] The dictator of a country is killed; in their first edition, newspapers print the story, but later all the country's newspapers and other media deny the story, falsely. Everyone who encounters the denial believes it (or does not know what to believe and so suspends judgment). Only one person in the country fails to hear any denial and he continues to believe the truth. He satisfies conditions 1 through 3 (and the causal condition about belief) yet we are reluctant to say he knows the truth. The reason is that if he had heard the denials, he too would have believed them, just like everyone else. His belief is not sensitively tuned to the truth, he doesn't satisfy the condition that if it were true he would believe it. Condition 4 is not satisfied.[14]

There is a pleasing symmetry about how this account of knowledge relates conditions 3 and 4, and connects them to the first two conditions. The account has the following form.

(1)
(2)
(3) not-1 → not-2
(4) 1 → 2

I am not inclined, however, to make too much of this symmetry, for I found also that with other conditions experimented with as a possible fourth condition there was some way to construe the resulting third and fourth conditions as symmetrical answers to some symmetrical looking questions, so that they appeared to arise in parallel fashion from similar questions about the components of true belief.

Symmetry, it seems, is a feature of a mode of presentation, not of the contents presented. A uniform transformation of symmetrical statements can leave the results nonsymmetrical. But if symmetry attaches to mode of presentation, how can it possibly be a deep feature of, for instance, laws of nature that they exhibit symmetry? (One of my favorite examples of symmetry is due to Groucho Marx. On his radio program he spoofed a commercial, and ended, "And if you are not completely satisfied, return the unused portion of our product and we will return the unused portion of your money.") Still, to present our subject symmetrically makes the connection of knowledge to true belief especially perspicuous. It seems to me that a symmetrical formulation is a sign of our understanding, rather than a mark of truth. If we cannot understand an asymmetry as arising from an underlying symmetry through the operation of a particular factor, we will not understand why that asymmetry exists in that direction. (But do we also need to understand why the underlying asymmetrical factor holds instead of its opposite?)

A person knows that p when he not only does truly believe it, but also would truly believe it and wouldn't falsely believe it. He not only actually has a true belief, he subjunctively has one. It is true that p and he believes it; if it weren't true he wouldn't believe it, and if it were true he would believe it. To know that p is to be someone who would believe it if it were true, and who wouldn't believe it if it were false.

It will be useful to have a term for this situation when a person's belief is thus subjunctively connected to the fact. Let us say of a person who believes that p, which is true, that when 3 and 4 hold, his belief *tracks* the truth that p. To know is to have a belief that tracks the truth. Knowledge is a particular way of being connected to the world, having a specific real factual connection to the world: tracking it.

One refinement is needed in condition 4. It may be possible for someone to have contradictory beliefs, to believe p and also believe not-p. We do not mean such a person to easily satisfy 4, and in any case we want his belief-state, sensitive to the truth of p, to focus upon p. So let us rewrite our fourth condition as:

(4) $p \rightarrow$ S believes that p and not-(S believes that not-p).[15]

As you might have expected, this account of knowledge as tracking requires some refinements and epicycles. Readers who find themselves (or me) bogged down in these refinements should move on directly to this essay's second part, on skepticism, where the pace picks up.

Ways and Methods

The fourth condition says that if p were true the person would believe it. Suppose the person only happened to see a certain event or simply chanced on a book describing it. He knows it occurred. Yet if he did not happen to glance that way or encounter the book, he would not believe it, even though it occurred. As written, the fourth condition would exclude this case as one where he actually knows the event occurred. It also would exclude the following case. Suppose some person who truly believes that p would or might arrive at a belief about it in some other close situation where it holds true, in a way or by a method different from the one he (actually) used in arriving at his belief that p, and so thereby come to believe that not-p. In that (close) situation, he would believe not-p even though p still holds true. Yet, all this does not show he actually doesn't know that p, for actually he has not used this alternative method in arriving at his belief. Surely he can know that p, even though condition 4, as written, is not satisfied.

Similarly, suppose he believes that p by one method or way of arriving at belief, yet if p were false he wouldn't use this method but would use another one instead, whose application would lead him mistakenly to believe p (even though it is false). This person does not satisfy condition 3 as written; it is not true of him that if p were false he wouldn't believe it. Still, the fact that he would use another method of arriving at belief if p were false does not show he didn't know that p when he used this method. A grandmother sees her grandson is well when he comes to visit; but if he were sick or dead, others would tell her he was well to spare her upset. Yet this does not mean she doesn't know he is well (or at least ambulatory) when she sees him. Clearly, we must restate our conditions to take explicit account of the ways and methods of arriving at belief.

Let us define a technical locution, S knows, via method (or way of believing) M, that p:

(1) p is true.
(2) S believes, via method or way of coming to believe M, that p.
(3) If p weren't true and S were to use M to arrive at a belief whether (or not) p, then S wouldn't believe, via M, that p.
(4) If p were true and S were to use M to arrive at a belief whether (or not) p, then S would believe, via M, that p.

We need to relate this technical locution to our ordinary notion of knowledge. If only one method M is actually or subjunctively relevant to S's belief that p, then, simply, S knows that p (according to our ordinary notion) if and only if that method M is such that S knows that p via M.

Some situations involve multiple methods, however.

> *First Situation:* S's belief that p is overdetermined; it was introduced (or reinforced) by two methods, each of which in isolation would have been sufficient to produce in S the belief that p. S's belief that p via one of these methods satisfies conditions 1–4. However, S's belief that p via the second method does not satisfy conditions 1–4, and in particular violates condition 3.

A case of this sort is discussed by Armstrong.[16] A father believes his son innocent of committing a particular crime, both because of faith in his son and (now) because he has seen presented in the courtroom a conclusive demonstration of his son's innocence. His belief via the method of courtroom demonstration satisfies 1–4, let us suppose, but his faith-based belief does not. If his son were guilty, he would still believe him innocent, on the basis of faith in his son. Thus, his belief that p (that his son is innocent) via faith in his son violates condition 3. Looking at his belief alone, without mention of method, his belief that p violates the third condition (namely, if p were false S wouldn't believe that p), which made no mention of method.

> *Second Situation:* S's belief that p via one method satisfies conditions 1–4. However, if p were false, S would not use that method in arriving at a belief about the truth value of p. Instead, he would use another method, thereby deciding, despite p's falsity, that p was true. S's actual belief that p is in no way based on the use of this second method, but if p were false he would believe p via the second method. (However, if p were false and S were to decide about its truth value by using the first method, then S would not believe that p. To be sure, if p were false S wouldn't decide about it by using that first method.) The truth value of p affects which method S uses to decide whether p.

Our earlier example of the grandmother is of this sort. Consider one further example, suggested to me by Avishai Margalit. S believes a certain building is a theater and concert hall. He has attended plays and concerts there (first method). However, if the building were not a theater, it would have housed a nuclear reactor that would so have altered the air around it (let us suppose) that everyone upon approaching the theater would have become lethargic and nauseous, and given up the attempt to buy a ticket. The government cover story would have been that the building was a theater, a cover story they knew would be safe since no unmedicated person could approach through the nausea field to discover any differently. Everyone, let us suppose, would have believed the cover story; they would have believed that the building they saw (but only from some distance) was a theater.

S believes the building is a theater because he has attended plays and concerts inside. He does not believe it is a theater via the second method of reading the government's cover story plus planted spurious theater and concert reviews. There are no such things. However, if it weren't a theater, it would be a nuclear reactor, there would be such cover stories, and S would believe still (this time falsely and via the second method) that the building was a theater. Nonetheless, S, who actually has attended performances there, knows that it is a theater.

To hold that a person knows that p if there exists at least one method M, satisfying conditions 1–4, via which he believes that p, would classify the father as knowing his son is innocent, a consequence too charitable to the father. Whereas it seems too stringent to require that all methods satisfy conditions 1–4, including those methods that were not actually used but would be under some other circumstances; the grandmother knows her grandson is well, and the person who has attended the concerts and plays knows the building is a theater. It is more reasonable to hold he knows that p if all the methods via which he actually believes that p satisfy conditions 1–4. Yet suppose our theatergoer also believes it is a theater partly because government officials, before they decided on which use they would put the building to, announced they were building a theater. Still, the theatergoer knows the building is a theater. Not all methods actually used need satisfy conditions 1–4, but we already have seen how the weak position that merely one such method is enough mishandles the case of the father.

We are helped to thread our way through these difficulties when we notice this father does not merely believe his son is innocent via the route of faith in his son; this defective route, not satisfying 1–4, also outweighs for him the method of courtroom demonstration. Even if courtroom demonstration (had it operated alone) would lead to the belief that his son is guilty, that not-p, still he would believe his son innocent, via faith in his son. Although it is the method of courtroom demonstration that gives him knowledge that p if anything does, for the father this method is outweighed by faith.[17] As a first try at delineating outweighing, we might say that method M is outweighed by others if when M would have the person believe p, the person believes not-p if the other methods would lead to the belief that not-p, or when M would have the person believe not-p, the person believes p if the other methods would lead to the belief that p.

This leads us to put forth the following position: S knows that p if there is some method via which S believes that p which satisfies conditions 1–4, and that method is not outweighed by any other method(s), via which S actually believes that p, that fail to satisfy conditions 3 and 4. According to this position, in some cases a person has knowledge even when he also actually believes via a method M_1 that does not satisfy 1–4, provided it is outweighed by one that does; namely, in the overdetermination case, and in the case when M_1 alone would suffice to fix belief but only in the absence of a verdict from the M he also uses which does satisfy 1–4.

S knows that p if and only if there is a method M such that (a) he knows that p via M, his belief via M that p satisfies conditions 1–4, and (b) all other methods M_1 via which he believes that p that do not satisfy conditions 1–4 are outweighed by M.[18]

We have stated our outweighing requirement only roughly; now we must turn to refinements. According to our rough statement, in the overdetermination case, method M_1, which satisfies 3 and 4 and which is what gives knowledge if anything does, wins out over the other method M_2 in all cases. The actual situation (Case I) is where M_1 recommends believing p as does M_2, and the person believes p. In this case we have made our answer to the question whether he knows that p depend on what happens or would happen in the two other cases where the methods recommend different beliefs. (See Table.) The first rough statement held that the person knows in Case I only if he would believe p in Case II and not-p in Case III. While this is sufficient for knowledge in Case I, it seems too stringent to be necessary for such knowledge.

	M_1 recommends	M_2 recommends	Does the person believe p or believe not-p?
Case I	believe p	believe p	believes p
Case II	believe p	believe not-p	?
Case III	believe not-p	believe p	?

An alternative and more adequate view would hold constant what the other method recommends, and ask whether the belief varies with the recommendation of M_1. Since M_2 actually recommends p (Case I), we need look only at Case III and ask: when M_2 continues to recommend p and M_1 recommends not-p, would the person believe not-p? Despite his faith, would the father believe his son guilty if the courtroom procedure proved guilt? That is the relevant question—not what he would believe if the courtroom showed innocence while (somehow) his method of faith led to a conclusion of guilty.

Consider how this works out in another simple case. I see a friend today; he is now alive. However, if he were not alive, I wouldn't have seen him today or (let us suppose) heard of his death, and so still would believe he was alive. Yet condition 3 is satisfied; it includes reference to a method, and the method M_1 of seeing him satisfies 3 with respect to p equals he is alive at the time. But there also is another method M_2 via which I believe he is alive, namely having known he was alive yesterday and continuing to believe it. Case III asks what I would believe if I saw the friend dead (though I knew yesterday he was alive); our position holds I must believe him dead in this case if I am to know by seeing him that he is alive in Case I. However, we need not go so far as to consider what I would believe if I had "learned" yesterday that he was dead yet "saw" him alive today. Perhaps in that case I would wonder whether it really was he I was seeing. Even so, given the result in Case III, I know (in Case I) he is alive. Thus, we hold fixed the recommendation of the other method, and only ask whether then the belief varies with the recommendation of method M_1.[19]

Our test of looking at Case III cannot apply if M_1 is a one-sided method, incapable of recommending belief in not-p; it either recommends belief in p or yields no recommendation. (Perhaps M_1 detects one of a number of sufficient conditions for p; not detecting this, M_1 remains silent as to the truth of p.) What are we to say about his knowing if a person's belief is overdetermined or jointly determined by a one-sided method M_1 plus another method M_2 which fails to satisfy condition 3? Should we now look at Case II, where M_1 recommends belief in p and M_2 recommends belief in not-p, and say that believing p in this case is sufficient to show that M_1 outweighs M_2? That does not seem unreasonable, but we had better be careful to stipulate that this Case II situation is a sufficient condition for M_1's outweighing M_2 only when the Case III situation is impossible, for otherwise we face the possibility of divergent results. (For example, he believes p in Case II and in Case III, yet believes not-p when both methods recommend not-p; here the result in Case II indicates M_1 outweighs M_2 while the result in Case III indicates M_2 outweighs M_1.) It is Case III that should predominate.

One final remark about method. Suppose a method is good for some types of statements but not others; it satisfies 3 and 4 for the first type but not for the second. However, S believes the method is good for all types of statements and applies it indiscriminately. When he applies it to a statement of the first type which he thereby comes to believe, does he know that it is true? He does, if he satisfies conditions 3 and 4. Hesitation to grant him knowledge stems, I think, from the fact that if p were false and were of the second type, he might well still believe it. Whether or not this undercuts condition 3 for knowledge depends upon the disparity of the two types; the greater the gulf between the types, the more willing we are to say he knows a statement of the type where M works.

In explaining the nature of knowledge by reference to a method or way of believing, we leave large questions open about how to individuate methods, count them, identify which method is at work, and so on. I do not want to underestimate these difficulties, but neither do I want to pursue them here.[20] Still, some clarifying remarks are needed.

A person can use a method (in my sense) without proceeding methodically, and without knowledge or awareness of what method he is using. Usually, a method will have a final upshot in experience on which the belief is based, such as visual experience, and then (a) no method without this upshot is the same method, and (b) any method experientially the same, the same "from the inside", will count as the same method. Basing our beliefs on experiences, you and I and the person floating in the tank are using, for these purposes, the same method.

Some methods are supervenient on others, for example, "believing what seems to be true to you" or "believing what seems true given the weighting of all other methods". The account of outweighing is not to apply to such supervenient methods, otherwise there always will be such a one that outweighs all the others. There are various gerrymandered (Goodmanesque) methods that would yield the same resulting belief in the actual situation; which method a person actually is using will depend on which general disposition to acquire beliefs (extending to other situations) he actually is exercising.[21]

Although sometimes it will be necessary to be explicit about the methods via which someone believes something, often it will cause no confusion to leave out all mention of method. Furthermore, some statements play a central role in our continuing activities, or in our picture of the world or framework wherein we check other statements, for example, "I have two hands", "the world has existed for many years already"; it is misleading to think of our coming to believe them via some delimited method or methods.[22] So nested are these statements in our other beliefs and activities, and so do they nest them, that our belief or acceptance of them is (for almost all purposes) best represented apart from any particular methods. In considering our knowledge of them we may revert to the earlier simpler subjunctives

(3) not-p → not-(S believes that p)
(4) p → S believes that p.

The very centrality of the specific p means that 4 will be satisfied without reference to a specific method or way of believing. In contrast, I know there is a pair of scissors on my desk (in front of me) now; but it is not accurate simply to say that if there were a pair of scissors there, I would believe there was. For what if I weren't looking, or hadn't looked, or were elsewhere now? Reference to the method via which I believe there are scissors on the desk is needed to exclude these possibilities. With the most central statements, however, there is no similar "what if"; their centrality ensures they will not escape notice.

Knowledge of Necessities

Otherwise plausible accounts of knowledge often stumble over mathematical or ethical truths. Though they can seek safety by restriction to "empirical" truths, it seems desirable to offer a unified account of knowledge of all types, even if the distinctions among truths bring differences in how the one account applies.

Assume, as does the literature, that statements of mathematics when true are necessarily true. Our third condition of tracking speaks of what the person would believe if p were false, but in the case of mathematical truths p, this is a necessarily false supposition, an impossible one. When p is necessarily true, the antecedent of condition 3 is necessarily false. Perhaps a theory of subjunctives can be constructed to cover such cases—none has yet been proposed that is remotely satisfactory—but we should try to avoid such a desperate expedient.

Since condition 3 does not come into play for necessary truths p, the account of tracking for these statements, when truly believed, reduces to

(4) If p were true and S were to use method M to arrive at a belief whether (or not) p, then S would believe, via M, that p.

When M is the method of coming to believe something on the basis of a mathematical proof then, since this method guarantees truth, it is p that will be believed and so 4 is satisfied.[23] However 4 is not satisfied by someone's method of dogmatically believing what his parents told him, in this case the necessary truth p, even though p will be true in all close situations or worlds. For if there are close worlds in which his parents told him not-p, the method leads to false belief in those worlds, so it is not actually true of him that he would believe the truth by that method. It is not enough for the dogmatist to firmly believe something; he must come to the belief in a way that not only does but would yield a true belief (when it yields any belief at all).

Although methods of mathematical proof may guarantee truth, through the formal relations they specify,[24] we are fallible creatures who can make mistakes in our application of such methods. Do we know mathematical truths via our application of these methods? (When correctly followed the recipe always leads to an exquisite dish, but success lies in the execution.) That depends not on whether a mistake is logically possible but whether we would or might make one under those conditions.

Many mathematical statements we believe on the basis not of proofs but of authority or hearsay: we have been told they are true. Here, the question is whether our source is tracking the truth and whether the particular channel via which we learn it preserves tracking. More generally, a channel of communication C will transmit knowledge that p if C counts as a method of knowing: if S's belief via C that p satisfies the four conditions (when applicable) for S's knowing via M that p, and if the channel outweighs any other methods actually operating which do not satisfy 3 and 4. Believing via a channel of communication is just a particular case of believing via a method or way of believing. Channels include reading books, being told something by another, and so on. It is the channel condition that describes how we can learn from others and acquire knowledge from them. Mathematical truths raise no special questions about learning from others.*

---

* There is another interesting question, though, about channels. It is natural to regard a channel as follows: someone else knows that p and does something (writes, speaks, or whatever) to transmit that knowledge to me. A theory of my acquiring knowledge becomes a theory of the conditions under which his knowledge, already there, flows to me. If he doesn't know that p, he has no knowledge that p, and so no knowledge to transmit; I cannot acquire knowledge that p from him if he doesn't already know p. (I am imagining that the content of p is not about his transmitting. If he says, "I am speaking boringly", or "I am speaking loudly enough for you to hear", but doesn't believe it, still, you may come to know it from his saying it.)

Consider a situation where the person believes that p, yet does not track that fact: if p were false, he still would believe that p. However, suppose that actually if p were false, he wouldn't convey his belief to me. (He is ill and says he took his special pill; but another one similar in appearance was next to it, and if he had taken that one, he still would believe he'd taken the special one. If he had not taken the special pill, though, he wouldn't have said anything to me at all, not because he is especially scrupulous about what he says but because the special pill has the effect of giving him enough energy to talk. So if he had not taken it, I wouldn't believe he had.)

Thus, we see two ways the falsity of p can stop his transmitting the statement that p to me: by getting him not to believe p, and by getting him (though believing p) not to transmit his belief. In this second case, do I come to know via his transmission? Not if the method via which I come to believe it involves inferring it from the statement that he knows it.

Cases and Complications

In the case of necessary truths, we have said, condition 4 is enough for tracking and for knowledge when there also is true belief, even though condition 3 does not apply. Now we face a puzzle. If 4 without 3 is enough in these cases, why not make 4 (along with 1 and 2) the whole account of tracking for other cases as well? Why is 3 needed even for those cases where it is able to apply, if 4 alone is sufficient where 3 cannot apply? Why not simply say that for any true statement p (and not merely necessary ones) a person knows that p when: if p were true he would believe it.

Recall that the root notion of knowledge we have uncovered is one where not only does a person truly believe that p, but he would truly believe that p, and he wouldn't falsely believe that p. When p is a necessary truth, this last part drops away—we needn't worry about his falsely believing that p, since p (necessarily) cannot be false. With contingent truths, however, it is not enough that the person would truly believe it. For when some not-p world could easily be (or have been) the case, if the person would believe p even then, he doesn't actually know that p; he would or might falsely believe that p. Thus, it is clear why we cannot merely require condition 4 in the case where p is contingently true: 4 alone does not show the person wouldn't or mightn't falsely believe that p.[25]

In the Gettier example where a person believes someone in his office owns a Ford, neither of the two conditions for tracking was satisfied, and so this did not count as knowledge according to our account. It was not true that if no one in the office owned a Ford, the person wouldn't believe that someone did. For if the friend had come in without the stranger, which might have happened, then the person still would believe that someone in the office owned a Ford. Suppose we modify the example somewhat, so that the friend would not come to the office unless the stranger did, and so wouldn't have been there alone. Still, the stranger might not have owned a Ford, and in that case the person still would believe that someone in the office did. Modify the case still further: suppose that (for whatever reason) the friend would not come into the office unless accompanied by someone with a Ford. Isn't 3 now satisfied? Still, 4 is not, for if the stranger were there alone, the person wouldn't believe that someone in the office owned a Ford. Modify the case still further:

suppose also the stranger would not come to the office without the friend, neither would come without the other. It is not clear, even in these cases, that the subjunctives 3 and 4 hold true; that would depend upon the constituent subjunctives being transitive, which is not always so. Moreover, the examples thus far ignore the method via which the person comes to believe the statement.

Gettier-type examples often involve inferring a truth from a (justifiably believed) falsehood.[26] While condition 3 without mention of method excludes many of these cases, there may seem to be other cases of nonknowledge that do satisfy condition 3 because the person wouldn't have been led to have the false belief q from which he infers p, unless p were true.*

Gilbert Harman formulates a requirement that "the lemmas be true" to explicitly rule out such inferences from falsehood. Perhaps our account can yield this result, by treating "infers it from q" as the method the person uses to arrive at his belief that p. When q is false, the person using this method will not satisfy condition 3; for if p were false and the person arrived at his belief about the truth value of p by inference from q, he still would believe p. Therefore, he does not know p unless he also uses some other method M_1 satisfying 3 and 4 that outweighs this defective one.

In this case imagined, however, the person would not use the method if p were false. Nevertheless, we are holding the method fixed and asking what the person would believe, via this method, if p were false.[27] Many of the counterexample cases to simpler conditions involve situations where even though the method does not satisfy condition 3, if p were false the person would not be using that method and so would not be believing p. This may give rise to the illusion that 3 is satisfied; but according to our formulation, it is not.

Let us take a quick run through some examples presented in the literature, to illustrate and test our account.[28]

---

* Here is an example suggested to me by Eddy Zemach. A Persian child is brought to Nazi Germany in the 1930s as part of an Aryan ingathering, and grows up there thinking himself German, and learns the concept Aryan. He believes all Germans are Aryans, believes (falsely) that he is German, and so believes that he is Aryan. Condition 3 is satisfied because if he were not Aryan, he wouldn't have been gathered in by the Germans and so would not have come to believe he was Aryan. (To suppose condition 4 satisfied, we would have to suppose also that in varying circumstances he would be gathered in by the Germans.)

(a) As an effect of brain damage a person is led (irrationally) to believe he has brain damage, which he would not believe if he didn't have brain damage.[29] However, condition 4 is not satisfied: if the brain damage had been slightly different, though using the same route to belief he would not believe he had it.

(b) A magician in mid-routine moves a coin blatantly, but those who have been watching do not believe it, having been fooled so frequently during his performance. A person who wanders by just then, not knowing a magician is performing, sees him move the coin and believes he moved it.[30] He does not know the coin has been moved. For if it had not been moved he might well believe it had (if the magician had done a trick), so 3 is not satisfied; also, it might be that it was moved yet he would not believe it (either because he had seen the act from the beginning or because the magician tricked him), so 4 is not satisfied either.

(c) A person comes to believe a vase is in a box by seeing an illuminated hologram, part of a machine that alternates between displaying the hologram and the real vase contained in the box.[31] The person does not know, even when seeing the vase (a case suggested by Shope), for if it weren't there, he would see the hologram and still believe it was. Modify the example so that the machine, in alternate time periods, displays a hologram of a vase only when a vase is pressing down on a lever (it somehow detects a vase and not another thing). Hence if there weren't a vase there, he wouldn't believe there was one; and if there were one, he would come to believe, by looking, that there was. Thus, our account has the consequence that he knows a vase is there, even when he is seeing the hologram but thinks he is seeing the vase. This consequence is somewhat counterintuitive; however, we certainly do not want to hold that a person knows that p only if he has no false beliefs about the process via which he comes to believe that p. The Greeks had many false beliefs about the visual process.

(d) Talking to her on the telephone, a man believes his friend is wishing him a happy birthday. Unsuspected by the man, his psychiatrist was concerned that the friend would not call and so hired an actress who can perfectly imitate the friend's voice; this actress was attempting to get through on the telephone at the same time as the friend spoke, and would have performed if the friend had not called.[32] Supposing the actress could do the imitation undetected, in this case, the man does not know he is talking to his friend; if he weren't talking to her he still would believe he was.

Consider another case, of a student who, when his philosophy class is canceled, usually returns to this room and takes hallucinogenic drugs; one hallucination he has sometimes is of being in his philosophy class. When the student actually is in the philosophy class, does he know he is? I think not, for if he weren't in class, he still might believe he was. (Is this made more plausible if we add that he knows he sometimes hallucinates his being in a philosophy class?) Two students in the class might be in the same actual situation, having (roughly) the same retinal and aural intake, yet the first knows he is in class while the other does not, because they are situated differently subjunctively—different subjunctives hold true of them. Suppose, in addition, that a hypnotist is going around and hypnotizing some students outside class into thinking they are in class. He has never encountered the first student, but does his prowling nearby change which subjunctives hold of this student, so that he no longer knows he is in class?

(e) Faced by one of two identical twins, Judy and Trudy, a person believes it is Judy before him, but only because he has bumped his head which (somehow) gave him the idea that Judy has a mole; coincidentally, Judy just developed a mole.[33] He doesn't know it is Judy who is before him. Condition 4 is not satisfied; if Judy were before him, but in the very close situation of not having developed the mole, he wouldn't believe it was she. (And does condition 3 also block it, since it might have occurred that Trudy had developed a mole and stood before him?)

(f) You see a man named Tom remove a book from the library, concealing it in his coat, and you believe truly that Tom took the book. Unbeknownst to you, Tom's mother is across the library room, telling someone else that Tom is out of town, and it is his identical twin John whom they are looking at in the library. Do you know that Tom took the book? Now add the fact that Tom's mother is a pathological liar, and he has no twin brother; next alter the fact that she was in the library, and place her across town saying that Tom is out of town, and his twin John is in the library. In each of those cases, do you know that Tom is taking the book?[34]

Condition 3 is satisfied; if it were not Tom then (since there is no twin), you wouldn't believe it was. But is condition 4 satisfied? Do

191

the similar situations in which you must, by seeing him, believe it is Tom, include overhearing the mother (something you easily could have done)? Our answer here about the application of 4 may be unclear, as it should be if the epistemological status of the example also is unclear.

There are two types of philosophical accounts of a notion N. The first type classifies cases exactly as they are classified under the notion N, correctly classifying clear cases of N and clear cases of non-N, while leaving the unclear cases unclear. In terms of the conditions of the account, one can understand why the clear cases fall as they do, and why the unclear cases are unclear, either because different conditions of the account conflict, or because we can see why some of the account's conditions do not apply clearly. The second type of account sharpens up the notion; it classifies the clear cases correctly and moreover classifies the cases whose status was left unclear by the notion N itself, thereby making N more serviceable for some purposes. Accounts also can mix these features, reclassifying some previously unclear cases while leaving others to their old status. Our account of knowledge is of this last mixed sort, and the present example is, I think, an unclear case which it leaves so. For it is unclear how far afield the subjunctive condition 4 is to travel in such cases. Similar remarks probably should apply to the question whether there is knowledge in the case[35] where someone some distance away sees and hears a stationary sheep, but does not hear the farmer nearby playfully deceiving the city-person he is then speaking to, telling him that out in the field is a carefully contrived wooden replica covered with wool and containing an electronic bleater.

(g) You see a light on in a neighbor's house and conclude (on the basis of this plus other evidence) that it is lit by electricity supplied by the electric company; it is, but this homeowner has an alternate power generator that would switch on and supply electricity to the light even if there was some failure in drawing power from the electric company.[36]

Assume the case can be specified so that condition 3 is violated; if it weren't supplied by the company, you would still believe it was. So you do not know it is. The probability of a central power failure is very small; does this affect the matter? We shall consider issues about probability below; such issues also enter into whether condition 4 is satisfied: if the electricity were supplied centrally (and he had told you of his own power generator) would you still believe it was centrally generated, or only that it probably was?

(h) The reference to method helps with the case where the person might not happen to use it, for example, he might not have glanced that way and so might not have seen the criminal escaping. Still, he knows when he sees. What of the cases where what is seen (rather than his looking) is a matter of happenstance;[37] for example, the bank robber's mask slips off as he is escaping and the bystander sees it is Jesse James, whose picture is on many wanted posters. (This example will not work with the Lone Ranger for, leaving aside the issue of whether he would rob a bank, we recognize him only when his mask is on.) The bystander knows that Jesse James is robbing the bank. Condition 3 is satisfied, but is condition 4, even with the method explicit? If Jesse James were to rob the bank would he know it via that method? His method is looking and concluding it is Jesse James on the basis of seeing certain things. By that method (applied in this way) he would know in other cases also. To be sure, some other situations might not allow that method to be used—these situations do not yield any belief (see the discussion above of knowledge via methods and of the importance of holding the method fixed)—but that causes no difficulty for condition 4, properly understood.

Since we have not specified a precise theory of subjunctives or specified precisely how to identify a method and tell when it is held fixed, there is some leeway in our account. It may be this leeway that enables the account to cope with these examples and other cases, by using the constituent notions loosely and intuitively. This is not an objection but a reason to think the notions can be specified more precisely to handle the cases—a condition on their specification is that they handle the cases adequately—provided the discussion of the cases did not exploit the leeway or wobble inconsistently, first leaning in one direction, then in another.

Until now we have considered only temporally local conditions for knowledge, ignoring any problems raised by wider contexts. Consider a situation where p contains the term "now" and the truth value of p keeps changing, as do the truths of the subjunctives 3 and 4. However, from the observer's own point of view, there is no apparent change. Some of these cases we would not hold to exhibit knowledge, but the intricate problems and considerations these raise are best set aside; perhaps some additional condition is needed—but whatever additional intricate contextual condition is appropriate can be plugged into our structure.

Another issue about the temporal width of application of the conditions can be discussed usefully now. Suppose at time t_1 S knows that p and also knows that at a later time t_2 others will attempt to brainwash him into believing not-p. So between times t_1 and t_2 S unalterably fixes in himself the belief (that p) he already has, perhaps through psychosurgery. At time t_2, does S know that p? We might say not, for if p were false at t_2 then S still would believe p; or we might hold that S does know that p then, for if p were false he would not have cemented that belief in. Should we view the method by which S at t_2 believes p as "cementing", which fails to satisfy condition 3, or as "cementing after knowing (that is, believing in the way he did)", which does satisfy 3?

There is reason for not insisting upon the narrowest time interval. Many of us may have become cemented into some of our beliefs; as we become older, it is said, we can less easily learn new tricks or unlearn old ones. According to the interpretation of the condition as locally focused, much of our knowledge therefore would be passing into mere belief.* Second, evolution, which doth make trackers of us all, would select for global tracking rather than especially favoring the local version. (Also, in this particular example, might cementing be the person's way of satisfying condition 4?)

Therefore, I lean toward calling such cases knowledge; yet since now if p were false S still would believe p, I am reluctant to say simply that he knows. Thus, the general issue of local versus global analysis that crosses so many philosophical problems, as seen in the first chapter, comes into play again. Perhaps it suffices here to note the sources of the contrasting pulls, which subjunctives hold and which ones do not, and to note that 3's holding as a local subjunctive is better than 3's holding as a global subjunctive which in turn is better than 3's not holding in any version at all.

There are variations also in the ways 3 can hold globally. Consider another case: a parent, knowing that p and knowing that an attempt

---

* We have focused on methods of arriving at beliefs, but not on methods (including inertia) of retaining them. If the method via which someone now has a belief is a combination of the acquiring and the retaining methods, clearly an adequate account of the conditions under which he knows now will have to incorporate details about subjunctives including these joint methods.

will be made to brainwash his child at time t_2, acts before time t_2 to cement in the child the belief that p. At time t_2, does the child know that p? Here again, we can note which subjunctives hold and which ones do not; without attempting to decide whether this is a case of knowledge, we can say that 3's holding globally in this way is better than its not holding at all, but worse than its holding due to an earlier choice to cement the belief made by the person himself. I am content here to rank order these global cases without forcing a classification as knowledge or not, especially since my interest lies in the examples of action corresponding to them which we shall encounter in the next chapter as we pursue the parallel of action to knowledge. Note, though, that the issues we mention here are the ones underlying the question of whether innate beliefs instilled by a process that tracks their truth constitute innate knowledge.[38]

A belief that p may be true in some situations because the person believes it, rather like a "self-fulfilling prophecy". For example, suppose my children (through a misunderstanding or however) believe I will get them a puppy and, discovering they believe this, I do so in order to avoid their being disappointed. If they didn't believe it, I would not get the puppy. It may be true that for all close-by situations where p is true, they believe it; for those p situations are precisely the ones where they already believe it and I get one (there is no other reason I would choose to do so) in order to make their belief come true. Yet, though it seems that conditions 3 and 4 are satisfied, the children do not know I will get them a puppy. (It would be a different situation where the children manipulate me into getting one, knowing I will make their expressed belief come true, and so expressing it and, indeed, therefore believing it.) We might reach the result that the children do not know they will get a puppy by holding that 3 is false. For there are very close situations where I don't learn of their belief, or decide not to get them the puppy; so they would believe they were going to get it even if they were not.

Consider another case, which David Armstrong discusses, of a sick person who believes he will recover and thereby does so.[39] Suppose that if it were true, he would believe it; for there is no way he could recover from this illness except via the effects of believing he will. Is it also the case that if it weren't true, he wouldn't believe it? Well, at least, if it weren't to be true, he wouldn't have been believing it. (But wouldn't he also believe in his recovery, even if his condition differed slightly so as to be unimprovable via this belief?)

These seem to be cases not of a belief's tracking the truth, but of the truth's tracking a belief. Yet we do not simply want to require that believing it does not make it true; consider "I believe something now." Perhaps a sharper theory of subjunctives, a better understanding of how they function, will show clearly that 3 and 4 are not satisfied in these cases. Or perhaps the difficulty lies in the fact that if it weren't believed it wouldn't be true, where a better understanding of subjunctives might enable us to add a condition denying this, namely not-(not-believing $p \to$ not-p), without undercutting the truth of the subjunctives 3 and 4. Or perhaps it will turn out, on any theory of subjunctives, that this is cutting things too finely. In that case, one might add a further condition about why conditions 3 and 4 hold, requiring it not be the case that 3 or 4 hold solely because: not-believing $p \to$ not-p, or believing $p \to p$. These are matters I must leave open here. There is some attraction, in any case, to including within our account of knowledge some further condition on why subjunctives 3 and 4 hold true: this also may aid with previous and further problem cases.[40]

One last remark. Suppose that though the person's belief that p is tracking the fact that p, yet the person believes it is *not*. We might doubt in this case that he knows. While it would be too strong to require the belief that 3 and that 4 in order for the person to know—don't children know?—perhaps it is appropriate to require that he not believe the negations of 3 and 4.[41]

We are now ready to turn to the subject of skepticism. Even readers who find difficulties with the account of knowledge, with the precise way the subjunctive conditions are formulated, should read on.* The points made in applying the account to issues about skepticism might well still hold, invariant under whatever changes are needed to meet the difficulties.

---

* In the second part of the next chapter, we return to this chapter's opening question: whether actions can be connected to something in the same way belief is connected to the truth when there is knowledge. If the parallel between beliefs and actions is an illuminating one, we should expect illumination to be cast in both directions. Therefore, we should be especially alert to see whether any additional considerations brought forth as we apply (analogues of) the notion of tracking and conditions 1–4 to actions do not apply also in the area of knowledge. Especially gratifying would be to discover features of knowledge we would not notice at all without pursuing the parallel to action.

II. SKEPTICISM

The skeptic about knowledge argues that we know very little or nothing of what we think we know, or at any rate that this position is no less reasonable than the belief in knowledge. The history of philosophy exhibits a number of different attempts to refute the skeptic: to prove him wrong or show that in arguing against knowledge he presupposes there is some and so refutes himself. Others attempt to show that accepting skepticism is unreasonable, since it is more likely that the skeptic's extreme conclusion is false than that all of his premisses are true, or simply because reasonableness of belief just means proceeding in an anti-skeptical way. Even when these counterarguments satisfy their inventors, they fail to satisfy others, as is shown by the persistent attempts against skepticism.[42] The continuing felt need to refute skepticism, and the difficulty in doing so, attests to the power of the skeptic's position, the depth of his worries.

An account of knowledge should illuminate skeptical arguments and show wherein lies their force. If the account leads us to reject these arguments, this had better not happen too easily or too glibly. To think the skeptic overlooks something obvious, to attribute to him a simple mistake or confusion or fallacy, is to refuse to acknowledge the power of his position and the grip it can have upon us. We thereby cheat ourselves of the opportunity to reap his insights and to gain self-knowledge in understanding why his arguments lure us so. Moreover, in fact, we cannot lay the specter of skepticism to rest without first hearing what it shall unfold.

Our goal is not, however, to refute skepticism, to prove it is wrong or even to argue that it is wrong. In the Introduction we distinguished between philosophy that attempts to prove, and philosophy that attempts to explain how something is possible. Our task here is to explain how knowledge is possible, given what the skeptic says that we do accept (for example, that it is logically possible that we are dreaming or are floating in the tank). In doing this, we need not convince the skeptic, and we may introduce explanatory hypotheses that he would reject. What is important for our task of explanation and understanding is that *we* find those hypotheses acceptable or plausible, and that they show us how the existence of knowledge fits together with the logical possibilities the skeptic points to, so that these are reconciled within our own belief system. These hypotheses are to explain to ourselves how knowledge is possible, not to prove to someone else that knowledge *is* possible.*

Skeptical Possibilities

The skeptic often refers to possibilities in which a person would believe something even though it was false: really, the person is cleverly deceived by others, perhaps by an evil demon, or the person is dreaming or he is floating in a tank near Alpha Centauri with his brain being stimulated. In each case, the p he believes is false, and he believes it even though it is false.

How do these possibilities adduced by the skeptic show that someone does not know that p? Suppose that someone is you; how do these possibilities count against your knowing that p? One way might be the following. (I shall consider other ways later.) If there is a possible situation where p is false yet you believe that p, then in that situation you believe that p even though it is false. So it appears you do not satisfy condition 3 for knowledge.

(3) If p were false, S wouldn't believe that p.

For a situation has been described in which you do believe that p even though p is false. How then can it also be true that if p were false, you wouldn't believe it? If the skeptic's possible situation shows that 3 is false, and if 3 is a necessary condition for knowledge, then the skeptic's possible situation shows that there isn't knowledge.

So construed, the skeptic's argument plays on condition 3; it aims to show that condition 3 is not satisfied. The skeptic may seem to be putting forth

R: Even if p were false, S still would believe p.[43]

---

* From the perspective of explanation rather than proof, the extensive philosophical discussion, deriving from Charles S. Peirce, of whether the skeptic's doubts are real is beside the point. The problem of explaining how knowledge is possible would remain the same, even if no one ever claimed to doubt that there was knowledge.

This conditional, with the same antecedent as 3 and the contradictory consequent, is incompatible with the truth of 3. If 3 is true, then R is not. However, R is stronger than the skeptic needs in order to show 3 is false. For 3 is false when if p were false, S might believe that p. This last conditional is weaker than R, and is merely 3's denial:

T: not-[not-$p \rightarrow$ not-(S believes that p)].

Whereas R does not simply deny 3, it asserts an opposing subjunctive of its own. Perhaps the possibility the skeptic adduces is not enough to show that R is true, but it appears at least to establish the weaker T; since this T denies 3, the skeptic's possibility appears to show that 3 is false.[44]

However, the truth of 3 is not incompatible with the existence of a possible situation where the person believes p though it is false. The subjunctive

(3) not-$p \rightarrow$ not-(S believes p)

does not talk of all possible situations in which p is false (in which not-p is true). It does not say that in all possible situations where not-p holds, S doesn't believe p. To say there is no possible situation in which not-p yet S believes p, would be to say that not-p entails not-(S believes p), or logically implies it. But subjunctive conditionals differ from entailments; the subjunctive 3 is not a statement of entailment. So the existence of a possible situation in which p is false yet S believes p does not show that 3 is false;[45] 3 can be true even though there is a possible situation where not-p and S believes that p.

What the subjunctive 3 speaks of is the situation that would hold if p were false. Not every possible situation in which p is false is the situation that would hold if p were false. To fall into possible worlds talk, the subjunctive 3 speaks of the not-p world that is closest to the actual world, or of those not-p worlds that are closest to the actual world, or more strongly (according to my suggestion) of the not-p neighborhood of the actual world. And it is of this or these not-p worlds that it says (in them) S does not believe that p. What happens in yet other more distant not-p worlds is no concern of the subjunctive 3.

The skeptic's possibilities (let us refer to them as SK), of the person's being deceived by a demon or dreaming or floating in a tank, count against the subjunctive

(3) if p were false then S wouldn't believe that p

only if (one of) these possibilities would or might obtain if p were false; only if one of these possibilities is in the not-p neighborhood of the actual world. Condition 3 says: if p were false, S still would not believe p. And this can hold even though there is some situation SK described by the skeptic in which p is false and S believes p. If p were false S still would not believe p, even though there is a situation SK in which p is false and S does believe p, provided that this situation SK wouldn't obtain if p were false. If the skeptic describes a situation SK which would not hold even if p were false then this situation SK doesn't show that 3 is false and so does not (in this way at least) undercut knowledge. Condition C acts to rule out skeptical hypotheses.

C: not-p → SK does not obtain.

Any skeptical situation SK which satisfies condition C is ruled out. For a skeptical situation SK to show that we don't know that p, it must fail to satisfy C which excludes it; instead it must be a situation that might obtain if p did not, and so satisfy C's denial:

not-(not-p → SK doesn't obtain).

Although the skeptic's imagined situations appear to show that 3 is false, they do not; they satisfy condition C and so are excluded.

The skeptic might go on to ask whether we know that his imagined situations SK are excluded by condition C, whether we know that if p were false SK would not obtain. However, typically he asks something stronger: do we know that his imagined situation SK does not actually obtain? Do we know that we are not being deceived by a demon, dreaming, or floating in a tank? And if we do not know this, how can we know that p? Thus we are led to the second way his imagined situations might show that we do not know that p.

Skeptical Results

According to our account of knowledge, S knows that the skeptic's situation SK doesn't hold if and only if

(1) SK doesn't hold
(2) S believes that SK doesn't hold
(3) If SK were to hold, S would not believe that SK doesn't hold
(4) If SK were not to hold, S would believe it does not.

Let us focus on the third of these conditions. The skeptic has carefully chosen his situations SK so that if they held we (still) would believe they did not. We would believe we weren't dreaming, weren't being deceived, and so on, even if we were. He has chosen situations SK such that if SK were to hold, S would (still) believe that SK doesn't hold—and this is incompatible with the truth of 3.[46]

Since condition 3 is a necessary condition for knowledge, it follows that we do not know that SK doesn't hold. If it were true that an evil demon was deceiving us, if we were having a particular dream, if we were floating in a tank with our brains stimulated in a specified way, we would still believe we were not. So, we do not know we're not being deceived by an evil demon, we do not know we're not in that tank, and we do not know we're not having that dream. So says the skeptic, and so says our account. And also so we say—don't we? For how could we know we are not being deceived that way, dreaming that dream? If those things *were* happening to us, everything would seem the same to us. There is no way we can know it is not happening for there is no way we could tell if it were happening; and if it were happening we would believe exactly what we do now—in particular, we still would believe that it was not. For this reason, we feel, and correctly, that we don't know—how could we?—that it is not happening to us. It is a virtue of our account that it yields, and explains, this result.

The skeptic asserts we do not know his possibilities don't obtain, and he is right. Attempts to avoid skepticism by claiming we do know these things are bound to fail. The skeptic's possibilities make us uneasy because, as we deeply realize, we do not know they don't obtain; it is not surprising that attempts to show we do know these things leave us suspicious, strike us even as bad faith.* Nor has the

* Descartes presumably would refute the tank hypothesis as he did the demon hypothesis, through a proof of the existence of a good God who would not allow anyone, demon or psychologist, permanently to deceive us. The philosophical literature has concentrated on the question of whether Descartes can prove this (without begging the question against the demon hypothesis). The literature has not discussed whether even a successful proof of the existence of a good God can help Descartes to conclude he is not almost

skeptic merely pointed out something obvious and trivial. It comes as a surprise to realize that we do not know his possibilities don't obtain. It is startling, shocking. For we would have thought, before the skeptic got us to focus on it, that we did know those things, that we did know we were not being deceived by a demon, or dreaming that dream, or stimulated that way in that tank. The skeptic has pointed out that we do not know things we would have confidently said we knew. And if we don't know these things, what can we know? So much for the supposed obviousness of what the skeptic tells us.

Let us say that a situation (or world) is doxically identical for S to the actual situation when if S were in that situation, he would have exactly the beliefs (*doxa*) he actually does have. More generally, two situations are doxically identical for S if and only if he would have exactly the same beliefs in them. It might be merely a curiosity to be told there are nonactual situations doxically identical to the actual

---

always mistaken. Might not a good God have his own reasons for deceiving us; might he not deceive us temporarily—a period which includes all of our life thus far (but not an afterlife)? To the question of why God did not create us so that we never would make any errors, Descartes answers that the motives of God are inscrutable to us. Do we know that such an inscrutable God could not be motivated to allow another powerful "demon" to deceive and dominate us?

Alternatively, could not such a good God be motivated to deceive itself temporarily, even if not another? (Compare the various Indian doctrines designed to explain our ignorance of our own true nature, that is, Atman–Brahman's or, on another theory, the purusha's nature.) Whether from playfulness or whatever motive, such a good God would temporarily deceive itself, perhaps even into thinking it is a human being living in a material realm. Can we know, via Descartes' argument, that this is not our situation? And so forth.

These possibilities, and others similar, are so obvious that some other explanation, I mean the single-minded desire to refute skepticism, must be given for why they are not noticed and discussed.

Similarly, one could rescrutinize the *cogito* argument. Can "I think" only be produced by something that exists? Suppose Shakespeare had written for Hamlet the line, "I think, therefore I am", or a fiction is written in which a character named Descartes says this, or suppose a character in a dream of mine says this; does it follow that they exist? Can someone use the cogito argument to prove he himself is not a fictional or dream character? Descartes asked how he could know he wasn't dreaming; he also should have asked how he could know he wasn't dreamed. See further my fable "Fiction", *Ploughshares*, Vol. 6, no. 3, Oct. 1980.

one. The skeptic, however, describes worlds doxically identical to the actual world in which almost everything believed is false.*

Such worlds are possible because we know mediately, not directly. This leaves room for a divergence between our beliefs and the truth. It is as though we possessed only two-dimensional plane projections of three-dimensional objects. Different three-dimensional objects, oriented appropriately, have the same two-dimensional plane projection. Similarly, different situations or worlds will lead to our having the very same beliefs. What is surprising is how very different the doxically identical world can be—different enough for almost everything believed in it to be false. Whether or not the mere fact that knowledge is mediated always makes room for such a very different doxically identical world, it does so in our case, as the skeptic's possibilities show. To be shown this is nontrivial, especially when we recall that we do not know the skeptic's possibility doesn't obtain: we do not know that we are not living in a doxically identical world wherein almost everything we believe is false.[47]

What more could the skeptic ask for or hope to show? Even readers who sympathized with my desire not to dismiss the skeptic too quickly may feel this has gone too far, that we have not merely acknowledged the force of the skeptic's position but have succumbed to it.

The skeptic maintains that we know almost none of what we think we know. He has shown, much to our initial surprise, that we do not know his (nontrivial) possibility SK doesn't obtain. Thus, he has shown of one thing we thought we knew, that we didn't and don't. To the conclusion that we know almost nothing, it appears but a short step. For if we do not know we are not dreaming or being deceived by a demon or floating in a tank, then how can I know, for example, that I am sitting before a page writing with a pen, and how can you know that you are reading a page of a book?

However, although our account of knowledge agrees with the skeptic in saying that we do not know that not-SK, it places no formi-

---

* I say almost everything, because there still could be some true beliefs such as "I exist." More limited skeptical possibilities present worlds doxically identical to the actual world in which almost every belief of a certain sort is false, for example, about the past, or about other people's mental states. See the discussion below in the section on narrower skepticisms.

dable barriers before my knowing that I am writing on a page with a pen. It is true that I am, I believe I am, if I weren't I wouldn't believe I was, and if I were, I would believe it. (I leave out the reference to method.) Also, it is true that you are reading a page (please, don't stop now!), you believe you are, if you weren't reading a page you wouldn't believe you were, and if you were reading a page you would believe you were. So according to the account, I do know that I am writing on a page with a pen, and you do know that you are reading a page. The account does not lead to any general skepticism.

Yet we must grant that it appears that if the skeptic is right that we don't know we are not dreaming or being deceived or floating in the tank, then it cannot be that I know I am writing with a pen or that you know you are reading a page. So we must scrutinize with special care the skeptic's "short step" to the conclusion that we don't know these things, for either this step cannot be taken or our account of knowledge is incoherent.

Nonclosure

In taking the "short step", the skeptic assumes that if S knows that p and he knows that 'p entails q' then he also knows that q. In the terminology of the logicians, the skeptic assumes that knowledge is closed under known logical implication; that the operation of moving from something known to something else known to be entailed by it does not take us outside of the (closed) area of knowledge. He intends, of course, to work things backwards, arguing that since the person does not know that q, assuming (at least for the purposes of argument) that he does know that p entails q, it follows that he does not know that p. For if he did know that p, he would also know that q, which he doesn't.

The details of different skeptical arguments vary in their structure, but each one will assume some variant of the principle that knowledge is closed under known logical implication. If we abbreviate "knowledge that p" by "Kp" and abbreviate "entails" by the fish-hook sign "$\dashv$", we can write this principle of closure as the subjunctive principle

P: $K(p \dashv q)$ & $Kp \rightarrow Kq$.

If a person were to know that *p* entails *q* and he were to know that *p* then he would know that *q*. The statement that *q* follows by modus ponens from the other two stated as known in the antecedent of the subjunctive principle P; this principle counts on the person to draw the inference to *q*.

You know that your being in a tank on Alpha Centauri entails your not being in place X where you are. (I assume here a limited readership.) And you know also the contrapositive, that your being at place X entails that you are not then in a tank on Alpha Centauri. If you knew you were at X you would know you're not in a tank (of a specified sort) at Alpha Centauri. But you do not know this last fact (the skeptic has argued and we have agreed) and so (he argues) you don't know the first. Another intuitive way of putting the skeptic's argument is as follows. If you know that two statements are incompatible and you know the first is true then you know the denial of the second. You know that your being at X and your being in a tank on Alpha Centauri are incompatible; so if you knew you were at X you would know you were not in the (specified) tank on Alpha Centauri. Since you do not know the second, you don't know the first.[48]

No doubt, it is possible to argue over the details of principle P, to point out it is incorrect as it stands. Perhaps, though Kp, the person does not know that he knows that *p* (that is, not-KKp) and so does not draw the inference to *q*. Or perhaps he doesn't draw the inference because not-KK(p -3 q). Other similar principles face their own difficulties: for example, the principle that $K(p \rightarrow q) \rightarrow (Kp \rightarrow Kq)$ fails if Kp stops $p \rightarrow q$ from being true, that is, if $Kp \rightarrow$ not-$(p \rightarrow q)$; the principle that $K(p \text{ -3 } q) \rightarrow K(Kp \rightarrow Kq)$ faces difficulties if Kp makes the person forget that (p -3 q) and so he fails to draw the inference to *q*. We seem forced to pile K upon K until we reach something like $KK(p \text{ -3 } q) \text{ \& } KKp \rightarrow Kq$; this involves strengthening considerably the antecedent of P and so is not useful for the skeptic's argument that *p* is not known. (From a principle altered thus, it would follow at best that it is not known that *p* is known.)

We would be ill-advised, however, to quibble over the details of P. Although these details are difficult to get straight, it will continue to appear that something like P is correct. If S knows that '*p* entails *q*' and he knows that *p* and knows that '(*p* and *p* entails *q*) entails *q*' (shades of the Lewis Carroll puzzle we discuss below!) and he does draw the inference to *q* from all this and believes *q* via the process of drawing this inference, then will he not know that q? And what is wrong with simplifying this mass of detail by writing merely principle P, provided we apply it only to cases where the mass of detail holds, as it surely does in the skeptical cases under consideration? For example, I do realize that my being in the Van Leer Foundation Building in Jerusalem entails that I am not in a tank on Alpha Centauri; I am capable of drawing inferences now; I do believe I am not in a tank on Alpha Centauri (though not solely via this inference, surely); and so forth. Won't this satisfy the correctly detailed principle, and shouldn't it follow that I know I am not (in that tank) on Alpha Centauri? The skeptic agrees it should follow; so he concludes from the fact that I don't know I am not floating in the tank on Alpha Centauri that I don't know I am in Jerusalem. Uncovering difficulties in the details of particular formulations of P will not weaken the principle's intuitive appeal; such quibbling will seem at best like a wasp attacking a steamroller, at worst like an effort in bad faith to avoid being pulled along by the skeptic's argument.

Principle P is wrong, however, and not merely in detail. Knowledge is not closed under known logical implication.[49] S knows that p when S has a true belief that p, and S wouldn't have a false belief that p (condition 3) and S would have a true belief that p (condition 4). Neither of these latter two conditions is closed under known logical implication.

Let us begin with condition

(3) if p were false, S wouldn't believe that p.

When S knows that p, his belief that p is contingent on the truth of p, contingent in the way the subjunctive condition 3 describes. Now it might be that p entails q (and S knows this), that S's belief that p is subjunctively contingent on the truth of p, that S believes q, yet his belief that q is not subjunctively dependent on the truth of q, in that it (or he) does not satisfy:

(3') if q were false, S wouldn't believe that q.

For 3' talks of what S would believe if q were false, and this may be a very different situation than the one that would hold if p were false, even though p entails q. That you were born in a certain city entails that you were born on earth.* Yet contemplating what (ac-

* Here again I assume a limited readership, and ignore possibilities such as those described in James Blish, *Cities in Flight*.

tually) would be the situation if you were not born in that city is very different from contemplating what situation would hold if you weren't born on earth. Just as those possibilities are very different, so what is believed in them may be very different. When p entails q (and not the other way around) p will be a stronger statement than q, and so not-q (which is the antecedent of 3') will be a stronger statement than not-p (which is the antecedent of 3). There is no reason to assume you will have the same beliefs in these two cases, under these suppositions of differing strengths.

There is no reason to assume the (closest) not-p world and the (closest) not-q world are doxically identical for you, and no reason to assume, even though p entails q, that your beliefs in one of these worlds would be a (proper) subset of your beliefs in the other.

Consider now the two statements:

p = I am awake and sitting on a chair in Jerusalem;
q = I am not floating in a tank on Alpha Centauri being stimulated by electrochemical means to believe that p.

The first one entails the second: p entails q. Also, I know that p entails q; and I know that p. If p were false, I would be standing or lying down in the same city, or perhaps sleeping there, or perhaps in a neighboring city or town. If q were false, I would be floating in a tank on Alpha Centauri. Clearly these are very different situations, leading to great differences in what I then would believe. If p were false, if I weren't awake and sitting on a chair in Jerusalem, I would not believe that p. Yet if q were false, if I was floating in a tank on Alpha Centauri, I would believe that q, that I was not in the tank, and indeed, in that case, I would still believe that p. According to our account of knowledge, I know that p yet I do not know that q, even though (I know) p entails q.

This failure of knowledge to be closed under known logical implication stems from the fact that condition 3 is not closed under known logical implication; condition 3 can hold of one statement believed while not of another known to be entailed by the first.[50] It is clear that any account that includes as a necessary condition for knowledge the subjunctive condition 3, not-$p \rightarrow$ not-(S believes that p), will have the consequence that knowledge is not closed under known logical implication.[51]

When p entails q and you believe each of them, if you do not have a false belief that p (since p is true) then you do not have a false belief that q. However, if you are to know something not only don't you have a false belief about it, but also you wouldn't have a false belief about it. Yet, we have seen how it may be that p entails q and you believe each and you wouldn't have a false belief that p yet you might have a false belief that q (that is, it is not the case that you wouldn't have one). Knowledge is not closed under the known logical implication because "wouldn't have a false belief that" is not closed under known logical implication.

If knowledge were the same as (simply) true belief then it would be closed under known logical implication (provided the implied statements were believed). Knowledge is not simply true belief, however; additional conditions are needed. These further conditions will make knowledge open under known logical implication, even when the entailed statement is believed, when at least one of the further conditions itself is open. Knowledge stays closed (only) if all of the additional conditions are closed. I lack a general nontrivial characterization of those conditions that are closed under known logical implication; possessing such an illuminating characterization, one might attempt to prove that no additional conditions of that sort could provide an adequate analysis of knowledge.

Still, we can say the following. A belief that p is knowledge that p only if it somehow varies with the truth of p. The causal condition for knowledge specified that the belief was "produced by" the fact, but that condition did not provide the right sort of varying with the fact. The subjunctive conditions 3 and 4 are our attempt to specify that varying. But however an account spells this out, it will hold that whether a belief that p is knowledge partly depends on what goes on with the belief in some situations when p is false. An account that says nothing about what is believed in any situation when p is false cannot give us any mode of varying with the fact.

Because what is preserved under logical implication is truth, any condition that is preserved under known logical implication is most likely to speak only of what happens when p, and q, are true, without speaking at all of what happens when either one is false. Such a condition is incapable of providing "varies with"; so adding only such conditions to true belief cannot yield an adequate account of knowledge.[52]

A belief's somehow varying with the truth of what is believed is not closed under known logical implication. Since knowledge that p

involves such variation, knowledge also is not closed under known logical implication. The skeptic cannot easily deny that knowledge involves such variation, for his argument that we don't know that we're not floating in that tank, for example, uses the fact that knowledge does involve variation. ("If you were floating in the tank you would still think you weren't, so you don't know that you're not.") Yet, though one part of his argument uses that fact that knowledge involves such variation, another part of his argument presupposes that knowledge does not involve any such variation. This latter is the part that depends upon knowledge being closed under known logical implication, as when the skeptic argues that since you don't know that not-SK, you don't know you are not floating in the tank, then you also don't know, for example, that you are now reading a book. That closure can hold only if the variation does not. The skeptic cannot be right both times. According to our view he is right when he holds that knowledge involves such variation and so concludes that we don't know, for example, that we are not floating in that tank; but he is wrong when he assumes knowledge is closed under known logical implication and concludes that we know hardly anything.[53]

Knowledge is a real factual relation, subjunctively specifiable, whose structure admits our standing in this relation, tracking, to p without standing in it to some q which we know p to entail. Any relation embodying some variation of belief with the fact, with the truth (value), will exhibit this structural feature. The skeptic is right that we don't track some particular truths—the ones stating that his skeptical possibilities SK don't hold—but wrong that we don't stand in the real knowledge-relation of tracking to many other truths, including ones that entail these first mentioned truths we believe but don't know.

The literature on skepticism contains writers who endorse these skeptical arguments (or similar narrower ones), but confess their inability to maintain their skeptical beliefs at times when they are not focusing explicitly on the reasoning that led them to skeptical conclusions. The most notable example of this is Hume:

> I am ready to reject all belief and reasoning, and can look upon no opinion even as more probable or likely than another . . . Most fortunately it happens that since reason is incapable of dispelling these clouds, nature herself suffices to that

purpose, and cures me of this philosophical melancholy and delirium, either by relaxing this bent of mind, or by some avocation, and lively impression of my senses, which obliterate all these chimeras. I dine, I play a game of backgammon, I converse, and am merry with my friends; and when after three or four hours' amusement, I would return to these speculations, they appear so cold, and strained, and ridiculous, that I cannot find in my heart to enter into them any farther. (*A Treatise of Human Nature,* Book I, Part IV, section VII)

The great subverter of Pyrrhonism or the excessive principles of skepticism is action, and employment, and the occupations of common life. These principles may flourish and triumph in the schools; where it is, indeed, difficult, if not impossible, to refute them. But as soon as they leave the shade, and by the presence of the real objects, which actuate our passions and sentiments, are put in opposition to the more powerful principles of our nature, they vanish like smoke, and leave the most determined skeptic in the same condition as other mortals . . . And though a Pyrrhonian may throw himself or others into a momentary amazement and confusion by his profound reasonings; the first and most trivial event in life will put to flight all his doubts and scruples, and leave him the same, in every point of action and speculation, with the philosophers of every other sect, or with those who never concerned themselves in any philosophical researches. When he awakes from his dream, he will be the first to join in the laugh against himself, and to confess that all his objections are mere amusement. (*An Enquiry Concerning Human Understanding,* Section XII, Part II)

The theory of knowledge we have presented explains why skeptics of various sorts have had such difficulties in sticking to their far-reaching skeptical conclusions "outside the study", or even inside it when they are not thinking specifically about skeptical arguments and possibilities SK.

The skeptic's arguments do show (but show only) that we don't know the skeptic's possibilities SK do not hold; and he is right that we don't track the fact that SK does not hold. (If it were to hold, we would still think it didn't.) However, the skeptic's arguments don't show we do not know other facts (including facts that entail not-SK) for we do track these other facts (and knowledge is not closed under known logical entailment.) Since we do track these other facts—you, for example, the fact that you are reading a book; I, the fact that I am writing on a page—and the skeptic tracks such facts too, it is not surprising that when he focuses on them, on his relationship to such facts, the skeptic finds it hard to remember or maintain his view that he does not know those facts. Only by shifting his attention back to his relationship to the (different) fact that not-SK, which relationship is not tracking, can he revive his skeptical belief and make it salient. However, this skeptical triumph is evanescent, it vanishes when his attention turns to other facts. Only by fixating on the skeptical possibilities SK can he maintain his skeptical virtue; otherwise, unsurprisingly, he is forced to confess to sins of credulity.

Skepticism and the Conditions for Knowledge

We have considered how the skeptic's argument from the skeptical possibilities SK plays off condition 3: if p weren't true S wouldn't believe that p. His argument gains its power by utilizing this condition ("but even if SK held, you still would believe it didn't, so you do not know it doesn't"); the deep intuitive force of the argument indicates that condition 3 (or something very much like it) is a necessary condition for knowledge. Similarly, are there any skeptical arguments or moves that play off condition 4: if p were true then S would believe that p (and wouldn't believe that not-p)? If condition 3 specifies how belief somehow should vary with the truth of what is believed, condition 4 specifies how belief shouldn't vary when the truth of what is believed does not vary. Condition 3 is a variation condition, condition 4 is an adherence condition. Both conditions together capture the notion that S (who actually truly believes p) would have a true belief that p. He wouldn't have a false belief that p if p weren't true (condition 3), and he would have a true belief that p if p were true (condition 4). Just as the skeptic argued earlier that the belief wouldn't vary when it should, he also can argue that it would vary when it shouldn't, concluding both times that we don't have knowledge.

We would expect skeptical arguments playing off condition 4 to be less powerful and compelling than ones playing off 3. Condition 3 requires that we wouldn't falsely believe p, and we can be led to worry not only whether we might but whether we do. While condition 4 requires that we would truly believe p (and wouldn't falsely believe not-p), and though we might worry whether we might violate this, we need have no fear that we are—for we know we are believing p and are not believing not-p. Skeptical arguments playing off condition 4, unlike those with 3, cannot make us wonder also whether we violate the condition's indicative version.

Condition 4 is an adherence condition, so the relevant doubts concern how securely you are tied to the truth. For many (most?) of the things p you believe, if a group of people came and deceitfully told you not-p, you would believe them and stop believing p. (Relevant experiments frequently have been done by social psychologists.) So do you really know p? If physicists told you that Newton's theory turns out to have been correct after all, wouldn't (or mightn't) you believe them? So do you really know Newtonian theory is false?

But, as before, the mere possibility of its being true while you do not believe it is not sufficient to show you don't actually know it. That possibility must be one that might arise. Call this possibility of p's being true while you don't believe it: sk. (Lowercase "sk" is p's being true and your not believing it, while capital SK is p's being false and your believing p.) Possibility sk need not concern us when: if p were true, sk wouldn't hold; $p \rightarrow$ not-sk; sk is false throughout the first part of the p neighborhood of the actual world. It is fortunate for my knowing that p that there wouldn't be people who trick me, just as it is fortunate for my knowing I am in Emerson Hall that whatever would occur if I weren't there does not include people tricking or hypnotizing me into believing I am there.

Suppose I present a certain argument to someone who believes (truly) that p, and he is convinced by it and comes to believe not-p. Look how easily he can be moved from believing p to believing not-p. Suppose it happens that I do not present the argument to him, so he does not start to believe not-p, and he continues to believe p. Does he know that p? Is it merely the case that his knowledge is insecure, or does such instability show it is not knowledge after all?

A skeptic might argue that for almost each p we (think we) know, there is an argument or happening that would get us to believe not-p even though p was true. We reply to this skeptic as before—the fact that some possible argument or happening would get us to believe

212

not-p when p doesn't show that it is false that 4: if p were true then S would believe p and S wouldn't believe not-p. To show the falsity of 4, the skeptic would have to refer to something that might occur if p were true; if it wouldn't hold if p were true, what he refers to is irrelevant.

Among the arguments that get people to stop believing things are the skeptic's arguments themselves. These arguments often puzzle people, sometimes they get people to stop believing they know that p. They do not know that they know. Should we describe this as a case of people who first know that they know but who, after hearing the skeptic's arguments, no longer know that they know because they no longer believe that they know (and knowledge entails belief)? Our present view is that such people did not know that they knew that p, even before hearing the skeptic. For their previous belief that they knew that p would vary when it shouldn't, so it violates condition 4. Similarly, some people who never have heard the skeptic's arguments would (if they heard them) become convinced that they don't know that p. It is pleasant to grant the skeptic a partial victory after all, one gained by the plausibility of his arguments, not their cogency. Because of the skeptical arguments, some people would falsely believe they don't know that p, and these people do not know they know it. The existence of skeptical arguments makes one type of skeptical conclusion (that we don't know we know things) true of some people—those the shoe fits have been wearing it.

Meno claimed he could speak eloquently about virtue until Socrates, torpedolike, began to question him. He did not know what virtue was, for Socrates' questions uncovered Meno's previously existing confusions. Even if it had been a sophist's questions that bewildered Meno, getting him to believe the opposite, what he previously had would not have been knowledge. Knowledge should be made of sterner stuff.[54]

Thus, some skeptical arguments play off condition 3, others off condition 4. In addition to these conditions, our (full) account of knowledge formulates a condition about outweighing to cover the situation when multiple methods, not all satisfying 3 and 4, give rise to the belief. Do any skeptical arguments play off this outweighing condition? Here, presumably, would fit various attempts at unmasking the dominant sources of our belief as methods that do not track:

faith, prejudice, self-interest, class-interest, deep psychological motives. The outweighing view involves subjunctives, but does anything here correspond to the skeptic's focusing upon a possibility that is so far out that it wouldn't occur, even if p were false? Perhaps the following is comparable. Recall that it was not necessary for the tracking method to win out against the combined opposed weight of all other methods; the person's belief merely had to vary with the verdict of the tracking method when the recommendations of every other way used to arrive at belief were held fixed. (It was only Case III in the chart that needed to be examined.) Any actual split in the verdict of nontracking methods will be welcome support. The skeptic should not load the other methods against what tracking recommends, any more than they actually are; to suppose more counts as too far out.

Some skeptical arguments play off condition 3, some off condition 4, some (perhaps) off the outweighing condition when multiple methods are involved. Still other skeptical arguments play off the methods themselves, off the fact that knowledge is gained via methods or ways of believing. In the situations when we are aware of what methods we are using, do we know we are using those methods? To decide whether we know this, according to condition 3 we must consider what we would believe if we weren't using the methods. Would we then still believe we were? If so, condition 3 is violated, and so we did not actually know we were using the methods.

Along this pathway lies trouble. For if we weren't using that method, the very method we use to track various facts—a situation we have to contemplate in applying condition 3—who knows what we would believe about what methods we are using? That method M we are using to track various facts may be the very method via which we believe that we are using method M. This is likely if (and only if) M is described widely and deeply enough, for example, as the sum total of our (rational or effective) methods. But then, how are we to treat the question of what we would believe if we weren't using that method M, a question condition 3 pushes at us in order to decide if we know we are using M? "If I weren't using M, would I still believe I was?" What methods of believing am I left by this question? After all, condition 3 when fully formulated says: not-p and S, via M, comes to a belief about the truth of $p \rightarrow$ not-(S believes that p). And the method M of condition 3 is the very one said to be actually utilized, in condition 2: S believes, via M, that *p*.

Yet now we face the situation where S believes of himself that he is applying method M, via an application of method M itself;[55] moreover, in this situation the statement *p*, which we are trying to decide whether S knows, is: S is using method M. The result of substituting this *p* in the full condition 3 is: If S weren't using method M, and S, via using M, were to decide about the truth of 'S is using method M' then S would not believe 'S is using method M'. But the antecedent of this subjunctive is supposing both that S is not using method M (this supposition is the not-*p* of the antecedent of condition 3) and that S is using method M (he uses this method in 3 to decide whether or not *p*, since that is the method via which, in condition 2, he actually believes *p*). We have no coherent way to understand this.*

Yet if we cannot simply include the use of method M in determining what S would believe if he were not using M, neither can we simply suppose (for the purposes of condition 3) that S is using some other method to arrive at a belief about this matter. We saw earlier, in considering a range of examples, the great importance of holding the method fixed in deciding questions about knowledge. Recall the grandmother who sees her grandson visit her and so believes he is healthy and ambulatory; yet if he weren't ambulatory, other relatives would tell her he was fine to spare her anxiety and upset. She sees her grandson walking; does she know he is ambulatory? According to condition 3 we must ask what she would believe if he weren't ambulatory. If the method via which she believes is not held fixed, the answer will be wrong. True, if he weren't ambulatory, she would then believe he was (via hearing about him from other relatives). But the relevant question is: what would she believe if he weren't ambulatory and (as before) she saw him and spoke to him. Thus, to reach the correct answer about her knowledge, the method must be held fixed—that is one of the reasons why we introduced explicit reference to the method or way of believing.

How then are we to treat the question of whether the person

---

* Similar questions arise about our knowledge of other statements such that if they were false, we would not be using the methods via which we know they are true, for example, "there are eyes", "I am alive", "I am sentient", perhaps "I sometimes am tracking something".

knows he is using method M, when he believes he is via that very method M? If he knows he is, then his belief that he is tracks the fact that he is, and varies with that fact. To determine whether it so varies, we must look to the question of what he would believe if p were false, that is, if he weren't using method M. How are we to understand this question? It seems we must hold fixed the method M via which he believes, in order to reach the correct answer about knowledge (as is shown by the case of the grandmother), and that we cannot hold the method M fixed, for then we have the (apparently) incoherent supposition that he is applying the method to the situation where he is not using it, in order to determine whether or not he is—and this supposes that he both is and isn't using the method.

This problem does not arise when we know via another method that we are using some particular method; it arises only for our knowledge of our use of our deepest methods, though not for shallower specifications of these methods in specific instances. Still, what should we say about our knowledge of these deepest methods or of the conditions in which we apply them. Do you know you are rational, do you know you are sane? If you were irrational or insane, mightn't you think you were rational and sane? Yes, but not by applying methods under (fixed) conditions of rationality and sanity. We cannot conclude simply that condition 3 is not satisfied so you don't know you are rational or sane; for that condition is not satisfied only when the method is allowed to vary. It would be best to be able coherently to discover whether or not that method is being used. I can use M to discover whether you are using M (if you weren't, I wouldn't believe, via M, that you were), or whether I was using M in the past (if I hadn't been, I wouldn't now believe, via M, that I had been). The difficulty is to make sense of saying that M, if currently used, would detect that it was not being used (if it weren't). And while I do not think this simply is incoherent, neither is it pellucidly clear.*

Questions about knowing one is rational or sane need not depend on varying the method used. If what we have to go on as we apply methods is the appearance of rationality and sanity, then mightn't we

---

* Should we say for these cases discussed in the text that condition 3 does not apply, so that, as in the previous case of necessary truths, the whole weight of tracking devolves upon condition 4? The issue then simply turns on whether in similar situations where the person uses method M, he also would believe he does.

appear sane and rational to ourselves even if we are not? So how do we know we are? We do have more to go on than how we appear to ourselves; there also is the agreement with others. Let us leave aside the possibility that all those others also might be insane and irrational, or be engaged in a plot to convince me (falsely) that I was rational and sane. Neither of these is what (actually) would or might occur if I weren't rational or sane. Might an insane and irrational person also be mistaken about whether others are agreeing with him, though, interpreting their disagreement as concord? If a person were insane or irrational in this way then others would appear (to him) to agree with him, and so he would appear sane and rational to himself. Things would appear qualitatively indistinguishable to him from the situation where he rationally and sanely judges the world. There appears to be no shift in method here, at least insofar as how using the method is experienced internally by the user. Do you know, then, that you are not in that particular skeptical situation SK? Perhaps not, but (as before) from our not knowing that particular not-SK it does not follow that we don't know other things, including that we are being sane and rational in particular situations in particular ways. For if we weren't, we wouldn't believe we were; if we weren't then sane and rational in those particular ways, what would or might obtain is not this skeptic's possibility SK. These points emerge even more clearly if we consider positions skeptical not about (almost) all knowledge in general, but about particular kinds of knowledge.

Narrower Skepticisms

The skeptical arguments we have examined thus far apply to knowledge in general. Other skeptical arguments focus upon particular kinds of knowledge, upon a particular type of statement or one arrived at in a particular way. Thus, in addition to general skepticism there are narrower philosophical skepticisms: about other minds, about a world existing unperceived, about induction, and so on.

Our account of knowledge says of these more particular skepticisms what it said of general skepticism: though the sweeping (skeptical) conclusion is too broad, the skeptic is not to be dismissed. He is correct in saying there are some things we do not know, even though unreflectively we might have thought we did; but while it might appear that much knowledge depends on having this first knowledge (which we don't have), this appearance is misleading.

Let us begin with the problem of other minds.[56] How can we know another person is in pain, or thrilled, or overcome with emotion, or thinking about philosophy? All we have to go on is her external behavior and speech, yet such behavior does not entail the existence of the felt psychological state. It is logically possible that accompanying the behavior we have observed is a very different felt state, or even no feeling at all. So how can we know what anyone else feels, or that they feel or experience anything? Can you know you are not surrounded by unfeeling bodies in motion?

Suppose a terrorist bomb explodes nearby and I am singed by the heat. I rush forward to help and find someone on the ground, bleeding, writhing, and screaming. Others are moaning. I know the person is in pain. The situation is the sort that can cause extreme pain, and I see a victim writhing and screaming (in pain). I believe it because of what I see and other things I know, for example, that I am not in Los Angeles on a movie set. The person is in pain, and my belief that the person is tracks the fact that he is. If the person were not in pain he wouldn't be behaving like that, and so I wouldn't believe he was in pain; moreover, if he were in pain I would (in this situation, via this way) believe he was. My belief that my children are happy, as they play with the animal, tracks the fact that they are; my belief that my friend is depressed tracks the fact that he is—I know my children are happy, I know my friend is depressed. The conditions for knowledge are satisfied in these cases, so our account yields the result that I do know what these people are feeling then, and so do have this knowledge of other minds. Nothing said by the skeptic shows that I am not in fact tracking (the state of) other minds in these cases; no general skepticism about (all) knowledge of other minds is justified or true.

But could it not be that the person on the ground is an actor in a film, my friend is out to trick me, my children are pretending to enjoy playing with the animal, or even that all of them, and all others as well, are extraterrestrials without human feelings or are cleverly constructed robots without any feelings at all—humanoid automata? Do I know this is not the case?

Let p be the specific statement about another's experience, and let SK be some skeptical scenario wherein although my belief that p is based exactly as it actually is apart from the scenario (for example, upon the behavior of others and the way the setting appears), p is false nonetheless. Do I know that SK does not hold, do I know that not everyone else on earth is a feelingless robot cleverly constructed by beings from another galaxy in whose psychological experiment I am a participant? (You know this is not true of yourself but do you know it is not true of others, including me?) How could I know that SK doesn't hold? If it held, things would seem exactly the same to me as they do now. (If things wouldn't seem exactly the same, it is not the right possibility SK.) So I don't know that not-SK; condition 3 for knowledge of not-SK is not satisfied. If SK were true I (still) would believe not-SK. My belief that not-SK does not track the fact that not-SK, so I don't actually know that not-SK. Since SK is incompatible with p, and I realize this, how can it be that (not knowing not-SK, still) I know that p? My belief that p does track the fact that p, and knowledge is not closed under known logical implication.

The situation exactly parallels our earlier discussion of knowledge and a general skepticism based (for example) upon the logical possibility of being immersed in the tank near Alpha Centauri. The skeptic is correct in saying we don't know particular skeptical possibilities SK do not hold, but he is wrong in concluding from this that we don't know anything of a particular sort, about other minds, for instance. The skeptic's alternative SK is not what actually would or might obtain if p did not; so, we can track and therefore know p without tracking or knowing not-SK. The dream hypothesis is similar. I can know I am not now dreaming if: if I were dreaming I wouldn't be dreaming this. Yet I don't know I'm not dreaming *this*, for if I were things would seem exactly the same. Still, though not knowing this I now do know I am sitting before paper and writing, and so on.

Do I really mean to say I don't know my children are not feelingless automata? (How will they feel when they read this?) I know their feelings when they are happy, sad, proud, embarrassed, frightened. I track these feelings and sometimes cause them. Furthermore, I know I don't have children who are feelingless robots. The (closest) world in which I (would) have children like that is a world in which, for example, I volunteered to adopt a robot or to participate in a genetic-engineering experiment that risked that eventuality, and I know that nothing of this sort is the case. But do I know that the skeptic's alternative SK doesn't hold, in which, among other things, I have automata children; of this SK whose obtaining would not reflect itself back into the evidence available to me, do I know it does not hold? Of course not. How could I? Do I believe it doesn't hold? Of course. (Don't worry, children.) Would I stake my life on its not holding? I have.

Consider Wittgenstein's view (in the *Philosophical Investigations*) of how stage setting and context are crucial to the application of a mental term, to the situation's fitting the term. (So he often points out what else will have to be true for something to be a case of, for example, understanding or reading or—the most difficult case for his view—pain.) The behavioral evidence does not entail the occurrence of the particular mental state, for there could be a wider context including this behavioral 'evidence' that shows the person wasn't in that specific mental state. Similarly, feelings of understanding will not constitute *understanding* unless they are embedded in an appropriate wider context. In both cases, each appropriate wider context could be undercut by a still wider context (which itself could be undercut by a yet wider one); that is why there's no entailment, why Wittgensteinian criteria are not logically sufficient conditions.[57] Wittgenstein's view structures mental predicates in the global closest relation mode, to invoke a category from Chapter I above; these terms involve a negative existential quantifier excluding a certain wider context. This seems not only to leave room for but to invite skepticism. For to know on some basis that a mental term applies to someone, won't I have to know also that there is no wider context (which includes that basis), itself not undercut, that undercuts the application of the mental term in question? And how can I know this? Is it not always possible that there is such a wider context, undetectable from where we stand and look?

Our comment follows a now familiar path. In applying a mental term to someone, I don't know that such a wider context does not obtain (for I don't track the fact that it does not). Yet I do know (for I track the fact that) the mental term applies in a particular case; if it didn't apply, I wouldn't believe it did. For if it weren't to apply, that would not actually be (because of) the undetectable wider undercutting context.

Wittgenstein's points about context and stage-setting apply not only to our application of mental terms to others, but (as he emphasizes) to ourselves as well. This might give rise, for each of us, to a problem of our own minds, parallel to the problem of other minds. Do I know a particular mental term currently applies to me, do I know the wider context will not undercut it, or that the earlier unre-membered context hasn't already done so? And so on.

We can imagine even a problem of "my own mind" similar to the traditional "other minds" problem discussed earlier, which did not focus on issues of context. Do I know on a particular occasion that I am in pain? Yes. My belief that I am tracks the fact that I am. Indeed, the relation between my belief and the fact seems stronger than tracking. The two vary together across (almost?) all possible worlds, not merely the closest ones. So it is not surprising that theorists searching for a foundation for knowledge found such psychological statements especially appropriate. Freud claimed that not all occurrent psychological facts are tracked by belief, so only some would remain for foundationalist purposes. But even of this subclass one might imagine skeptical possibilities. Perhaps I am so wired up that I say and think there is a felt phenomenological quality, although there really isn't any such thing but merely a connection of physical states to my speech and thoughts and reports of "introspection".[58]

If some clever skeptical alternative SK can be specified to drop out the felt quality yet leave everything else as it is, then I will not know that not-SK. Skepticism about minds begins at home. Still, I will know that I feel pain, and that it phenomenologically feels that way. If it didn't, I wouldn't think it did; the skeptic's alternative SK (in which nothing feels that way yet I do think and say that something does) is not what would or might occur if p were false, if I weren't feeling a pain of a certain phenomenological sort.

We can proceed more quickly with the next example of a skepticism narrower than total skepticism, for our points are the same as before. (This saves time and intellectual effort, yet leads to a certain mechanical quality in the writing and—no doubt—in the reading. I apologize.) Do I know that my desk continues to exist when I am not perceiving it? Yes, you see it then and tell me it does. Do I know it continues to exist during a time when no one is perceiving it? Yes, for examination shows the rebound rate of the carpet tuft underneath the desk to be the same as the rebound speed of the carpet underneath a desk continuously observed for that length of time, and if the unperceived desk had not been there all the time, its (downtrodden) piece of carpet wouldn't have behaved like that; so I know it was there continuously. Do I know the carpet ever exists when it is not perceived or filmed? Yes, because I did see the table on it, and when I later examined the tuft, its rebound speed indicated that that part of the carpet had been under pressure for three hours, though it was observed for only one half hour. Do I know that anything ever exists when it is neither perceived nor known to be connected with other perceived things; rather (to leap to it) do I know that some skeptical possibility SK doesn't hold, under which some unperceived things undetectably are not there temporarily? Some such skeptical possibility SK can be specified, I suppose; if so, I do not know it doesn't hold. Consider next the statement that there is a chair behind me now at the other end of this room. I know that statement is true. If it weren't there now, that would be because it wasn't there before (but I saw it then) or because someone removed it since then (but I would have heard that). "But couldn't Martians have silently and invisibly entered to remove it, or couldn't the skeptic's possibility SK hold, with this being one of the moments the chair is not there?" Since these skeptical possibilities are not what would or might obtain if the chair weren't there now, they don't show I am not tracking the fact that it is. I can know that p even though I don't know these skeptical possibilities (each known to be incompatible with p) do not hold; knowledge is not closed under known logical implication.

Let us turn to the third of the particular skepticisms: skepticism about induction, about knowledge of the future or about any inference from sample to population or to facts outside the sample. We hold a belief p about the future on the basis of some current and past facts. Do we know that p? Only if our belief that p tracks the fact that p. Since our belief that p is based on current and past facts, we know that p only if these current and past facts track the fact that p. That is, only if: if p weren't true, this actually would have been reflected back so that some of the current and past facts wouldn't have held. Do we know that the sun will rise tomorrow, that the earth will continue to rotate on its axis during the next 24-hour period? If the sun were not going to rise tomorrow, would we have seen that coming, would that alteration in the earth's rotation have been presaged in the facts available to us today and before? If so, then we do know the sun will rise tomorrow; our belief that it will tracks the fact that it will, by being based on facts that would have been different otherwise.*

But isn't it logically possible that everything was as it was until now, yet the earth will not continue to rotate tomorrow? Yes, there are such skeptical logical possibilities SK: the bread no longer nourishes us, the sun stops in the sky, an event of a certain sort no longer continues to produce its usual effects. If they are elaborated suitably, so that everything we can detect up until now would have remained the same, then we don't know they do not hold. The skeptic about induction is right to say we don't know these possibilities do not hold, but he is wrong to deny we know those particular results of inductive inference whose falsity would have been reflected back and presaged in the facts upon which we based the inference.

These very general remarks are not restricted to particular modes of inductive inference. What matters for such inferential knowledge is that the evidence upon which we base our beliefs actually be subjunctively connected in a suitable way with the facts inferred. (We shall return to this point, and to induction, later when we discuss the theory of evidence.) Specific patterns of inductive inference are to be judged by their mesh with subjunctive relations. There is no reason in principle, though, why our knowledge must be limited to facts about the past and present, no reason in principle why our tracking and our knowledge must be limited to our sample.

Let h be some statement believed on the basis of evidence e. One question is whether I know h; here the answer might be "yes, on the

---

* Therefore, the relevant not-p world is not a world identical to the actual one until now and then diverging so as to produce not-p. There are delicate questions about how best to construe subjunctives that reach back in time, of the sort: if p weren't (to be) the case, q wouldn't have been the case. If determinism holds true, the (supposed) falsity of p might send ripples of change all the way back to the initial conditions of the universe, and with these antecedently changed, forward again through time, leading to (who knows what) enormous changes in the present. Perhaps the matter should be handled by saying the changes in the current evidence (the q that wouldn't have been the case) have to come as part of the rippling changes on the way back from the supposition that not-p, rather than as part of the forward movement of change from even more extensive backtracking. No doubt, a more complicated theory will be needed; my hope is that any such theory can be plugged into the text above, producing only minor modifications in it. For a recent discussion, not jibing with the tenor of this footnote, see David Lewis, "Counterfactual Dependence and Time's Arrow", Nous, Vol. 13, 1979, pp. 455–476.

basis of e," when e is subjunctively connected with h in a way so as to yield knowledge of h (when believed on the basis of e). A second question is whether I know it's not the case that e and not-h, or know that not-SK (where SK entails e and not-h); here the answer might be "no". From this last, however, it does not follow that I do not know that h; for my belief that h, based upon e, might still track the fact that h, since e itself might track h.

There is one question, though, that appears to fall between these two, being like the first in apparently asking whether h is known, and being like the second in depending upon whether not-(e and not-h) is being tracked. This question is: *given* that e is true, do I know that h? Given that the person is behaving in that way (writhing, screaming, complaining), do I know he is in pain? Given that I saw the chair before and hear no noise now, do I know the chair now is behind me? Given that the earth has rotated on its axis as it has previously and given all the other astronomical facts holding today and before, do I know the earth will rotate tomorrow? Given that e, do I know that h?

The "given that e" in the question holds e fixed; it holds fixed (among that which is accessible to me) what would vary if h were false. Thereby it blocks the answer, "I know h, because if h were false, e wouldn't hold true", for that answer seems directed to another question, and does not speak to whether given that e, I know that h. To the question "given that he is behaving that way, do you know he is feeling pain?" we cannot answer "yes, for if he weren't feeling pain he wouldn't be behaving that way." Holding e as fixed and given allows only h to vary, or h along with some other things that do not include e. "Given that e, do you know that h?" To answer this we must consider whether condition 3 is satisfied, and so examine what you would believe if h were false. But the "given that e" requires that in considering the situation where h is false, we hold e true; so it requires us to consider an e and not-h world. What we believe in that world cannot be determined by e's not holding there because h does not, for e does hold there—that is given. To ask "given that e, do you know that h?" seems to ask merely whether we know that h, noticing by the by that e is true. However, really it asks whether we know that not-(e and not-h), a different question, and one that may merit a negative answer. Though it is an easy slide from this negative answer—"we don't know that not-(e and not-h)"—to the conclusion that therefore we don't know that h, this move should be resisted.

If the answer to "given that e, do you know that h?" is negative, then: given that e, I do not know that h. Since e is (let us suppose) true, it seems an easy step to detaching the simple conclusion: I do not know that h. Even if that cannot legitimately be inferred from e, how can it be that I do know that h? If I do, that must be on the basis of e which is all the evidence I have, and we already have seen that: given that e, I do not know that h. Although given that e I don't know that h, still, I can know (on the basis of e) that h. For I do not live in a world in which e is given, in which e is fixed and must be held constant. So I can know that h on the basis of e, on the basis of the e which is able to vary and so, because it hasn't, shows me that h is true. If h were false, e wouldn't hold either, and so I would not believe h. Thus, condition 3 can be satisfied and I can track h.

To speak of knowing h given that e forces us to look at a not-h world (in considering condition 3) which is not one that would or might hold if h were false, for it forces us to look at a not-h world which also is an e world; it forces us to look at an e and not-h world. The linguistic device "given that" holds things constant, and by preventing certain variations may force us to consider worlds farther out. Other linguistic devices, such as demonstratives, also may fix things as constant; so sentences containing these also may be like "given that" sentences in really being about a (skeptical) world farther out than the closest not-h world, while apparently being simply about h. It is not my purpose to pursue the theory of demonstratives, merely to note and illustrate the complication. Do I know I am holding in my hand the pen my children bought for me in the Harvard Coop as a Chanukah gift? Yes, if I wasn't holding it in my hand, I wouldn't think I was. (Either my hand would be empty, or I would be holding something other than a pen, or another pen but then I would notice it wasn't red.) Do I know that this red Parker $2.98 ballpoint pen is the one my children bought for me? Yes, it has a bent clip, resulting from my clumsiness soon after I got it. Do I know that this red Parker $2.98 ballpoint pen with the bent clip and these certain marks is the very pen my children bought in the Coop for me as a Chanukah gift? Perhaps not. If this were not that very pen, then I would still think it was; how, after all, would I tell the difference? All the features by which I am able to tell it is the original gift pen are held constant by the question "given that it has these stated characteristics do I know it is the pen my children bought me?" and also by the question "do I know that this red Parker with the bent clip is the very pen my children bought me?" The two questions "given that e, do I know that h?" and "do I know that this e thing is h?" each hold e fixed and thus appear to force the skeptical answer that h isn't known—when actually it is not-(e and not-h) which isn't known.

When e is all our evidence for h yet does not entail h, the skeptic asks whether given e we know that h. A negative answer to this question does not require us to conclude we don't know that h. The skeptic has more to say, however, about his particular skepticisms. He points out that our evidence e falls into one class or type of statement while the h we conclude falls into another, and that no amount of evidence taken from the first class can yield an affirmative answer to "given the evidence, do we know that h?" The evidence consists completely of statements about behavior, or about objects when they are observed, or about the past and present, or about the sample; and each time we go to an h beyond, we run risks. We acknowledge the risk due to the fact that h is not entailed by e but stands in subjunctive relations to it. (The skeptic also will ask whether and how we know these subjunctive evidence relations hold, a topic we leave for a later section.) Some skeptical partitionings of the statements into two classes are more illuminating than others, marking a natural distinction among types of statements with stable membership. Such is the distinction between statements about behavior in a setting and statements about felt psychological states. The skeptic's division is less illuminating when it simply reduces to the general point about whether given e we can know h, or gerrymanders the contours of the statement-classes solely to make the skeptical point, or when a statement can shift from one class to another with ease, for example, from being about the future to being about the past, from being about something unobserved to being about it when observed, from being about the front of a surface to being about an undistinguished area.[59] Even the general point, though, is worth making; but correctly understood it is a point about our lack of knowledge (when e is all the evidence we have for h) that not-(e and not-h), not a point about our lack of knowledge that h. Furthermore, when e is just part of the evidence we have for h, even holding e fixed we may well know that h (given that e) and also know that not-(e and not-h), provided the rest of the evidence for *h* would vary with the truth of *h*, thereby indicating *h*'s truth-value.

Details of Nonclosure

Knowledge is not closed under known logical implication; therefore some specific rules of inference also must exhibit nonclosure. Let us investigate a few details.

Knowledge is not closed (in general) under a known application of the principle of universal instantiation, which licenses the inference from 'For all x, Px' (written as "(x)Px") to '*a* is P', for arbitrary *a* (written as "Pa"). For if knowledge were closed under the known application of this more limited rule, it also would be closed under known logical implication in general.[60]

This result appears surprising, that someone may know that for all x, Px, without knowing that Pa for some particular *a* (he knows to exist). If a person knows that something is true of everything, won't he also know it is true of each particular thing?[61]

We can gain an intuitive understanding of how a person can know that everything is P without knowing of some particular specified thing that it is P, by recalling that knowledge involves a belief that somehow varies with the truth of what is believed. It might be that a person's belief that everything is P somehow varies with the truth of that, yet his belief that *a* is P, does not vary with the truth of *that*. If "everything is P" were false, then in that situation which would obtain, he wouldn't believe that everything is P. Suppose or assume that the situation that would obtain if "everything is P" were false is not the situation where *a* isn't P—rather it is one where something else *b* isn't P—and suppose that the person would realize then that *b* is not P, and so not believe that everything is P. Thus, he satisfies condition 3 for knowing that everything is P. Yet even so, he might fail to satisfy condition 3 for knowing that *a* is P; for it might be that if *a* weren't P, the person would still believe it was, and so he does not know *a* is P. The truth of the universal generalization that everything is P can vary without the truth of *a* being P varying, precisely in the case when if something weren't P, it would be something other than *a*. (If something weren't P, then that something, which was not P and which made (x)Px false, would be something other than a.) Thus, we have an intuitive argument for the result that not only is knowledge not closed in general under known logical implication, it is not (always) closed under known application of the rule of universal instantiation (even when this is known to be a valid rule). A person may know that everything is P without knowing that a is P, even though he realizes that Pa follows logically from (x)Px. There is a difference between knowing that everything is P, and knowing of each and every thing that it is P.[62]

Similarly, a person may know a conjunction without knowing each of the conjuncts. The knowledge of q, Kq, does not follow from K(p&q) and K(p&q $\rightarrow$ q). It may seem that this is an especially clear and close logical consequence and that knowledge should follow along with it when this entailment is known. But if we grant this, and maintain that knowledge is closed under known logical equivalence, then we will have the (undesired) result that knowledge is closed under known logical implication generally.[63]

S's belief that p & q tracks the fact that p & q; if it were true he would believe it, and if it were false he wouldn't believe it. It may be that if the conjunction p & q were false, it is the first conjunct p that would be false, and in that situation the person wouldn't believe p and so wouldn't believe p & q. However, it does not follow that his belief in q tracks the fact that q; for if q were false (which is not what would or might be the case if the conjunction were false—p would then be the culprit) he might still believe q. We can satisfy condition 3 for a conjunction by satisfying it for its most vulnerable conjunct, the one that would be false if the conjunction were false; it does not follow that we satisfy condition 3 for the other conjuncts as well.

So, we must adjust to the fact that sometimes we will know conjunctions without knowing each of the conjuncts. Indeed, we already have adjusted. Let p be the statement that I am in Emerson Hall, not-SK be the one that I am not on Alpha Centauri floating in that tank; since p entails not-SK, p is (necessarily) equivalent to p & not-SK. I know that p, yet I do not know that not-SK.

Also, it is possible for me to know p yet not know the denial of a conjunction, one of whose conjuncts is not-p. I can know p yet not know (for I may not be tracking) not-(not-p & SK). I know I am in Emerson Hall now, yet I do not know that: it is not the case that (I am in the tank on Alpha Centauri now and not in Emerson Hall).

However, we have seen no reason to think knowledge does not extend across known logical equivalence. When p entails not-SK and hence is known to be equivalent to p & not-SK, the person who knows p will know p & not-SK. I know I am in Emerson Hall now and not floating in that tank on Alpha Centauri; I believe it, and my belief tracks that conjunctive fact. If the conjunction weren't true, it is p that would be false (rather than SK's being true) and in that situation I would not believe I was in Emerson Hall. But, though I believe the second conjunct, not-SK, my belief in that (alone) doesn't track the fact; if SK were true, I would still believe not-SK. So I don't know not-SK.

Some people are convinced that the skeptic is wrong even in saying we don't know not-SK. Perhaps their conviction stems from the fact that we do know (and track) conjunctions that include not-SK. (It is perfectly true to say "I do know I am in Emerson Hall in Massachusetts and not in that tank on Alpha Centauri.") However, we cannot detach that conjunct; knowledge is not closed under inference of a conjunct. The feeling that the skeptic is wrong about our not knowing not-SK may stem from our focusing on wider conjunctions we do know which include not-SK. Earlier, we said the skeptic could maintain his belief that we know practically nothing only when he attends to the possibility SK; when he focuses upon other statements p (other than not-SK) which we do track, he too falls into thinking he knows it, until he attends again to his skeptical arguments and shifts his focus of attention to SK and to the specific belief that not-SK. Similarly, I think, the person who denies everything the skeptic says maintains his belief only by a shift of attention. He maintains his belief that he knows even not-SK only by shifting his attention to some other p (incompatible with SK) that is tracked, or to some tracked statement that includes not-SK as a conjunct. It is easier for the nonskeptic to shift his attention supportively than for the skeptic to shift attention to SK. There are so many different things the nonskeptic can focus on other than the isolated not-SK, thereby maintaining his position; while the skeptic has to stay with attention fixed on SK (or on the belief that not-SK) to maintain his position. Still, the position of each involves a shift of attention, an averting of gaze; only this slide into misfocus enables each to maintain his uniform position, be it that knowledge extends everywhere or nowhere.

Proof and the Transmission of Knowledge

We have seen that knowledge is not (in general) closed under the inference of a conjunct (called in the literature "simplification") or under the rule of universal instantiation, inferring an instance from a universal generalization, itself a kind of simplification. Is knowledge closed under the inference of existential generalization, inferring from 'Pa' the statement 'there is an x such that Px'? It seems that a person can track 'Pa' without tracking 'there is an x such that Px'. Condition 3 can be satisfied for one yet not for the other. If a weren't P, the person wouldn't believe it was; yet if there were not any x such that Px, perhaps he still would believe something was P (though he wouldn't believe this of a). But this apparent nonclosure result surely carries things too far.[64] I am now writing with a blue pen. I know the pen is blue. I realize this entails that something now is blue, and I know that something now is blue, even solely on the basis of this inference.

These last points about nonclosure under existential generalization (or under addition, inference of a disjunction that includes a premiss) cut things too finely. Surely our knowledge that p does not stand in such splendid isolation from knowledge of other things so closely connected to p. There is a further difficulty. The general view of knowledge as not closed under known logical implication appears incompatible with the fact that sometimes we come to know something via a deduction or proof. What a proof shows us is that the premisses logically imply the conclusion; but if knowledge is not closed under known logical implication then how could we ever come to know something via a proof? However, we have not said knowledge is never closed under known logical implication, that knowledge never flows down from known premisses to the conclusion known to be implied, merely that knowledge is not always so closed, it does not always flow down. This leaves room for sometimes coming to know something via a proof, for situations where because the premisses are known and known to logically imply the conclusion, the conclusion also is known. We need to identify and delineate which situations these are.

Under what conditions is knowledge transmitted from the premisses of a proof to its conclusion? (Of course, truth is transmitted always if the proof is valid.) It is not fruitful to look for a subset of the formal rules of proof that always preserves knowledge; whether knowledge is preserved will depend on what subjunctives are true of each step. It would be inadequate, though, merely to say that knowledge is preserved in cases where the proof is valid and the statement to be proven also is known in that it too satisfies the four conditions for knowledge. This would fail to explain how sometimes we can come to know something via a proof.

Let us adapt the four conditions for knowledge to our current concern of inferring q from p. S knows via inference (from p) that q if and only if

    (1) S knows that p
    (2) q is true, and S infers q from p (thereby, we assume, being led to believe that q).

If S is to know q via this inference, the third condition for knowledge will have to be satisfied, namely: if q were false then S wouldn't infer q from p. Most notably for our purposes, this will hold when and because: if q were false S wouldn't believe p (from which to infer q). Alternatively, it might be that if q were false S, though believing p, wouldn't make the inference of q from p. The following condition (call it "I" for *inference*) specifies when the inference of q from p (which is known) yields knowledge that q.

    I: if q were false, S wouldn't believe p (or S wouldn't infer q from p).

When, for some skeptical hypothesis SK, an inference is made to not-SK from another statement p which is tracked and known, this condition I is not satisfied, and so one does not come to know that not-SK through that inference. Let q be the statement (not-SK) that S is not in the (relevant) tank on Alpha Centauri, and let p be the statement that S is sitting and reading in Massachusetts. S knows that p entails q, and infers q from p (and from many other things as well, but we may leave these aside, or imagine them included in the premiss p which becomes a very large conjunction). If q were false and he were floating in that tank, he still would believe p (and infer q from p). Thus, to show the inference to a conclusion q from a known premiss p yields knowledge that q, the condition I (for transmission of knowledge via inference) will have to be satisfied. In this case, in particular, we will need: if q were false S wouldn't believe p.* If the conclusion of the inference were false, he wouldn't believe the premisses.

This additional condition will be needed if the method of inferring q from p is to yield knowledge that q. But can't we view the method of arriving at belief that q as: inferring q from p which is tracked, that is, known to be true? When p entails q, if q were false the person would not be using *that* method to arrive at a belief that q, and so would not believe q via that method. So doesn't he thereby satisfy the third condition for knowledge that q: if q were false he wouldn't believe q via that method? The problem is that the method of inferring q from known p is indistinguishable by the person from the method of inferring q from (believed) p. We have said that knowledge is a real connection of belief to the world, tracking, and though this view is external to the viewpoint of the knower, as compared to traditional treatments, it does treat the method he uses as identified from the inside, to the extent it is guided by internal cues and appearances. Is he, basing his belief in the way he does (from the inside), actually in a subjunctive connection with the truth? But if we are willing to look at the actual factual connection externally, why don't we similarly view his method of arriving at belief on a particular occasion not from his viewpoint (from the inside), but as it really is externally? The notion of knowledge holds the method fixed (recall the grandmother case) but not that fixed—fixed enough only to

* There are additional imaginable routes whereby if q were false the person would not infer q from p, thereby satisfying condition I and also the third condition for knowledge. One is that the inferential relation from p to q itself depends upon the truth of q, and so if q were false the inference could not be made. Since deductive relations are not dependent in this way, this consideration is irrelevant to our present concerns. Under the second additional route, if q were false the inference from p to q would not actually be made; if q were false the person wouldn't apply his inferential power to p or to the question of q's truth, and so on. Here, however, the method is not held fixed. More relevant is the case where the person would apply his deductive powers but, if q were false, would not perceive the deductive connection between p (which he believes) and q. However, these additional considerations are so messy that, while a completely adequate theory would have to include them, the specification of condition I as

not-q → not-(S believes p)

is good enough for all our present purposes.

exclude differences the person would detect, believing it to constitute a difference. The method used must be specified as having a certain generality if it is to play the appropriate role in subjunctives. This generality is set by the differences the person would notice; the methods are individuated from the inside. Otherwise, you needn't reach to inference to establish your knowledge that you are not floating in the tank on Alpha Centauri. You see you are not on Alpha Centauri, and via this method, externally specified, you track the fact that you are not—even though if you were it would seem perceptually the same as it does to you now. That perceptual seeming, though indistinguishable internally from your actual current seeing, is distinguishable externally as a distinct method, if such external individuation of methods is allowed to count. Would even Dr. Johnson have said, "How do I know I am not dreaming? By seeing what is in front of me"?

A person uses method M_1 to track the fact that p and uses M_2 to deduce from p the conclusion that not-SK. He comes to believe not-SK via the method $M_1 + M_2$. But this (combined) method doesn't yield his tracking not-SK; for if SK were true, he still would believe, via $M_1 + M_2$, that not-SK.

Thus, if S is to know that q when he infers it from p, if the third condition for knowledge that q is to be satisfied (namely, not-$q \rightarrow$ not-S believes, via M, that q), then so must the following further condition: not-$q \rightarrow$ not-S believes p. A similar treatment is needed for the fourth condition on knowledge that q: $q \rightarrow$ S believes, via M, that q. If knowledge that q is to be gained by the inference of q from p, these additional conditions must be satisfied: $q \rightarrow$ S believes, via M, that p (or at least, not that if q were true S wouldn't believe via M that p); and also $q \rightarrow$ S, inferring q or inferring not-q from p, infers q from p. Previously, we said the person wouldn't believe the premiss if the conclusion were false; now we add: the person would believe the premiss (or at least: wouldn't stop believing it) if the conclusion were true.[65]

We do sometimes come to know something via a proof from known premisses, namely, when we wouldn't believe the premisses if the conclusion were false and we would (continue to) believe them if the conclusion were true. (I assume this case is one where we come to believe the conclusion via inferring it from the premisses.) These two conditions for knowledge being transmitted in the inference of q

from p

not-q → not-(S believes that p)

q → S believes that p

are tracking conditions, like conditions 3 and 4 for knowledge, except that they state that S's belief that p tracks the fact that q. An inference yields knowledge of the conclusion, we now see, when the belief in the premisses tracks the truth of the conclusion.[66]

When the belief in the conclusion is based upon (because inferred from) the belief in the premisses, if this belief in the premisses does not track the truth of the conclusion, then the belief in the conclusion will not track its truth either. The belief in the conclusion will not be knowledge, will not track the fact, unless the belief in the premisses (from which it is inferred) tracks that very (conclusory) fact. It is not enough for the belief in the premisses to track some other fact, even if that other fact is the very fact stated in the premiss —that gives us knowledge just of the premiss, not of the conclusion.

The skeptic specifies possibilities SK so that, even when we deduce not-SK from some p, we violate the condition that SK → not-(S believes that p). In fact, they have been carefully designed so that SK → S believes that p; if SK were true, S still would believe p (and also believe not-SK). The inference from p to the nonskeptical conclusion not-SK does not yield knowledge, for the belief in the premiss (upon which the belief in the conclusion is based) does not track the truth of the conclusion.

We have said that when a person knows p and infers not-SK from p, where SK is the skeptic's possibility incompatible with p, then he does not know not-SK. His belief that not-SK does not track the fact that not-SK, nor does his belief that p. A person can know that p without knowing of "far out" possibilities incompatible with p, that they do not hold. It is otherwise with possibilities incompatible with p that are closer, for example, a possibility q_1 which would or might hold if p were not to hold. Call such a q_1, a first subjunctive alternative to p; p entails not-q_1, and if p weren't the case q_1 would be the case or at least might be; not-p → q_1, or at least not-(not-p → not-q_1). A second subjunctive alternative to p is a q_2 incompatible with p which would or might obtain if both p and q_1 did not. If a person knows that p is true, mustn't he also know that the first subjunctive alternative q_1 to p doesn't hold; mustn't he at least know of that alternative incompatible with p (as he doesn't know of SK) that it does not hold? We would not want to require or suppose that in order to know that p a person must know independently, apart from inferring this from p, that its first subjunctive alternative q_1 doesn't hold. That requirement would threaten to move us all the way up the line; to know that not-q_1 is also to know that its first subjunctive alternative doesn't hold, and so on. Or is this regress stopped by the simple knowledge that not-q_1?

Although the person who knows p need not know that not-q_1 independently of p, he will know it if (realizing that p entails not-q_1) he infers it from p. That inference puts him into a position of tracking not-q_1.[67] However, we cannot move up the line to more remote subjunctive alternatives q_m to p, to knowing that not-q_m by inferring it from p. For the inference to not-q_m from p will not preserve knowledge unless $q_m \rightarrow$ not-(S believes p). This last condition earlier set a limit to the transmission of knowledge via deductive inference; here it limits how remote are the subjunctive alternatives a person will know don't hold, via the deductive inference from p. However, our theory does have the consequence that when S knows that p, he can know, by inferring this from p, that p's first subjunctive alternative q_1 does not hold. Knowledge is not closed under known logical implication, yet the knowledge that p is not cut so finely that a person does not know, when he infers it, that the first subjunctive alternative to p doesn't hold. Under that inference (to the denial of what is a first subjunctive alternative—the person needn't identify it as such) knowledge is preserved.*

Return now to the inference of existential generalization. Earlier, the view of knowledge as tracking apparently led to the consequence that someone might know a is P, infer from this that something or other is P, yet not know (because he doesn't track) that. It was this unsatisfactory consequence that led us to worry that nonclosure involved too fine a delineation of our knowledge, and led us to investigate how (and under what conditions) it was possible to acquire

---

* One might feel that tracking p does not give us knowledge when we don't know that all alternatives incompatible with p don't hold. For in that case, how can we find out that p holds? But "finding out" that p, is a notion like tracking; where q is some alternative incompatible with p which wouldn't hold even if p did not, we can find out that p without finding out that not-q.

knowledge via a deductive proof or inference, given that knowledge is not always closed under known logical implication. The crucial condition, we saw, is that the belief in the premisses track the truth of the conclusion of the inference. Let us apply this now to the inference of existential generalization. Suppose that S knows (and tracks) Pa, by some method M_1, and let M_2 be his method of coming to believe 'there is something that is P' by (realizing it follows and so) inferring it from Pa. S knows 'there is something that is P' by the combination of the methods $M_1 + M_2$. If there weren't anything that was P, this combined method wouldn't yield his believing there was, or that Pa, for in that case of there being no P's, 'Pa' would be false, and since (by hypothesis) his belief that Pa tracks the fact that Pa, he wouldn't then believe that Pa—I leave aside a complication here—and so wouldn't then use it as a premiss from which to infer "there is something that is P". His belief in the premiss Pa tracks the truth of the conclusion "something is P", and so when he infers this conclusion, he thereby comes to know it. Knowledge, almost always, will be closed under existential generalization.[68] Similar remarks apply to inferring a disjunction from a disjunct. In contrast, we can believe a conjunction without our belief tracking the truth of one particular conjunct; we can believe a universal generalization without our belief tracking the truth of one particular instance. (Here, I use "tracking" to refer to condition 3.) With these latter inferences, of course, sometimes the belief in the premisses will track the truth of the conclusion; in those cases the person will come to know the conclusion is true via the inference from the known premisses.

Knowledge also seems to be (always) closed under (known application of) adjudication: the inference from the two premisses p, q to the conjunctive conclusion p & q. Contrast evidential theories of knowledge which set a limit to how low the probability of a statement may be if it is to be known; it is known that under these theories adjudication can fail, since a conjunction (each of whose conjuncts has a probability less than unity) will have a lower probability than either of the conjuncts, and this lessening of probability may send it below the lower cutoff limit.

The fact of the nonclosure of knowledge under various known implications and entailments, at first surprising, has the side effect of helping to solve a little puzzle about evidence. I take this to support a theory of knowledge incorporating such nonclosure; it is difficult to see how else to solve the puzzle (while maintaining knowledge exhibits closure) without conceding too much to the skeptic.

This conundrum is due, I believe, to Saul Kripke.[69] Why should one look at or listen to arguments or evidence against what one knows? If p is true then all evidence showing (or tending to show) that p is false will be misleading. Someone who knows this and who knows that p is true will therefore know that all evidence against p is misleading. So wouldn't it be perfectly all right for him to ignore any evidence against p, to refuse to consider any evidence against p, for doesn't he already know that such evidence will be misleading? Why is it not all right for him to ignore such evidence? An adequate view of knowledge should illuminate and dispel this conundrum.

Rather than rest our discussion upon some particular theory of the evidence relation, let us suppose instead that all evidence relations are deductive. This simplification certainly does not make it easier to deal with the conundrum. For if such relations were all deductive, the case appears even stronger that a person may ignore such evidence, may ignore propositions entailing (and not merely otherwise supporting) the negation of what he knows. On the deductive view of evidence, adopted here only temporarily, we interpret evidence against p as statements that entail not-p. On this view, to say all evidence against p is misleading is to say $(r)(r \dashv 3 \text{ not-}p \supset \text{not-}r)$, which is logically equivalent to p. A person who knows one will know the other, and so we can assume that $K(r)(r \dashv 3 \text{ not-}p \supset \text{not-}r)$.

It will be legitimate for the person to ignore evidence e (against p) only if he knows that (considering) evidence e will be misleading. A person may know that p is equivalent to: all evidence against p will be (to the extent that it is against p) misleading, in that it tends to get him to believe something false (not-p) or not believe something true (p). Since we are assuming knowledge is closed under known mutual entailment, he will know this latter general statement that all evidence against p is misleading. However, he may not know of some particular evidence e that it will be misleading (even though he thinks of it and sees it conflicts with p); he can infer this instance from the general statement by the rule of universal instantiation, but knowledge is not always closed under known applications of this rule. So he does not know that e is misleading merely by virtue of inferring this from the general statement (by universal instantiation); it does not follow merely from his knowing the general statement that he has this particular knowledge.

Does he know of the evidence that it would or will be misleading? Does he know of e that ignoring it would not or will not be misleading? If he does not know these things, it is not legitimate for him to ignore the evidence e. Therefore, the nonclosure of knowledge under known logical implication leaves room for a solution to the conundrum, showing how the person may know p yet may not legitimately ignore evidence e against p. Simply pointing to this room, however, does not constitute a solution to the conundrum. For though knowledge is not always closed under known logical implication, perhaps this is one of the cases where knowledge is transmitted down to the inferred conclusion.

Whether he knows of this evidence e that it would or will be misleading depends on whether his belief that p tracks the truth of this conclusion, tracks the fact that the evidence is misleading. This is the crucial factor in determining whether, in inferring the conclusion from the premiss, he knows the conclusion is true. Here, we have to investigate what he would or might believe if the evidence weren't misleading: would or might he continue to believe p, would or might he continue to believe the evidence was misleading? Only then can we see whether condition 3 is satisfied, whether he knows the evidence is misleading. The details showing he does not know this consequence are messy, and left as an exercise for excessively masochistic readers.

Not knowing of e that it is misleading, he may not legitimately simply ignore it, refusing to consider it as evidence against p. Various statements about counterevidence to p do follow from the truth of p, but since knowledge is not closed under known logical implication, these are pruned away; what he knows is simply p, and this knowledge does not make it legitimate for him to ignore counterevidence.

Our view that knowledge is not closed under known logical implication has yielded, as a side effect, a way of handling the conundrum. Other views of knowledge must show that they too can avoid its snares, without saying that we don't really know that p, or that we can ignore evidence only if we know we know that p but we never do, or any other similar skeptical move.

We should not conclude, however, that we can never ignore (purported) evidence against what we know. For example: we (or one of us) must examine evidence presented by the critics of the Warren Commission Report who hold that John Kennedy was killed by a conspiracy, but surely we can refuse to examine someone's presented evidence that Kennedy was killed by a conspiracy from Sirius. We need not examine every conspiracy or paranoid or crackpot batch of evidence; to delineate which (type) we may ignore is the job of a general theory of evidence.

We have said that whether knowledge is transmitted from premisses down to an inferred conclusion depends not only on whether the conclusion follows, but also on whether the belief in the premisses tracks the truth of the conclusion. Whether or not this (further) condition is satisfied is not settled by the formal character of the rule of inference. If a proof is something that always transmits knowledge (in contradistinction to truth, which is transmitted by valid deduction—of which there is a formal theory) then there is no formal theory of proof.[70]

Let us look more closely at this notion of proof. A proof, we have said, transmits knowledge. If there is to be a proof to S of q from p it must be that

(1) S knows that p.

Otherwise, there is no knowledge to transmit. Second, it must be that

(2) not-q → not-(S believes that p).

Otherwise, we have seen, knowledge will not be transmitted by the sequence of deductive or inferential steps, though truth may be, even when

(3) p entails (or logically implies) q.

However, an argument for q may satisfy all these conditions, yet still not be a proof that q, because it begs the question. An argument begs the question (as a proof) when, if S didn't know the conclusion, he wouldn't know (one of) the premisses. We need to add the further condition

(4) not-(S doesn't know that q → S doesn't know that p).

A proof must pick its premisses carefully; it must have premisses which wouldn't be believed if the conclusion were false (point 2), but which might be known even if the conclusion weren't known (point 4).[71]

The subjunctive 4 talks of a particular person's knowledge; let us say that a proof begs the question for S when: if S weren't to know that q, he wouldn't know that p. And let us say that a proof is circular when it would beg the question for everyone, when it is and would be true for every person S that if he weren't to know that q then he wouldn't know that p.

Since the aim of a proof is to bring knowledge, the conditions for a proof's being circular or begging the question are stated in terms of knowledge. However, the goal might be to bring or transmit some thing other than knowledge; an argument, for example, aims at producing and transmitting belief or perhaps conviction. We may say that an argument from p to q begs the question for S when: if he weren't to believe q, he wouldn't believe p—and that an argument is circular if it would beg the question for everyone. Justification, on most views, aims at producing something else: rational or justified belief.[72] A similar account can be offered of when a justification of q from p begs the question for a person, or is circular. These elucidations leave open the possibility that the very same movement from p to q may beg the question for one person but not for another, or may beg the question for someone as one of these things but not as another, as a proof but not as an argument, for instance.[73]

Skepticism Revisited

Knowledge is not closed under known logical implication. There are two ways to extend our notion of knowledge, as specified by conditions 1–4, in order to insure closure: the way of the skeptic and that of the anti-skeptic. Retaining "know" for our ordinary notion, the skeptic introduces a notion 'know*' that satisfies the following conditions:

(1) if S doesn't know that p, he doesn't know* that p

(2) if S knows that p entails q and S doesn't know that q, then S doesn't know* that p.

His notion 'know*' is closed under known logical implication; under it we know* almost nothing. The skeptic might obtain his notion by requiring that

$$\text{not-}p \rightarrow \text{not-(S believes that } p)$$

is true only if S wouldn't believe p both in the not-p situation or world that would obtain if p did not, and also in all not-p worlds doxically identical to the actual world. After all (he might say) we don't know we are not in one of those worlds.

On the other hand, the anti-skeptic introduces a notion 'know^' that satisfies these conditions:

(1) if S knows that p then S knows^ that p

(2) if S knows that p and S knows that p entails q then S knows ^ that q.

His notion 'know^' is closed under known logical implication; under it we know^ quite a lot, including that we are not floating in that tank, and so forth.

Neither of these deductively closed notions is our own. Still, we can raise the question: if knowledge *were* deductively closed under known logical implication, would it be more like know* or like know^? If there were a notion N such that S N's that p if and only if

(a) p is true

(b) S believes p

(c) not-p → not-(S believes that p)

(d) p → S believes that p & not-(S believes that not-p)

and N were closed under N-ed implication (that is, if S N's that p and S N's that p entails q then S N's that q), then would we N quite a lot or almost nothing?

Perhaps we suspect the skeptic to be right subjunctively; perhaps we are troubled by the suspicion that if there were a notion worthy of being called KNOWLEDGE—I am tempted to write, in Hyman Kaplan fashion, K*N*O*W*L*E*D*G*E—the skeptic would be right about that notion. Do we think (why?) that for knowledge to be all it should be, it would have to be closed under known logical implication? For condition 3 to be so closed, whenever p entails q, the not-q situation or world that would obtain (if q did not) would have to be no farther from the actual world than the world that would obtain if p did not (the closest not-p world). But when this entailed statement q

is not-SK, the statement that the skeptic's doxically identical world doesn't obtain, this would mean that SK is no farther from the actual world than any other not-p world is. In that SK world, we would continue to have the beliefs we do (almost all of them then being false); this has the consequence that almost all subjunctives of the form of 3, not-$p \to$ not-(S believes p), are false, thereby eliminating almost all cases of knowledge. Knowledge would be deductively closed only if the skeptic's imagined worlds SK would or might obtain if p weren't true; but then we would or might believe p even if it were false, and so we do not know that p.[74] Thus, if our notion of knowledge was as strong as we naturally tend to think (namely, closed under known logical implication) then the skeptic would be right. (But why do we naturally think this? Further exploration and explanation is needed of the intuitive roots of the natural assumption that knowledge is closed under known logical implication.)

The skeptic might ask whether we know he is not right. If he says

s: we know practically nothing

then I do know that not-s. I correctly believe s is false; and if s weren't false, if it were true, I wouldn't then believe not-s. For if s were true, it wouldn't be because some doxically identical world existed; in the not-s world that would obtain if s were false (which is not the skeptic's imagined world SK) I wouldn't continue to believe not-s.* However, suppose I am wrong about this; suppose that if s were true (not-s were false) it would be a skeptic's doxically identical world SK that obtained wherein I would continue to believe not-s. So I don't know not-s; I don't know it is false that we know practically nothing. Yet it does not follow from this that I don't know that I am now sitting while writing on paper, for instance—call this p. Perhaps if not-s were false I still would believe not-s. Be that as it may, still, if p were false, I wouldn't believe p. (Even if the skeptic's doxically identical world SK would obtain if not-s were false, that does not mean it, SK, would obtain if p were false.)

The skeptic need not merely put forth s, of course. He may also put forward a full-blown skeptical theory SK which includes s and which is doxically identical to the actual world (as s alone is not)—

* But do I know: no doxically identical world of that sort obtains? No, but this is just one isolated thing I do not know, another not-SK.

and we will not know this skeptic's theory SK is wrong. However, it will not follow from this that you don't know you are now reading a book, for example, any more than that followed from your not knowing other not-SK's, such as that you are not floating in that tank. One skeptic says we don't know we are not floating in the tank and therefore we don't know that *p*. That skeptic's "therefore" is wrong. Another skeptic may actually put forward as true the hypothesis that I am in a doxically identical world SK in which almost everything I believe is false. I do not know his hypothesis is false—but still I know that *p*. This skeptic may say: "if you don't know my hypothesis is false, then perhaps you know that *p*; but you certainly don't know that you know. How can you know you know that *p*, unless you know that my skeptical hypothesis SK does not hold? Perhaps skeptical arguments don't show you know practically nothing, but they do show you don't know you know much of anything."

This skeptical argument trades on some purported closure property of knowledge; our suspicions should be aroused, therefore. I interpret this skeptic's argument (where SK is his skeptical possibility about person S) as beginning with

(a) SK → not-(S knows that *p*).

If S is floating in the tank, he does not know that *p* (whether or not *p* is true); if S is dreaming, he does not know that *p*, even if *p* happens also to be true. (G. E. Moore refers to the story of someone who dreamed he was speaking in the House of Lords only to wake up and discover that he was speaking in the House of Lords.)[75]

Moreover, the skeptic assumes the person S knows proposition a, and also that he knows the contrapositive of it. So we have the skeptic's second assumption:

(b) S knows (S knows that *p* → not-SK).

His third assumption is the (correct) hypothesis:

(c) not-(S knows that not-SK).

From these, the skeptic could derive the conclusion that

(d) not-(S knows that S knows that *p*)

if he had use of the closure principle:

S knows that (S knows that $p \rightarrow r$) & S knows that S knows that $p \rightarrow$ S knows that r.

This principle may have more appeal than the simple closure principle (of which it is a special instance): S knows that 'p entails q' and S knows that $p \rightarrow$ S knows that q. However, it fails because (and when) the skeptic's possibility SK is not the first subjunctive alternative to S's knowing that p. It is possible for a person's belief that he knows, his belief that Kp, to vary subjunctively with the truth of Kp, while his belief that not-SK does not vary subjunctively with the truth of not-SK.

It is worth noting that, and why, the skeptic tries to prove something stronger than is necessary for the truth of his thesis. We will not know p if there is a q incompatible with p such that we don't know that not-q, while yet if p were false q might be true. Whether or not we could know not-q, if we actually don't know not-q, we do not know p.

We will know almost nothing if this situation holds true of almost everything we believe, that is, if

    I. For almost all p, there exists a q such that q entails not-p and q might be true if p were false, and we do not know that not-q.

This says that for each p, there is some q or other which . . . ; it need not be the very same q for every p. The skeptic however attempts to prove I by introducing his skeptical possibility SK—this one possibility is to do the job for almost every p. That is, the skeptic argues for

    II. There is a q such that for almost every p, q entails not-p and q might be true if p were false, and we do not know that not-q.

He suggests SK is such a possibility q, serving for all p. Statements II and I are very similar, but with the order of the quantifiers reversed. Statement II is stronger than I, and implies it; if the skeptic's argument did establish II, he also would have shown that I holds. The problem, as we have seen, is that in specifying one possibility SK to do the job for almost every p, he has specified one so remote that it would not hold even if p did not; he has specified an SK such that not-$p \rightarrow$ not-SK. Thus, his possibility SK does not satisfy the middle clause of II (that the possibility might hold if p were false), and so does not show that II is true. The economical way to establish I is by producing one q that makes it true, that is, to show the truth of II. It is not surprising that no example serves to show II is true; any q that is incompatible with almost every p and is not known to be false will be so remote that the middle clause will not be satisfied. There is no one q incompatible with most of what we know such that for each piece of our knowledge, that q also would or might obtain if the thing known did not obtain.

The skeptic needs, yet cannot find, an SK incompatible with almost every (supposedly known) p, that also is a first subjunctive alternative to each and every one of these p's. No wonder he cannot find a possibility that establishes his point in one fell swoop.

Since the argument for I via II is bound to fail, the skeptic must seek an argument for I that does not go through II. It is not clear what such a general argument would be like—one almost would have to believe there was an actual demon who strewed the world with different pitfalls q_i, one for each p_i we believe. The prospects are not bright for less bizarre skeptical arguments, in view of our earlier observation that if S knows (and tracks the fact) that p, and S infers not-q_1 from p, where q_1 is the first subjunctive alternative to p, then S knows that not-q_1.

Knowing That One Knows

The topic of knowing that one knows is interesting in its own right, apart from the skeptical arguments purporting to show this knowledge almost never occurs. According to our account of knowledge as tracking, to know that one knows that p is to truly believe that one knows that p, and to have this belief track the fact that one knows. Spelling it out further, this belief that one knows tracks the fact of tracking that p; that is, the belief that one knows tracks the fact that one's belief that p tracks the fact that p. Thus, with knowledge that one knows that p, there is tracking embedded in tracking—a particular tracking is tracked.

Some writers have put forth the view that whenever one knows, one knows that one knows. There is an immediate stumbling block to this, however. One may know yet not believe one knows; with no existing belief that one knows to do the tracking of the fact that one knows, one certainly does not know that one knows.* Even the weaker thesis that S knows he knows that p whenever he believes truly that he knows that p fails. Nor is this surprising. We have held that knowledge is a certain factual relationship of the belief that p to the fact or truth believed, a relationship specified by the subjunctive conditions 3 and 4. To know that p is to actually be related to the world in a certain way, namely, to track it. But the nature of the tracking relation is such that you can track the fact that p without also tracking the fact that you are tracking p. Your belief that p may somehow vary with the truth of p even though your belief that you are tracking does not vary with truth of "you are tracking p". If knowledge is a real relationship in the world, such as tracking, then it will be a fact that you stand in that relationship to p; so room will be left for failing to stand in that very (tracking) relationship to the fact that you stand in it to p. If the knowledge relationship is a stringent one, not easily satisfied, there will be many cases of knowing without knowing that one knows.

Is there some argument of the skeptic which, while failing to show lack of knowledge that p, at least shows lack of knowing one knows that p? We might imagine two skeptics: the first claims that for almost all the p you think you know, you do not, while the second claims that for almost all the p you think you know, you do not know you know it. The first skeptic's problem was that since knowledge is a real relationship in the world, that of tracking, his imagined possibility doesn't show that relationship does not hold. The second skeptic faces a similar problem. How can his imagined possibility show a real relationship (of tracking) does not hold to another fact: that tracking holds to p? The skeptic's doxically identical possibility SK, for example, of an evil demon or of floating in a tank, did not show the falsity of condition 3, not-p → not-(S believes that p). For even if p were false his possibility SK wouldn't hold, anyway. Similarly, his possibility will not show the falsity of

not-3 → not-(S believes that 3)

* A person who knows that p might not believe he does because he doesn't believe he satisfies conditions 3 and 4, even though he does actually satisfy these conditions. We might say that someone S is a stickler about his beliefs if for all p, S believes that p → S believes that he knows that p, or at least, for all p, S believes he doesn't know that p → S does not believe that p. A stickler about his beliefs would not believe something he didn't think he knew, or at least, that he thought he didn't know.

when even if 3 were false his possibility SK also wouldn't hold; that is, when

not-3 → SK does not hold.

The skeptic's possibility SK can show that a certain (purportedly real) subjunctive relationship does not hold in the world, only when SK is the first subjunctive alternative to the antecedent of that subjunctive relation, that is, only if SK would (or might) hold if the antecedent didn't. To show the factual (subjunctive) relationship does not hold, he would have to show that SK is the relevant first subjunctive alternative. Even if it is not, his possibility SK might show that the person doesn't know he knows . . . he knows, that is, that there is some limit to the iteration of the knowledge operator K.[76]

Some remarks are in order about the n-fold iteration of K, K^n. People who know that p will differ in the n up to which they K^n that p. Perhaps some differences between people in their depth of understanding p are reflected in differences in the n up to which they K^n that p. And some channels that can transmit knowledge (K^1) from one person to another need not be able to transmit a person's full knowledge, his full K^n. People sometimes speak not merely of knowing that p, but of knowing for certain that p. Perhaps this should be interpreted as claiming an even stronger relation of tracking than 3 and 4 put forth. But there is another possibility, that of interpreting "knowing for certain that p" as meaning KKp. On this view, even to know for certain that p would not exclude all (distant) possibility of mistake.

It may seem strange that on our view a person can know up to a certain level, without knowing exactly up to which level he knows. Suppose $K^3p(= KKKp)$, yet not-K^4p. Suppose also that the person knew that he was at exactly this third level, KK^3p & K not-K^4p. But KK^3p just is K^4p, which we already supposed was false. If we knew precisely where we were, we would not be there but up one more level instead. Therefore, we should expect that if we are at some finite level K^np, we will not know exactly at which level we are. The width of the interval in which one can know one falls must be greater than one, greater than an exact position; we shall not undertake to investigate various conditions that might limit the width this interval can take.

III. EVIDENCE

In treating knowledge as a real subjunctive relation between belief and fact, holding in the world, we have said nothing thus far about evidence or justification, topics other views take to be central to the subject of epistemology, if not to constitute it. These other views sometimes view knowledge simply as justified true belief or true belief on the basis of (adequate) evidence. The tradition cannot have been wholly mistaken. These notions surely have something to do with knowledge, and an adequate theory of knowledge as tracking should delineate, at least roughly, what this linkage is, and show why it was plausible to take evidence and justification as definitive of knowledge. What follows is only a sketch of the domain, as it connects with the tracking view of knowledge; we ignore much of the relevant technical details, hoping these will not require a significant alteration in the following overview. Although an adequate view of knowledge as tracking will say something about evidence, it need not, we should emphasize, say what follows. This part of the chapter is one way of elaborating the first two parts—it does not underlie them.

The Evidential Connection

What is evidence, what is the connection between evidence *e* and a statement or hypothesis *h* for which it is evidence? The evidential connection is a subjunctive one. Let us begin with the simplest model, then work our way to slightly more complicated cases.

Evidence for a hypothesis is something that would hold if the hypothesis were true. If *e* is evidence for *h*, then

(a) $h \rightarrow e$; if *h* were the case *e* would be the case.

However, this is not sufficient for an evidential connection between *e* and *h*; for perhaps *e* would hold anyway, even if *h* were not true. In that case, *e*'s holding is no evidence for the truth of *h*. Let us add, then

(b) if *h* weren't true, *e* wouldn't hold; not-*h* $\rightarrow$ not-*e*.

In this situation, where e would hold if h did and would not hold if h did not, let us say that e is strong evidence for h.

From conditions a and b, along with the statement that the evidence does hold,

(c) e,

we can deduce the hypothesis h. From the holding of the evidence, plus the fact that that evidence is strong evidence for the hypothesis, the truth of the hypothesis (logically) follows.

The subjunctive conditions a and b are tracking conditions; they specify that evidence e stands in the same relationship to the hypothesis as belief does to the truth when belief tracks the truth. Conditions a and b correspond to conditions 4 and 3, respectively, in our account of knowledge. Strong evidence tracks the truth of what it is evidence for; let us say it strongly tracks the truth of that for which it is evidence.

Consider someone who believes h on the basis of his belief in (what is) strong evidence e; his belief that h depends upon (and varies with) his belief that e. And let us suppose he knows the evidence is true, his belief that e tracks the fact that e. In this case, his belief that h tracks his belief that e (because it depends on it) which in turn tracks the fact that e (because he knows that e) which in turn tracks the fact that h (because, by hypothesis, e is strong evidence of h). Thus, there is a tracking chain. Although tracking sometimes can fail to be transitive, with the relevant qualifications and details filled in, transitivity will obtain. The person's belief that h, because it tracks e which tracks h, will track the fact that h. Since his belief tracks the fact, the person knows that h. To believe something h on the basis of (what is) strong evidence e, where e is known, is to know h.

Consider the (nondeductive) inference from e to h. Under what conditions will a person know h which he infers from known e? We have seen that knowledge is not always closed under known logical implication; the critical condition for the transmission of knowledge down to the conclusion, in a deductive inference, was that the belief in the premisses tracked the truth of the conclusion. Although deductive implication preserves truth its crucial feature in transmitting knowledge is this tracking condition. Knowledge also can be transmitted by a nondeductive inference (treated as the employment of a method M) provided that belief in the premisses tracks the truth of the conclusion. In evaluating nondeductive inferences, we consider how (well, frequently, and so on) the belief in the premisses tracks the truth of the conclusion; the standard for evaluating particular nondeductive inferences, and general modes of nondeductive inference, is a complicated one which makes reference to tracking. When e is known and e is strong evidence for h, the inference of h (from e) yields knowledge that h; the belief in the premisses (the evidence) strongly tracks the truth of the inferred conclusion (the supported hypothesis). The subjunctive conditions written as plausible for the relation of strong evidence to hypothesis turn out to be the very conditions crucial for the (knowledge-preserving) validity of the inference from evidence to hypothesis.

Unfortunately, the evidence we have for hypotheses is not usually strong evidence; too often although the evidence would hold if h were true, it also might hold if h were false. Earlier, we said that if e would hold also if h were false, if not-$h \rightarrow e$, then e is not evidence for h at all. The denial that e would hold (also) if h were false, is:

(b') not-(not-$h \rightarrow e$); if h were false, e might be false.

This b' is weaker than the earlier b which said that if h were false, e would be false; under b' e only *might* be false (if h were false). When b' holds but the stronger b does not, if h were false then e might be true and might be false. When conditions a and b' both hold, the evidence e would obtain if h were true and might not obtain if h were false. Let us say in this situation that e is weak evidence for h, and that this evidence e weakly tracks h.[77]

Consider the notion of a test of a hypothesis. To test a hypothesis h is to look for data that would not hold if h were true. Finding that data, call it not-e, counts against the truth of h—h fails the test. To say data not-e would not hold if h were true is to say

(a) $h \rightarrow e$; if h were true e would hold.

It would not be a real test of h to look for particular data not-e that wouldn't hold even if h were false—failure to find that (held) would not signify that h had passed any test. Someone who looks only for those not-e's that are so outlandish that even if h were false they wouldn't hold runs little risk of discovering h is false. To test h is to look for data not-e that might actually hold if h were false, that is, to look for data not-*e* such that

    (b') not-(not-*h* → *e*); if *h* were false, *e* might be false, not-*e* might hold.

A severe test will look not only for data not-*e* that might hold if *h* were false; it will look for data not-*e* that would hold if *h* were false. A severe test satisfies a condition stronger that (b'), namely,

    (b) not-*h* → not-*e*; if *h* were false, not-*e* would hold, and *e* would not.

To test *h* severely is to look in just the place where *h* would (turn out to) be false if it were false. And *h* fails the test if data not-*e* is discovered to hold true; it passes the test if *e* is discovered to be true.

These conditions for a test, and for a severe test, are the very same conditions as the ones for evidence, weak and strong. A test of *h*, however, seeks the opposite of evidence; it seeks data not-*e* while the evidence (for *h*) would be *e*. A test of *h* looks for the falsity of what, if true, would be weak evidence for *h*; a severe test looks for the falsity of what, if true, would be strong evidence for *h*.* Experimental science is a testing of hypotheses, manipulating conditions (and controlling other variables) so that the subjunctives (or their probabilistic variants) hold true; artificial conditions are created so as to connect a particular hypothesis *h* with observable data by the subjunctive evidential relations.[78]·

Evidence Based on Probability

We have seen that the inference of *h* from (known) evidence *e* that is weak does not yield knowledge that *h*; in this case, the belief in the

---

* Evidence need not be obtained in the course of a test, of a procedure intending to test (although how it is obtained will affect the probabilities to be mentioned below). What is crucial about evidence, and the inferences based upon it, is which subjunctives hold. We seek facts for which such subjunctives hold, that is, we test and sometimes severely; but its being evidence does not depend on our seeking it—we can just stumble across evidence. If the evidential effects of tests could be had only by searching, then we could not ever have evidence for a hypothesis about a phenomenon that includes (postulated) interaction effects with an observer so that the phenomenon does not occur when the hypothesis is tested. We can come across such evidence unsought, though.

premisses (the evidence) does not (strongly) track the truth of the conclusion (the hypothesis h). When evidence e weakly supports h, how weak is the support it provides? To answer intuitively, that depends on whether the 'might or might not' applying to e when h is false is closer to a 'would' or to a 'would not'. Just as e is not evidence for h when e would hold even if h were false, so too e is not very significant evidence for h when, if h were false, although e *might* not hold it almost certainly or most probably would. Leaving the notion unexplained for now, let us write "prob (e, h)" for the probability that e would hold (occur, be true) given that h is true.[79]

Our first condition (a), $h \rightarrow e$, can be represented as

prob $(e, h) = 1$;

while the second condition (b) for strong evidence, not-$h \rightarrow$ not-e, can be represented as

prob $(e, $ not-$h) = 0$.*

Tentatively, let us specify a measure of support as follows:

support $(e, h) =$ prob $(e, h) -$ prob $(e, $ not-$h)$.

The support of e for h is the difference between the probability of e given h and the probability of e given not-h. This degree of support has an upper value of 1, when the first probability is 1 and the second zero. It is equal to zero when the two probabilities are equal, in which case e gives h zero support. However, when the probability of e given not-h is greater than the probability of e given h, then the support (e, h) takes on a negative value, and can reach as low as -1.[80]

The answer to our question of how much support weak evidence gives to its hypothesis, when condition b$'$ holds, depends on the probability of e given not-h, prob $(e, $ not-$h)$. The smaller this is, the greater the support that e gives to h.

Just as we have weakened condition b to consider b$'$, where e might or might not occur if not-h were true, so also we can consider a

---

* In treating a probability of 1 or 0 as identical to its being the case that an event would or would not occur, I ignore sets of measure zero. Though I am writing as if numerical probability values can be assigned, much of what I say below can be reformulated using only the qualitative terms "almost certain", "almost impossible".

relationship weaker than '$h \to e$' as the relationship between the hypothesis and evidence for it. We can, that is, consider situations where it is not guaranteed that if h were true, e would hold; however, although e might not hold, it almost certainly would. In these situations, the prob (e, h) is less than 1 but very close to it. Such cases are common in statistical practice; for example, h may be a hypothesis about a proportion of something or other in a population, or about a chance mechanism having a certain outcome (a coin coming up heads), while e is evidence about the proportion of something or other in a sample drawn (in a specified way) from the population, or about the results of a certain number of operations of the chance mechanism (the proportion of heads in a certain number of tosses of that coin). These are not situations where if the hypothesis h were true then the evidence would (definitely) have a specified character; rather, there are various probabilities of obtaining various outcomes or data if the hypothesis were true. If the coin were "fair", having an equal probability of giving heads or tails on each toss, then it would be very likely that 100 heads would not be tossed in a row on the first hundred tosses—it would be very unlikely that tosses of that character would be made. Such tosses would be evidence against the coin's being fair.

Thus, we are set adrift on the perilous more general case where neither $h \to e$ nor not-$h \to$ not-e holds, yet these are approximated by the probabilities, prob (e, h) and prob (e, not-h), so the degree of support of e for h is very high.[81]

Let us pause to say a word about how 'not-h' is to be treated here. Since it appears in subjunctives (or subjunctively related statements), it is to be understood as what would or might be the case if h were false; 'not-h' includes all those h_i which might hold if h were false, all the h_i such that not-(not-h $\to$ not-h_i). How are we to understand the probability of e given not-h? Suppose that e would occur if one of the h_i held, say h_1, but would not occur if any of the other h_i (which are first subjunctive alternatives to h) held. The probability of e given not-h then depends on (and is equal to) the probability of h_1 given not-h. And though prob (e, h_1) is (we are supposing) equal to 1, the prob (e, not-h) is very small, because prob (h_1, not-h) also is very small. In assessing by how much evidence e supports hypothesis h, we shall have to take account of such a possibility h_1, even though it is buried in not-h.[82] But let us leave that matter aside for now.

Inference Based on Probability

We have formulated a measure of the degree of evidential support of *e* for *h*, but what are we to do with this measure, what use are we to make of it? We wish to see how a person might base his belief that *h* on the evidence for it, the evidential support. For other purposes, one might need only a procedure for assigning degrees of belief to various hypotheses or for acting in situations of uncertainty or risk; however, for our purpose here, the upshot is to be belief that *h*.

It has seemed reasonable to many that we should believe *h* when its support is very high, close to 1. When evidence *e* is obtained (and we have no other evidence) that is very likely if *h* were true, and very unlikely if *h* were false, then it has seemed plausible to propose that we should believe (on the basis of *e*) that *h* is true. Taking a probability of .05 to demarcate 'almost impossible', and .95 to demarcate 'almost certain', the following is the inference proposed:

From   prob (e, h) $\geq$ .95
       prob (e, not-h) $\leq$ .05
       e
infer h.

Evidence *e* has been obtained, but if not-*h* held it would be very unlikely ($\leq$ .05) that *e* would obtain; on the other hand, *e*'s obtaining is very likely ($\geq$ .95) if *h* were true—we therefore conclude, on the basis of *e*, that *h* is true. If not-*h* were true, then *e*'s holding would be the holding of a very improbable thing. It seems reasonable to conclude that nothing so improbable has occurred in this situation, and therefore that not-*h* is false, *h* is true. Note that it is not enough merely that *e* be very improbable given not-*h*, that prob (*e*, not-*h*) $\leq$ .05. For perhaps *e* is very improbable no matter what, including given *h*. In that case, clearly, we should not conclude that not-*h* is false, merely because *e* (which occurred) was very improbable given not-*h*. The premiss that prob (*e*, *h*) $\geq$ .95 also is needed in the inference.

Although this specified inference looks quite plausible, we must scrutinize it more carefully. Merely from the facts we have been given

e
prob (e, h) $\geq$ .95
prob (e, not-h) $\leq$ .05

can we reasonably conclude, does it follow, that e most probably arose from h (rather than not-h)? We cannot. How it is most likely that e arose depends also on how probable h was, and how probable not-h was, apart from e. Even if it is very improbable that e given that not-h, if it is much more improbable that h holds at all, then it may well be that e arose from not-h after all. Letting $prob_0$ (h) represent the initial or otherwise determined probability of h, and $prob_0$ (not-h) that of not-h (where these sum to one), then the probability of e occurring is the sum of its conditional probabilities of occurring, as weighted by the probabilities of that upon which it is conditional. Thus prob (e) = prob (e, h) × $prob_0$ (h) + prob $(e,$ not-h$)$ × $prob_0$ (not-h). Which way it is most probable that e arose depends on which of the two weighted conditional probabilities is greater, prob (e, h) × $prob_0$ (h) or prob $(e,$ not-h$)$ × $prob_0$ (not-h). So it is rash to make the previously proposed inference without taking any account of information about the probabilities of h and of not-h themselves— (as they are called in the literature) the prior or a priori probabilities of h, and of not-h.

There is a developed body of theory, Bayesian statistics and decision theory, which takes such prior probabilities heavily into account. From the point of view of a methodology to arrive at belief (rather than merely degrees of belief, or optimal actions under risk or uncertainty), belief that is to be closely connected with knowledge (tracking), this Bayesian emphasis on prior probabilities is too heavy.*

* Some philosophers have based theories of the acceptance of hypotheses upon Bayesian or more general decision-theoretic considerations in another way. Taking the rule of maximizing expected utility from decision theory, these theorists delineate epistemic or cognitive utilities whose expected value is then to be maximized by a decision about acceptance of a hypothesis. (The most elaborate development and exposition of such a view is found in Isaac Levi, *Gambling with Truth*, Knopf, New York, 1967; that project is continued in Levi's *The Enterprise of Knowledge*, MIT Press, Cambridge, 1980, to which also the strictures of this note apply; see especially his chapters, 2, 4–8.) However, one cannot simply assume that it is the expected value of epistemic utilities that is to be maximized. Within writings on decision, it was a matter of some controversy whether (higher moments of) variance also should be taken account of in a decision rule.

It was the accomplishment of John von Neumann (in the appendix to the second edition of his work with O. Morgenstern, *Theory of Games and Economic Behavior*, Princeton University Press, Princeton, 1947) to show that the (interval scale) measurability of utility followed from a set of plausible normative conditions on preference among probability mixtures, and that

Rather than incorporate Bayesian considerations into (the previous conditions in) the principle of inference, we can impose them as a constraint upon the principle. The intuitive rationale behind the previously formulated principle was that we should conclude something very unlikely was not happening; since *e* was very unlikely given

preference went along with the expected value of this defined function, utility. Essentially, utility was *defined* as that function whose expected value was to be maximized. To take the simplest case, where *a* is the most preferred alternative and *z* is the least, it follows from the conditions, when *m* is an intermediate alternative, that there is a unique probability *p*, between zero and 1, such that the person is indifferent between the option of *m* (for sure) and the probability mixture of *a* with probability *p* and z with probability (1-p), written pa, (1-p)z. Utility numbers are assigned to *a* and *z* arbitrarily, subject only to the constraint that u(a) > u(z), and the utility of *m*, u(m), is defined as $p \times u(a) + (1-p) \times u(z)$. Similarly for the utility of any other intermediate alternative. The rest of the von Neumann conditions function to guarantee that everything works out, multiplies through all right, and so on. It might seem to trivialize the rule of maximizing expected utility to define utility as that function whose expected value is to be maximized. What was not trivial was to formulate conditions which guaranteed the existence of a function that behaved appropriately so that the (trivial) definition then could be offered.

Von Neumann's theory essentially ended the controversy over whether it was expected utility that should be maximized—although some bit continued in discussions of whether the underlying conditions on preference among probability mixtures should be satisfied, in discussions of the utility of gambling, and so on. Other writers were not in a position to say there is (a coherent notion of) utility, but that its expected value should not be maximized. The only coherent notion in the field was that defined and specified so as to fit the rule of maximizing expected utility, which rule thus flourished and won theoretical adherents. Other axiom systems for measurable utility were proposed which involved direct ordering judgments of differences (see Chapter 5 below, note 87); these left open the question whether it was the expected value of utility, thus measured, that was to be maximized in situations of risk.

When some other things are specified as goals on the basis of cognitive criteria, such as informativeness, and these somehow are measured so that numbers are assigned, it cannot be assumed that (in probabilistic situations) it is the expected value of these things that is to be maximized. Calling these other desirable things (cognitive or epistemic) utilities does not help. Since these "utilities" are specified independently of the von Neumann conditions and hence independently of the rule of maximizing expected utility, there is no reason to think this rule should be applied to these things. Since the question of the appropriate decision rule for these things is left completely open, the old controversies will return (along with some new ones).

The moral of this story is that though technical results can provide suggestive analogies elsewhere, when they are moved out of their home area they do not carry with them their support or authority, perhaps not even their meaning.

not-h, and was likely given h, we should, the principle said, conclude not-h was not true. However, if the guiding (rough) intuition is that the very unlikely is not happening, then we shouldn't conclude that not-h is false and therefore that h is true without first checking to see whether h also isn't very unlikely (in that it has a very low prior probability).

The revised principle of inference, then, is the following.

From prob (e, h) $\geq$ .95
prob (e, not-h) $\leq$ .05
e
$prob_0$ (h) > prob (e, not-h)
infer h

If $prob_0$ (h) is low, yet e has occurred, then something unlikely holds true, either e or h. It seems reasonable to conclude that h is true in this situation only when it is the lesser improbability, when it is more probable that h than that e given not-h.

This revised principle of inference gives some role to judgments of prior probability, as a constraint on when we can conclude that something with a low probability or plausibility is true. However, though the revised principle allows prior probabilities sometimes to block beliefs, it does not allow them a central role in giving rise to beliefs. It is a defect of Bayesian procedures that very high but uninformed prior probabilities will lead (when the evidence is not heavily against them) to high posterior degrees of belief. Our principle does allow prior probabilities to thwart believing what the evidence supports, but not to require believing what the evidence is neutral toward or opposes. The principle we have formulated, a sufficient condition for belief, makes evidence the central factor in producing belief.[83] It is some such principle, mirroring subjunctive tracking relations, that is an appropriate principle of inference.

However, I would not want to rest much on precisely what is sketched here. My departmental colleagues are meticulous intellects who instill in students the importance of mastering all the details whereof they speak; while I think it important for students also to learn how (and when) to *fake* things, to glide over topics with a plausible patina, trusting (fallible) intuitions that something like what they say, something of that sort, can be worked out—preferably by someone else. I agree, of course, that sometimes gliding over the

257

details shields one from seeing that one's general conception just cannot be worked out, and a very different one is needed. (I learned this lesson as a graduate student from C. G. Hempel, who did not glide over details.) On the other hand, often the details merely reinforce a picture, adding nothing of real philosophical interest. What then can one do but follow one's hunches? I mention this now, because of a special worry: while I think the general subjunctive picture of evidence is correct, and that some principle of inference embodying it is appropriate, I also believe that serious flaws may be uncovered in the particulars of the proposals here. It is many years since I have thought carefully about probabilistic inference, then along different lines than now, so I feel on very shaky ground in this section, suspecting that even points and details I previously knew might overturn things I say here.

We now need, I think, to introduce explicitly the alternative hypotheses $h_1, h_2 \ldots$ which fall under not-h, which might hold if h were false. One way would be to use the previous principle only when: there is no h_i that might be true if h were false that also satisfies the conditions of the principle, so that

prob $(e, h_i) \geq .95$
prob $(e, \text{not-}h_i) \leq .05$
$\text{prob}_0 (h_i) > \text{prob} (e, \text{not-}h_i)$.

More to the point is to add: and there is no h_i that might be true if h were false, that also is unexcluded by previous applications of the principle (that is, not-h_i hasn't already been concluded via the principle), such that prob $(e, h_i) < .05$. This is a stringent addendum: no other unexcluded h_i that might hold gives e a probability greater than .05. (But the path of weakening it ends at a Bayesian assignment of degrees of belief.)

In specifying the principle of inference, we have required that prob (e,h) be $\geq .95$, and that prob $(e, \text{not-}h)$ be $\leq .05$. This guarantees that the support of e for h, defined as the difference between the two conditional probabilities, is at least .9. Perhaps it is sufficient to require simply this, that support $(e, h) \geq .9$; this would allow prob (e, h) to dip below .95 toward .9 provided the prob $(e, \text{not-}h)$ dipped correspondingly.

When support $(e, h) \geq .9$, we have a situation which approximates (strong) tracking. So the method of inference (when the premisses all are made explicit, and hold true) gets us close to (strong) tracking. That prob (e, h) ≥ .95 is almost like 'h → e' (especially since we are imagining that some account of the probability of e given h is given that builds on the nature of subjunctive conditionals and is designed to approximate them); that prob (e, not-h) ≤ .05 is almost 'not-h → not-e'. Should we say that a person who infers h from e in such a situation knows that h is true (when h is true)? It seems to me more accurate to say—and why should we not?—that the person almost-knows. On the basis of the information about the tosses of the coin, or the properties of the sample, we do not know the coin or population has a certain specified other feature, as connected in the inference, but we almost-know it. In almost-knowing, our belief stands in a real, probabilistic connection to the fact, a connection that barely falls short of tracking. In failing only by a little to know, we succeed in something almost as good. Some problem cases the tracking account excluded, with discomfort, from knowledge now can get classified as almost-knowledge.

Let me say a brief word about how these very general considerations connect with current approaches to statistical theory. Our concept of evidence is a likelihood concept, based on the probabilities of the evidence on various hypotheses.[84] The principle of inference we formulate, a sufficient condition for believing h, uses this likelihood notion. We constrain the operation of this principle (as a sufficient condition) by the requirement that the prior probability of h be greater than the probability of e on not-h. Although this Bayesian consideration constrains our principle, we have not put forward a program of determining degrees of belief by application of Bayes Theorem, a process heavily dependent on the choice of prior probabilities; high prior probabilities cannot fix belief by themselves in the absence of sufficient empirical evidence.

The principle of inference takes as premises prob (e, h) ≥ .95; prob (e, not-h) ≤ .05. These probability values within the principle are meant to approximate the nonprobabilistic subjunctives h → e and not-h → not-e. How closely to zero and one these values are set is to some degree arbitrary; how close is a "good enough" approximation to the subjunctives? However, this degree of approximation is not part of a decision problem, to be fixed by various practical losses or gains. Though these numbers resemble the Neyman-Pearson values for errors and nonerrors,[85] their rationale as an approximation of the

EPISTEMOLOGY

nonprobabilistic evidential subjunctives is different. Still, external to the formulated principle of inference, we can ask what the probabilities are that it will be utilized to accept *h* when *h* is false (a type II error) or to fail to accept *h* when it is true (a type I error). Since our principle is a sufficient condition for belief, into which different evidence can be fed, the issue is more cloudy than it appears at first. With *h* fixed, what is the probability that some evidence or other *e'* will be found such that prob (e', h) ≥ .95, and so forth, while yet *h* is false? When a particular *e* is specified in advance, discussions of the likelihood relations need to distinguish *e* holds true, from *e* is found or known to be true but not as part of a test procedure wherein the character of *e* is fixed in advance, and from *e* is found to be true within such a specified test procedure. Each of these can have a different probability given *h* (or given not-*h*), and so the evidential likelihoods will depend on precisely which evidence it is.

Even if things about the type of evidence *e* are dovetailed correctly, we cannot conclude simply from the premiss within the inference (to *h*) that prob (e, not-h) ≤ .05, to the conclusion about this inference that it will have a probability of type II error (accepting *h* when it is false) of less than .05. The relevant question is not one about the probability given not-*h*, that this principle will lead to the acceptance of *h*. Rather, since *e* already has been found and *h* already has been accepted, the question is: given that *e* and that *h* has been accepted according to the principle, what is the probability that *h* is false, that not-*h* is true? The probability of type II error cannot be simply computed from the application of the principle of inference, without more precise knowledge of the prior probabilties (via Bayes Theorem).[86] Here the Neyman-Pearson theorist enters, saying we should not use a principle of inference unless its probabilities of type I and type II errors can be fixed at certain magnitudes.[87] And so on into the controversies of current statistics. My purpose is not to solve these controversies and issues, merely to show the relation of our notion of evidence to them—strong evidence avoids them altogether while being sufficient for tracking and knowledge, weak evidence (unfortunately) encounters them.* Probability numbers enter

* The tracking account of knowledge was formulated without having statistical errors in mind, but conditions 3 and 4 can be (roughly) put as: the person wouldn't commit a type II error about *p*, and he wouldn't commit a type I error about *p*. In contrast to Neyman-Pearson testing, our discussion of knowledge (though not the mere statement of the conditions, each of which

into the discussion in two places, within the premises as likelihoods, and in evaluations of the principle of inference as (estimates of) the probabilities of type I and type II errors. These numbers are not unconnected, but they have different rationales and play different roles.[88]

The Contingency of the Evidential Tie

The evidential connection is a subjunctive one, a real factual relationship which holds in the world. Whether or not e is evidence for h depends on what factual empirical connection holds between e and h. The dominant view on the evidential relation in the philosophical tradition, however, has held it is a logical connection, one which holds necessarily if it holds at all. Hilary Putnam has pointed out that such views (unrealistically) assume evidence is assessed relative to the best possible formulatable theory.[89]

Whether we hold e is evidence for h depends on what other theories we accept connecting e and h; we assess (whether something is) evidence for h against a background of theory, other beliefs, and so on. If relative to these other theories and beliefs that we accept, the relevant subjunctives (or probabilistic connections) hold between e and h, then we will hold that e is evidence for h. If later we discover that one of our background assumptions is false, so that the relevant subjunctive connections did not actually hold, we will say that e was not evidence for h after all, though we thought it was; just as when we later discover some p is false, we will say we didn't know that p, but only thought we knew it. This is not to say that there can never be evidence for something false. Perhaps e did arise from not-h, even though prob (e, h) is very much greater than prob (e, not-h), even though e is evidence for h. The fact upon which e's being evidence depends is not h's being true, but e's standing in a factual probabilistic relation to h (were it to hold), and also in one to not-h, of lesser magnitude. If we discover that (by our best later ac-

_____

was given equal weight as necessary conditions) seemed to make avoiding type II errors more crucial than avoiding type I errors, so that in their terminology, the power of a test should be fixed as high, and the level of significance minimized subject to that.

cepted theory) actually prob (e, h) ≤ prob (e, not-h), we will, in look-ing back, say that e was not evidence for h after all.

Granting that these factual probabilistic and subjunctive connec-tions between e and h are crucial to the evidential status of e, cannot we still treat 'evidence for' as a formal logical relation simply by making explicit the background beliefs and theories, by including them in? First, it is unclear whether those background theories will entail the subjunctives or probabilistic connections, but second, into where are they to be built? If into the evidence, added to e to form a new conjunction e', then this plays havoc with foundationalist hopes in epistemology, a major motive for the construction of formal induc-tive logics; while if the theory and other beliefs are to be added to the hypothesis, forming a new conjunctive hypothesis, it is difficult to see how such hypotheses will get supported by such meager evi-dence e. Still, perhaps these points can be handled by ingenious technical devices. The major objection to the program of formulating an inductive logic within which evidential relations are formal or logical or necessary still stands. The evidential relations really are factual and contingent; the point of making the background context and theories explicit would be to guarantee these factual connections hold. But this strategy will not work, for even if these connections do hold in the wider context, this context can be embedded in a still wider one that undercuts the subjunctive's holding, a context relative to which there are different factual probabilistic connections be-tween h and e.[90] This kind of contingency of the relevant evidential subjunctives is not adequately handled by the (at least) two relativi-ties already present within inductive logics: that probability is rela-tive to evidence, and that some principle of total evidence is to be utilized in applications of probability statements.

Other formalist attempts have been made, apart from inductive logic, to specify evidential relations, for example, that data e is evi-dence for what would explain e.[91] When the appropriate explanatory connection holds, the subjunctive ones also will, and it is on the latter that the evidential connection rests. There are many instances of an evidential connection without that explanatory one: seeing lightning is evidence that a sound of thunder will follow, though it is the former that explains the latter; seeing one of a disease's unique symptoms is evidence for the presence of another one, although nei-ther explains the other—each is explained by a third thing. I do not deny that explanatory connections somehow weave through the fabric of the subjunctive and probabilistic connections; although if there is some fundamental correlational law, irreducibly probabilistic, between the two features connected thereby there will be no explanatory link—yet each is evidence for the other. (Don't say the correlational law makes each the explanation of the other.)

Only if the factual subjunctive or probabilistic relations actually hold between e and h is e evidence for h; whether these do will not depend on formal features of e and h, but on what other truths hold, what specific deeper explanatory theories, and so on. But might there not be some very general contingent truths whose holding is sufficient to establish the requisite factual subjunctive or probabilistic connections between statements as specified on the basis of their formal features and relations; mightn't the general statement show (given it) that certain formally related statements also are factually related? It is as attempts at this that we should see Keynes' principle of limited variety, principles of the uniformity of nature, and other postulational or presuppositional approaches to induction.[92]

Is There Evidence for Skepticism?

Let us pause to note the relevance of this notion of evidence to skeptical hypotheses SK. The skeptic produces a hypothesis SK relative to which everything still would seem the same to us, including all of the evidential data e we have, our observations and so on. Is the sum total of this evidential data evidence for the skeptical hypothesis SK? It fits the skeptical hypothesis, for the skeptical hypothesis was designed to fit it. If the skeptical hypothesis were true, this data e (still) would hold:

(a) $SK \rightarrow e$.

However, this does not settle the question of whether e is evidence for SK, for perhaps e would or might hold even if SK did not. We need, that is, to consider whether

(b) $not\text{-}SK \rightarrow not\text{-}e$;

only if b holds will e be strong evidence that SK. Clearly, b does not hold, however; for one other thing that might hold if SK did not is the usual situation, the situation as we nonskeptics usually view it, and in this case e also would hold. There is no strong evidence for the skeptical hypothesis SK. Is there any weak evidence? Here, we have to consider whether

(b′) if SK were false, e might not hold; not-(not-SK → e);

and if b′ does hold, we must consider whether

prob (e, SK) − prob (e, not-SK) > 0.

The skeptic's alternative SK is specified so that prob (e, SK) = 1; but there is a similar nonskeptical alternative h specifiable (though not specifiable simply as not-SK) which might hold if SK did not, such that the probability of e given it also is 1. There is an asymmetry, however, for this alternative h might (indeed perhaps would) hold if SK did not, while SK *wouldn't* hold even if h did not.

Thus, assuming the subjunctives are as we think, there is not evidence for the skeptic's hypothesis SK, even though this hypothesis is in conformity with all the data and would yield it. But although there is no evidence for the skeptic's hypothesis SK, and there is evidence for h (since SK is not, we assume, something that might hold if h did not), still, we do not know not-SK. Our belief that not-SK does not track that fact, and we have no evidence that not-SK. (Such evidence would have to be something that wouldn't also hold if SK did; but SK leaves all our observations the same.) The subjunctively constituted notion of evidence, too, exhibits nonclosure under logical implication.[93]

Knowledge, Evidence, and Justification

In contrast to more traditional treatments of justification, some recent writing has held that a person's belief is justified if the method via which the person arrives at the belief is reliable, is likely to produce mostly true beliefs.[94] It is a delicate task to state adequately this probabilistic fact about the method M via which the belief is arrived at, to specify the propensity interpretation of probability or the appropriate narrow reference class.* However, our purpose is not to linger

---

* Which is the reference class of belief acquisitions within which the method is reliable and has a high proportion of successes? Not the class of actual belief acquisitions thus far, for an unreliable method may be accidentally lucky until now, or a reliable one unlucky so far; not the class of all possible belief acquisitions, for a method's reliability is unaffected by the

over the details, but to notice that this view of justification externalizes it, just as we already (in comparison to traditional epistemological writings) have externalized knowledge and evidence.

On this account, when a belief is arrived at by a method that usually (more than half the time) is right, or at least is likely to be right, the belief is probably true and the person is justified in holding it. More generally, one might say the person is justified to degree n in his belief if the method is reliable to degree n, having that probability of yielding the truth.

We shall follow the externalized treatment of justification as reliability, but without holding that some particular degree of reliability is either sufficient or necessary for the belief's being justified. Even if a method M_1 has a reliability with regard to p of greater than $\frac{1}{2}$, if it is not the most reliable method available to the person (with regard to the salient type of belief which p is) then the person is not justified in believing p. (I here omit considerations of cost; perhaps the other more reliable method takes much time and energy to apply.) To be justified in his belief, the person must reach it by the most reliable appropriate method. Second, if this method has a degree of reliability less than $\frac{1}{2}$, but still is more reliable than yet other methods, a person will be justified in believing on its basis. Scientific methods need not yield true theories more than half the time for us to be justified in believing their results—they just have to be better methods than anything else available to us.† (Notice that we

---

fact that it would frequently fail in situations that would not arise. Is the appropriate reference class those situations that might arise in the actual world, and how is this to be spelled out? Thus, there are problems in specifying the reference class, even apart from the difficult ones about delineating appropriate narrowness.

It might also be worth investigating a stronger notion of reliability, one wherein the application of a method reliably yields knowledge (tracking) rather than simply truth.

† Better for reaching narrowly specific beliefs; otherwise a more reliable method might be to believe not-p when scientific methods yield particular p's.

Consider also the case of newspaper stories. Every story about which I have had firsthand knowledge I have known to contain errors of fact. I believe therefore that almost every newspaper story does. Still, when I read a story, I believe each statement (and also the conjunction); I do not know which the falsehoods are, or in which direction the story is false, so, for lack of a better alternative for arriving at such beliefs, I believe the story as written.

have structured the notion of justification in the best instantiated realization mode.)

There was evolutionary selection for believing via particular methods when that was the best available, even if the reliability was less than ½; also, against believing by methods with reliability greater than ½ when even better are available. None of the rest of our discussion, though, will depend on this point that arising via the most reliable method is necessary and sufficient for a belief's being justified.

The reliability of a method is its probability of yielding true beliefs. A statement about reliability looks at the body of beliefs yielded and says something about the percentage which is true, rather, about the probability that each is true. Reliability is a connection between belief (by the method) and truth, in the direction from belief to truth: if belief (by the method) then probably true. This direction is opposite to the direction of tracking, of subjunctive conditions 3 and 4 which have truths in the antecedents and belief or lack of it (by the method) in the consequents. When tracking holds, if it is true (false) you would (not) believe it—when reliability holds, if it is believed (by the method) then it (probably) would be true. It is important to keep these directions distinct, as it is to be clear about the direction in assessing type I and type II errors. There is a distinction between the probability that a specified method gets you to believe p given that it is false, and the probability that p is false, given that a specified method has persuaded you to believe it. The first concerns whether the method approximates tracking, the second concerns its reliability. (Recall now the principle of inference we formulated, and consider the directions of the likelihood probabilities within the premises, and of the type II error evaluations about the mode of inference.)

Let us briefly consider some questions about the relationships among knowledge, evidence, and justification. Can one know without evidence? A person can believe without having inferred it from anything else; a person might wake up each morning with a belief about which horse will win a horse race that day.[95] If the subjunctives do hold, although we may not understand the mechanism whereby they do, he knows—and not by (even let us suppose unconscious) inference from evidence. Still, when a person knows that p there is a fact available to him that is evidence that p. For when he knows that p, his belief that p tracks the fact that p. Thus, the fact that he believes that p (a fact I assume is accessible to him) is strong evidence that p. Conditions 3 and 4 for tracking in our account of knowledge

not-$p \rightarrow$ S does not believe p

$p \rightarrow$ S believes p

are also the conditions for S's believing p being strong evidence that p. Hence, whenever someone knows that p, he "has" strong evidence that p, namely, the fact that he believes that p; but this will not be evidence *from* which he arrives at his belief. In the horse race example, knowing of his past history of successes, the person might use the fact that he has a belief as an indicator, as evidence on which he bases very strong confidence—which he did not have before— about which horse will win the race.

A person may believe that p on (weak) evidence that p without knowing that p. However, perhaps there is this connection between evidence and knowledge: though truly believing on (perhaps weak) evidence does not entail knowledge, it is evidence for knowledge. For it seems plausible that truly believing p on the basis of e which is evidence for p, itself stands in the subjunctive evidential relation to conditions 3 and 4 for tracking.

Justified true belief is not sufficient for knowledge (recall the Gettier examples); a true belief may be arrived at by a reliable method without the belief tracking the truth. What about the other direction —whenever someone knows that p will he also have a justified true belief that p? Not if a person can believe via a method that is highly unreliable (and less reliable than others available to him) yet which not only yields the truth that time but also tracks that one time. However, since tracking involves some generality to other (subjunctive) situations, it seems plausible that whenever a person knows, there will be some reliable submethod via which he knows. So it seems plausible that justified true belief is a necessary condition for knowledge; but I prefer to leave this question unsettled. A further relation is worth mentioning: although justified true belief is not sufficient for knowledge, it does seem to be evidence for knowledge, to stand in the evidential relation to the holding of the tracking conditions 3 and 4.

What of the relationship of evidence and justification—is believing something on the basis of evidence a reliable method, a method that yields justified belief? When the inferential method based upon evidence is the principle we put forth earlier, with prob (e, h) ≥ .95 and prob (e, not-h) ≤ .05, then when the prior probability of h is greater than .05, the posterior probability of h (on e) will be greater than $\frac{1}{2}$. But we cannot say that principle is reliable (to degree greater than $\frac{1}{2}$) when it accepts an h whose prior probability is greater than .05, for factual probabilities and subjective priors cannot be combined in this way.[96] However, according to our earlier view of justified belief as one based on the most reliable relevant method, the question is whether believing on evidence is the method most reliable.

Evidence for the Evidential Relation

We do have some evidence that believing on evidence is the most reliable method, namely, this method's past track record as compared to that of other methods we know. It is likely, though, that this inference itself yields the truth only if the method of belief on evidence is reliable—and that is the very statement which was in question. So isn't the procedure of supporting the conclusion that the method of evidence is reliable, by evidence (and so concluding this conclusion is more likely to be true than one arrived at by some other method), circular? We should not scorn such circularity; we certainly want a method that does support itself in this way rather than one that does not, but since many methods do, we cannot uniquely justify a method by its possession of this self-supporting property.[97] Clearly, we are about to become entwined in issues about inductive justifications of induction, inductive support for the reliability of inductive inferences.[96]

Let me emphasize that nothing about the views of knowledge or evidence we have presented depends upon how we treat these further issues of induction. To avoid drowning in the details, we shall keep our discussion at the most general level. In order not to tie our discussion to the particular subjunctive or probabilistic account of evidence we already have offered, let us write "eRh" for the evidential relationship, whatever it is, between evidence and hypothesis. When the correct theory of this relationship is discovered, it can be plugged into the following discussion.

The existence of evidence for a hypothesis shows something meritorious about the hypothesis, that it is true (in the case of strong evidence), or that it probably is true, or that it might be true, or whatever. Without specifying here what that meritorious feature of the hypothesis is, a task for a detailed theory, let us assume it has already been specified by some general statement

H: For all e and for all h, when e is true and eRh then . . .

where the statement continues describing some desirable feature of h.

One type of theory would continue the general statement with something entailed by the antecedent of the conditional, thereby making of H a logical or necessary truth. The facts that e and that eRh each would be empirical, and the statement H would spin out some necessary implication of these facts.

I am imagining something different: that the general statement H itself is a contingent statement. Perhaps the main 'if then' in H itself is subjunctive, perhaps a probability operator governs what follows the quantifiers, perhaps H concludes with a statement that h might be true, making H a negated subjunctive conditional. Whatever, the statement H is an empirical statement specifying what is good about evidence; it is logically possible that evidence does not have that good upshot for the hypothesis for which it is evidence.[99]

Of any such general theoretical statement about the merit of (hypotheses supported by) evidence, we can ask whether there is any evidence for it. Let us suppose there is some evidence for this general theory H, and let us call this evidence (for H) E. Since H is a general theory about evidence, it specifies the general evidential relationship 'R'—since E is evidence for H, E will stand in the evidential relationship R to H. If there is evidence E for a (correct) general theory H of evidence, then ERH. Like other facts of evidential connection, the fact that ERH is itself a real (subjunctive) fact holding in the world.

This raises the first issue of "circularity" we shall consider. An evidential relationship between evidence e and hypothesis h is a real fact in the world. That fact, like other facts, may depend upon something's holding true, and in particular it may depend upon the very hypothesis h which the evidence is evidence for, in that either the hypothesis h is the explanation of the holding of that particular evidential relation, of the fact that eRh, or at least if the hypothesis h

were not true the evidential relation wouldn't hold: not-h → not-(eRh). For some hypothesis it might even be true that the holding of all the evidential connections for that hypothesis depends upon the truth of the hypothesis. In particular, it might be that the evidence E for the most general theory of evidence H is such that the fact that it is evidence for H depends upon the truth of H, so that not-H → not-(ERH).

There is a difference worth noting between the evidential fact's being explained by the hypothesis (which the evidence is evidence for), and its depending on the truth of the hypothesis. Suppose there were a correct unified field theory U of everything. Any evidential fact eRh would be explained by the unified theory U and so therefore would the evidential fact eRU; but it does not follow that the evidential fact eRU would depend on U; it does not follow that not-U → not-(eRU). Even if U were false, whatever then was true might provide the background against which the subjunctives eRU would hold true (though U wouldn't hold and neither, probably, would e). To seek dependence of the evidential fact on the contained hypothesis, look to weaker hypotheses: the weaker the hypothesis, the stronger its denial and so the more likely that denial is to overturn evidential relations.

Clearly, there is one weak statement whose denial overturns all evidential relations, namely, the (existentially quantified) statement that something is evidence for something else:

W: There is an h and there is an e such that eRh.

Any evidence for the statement W, for there being evidence, will stand in the relation R to W, and its evidential status will depend upon the truth of W; if W were false, that (previous) evidence would not stand in the relation R to W.

This example is not perfect for our purposes. The existence of evidence for W entails the truth of W, since W says simply that something is evidence for something else; so the falsity of W entails the falsity of anything's standing in R to W. We want, instead, an example of a hypothesis where something's—or better, anything's—being evidence for the hypothesis depends subjunctively (but not logically) on the truth of the hypothesis.[100] Since this subjunctive dependence of the evidential relationship on the truth of the hypothesis is factual (and not a matter of entailment), we cannot easily generate an example. But the following question is an interesting one for the theory of evidence: are there any statements upon whose truth all evidential connections subjunctively (but not logically) depend, in that if they were false, nothing would be evidence for anything else?[101]

Let us return to the general hypothesis H about the desirable feature any hypothesis has when some true evidence E stands in the evidential relation R to that hypothesis; and let us return to the evidence E for H. It is unlikely, I think—but in any case not troubling—for the fact that ERH to depend upon the full strength of H. It may depend upon the truth of an instance of H, on some true factual instantiation of H to the effect that when e_1Rh_1 and e_1 hold true then h_1 has some desirable feature. But this is unobjectionable.

It is all very well that some true E stands in the evidential relation R to H—a proponent of H would have it no other way—but what does this tell us about H? Here looms the more serious issue of circularity.

If H is true, then when some true E stands in R to H, H will have the desirable feature it speaks of, one that (it says) every evidentially supported hypothesis has. This feature, it seems, can at best be 'truth'; it may also be 'probably true' or 'might be true' or some such thing. If the full strength of the general H holds true, which speaks of all evidence and all hypotheses, then this particular instance of it will hold also:

I: if E is true and ERH then H has some desirable feature.

We do not, however, seem to be gaining any ground by starting with the assumption that H is true, deducing the instance I, adding the facts that E and that ERH, and finally, after all this, concluding that H has some desirable feature which at best is 'truth' and may well be something worse such as 'probable truth' or 'might be true'. Starting with the assumption that H is true, we get round again, at best, to the conclusion that H is true—not much of a gain. (Still, it is good that not so much ground was lost, and we did not reach the conclusion that H was (probably) false.)

However, this conclusion does not depend upon the truth of the full strength of H; it depends only on the instance I. The fact that E and that ERH bestows some desirable feature on H only if I is true. But if the instance I can hold true even though the full strength of H does not, if not-(not-H → not-I), then the conclusion on the basis of

E that H has some desirable property need not depend on assuming the truth of H.

Consider now someone who wonders (aloud) whether H is true, and is presented with the evidence E for H. Let us suppose for now that this person does not doubt that E, or that ERH. His question was why he should believe that the evidential relation R is worth anything, why believe it bestows a desirable feature on what is R-supported. Must it be that presenting him with evidence E begs the question, begs his question?

Recall our earlier discussion of 'begging the question', according to which a premiss from which a conclusion is to be inferred begs the question if the person would not believe the premiss unless he (already?) believed the conclusion. Let us (properly) extend the notion: an argument, presenting of evidence and so forth, begs the question for a person not only if he wouldn't accept (one of) the premisses if he didn't accept the conclusion, but also if he wouldn't make (embark on) that move from those premisses to the conclusion unless he (already?) accepted the conclusion. If this presentation of evidence E begged the question about H, it would do so in the latter way: someone would not move from E to concluding that H had some desirable feature unless he (already) accepted H.

However, we have seen that the move from E to the conclusion about the desirable feature of H doesn't depend on (and need not presuppose) the (full) truth of H, only H's weaker instance I. Starting with that weaker instance, and given E, one can reach the conclusion about H. This will beg the question for the person only if he wouldn't accept I or inferentially move in accordance with it, unless he (already) accepted H. This need not be the case, for he might accept (the weaker) I without yet accepting (the full) H. So it need not beg the question for him. Since the proffering of evidence E for H will not beg the question for everyone, it is not circular.

We now see an important ambiguity in the person's wondering about H; he might be wondering whether the evidential relation R always (as H claims) bestows some desirable feature on an R-supported hypothesis, or he might be wondering whether it ever does. In the second case his wondering would extend to all instances of H, including the instance I; but in the first case it would not, and so the proffering of evidence E (whose truth is not guaranteed merely because the conditional I holds) can answer the question without begging it. Furthermore, a person who begins without accepting I, but who doesn't wonder whether the evidential relation R *ever* bestows some desirable feature on a hypothesis, might be brought to accept I by some evidence e_I for it. His acceptance of the following (instance of H)

if e_I is true and e_IRI then I has . . . (some desirable feature)

does not depend on his already accepting I, or already accepting H. Thereby, he might be brought to accept I on the basis of e_I, and then H on the basis of E. He can "bootstrap" his way up the line.

Suppose, however, the person in wondering about H is wondering whether it ever is true, whether it is not rotten to the core so that all of its instances are false. For such a person, any evidence for H would beg the question, and he cannot be brought to accept H by a bootstrapping series of evidential (of R-evidential) steps. This person wonders whether H has any true instances; he wonders whether

S: there is an *e* and an *h* such that if *e* were true and eRh then *h* would have . . . (some desirable feature).

If any evidence is to support S and bestow some desirable feature on it, then that fact of evidential support and bestowal will depend (logically) upon the truth of S. If S were false, then no evidence could bestow anything on S, or on any other hypothesis—the falsity of S entails that nothing good ever is bestowed by evidence. (Compare S to the earlier statement W which said that something stands in the evidential relation R to something else.)

It is not surprising that any evidence for S, for the existence of some evidential bestowal sometime, would beg the question. No one who thought there was never such bestowal would be moved to accept S by something that purported to bestow upon S.[102] No evidence can be produced for S without begging the question because S has been devised to just this effect. From this, though, it does not follow that evidence cannot be produced for other things, including H, without begging the question; as indeed it does not follow that there isn't any evidence for S itself that bestows some desirable feature on it—although, to be sure, that person will not recognize the bestowal. Still, though S was devised in order to reach the result about begging the question, it is of interest that there is some statement for which the result can be reached, a statement as fundamental as one that holds the general evidential relation sometimes bestows something desirable.

Consider now the question of whether we know that S is true, that the (empirical) evidential relations sometimes are worth something. Suppose we believe S via a method which utilizes evidence and applies our belief that the evidential relation sometimes bestows something desirable upon a hypothesis. Even if accepting S so infuses our lives that no talk of a delineated method is appropriate, it yet might be the case that if S were false, we still would accept S (whether by a delineated method or not). Then the third condition for knowledge, the tracking condition not-p → not-(S believes that p), is not satisfied, and we do not know that S. However, it doesn't follow that we do not know of a particular pair (e, h) that if eRh then e bestows on h, or simply that a particular e bestows some feature on a particular h. For if it did not, that would not be because S was false, but because in particular not-(eRh); the first subjunctive alternative to e's bestowal on h is a specification of not-(eRh)—it isn't not-S.

But cannot we infer the existentially quantified statement S, evidence sometimes bestows, from a particular case where we know it does? This inference will preserve knowledge (we have seen) only if our belief in the premises tracks the truth of the conclusion. So if we don't know the existentially quantified statement S, if we don't know that evidence bestows some desirable feature, this must be because if evidence didn't, things would be the same as they are now, or at least similar enough so that we still and nonetheless would believe S and the particular case as well. But it is highly unlikely that if evidence didn't bestow this desirable feature, the past would seem the same to us or that we, who base belief on the evidential relation R (and are descended from those who did), would be here at all.

The relevant record of the past, such as it is, fits the view H that the evidential relation R bestows some desirable feature, but does it support that view, is it evidence for it? Only if the appropriate subjunctive or probabilistic connections hold between the past record and H. Is prob (past record, H) > prob (past record, not-H)? One would think so. The probability of the past successes when basing belief on evidence is greater given H than it is given not-H. (Still, the successes are limited, and so the feature bestowed also must be limited.) Of course, there is a hypothesis h_{SK} that says the evidential relation R used to bestow, but will not any longer; and this hypothesis also fits the past record, the past record fits it. But is this h_{SK} something that (actually) would or might hold if H did not? If not, it is not a first subjunctive alternative to H, and so the past record is evidence for H; similarly, the past record is not evidence for h_{SK}.

How can the past record show any connection between the evidential relation R and the bestowal of some desirable feature? One of the things to be connected (to bestowal) is the evidential relation holding between h and e, either the relevant subjunctives or the probability inequality. But where do we find these subjunctives or probabilities in the record? Even high correlations in the past do not show probabilistic connections; the probabilities could be very different (or completely nonexistent), the observed relative frequency just an accident. So evidential connections are used to get to beliefs about the probabilities. People made inferences from fact e along with subjunctives or probabilistic inequalities which they thought held, on the basis of other theories they accepted or presupposed— but how did they arrive at these, what evidence did they have for them?

The contingent empirical character of the evidential relation has already been emphasized. We think evidential connections hold when we think the relevant subjunctives or probabilities do, and we will think this on the basis of other beliefs or presuppositions. (Compare the role in the statistician's practice of the theory of probability and the model of the experiment.) For many of these other beliefs we also will have evidence, that is, know facts related by the evidential relation R to these other beliefs, according to yet further beliefs, presuppositions, and components of a general picture of the world. Our task, fortunately, is not one of providing foundations for knowledge, of showing how all of our knowledge can be built up by the principle of inference out of known evidence that supports it (and is known to do so). We simply are delineating the place of evidence within the fabric of our knowledge, not underneath it.

How the Regress Stops

When e is evidence for h, eRh; if the person also has evidence for this, for e's being evidence for h, then he knows an e' such that $e'R(eRh)$.[103] This further statement itself is contingent and he will have evidence for it only if he knows an e'' that stands in R to it. We seem embarked on a regress of evidence for something's being evidence. Since our task is not to provide foundations for knowledge, it is no worry if some evidential connection holds but is left dangling in that the person has no evidence for it. Still, it is worth looking to see how the regress might (in principle) stop.

The evidential connection R is contingent; the evidence e' for eRh will stand in R to the fact that eRh, and the evidence e'' will stand in R to the fact that e'R(eRh), and so on. There is no necessity, I think, that this be different evidence each time. The regress can be brought to a halt if there is reached some evidence which is evidence for two contingent statements: a particular statement, and also the statement that this evidence stands in R to that particular statement. Thus, suppose eRh, and also e'R(eRh). If it also is the case that e'R[e'R(eRh)], then the regress is brought to an end. Some evidence e' is subjunctively or probabilistically related (by R) to two facts, first the fact eRh, and second the fact e'R(eRh). The regress would be stopped even earlier if for some h, not itself about R holding, the evidence e for h (so that eRh) also stands in R to eRh—so that eR(eRh). What stops the regress is evidence that does double duty, being evidence for something while also being evidence that it *is* evidence for that thing. Indeed, what is needed to stop the regress is something which does n-tuple duty all the way up the line—evidence for something which also is evidence for its being evidence, and is evidence for its being evidence for its being evidence, and so on.

Compare Lewis Carroll's problem about Achilles and the Tortoise.[104] Here, the tortoise accepts

(1) If p then q
(2) p

but from these does not accept or infer q, claiming that to infer q he must first accept

(3) If (if p then q) and p, then q.

This additional premiss (3) is: if 1 and 2 then q. Still he balks at q, saying he will not (be forced to) infer q unless he also accepts

(4) If 1 and 2 and 3 then q.

Yet still he is not forced to infer (accept) q, he says, unless he accepts

(5) If 1 and 2 and 3 and 4 then q.

And so on.

What stops the regress? Some views do not let it begin, claiming that to write 3 down as a needed premiss confuses premisses with principles of inference; other views let it begin and cannot stop it. Our third position holds that the regress stops when a premiss is introduced which is of the same form (and which would license all the inferences) as the further premisses that apparently have to be introduced. Thus, 3 does get written down as a premiss, but 4 need not be, being merely an instance of 3. Note that the introduced premiss must incorporate as instances not only the next one to be introduced as the apparent regress proceeds, but all future ones as well. (This position on the regress must ignore Wittgenstein's problems, discussed in Chapter 2 above, about what fixes how statements apply: what fixes it that premiss 3 is to be applied so as to cover all instances of 4 as well; what fixes the meaning of 3 so that the application under 4 must be included?)

The regress is stopped when there is a general premiss P_G such that

   (a) the inference to the conclusion q from the other premisses P falls under it,

and also

   (b) the inference to the conclusion q from premisses P & P_G falls under it.

The Lewis Carroll regress is stopped when there is a premiss that does double (really, n-tuple) duty; similarly, the regress of evidence is stopped when there is evidence that does double (n-tuple) duty.

Consider now the general theory H, of bestowal of a desirable feature by the evidential relation R. We have supposed there is evidence E for H which bestows on H (in accordance with the instance I of H); so ERH. What is the evidence that ERH? Perhaps none is available to us, perhaps it is another E′, but if the regress is to stop, and stop here (rather than only stopping later, at a higher level) then it also will be the case that ER(ERH).

Recall now the earlier issue of whether producing the evidence E for H begs the question. It is not that the person would not have any evidence that E is evidence for H unless he first or already had evidence that H. If E does double duty, it does its duties simultaneously; the person has evidence both that H and that his evidence is evidence that H in one fell swoop.

When H is a correct general theory of evidence, then any evidence E for it will instantiate it; and if the regress of evidence is to stop there, the evidence E for it also will be evidence for its being evidence. These are not undesirable circles; rather, this structure holds when evidence has the highest degree of evidential grounding, when not only is it true that the factual evidential relations bestow, but there is evidence that they do—all the way down the line.

Remarks similar to these on evidence apply to justification, too. We want the most general principle of justification J, whatever it is, to be justified in a way that is an instance of J; we want the statement that something justifies J itself to be justified, and so forth—and we want there to be no regress. We want to find a principle of justification like this; perhaps some will not rest content until they find one. It will not do, then, if one is found, to thereupon proclaim a crisis for philosophy because the principle of justification itself cannot be (noncircularly) justified.

Let us recall what we said in the previous chapter, in reference to fundamental explanatory principles. One central task of philosophy is to uncover and delineate the fundamental general evidential and justificatory principles (perhaps also explanatory ones) that underlie (and explain) the more limited ones. One goal of philosophy should be to uncover these. Perhaps it cannot be shown that specific principles are fundamental, but a sign that they are (a fallible sign, to be sure) is that they fall under themselves, as instances, and they subsume other things standing in the relevant relation (evidential or justificatory), including to themselves. Note that this self-subsumption is a mark not of truth (quite false principles can exhibit it) but of fundamentality.

Philosophers usually are discouraged when they investigate what underlies a truth or principle (whether as evidence, justification, or explanation) and find that very same principle reappearing in the course of their investigation. When our focus is narrow, or upon derivative principles, we want the investigation to lead to different (and deeper) principles. Looking at the overall structure, however, we seek just such "circles". It is not surprising that some features objectionable in intermediate connecting links within a structure might be desirable in fundamental principles that underlie the whole structure. Local vices, global virtues. It is desired that there be principles which underlie and yield the rest, which subsume themselves and so do not dangle or lead to infinite regress. The discovering and uncovering of such fundamental truths is not a crisis or trauma for philosophy, but a triumph. Would it be better if there were not such truths, or if they were not found? (Does our uneasiness with this view of what constitutes a success for philosophy stem from long, and misguided, training in seeing things differently?)

Note that though something may be fundamental in one type of structure, it need not be in all others. A fundamental evidential principle needn't be a fundamental explanatory one, and so it can have some other ("noncircular") explanation; while a fundamental explanatory principle needn't be a fundamental evidential one, so it can be supported by "noncircular" evidence. In the different realms, evidential, justificatory, and explanatory, the same facts or statements can stand in different relations, orders, connections. Something might be fundamental, then, only in one aspect; even the true fundamental principles that apply to and yield themselves need not stand as utterly ultimate, unyielded and primary in every way. (What might a unified philosophical theory look like, which held that one principle was fundamental in all—important?—realms?)

Perhaps we will not succeed in discovering fundamental evidential (or justificatory) principles. The regress might be blocked only at some high level, beyond our capacity to examine, or perhaps it is not blocked at all. The evidential relation R is a factual relation, and the general evidential principle H is a contingent principle; whether the regress is blocked (and if so at what level) depends on what the facts actually are. There are even more complicated possibilities, variants of omega-inconsistency, for example. It might be that the evidential relation R is such that the regress is stopped for all true particular statements eRh, and for every instantiation, but not for the statement H itself of a general evidential principle. Also, since the evidential relation R is a real relation in the world, it seems possible for some e to stand in that relation to a statement h, even to a general theory H of the evidence relation, without e or any statement we know standing in that relation to the fact that e stands in R to h (or to H). This resembles the situation with the tracking relation

—a real relation in the world; it is possible to track some fact f without tracking the fact that you track it. You can know that p without knowing that you know that p, and you can have evidence that h (or that evidence bestows) without having evidence that you so have evidence. In pointing out how the regress might be blocked, I do not mean to say that it is blocked, or that unless it is blocked (either in the case of a particular e and h, or the general theory H) we don't have any evidence at all.

We might transform the problem of justifying induction into the following: given the evidential relation R, or the justificatory relation, and given the fundamental evidential principle H, or the fundamental justificatory one, show that the regress is stopped. Perhaps the formal properties of these relations and principles suffice to determine whether the regress is ended or not. But since the evidence and justificatory relations are real factual (subjunctive) relations, and since the principles hold contingently, it may well be an empirical question which possibility holds—whether the regress is stopped at a low level, a high one, or not at all. Under this construal of the problem, whether or not induction can be justified may be an empirical question. To be sure, one cannot begin to answer this question without specifying precisely the evidential and justificatory relations and principles, something we have not done. Even so, simply presenting the view of evidential relations and principles as factual and contingent, and proceeding explicitly within a global framework, has the beneficial effect, I think, of transforming some traditionally obdurate questions, giving them a fresh look.

Knowing Inside Out

The account we have offered treats knowledge as a real subjunctive relation in the world, tracking, and it treats evidence as a real factual (subjunctive or probabilistic) relation in the world. Moreover, we have referred to an account of justification as the factual (dispositional) reliability of the method via which something is believed. These accounts are all external; what has become of epistemology, the subject which treats how, as things appear from the inside, a person builds up his body of knowledge?[105] About each such external fact, concerning the tracking or reliability or evidential connection of our belief, it is logically possible that we could be mistaken; we could think the fact holds when it does not really, and it could hold when we don't think so. So we seem as distant from these facts of tracking, reliability, and evidential connection, as we were from the fact that p. Knowledge was supposed to connect us closely with the fact that p, yet apparently it turns out that the connections of knowledge (tracking, reliability, evidence) are no clearer to us than p was. What we want is some connection with the fact that p that links it all the way to us, all the way to us on the inside. Given the skeptical arguments, it seems that nothing else could show us that we know. (Did he not show me his new baseball glove, because the glove was *out there*?)

These notions of 'inside' and 'external' are unclear but evocative. We might describe an internalist, more precisely, as someone who believes that if q is (known to be) entailed by S's knowing that p, and if S does know that p, then S knows that q also. If the internalist is right, we know each and every precondition of our knowing—whenever we know we also know that we know, and so on. Notice that so delineated, internalism goes beyond the condition of deductive-closure extensively discussed earlier; under internalism not only does the person who knows that p know every consequence (known to be one) of p, he also knows every consequence (known to be one) of knowing p.

Let us not, however, overemphasize the externality of our accounts. It is your belief that is connected by the tracking relation to the facts; moreover, when a method shows an inner face, tracking via the method depends on what would happen in other situations identical in inner cues. And the notion of justification (in contrast to that of tracking) starts from the belief end and works toward the facts.

Still, although the (external) fact that p is linked to us, even to something internal (such as belief might be), the connecting link itself is external to us. So this linkage is out of our (let us say) ken; even if we have a belief about this linkage which tracks it, *that* tracking linkage is out of our ken.

How could things be otherwise? If there is an external fact to which we are linked, then eventually the linkage must turn external. (Or else there must be an external gap between the end of the connecting link and the fact—but then are we linked to *it*?) You can't get there from here, by staying here. And it is certainly there that we want to get; when various philosophical reductionisms (such as Berkeley's and phenomenalism) make there a version of here, we say they have not gotten us to where we want to be, to an external reality that exists independently of us. Neither do we want the gap closed by the externalization of ourselves, omitting reflexive self-consciousness, so that we were there all the time.

Any theory of knowledge that succeeds in connecting us with some external fact (we know) will make some part of the linkage external. Different theories may draw the boundary in different places, but each will countenance some externality—this in virtue of not flaws in us as connectors but the character of that to which we are to be connected. The transition to externality may be camouflaged, there may be internal glimmerings of the closest external portion, but (at least part of) the linkage between these internal glimmerings and the external portion itself will be external. Even if some internal item said of itself that it was connected with something external, there would be the question (marking a gap) of whether it was—unless the saying made it so. (A performative account of externality seems unpromising, but could one be offered of the epistemological connection itself?) The solipsist who is happy in his solipsism will face an opposite predicament, worrying that perhaps it happens that he *is* linked externally. Can anything internal show him he is not?

Perhaps it is the narrowness of the tracking relation that makes externality seem so salient. If belief varied with the fact across a wider range of possible situations than the tracking subjunctives specify, would our connection to the fact seem closer? If it varied with the fact in all possible worlds, would it be close enough? Or would we need also to believe in this wider or complete variation, and also to have that belief widely or completely vary with its truth, and so forth?

Yet if we had that complete linkage, would it be with something external? When something is external, isn't there a gap between us and it, and so room for something (else) to intervene and prevent complete covariation across all possible situations between it and, say, our belief? And is this lack of complete and universal covariation a consequence of externality, involving (as it does) a gap, or is it a defining feature of externality? Is something external in virtue of its lack of universal covariation?[106] Still, though we want some failure of covariation, we might prefer that our beliefs covaried far more widely with the facts than is specified by the tracking subjunctives.[107] Yet this would not check or satisfy the internalist desire of the epistemologist, who insists on having his external reality and eating it too. We shall see the tension between external connection and internality (of one sort or another) recur as a theme in various contexts. For now, let us turn to examine the value of the particular delimited relation of tracking.

What's So Special about Knowledge?

Our account of knowledge places it somewhere between true belief and a belief that p which covaries with p in all possible situations, all logically possible worlds. There are other alternatives: for example, the two notions we glanced at earlier, know* and know^, which made knowledge closed under known logical implication. What is important about knowledge as we have explained it? Why are the contours of an important notion delineated precisely there?

The first question does not concern the geometric contour of the figure of knowledge in the space of possible worlds, but its size. Among all the similarly contoured figures of different sizes, why is knowledge that one which goes with subjunctive connections, rather than one somewhat larger or somewhat smaller? Once we have the notion of a belief's varying with or being sensitive to the truth-value of what is believed, we see there are differing degrees of such sensitivity or covariation. (The skeptic demands absolute sensitivity.) What rationale picks out precisely that degree of sensitivity possessed by the subjunctive notion? Second, we can ask what is so special, among the different notions expressible via subjunctive conditions, about our notion of tracking? Given that knowledge will be (of the dimensions of) a subjunctive notion, why is it that particular subjunctive notion?

Let us begin by asking what is wrong with or defective about mere true belief. Perhaps some function of belief is not served by merely true belief; however, for our purposes now, we need not suppose anything is wrong with merely true belief. The problem is: how are people in a diverse and changing world to reach the state of having (merely) true beliefs? Imagine yourself in the position of God wanting to create organisms who would have (merely) true beliefs in a diverse and changing world. The ways to accomplish this are to: (a) constantly intervene: start them with true beliefs and intervene to change their beliefs each time the world changes; (b) determine what the whole future will be, and create each being with a preprogrammed sequence of beliefs to fit his changing situation in a preestablished harmony; (c) create beings able to detect changes in facts, who will change their beliefs accordingly. It is unnecessary to create beings able to detect all possible facts or changes. Their detection capabilities need only detect the facts that will obtain, the changes of fact that will occur.

Next, consider how true beliefs fare under the evolutionary process. Not all organisms will have beliefs or the cognitive equipment beliefs involve, but some will. We may suppose that possessing the biological preconditions of belief has been an adaptive advantage, connected with the advantages of having true beliefs. There would be evolutionary selection for better capabilities to detect facts and to have true beliefs, including theoretical beliefs. Not every false belief leads to extinction before the age of child-bearing or rearing; but the better belief capacities and capabilities give an advantage. Here, betterness of capacity (presumably) is some function of the ratio of true beliefs to total number of beliefs, weighted by the importance of the beliefs (individually or by type?) to survival and to the bearing and rearing of progeny. Some sacrifice in the total ratio of true beliefs would occur to achieve a higher ratio of important true beliefs; specialization of belief capabilities would occur to fit the contingencies of the environments the organism occupies.

Each environment includes a range of variation of situations, a probability distribution over situations, to which the organism must adapt its behavior; over time, what range of variation environments include also can change. A population will not continue without sufficient genetic heterogeneity to contain or produce organisms adapted to the new range of variation. However, capabilities suitable for much beyond the range of variation would constitute a significant energetic cost.

Our belief capabilities are more supple than our perceptual ones— we can believe what we do not perceive, and can disbelieve the evidence of our senses. Also, our perceptual capacities damp down some changes, as in object constancy. It is unclear whether these belief capacities and capabilities are supple enough to arrive eventually at some truths in any world, no matter what it is like,* but even if so, clearly some different mechanism of belief (at least in its details) would serve more efficiently in some other worlds (just as a different world would be suited best by different Carnapian c-functions). We can imagine that changes in environments lead to the evolution of new types of belief mechanisms which replace previous ones, and that this will happen also to the ones we now have—they, and we, will become obsolete.[108]

The evolutionary process can give organisms true beliefs (in a changing world) only by giving them the capability to have true beliefs: so, it will give them more than (merely) true beliefs. In giving them a capability for true beliefs, it makes their beliefs (sometimes) vary somehow with the truth of what is believed; it makes their beliefs somehow sensitive to the facts. However, the evolutionary process will not bestow upon them a capability for true beliefs so powerful that in no logically possible situation would their beliefs be mistaken. Even if such a capacity could arise by random mutation (and even if it did not have greater energetic requirements so that there would be selection against it), there would not be strong selection for it; there would be no selection against those other organisms whose lesser capacities function just as well in the actual range of situations.† A being with (some of) God's traits could arise (and be maintained) by an evolutionary process only in a very tough environment.

Thus, the belief capability instilled by the evolutionary process will yield beliefs of status intermediate between a belief that (merely) is true in the actual world, and a belief that varies with the

---

* Consider a counter-rational world which frustrates rational belief formation there, in that when sufficient evidence has been presented to lead us to conclude h, not-h then starts being true. Each pattern changes at precisely the time it becomes rational to (tentatively) believe it holds. Finally, incredible as it seemed at first, it becomes rational to believe

D: There is a preestablished disharmony under which at the time it becomes rational to tentatively accept any hypothesis h, h starts being false.

What happens at the time when it becomes rational to believe D, if the disharmony is so thoroughgoing that D applies to itself?

† So there is a puzzle about the oft-repeated remark that we make use of only a fraction of our brain's capacity. Of what adaptive advantage was such excess capacity, and why (especially given the disadvantage of its greater energetic requirements) was it selected for in the process of evolution?

truth in all possible worlds. It will instill a capability that works well enough in the range of actual situations that occurred in the evolutionary history of the organism; and the crudity of "technology" may leave it not just precisely specialized only for these. Similarly, our belief capacities may compromise getting things exactly right in order to widen the range within we get things roughly right, thereby improving our functioning in more actual situations—as well as in a wider range of changed ones that might occur.[109]

This appears within shouting distance of "the situations that would or might arise", and so locates us not impossibly far from our account of knowledge. However, evolutionary considerations at this high level of generality will not converge precisely to only that account. It would be interesting to investigate the question of what type of variation of belief with the truth, what type of sensitivity of belief to fact, would be predicted solely on the basis of evolutionary theory; rather, what (according to evolutionary theory) would be the optimum type of variation or sensitivity? There is some reason to think such an investigation within evolutionary theory would end reasonably close to our account of knowledge. It seems plausible that the notion of tracking will have its analogue in an account of 'perceiving that p', that analogues of the subjunctive conditions 3 and 4 will fit such perception. Since the evolutionary process did lead to our perceptual capacities and those of lower organisms, it seems that something like tracking, something like 3 and 4, is of the right magnitude, the right degree of strength, to be yielded by the evolutionary process—for it was yielded by that process as it produced perceptual capabilities. Therefore, it seems plausible to suppose tracking might be yielded for belief-capabilities as well. I do not mean merely: knowledge exists, so it must have been produced by evolution. That remark could not help to answer or illuminate the question of why the boundaries marked off by our account of knowledge are important, why something of the order of magnitude of tracking is important. However, to say "knowledge, that is, something of the order of magnitude of tracking, is what (on theoretical grounds we should expect) evolution would produce" *is* an illuminating answer—or rather, it would be one if detailed investigation could show it was true.

Although it hardly has been hidden thus far, let us close this chapter by recapitulating explicitly the explanation we are offering of how knowledge is possible. The explanatory hypothesis, which reconciles the existence of knowledge with the possibilities the skeptic points out, holds that we have, and often exercise, the capacity to track facts; this hypothesis is plausible on evolutionary grounds. The skeptic is correct that we do not track some particular things, such as the facts that not-SK. However, we do track many others. It is for empirical science to investigate the details of the mechanisms whereby we track, and for methodologists to devise and refine even better (inferential) mechanisms and methods. But the mere existential hypothesis that we (often) do track (by some means or other), that we do satisfy the subjunctive conditions 3 and 4, is sufficient to reconcile the skeptic's logical possibilities with our possessing knowledge (not all we previously thought we had, though) and thereby to explain how knowledge is possible. This is not a proof that we have knowledge—it would not (nor is it designed to) convince the skeptic. He will not accept the statement that we do track, he will ask whether we know we do, how we know we do, whether we could not be mistaken, and so on.

However, the hypothesis that we track, while unacceptable to the skeptic, helps us with our own explanatory task of explaining how knowledge is possible. The nonclosure of tracking (under known logical implication) enables us to meet the skeptic (partly) on his own ground, while standing (mostly) on our own.

It may seem quite unexciting—too paltry to be worth the bother—to say that what we do is track facts. (Though it is not trivial to find something which handles cases correctly, including problem cases, fits in with evolutionary considerations, and illuminates the issue of skepticism.) We would prefer a theory of knowledge that specified procedures to determine whether or not any particular case *is* a case of knowledge. However, not every account of a notion specifies such procedures to decide its application; not every notion is recursive or even recursively enumerable. Although the view of knowledge as tracking does not tell us how to find out whether a particular belief that p is knowledge, it does illuminate the pattern and structure of knowledge.[110] I find the account of knowledge as tracking illuminates and explains how knowledge is possible—something I did not understand before (though I didn't doubt that it was possible or, indeed, actual). Knowledge is a real relationship to the facts, subjunctively contoured. That we have this type of real connection to reality, instanced in this case by beliefs tracking truth but holding, somewhat differently, for other cases too, is a fact of great interest we shall explore later as we consider the modes, knowledge being just one, of our connecting to reality.

VALUE

Chapter

Four

FREE WILL

Philosophers often treat the topic of free will as a problem about punishment and responsibility: how can we punish someone or hold him responsible for an action if his doing it was causally determined, eventually by factors originating before his birth, and hence outside his control? However, my interest in the question of free will does not stem from wanting to be able legitimately to punish others, to hold them responsible, or even to be held responsible myself.

Without free will, we seem diminished, merely the playthings of external forces. How, then, can we maintain an exalted view of ourselves? Determinism seems to undercut human dignity, it seems to undermine our value.

Our concern is to formulate a view of how we (sometimes) act so that if we act that way our value is not threatened, our stature is not diminished. The philosophical discussion focusing upon issues of punishment and responsibility, therefore, strikes one as askew, as concerned with a side issue, although admittedly an important one.

The task is to formulate a conception of human action that leaves agents valuable; but what is the problem? First, that determinism seems incompatible with such a conception; if our actions stem from causes before our birth, then we are not the originators of our acts and so are less valuable. (We shall look later at what assumptions about value underlie this reasoning.) There is an incompatibility or at least a tension between free will and determinism, raising the question: given that our actions are causally determined, how is free will possible?

Some would deny what this question accepts as given, and save free will by denying determinism of (some) actions. Yet if an uncaused action is a random happening, then this no more comports with human value than does determinism. Random acts and caused acts alike seem to leave us not as the valuable originators of action but as an arena, a place where things happen, whether through earlier causes or spontaneously.

Clearly, if our actions were random, like the time of radioactive decay of uranium 238 emitting an alpha particle, their being thus undetermined would be insufficient to ground human value or provide a basis for responsibility and punishment. Even the denier of determinism therefore needs to produce a positive account of free action. On his view, a free action is an undetermined one with something more. The problem is to produce a coherent account of that something more. Once that account is formulated, we might find it does all the work, and that it is compatible with determinism and sufficient for our value purposes; in that case, the something more would become the whole of the account of free will.

How is free will possible? Given the tension between causal determination and randomness on the one hand, and valuable agenthood on the other, how is valuable agenthood possible? The problem is so intractable, so resistant to illuminating solution, that we shall have to approach it from several different directions. No one of the approaches turns out to be fully satisfactory, nor indeed do all together.

One line of approach motivated the previous chapter's investigation of knowledge. Couldn't action be connected to something exactly as belief is to the truth when it constitutes knowledge? We want our beliefs to track facts, and the desirability of this is not undercut (but indeed may be aided) by our belief's being caused in a certain way. Wouldn't it be similarly desirable if our actions also were connected to something, tracking it? Might not the causation of action too aid rather than undercut this tracking and so contribute to the desirable mode of action or at least be compatible with it? If this is to be plausible, what the action tracks will have to be some evaluative fact or characteristic. We shall pursue this line of thought to (see to what extent we can) defang determinism without denying it, in the second part of this chapter. In the third and last part, we shall investigate issues of punishment (despite their not being central to the free will problem); in particular, we will formulate a rationale underlying punishment in retribution for a wrong.

First, however, we shall try to delineate an indeterminist view of free will. If some such view could be made to work, we would welcome it most. Seeing its difficulties might prepare us to view what the second part lays out, although causally determined and hence "second best", still as desirable and a form of free will nonetheless, the best instantiated realization of it. On the other hand, if the parts of this chapter came in a different order so that we first saw the inadequacies of the determinist picture, this might induce more tolerance of the indeterminist account, difficulties and all. Parts I and II of this chapter, it is only fair to warn the reader, contain more thrashing about than any other chapter of this book. Over the years I have spent more time thinking about the problem of free will—it felt like banging my head against it—than about any other philosophical topic except perhaps the foundations of ethics. Fresh ideas would come frequently, soon afterwards to curdle. (This is especially evident in Part II.) The presentation of many of these ideas and approaches may spur the reader to a success that has eluded me, or at least lift her spirits temporarily on this most frustrating and unyielding of problems. We approach the issue of free will from many directions. If we cannot solve the problem, at least we can surround it.

I. CHOICE AND INDETERMINISM

Weigh(t)ing Reasons

Making some choices feels like this. There are various reasons for and against doing each of the alternative actions or courses of action one is considering, and it seems and feels as if one could do any one of them. In considering the reasons, mulling them over, one arrives at a view of which reasons are more important, which ones have more weight. One decides which reasons to act on; or one may decide to act on none of them but to seek instead a new alternative since none previously considered was satisfactory.[1]

After the choice, however, others will say we were caused to act by the considerations which were (or turned out to be) more weighty. And it is not just others. We too, in looking back at our past actions, will see which reasons swayed us and will view (accepting) those considerations as having caused us to act as we did. Had we done the other act, though, acting on the opposing considerations, we (along with the others) would have described those considerations as causing us to do that other act. Whichever act we do, the (different) background considerations exist which can be raised to causal status. Which considerations will be so raised depends upon which act we do. Does the act merely show which of the considerations was the weightier cause, or does the decision make one of them weightier?

The reasons do not come with previously given precisely specified weights; the decision process is not one of discovering such precise weights but of assigning them. The process not only weighs reasons, it (also) weights them.[2] At least, so it sometimes feels. This process of weighting may focus narrowly, or involve considering or deciding what sort of person one wishes to be, what sort of life one wishes to lead.

What picture of choice emerges if we take seriously the feeling that the (precise) weights to be assigned to reasons is "up to us"? It is causally undetermined (by prior factors) which of the acts we will decide to do. It may be causally determined that certain reasons are reasons (in the one direction or the other), but there is no prior causal determination of the precise weight each reason will have in competition with others. Thus, we need not hold that every possible reason is available to every person at every time or historical period. Historians and anthropologists delineate how certain ideas and considerations can be outside the purview of some societies, some of whose reasons would not count as reasons for us. (Yet, there does remain the question of whether an innovator couldn't have recognized as a reason something outside the purview of others in his society.) Psychology, sociobiology, and the various social sciences, on this view, will offer casual explanations of why something is or is not a reason for a person (in a situation). They will not always be able to explain why the reasons get the precise weights they do. Compare the way art historians treat style; not every style is equally available to every artist in every period, yet within a style creative choices are made, and some artistic revolutions introduce new stylistic possibilities.

It is neither necessary nor appropriate, on this view, to say the person's action is uncaused. As the person is deciding, mulling over reasons R_A which are reasons for doing act A and over R_B which are reasons for doing act B, it is undetermined which act he will do. In that very situation, he could do A and he could do B. He decides, let us suppose, to do act A. It then will be true that he was caused to do act A by (accepting) R_A. However, had he decided to do act B, it then would have been R_B that caused him to do B. Whichever he decides upon, A or B, there will be a cause of his doing it, namely R_A or R_B. His action is not (causally) determined, for in that very situation he could have decided differently; if the history of the world had been replayed up until that point, it could have continued with a different action. With regard to his action the person has what has been termed contra-causal freedom—we might better term it contra-deterministic.*

* The notion of contra-causal human freedom (though not the term) originated with Philo. In his view, God, in creating the world, reserved for himself the power to upset laws by working miracles, and gave to man a portion of that same power—although man's 'miracles' are not worked with respect to laws that he himself created. (See Harry A. Wolfson, *Philo*, Harvard University Press, Cambridge, 1947, Vol. I, pp. 431, 436.) The Epicureans denied causality altogether, and Chrysippus held that causality, by its nature, stopped at the will of man. The Philonic view is the first to place absolute

VALUE

Thus, we draw a distinction between an action's being caused, and its being causally determined. Some philosophers would deny this distinction, maintaining that whenever one event causes another, there holds a general law in accordance with which it does so: some specification of the first event (along with other conditions which hold) always is and would be followed by an event of the same type as the second. It is a metaphysical thesis that the root notion of causality, producing or making something happen, can operate only through such lawlike universality. If this were correct, and if a law could not hold only at that (moment of) time, then causality necessarily would involve causal determination: under exactly the same conditions repeated, exactly the same thing would have (again) to happen. According to the view that distinguishes causality from causal determination, an act can be done because of something and have a cause even though in exactly the same conditions another act could have been done. It is common, in retrospect, to see what caused us to act as we did. Although we can retrospectively identify a cause, this does not mean our action was causally determined; had we acted differently in that situation (as we could have) we retrospectively would have identified a different cause—R_B instead of R_A.

The weights of reasons are inchoate until the decision. The deci-

---

free will within a world of some causality which otherwise would apply and which is suspended. (See H. A. Wolfson, *Religious Philosophy*, Harvard University Press, Cambridge, 1961, p. 196; *The Philosophy of the Kalam,* Harvard University Press, Cambridge, 1976, p. 733.) It became a matter of controversy within Christian theology whether humans naturally retained this gift of free will from God, or whether, after Adam's fall, God withdrew it as a matter of course and bestowed it only as a matter of divine grace. (See H. A. Wolfson, "St. Augustine and the Pelagian Controversy" in his *Religious Philosophy*, pp. 158–176.)

It is instructive to apply to these matters the notion (developed in Chapter 2 above) of an inegalitarian theory, wherein there is marked out a natural state, deviations from which have to be explained by special forces or reasons. There are at least three views: (1) Philo's view: man has free will as a gift from God, a gift bestowed in creating man's nature; hence free will is man's natural state, and could not be altered by Adam's sin; (2) man's natural state was unfree, but in one act God gave all men free will as a donation of some of his powers; (3) in response to Adam's act God altered man's natural state (if 1 had been true) or revoked his general gift; he now has to bestow free will upon each person individually. (This last is Augustine's view.) Notice that proponents of each of these views can agree that all people have free will, yet disagree about its explanatory status or explanation.

296

sion need not bestow exact quantities, though, only make some reasons come to outweigh others. A decision establishes inequalities in weight, even if not precise weights.[3]

These bestowed weights (or comparative weightings of reasons) are not so evanescent as to disappear immediately after the very decision that bestows them. They set up a framework within which we make future decisions, not eternal but one we tentatively are committed to. The process of decision fixes the weights reasons are to have. The situation resembles that of precedents within a legal system; an earlier decision is not simply ignored though it may be overturned for reason, the decision represents a tentative commitment to make future decisions in accordance with the weights it establishes, and so on.[4]

The claim that we always do what we most prefer or always act from the strongest motive is sometimes said to be empty of content, since the preference or the strength of motive is identified by what the person does. If the claim is to have empirical content, it must sometimes be possible to discover what a person's preference or strongest motive is via some other situation, to independently identify it in order then to check in this situation whether the person is doing what he most prefers or has the strongest motive to do.[5] Defenders of the claim do point out other situations (of choice or answering questions) where the relevant preference or motive can be identified; so the truth of the claim in this decision situation is testable, given the assumption that the preference or motive is stable from the one situation to the other.[6] However, if our conception of the bestowal of weights (with a commitment that lingers) holds true, then these independent "tests" are to be interpreted differently. We do not always act on what was a preexistingly strongest preference or motive; it can become strongest in the process of making the decision, thereafter having greater weight (in other future decisions) than the reasons it vanquished. The prior independent test of a preference therefore need not discover one that existed; it may establish a preference which then consistently carries over into a new decision situation. The testing procedure cannot show that we always act on a preexistingly strongest preference or motive.[7]

Only when there are opposed reasons for different actions is it necessary to arrive at a weighting; otherwise, one can just do what all the reasons favor. However, neither group of these opposed reasons need be moral; decisions that involve a conflict of duty or other moral motives with (nonmoral) desires are only a subclass of the free decisions.[8] Shall we say, though, that every free decision involves a conflict of some sort, with reasons pulling in different directions? The reasons in conflict need not then have indeterminate weight, for a free decision may "act out" an earlier weighting decision as precedent. (But is there always present a reason of indeterminate weight to reexamine and overturn an earlier precedent, which reason itself must be given a determinate lesser weight in the decision to follow the precedent?) Even though it will include no interesting cases we especially want to judge, still, we may formulate the theory to avoid the uncomfortable consequence that actions in the face of no contrary reasons are not free ones.

Is this conception of decision as bestowing weights coherent? It may help to compare it to the currently orthodox interpretation of quantum mechanics. The purpose of this comparison is not to derive free will from quantum mechanics or to use physical theory to prove free will exists, or even to say that nondeterminism at the quantum level leaves room for free will. Rather, we wish to see whether quantum theory provides an analogue, whether it presents structural possibilities which if instanced at the macro-level of action—this is not implied by micro-quantum theory—would fit the situation we have described. According to the currently orthodox quantum mechanical theory of measurement, as specified by John von Neumann, a quantum mechanical system is in a superposition of states, a probability mixture of states, which changes continuously in accordance with the quantum mechanical equations of motion, and which changes discontinuously via a measurement or observation. Such a measurement "collapses the wave packet", reducing the superposition to a particular state; which state the superposition will reduce to is not predictable.[9] Analogously, a person before decision has reasons without fixed weights; he is in a superposition of (precise) weights, perhaps within certain limits, or a mixed state (which need not be a superposition with fixed probabilities). The process of decision reduces the superposition to one state (or to a set of states corresponding to a comparative ranking of reasons), but it is not predictable or determined to which state of the weights the decision (analogous to a measurement) will reduce the superposition. (Let us leave aside von Neumann's subtle analysis, in Chapter 6, of how any placing of the

"cut" between observer and observed is consistent with his account.)
Our point is not to endorse the orthodox account as a correct account
of quantum mechanics, only to draw upon its theoretical structure to
show our conception of decision is a coherent one. Decision fixes the
weights of reasons; it reduces the previously obtaining mixed state or
superposition. However, it does not do so at random.

Nonrandom Weighting

Granting the coherence of the conception wherein the process of decision bestows weights, still, is that free will? An action's being non-
determined, we saw earlier, is not sufficient for it to be free—it
might just be a random act. If we acted in the way uranium 238 emits
alpha particles, determinism would be false but (unless we are
greatly mistaken about uranium 238) we would not thereby have free
will. What makes the bestowal of weights on reasons any different?
If that too is a random act, then is acting on those weights in that
very decision other than random? Acting on those same weights later
will not be random, but is it better than any other determined act if it
traces its history back not to causes before birth but to a recent random weighting of reasons?

How can the giving of weights be other than random? Since (by
hypothesis) there is no cause for giving or bestowing these particular
weights on reasons rather than other weights, must it be merely a
random act when these are bestowed? (Let us leave aside for the
moment the distinction between 'caused' and 'causally determined'.)
If the absence of causation entailed randomness, then the denial of
(contra-causal) free will would follow immediately. However, 'uncaused' does not entail 'random'. To be sure, the theorist of free will
still has to explain wherein the act not causally determined is
nonrandom, but at least there is room for this task.

In what way is the bestowal of weights not simply random? There
may be causes limiting the reasons on which (nonzero) weight can
be bestowed, and the interval within which these weights fall may
similarly be limited. However, although it is not a random matter
that the weights bestowed fall within this range, neither is that decided by the person. The question remains: how is her decision

among the alternatives causally open to her (the alternatives it is not causally determined she won't choose) not simply a random matter?

First, the decision may be self-subsuming; the weights it bestows may fix general principles that mandate not only the relevant act but also the bestowing of those (or similar) weights. The bestowal of weights yields both the action and (as a subsumption, not a repetition) that very bestowal. For example, consider the policy of choosing so as to track bestness: if the act weren't best you wouldn't do it, while if it were best you would. The decision to follow this policy may itself be an instance of it, subsumed under it.

Another issue shows how an act of decision can refer to itself. In contrast to optimizing models of decision, which see the agent as maximizing some objective function, Herbert Simon has presented a *satisficing* model of decision (to use his term): an agent will do an action that is "good enough", but failing to find one among his alternatives he will search for still others; repeated failure to find a suitable one will change his view of what is good enough, lowering his level of aspiration. It is natural to try to embed these considerations within an optimizing model that includes the costs of searching for new alternatives, gathering further information, as well as estimates of the probability of finding a new better alternative. The optimizing model would view 'searching for another alternative', or 'searching for more information about the other alternatives' as (always) among the actions or options already available. It therefore sees the choice among these available alternatives as involving maximization (under risk or uncertainty).[10] This faces the following difficulty, however. In making that choice among those alternatives on the basis of that information, was the structuring of that choice situation based on a previous optimizing decision or upon a satisficing decision that the structuring was "good enough"? Whichever, is not a decision made, at some point, which includes estimates of the costs and benefits of gathering more information in *that very* choice situation? Won't there be some decision, whether optimizing or satisficing, whose scope covers all costs including its own?[11]

Consider a self-subsuming decision that bestows weights to reasons on the basis of a then chosen conception of oneself and one's appropriate life, a conception that includes bestowing those weights and choosing that conception (where the weights also yield choosing that self-conception). Such a self-subsuming decision will not be a random brute fact; it will be explained as an instance of the very conception and weights chosen. (I do not say that all of one's choices or all that bestow weights are self-subsuming in this way; however, the other ones that are based on weights previously given in such decisions, revokable weights, will inherit autonomy.) It will no more be a random brute fact than is the holding of a fundamental deep explanatory law that subsumes and thereby explains itself. (See Chapter 2 above.) A self-subsuming decision does not happen inexplicably, it is not random in the sense of being connected to no weighted reasons (including the self-subsuming ones then chosen). But although it doesn't happen just randomly, still, there are different and conflicting self-subsuming decisions that could be made; just as there are different fundamental, self-subsuming laws that could hold true, could have held true. Is it not arbitrary then that one self-subsuming decision is made rather than another? Won't it be left inexplicable why this one was made (rather than another one)?

Understanding and Explaining Free Choices

First, a word about explanation and intelligibility. When deductive explanations subsume an event under a covering law, then we understand why that event occurred rather than any other. (It is another question why that covering law held rather than another; given that it did, we understand why the particular event occurred.) The situation is different with statistical explanations. Suppose a fundamental law states that the probability that anything has property Q given that it has property P is .95; if we wish to explain why some entity has property Q, we cannot deduce this fact from the entity's having property P plus the probabilistic law. Nevertheless, many have thought the statistical law does enable us to explain why the entity has property Q. Hempel has held that high probability events are explained by subsuming them under probabilistic laws; the high-probability probabilistic explanation is an approximation to a deduction.[12] What of the low probability event, though; when we encounter an entity that is P but isn't Q, can we explain why it is not Q? There is no way to do this on Hempel's view. True, if many P's are observed, then it can be very likely that one or another of them will not have property Q; we expect (as our best estimate) only 95 percent of the P's to have property Q, so there is a high probability that one of the very many P's we encounter will lack Q. When this one lacks Q, isn't the explanation simply that some (small) percentage of the P's will lack Q, and this is simply one of the ones that do? Strictly, on Hempel's view we have only an explanation that some P or other will lack Q, for that fact has a high probability; but we do not have an explanation of why, for example, this entity E lacks Q even though it has P. But even though we cannot deduce or yield with a high probability that it, entity E, will lack property Q, still, when we encounter it don't we know the explanation of why it does? We know there exists a system, a chance mechanism or whatever, that generates some P's that are not Q's, and we explain why this P is non-Q, by its being one of the things spewed forth by the operation of the chance mechanism.[13] The alternative (if there are some fundamental probabilistic laws) is to say these low probability events are unexplainable.

The moral I wish to draw is this: we can have an explanation and understanding of why something occurred even when we do not know of any reason why it, rather than something else, occurred that time, in that instance. Even when the event is random, its occurrence need not be inexplicable; it can be seen as an event, one of a type to be expected, arising from a mechanism or system that, in a way we may have better or worse understanding of, yields such events among others.

I am not suggesting that free decisions are random happenings from a chance mechanism with a well-defined probability distribution (whether flat or otherwise) over the various alternative actions. The process of choice among alternative actions is different; there are not fixed factual probabilities for each action, there is no such dispositional propensity or limit of long-run frequencies or whatever. Rather, there is a process operating wherein each alternative action could be yielded, and one of them was. This time, the process gave rise to that particular alternative. (Compare: this time the random system yielded that particular event.)

To be sure, we do not want to say simply that there is a process which could give rise to any of the alternative actions—we want to know more about the process, we want to delineate and understand it, we want to know how it works.

According to the view currently fashionable, we adequately understand a psychological process only if we can simulate that process on a digital computer. To understand a psychological notion is to know a set of quadruples that would place a Turing machine under the notion. Any process of choosing an action that could be understood in this sense would appear not to be a process of free choice. Suppose that this is so.[14] Does the fact that we cannot, in this sense, understand what a free choice is, indicate some defect in the notion of a free choice or rather is the defect in the view that this mode of understanding is the sole mode? Is the result, that we cannot understand what a free choice is, an *artifact* of this method of understanding?[15]

In what other way, if not simulation by a Turing machine, can we understand the process of making free choices? By making them, perhaps. We might interpret those theorists who pointed to our choices not as trying to prove that we made free choices but as ostensively explaining the notion, showing its intelligibility. Were they saying that we understand free choice and agency by virtue of making free choices as agents? To accept a (restricted) form of knowledge by self-acquaintance, encompassing knowledge of a mode of action and of ourselves, runs afoul of views that we know something only when (and to the extent that) we know the laws it obeys.[16] However, even if such views are rejected, the nature of this other mode of knowledge, by self-acquaintance, is unclear;* an adequate theory, showing how it is possible, would take us into issues far removed from our present concern without helping us especially with the topic of free will. Our problem is that we are puzzled about the nature of free choices, so any inside knowledge we may have of such choices due to and in making them obviously hasn't served to clear up our puzzles about their nature. It is tempting to say our puzzlement stems from supposing we must be able discursively to say or describe what a free choice is like, yet the fact that we cannot, when we are directly acquainted with them, doesn't interfere with understanding them. But too many ineffabilities spoil the philosophical

---

* "How can we know in that way, without reflective conceptual scrutiny? And will not all the knowledge be in the reflective scrutiny?" For a presentation of a view that avoids this philosophical picture but leaves much obscure (at least as judged by the mode of knowledge it claims is not the only one) see Aurobindo, *The Life Divine*, Book II, pt. I, ch. X, "Knowledge by Identity and Separative Knowledge".

broth. Since I do not myself have even the feeling of understanding, I will continue the (discursive) attempts at explanation.

We can explain an action as an intentional doing arising out of a process of choice among alternatives, if we can illuminate this process; however, we need not offer a Turing machine model, a computer simulation of the process of decision that matches which alternative the person chooses. We have said already that the decision process (sometimes) bestows weights on the reasons for and against the various alternatives, and that this bestowal of weights is self-subsuming and so to that extent not random. Still, there can be different self-subsuming bestowals of weight. Although after one occurs we will be able retrospectively to give a reason as the cause (though without causal determination), can anything be said about why that one self-subsuming decision is made rather than another? No, the weights are bestowed in virtue of weights that come into effect in the very act of bestowal. This is the translation into this context of the notion of reflexivity: the phenomenon, such as reference or a law's holding, has an "inside" character when it holds or occurs in virtue of a feature bestowed by its holding or occurring.

The free decision is reflexive; it holds in virtue of weights bestowed by its holding. An explanation of why the act was chosen will have to refer to its being chosen. However, not every act you do is a minor miracle of reflexive self-subsumption, only the ones involving choice of fundamental principles and self-conception. (Yet since such a choice is revokable, do later choices reaffirm it, and so also involve reflexive self-subsumption?)

Suppose a process of decision can have these features, bestowing weights in a self-subsuming fashion which is reflexive. The decision then does not simply dangle there at random—we can see the many ties and connections it has (including internal ones); the particular decision is not inexplicable—we see it as something that could arise from a process of this sort.

More might be demanded, however; it might be demanded that the theorist of free will show how the decision is causally determined. Otherwise, it will be said, the character and nature of the decision will remain mysterious. But clearing up any mystery in that way would come at the cost of the act's contra-causal freedom. No adequate condition on explanation or understanding necessitates either causal explanation or Turing machine delineation. Free will is to be explained differently, by delineating a decision process that can give rise to various acts in a nonrandom nonarbitrary way; whichever it gives rise to—and it could give rise to any one of several—will happen nonarbitrarily. These remarks are independent of the particular process we have delineated here, involving the bestowal of weights, reflexive self-subsumption, and so on. What is inappropriate is to demand that a free choice be explained in a way that shows it is unfree.

The theme of the bestowal of weights to reasons, in a situation of no preexistingly determinate weights, seems to me phenomenologically accurate[17] and proper to emphasize. I have more worries about terming this bestowal nonarbitrary and nonrandom because it is self-subsuming and reflexive. This position has too much the flavor of applying shiny new tools and ideas everywhere, as a magic key—except that some of the applications depend, perhaps, upon these ideas being not so well understood, not so shiny. So we should be somewhat wary of this use of the themes of self-subsumption and reflexiveness to delineate the nonarbitrary nature of a free choice. They do have the right flavor, though. For example, consider all the talk (in the literature) of "stepping back" to reconsider any previous commitment or self-conception. Is this merely the analogue of Peirce's point in epistemology that anything can be doubted but not everything at once—any motive or reason can be examined though not every one simultaneously? To where do we step back? In the case of a free choice, it seems appropriate that it be to somewhere such that (the act of) stepping to there is an instance of being there, which you are in virtue of a feature of your being there. "Stepping back", at least sometimes, is not like moving up to different levels in a type theory hierarchy; rather, it is self-subsuming and reflexive.

There are other issues that need to be explored, but will not be here: how the later (possible) revocation of bestowed weights works; whether there is causal leeway not only in bestowing weights on reasons, but also in the generation of alternative actions;[18] how the later less fundamental choices, which spin out the previously bestowed weightings, inherit autonomy. One further word can be said about the commitment involved in the bestowal of weights. Acting later on those weights anchors your later choices to them, and them to the later choices. Part of this nonrandom character of the weighting is shown by the life built upon them; perhaps it not merely is exhibited there but exists there.[19] If this is too strong, at least we may see the later adherence to weights as an indication of their nonrandom character; if the choice of these weights was simply random and arbitrary, would they win continued adherence?

Could One Have Bestowed Otherwise?

In the first chapter we saw how, within a closest-continuer framework, the self weights dimensions to yield a measure of closeness for itself, in accordance with its own self-conception, and saw how this weighting, including of plans, desires, and values, can be an important component in reflexive self-synthesis. Another way in which bestowal of weight upon reasons can be nonarbitrary is that the self can synthesize itself around this bestowing: "I value things in this way." If in that reflexive self-reference, the I synthesizes itself (in part) around the act of bestowing weight on reasons, then it will not be arbitrary or random that *that* self bestowed those weights.*

The process of decision can yield the intentional doing of different actions, and it would have if different weights had been assigned, which could have happened. But does it follow that the person could have done otherwise, that it was within the person's power to bestow different weights, as opposed to that merely happening? In what way could the person have *done* otherwise, not merely been the arena in which otherwise happened?

It would be fruitless to embark upon the theoretical regress wherein a different intentional action of bestowing weights occurs with its own separate weights which have to be bestowed by a still separate act.[20] And why is it asked only if another bestowal could

---

* Does this have the consequence that that self could not have bestowed weights differently? Not if the bestowal itself receives only a limited weight in the actual self-synthesis, and if the alternative syntheses involving different bestowals would then have been the closest continuers of the same earlier self, the one the actual synthesized self most closely continued. By most closely continuing the same earlier self, the other (possible) syntheses around other bestowals would have been that self later, just as the actual synthesized self is. So the particular bestowal isn't essential to the self with the consequence that the self couldn't have done otherwise, yet as a weighted component of a self-synthesis, neither is it random and arbitrary in relation to that self.

have been done; why is it not similarly asked whether the bestowal that did occur was a doing or merely a happening? Maybe it is possible for weights somehow to just happen to get bestowed on reasons; however, when the bestowal is anchored and tied in the way we have described, to a formed self-conception (even if formed just then), if it is self-subsuming and reflexive, leading to later (revokable) commitment, then it is a doing, not a happening merely. If all that context and stage setting (compare Wittgenstein) does not make it an action, what alternative conception of action is being presupposed? The actual bestowal of weights on reasons is a doing and not merely a happening; another and alternative bestowal of weights on reasons could have occurred instead—this one wasn't causally determined, and others aren't causally excluded—with all of the accompanying context and stage setting appropriate to it, so that alternative bestowal too would have been a doing and not merely a happening. The person could have bestowed differently.

Why Free Will, and How?

We have sketched a view of how free will is possible, of how without causal determination of action a person could have acted differently (in precisely that situation) yet nevertheless does not act at random or arbitrarily. (I admit the picture is somewhat cloudy.) Are there considerations that make this view plausible, not proving it true but indicating enough plausibility so that we do have an admissible (possible) explanation of how free will is possible? We might try to place free will within an evolutionary framework, thereby making it scientifically respectable. This could occur even without understanding how free will works, how weight is bestowed on reasons; if we could understand its adaptive value, understand why once it came to exist it would be selected for, then it would be placed within the network of scientific theory.[21]

What is the adaptive advantage to bestowing weights upon reasons in a self-subsuming reflexive fashion with a result that is not determined causally, so that if this capacity arose (at random) and was (to some significant degree) heritable, it would be selected for in the evolutionary process? It will be plausible that we do bestow weights on reasons (the particular bestowal not being causally determined) if both we naturally think (or feel) we do, and this would have been selected for, had it arisen, in the evolutionary process. It is not difficult to see the advantages for an organism of being able to behave in new ways in new situations, not just random thrashing and done only when it is appropriate or needed. The self-subsuming character of the decision may limit the thrashing; only some candidates (but more than one) will pass this test. But among these candidates, why is the choice not simply random, with an equal probability of choosing any one; what adaptive advantage does a nonrandom choice have over a random one here? Unfortunately I have not myself been able thus far to demarcate the special adaptive advantage free will might have; nonetheless, the evolutionary framework is a useful one to mark for further pursuit.

It is quite extraordinary that (some of) our decisions should escape the lattice of causal determination. Supposing or granting that there would be a function to their doing so, how does it manage to happen? What is it about (some of) our decisions, what feature do they have, that lifts them from the nexus of causal determination? Here, I can only offer a vague speculation. Reflexive self-subsuming acts have an intrinsic depth; the way they turn back on themselves, refer to themselves, refer reflexively "from the inside", gives them an unlimited (infinite?) semantic depth. Might it be that this cannot be caused, so the very feature that makes the decision nonrandom, reflexive self-subsumption, by its character eludes being caused by something else?[22]

Why cannot something reflexively self-referring be causally determined; even if it has unlimited (semantic) depth, why can it not be caused by something else which is (at least) equally deep? Descartes utilized a principle—one I don't understand well—that an effect cannot have a greater degree of "reality" than its cause.[23] We seem to be dealing with a similar type of principle here, that an effect cannot have a greater semantic depth than what causally determines it; that aspect of the effect, its semantic depth, cannot be causally determined by anything of lesser semantic depth. Semantic depth doesn't arise out of nothing; at least, it is not causally determined out of nothing or even less than itself. This principle is more modest (and plausible) than one that says reflexively self-subsumptive semantic depth cannot be causally determined at all, even by something of equivalent depth. Various philosophical controversies about reduction seem to hinge on this general principle; for example, whether intentional contexts can be reduced to nonintentional ones.[24] The principle, if correct, would delimit a barrier to explanatory or causal reductions: no reduction of the deep to the shallow.

Free decisions, then, would be an instance of this more general principle, a principle for whose own explanation we would have to seek deeper yet. More accurately, the principle says reflexive self-subsumptive decisons will not have causes of a certain sort, of lesser depth. But cannot one of mine be caused by someone's saying, "make that particular reflexive self-subsumptive decision or I will shoot you"?[25] Would this reference by the threatener to my decision have at least the same depth as the decision and so be able to cause it? Here, perhaps we have a further explanation of why theorists of coercion focus upon the interpersonal situation where someone else intentionally threatens you, placing their intentions about your action (and choice?) within your decision. In contrast to a fact of nature such as an electrical storm that gives the same probability distribution over relevant consequences, and to another's act that accidentally alters the probability distribution you face, this intentional interpersonal case has the requisite degree of depth to causally determine your (even semantically deep) act, perhaps. Still, one can decide to resist a threat, one can weigh it and go against it. Is one's decision deeper than the threat in that one "steps back" from it and weighs it? Yet why cannot the threat also refer to itself ("do that action on this very threat or else"), and so achieve the same depth as the decision that weighs it?[26] But can it achieve the same depth as a decision that weights it?

The principle of nonreduction to lesser semantic depth, and no causal determination by it, is an interesting one, whose consequences (and possible explanations) are worth exploring. However, it is not a principle I can put forth with any confidence or accept yet, even very tentatively.[27] I mention it merely to help explain how a free decision might be possible, how it is possible that it is possible. We have not produced any very good reasons for thinking the principle true,[28] nor any for thinking that (some) indeterminism does hold true, as opposed to speculating how it might possibly hold.

Is Free Will Valuable?

How important is it to this picture that our decisions not be causally determined? Suppose that in certain types of situations, we did reconsider our weighting of reasons, our self-conception, and our lives, but the new position we arrived at was causally determined—we always would arrive at precisely that position in precisely those circumstances. How different would this really be from the indeterministic situation described earlier, especially if others (and we ourselves) could not reliably predict the new position? How significant is the difference between this deterministic situation and its indeterministic mate?

How does determinism threaten (to undercut) our value? One can have various pictures: our being simply an arena in which causes play out their effects,* or our being puppets—marionettes moved by the causes at the other ends of the strings. It will be pointed out that we are not extremely simple input-output devices, much internal processing takes place, involving feedback loops and other delightful "software"; however, does that not make us merely more complicated puppets, but puppets nonetheless? True, much of these causes occur "inside" us—is it better to be a hand puppet than a marionette?

If we are caused to be aligned with correct value, to track some value trait such as bestness or rightness, there will be a value we have in virtue of this. Being aligned with correct values, tracking them, itself is a valuable thing, the connection itself is valuable. (In the next chapter, we will want a theory of value to explain or have the consequence that this connection with value itself is valuable.) However, it seems this value is not due to us, even if we play some part in it. On the causal determination view, though the connection involves us, the value of connecting to correct values just unrolls from the previous causes, so we do not add any value. We do not originate any value.

A daub of paint or a brushstroke in a painting may increase its aesthetic value, but that paint does not bring new value into the

---

* Compare the sociobiological view that we are simply the arena, the vehicle that genes use to reproduce others like themselves (see R. Dawkins, *The Selfish Gene*, Oxford University Press, 1976), or for that matter Samuel Butler's remark that a chicken is an egg's way of making another egg.

world; the value added in the placement of paint is added by the painter. Yet if he has no more autonomy than a paint blob, then although he is the vehicle through which value is added, and though his act of painting may be a component that is valuable, he does not originate any new value. The process of adding value occurs through his act, but that act does not change or alter the probability (or certainty) that there will be that value in the world. That probability is fixed beforehand and independently of the act, then is played out through the act. The probability of a strike at bowling is not altered by anything the ball does; that probability is fixed by other events: the precise release, condition of the lane, adhesions on the ball and so on. (Nor is the probability altered by the bowler's body movements after the follow-through, when the ball is more than halfway down the lane; follow-throughs in sports are designed to affect, by being headed for, some earlier motions.) The strike occurs through the action of the ball, but the ball's action does not add any new value that (to mix metaphors) was not in the cards already.

We can demarcate four sorts of value something such as an action, thing, event, or state of affairs might have. First, its intrinsic value, the value it has in itself apart from or independently of whatever it leads to or its further consequences. Second, its instrumental value, which is a function and measure of the intrinsic value it will lead to: either the sum of the intrinsic values of the different things it actually will lead to (if these intrinsic values are independent) or some measure of the different intrinsic values it might lead to as weighted by the probabilities that it will, such as the expected intrinsic value. (Or, if there are not even fixed probabilities, a measure appropriate for the uncertainty situation.) Something of instrumental value need not be valuable in itself, it needn't have its own intrinsic value; its instrumental value is measured by the value to which it leads. (We can let considerations of overall theoretical simplicity decide whether something of intrinsic value also has at least its own weight in instrumental value since the probability that it occurs, given that it occurs, is one.) These first two types of value are familiar from the literature.

Third, there is something's originative value which is a function of the value it newly introduces into the world, the new instrumental or intrinsic value it introduces that was not presaged by or already fully counted in previous instrumental value. An intermediate stage of a causal process has instrumental value in that it leads to some later intrinsic value, but it lacks originative value; the probability distribution over future intrinsic value was exactly the same beforehand and it is unchanged by the occurrence of this causally intermediate event. Anything may have all three kinds of values combined, intrinsic, instrumental, and originative. Note that a randomly occurring event of instrumental value, leading to further intrinsic value, can have originative value, as this notion was just explained. Perhaps we want to formulate a still tighter notion; but causal determinism denies us even this originative value. Puppets and marionettes lack originative value (except in fairy stories), and the way we resemble them, if causal determinism is true, is that we lack originative value too.[29]

A being with originative value, one whose acts have originative value, can make a difference. Due to his actions, different value consequences occur in the world than otherwise would; these were not in the cards already (with the person's action being one of the cards). It is clear, I think, that a proponent of free will means the choice that is up to us is among actions differing significantly in value. She does not think we can do simply anything at all; our (current) range of choice is limited, for example, to actions that don't involve travel at faster than the speed of light. But neither would she be happy to be told that someone did have a nonunit range of choice but that none of the actions in that range differed significantly. If a murderer was free to choose between stabbing with a knife in one hand and stabbing with it in the other, or to choose between stabbing and shooting, but all the actions he could choose among involved murder of some sort or another, then this would not be a freedom of decision worth having. What is wanted is that we be free to choose among actions that differ significantly in value, or at least in value profile—in the kinds of values they realize, if not in total value score. We want our decisons to make a value difference. Actions of instrumental nonoriginative value do make some difference too when, if they weren't to occur, the later intrinsic values wouldn't materialize. But although such actions make a difference in that they participate in one, they are the vehicles of one, they do not start any difference off, they do not originate one. A paintbrush or a palate knife used by a great painter contributes to some further effects, it is the instrument whereby they are effected but, unlike the painter, it does not originate any. The palate knife may have its own peculiarities, though, so that the same effects would not occur if another were used. The probability distribution over future effects then must take account of features of the palate knife. (Or need it consider only the factors that give rise to those features?)

Another notion of what difference something makes focuses upon what would have been the case if it had not existed or occurred, but other factors were reorganized to minimize its absence. Here, its value contribution is subjunctively defined by the difference between the actual situation of its presence and the reorganized one in its absence, not by what it leads to causally as a vehicle. Something can be necessary for the production of a certain value, even if it is not an originative factor. One thing we want is that our actions make a value difference, not merely that value be produced via them but that they be necessary for that production: the slack of their absence would not be taken up by other factors so that the same value got produced anyway. Let us term this value difference something makes—the value (amount) that wouldn't be there if it weren't—its contributory value. We certainly want our actions to have contributory value.

Causal determinism sometimes is misread as fatalism, as saying that our actions have no contributory value because the same (future) thing will happen anyway no matter how we act.[30] However, causal determination does allow contributory value; without our actions the future would be different. What causal determinism does not allow is originatory value. The worry about determinism, I think, is that it leaves us no originatory value. The "soft determinist" assures us that contributory value is enough. Yet a puppet can have contributory value also if in no other way could the children be brought to laugh so; although that is value indeed, it is not value enough, of the right sort. We want it to be true that in that very same situation we could have done (significantly) otherwise, so that our actions will have originatory value. The philosophical task is to explain how this is possible.

In explaining the kinds of value, we explained intrinsic value first, then instrumental, originatory, and contributory by the different ways these are related to the intrinsic value that follows them. In the next chapter, we will investigate the special worth of originatory value, which does not lie merely in its contribution to other intrinsic value. For now, let us note that something can be instrumental to later originatory value, or originate another thing of originatory value, as when parents decide to have children. (When you create certain decision opportunities for others who can freely choose whether to utilize them, how is the originatory value of your act to be calculated?) One standard position on the problem of evil is that God created beings (people or angels) with free will, and that this had value even though it opened doors to the production of evil; on this view (in our terminology) God created beings of originatory value and this made the originatory value of his act of creation higher than it otherwise would have been.

The free decision, bestowing weights on reasons of previously indeterminate weight, has originatory value; and as we shall see in the next chapter, it has intrinsic value as well. Presumably, what we would most want are decisions of originatory value that track bestness, ones connected to bestness (though not causally) as belief is to truth when it constitutes knowledge. If there was a conflict between the originatory and contributory values of a decision, which would we favor, what tradeoff would we make? How much originatory value would we sacrifice for (how much) caused increase in the amount bestness is tracked—either in the amount which is tracked or in the fidelity with which it is tracked? And would we want this choice about the tradeoffs we make to be an originatory choice or simply one caused to be aligned with value, a self-subsumptively originatory or a caused tracking choice?

Let us close this section by considering how we naturally tend to express our worry about determinism: if all of our actions are causally determined, eventually going back to causes occurring before we were born, then. . . . Why is that addendum made about causes before we were born, why is it so natural—rather, what function does it serve, what other possibility is it introduced to block or to cut off? Well, it is clear, isn't it, that if the causes go back to a time before we were born, then we don't control them and so, since they control our decision, we don't control our action. But is the notion of control transitive? Even if so, it does not follow that only the first event, and nothing intermediate in the chain, controls the last event. Even if I build, install, and set a thermostat, controlling it and controlling its controlling the temperature in my house, still, it does control the temperature in the house. (No one has ever announced that, because determinism is true thermostats do not control temperature.) My decision can control an action decided upon, as an instrumental control and as a contributory control—to adapt the terminology of the earlier value distinctions. The phrase "due eventually to causes existing before I was born" is meant to exclude my being in originatory control, initiating a new causal chain that was not already in progress. If, on the other hand, the causes of my current action went back only to last week or last year, then I might control those causes; I might have originated them by some earlier act or decision of mine. To ensure that the causal chain leading to my action isn't itself under my control, the point is added about going back to causes before I was born. For surely I do not control those. No decision or action of mine could originate things occurring before I was born.

Thus, mention of causes going back to before I was born is supposed to make plain that my decision (and I too) can have no originatory value. On the view we have presented, however, some actions are not causally determined, though they are, we correctly say in retrospect, caused by the reasons upon which the greater weight was bestowed in that very decision; so the causes may go back a long time, even to before birth, yet nonetheless the person still can originate actions. For which action she does, A or B, is under her originatory control, and though the occurrence of the reasons for each, R_A and R_B, are not under her control, the fact that one of them causes (though doesn't causally determine) her act—which one does so—is under her control. She can choose A or B; if she chooses A she makes it true that R_A caused A while if she chooses B she makes it true that R_B caused B. The existence of the cause is not under her control and doesn't originate with her, but the fact that it causes her act is and does.

This probing of why we so quickly slide to speaking of causes before we were born fits with the view that it is originatory value that is crucial to the problem of free will.* It is difficult to feel any confi-

---

* Yet, I have the feeling there is more to be discovered here, that that natural move to talking of causes before one was born covers and masks a deeper fact (perhaps a nonclosure to match that exhibited by tracking)—one whose delineation has eluded me, thus far.

dence, though, that this Part I has succeeded in delineating a coherent concept of free action, undetermined yet nonrandom, ascribing originatory value to us. (This apart from the question of whether that conception, if coherent, actually is realized.) If indeterminism seems like intellectual quicksand, can we do any better on the more solid but frozen ground of determinism?

II. DETERMINISM AND ALIGNING WITH VALUE

Tracking Bestness

There are two reasons to investigate the notion of an action's tracking bestness. First, that is what we want the upshot of the indeterminist free decision process to be; we want the person who makes free decisions to end up tracking bestness. Second, if determinism is true, no person or action will have originatory value. What remains as the most valuable possible mode of action, in that case, is (to be determined) to do the action that is the best of those available to us; moreover, that this doing what is best or most valuable not be an accident, like true belief, but rather that the action tracks value or bestness. Thereby, we and our actions would be connected to value by the subjunctive tracking relation, and to that extent exhibit a valuable mode of action; we would be valuable although not originatory of value.

Yet determinism threatens even this, apart from any doubts (which we shall investigate in the next chapter) about the objective status of value. Even if there is value, can our actions track it; will causal determination not attune actions to other (nonevaluative) characteristics? Is causal determination compatible with saying, for example, that if the value of the act were different the person would act differently? Our task, therefore, is not only to delineate what an action's tracking value would be like, but also to see whether and how tracking value or bestness is possible given causal determination of actions.

We investigated knowledge in Chapter 3, delineating how belief is therein connected to truth. We found that a person's belief that p is knowledge when it is subjunctively connected, in a specified way, to the fact that p: he knows that p when his belief that p tracks the fact that p. (Leave aside, for the moment, the additional complications of the reference to methods.) A belief's being causally determined does not undercut the desirability of the tracking connection, and might well underlie that connection. Mightn't a mode of action parallel belief in this way, tracking something desirably in a way that also is not undercut by causal processes?

Beliefs track facts or truths; what are actions to track, and how? If our actions are to track anything, we want that to be some evaluative fact; we want the doing of the act to be responsive to and track some evaluative feature the act has. Just as we want our believing p to be responsive to its truth, so we want our doing A to be responsive to its rightness or goodness, for instance, or to the fact that it is the best one of the actions available. We want doing an act to be responsive to the most important evaluative property of action (perhaps a weighted sum or profile of several evaluative properties), whatever that is, as this enters some appropriate principle of choice.

The philosophical tradition, by and large, has considered the crucial evaluative properties of action to be moral ones, holding that moral principles are (or should be) the most fundamental and overriding principles of choice. Thus, Kant held that a free action is one done because it is right (by someone who, from his rational nature, wills the moral law to himself and acts out of a respect for this moral law). There are exceptions, however: Kierkegaard (in *Fear and Trembling*) speaks of Abraham's "teleological suspension of ethics"; arguably, Nietzsche intended his transvaluation of values to transcend the realm of morality altogether, not merely to substitute another morality for the reigning one; other writers have held self-realization or self-perfection to be the central evaluative goal, one that might conflict with ethics.

If our action is to track and be responsive to some evaluative facts, we need to know which ones. It is a particular claim, difficult to show true, that the most important evaluative dimension of action is a (perhaps complicated) moral one. Does any comparable problem arise for belief, can there be any question that belief is to track the truth? Even here, there may be competition to guide belief from different cognitive goals such as explanatory power, simplicity, theoretical fruitfulness, capacity for problem solving, even perhaps interestingness. (Therefore, a wedge might be driven between believing p and believing that p is true.)

Let us leave open for now which evaluative aspect of action is the appropriate one. (Also leave open how or whether a person is to exercise choice over which of the evaluative dimensions his actions track.) It will be inconvenient always to refer to "the most important evaluative feature". For brevity, then, we shall speak of "bestness" or (following Kant) of "rightness". This is not meant to fix the evaluative dimension, merely to enable us to get on with exhibiting the tracking structure. (We deliberately ignore, for now, conflicts between different dimensions, or their differing stringencies even when they are compatible.) Our actions, then, are to be sensitive to bestness or rightness; they are to track these.

Let us spell out the conditions for an action to track rightness or bestness, in parallel to the conditions in the account of knowledge wherein belief tracks the truth. In the conditions for knowledge from Chapter 3, we substitute 'intentionally doing' for 'believing', 'rightness' for 'truth'. Person S's (doing of) act A tracks rightness when

(1) Act A is right
(2) S intentionally does A
(III) If A weren't right, S wouldn't intentionally do A.
(IV) If A were right, S would intentionally do A.

We would proceed similarly for tracking bestness instead of rightness. The notion of right is ambiguous between permissible (all right) and mandatory (impermissible not to do). A similar ambiguity arises for "best", which may mean "none better" and so countenance ties for the top spot, or may mean "better than all others". (Mathematicians mark the ambiguity by using the term *maximal* for 'none greater' and *maximum* for 'greater than all others'.) However, resolving the ambiguity and then using one nonambiguous sense to (uniformly) interpret both III and IV leads to difficulty.[31] We need to use the weaker notion to interpret condition III and the stronger one for IV. That gives us

(3) If A weren't permissible, S wouldn't intentionally do A
(4) If A were mandatory, S would intentionally do A.

Similar elaboration of the conditions for tracking bestness yields: person S's (doing of) act A tracks bestness when

(1) Act A is best (maximal at least, perhaps maximum)
(2) Person S intentionally does A
(3) If act A weren't as good as any other action available (if it weren't maximal) person S wouldn't intentionally do it
(4) If act A were better than any other action available (if it were maximum) person S would intentionally do it.[32]

Just as in our discussion of knowledge we introduced explicit reference to a way or method M of believing, so too here we can introduce explicit reference to a motive M for acting (or a type of reason for acting or way of being brought to act) in conditions 2–4. This helps clarify the Kantian issue of when we act from the moral law (to use his terminology). As often has been noticed, it is excessively stringent to hold (and doubtful that Kant did so) that if we are to act from the moral law, acting morally as opposed merely to doing what happens to be moral, then no nonmoral motive may be present. To allow overdetermination of the action, provided the moral motives actually do the pushing, would not satisfy Kant, however. It leaves open the possibility that if the act were contrary to the moral law, the other nonmoral motives, if present, would suffice to get the person to do the act. Kant's purposes would better be served by the simple subjunctive conditions 3 and 4: if A were not permissible, S wouldn't do it; if A were mandatory then S would do it. More complicated subjunctives would serve him better yet. Recall the grandmother case in the previous chapter: she knows her grandson is ambulatory, but if he weren't she would believe he was anyway because her relatives so would inform her. Recall also the person who knows a building is a theater by going into it, yet if it were not a theater he would believe it was anyway, via another route. Similarly, someone might perform a mandatory action after carefully considering its rightness, yet if it weren't right, the issue of its moral quality would never have arisen for him or come to his attention, so still he would have been led to decide to do it, only that time without considering its (having or lacking) rightness. Despite this subjunctive, suppose he did actually consider the act's rightness, concluding it was right and acting accordingly; and also suppose that once he was engaged in considering its rightness, these subjunctives would hold: if the act weren't right he would have concluded that and so not done it; if the act were mandatory he would have concluded it was, and done it. Surely this together meets all Kantian requirements.

Comparable issues about belief led us away from the simple subjunctive view to one that not only explicitly mentioned methods but included an outweighing condition about which method was predominant. A similar structure fits here as well. A person satisfies the Kantian requirement of acting from the moral law when there is a motive M via which he does A which satisfies conditions 1–4, and any other motive M' via which he does A which fails to satisfy 3 or 4 is outweighed by M.[33]

How the Tracking Is Mediated

When S's action tracks rightness or bestness, how is this related to S's belief that A is right or best? It seems plausible to think that the only way an action can track an evaluative fact is via the person's evaluative belief that tracks the fact; that is, via the person's knowledge of the fact. When

(1) A is right
(2) S believes that A is right,

then S's belief tracks that truth when

(3) If A weren't right, S wouldn't believe A was right
(4) If A were right, S would believe it was.

Under these conditions, S knows that A is right. Substituting "permissible", "mandatory", "maximal", or "maximum" in the account of knowledge gives us accounts respectively of S's knowing that act A is permissible or mandatory or maximal or maximum.

How is doing the action to be connected with S's belief (which tracks the truth) that A is right? To say that S acts because of his belief faces a familiar problem: causes can act in funny ways. What seems needed is that S's doing of action A track his belief that A is right, namely

(5) S intentionally does A
(6) If S weren't to believe that A is permissible then S wouldn't intentionally do A
(7) If S were to believe that A is mandatory then S would intentionally do A.

Similar conditions can be formulated for his action tracking his belief that A is best. These conditions 5–7 are the conditions for S's action A tracking his belief that A is right (either permisssible or mandatory). When his belief that A is right is true and tracks the fact, so that he knows A is right, we also might say he does A because he knows that A is right. He does A because he knows it is right, when conditions 1 through 7 hold, when he does A because he believes it is right and believes it because it is.[34] To say S did A because he knew that *p* is to say he did A because *p*, and that the *p* operates in a certain restricted way, namely, through beliefs that are tracking. (Ruled out are certain modes of "because", for example, that in the tank cases and in the case of the newspaper's false denial.) When the p does operate in this restricted way, shall we say that S does A because p, or shall we say he does A because he believes that p? Since the belief tracks p, we would need a special occasion to distinguish between these.[35]

Condition 3 connects doing an act (or in the case of knowledge, believing the act is right or best) with the act's being right or best; it considers what the person would do (or believe) if the act were not right or best. How are we to understand that? Not, I think, as postulating some grand moral change in the universe, so that the type of thing which (at the deepest level) was right is now supposed not to be. The case of "best" is easiest; since this is a comparative notion, we need only suppose that some other (even better) alternative also is available. In the case of rightness the supposition will be more modest. The actions are not identified by their moral quality; even if that is how they are identifyingly referred to, that moral quality of rightness is not part of their essence. So what the antecedent of 3 supposes is that something is different about the act or about the context in which it is done, so that the act then is not right—however, it is not supposed that the nature of rightness itself has changed in any way. To be sure, this will involve some theory wherein an act could have a different moral character (in another situation, say) while yet being the same act. A utilitarian view would suppose a situation in which the act had different consequences, for example. The problems about knowledge of general (perhaps fundamental) moral principles are more difficult. Here it may be quite unclear what situation is contemplated in supposing the principle were false. As in the case of knowledge of mathematical or other necessary truths, given true belief, tracking moral principles may reduce to the fourth condition: S would believe p if it were true. Even if general moral principles have a necessary character and cannot coherently be supposed to be false, still, knowledge of such general moral principles raises no problems special to ethics, not arising also in the epistemology of mathematics. In any case, the notion of an action's tracking rightness or bestness does not seem directly to involve any such (general) knowledge best construed as necessary.

When a person's action tracks his belief that A is right, is the intention to do A produced simply by the belief that A is right? Don't we also need the desire to do what is right, or the general intention or policy to do what is right? Let us suppose that an action's tracking rightness requires not only the belief that A is right, but also the desire to do whatever is right. That desire may be present, steadily enough so that it provides the background for the subjunctives connecting action with belief about rightness. In these subjunctives the desire need not be mentioned explicitly, either as actual or in those situations that would obtain if the antecedents held. Still, whether stated explicitly or only presupposed, this desire to do what is right must be present.

In the case of belief, we did not introduce any corresponding desire to believe what is true. Yet such a desire plays a role there as well. Consider a situation where not merely is this desire absent, but a contrary desire operates. Suppose someone can arrange for himself to have certain beliefs in the future, by planting clues in advance or by machine implantation. He knows now that later he will not remember his own earlier role in bringing about the beliefs. Let us suppose the primary question for this person is what it will make him happy to believe. Some false beliefs would lead to trouble and unhappiness (when he acted on them), so he will not decide to implant those. However, there is great leeway, he realizes, to increase his own future happiness by giving himself some other false beliefs; for example, in those cases where the fact that p doesn't act on him directly but makes him unhappy only through knowing of it, only through his *belief* that p. So he proceeds to make himself happy in the future by implanting (in such cases) the beliefs that not-p, currently having good grounds for thinking he will not discover the falsity of these not-p beliefs when he later has them.[36]

Let us postpone moral judgment of someone who engages in such self-deception. (Still, note that a person, without moral discredit, may not want to believe all truths. There are costs in acquiring beliefs or in cluttering up the mind; furthermore, many truths are too trivial to care about believing, even if costless.) Our current concern is to judge this happiness-seeker epistemologically, not morally. When he acquires beliefs in this fashion can he know they are true? Suppose the belief is true, the person now knows that p, and decides to give himself the future belief that p on the grounds that believing p will serve his happiness better than believing not-p. This need not be an accident; belief in p when it is untrue might not serve his happiness. So he would not believe p if it weren't true, and (given the close connection for this type of statement between happiness and true belief) if it were true he would believe it. Still, in the future he will not know that p; although subjunctively connected to the truth, his belief is not based on the desire to believe the truth but on a different and sometimes contrary desire to believe what will make him happy.

If a belief's being knowledge is dependent upon some desire to believe what is true, this desire need not be the universal desire to believe all truths. It will suffice if it is the desire to believe truths of a particular sort, in an area that includes the p in question. Notice that the desire to believe what is true (in an area, about a subject) is not merely, when p is true, the desire to believe p. It is the desire to believe whatever is true, whether p or not-p: the desire to believe p if p were true and to believe not-p if not-p were true. Knowledge involves a desire to believe the truth, when the method M via which a person believes that p involves the desire so that his coming to the belief or maintaining it is in application of the desire.

Strictly, is it necessary to introduce the desire to believe what is true? If a person cannot help believing what is true, yet does not desire to do so, cannot he have knowledge? (Can't animals have knowledge, though they lack the desire to believe the truth?) Since the original trouble was caused by the active role of another contrary desire, the desire to believe whatever will make one happy, perhaps it suffices merely to exclude such other desires from operating in the absence of a desire to believe the truth. Under this account, a person can know that p without the desire to believe what is true. However, if other desires do play a significant role in his belief, then he will know only if the desire to believe the truth also operates, outweighing these other desires.

The idea is that a person without desires about his beliefs may actually be aimed at the truth; but if he himself aims his beliefs at something else (other than truth) then this will deflect him from knowledge, unless he also aims, in a predominant way, at believing what is true. Although I have spoken thus far only of truth, I mean to include other appropriate cognitive aims too, such as explanatory power, depth of theory, and understanding. It is a delicate question which aims are relevantly noncognitive and so have to be outweighed. For example: is a desire for an elegant theory an appropriate cognitive aim or one to be outweighed? are some pragmatists who speak of truth really speaking of another aim which interferes with knowledge? My purpose here is not to present a full normative theory of belief. It is enough to point to these issues, drawing a rough distinction that, though crude, can say that someone does not know who believes mainly because he wants to believe what will make him happy or what will best fit in with his political beliefs. An ideologue doesn't *know* the truth, because inappropriate desires which are not outweighed enter into the method M via which he believes.*

We need not claim that the desire to believe what is true must be a fundamental and underived desire, not subordinate to any other. It suffices if any other more fundamental desire that operates in the method M, operates through the desire to believe what is true. But this does raise the possibility that someone who reconstructed her methods of arriving at belief so that her fundamental underlying desires and values predominated, and acted without passing through the subordinate desire to believe what is true, would bypass knowledge. Perhaps she would view herself as transcending knowledge. It

* Some people are prone to become committed to beliefs they publicly have proclaimed; having arrived at the belief (let us suppose) objectively, they then *want* it to turn out to be true, they hope to find further evidence for it, and so on. Such people must be especially careful not to slip into being ideologues and letting those derivative desires, which stem from the previous reaching and defending of conclusions, infect the way they arrive at beliefs and evaluate evidence now. (Compare the predictions of Festinger's cognitive consistency theory, but note the cautions in Janis and Mann, *Decision Making*.)

Even someone who succeeds in avoiding this pitfall may succumb to another. Consider racism: a racist is not simply someone who believes there are or may be racial differences along dimensions of value—whether or not there are is an empirical question. A racist, I am inclined to say, is someone who wants there to be racial differences along dimensions of value, and who wants these differences to go in a certain direction. (He is not merely a lover of variety in the world, however it happens to fall out.) Some might argue that the empirical evidence for such racial differences is so slight that only someone who wants them to exist would conclude that they do, so that such a person would be a racist ideologue. Others might argue that the evidence is at least as strong as we find acceptable in other social scientific investigations, and so only the want that there not be such racial differences leads those who have looked at the evidence to refuse to accept the conclusion, making them nonracist ideologues. Yet to avoid falling into wanting there to be such racial differences (which by the earlier plausible criterion is the mark of being a racist), we might avoid reaching a conclusion or (especially) a stand on the issue.

is strange that philosophical investigations of norms about belief have not placed more emphasis on the purpose of beliefs. In addition to putting the philosophical issues in a different perspective, a teleological theory of beliefs might raise the possibility that believing is an inappropriate means to the goal—believing itself might be transcended. Some theorists treat beliefs as an abstraction made in order to explain facts about the behavior of organisms. Why then should fundamental norms be formulated about beliefs rather than about that from which the beliefs are abstracted: the ongoing life of the organism and the way it lives?

The role of desire is more salient, the issue about it arises more naturally, with action than with belief. Why? Our usual situation is to act upon desires which vary from situation to situation. (Some eastern disciplines do envision acting with no desire or attachment at all.) Since our acts depend so precariously on particular desires, we are led immediately to notice the importance for action of those particular desires. Thus we notice how important it is not simply to believe that some act is right, but to desire to do what is right or best, and to have this predominate in the face of other desires. Whereas with belief, there are (or appear to be) many cases where existing desires about beliefs play no role in arriving at the beliefs. Only when we explicitly consider beliefs acquired or maintained through the (predominant) operation of other contrary desires are we led to notice the role of the desire to believe what is true.

How Illuminating Is the Parallel?

The situation where our actions track rightness or bestness is desirable and valuable, one we certainly want to obtain. Moreover, it offers hope of a desirable mode of action compatible with determinism, although without orginatory value. As in the case of belief, determinism, rather than undercutting the subjunctives, may be their substratum. Yet the parallel of action to belief will be fully illuminating only if here too, as in the case of knowledge, the structural features of tracking have interesting and illuminating consequences. Do these structural features help us to understand issues of free will, as before they cast light on skepticism? We have seen in Chapter 3 how skeptical arguments play off the subjunctives, gaining force from the subjunctive account but only a limited force, without the sweeping and all-embracing consequences the skeptics claim. We need the tracking account of free action to do some work too: the distinction between subjunctives and entailments to make a difference; or some nonclosure feature of the subjunctive structure to cut deeply, showing that although we are not free in some things, we are free in others closely connected; or something to parallel knowing that one knows, with a corresponding lack somewhere up the line if not at the beginning. The tracking account of knowledge, which fit cases naturally, had powerful consequences that cut deeply; the notion of an action's tracking value, although certainly describing something desirable, does not fit intuitions about freedom naturally. All the more must its consequences cut deeply into the way we discuss that issue. Otherwise, it simply will be a nice description of something else, something we might be happy to have or exhibit, but not free action.

True, one important strand of the intellectual tradition does speak of freedom along these lines.[37] Also, we might draw upon Chapter 1's list of modes of structuring a philosophical concept. If tracking bestness is the best instantiated realization of the concept of free will (that is, is the best we actually do in the free will area) then is it not reasonable to offer that as an account of free will? That is reasonable (only) if tracking bestness is not only the best instantiated realization but also a good enough realization to count as (a version of) free will. There are reasons for holding it is a good enough realization of something important. Tracking bestness is a valuable and desirable state; it also is the goal to which we would want to direct any process of free will. We can highlight its virtues by supposing that it cannot be achieved along with or through the relevant free will process; if you utilize that process you consequently will fail to track bestness or rightness. Avoiding metaproblems, let us ask which you would choose for yourself: tracking bestness (without the process) or the process of free will (without tracking bestness).* Our difficulty simply in choosing the second indicates the value of the first, of tracking bestness. (Remember, "tracking", as we use it, denotes the holding true of certain subjunctives, not the occurrence through time of some process.)

* Dostoyevsky's underground man would choose the process rather than tracking bestness. He wants to go against the tyranny of reason, in order to be free. In thus having a reason and important motivation, though, he does not go against (the tyranny of?) metareason.

And yet, granting all this, there remains the feeling that a switch is being pulled. Only if the structural consequences of this notion of tracking illuminate the conflicting ways we are pulled on (what is unquestionably) the topic of free will—as happened previously with the topic of knowledge—will it be clear that tracking bestness is a theory of free will. Only then will tracking bestness be a candidate for a complete explanatory theory of free will, even without any indeterminist component such as weighting reasons.* Do the structural features of tracking cut to the heart of our quandaries about free will?

The situation, I think, is that though the structural features of tracking do have consequences for action, these consequences do not cut deeply enough. For example, a subjunctive is not a statement of entailment. Hence, the existence of a logically possible situation where A is wrong yet the person still does A does not show the falsity of

(3) If A weren't right, S wouldn't do A;

while the existence of a logically possible situation where A is mandatory yet the person doesn't do it does not show the falsity of

(4) If A were mandatory, the person would do A.

We can formulate arguments which do make these mistakes of thinking 3 or 4 is thus shown false. One example is the argument that if there are physiological causes of the action then the person is not tracking rightness, since it is possible that those causes occur when the action is not right yet still the person acts. (But these causes might not be subjunctively independent of the act's moral quality: if the act weren't to have this moral quality, those causes wouldn't have occurred.) A second example: there might possibly be other motives for doing the action, perhaps unconscious ones, so that even if the action were wrong, the person still would (be driven to) do it, whereas if it were right but those unconscious motives were absent, he wouldn't do the act in opposition to other motives. So, it is concluded, he is not tracking rightness. (But is that motivational situation, unconscious or otherwise, one that actually would obtain if the

---

* However, I did not foresee such deep illumination of the issues about skepticism when I first began to formulate the tracking account of knowledge, in order to find what action should parallel. Thus does level of aspiration rise.

act had a different moral quality, or were to have the same one; is it a first subjunctive alternative, or close enough to the rightness of the act?)

"No one acts morally; everyone has his price." But for some act A the person does which is right, even if there is some price or other that will get him to do it when it is wrong or omit it when it is mandatory, it does not follow that that price would or might actually be so offered; it might be offered only in some more distant situation. So it still can be true of a person whose act has a price that he would not (actually) do it if it were wrong because—fortunately or unfortunately for him—that would not be the situation in which the price was offered. It is also worth noting that the order of the quantifiers is important. Even if every act has its price, it does not follow that some one price suffices to buy each and every act. A person has integrity of a sort if, for any given price (however high), there are some acts or other that it will not buy from him. Although this is considerably weaker than there being some acts that simply cannot be bought, it still is something. (But even if it were the best instantiated one, would it be a good enough realization to constitute integrity?)

There are these issues which do play off the subjunctive character of the tracking conditions, and are illuminated by them, but these do not seem to be the central issues and quandaries about free will. It is more plausible to see in the tracking conditions an account of acting morally, as opposed to simply having what one does happen to fit what is right. (To this compare merely true belief). Perhaps it does illuminate deep worries about whether anyone ever acts morally; we even find a kind of nonclosure here.* If S does A, this entails that he didn't accept a specific price not to do A. Yet though he acted morally in doing A, it doesn't follow that he acted morally in (what was entailed, namely) not accepting that price not to do A. He didn't accept it because it was not offered; if it had been offered he would

---

* In the case of belief, the nonclosure was that knowledge, a belief's tracking the truth, was not closed under known logical implication: it could be that a person's belief that p tracks the truth that p, the person knows p logically implies or entails q, and the person does believe q, yet his belief that q does not track the truth that q. This structural possibility played a crucial role in understanding skepticism about knowledge, leading to the view that the skeptic is right in claiming we do not know certain things we thought we did know (namely, that certain skeptical possibilities don't hold), yet is wrong in concluding from this that we know almost nothing.

have accepted. This nonclosure of "acting morally" depended on his not having an opportunity (to accept the offer). Another nonclosure does not depend on this.

Doing A may entail doing B, and while doing A tracks its rightness, doing B need not track B's rightness; although the person does B, he doesn't act morally in doing so, for he would do B (but not A) even if it were wrong. My going out this afternoon to the library entails that I go out from my home sometime in the decade, and though I would not do the former if it were wrong, I still might do the latter even if (somehow) *it* were wrong. If, however, it were wrong for me to go out to the library this afternoon, that would not (actually) be because it was wrong for me to go out anytime at all during the decade. So still, if this going to the library were wrong, I wouldn't do it. The act of going to the library tracks its rightness, yet another act whose doing is entailed by the first, going out during the decade, though it is right, does not track its rightness. However, though there is this sort of nonclosure there to be noticed, it has not played any deep role in the free will issue. Is there any nonclosure exhibited by tracking bestness or rightness that cuts to the depths of the free will quandaries?

The nonclosures I have been able to discern do not have the theoretical fruitfulness of the one concerning knowledge. There are the following (in addition to the one already mentioned).

(a) It is false that whoever freely wills the end also freely wills the means. The person's doing A may track A's rightness, and though he realized that B was a means toward A and he did B, his doing of B did not track B's rightness; when B is the activity of staying alive through the time of doing A, the person would have done it even if it were wrong.

(b) A person may intentionally do A, realize that if he does A then he does B, yet not intentionally do B. Yet there is no hint of paradox here.

(c) Doing A may track rightness and entail not doing B, yet though not doing B is right, the person need not thereby be tracking rightness; perhaps he wouldn't do B even if it were right to do B.

(d) That A is right may entail B is right, and his doing A may track the rightness of A, yet he may do B without thereby tracking the rightness of B.

(e) This nonclosure, strictly, is not about action but about knowledge of moral principles itself. A person doing particular acts that instance a moral principle may track their rightness (if the acts were wrong, that is, had different factual features of moral weight, he wouldn't do them); yet his assenting to and following the fundamental moral principle itself does not track its rightness (if it were wrong, he would not realize that).

None of these facts of nonclosure underlies anything very deep about the issue of free will; none is especially connected to any issue about causality. The next one begins, at least, to have the flavor of free will problems.

(f) An act A may track the rightness of A, and X be the cause of doing A without the occurrence of X tracking the rightness of X. X might occur by accident, or whatever, and cause the person to track rightness in acting. Accidental factors could shape the person's character into that of someone who desired to track rightness and could recognize its presence.

The causes of your tracking rightness may go back to a time before you were born, without undercutting the fact that you are tracking rightness. Similarly, there is the nonclosure exhibited by the notion of control, mentioned in the first part of this chapter: a person may control X without controlling everything else that controls X or that controls his controlling it. (Though I keep pecking at the "back to causes before you were born" theme, I have not been able to make my hunch that it marks some illuminating nonclosure or nontransitivity pay off.)

The final theme to consider paralleling is knowing that one knows, where some skeptical doubts might have application farther up the line of knowing that one knows one knows. One parallel might be this: a person tracks bestness, monitors the fact, and bases another action on (so that it tracks) the monitoring. A more direct parallel, though, is the following. A person S's act A tracks bestness; let us write this as TA. ('T' for tracking bestness.) Consider now the activity of his tracking bestness in doing A; does that itself track bestness? If so, let us write that as TTA; A's tracking bestness tracks bestness. How far up the line will it go; are there cases where it does not take the next step after TA? (True, if A weren't best you wouldn't do it, so

331

A tracks bestness, but is it also true that if that tracking bestness weren't best, you wouldn't do *it*?) Consider the policy of doing whatever tracks bestness: for all courses of action A, if A tracks bestness then do A. Does the course of action of adhering to this policy itself track bestness, and is it a self-subsumed instance of itself? And so forth. Yet once again, it is difficult to foresee anything very illuminating about the free will issues arising from the elaboration of such an iterated structure. (However, the last self-subsuming possibility is relevant to ethics and to the indeterminist view of free will as weighting reasons.)

Unhappily, then, I must say that the parallel of action to belief, invoking the structural consequences of an action's tracking rightness or bestness, has not illuminated the deep quandaries and worries about free will; we are left with the feeling that the notion of 'tracking bestness or rightness' has not gotten to the heart of the free will problem. This should send us back to the indeterminist account of weighting reasons, offered earlier. However, there is the possibility that considerations added to the notion of tracking bestness, dovetailing with it and not replacing it, will yield the desired illumination. Of course, the indeterminist weighting of reasons also might dovetail with tracking bestness.

Though it leaves the issues of free will dark, nevertheless, the situation of tracking bestness or rightness may be a very desirable and valuable mode of action, the best we can hope to achieve. But can we even hope for that? There are two types of causal considerations that appear to undercut (the possibility of) our actions' tracking rightness or bestness. It is to these considerations we now turn. (Thus does the level of aspiration fall.)

Does Neurophysiological Reduction Undercut Tracking?

There are two components to an act's tracking rightness or bestness: first, the doing of the act tracks the belief that it is right or best; second, the belief that the act is right or best tracks the fact that it is. Correspondingly, there are two sorts of reasons to think our actions cannot or do not ever track rightness. The first holds that our actions cannot or do not track our beliefs about rightness or bestness. The second holds that our beliefs do not track the facts about rightness; in the next section, under this rubric, we discuss such "blind" explanations of our holding ethical beliefs as might be offered within evolutionary theory and theories of operant conditioning. Another reason for thinking our actions cannot or do not ever track rightness or bestness would follow from the view that there are no facts about rightness or bestness to track. Unlike the first two mentioned, this view doesn't threaten one of the two links—it denies the existence of the endpoint. We shall take up this view in the next chapter.

The most radical form of the first claim, that our actions don't track our beliefs about rightness or bestness, holds that our actions do not track any of our beliefs; it claims the causal explanation of our actions need not bring in beliefs at all. In its most plausible form, this view is not the cynical one that all beliefs are rationalizations; rather it holds that all of our actions are physically determined. If beliefs do come into the causal generation of an action, this is because holding a belief just is being in a certain physical state, and that state causes the action. If it is no part of the causal story that that physical state is the state of holding a true belief or any belief at all, if the physical state does not enter the causal explanation qua being a holding of a true belief, if that aspect of the state plays no explanatory role, then the action does not track the (true) belief. On this view, being in certain belief and desire states is identical with being in certain physical states, and at this physical level the (movements of the) action can be explained completely. Beliefs and desires are the froth of the underlying causal process.

Given physical causality, how can one find room for actions tracking rightness or bestness, for speech or actions being affected by rational reasons qua rational reasons? (Karl Popper calls this Compton's Problem; we might better call it Kant's Problem.) There are at least three possibilities.

First: Within the physical world there is indeterminism. This physical world is not a closed system; reasons and rational considerations can act upon the physical world within (and only within) the interstices marked by indeterminism. This is the view of Karl Popper.[38]

Second: The physical world is a thoroughly deterministic system; (therefore) it is a closed system in that no nonphysical influences act upon it to produce particular events. However, it is not a unified system (in the sense of "unified science"). Some physical causal laws governing human beings are emergent in that these laws cannot be explained by, deduced from, or reduced to underlying general physical principles of unrestricted application (plus boundary conditions). The causation of human action is physical causation, but it operates unlike other physical causal processes. Even supposing the identity theory of mind-body relations to be true, when a physical state that microreduces accepting certain reasons and having certain desires causes the doing of an action, this causal relation is not deducible from general causal laws applying to physical states that are not microreductions of beliefs and desires. The only causal laws that subsume this particular causal relation are causal laws of action. The realm of (rational) action is emergent; this emergence leaves room for rational principles to determine or constrain the character of physical laws. It is the rational connections of action and reasons, the rational content that makes those specific causal laws hold, and this reflects itself within the physical realm in the irreducibility and emergence of those causal laws that apply especially to those physical movements that compose rational actions. This possibility marks how an action may track beliefs and reasons.

Third: The physical world is deterministic, closed, and unified in that no causal relations concerning human behavior are emergent relative to more general physical principles. Even within such an austere environment we can try to find a place for tracking rightness or bestness, for an action's being dependent upon rational considerations qua rational considerations. Let R be the rational considerations sufficient for doing act B; let r be the physical state that microreduces "accepting R", and let b be the physical happenings and movements involved in (one way of) doing B. Within our austere assumptions, the rational reasons will play a role in a person's doing B only if r causes (or is part of the cause of) b. Is this sufficient for rational considerations to affect his actions, for his actions to track them? Does it follow that if it weren't for the rational considerations, he wouldn't do B?[39]

It follows, let us suppose, that if he weren't in the state r, which is the (physical) state of accepting reasons R, he wouldn't do B. The person, then, is affected by what are rational reasons; for under the micro-reduction, r is accepting those reasons. It does not follow, however, that the person is affected by rational reasons qua rational reasons. True, if he did not accept those reasons he wouldn't do B; but is it true that if those reasons were not reasons for doing B he

334

wouldn't do B, that if he didn't have rational reasons for doing B he wouldn't do it? We are supposing the fact that physical state b causes physical state r is deducible from general laws of physics plus boundary conditions—so it seems that r would cause b even if r reduced accepting that reason R but that reason was not a (rationally) sufficient reason for doing B, or if r reduced accepting another reason, or if r did not reduce accepting a reason at all. (Some will hold this identity of r with accepting R to be necessary if true; they will think only the first disjunct is possible.)

Since r is a neurophysiological state, we may imagine hospital laboratory instruments that detect r's presence and measure it. When the person is hooked up to the measuring instrument, r causes certain effects in it. However, r does not produce these effects in the detecting and measuring instrument qua rational reason for doing B, any more than low blood pressure produces its effects in a sphygmomanometer qua sign of acute fever or heart failure or Addison's disease or hypothyroidism or anemia or hyperinsulinism or intense hemorrhage. Its aspect of being a rational reason for doing B plays no role in r's production of those effects detected by the instrument, no role in the measurement process. Now r has other effects as well; it causes b, for example.

The third view described above has not provided any way to differentiate this effect, b, from the effect on the measuring instrument, so it hasn't (yet) shown that (in the austere deterministic world) rational considerations can affect actions, qua rational considerations.

If actions track rightness, bestness, rational reasons, something further must make the action dependent upon the rational content of the reasons. This further factor is needed to reach the result that if R weren't a rational reason for the person's doing B, he wouldn't do B.*

* Note that the following approach will not give us this result. It might be said that it is a condition of adequacy on a micro-reduction that when movement b is to be explained, the theorist find an r causing b and assign contents "accepting R" and "doing B" to r and b respectively so that R is (plausibly held to be) a rational reason for B. Thus, some version of what philosophers of language call the "principle of charity" is built into micro-reducing practice so that the connections come out rational. A rational patina thus is provided for the underlying causal process. However, this does not yield the subjunctive needed. It gives: if R weren't a rational reason for doing B, then "accepting R" would not be assigned as the to-be-reduced content of physical state r. Rewriting, it gives: if R weren't a rational reason for doing B, then r would not be "accepting R". But it does not yield: if R weren't a rational reason for

The person performs b because he is in state r. To obtain the subjunctive

> S: if R weren't a rational reason for doing B (and there were no other rational reasons for doing B) then he wouldn't perform B (or b)

we need either:

(1) if R weren't a rational reason for B then it wouldn't be that r causes b, or
(2) if R weren't a rational reason for B then he wouldn't have been in state r.

Strictly, we need: if R weren't a rational reason for B then it would not be that both the person is in r and r causes b.

Perhaps the emergentist position described in the second possibility above can yield 1. Under that position, "r causes b" would not be deducible from general physical causal laws that apply as well to unintelligent matters. (I mean to play on the ambiguity.) So room would be left for an explanation of why r causes b that involves R's being a rational reason for doing B. If Kant held that the noumenal self chose the whole phenomenal world including the laws of causality that held in the physical world,[40] and it holds that if R weren't a rational reason for doing B then the noumenal self wouldn't have chosen causal laws under which r causes b, then the subjunctive 1 would follow from this view. Indeed, within this Kantian view the subjunctive 1 would follow even without some causal laws being emergent.

Let us now concentrate on subjunctive 2: if R weren't a rational reason for B then the person wouldn't have been in state r. This is more specific than suits our present purposes; let us consider rational

---

doing B (and there were not other rational reasons for doing B) then he wouldn't perform b. Only with some subjunctive such as this is there tracking wherein rationality qua rationality plays a role. Therefore, subjunctive questions are needed to give questions about rationality some content—for any actual doings, *some* rational content could be devised. And it is only particular sorts of subjunctives that give edge to the issue of rationality.

A satisfactory result requires that rationality, bestness, rightness, truth, and so on, have some subjunctive power over what physically happens. It is not enough that content can be gerrymandered so as to make whatever physically happens rational.

reasons in evolutionary perspective. It seems reasonable to assume there has been some evolutionary advantage in acting for (rational) reasons. The capacity to do so, once it appeared, would have been selected for. Organisms able and prone to act for (rational) reasons gained some increased efficiency in leaving great-grand-progeny.

Selection for acting for (rational) reasons does the following: it selects for organisms so structured that they interact with environments E_B in which doing an act B is rational, by going into a physical state that causes them to do B (or b). Not every organism will go into such a b-causing physical state (call it r) in environments E_B; those physically constituted so as to do so, other things being equal, will be differentially favored. Evolution operates to filter out those organisms whose physical constitution fails to embody a rational pattern, that is, whose physical constitution leads them in environments E_B to be in physical states (r') that cause them to do some b' which is not a rational or effective thing to do in those environments.[41]

An organism's physical constitution may, for a wide range of environments, put it into a physical state that causes it to do something rational, appropriate, or effective in those environments. If also certain other important considerations are satisfied, we can say this organism, its brain or the physical constitution itself, reduces rational considerations; there is evolutionary selection for organisms (brains, constitutions) that reduce rational considerations.[42] Let us make the favorable supposition that this line of thought will hold up under further elaboration. Even so, it does not follow, about a particular organism of particular constitution, that if R weren't a rational reason for B then the organism wouldn't be in r, that is, would be in some physical state other than r. If R weren't a rational reason for B (and similarly for enough of its states and behaviors) then organisms of that type of constitution would not exist at all, and so neither would that particular organism. It is not that if R weren't a rational reason for B then the organism would behave differently; it simply would not be here to behave. The evolutionary explanation does not explain why r causes b. It explains why an organism of that type of constitution exists, an organism that goes into r under environment E_B, and also it explains why the organism goes into r under E_B.[43] If the organism did not reduce rational considerations, it would not exist. If R weren't a rational reason for B, then that organism and others of its kind which go into r under environments E_B, would not exist. However, we cannot say that if R weren't a rational reason for B then that organism (would exist and) would not be in r. Still, what we have been able to say seems sufficient for rationality to be operating in the world qua rationality. If the organism's being in r were not rational, it wouldn't be in the world; the world would be different. The way rationality qua rationality operates in the physical world, according to our line of argument, has been termed "downward causality".[44]

Our discussion of how rationality qua rationality operates in the world, of how a piece of physical reality can track the rationality of a reason, has focused on a subjunctive corresponding to the third condition for tracking. To show how a physical state can track rationality, we also need a subjunctive corresponding to the fourth condition for tracking: if R were a rational reason for B in environment E_B, then the organism would (have a constitution leading it to) do B (or b) in that environment. Evolutionary considerations do make this plausible as well. True, not every possible ecological niche gets filled, some exclude others, but since our topic is the impact of rationality qua rationality on actual happenings (namely, our own behavior), and since that ecological niche has been filled actually, the subjunctive that it would be filled with that constitution is given plausibility.

When an evolutionary explanation shows how some item's having a certain feature contributes to the inclusive fitness of the organism with that item, then (provided certain other conditions are met specifying the role of the feature in contributing to inclusive fitness) on some views this is sufficient to show that having that feature is the, or at least a, function of the item. On these views, then, a function of having the physical constitution discussed above is to reduce rationality considerations; a function of (being in) physical state r is to reduce a rational reason for doing B. Not only do various physical things (physical constitutions and states) happen to reduce and thereby embody rationality considerations, their function is to reduce and embody these rationality considerations. Rationality qua rationality thereby operates in the world.[45]

Hilary Putnam has suggested that mental states are not identical with an organism's physical states, but rather are functionally related states, one (but not the only possible) realization of which is the organism's physical states and their causal relations.[46] The essence of functionally related states, their only identifying characteristic, is their property of being related to other states and behavior in specified ways. Any physical (or even nonphysical) realization of these relations will be these mental states. A view suggested by our discussion thus far is that the biological function of the physical states is to be a realization of (particular rational instances of something like Putnam's) functional connections. (The previous sentence used two senses of "function".) This view is compatible with Putnam's position on the mind-body question, and also it is compatible with the mind-body identity theory.

Putnam is correct in saying that the particular material basis is not important, that beings made of different stuff could be in the same mental states as we. However, it does not follow that nothing about the material basis is essential, provided only that the functional interconnections hold. If a marble rolling up and down a channel in the head of a Martian had the functional interconnections that pain has for us, it would not follow that when in this marble-rolling state the Martian was in pain. (Recent philosophical literature uses "Martian" to refer to any alien intelligent life form.) In addition to Putnam's macro-requirement of functional isomorphism, two micro-conditions must be satisfied: first, that the corresponding states under the functional isomorphism are themselves isomorphic in internal structure; and second—what gives the first content—that these corresponding states perform their role in the functional macro-isomorphism in a way that is dependent upon their (isomorphic) internal structures. The structure that the states isomorphically share is what explains each carrying out its macrorole in the functional isomorphism. Martians can be made of sterner stuff, but if they are to have the same mental states we do, their physical states have not only to perform the same external functional role but also to be (internally) configured in the same way as ours.[47]

The view suggested above, combining this modification of Putnam's theory with biological functionality, holds that mental states are (physical) states of the organism whose (biological) function is to help realize certain abstract relationships and interconnections. Martians whose states differ from ours in the internal configurations that explain their performing the same roles in the macro-functional isomorphism are in different mental states. Yet even Martians in the same physical state as we, the same internal physical configuration performing the same macro-functional role, realized in the same material stuff, are in different mental states when those physical states of theirs do not have the same biological function as ours do: to help realize and instantiate those particular abstract (rational) relationships. They will not exhibit our mental states if their same physical state (though linked in the macro-relations) has no function at all, or has a function different from ours.

Two types of functions have been distinguished: the first (following Putnam), something's (functional) role at the macro-level; the second, the biological function of a physical state. We should not restrict this second type of function to those based on evolution. A component of artificially created life also may have a function, most clearly when the designers placed the component there in order to do a certain thing. We have emphasized that the two functions may be linked: performing the (first) macro-functional role may be the (biological) function of a physical state. They need not be, however; a state might participate in the web of macro-functional relations without that fact explaining (whether through intended purpose or evolutionary selection) why that state exists or has the features it does. In that case, the state would have a function (of the first sort) within the macro-web of relations, yet it would not be its function (of the second sort) to be within that web. A Martian's state must match ours in both functions, we have said, if his state is to be the same as ours. There is a difficulty in insisting upon this double functionality if a particular Martian's physical state has no (second type) function at all, if no selective pressure or designer led to or maintains that state's existence. Still, won't the Martian's state be ours—pain or wondering, for example—if his state performs the same role as ours at the macro-level due to the same internal configuration? True, the probability is miniscule that his state just got plunked into its world and web of relationships by accident, with no functional point to it. Nevertheless, the possibility inclines me to think that perhaps the physical realization of what plays the macro-role need not have as one of its (second type) functions, realizing that role.[48]

We hold that a Martian is in the same state as we when he is in a state with the same functional interconnections, and the configuration (if any) in virtue of which his state realizes this role is the same as the configuration whereby ours does, provided (?) his state has the same function of realizing this role as ours does. Note that we take precedence in fixing the state, its two functions and internal configuration; it is fixed as what we have. (Here we apply the views of Kripke and Putnam on the fixing of reference.) If we humans differ among ourselves in the functionally relevant internal configuration, then there will be serious questions about whether we are in the same mental states.

All this says little, however, about the mind-body problem: how is consciousness, felt awareness and experience, related to the bodily happenings? We have not said that conscious awareness qua conscious awareness is irrelevant to mental states; one would think conscious awareness is intertwined in the functional interconnections and in how the physical states manage to realize certain functional roles. So far as I know, little illumination thus far has been shed on the evolutionary adaptive advantage of conscious awareness. Is conscious awareness necessary for certain other things, or instead is it an efficient facilitator of them? Although other nonconscious routes to achieving or doing them are imaginable, perhaps these other things actually would not have happened without the evolution of conscious awareness. It would be helpful to see specific features and functions of conscious awareness discussed in an evolutionary context. Still, to know that and how physical states were selected for as realizers of conscious awareness does not tell one how conscious awareness is related to the physical state realizing it. Evolutionary selection would operate even if the physical states and the conscious ones simply were reliably correlated.*

Our account of how rationality qua rationality can operate in the physical world within a causal deterministic framework gave a central place to evolutionary theory. It is evolutionary selection that gave the states r the function of reducing rational considerations. Can the account be extended so that not only rationality but also rightness or bestness acts in the world? Is an evolutionary basis needed here as well, and does this turn out to support the claim that we track rightness qua rightness, or does it undermine that claim?

* Should it surprise us that the problem of the mind-body relationship thus far has proven to be intractable? It has been approached only from one end— by the mind from its standpoint. The body end comes in only when the mind takes a look at the body. Perhaps it is not enough to put our minds to the mind-body relationship; perhaps we have to put our bodies to it too, in the right way.

Does Sociobiology Undercut Tracking?

We have shown how rational considerations might act, qua rational considerations, within the physical world. In removing one general objection to thinking that actions can track rational considerations, however, we have not thereby shown how actions might track rightness or bestness. The evolutionary factors considered thus far do not indicate how the tracking of such evaluative properties might possess adaptive value. Indeed, such evolutionary considerations, far from showing their adaptive value, seem to eliminate evaluative facts. There is adaptive value in tracking truth and rationality; an evolutionary explanation will give a role to truth and rationality or to some closely linked surrogates. However, an evolutionary explanation of social or ethical behavior threatens to bypass moral rightness or bestness completely.

An evolutionary explanation threatens to snap a component connection in an action's tracking rightness, between the belief that the act is right or best and the evaluative facts. It does this by attempting to explain our evaluative beliefs without at any point bringing in evaluative facts, and so denies that the evaluative beliefs track these facts. Even if the action tracks the belief, then, it too does not track the evaluative facts. This type of explanation does more than threaten the link wherein our beliefs track evaluative facts; if successfully carried through, it also would seem to show that it is unreasonable to believe there are any such (objective) evaluative facts at all. It seems to show not only that we have not been tracking them and so don't know them, but that it is unreasonable for us to think any such facts exist. Given the absence of any demonstration or strong argument that there are such facts, despite repeated attempts by philosophers, if also all of our ethical behavior and beliefs can be explained without in any way assuming their existence, then it would seem unreasonable to continue to think there are these facts—especially if and when our supposing they exist also can be explained without assuming they do.

Not every social scientific explanation of our ethical beliefs and behavior undercuts the reasonableness of believing that objective ethical facts exist. For example, the explanation that we hold certain ethical beliefs because we were brought up to do so, and socialized into doing so, leaves open the possibility that those who inculcated such beliefs in us did so intentionally because they realized that the beliefs were true. Most of us believe many mathematical statements simply because we were taught they were true; this alone doesn't show there are no objective mathematical facts, or that our belief can be explained without reference to them. It depends on whether, back in the chain of teachers of teachers, we find someone whose belief we must explain by reference to the truth of what is believed. Similarly, to explain why that particular ethical socialization got started or continues, we may need to refer to the truth of the ethical statements. To be sure, we cannot yet specify, even roughly, how we know ethical truths. However, our inability thus far to develop an adequate epistemology for mathematics, to specify how we can know *those* truths, has not pushed us to conclude that there are no such truths. Why should things be different with ethics? For example, intuitionist epistemological views about ethics should not be dismissed on the basis of types of arguments that clearly do not refute the corresponding epistemological position about mathematics, one defended by Kurt Gödel.[49]

A social scientific explanation will threaten the rationality of believing in the existence of such objective facts when, unlike the socialization explanation, it leaves no room for saying "but perhaps that all got started because someone realized the facts were true." The threatening explanation, that is, must be an invisible hand explanation which shows how the facts arose from some blind mechanism that in no way had the facts in mind or presupposed the truth.*

Prime examples of invisible hand explanations are evolutionary explanations, and these have begun to be applied to ethics and social behavior.[50] Since these attempts are in their infancy, as one would expect, slips are made and factors are overlooked.[51] However, the particular slips do not obviate the fruitfulness of the approach; and some mistakes can point to further fruitful development.[52]

In presenting invisible hand explanations of ethics, we are not lim-

---

* The notion of invisible hand explanations is delineated in my *Anarchy, State, and Utopia*, pp. 18–22. Even an invisible hand explanation of why we accept *p* does not absolutely preclude introducing the truth of *p* at a deeper level, for perhaps the whole invisible hand process (which yields our believing *p*) exists only because someone realized *p* was true and so instituted an invisible hand process that would yield our belief that *p*. In such a way, a theologically based ethical view might withstand an invisible hand explanation while admitting its correctness so far as it goes.

ited to evolutionary ones. The theory of operant conditioning offers another invisible hand explanation suitable for these purposes: a behavior pattern can arise and be maintained by contingencies of reinforcement which in no way envision or try or intend to bring about such patterns.[53]

Let us roughly sketch the program of explaining ethical beliefs and behavior in invisible hand fashion utilizing evolutionary theory, the theory of operant conditioning, and whatever other "blind" theories might fit in with the project. The theory of operant conditioning will imagine behavior B in interpersonal situations performed for other reasons yet having as a side effect the shaping of the behavior of others. In some mutual process, everyone's behavior gets shaped into a pattern P. (Note the importance of that shaping being a side effect of the people's behavior. Otherwise there would remain the question of why they wanted to get others to act in accordance with the pattern P.) Even this explanation of P would be entangled with evolutionary explanations of P if the tendency to perform B was selected for (partly) because it leads to P's being instituted. The invisible hand explanation of an adult behavior pattern will show how it arises from innate behaviors via a blind shaping process wherein the shaping behavior of others also has an invisible hand explanation. Thus, we would expect such explanations to have a recursive structure.[54]

Invisible hand explanations seem to undercut the objective status of ethics by showing that ethical behavior can be explained without in any way introducing ethical truths. If ethical behavior is adaptive, if that behavior increases inclusive fitness, and is genetically based and heritable, over the generations it will spread more widely. Ethically behaving individuals will leave more great-grandchildren or (given kin selection) great-grandnephews and nieces similarly disposed.

However, this explanation of the spread of ethical behavior, of the increasing ratio in the population of those who behave ethically, does not undercut the (possible) role of ethical facts in the origin of that behavior, or in its performance in the later generations. To see this point, suppose that a knowledge of rudimentary truths of number theory has adaptive value, because of the advantages it gives in warfare, the hunt, domestic activity, or whatever. If the capacity to recognize such truths and the predisposition to act on them is genetically based and heritable, these capacities will spread in the population so that a higher proportion of the organisms will come to take account of arithmetical truths in their behavior. But though the spread is explained "blindly", each individual's behavior is not. The first individuals recognized that $2 + 2 = 4$ and similar such facts; to explain their behavior, and its success, we have to introduce the fact that these arithmetical statements are true. Because of the advantage bestowed, these individuals left more descendants with similar arithmetical capacities. Their behavior too is to be explained in terms of their recognition of arithmetical truths. That those organisms are there to recognize those truths, and have the capacity to do so, receives an evolutionary explanation, but nonetheless the truths enter into explaining their behavior. Moreover, the truths enter into the evolutionary explanation of the spread of the capacities. The capacities are adaptive, as is the predisposition to act on the beliefs, because the beliefs are true and acting on the truth helps.

If ethical behavior increases inclusive fitness, this will explain the spread of such behavior in the population. Yet each individual's behavior, ancestor or descendant, might be explained by her recognizing certain ethical truths and acting on them. What spreads in the population can be the capacity to recognize certain (ethical) truths and the predisposition to act on this recognition. It is compatible with an evolutionary explanation of a capacity that it is a capacity to detect or to track some truths. Recall the last section of Chapter 3; not only does evolution not undercut the tracking of truths, it sometimes yields it.

Must *truth* be brought in? Cannot we explain beliefs in terms of the explicitly nonevaluative facts that underlie the moral truths, those in virtue of which the (supervenient) moral truths hold, without bringing the truth of the moral beliefs into the explanation? But then why the people come to have that moral belief under that factual situation would be left without any explanation, as a brute fact.*

* Would a continuity with animal behavior show that ethical behavior involved no recognition of ethical truths? No one should doubt that ethical behavior stems from a matrix of other behavior, transforming it, but this will show it is "no different" only to those who think an exploration of Shakespeare's literary sources and influences shows he did "nothing new". Also, we need not be committed to the view that no other higher animal can possibly exhibit the glimmerings of rudimentary ethical recognitions.

For selection to operate, there must be a correlation (constituting herita-

Will the explanation of why the ethical beliefs are selected for, of why the behavior is adaptive, bring in the fact that these beliefs are true? However the behavior increases inclusive fitness, won't this connection be independent of the truth of the beliefs? The ethical behavior will serve inclusive fitness through serving or not harming others, through helping one's children and relatives, through acts that aid them in escaping predators, and so forth; that this behavior is helpful and not harmful is not unconnected to why (on most theorist's views) it is ethical. The ethical behavior will increase inclusive fitness through the very aspects that make it ethical, not as a side effect through features that only accidentally are connected with ethicality.[55]

Thus, evolutionary theory may provide an explanation of why the capacity to recognize ethical truths has spread, showing some neurophysiological structures have the function of realizing that capacity, or a wider capacity that includes it. The explanation of the adaptedness of arithmetical capacities probably will not bring in the truth of the arithmetical beliefs much more than this. (Recall the tenor of pragmatic theories of truth; in explaining how a particular false approximation was of service, will one have to specify how close it was to the truth?) And in each case, arithmetical and ethical, the capacities of recognition selected for will reveal splendors beyond the then useful. The abilities especially to recognize, prove, or understand a proof that there is no greatest prime number or that every number has a unique prime factorization, I suppose, made no special contribution to survival. But the mathematical realm, once entered for narrow utilizable purposes merely, exhibits its own further structure and intricacies. Similarly, the capacity to recognize ethical truths unveils surprising structures, convolutions, refinements, modulations,

---

bility) between the traits of different organisms, indicating transmission from one to another. William Durham has pointed out that this correlation need not be genetically based but may stem from transmission by cultural means. ("Toward a Co-evolutionary Theory of Human Biology and Culture", in N. Chagnon and W. Irons, eds., *Evolutionary Biology And Human Social Behavior*, Duxbury Press, Scituate Mass., 1979, pp. 39–59.) So one cannot conclude merely from the fact that behavior serves inclusive fitness that it was transmitted genetically. This point is not undermined by continuity with behavior in subcultural animals, for once cultural transmission operates it allows genetic change to proceed underneath without adverse selection, since the behavior pattern gets maintained anyway, by other means.

and asymmetries. Reflective people, on their own or when presented with them, are led to recognize these features and give them some weight, features having little apparent connection with inclusive fitness or actual schedules of reinforcement and shaping. This is evidence of a realm with its own objective standing and characteristics.*

Mention of reflective thinking about ethics indicates a substantial stumbling block to carrying through an explanation of ethics in a thoroughgoing invisible hand fashion: consciousness, language, and self-consciousness. The question is not whether there will be evolutionary explanations of how consciousness, language, and self-consciousness arise and are selected for. The question is whether once these do arise by a blind process, they then operate and lead to some things unblindly. (Do percepts with concepts *stay* blind?) That there is an invisible hand explanation of our having our cognitive capacities does not mean there is an invisible hand explanation of my writing the contents of this book.

The advent of consciousness, language, conceptual abilities, and self-consciousness opens new possibilities: we can notice how we are behaving, decide to have our behavior conform to general principles of behavior, produce reasons for and against our beliefs and critically discuss them, weight these reasons, be inspired by moral figures and decide to emulate them, formulate conceptions of what we want ourselves to be like, notice what is getting us to behave in that way and consider whether we want to behave in that way or to continue to put ourselves under the influence of certain causes, and so on. It need no longer be true of our pattern of moral behavior (and beliefs) that no one tried to bring it about; it need no longer be true that the correct explanation of why it exists and continues is a blind explanation. Since what arises via a blind process need not itself be blind, this can lead to new things that cannot themselves be explained by an invisible hand explanation.[56]

These factors do not guarantee that our actions are sometimes tracking rightness or bestness, or that the explanation of some of our

---

* See the convolutions and asymmetries of the multileveled balancing structure described in Part III of the next chapter; or, for a different example, the literature on the doctrine of double-effect. I am aware that further biological investigation often shows the adaptiveness of apparently nonadaptive physical features; so caution is appropriate in claiming that on the face of it, certain features cannot be shown to be adaptive.

347

moral beliefs must eventually refer to their truth. These considerations do specify, though, what on any plausible view will be means through which tracking operates. And they do show that the total absence of tracking will not follow from the (successful) offering of some invisible hand explanations. There will remain the question of what explains the moral actions and beliefs of conscious persons who critically reexamine their own moral principles. Perhaps the explanation of how ethical actions, beliefs, and principles originate and endure will turn out not to refer to the truth of the principles believed; but in any case, that will not be purely an invisible hand explanation. Even pure invisible hand explanations, we already have seen, need not undercut the existence of ethical or evaluative truths or the fact of our tracking them.[57]

Acts in Equilibrium

The notion of tracking rightness or bestness has been specified independently of causality. The tracking might operate through causal processes or instead result from a decision process that is not causally determined, such as the one of weighting reasons described in the first part of this chapter. It is a virtue of the tracking account that it can fit both the indeterminist and the determinist backgrounds. This second part of the chapter mainly (though not solely) investigates tracking bestness against a presumed background of determinism. True, the causally determined agent and action will not have originative value; but there are ways one might reduce the sting of determinism.

Provided that our action is tracking bestness or rightness, why should it bother us that the particular act is caused, or that we are caused (in general) to track bestness? If we knew of the causes, would we want to behave any differently? When explanations tell us the causes of our holding certain beliefs or doing certain actions, this greater self-knowledge sometimes leads us to (want to) change the way we are. Knowledge of the causes of our doing an act may lead us to not do it (any more), or no longer to want to do it, or to want not to want to do it. The knowledge may change our action or our desire— or at least our desire about desire. Psychoanalytic therapy is said to depend on the assumption that knowledge and understanding of the

causes of certain desires or modes of behavior will lead to the alteration of these desires; the causes will lose their power.[58]

Let us say an act is in disequilibrium for a person if (a) he does (or
wants to do) it, yet (b) if he knew the causes of his doing or wanting
to do it, this knowledge would lead him not to do it, or not to want to
(or to want not to want to do it, or at least to a lessening of his want to
do it—I shall not keep repeating these latter clauses). When condition a is satisfied but b is not, the act is in equilibrium. An act in
equilibrium withstands knowledge of its own causes. Strictly, we
should say the act is in equilibrium not when b fails to hold but
when the opposing subjunctive holds: if he knew the causes of his
doing or wanting to do the act then he still would (want to) do it as
much.[59]

Clearly, it is desirable that the acts we do be in equilibrium, that
they (and we) be able to stand and withstand knowledge of their
causes. Would it not be very distressing to learn or believe that if you
knew why you were pursuing some major course of action, what was
causing you to do so, you wouldn't then choose to do it? Even if we
do not know an act's specific causes, can doing it withstand the (general) knowledge that that act is in disequilibrium? Carrying on philosophy (semi-)coercively as described in the Introduction is not, I
believe, in equilibrium.

The unmasking of motives depends upon this disequilibrium.
Nietzsche, for example, diagnoses self-contempt, insufficient love of
self, and a resentful envy of those recognized to be better and superior as at the heart of Christian "slave morality".[60] He assumes that
adherence to this morality cannot withstand an acknowledgment and
facing of its real (ignoble) motives. (Did he underestimate how ignoble people are willing to be?) That there are bad motives for a position does not show there *couldn't* be good motives for it; yet perhaps
no one whose bad motives were unmasked would have any good
reason (other than inertia?) for searching for further (good) motives to
motivate continuing the old position. Freudian explanations of creative or artistic activity as sublimation often are taken as demeaning
("if those are the motives, who would want to do that?"); but it also
is possible for them to be meant and read, as in the case of Erikson
on Gandhi, as delineating the wonderousness of the transformation
of lesser materials.[61]

One philosophical tradition held that freedom is knowledge of necessity. The puzzle is why knowledge of what one is stuck with should constitute freedom rather than, say, knowledge of unfreedom. May we read this tradition as saying that a necessary condition, at least, of freedom is that knowledge of necessity, knowledge of the causal conditions of an act, will not lead (perhaps as an additional causal factor) to the action's not being done or wanted? Put somewhat more tersely, a necessary condition, at least, of an act's being free is that it be in equilibrium. We would be able to maintain this if we could suitably connect the two notions expounded: an act's being in equilibrium, and an act's tracking rightness or bestness. Unfortunately, the details of the connection are not neat.[62]

It always has remained unclear what it would mean to say of man that he is naturally good. To say "he is caused to be bad" does not help much, if (when he is good) he is caused to be good also. Even if these are caused by different routes, in virtue of what is one of the routes natural? Under some circumstances we develop in one direction, under other circumstances in another. There seems to be no way to pick out which direction is natural without first picking out some circumstances as natural—a bewildering project, to say the least. An optimistic view would hold that people who pursue things other than bestness, for example pleasure or fame, would no longer want to (want to) as much, if they knew what caused them to track these. On this view, all badness is a deformation and the resulting partial desires and false values would be eliminated or weakened by knowledge of their causes. This is not to identify false values as those that are caused by situations we wouldn't want to be in; since Aeschylus, people have distinguished the worth of a lesson from the desirability of the school. The gloss on "man is naturally good", according to the optimistic view, is that being good is in equilibrium, while being bad is not: a good act is an unfrozen act in equilibrium. (This notion of naturalness might be of help in clarifying the notion of a sexual perversion.) The optimistic view might combine with theories that identify goodness with what would be chosen under specified conditions,[63] by adding to those conditions the additional one that, for each choice, the chooser knows what would be the cause of his making that choice. This addition assures that what is chosen under the canonical choice conditions will be in equilibrium (while perhaps the other conditions function to exclude those bizarre cases where badness is compatible with equilibrium).

Equilibrium is a subjunctive notion, specifying that something would stay the same if the person were to know its causes. Let us say, in the occurrent situation when the person does have the causal knowledge and the belief or action does stay unchanged, that the belief or action *socratizes*. Earlier we saw that equilibrium was not sufficient for tracking bestness or truth. Is socratizing?

We cannot be sure that anyone's act now is in equilibrium, much less socratizes. As we gain more knowledge, including scientific knowledge within psychology, sociobiology, and sociology, perhaps we will want to modify our current wants and character. Suppose these wanted changes were made, that people were transformed in the direction they chose as a result of knowing the causes of their own (previous) behavior. If they then are not yet in equilibrium, let the process continue. The good would be the (using the term in another sense) equilibrium this process reaches, if it reaches one. Perhaps we are only near the beginning of development with more to come, including moral development. Monism about goodness holds this iterated process has a unique equilibrium (at least as a limit), pluralism that there are multiple equilibria, and pessimism holds that there is no such equilibrium, no possible way we can withstand our knowing the causes of our being that way, so a socratic person is impossible.[64]

Are there at least some (unfrozen) desires that are in equilibrium? Consider a function representing how desires are transformed under knowledge of their causes. (If the universe is deterministic there will be such a function.) Let function t on ordered pairs D_i, C_i of desires and causes be such that $t(D_i, C_i) = D_j$, when desire D_j is the result of having had desire D_i and learning that C_i was its cause. Is there some desire D with causes C such that the desire remains under the new knowledge: $t(D, C) = D$? Do any plausible conditions suffice to prove that there must be a fixed point under the transformation t? Are the desires to track bestness or rightness, and to track the truth, fixed points under t? At least, is the desire to have beliefs and actions be in equilibrium, a fixed point under t? If so, are we not then in a position to deflect the complaint that since these desires are caused like any others, their holders are as mired as anyone else in the causal nexus?

Yet there is a problem, even with this. For if desires are caused, then so is "the desire to do act A knowing its (previous) causes".

Even if we require strong equilibrium and unfrozenness, cannot the causal process that instilled the desire to do an act also do such a thorough job that the desire withstands a knowledge of its own actual causes (yet would not withstand some other possible causal story, and so is unfrozen)? We should not be reassured completely, then, by a desire's being in equilibrium. However, though not sufficient for our not being a plaything of the causal processes, it is necessary. When combined with tracking rightness or bestness, it shows how we would want causal determination to proceed, given that it exists.* We would want our causally determined acts to be in (unfrozen) equilibria, tracking bestness.

Self-Choosing

The conception of a free act as one tracking rightness or bestness in equilibrium specifies freedom in terms of outcome—doing what is best and being subjunctively connected to bestness—rather than in terms of a process that is to lead to this (or some other) outcome. This outcome specifies what we would like to do with our freedom, what we would like it to result in; the ordinary view holds that a free action is one that results from a process of free choice, a process that can yield a wrong act too. To be sure, the tracking view leaves room for choice, deliberation and so on, as the mechanism whereby tracking is effected, but it does not specify any characteristic of the choice process in virtue of which it counts as free. In the first part of this chapter we presented such a view of the decision process, the indeterminist account of weighting reasons.

How close can we come to simulating this process deterministically? (Compare a digital simulation of an analogue process.) Here enter the various "software" techniques allowing some flexibility in the pursuit of goals, modifying some goals when they conflict with others, subordinating some goals to other more general or weighty ones, and so on. It is reasonably clear how all this might work with subsidiary goals. When they are seen (via cognitive mechanisms) no

* Unless one thought any level of causal determination was despotic and, not wanting to be a content slave, therefore didn't want any desire to sit happily alongside knowledge of its causes. But is that preference self-subsuming, so that it prefers even itself not to be in equilibrium?

longer to serve deeper purposes and goals, they are altered, replaced, submerged, overridden. We might imagine even that the
higher goal does not have absolute priority, that it can be replaced
and altered when it conflicts with a sufficient number and weight of
lower-level goals that originally perhaps merely were means to it.[65]
And we can throw in all sorts of arcana: loops, feedback loops, TOTE
and other hierarchies, precommitting devices, and private side bets
to govern behavior in the face of earlier greater reward.[66] All these
give greater flexibility. Even more flexibility might be introduced by
machinery for conceptual and goal gestalt switches, whereby (in
some situations) a discontinuous move, not itself falling under a previous consciously formulated concept or goal, is made to another system of concepts or goals.

It is not difficult to imagine how such capacities and capabilities,
the bread and butter of the free will theorist when he descends to
the specific, might have adaptive value and be selected for in the
process of evolution. Perhaps together they constitute the substratum
of the capacity to track rightness or bestness. However, these capacities will not lift us outside the causal nexus; when the flow diagram
is set out in detail, it will be clear how everything happens. The set
of ordered pairs of environmental inputs and resulting actions will
be recursively enumerable, if not recursive.

What we want to be able to do is to choose radically new goals,
and not be tied to modifications of the goals built into us. In terms of
what can we choose? What we really want is to be able to choose
ourselves, all the way up to our highest (order) flow diagram. How
can that be possible? The interest of this question is not restricted
merely to the determinist account; the indeterminist account of
weighting reasons also seems to fall short of this aspiration for total
self-choosing. Yet the contradeterminist theorist too feels the pull of
this aspiration—more so even—so he must investigate it, draw it
out.

One tradition, that of Locke and Hume, holds that we are not free
when our acts are caused by an independent source that operates
independently of our will and preferences instead of through them;
otherwise, we are free. A second tradition, Kant's, holds that we are
free when our acts are done in accordance with reason, when a law
of reason determines them. A third tradition holds that our acts are
free when they are not caused by any independent source at all, and

arise only out of our own essence. (Thus, Spinoza holds that God alone is free.) Hegel combines the second tradition with the third by following Aristotle in holding that reason and thought are of the essence of man. According to him, we are free when determined self-consciously by a law of reason, which is a principle constitutive of our essential nature.[67]

Is even Hegel's solution enough? Though an action stems from our essence, can't we be stuck with our essence and so to that degree be not autonomous? Need chains that don't arise from an alien source be any the less binding? It sometimes is useful to transform proposed bases for morality into explicitly hypothetical form. Why should I do that particular act which is right or moral? "Do it (if you want) to be moral!" But why should I (want to) be moral? "Do it (if you want) to be happy!" Must I want to be happy, is that a binding goal, is happiness everything? "Do what is right (if you want) to be rational!"*

Only a philosopher would think that this is a clincher. Who else would think that the ultimate insult is to be called irrational? So I'm not rational; why should I (want to) be rational? "Your essence is rationality: do what is right (if you want) to realize your essence!" Look, it's bad enough that this is my essence—must I encourage it? Why shouldn't I view my essence as an unfortunate handicap? "Your essence is you. Do what is right (if you want) to be really you!" First of all, I am myself without doing it. And if in that case I am not *really* I, must I want that? Is being I so wonderful that inescapably I must want it? Could I not rather be a star or the Messiah or God? "But you have no choice; you must be what you inescapably are!" Ah, so that is what you are offering me as freedom. I prefer to describe it differently.

It seems that to have an objective morality we must have something whose presence or claim or allure is inescapable; yet to have freedom, we must have something that does not bind us. A free being isn't just *stuck*. If these are incompatible requirements, as they

---

* On one reading this is Kant's view. "Kant's Categorical Imperative would permit of the following hypothetical formulation without any injustice to Kant's thought: do this, if you want to be rational! The condition here is of a kind that seemed to Kant sufficiently unique to warrant the name 'Categorical Imperative'" (Walter Kaufmann, *Nietzsche*, Princeton University Press, Princeton, 1950, p. 146). Another reading might see Kant as saying "do this (if you want) to be free."

seem, then there cannot be a free being with an objective morality. In the next chapter we shall return to this question.

Kant tells us that the law that does not bind is the law we give ourselves, a law not borrowed from nature but legislated by reason by the necessity of its own nature.[68] We have seen that our essence and the nature and necessities of reason may themselves be viewed as binding us. Kant also would hold that an autonomous being will choose to guide herself by the moral law, acting only out of reverence for the moral law; any other choice from another motive makes us passively subject to that motive and so not autonomous. But why doesn't reverence for the moral law also show us to be passively bound? If because it reflects or encapsulates our nature, cannot that too bind us? In any case, couldn't one act equally autonomously from another motive? (Kant does not want to call reverence for the moral law a motive, but its status in his theory is unclear and we may leave that issue aside here.) Imagine someone who decides to act on the principle of discovering what the categorical imperative or moral law requires, and then doing the opposite. "But what motive for this could he possibly have?" If we must attribute one, perhaps he acts purely from reverence for autonomy. The prospects are not bright for deriving morality from autonomy.

The moral law must not only be given to ourselves and so chosen, it must be given by something that itself is chosen. Only what arises from a chosen essence will not bind. But if that essence is chosen, in what way is it inescapable? Can we have our cake and choose it too? There is one essence that would not bind: being a self-chooser. The fullest autonomy is had only by a being whose essence is self-choosing.

We shall pursue this notion of self-choosing; but first we must pause to consider whether even this essence is indeed nonbinding. Although this essence perhaps is the minimal possible constraint and so the one that most nearly approaches full autonomy, still, would it not bind or constrain us somewhat? Is being a self-chooser so wonderful that everyone would want to be like that? Might not someone choose to be a non-self-chooser? Note that in choosing to be different, to be(come) a non-self-chooser, you would be exercising that self-choosing nature, and so, in virtue of that choice, you would be (at the fundamental level) a self-chooser. It is impossible to choose not to have your nature as a self-chooser, for in so choosing you express and exercise that very nature. The essence being a self-chooser does not constrain or bind any choices yet it is inescapable—as those who choose to escape it discover.

The person who has sold himself into slavery differs from someone else born into that status: the first has chosen to be a slave. An inalienable right is one you are stuck with, in contrast to a right that can be alienated by exercising it (or another) in a certain way; one is not stuck with an alienable right of freedom. Nevertheless, someone who sells himself into slavery is always stuck with once having been free. There is no way he can avoid that, and there is no way a self-chooser can avoid once having made a choice that led to his current non-choosing situation. There will always be that skeleton in the closet of his past. Might not someone dislike ever being a self-chooser, and although he cannot choose not to be a product of self-choice, can't he wish he were not?

To be a self-chooser constrains no future choices, and so that essence does not constrain freedom. However, someone might wish never to have been a self-chooser. Is "once to have been free" itself a constraint upon freedom? If so, it surely is less of one than its alternative, "never to have been free"; it is the minimal constraint imaginable. Perhaps it is not constraints upon freedom that someone most wishes to avoid, but rather constraints generally. Having a particular nature, or once having had it, is a limitation, an inescapable and unalterable fact about oneself. We might make it no longer hold true in the future, but we are stuck with it as a part of our past. (Even someone with the power to alter the past still has it as part of his altered away whatchimicallit.) We shall return in the final chapter to the desire not to be any particular thing, the desire to be unlimited.

Consider again the person who does not want to be a self-chooser. Though he cannot (successfully) choose not to be one, he regrets being one. Where did he get that desire not to be a self-chooser and why does he regret its not being satisfied? If he chose that desire and to act upon it, then at the fundamental level he is a self-chooser. So let us imagine him finding himself with the desire, and hence happy that he has it that way since he doesn't want to be a self-chooser. However, being happy he has the desire D means he has another desire D' to have D, one that he would act on in some appropriate choice situation. D' would lead him (in the appropriate choice situation) to choose to have D; presumably also it does lead him to refrain from altering the desire D with which he finds himself. Despite his desire D, he is coming close to some degree of self-choosing through D'.

People have higher order wants about what wants and desires to have, what they are to be like.[69] A desirable condition is that there be some level of desire such that the desires at all higher levels endorse this level. The most harmony would be exhibited if all desires above the first level endorsed the first level desires, that is, stand in the ancestral of the desiring-relation to the first level desires. We are considering a weaker condition, however, namely that starting from some level or other, there is harmony from then on up.[70] Instead of imagining an infinite number of levels, we can imagine that we reach a desire that desires some desire at the next lowest level and also self-subsumptively desires itself. Let us say that a desire dangles if no desire (including itself) desires it. We want not only that from some level up our desires are harmonious but also that no chain of desires up through the levels terminates with a dangling desire.

However, a person who wants not to be a self-chooser wants that the chain for each desire he has terminate in a dangling desire. But we can ask about this very want—call it W—would he act on it and so is he not to that extent a (potential) self-chooser? Also, it seems that having the want W prevents his desires at the end of the chain from dangling purely. Take any particular non-self-subsumptive desire d at the end of a chain; although there is no other desire to have it especially, W is a desire to have it or something like it. W yields d by existential instantiation. With no further preferences among the desires that would fit W, d does as well as any, and so can be viewed as maximally desired by W. Thus d is not just dangling, when W is present. Finally, is W itself a self-referring desire in that the person also wants W to be left dangling? Yet to want there to be no further desire for W is already to have some desire about the status of W and so to place W in a context of desire, a context so tight that it is self-referring. To recapitulate the path we have taken: we worried whether being a self-chooser did not limit autonomy somewhat, and noticing that someone could not (successfully) choose to be a non-self-chooser, we turned to consider the situation of someone, unable to choose it, who wants to be a non-self-chooser, only to encounter similar puzzles about his wanting to be a non-self-wanter. Let us return, then, to the relationship of self-choosing to free will.

There are two obvious problems in attempting to use the notion of a self-chooser to illuminate the problem of human free will. First, the notion is itself so obscure that we may doubt whether it is a coherent notion, and whether, if it is, it has sufficient (nonformal) content to yield a determinate result about what (else) a self-chooser would choose to be like. (Will a self-chooser, having no particular reason to be one determinate way, choose to realize all possibilities?) Can we say that if the notion is incoherent, then we shouldn't feel badly about falling short of that? Or is it worse if there is not any coherent satisfactory way to be, even one out of reach? Second, since it is clear that we are not self-choosers,* if only this ideal of the fullest autonomy would satisfy us, then we are doomed to fall short and remain unsatisfied. Even if a self-chooser is free, even if self-choosing is a sufficient condition for being free, how does that help *us*?

It might help in this way. Suppose there were or could be a self-choosing being; it shapes itself a certain way and also behaves a certain way. (Treat it as an idealization, an ideal type, a thought experiment.) Though we cannot be that being, perhaps we *can* track it, in certain respects. Though we are not self-choosing, it sets a standard for us; what it would do is what our actions (should) track. So in certain respects (but not in others) our behavior will resemble and be aligned with that of a self-choosing being.

The way in which we come to be so aligned is, let us assume, via some causal process, while the self-choosing being itself is not, let us further assume, caused to be that way. Our being causally determined to be that way, to track the actions of a self-choosing being, is in equilibrium, however. The knowledge of the causes of our being that way would not lead us to change our behavior or to want to change it or to want less to do it. By some causal process we simulate the behavior of a self-chooser, and our simulation behavior is in equilibrium; it withstands the knowledge of its causes. As belief is aligned with the facts when it constitutes knowledge, so our behavior is aligned with how a self-chooser would act. We want our behavior to track something, just as we want our beliefs to do so—what better to track than a self-chooser?

There is an ambiguity in the notion of tracking what a self-chooser

---

* A midrash tells us, "It is against your will that you are born . . . that you live . . . that you are bound to give account."

would do. It might mean (a) tracking the property: would be done by a self-chooser, or (b) tracking the property (such as bestness or rightness) that would be instanced or even tracked by the actions of a self-chooser, although we are not tracking it as "what a self-chooser would do". Perhaps, for now, the second is the most we can hope to track successfully.

Is this yet another outcome view of choice, holding that what is valuable about self-choosing is the outcome of the self-chooser's choice, an outcome we can strive to match and track in certain respects? If it is the process of self-choice itself that is valuable, though, then our most earnest efforts to track its results will fall far short.

What would a self-chooser choose to be like, what content can we give to the upshot of a self-chooser's choice? The most elaborate tradition of thought about self-choosers are those religious traditions that hold the divinity is self-choosing or self-determining. Certain features of these traditions are unhelpful in our context. That such a being would choose to be divine and all powerful gives us little we can track. More interesting is the religious view of such a being as a conscious self. A self-choosing being, I think, would choose to be a self. But what particular kind of self would it choose to be, and in particular what evaluative principles, if any, would it choose to conform to or track? Does a self-chooser itself ask what a self-chooser would do, and is that question any help to it in reaching a determinate choice? If so, our choice to imitate a self-chooser might not be so very different, in that way, from its choice. Kantian theory would hold that a self-chooser would choose to be moral. The tradition of German idealism, Fichte especially, would spin the world out of self-choice. Indian Vedanta seems to spin many worlds out; the self-chooser chooses variety and even, in playfulness, temporary ignorance and self-deception—whether it chooses ethics as we understand it, is less clear. *If* Kant were right, and a self-chooser would choose to be moral, then we could track what a self-chooser would do by tracking rightness. The fact that we ourselves were not self-choosers might seem to us less significant than that we can do this reasonably good imitation.

The grandiosity of speaking of a self-chooser causes trouble in two ways. A self-chooser chooses his own characteristics as part of a package, whereas we can hope to emulate only some of the characteristics. Perhaps those within our reach pale in isolation, perhaps even a self-chooser wouldn't choose them if he could not have the rest also. (See the writings by economists on the theory of 'second best'.) The fact that a self-chooser would (or wouldn't) choose to be ethical, as part of a gestalt, does not settle the question of whether it is best that we match that in isolation. Second, perhaps (no doubt?) a self-chooser would choose to be nothing like us, choosing instead to be immortal, indestructible, not in a gravitational field, and not physically continuous. Though one philosopher has claimed this is the best of all possible worlds,* none has claimed that *we* are the best of all possible beings. Most of the theory of a self-chooser seems irrelevant to us (except insofar as we hold that a self-chooser also would choose to create us). And that small isolated part within our realm of emulation raises very serious 'second-best' questions.

Narrower than the question of what a self-chooser would be like is: what would a self-chooser do or be like in my situation, compatible with being or staying me. Recall that the closest continuer theory of identity through time had three components: that the next day's person somehow arise from today's you; that it be close enough (according to the weighted sum of characteristics) to be you, if there existed no other continuer as close to you; and that there be no other continuer as close. The last component about the closest continuer is irrelevant here, so we may ask: in your situation, among those ways close enough to (continue to) be you, how would a self-chooser act or be?

Here, too, some responses are unhelpful: a self-chooser would not choose to be in my situation; the very fact that it is a self-chooser deciding makes it not close enough to be me; a self-chooser while maintaining the same consciousness would transform himself into something physically very different that could surmount my problems. Yet the more we constrain the self-chooser's choice, by building in our own limitations so as to make it more relevant to us, the less it looks like a model of freedom. The fact that a self-chooser, when confronted with a highwayman powerful and inescapable, also would hand over his money rather than his life, is cold comfort to someone actually stuck in such a threatening situation.

We have investigated the notion of a self-chooser to see to what

---

* Recall the joke: the optimist claims that this is the best of all possible worlds and the pessimist agrees. Economists tell a similar one about the world's being Pareto-optimal.

extent we, even if mired in the causal nexus, happily can match it; also, to see how far we fall short of this aspiration. If a self-chooser, although not caused to do so, would choose to track bestness or rightness, then we can be pleased that we are doing it or (if we are not) we can attempt to do it, attempting to match, in our way, the way a self-chooser would be. However, if we are (lucky enough to be) caused to track bestness or rightness, what we track is bestness or rightness in our situation. And while it is true that a self-chooser in our situation would track that too, it also is true that a self-chooser wouldn't let himself get into our situation. So, at best we can match the choices of a self-chooser only partially. Even if the self-chooser follows a general policy of tracking bestness or rightness, he may see its most important applications in choosing to stay out of situations like ours.

The ways in which we fall short of being a self-chooser might be less oppressive to us if the very obduracy of an external world, the very existence of external and internal constraints within which we operate, was crucial to our identity, so that any transformation of us into something unconstrained would be transformation into something not close enough to be us. Part of our essence, then, would be: not being a self-chooser. We already have seen that some philosophers hold we are free whenever we express our essence. It is unclear, though, why we cannot be stuck with an undesirable essence and why expressing *that* should count as freedom. (Would those philosophers be driven to hold that a being whose essence is being unfree, when it expresses that essence, is free?) Isn't one who accepts such an essence of his as valuable like a slave who has come to love his chains? That something is essential to the human condition does not make it or that condition valuable.

Neither do undetermined decisions, reflexive self-subsuming weighting of reasons as described in the first part of the chapter, transcend human limitations. Even such freedom under indeterminism leaves us limited to choosing only among those alternatives that are (fixed by external factors as) available to us. Still, it does leave us free to act within those external constraints; we have leeway in which weight to give to reasons, which (feasible) self-conception and self-subsuming weights to choose.

This is not negligible; perhaps even a self-chooser would choose partially to keep that status of a being who (without causal determination) bestows weights on his reasons. (In that case, if determinism is true we cannot match that process, though perhaps we can track some aspect of the upshot of those decisions.) Whatever the condition or character he might choose to acquire, consider the self-chooser's first choice of self. Surely it is undetermined, bestows weight on reasons, and is self-subsuming and reflexive. If the theory of free will presented in the first part of this chapter did fit us, to that extent at least (even if a poor second best in other ways) we would resemble a self-chooser, sharing its mode of choice.

Will a person's self-subsuming weighting of reasons track bestness, and is that standard of bestness an independently existing valid standard, or is it too something we choose self-subsumingly? Can we choose the contours of bestness itself, the weights of its components, even the components themselves? These questions are important, if not so much for the free process of decision or weighting reasons, then for the further topic of what (value) this process is to eventuate in, and how it is to do so. The next chapter will take up issues concerning the nature of bestness, of value, and its connection to choice. First, though, I shall consider a topic I deemed merely peripheral to the problem of free will: punishment. I do this partly to round off the discussion of free will, but mainly because the topic of punishment has an importance in its own right. And as we will see later, its themes intertwine with those of the next chapter.

III. RETRIBUTIVE PUNISHMENT

A Framework for Retribution

How can someone be held responsible or deserve punishment for an action he was causally determined to do? Even if wrongful actions are freely chosen, in what sense is punishment deserved and what purpose does its infliction serve? Is not the notion of deserved punishment, of retribution, primitive—a disguise for vengeful passions? To answer these questions, I shall outline a theory of punishment, one I imagine is to be combined with a theory of compensation to victims. A wrongdoer deserves punishment for a wrongful act, and he must compensate the surviving victims of his act.

The punishment deserved depends on the magnitude H of the wrongness of the act, and the person's degree of responsibility r for the act, and is equal in magnitude to their product, $r \times H$. The degree of responsibility r varies between one (full responsibility) and zero (no responsibility), and may take intermediate numerical values corresponding to partial responsibility. Thus, the punishment deserved is equal to H when the person is fully responsible for the act, when r equals one, and he deserves no punishment when his degree of responsibility is zero; otherwise H is discounted by (because multiplied by) the person's intermediate degree of responsibility. The magnitude H is a measure of the wrongness or harm, done or intended, of the act.[71]

The details of the theory of compensation are not our concern here; but note that the compensation owed to victims will depend upon (the degree of) causation of the harmful consequences, not upon the r value of the act, the degree of responsibility for it. If someone nonnegligently and accidentally causes damage to your property, he owes you compensation, but since his $r = 0$ he does not deserve any punishment for this.

The punishment (deserved) is to affect the wrongdoer, but not simply as he finds himself after doing the wrongful act; his ill-gotten gains (including psychic ones) are removed or counterbalanced before the infliction of the deserved penalty. Thus, the punishment deserved, $r \times H$, is imposed relative to a baseline that marks the situation the wrongdoer would have been in had he not committed the wrong. However, the process of making compensation to victims (so that they are no worse off than they would have been had the wrong not been done to them) may itself lower the wrongdoer from his baseline situation by some amount c.[72] If so, then the punishment still to be inflicted will be equal in magnitude to $(r \times H) - c$; thereby the process of extracting compensation followed by punishment leaves the wrongdoer $r \times H$ below his baseline situation. Someone who by preference lives without much monetarily gainful employment, if he commits an assault, may find the process of doing what is necessary to provide monetary compensation to his victim so unpleasant as to be lowered by the full degree $r \times H$ from his baseline situation; no further punishment is appropriate since the (magnitude of the) deserved punishment has been visited upon him in the course of his paying compensation. (I leave aside issues about deserving a punishment that matches the wrong.) Providing compensation may even leave the person more than $r \times H$ below the baseline; however, in this case full compensation still is extracted—why should it be the victim who bears the undeserved cost?—but no further penalty is visited.*

Retributive matching penalties are penalties that not only fit the magnitude of $r \times H$ but, when $r = 1$, do to the wrongdoer the same H, to the extent this is feasible, as he has done.[73]

There are difficulties worth mentioning in understanding what the same or a comparable penalty would be, to equal the magnitude of the wrong or harm done. If a millionaire steals \$100 from a poor person then, after restitution, the appropriate penalty is not \$100 from the millionaire. Rather it is some deprivation as severe for the

---

* Here, some of $r \times H$ may be used up in the process of compensation. In *Anarchy, State, and Utopia* (pp. 62–63), I pointed out that (some of) $r \times H$ may be drawn upon and used up at the time of the crime, in self-defense against the criminal. For what is necessary for successful defense may go beyond what is allowed by the principle of proportionality, which holds that what may be inflicted in defense is some function of H, but not of r. Both types of "drawings" upon $r \times H$ that take place must be counted in fixing how great a penalty, by itself, still remains to be visited. There being two types of drawings raises issues about how they interact; how, if at all, do the future compensations that will occur affect what "drawings" upon $r \times H$ a person may make in self-defense?

millionaire as a $100 loss is to the poor person he victimized. However, to set penalties at exactly the amount the victim's utility is lowered would set the penalty too low for theft from millionaires. Nor is it perfectly appropriate to set the penalty for a theft at the maximum of either how much utility the victim loses by the theft, or how much the thief would lose by a theft of that amount. In some special situation, losing that amount might have tremendous (but unforeseeable) disutility for the victim; this should not increase the punishment though it must be counted in the compensation stage. Rather, it seems appropriate to let the penalty be the maximum of the amount of disutility the victim reasonably could have been expected to undergo, and the amount of disutility the perpetrator would (reasonably be expected to?) undergo from that same act.

A Rationale Is Needed

Having set forth the r × H framework, we turn to delineating its rationale: what might underlie such a notion of deserved punishment, and what principles govern it? When the task is to examine some moral notion and the principles in which it is embedded, the distinction drawn in the Introduction between explanation and justification (or proof) becomes tenuous. Will not an explanation of why a moral principle holds, of why a moral notion has application, also provide a justification (or at least a pointer toward one) of the principle or notion? Won't this be provided even by an explanation of how such a (correct) principle or (correct) application is possible? An explanation of how something is possible will appeal to principles or structures not themselves known (or obviously seeming) to be false or inapplicable. The explanation will utilize apparatus that at least is a candidate for acceptability. Given our ability to think up objections to moral principles, to say a moral principle or underlying view is not immediately to be rejected is to say it has a certain plausibility, a certain moral force. So to show how or consider whether something of moral status follows from or is generated by a candidate moral principle is to be entered, willy nilly, in the arena of justification.

My aim is not to justify or argue for retributive punishment. It is true that I do think such a view is correct, that retributive punishment sometimes is appropriate, even called for. For this reason, I investigate how it can be so, what other truths underlie retributive punishment, what else would have to be true to require such punishment. I am trying to explain how it is possible that retributive punishment sometimes is appropriate or demanded. Those who think it never is suitable will think there is no such fact to be explained. They will see my explanatory efforts as useless theory, although perhaps constituting source material for a psychological theory of what might be involved when people accept retributivist views. Yet perhaps even these deniers can see the material that follows as providing (to invoke another distinction from the Introduction) understanding if not explanation, providing understanding of appropriate retributive punishment by placing it in an illuminating network of possibilities.

Is it necessary, though, to offer any explanation at all of retributive punishment? Perhaps its appropriateness is just a fundamental fact, with nothing further underlying it: people who commit wrongs simply deserve to be punished. However, as we shall see, the retributivist position is not, on the face of it, smoothly shaped. In the space of theory, it is not a perfect sphere. There are surprising contours, irregular dips and angles, about which performers of wrong acts are to be punished when. It is not at all plausible, I think, that fundamental facts having no further explanation would take *that* shape. There must be some underlying structure, nature, principles, connections with other things, that yield up precisely that irregularly contoured position.

Retribution and Revenge

The view that people deserve punishment for their wrongful acts in accordance with r × H, independently of the deterrent effect of such punishment,[74] strikes some people as a primitive view, expressive only of the thirst for revenge. Before pursuing the underlying rationale of retribution, punishment inflicted as deserved for a past wrong, we should consider some ways in which retribution differs from revenge.

(1) Retribution is done for a wrong, while revenge may be done for an injury or harm or slight and need not be for a wrong.

366

(2) Retribution sets an internal limit to the amount of the punishment, according to the seriousness of the wrong, whereas revenge internally need set no limit to what is inflicted. Revenge by its nature need set no limits, although the revenger may limit what he inflicts for external reasons.

(3) Revenge is personal: "this is because of what you did to my _____" (self, father, group, and so on). Whereas the agent of retribution need have no special or personal tie to the victim of the wrong for which he exacts retribution.

Do not say he exacts the penalty because of the injury done to his own moral code; that overextends the notion of personal tie. Steps sometimes are taken to exclude the personal tie from intruding in a process of retribution and clouding the nature of what is happening by blurring the distinctness of retribution from revenge. Thus, under a system of capital punishment, if the sister of the official executioner is murdered and the killer is apprehended, someone else will be substituted to perform that execution.

This third point has two aspects: revenge can be desired only by someone with a personal tie (others can desire that some such person inflict revenge, but their desire is not a desire for revenge), and it can be inflicted only by (the agent of) someone with a personal tie.* Retribution, on the other hand, may be desired or inflicted by people without such a tie. This personal factor also enters into the revenger's desire, noted below, that his connection to the victim for whom revenge is being exacted be known to the recipient of revenge.

(4) Revenge involves a particular emotional tone, pleasure in the suffering of another, while retribution either need involve no emotional tone, or involves another one, namely, pleasure at justice being done. Therefore, the thirster after revenge often will want to experience (see, be present at) the situation in which the revengee is suffering, whereas with retribution there is no special point in witnessing its infliction.

---

* Revenge may involve differing notions of linkage: (a) because of what you did to my _____; (b) because of what you did to me. If someone kills your father, under linkage *a* you kill him while under *b* you kill his father.

This connects with the previous point about the personal tie; one purpose of revenge may be to produce a psychological effect in the person who seeks revenge (that particular emotional tone, for example), while retribution has no such personal purpose.

(5) There need be no generality in revenge. Not only is the revenger not committed to revenging any similar act done to anyone; he is not committed to avenging all done to himself. Whether he seeks vengeance, or thinks it appropriate to do so, will depend upon how he feels at the time about the act of injury. Whereas the imposer of retribution, inflicting deserved punishment for a wrong, is committed to (the existence of some) general principles (prima facie) mandating punishment in other similar circumstances. Furthermore, if possible these general standards will be made known and clear in the process of retribution; even those who act in retribution against the guilty agents of a torturing dictatorship, keeping their own identities secret, will make the principles known.

In drawing these contrasts between retribution and revenge, I do not deny that there can be mixed cases, or that people can be moved by mixed motives, partially a desire for retribution, partially a desire for revenge, or that a stated desire can mask another one that is operative. Usually, it is charged that those favoring retribution really crave revenge; but this will be especially implausible in the absence of a special tie to the victim. (The charge never is made in the other direction, that some who call for revenge really are seeking retribution but are embarrassed at appearing moralistic.) The charge itself, though, recognizes the distinction, even as it seeks to blur it. That retribution can be distinguished from revenge and is, on its surface at least, less primitive neither shows that, nor explains why, retribution is justified. Nor does it explain why retribution and revenge so often have been confused.

Retribution and revenge share a common structure: a penalty is inflicted for a reason (a wrong or injury) with the desire that the other person know why this is occurring and know that he was intended to know. (In the comic books of my youth, the villain seeking revenge always was thwarted by his desire that the hero not merely die but realize why he was dying and at whose hand, in prolonged agony—

this gave the hero extended opportunity to escape.) I shall spell out that common structure as it is exemplified by retribution; this must be modified in accordance with the contrasts we have listed to obtain an account of revenge.

Under retributive punishment for S's act A (I speak here of the fullest and most satisfactory case):

(1) Someone believes that S's act A has a certain degree of wrongness

(2) and visits a penalty upon S

(3) which is determined by the wrongness H of the act A, or by $r \times H$,

(4) intending that the penalty be done because of the wrong act A

(5) and in virtue of the wrongness of the act A,

(6) intending that S know the penalty was visited upon him because he did A

(7) and in virtue of the wrongness of A,

(8) by someone who intended to have the penalty fit and be done because of the wrongness of A

(9) and who intended that S would recognize (he was intended to recognize) that the penalty was visited upon him so that 1–8 are satisfied, indeed so that 1–9 are satisfied.

If S wrongfully shoots another in a canyon and the sound of the shot causes an avalanche that maims or kills S, then this happens to S because of his wrong act but not because of the wrongness of the act. Since an act's moral qualities, qua moral qualities, seem to lack causal power, if something is to happen to someone because of the moral quality of his act, this must occur through another's recognition of that moral quality and response to it. Not every such response, even to wrongness, will count as retribution. If, on the cliff above, a witness sees the wrongful act and scrambles off to get forces of the law, thereby kicking loose some stones that cause an avalanche, the ensuing crushing of the killer still does not occur in retribution for his act. The conditions about intention are not satisfied. (Also, a more careful account than I offer here might use the notion of tracking rather than 'because of'.)

"Poetic justice" involves the wrongdoer's undergoing a consequence that appropriately could be visited upon him in retribution but which was not produced in that way, usually owing to the failure of one of the first two conditions of retribution. A system of karma, whereby the moral quality of acts produces effects automatically in (this or) another lifetime, is not a system of poetic justice. It is crucial to poetic justice that the (penalty) effect is not a result of the moral quality of the act, even though it appropriately would fit that moral quality. Thus, although very many poetically just things could occur, there could not be a system of poetic justice. The generality a system involves (supporting subjunctives about what would occur) could stem only from the (appropriate) effects being due to the moral quality of the acts, qua moral quality, and so the justice done would not be merely "poetic".

The conditions demarcating retribution explain what otherwise appears to be a ludicrous phenomenon. If someone sentenced to death falls perilously ill or is accidentally injured or attempts suicide the day before the scheduled execution, then the execution is postponed and measures are taken to bring the condemned person back to health so that he then can be executed. Although due-process reasons might be conjured up for this, I believe the reason is that his punishment is to involve something's being visited upon him by others because of the wrongness of his act. His death by natural causes or by his own hand would avoid this, so measures are taken to restore him for punishment.

The Message of Retribution

The complicated structure of the nine conditions for retribution, wherein something intentionally is produced in another with the intention that he realize why it was produced and that he realize he was intended to realize all this, fits the account of meaning offered by H. P. Grice.[75] Applying that theory, it follows that in retributively punishing someone we mean something. Retributive punishment is an act of communicative behavior. Revenge also fits this communicative structure, though with a somewhat different message; this provides an explanation of why the two are so often confused.

What is the message of retributive punishment, and why is it communicated in that especially forceful and unwelcome way? The (Gricean) message is: this is how wrong what you did was. Or, since

370

r × H may function as an upper limit to punishment and need not be inflicted fully: this is at least how wrong what you did was. In the case of retributive matching punishment where, to the extent feasible, the penalty inflicted on the wrongdoer is the same as the wrong or harm he did, perhaps the message then is: this is (precisely) the wrong you did.* But if our intention is to mean his act was that (magnitude of) wrong, why don't we just say so and spare him the penalty? (Don't say we first must get his attention.) What justifies us in inflicting upon him so unwelcome a mode of communication?

We may view different "theories" of punishment as focusing upon different aspects of communication: the sender of a message, the recipient of this message, the transmission itself. Some have pointed out that punishment has an expressive function, wherein the sender condemns the crime.[76] More frequently, the literature focuses upon the recipient. Under this rubric, we might see punishment as an attempt to demonstrate to the wrongdoer that his act was wrong, not only to mean the act is wrong but to *show* him its wrongness. Some retributive theorists see the showing as having a further goal: the moral improvement of the offender. Punishment is supposed to achieve this goal by bringing home to the offender the nature of what he has done, from which he is to realize its wrongness. Since these theorists see the central purpose of punishment in its further consequences, they have been termed teleological retributivists.[77]

Someone is shown something by being presented with it directly. If an act is wrong because of what it does to someone else, the most powerful way to show him what it does is to do the same to him. However, there are some things whose wrongness we cannot show by doing the same to him. If his act leads another person to waste his life, to punish such acts in retributive matching fashion would only make things irremediably worse. Also, we cannot so punish symmetrical consensual acts—the people involved already know what it is like.

* Even in retributive matching punishment, not every heinous act will be matched. And certainly, if the punishment is justified, the wrongness of the punished act will not be matched, that is, by us. By imprisoning a person we do place him in a dangerous environment where it is likely that wrongs will be done to him, but presumably this is not part of our intention in maintaining prisons. One must be careful in computing by how much incarceration lowers the totality of crime, as opposed merely to shifting its location and incidence.

To do to someone what he has done to another shows him what he has done. How does it show him that it is wrong? The hope is that the punished person will realize an act A is wrong when it is done to him. It is hoped that he will not universalize "Let A be done!" or distinguish his situation from that of his victim.[78] This is not to say that he won't be able to find distinguishing characteristics, or to state such morally irrelevant or insufficient characteristics in a principle. The hypothesis of teleological retributive matching punishment is that irrelevant moral distinctions are only skin-deep. When it is done to someone who knows his punishers think what is being done to him is what he did to others, he will realize it is the same thing, despite his ability to phrase principles distinguishing the cases.

Retributive matching punishment thus, in its teleological version, rests on an optimistic hypothesis about what another person will or can come to know. If someone is so far outside the moral community that there is no hope of bringing him to a realization of the wrongness of his acts by showing him them, perhaps there is nothing left to do but deter him. Deterrence theory treats everyone as outside the moral community. It does so, that is, unless deterrence is pursued under and within the retributive theory. A retributive theorist may worry that introducing deterrence considerations into a decision about whether to punish a person, and how much, uses the guilty person as a means. However, to be used as a means may be part of his retributive matching desert, since that is what *he* has done to another.

The hope of retributive matching punishment is that the wrongdoer will realize his act was wrong when someone shows him that it is wrong and means it. A person who is mentally defective so as to be incapable of learning or realizing that his act was wrong cannot be punished in this way, and so is an unsuitable object of such punishment. This also would account for the uneasiness retributivists feel about punishing someone who already realizes his act was wrong and is repentant, attempting to make amends, and so forth. The telos of the act of punishing has been removed, so it is left simply as a harmful act.* (Note that the deterrence theorist may well recommend a policy of punishing in such circumstances.)

---

* Another explanation would be that the wrongdoer's discomfort attendant on making amends is treated like that (discussed above) in making compensation, as a quantity to be subtracted from the deserved r × H.

Not only must a teleological retributive theory consider whether the goal justifies the actions (on which see below), it also must consider alternative and less unwelcome routes to the goal. Let us consider the most troublesome case for the teleological retributivist, one which appears to support nonteleological retributivism. Even were it possible to produce in him the realization that he acted monstrously and evilly, through his seeing films, reading novels, and hearing explanations of the causes of his behavior and the tales of his victims, but with tranquilizers administered to prevent his suffering at the realization of the enormity of what he had done, would we really want merely this to have been done to Adolf Hitler, had he been captured alive?

It is difficult to envision what it would be like to realize one's responsibility for the Holocaust and the other evils of Nazism, and to comprehend its moral character and so one's own. An anguished suicide would seem the only possible action, until one realized that this would turn off the knowledge of what one had done, and the accompanying emotions, and so would constitute tranquilizing oneself. Some acts, it seems to me, are so monstrous that a criterion of the agent's understanding their nature is that his realization itself involves (and leads to) a suffering comparable to what matching punishment would inflict. (I speak here of the end of the moral scale, and do not mean to encourage or endorse such, or indeed any, guilt feelings elsewhere.) If such a person is to be brought to know the nature of his act, then proportionate anguish or guilt might be taken as a criterion of such knowledge. We can see why matching penalties, inflicting on him where possible the very thing he did, would seem especially appropriate. By thus experiencing the quality of what he did to another, he would have intimate knowledge ("by acquaintance") of it. (Compare: "you don't really know what war is like unless you have been in one.")

Still, the view that punishment always will lead the person to realize he acted wrongly seems overly optimistic. (Many child batterers were themselves battered children; their defect is not ignorance of what it is like to be battered.) The teleological retributivist might grant that it will not always work, yet hold that we cannot tell in advance in any given case that it definitely won't. However, could not psychology advance so that such predictions could confidently be made in some cases, and would the retributivist really want to let such people go unpunished, those most hardened and resistant to recognizing that they acted wrongly? Yet the teleological retributivist might point out to a defense lawyer the danger of so giving up on someone's power of moral discernment, for in losing a trait that distinguishes him from a tiger, a person may lose part of his claim to be treated any differently.

The (Gricean) message of teleological retributive punishment is delivered in a way so that the delivery is evidence that or shows that it is true. (Compare a telegram that says "you have just received a telegram.") Receiving the message (sent that way), "this is how wrong what you did was", is supposed to convince one that it is true; the message, via its sending, is to be self-supporting. But why not transmit the evidence separately from the content of the message, via arguments, films, novels, and so on? Why are the content and the evidence and the showing so intermingled?

Connecting with Correct Values

I wish to present a different view of retributive punishment, conceiving of it nonteleologically, so that it is seen as right or good in itself, apart from the further consequences to which it might lead. These further consequences are not to be dismissed simply; but we shall see them as an especially desirable and valuable bonus, not as part of a necessary condition for justly imposed punishment. Rather, the consequences the teleological theorist seeks we view not as a disconnected bonus but as an intensification of what nonteleological punishment actually involves.

The wrongdoer has become disconnected from correct values, and the purpose of punishment is to (re)connect him. It is not that this connection is a desired further effect of punishment: the act of retributive punishment itself effects this connection.[79]

Consider three ways that correct values can have effect in our lives: (a) We can do acts because they are right or good, we can do them as right or good acts.* (b) Having acted wrongly, we can repent,

---

* Some economists writing on crime not only argue that all criminal activity is economically rational in its context but present the cynical view that crimes will be done whenever they are economically rational, and that moral beliefs have no influence on (nonverbal) conduct at all. Anecdotal evidence (for example, "I refrain from crime for moral reasons") carries little power in

and give this repentance effect in our lives, performing repentant actions and so forth. (c) We can have the connection imposed upon us, via punishment.

This third alternative is worse than the others, but although less desirable it is an alternative of the same sort. It is a way, an inferior one, of falling on the same dimension on which doing something because it is right falls. That dimension is: connecting with correct values.

Correct values are themselves without causal power, and the wrongdoer chooses not to give them effect in his life. So others must give them some effect in his life, in a secondary way. When he undergoes punishment these correct values are not totally without effect in his life (even though he does not follow them), because we hit him over the head with them. Through punishment, we give the correct values, qua correct values, some significant effect in his life, willy-nilly linking him up to them.[80] (Also, by our activity we illustrate and exemplify being connected to value as value, in addition to effecting this in him.)

Such an effect *on* him is not what the teleological retributivist seeks; he aims for an effect *in* the wrongdoer: recognition of the correct value, internalizing it for future action—a transformation in him. Not only is the nonteleological effect on the wrongdoer different, it is of lesser value and not as desirable. Yet still, it is of some consider-

---

such discussions, but there is one relevant economic fact we can adduce. Taking into account probability of apprehension, punishment, and so on, is the rate of return for criminal activity less than, equal to, or greater than that of noncriminal activity? If the rate of return for criminal activity is greater than for noncriminal activity, this requires an explanation. In an open market, the rates of return of different activities tend to equalize, so if there are persisting different rates of return we should look to some barrier to entry to one of the activities in order to explain the difference. One barrier, the sanctions of the criminal law (including an estimate of other social sanctions) has been included already in computing the rate of return of crime, and so it cannot be the relevant explanation of the (supposed) difference in rates of return. That leaves as the most plausible conjecture and hypothesis that the operative barrier to entry to crime is internalized moral belief; some people do not become criminals because they believe such activities are wrong. Thus, if empirical investigation shows different rates of return for criminal and noncriminal activities (with criminal having the higher rate), this would be empirical support for the view that people's moral beliefs do influence their behavior. (On the other hand, the cynical view would be supported if empirical investigation discovered equal rates of return.)

able value, much better than if the correct values qua correct values had no effect on him at all.*

The complicated structure of the nine conditions of retribution are a way to enable and ensure that correct values have an effect on the wrongdoer's life, qua correct values. In both canyon cases described previously, the avalanche crushes the murderer, but though this results from his act of murder, it is not due to the wrongness of the act; what happens to him does not happen as an expression of correct values. The complicated (Gricean) intentions enable us to act as a vehicle whereby correct values, qua correct values, act upon the wrongdoer. Only those complicated conditions enable the correct values to act upon him, in their nature as correct values. We transmit the message to him, shaping our intentions so as to transmit to him purely the effect of correct values as correct values. There now is no puzzle about why we do not simply speak or telegram the (Gricean) message, without adding a punishment. The punishment is central— that is the way the correct values which he has flouted have a significant effect on his life; while the Gricean conditions apply in order that it be those correct values qua correct values that have this significant effect. (Put too briefly, the Gricean conditions enable the correct values to communicate with him—through us.)

Retributive punishment is to effect two things: (a) connect the wrongdoer to value qua value (b) so that value qua value has a significant effect in his life, as significant as his own flouting of correct

---

* We wish to account for the irregular contours of deserved punishment and thereby not leave it a brute fact. But not only that; in seeing retribution alongside the other phenomena of connecting or linking with value, namely, acting rightly and repenting, in seeing it share some of their characteristics and also in seeing all such connections with value as part of an even more general category which includes the connection of knowledge, of belief tracking the truth, we place retribution in its widest context; in so seeing how it resembles other things of value, falling under the very same general categories, we do more than simply repeat that retribution is deserved.

To be sure, there are differences introduced when the link is to value. Responding to value qua value has a status and importance that tracking truth does not have. (See our discussion in the next chapter.) And the parallel to value qua value having some effect on a person's life willy-nilly, for the case of belief and truth—for example, someone's shouting truths at you which you won't accept, thereby disrupting your other activities—does not itself seem to be of importance or value. (I am indebted to Ronald Dworkin for raising this point.) Continuing the parallel with knowledge and belief, does deterrence leading to prudently doing what happens to be right establish some linkage comparable to true belief?

values. The punishment part is needed for the effect to be significant (this would not be served merely by telling him he was wrong), while the Gricean intentions in punishment are needed for it to be value qua value that acts through us on him. Value qua value acts on us as perceivers of it, but how does it get to act through us on him? By our (simultaneously) sending him, in punishing him, a message about value qua value. The hope is that delivering the message will change the person so that he will realize he did wrong, then start doing things because they are right—thus the teleological position. Yet, if it does not do this, still, punishment does give the values some significant effect on his life (even if not that of guiding his conduct) which is in itself good. The nonteleological position we have formulated does not replace the teleological one; it goes alongside it. More needs to be said about this relationship.

Retributive punishment, we have said on the nonteleological view, is to give correct values as significant an effect in someone's life as the magnitude of his flouting these correct values. For the most serious flouting of the most important values (for instance, intentionally and willfully murdering another), capital punishment is a response of equal magnitude. On the teleological retributivist view, this response cannot be justified, unless in terms of the changes that might be worked in the wrongdoer between sentencing and the completion of execution. Such a "justification" would seem a poor joke. Perhaps the prospect of so severe a penalty can work to bring the wrongdoer to concentrated moral clarity, but one would not think it occurs so very frequently; we know it has not with those who go to their death loudly unrepentant.

The nonteleological retributive view, which sees punishment as effecting a connection between the wrongdoer and the correct values that he has flouted, can look at capital punishment differently. The ending of a life is a very significant event in it (or of it, or on it), and can give the correct values an effect equal in importance to the magnitude of the flouting. I do believe that some deserve to die, to be killed, in punishment for their actions—to take an uncontroversial example, Hitler. Should the nonteleological retributivist then endorse capital punishment as an institution, provided the other issues that need to be considered in assessing it as an actually functioning institution (such as the probabilities of mistaken convictions) do not counterbalance the weighty fact that some people deserve death?

We have mentioned two connections with value that an act of punishment involves, that effected between correct values and the (life of the) punished person, and that between the punisher himself and the correct values when he acts as a vehicle for their having effect. In addition, there is a third connection: that between the punisher and the value of the person being punished. Generally, and not only in the case of capital punishment, there is a tension between you as punisher effecting his connection with correct values, and your connecting with and being responsive to *his* value qua value. Some acts, even if they effect his connection with correct values, may snap your connection with his value, so as to constitute your flouting his value. What prevents this flouting in an act of retributive punishment is the (genuine) teleological retributivist intention and hope; one is not simply intending to act on him, in disregard of his value, but also to act in him whom you recognize as a person capable of acknowledging correct values. Hence, capital punishment, involving as it does the dropping of the teleological intention, itself would involve a lack of connection with value, a flouting of his value. The person may deserve to die, may deserve correct values having that significant effect on his life, but this cannot be done at our hand if we are to be connected to (his) value and not flout it.* At any rate, so a nonteleological retributivist might claim. Thus, even the nonteleological retributivist position we have delineated need not endorse capital punishment, except perhaps in those truly monstrous cases (Hitler again) which drive one to conclude there is no value there to which to respond. Might not one hold, though, even for a case not involving a great monster, that our responding to the value of the victims he destroyed would involve visiting on him the most serious punishment? I myself have alternated on the issue of an institution of capital punishment, unable to reach a clear stable conclusion.

It is through the teleological aim that the nonteleological retributivist responds to the value of the punished person. This holds true, not only in refraining from capital punishment; it infuses the other punishments too. How, then, does our view differ from the simple teleological one; what role is played by the nonteleological component of the act of punishment itself connecting the punished person with correct values, apart from any further effect? Is *it* simply the bonus that comes to the teleological retributivist? The nonteleologi-

---

* Here then is a role for "poetic justice"; and though hoping for that might constitute lack of connection with his value, it does not constitute a *flouting* of it. (See the discussion below on the act requirement.)

cal retributivist effects a connection of the wrongdoer with correct values, and while he can pursue this as his purpose, he cannot pursue it alone; when pursued as the sole purpose, it flouts the value of the wrongdoer. However, this effecting is of value, and something of value is achieved when this connecting of the wrongdoer with correct value takes place, even if the further teleological result—his moral transformation—does not occur. There is a purpose to pursuing this connecting, even when the probability of the moral transformation is very small, almost nonexistent. (And when it is nonexistent, then have we reached a wrongdoer who does not possess a value that would be flouted by capital punishment, done for the purpose of bringing correct values qua correct values to have some significant effect on his life?) The nonteleological view of retribution is intertwined with the teleological view; they go together.

In terms of the connection with value effected by punishment we can understand some of the metaphors that stud retributivist talk. Wrong puts things out of joint in that acts and persons are unlinked with correct values; this is the disharmony introduced by wrongdoing. Punishment does not wipe out the wrong, the past is not changed, but the disconnection with value is repaired (though in a second best way); nonlinkage is eradicated. Also, the penalty wipes out or attenuates the wrongdoer's link with incorrect values, so that he now regrets having followed them or at least is less pleased that he did.

Some might put forth (though I myself do not) larger and more speculative metaphysical pictures, for example, that there is a realm of correct values that is thrown into disequilibrium by actions flouting them, and that punishing the wrongdoer, by connecting him with the flouted values, restores the equilibrium. Punishment of the wrongdoer then would be a kind of compensation or restitution to the values, restoring them to their previous state. (If the realm of value has its own re-equilibrating processes, taking longer to work with the more serious floutings, the greater disequilibriums induced, this would explain some features of statutes of limitations without the usual appeal to possible changes in the wrongdoer.)

We can isolate three aspects of the communicative linking of the wrongdoer with correct values. First, there is the effect in or on him of being linked: his being connected somehow to correct values. Second, there is the connection effected in those who punish; by so doing, they themselves link up with correct values. (Might they see failing to punish as a way of being disconnected with those values, or of flouting them?) Third, there is the fact of connection with correct values, whose rightness is not completely reducible to the effect in or on the parties involved. (Compare: a contract is signed and a person has an obligation to carry it out unless released. It is right that this occur, a rightness not located within either party but "between them", so to speak.)

Although the linking of the person with correct values effected by punishment does not depend upon some further effect as with the teleological retributivist, it can fail to occur, just as an ordinary act of communication can fail if the recipient is deaf, or does not understand the language. The linkage we are delineating corresponds to the recipient of a verbal message understanding the assertion; whereas the goal of the teleological retributivist corresponds to the recipient's accepting what is said. It is not so very difficult to get someone to understand that they are being punished because others view what they did as wrong, and intend for them to realize this is happening. Does the communicative success, the effecting of linkage, depend upon the recipient's believing that the punishers do believe the act was wrong and are acting for that reason? If, instead, a prisoner believes such assertions mask other motives, such as to crush him or to maintain power and privilege, then does the communication fail so that he is not linked up to correct values? Or is it enough for the linkage that the recipient understands the stated intention, even if he does not credit it?

The theory we have outlined of a communication that links the wrongdoer to correct values places intention within the institution of punishment, not simply behind it. Whose intention, then, is relevant: that of the prison guards (which shift?), the warden, the judge, the jury, the legislature, the citizenry? Or (like Durkheimean social facts), are certain intentions built into the institution, apart from the ascertainable intentions of particular participants? Such issues would have to be faced by a fuller development of the theory.

The Act Requirement

The rationale for retribution as effecting a connection or linkage with value qua value raises the question of why a wrongful act is required before the person is punished. Why not effect that value connection also with those who do not do wrong but who would under suitable circumstances? (Let us imagine that these circumstances might arise, so that the people were not tracking correct values.) They are not properly connected to value as value; nor are those who do the right thing but not for exactly the right reasons, or even from immoral motives. Have we presented a rationale that would condone constantly butting into people's lives in order to effect linkages to value? If being connected to value is the good we are demarcating, are we presenting a structure that mandates maximizing that good, and so does not require any prior wrongdoing to precipitate acts of linkage?

However, we are not morally permitted to go around demonstrating moral truths to all those ignorant of them, no matter what the means and what the person's willingness to be shown. What establishes these limits?

One possible explanation of the requirement that there be a wrongful act would refer to moral considerations outside the immediate area of punishment, namely, to the right of persons to be left alone and to live their own lives, provided they are not violating the rights of others. There are three major possibilities about punishment and the forcible imposition of moral instruction upon unwilling persons:

(1) punishment or moral instruction or value linkage may never be imposed upon anyone;

(2) punishment or moral instruction or value linkage may be imposed on everyone who might be improved by it, whether or not they have committed a wrongful act;

(3) punishment or moral instruction or value linkage may be imposed, but only on persons who already have committed wrongful acts.

The second possibility places people at the mercy of compulsory moral tutors, and violates their right to be left alone provided they have respected this right of others. There is an act requirement for punishment and other forms of moral teaching and moral connection because without one, people's rights would be violated, rights which are general and do not refer merely to punishment.

On this view, a person opens himself to moral instruction when he wrongs another. In that case, his moral condition is not solely his own private affair. (Therefore, alternative 1 is rejected.) Yet there are limits on the extent to which he has opened himself. It is only those of his character defects that eventuated in the wrongful action that are no longer his own private affair; any others remain private. Second, when the subject of legitimate external concern and action over his moral state, he does not thereby become a means that the deterrence practitioner may use to frighten others (except insofar as this is retribution for his having used others as means). Moreover, he deserves to have inflicted on himself no more than he has done to others. The matching requirement does not merely function to drive home the lesson; it sets an upper limit to the extent to which another is placed in our moral clutches. He has become our business but not our property. He may not be compelled to undergo thirty years of daily moral instruction and exhortation to learn how wrong it was when he once took a pencil by shoplifting.

This explanation of the act requirement is external in that it appeals to broader moral considerations, independent of the notion or theory of punishment itself.[81] If the rationale about effecting a linkage forces the retributivist to such external considerations, he loses an important advantage over other theories of punishment, deterrent and reformative, which notoriously have trouble in explaining why, given their goals, punishment should not be applied also to those innocent of wrongful conduct. (Would not penalizing an innocent person whom others will think guilty have the same deterrent effect, and be better than not finding the guilty party? Why not reform all who could use it?) For those theories too can appeal to external considerations that would constrain their practice of punishment. What is wanted is an internal explanation: from the theory of what is going on in retributive punishment itself it should follow that there is no reason or purpose in punishing an innocent person; the rationale of punishment itself should limit its exercise to those guilty of wrongful acts.

Flouting Correct Values

The person who acts wrongly flouts correct values, he goes against them. Not merely is he unlinked and unconnected to correct values, he is anti-linked and anti-connected. Perhaps we are unlinked when asleep or occupied with trivial amusements (unless a dispositional account of linkage is to be offered), but we are not anti-linked then. If linkage is good, unlinkage is not what is bad, anti-linkage is.

The clearest mode of flouting correct values is to pursue incorrect ones, to do something wrong because it is wrong. Less contrary is to pursue some goal (other than wrongness) that in this instance conflicts with rightness, and to act despite (but not for) the wrongness. Also, one can flout through negligence, acting wrongly without giving any consideration or attention to its wrongness. On the other hand, a person who does the right thing but for the wrong reasons, although unconnected to correct values, is not anti-connected: he is not flouting.

Consider how excuses function. Excuses show an act is not to be attributed to a defect of character, or not to as serious a one as might have been thought. The excuse does not show that the agent does not have a defect of character, even one that could lead to this act, but it shows that this act did not stem from that defect of character.[82] An action is done and its apparent explanation sees it as produced by a defect of character (explicitly so characterized, or by traits that constitute a defect), the act being an expression of that character disposition. Excuses undercut this explanation by pointing to another explanation of the action that involves either no character defect or a lesser one; this new explanation replaces the earlier one and its apparently (more serious) character defect.[83] An act is not attributable to a defect of character merely because it is evidence for one. If the person says, "I have a defect of character," that is evidence that he does have one (either the one he refers to or lying), and perhaps the explanation of his act refers to the character defect (he said it because he remembered he had one), but the action itself need not be an exercise of the character defect disposition. An excuse shows that an action which appears to be an exercise of that serious a character defect is not. (On the other hand, to say that appearances are deceiving, that an act appearing to be an exercise of a particular character defect really is an exercise of a more serious one, does not present an excuse, even though it replaces one explanation by another.)

If we punish acts only that stem from some or another character defect, then it appears that the crucial component is the defect of character. Why, then, do we need an action to precipitate punishment, why not simply punish the character defect which is there, even if it is unexercised? (Perhaps we can prove it is there, though we cannot prove anything done was an exercise of it.) Or, if we do require an act to trigger punishment, why punish only for that act as stemming from the character defect that produced it, rather than for all the character defects the person possesses, including those not involved in that particular act? (Anyway, is it so easy to isolate aspects of character?)

It is through actions that correct values are flouted; the actions constitute the flouting. (Is it part of our responding to correct values that we will not allow them to be flouted—that we allow them to be ignored, even anti-linked, but not flouted?) Since it is flouting that is to be punished, actions are required. However, consider the particular defective character disposition to do evil qua evil. Isn't such a person anti-linked with correct values, even if that disposition thus far goes unexercised? Anti-linked perhaps, but not flouting. More needs to be said, though, about why punishment is for flouting rather than simply for anti-linkage.

Punishment effects a connection with correct values for those who have flouted them. (The imbalance is rectified.) The system is not one of maximizing the good (connection with correct values) but of eradicating the bad (flouting of correct values) by replacing flouting with linkage. So the role of suffering in punishment is not merely to ensure a significant effect in people's lives, but, as mentioned earlier, to negate or lessen flouting by making it impossible to remain as pleased with one's previous anti-linkage.

Retributive Contours

The theory of punishment as connecting someone with correct values explains some responses of retributivists, some contours of retributive punishment alluded to earlier. First, consider someone who knowingly and willfully committed a wrong but who since has become insane or has suffered brain damage and so would be incapable of understanding, if punished, what was being done to him and why. He does not remember his act, and he would not understand the punishment or his punisher's reasons for acting. He deserved to be punished but does he now deserve to be punished, should we now punish him? Retributivists feel uneasy in answering "yes". Our theory accounts for this. Since the Gricean conditions cannot be satisfied with this person he cannot be connected up with correct values qua correct values. He should not have the penalty visited upon him because he is incapable of being the (knowing) recipient of retributive punishment, and so incapable of being connected (at least by the act of punishment) to correct values qua correct values.

Consider next a person who (before capture) sincerely repents of his wrongful act and, on his own, makes amends to the victims, goes off and does extraordinary good deeds—works in a leper colony or whatever—from a desire to add good to the world. Does such a person now deserve to be punished, should he be punished? Again, retributivists feel uneasy in saying so. (What would deterrence theorists say of these cases?) Our theory accounts for this; since the person already is connected up with correct values qua correct values, since these already have a significant effect in his life, there is nothing for punishment to do. The further consequence the teleological retributivist hopes for already is present, the link to be effected already holds. It is important, though, that the link with correct values make a significant alteration in his life, in what his life otherwise would have been, that it alter his life significantly, and negatively according to his previous view. (And also according to our view?) It is not necessary, though, that this person suffer or feel pain. Perhaps, we should say that the change in his life must involve as significant a loss in utility (as judged by his previous standards) as the (then) deserved punishment would have involved.

There exist ways other than punishment to connect people with correct values, to transform them and their lives. Recall how the lives of glowing and inspiring sages, such as Buddha, Aurobindo, the Baal Shem Tov, affect and transform others. However, such figures are scarce resources; there are not enough of them around to interact with and transform all flouters. Should we conclude that retributive punishment is right only in such morally impoverished epochs—all thus far; with enough agents of value-transformation able to effect a connection between others and value qua value, transforming their lives significantly, will punishment become unnecessary? Should we feel embarrassment that punishment is the best we can do now, since this indicates how we are not sufficiently connected with value qua value so as to be its powerful vehicle or channel?

These thoughts are alluring; yet there remains the question of suffering for great evildoers. We said previously that we would not and should not simply give Hitler treatment and send him happily on his rehabilitated way. The yoga tradition, we should note, holds that one cannot become fully transformed without moral purity; still, meeting an inspiring (and enlightened) figure could move one onto the right path of transformation. Would it have been enough for Hitler after the war to have met some spiritual sage, entered an ashram under a strict regimen, transformed himself morally and achieved bliss? (Note that according to samkhya yoga theory this could not happen; first, through many lifetimes, he would have had to work off all that karma. However, let us imagine it was possible immediately.) Still, don't we (rightfully) want him to suffer?*

We must probe somewhat more deeply into the rationale underlying retribution. We must investigate not only linking with correct values qua correct values but also responding to wrong as wrong.

First, there is the already mentioned consideration that suffering erases or attenuates the wrongdoer's being glad that he did the act. He would not similarly be sorry he had done the act if through it he was put on a transformed and blissful path. There also is a second line of thought, one about which I am unsure.

Under retribution, the wrongness of the act stands in a specific relation to the significant effect perpetrated in the wrongdoer. The punishment is contoured to the nature of the wrong, to its magnitude and character, so that punishment not only is responsive to correct values but also is responsive (negatively) to the wrong qua wrong. The morally inspiring figure who changes the wrongdoer does not contour his transforming behavior to the features of the wrong act, though his behavior may be triggered by the act's being wrong, and he does not respond to the act's wrongness as wrongness. In presenting an alternative, an inspiring example of right or saintly behavior, he is not being responsive to the specific wrongness.

---

* Might the suffering of the wrongdoer be required by the process of compensation to the victims, when only such suffering can compensate them or move them toward feeling as well off as if the wrong had not occurred? But can a victim's vengeful motives legitimately so enter the process of compensation? Perhaps according to the metaphysical picture mentioned earlier, great disequilibrium in the realm of values can be rectified only by a painful connection of the wrongdoer with value qua value, rather than via just any kind of connection. However, this seems ad hoc.

As a right action is done because it is right, connecting with and responding to correct values qua correct values, so an act of retribution is responsive to a wrong act as wrong. It effects a connection of the wrongdoer with correct values by being fully responsive to his wrong act in its character as a wrong act. It effects a connection with correct values through its recognition and response to wrongness as wrongness. The saintly exemplar effects the connection, when he does so, unmediated by a full response to wrongness as wrongness.

"So is it for the sake of the punisher that retribution is visited, in order that he can fully respond to wrongness as wrongness?" Retribution involves this, but only as one component. It also is right that significant portions of reality be responded to in suitable significant ways. To leave great wrongdoing unresponded to as wrong, substituting instead a beneficial transformation of the wrongdoer unrelated to the wrong in its content, is to ignore and be blind (in one's actions) to this significant portion of moral reality. At stake in addition to the punisher's response to wrongness as wrongness is the wrongdoer's response. Punishment links the wrongdoer with correct values, and is a vehicle whereby the nature and magnitude of his act's wrongness has a correspondingly significant effect in his life. (In addition, it is hoped that this effect will produce a change in character.) The purely beneficial and pleasant transformation, on the other hand, leaves the nature and magnitude of the person's wrong act as having no correspondingly significant effect in his life: he is not affected by the wrongness of his act as wrongness; he is left untouched in this significant way by the character of his act. Retribution gives significant effect in his life to correct values, and (not separately) gives his previous wrong act corresponding significant effect in its character as wrong. It breaks his anti-linkage with correct values, and it severs his (previously positive) linkage with wrong values by now connecting him with these values as wrong. (So, at any rate, runs this line of thought, about which I am unsure.)

We have offered an account, an interpretation, of retribution as effecting a linking of the wrongdoer-flouter with correct values qua correct values. Clearly, I believe that establishing such a linkage not only is involved in retribution, but also is (sometimes) appropriate, called for, and right. (Someone else could agree in interpreting retributive activity in this way, agree that is what is involved, yet hold that all such effectings of connection are wrong and never should be done.) There are further complicated questions in formulating the precise moral principles governing when it is right that retribution be done, best not pursued here. These principles will constitute (in part) an external theory of when punishment is to be done and for what. However, unlike the case of the act requirement, there is no reason to believe considerations internal to the very notion of punishment should yield the details of when it should be done, or the constraints on which acts should be punished.[84]

More on the r × H Structure

Our discussion began with the statement that the punishment deserved equaled r × H, where r was interpreted as the person's degree of responsibility for H. Note that this is a theory of punishment deserved, not a full theory of the institution of punishment. In addition to compensation as discussed earlier, which easily fits the theory, additional factors about feasibility, possible mistakes in conviction, personnel in penal work, and so on, may shape the designing of an institution. Furthermore, let me emphasize that I am not saying that any current penal practice is well designed and well functioning according to retributive criteria.

I now wish to reinterpret r as the degree to which the person *flouts* correct values, except for that component of his degree of flouting included in H. (If not all flouting stems from defects of character, perhaps we can say more generally that excuses show there was less flouting than there appeared to be.)

There is a bit more to be said about the r × H structure. H was said to represent the degree of harm or of wrong done or intended. There are two ambiguities here. The first is whether H represents harm or wrongness. Perhaps not all harming is wrong (even if a rejected suitor is harmed by a rejection, it is something the rejector has a right to do), and perhaps not all wrongs that are justifiably punished involve identifiable harm to others. It seems plausible to let H represent the amount that others are wronged, especially since, unlike revenge, retribution is done for a wrong rather than merely for a harm or injury (unless these are wrong). These are not matters I wish to pursue here, except to say that not all the wrongness of the act (as we normally conceive this) would be included under H; some would fall under r. In assessing how wrongly someone acted we look not only to what was done, but to the intention, motive, and so on.[85]

Should the H represent wrong done, or wrong intended or attempted? (This is the second ambiguity in the formula.) When the wrong done is greater than that intended, the punishment deserved is greater than what fits merely what was intended. (But is it so great as to fit fully what was done?) When the wrong intended is greater than what it turned out (through no virtue of the agent) was done, then the person deserves punishment greater than for merely what was done (which may be no harm at all). Most people agree, though, that this punishment should be less than for what was intended: punishment for attempts should be less than for successful crimes. One proposal would be to take some weighted sum of the two, perhaps the average of wrong done (H_D) and wrong intended (H_I). On this view

$$H = \frac{H_D + H_I}{2}$$

(Why take the average which is an equal weighting, rather than some differential weighting, and what considerations would specify the differential weights?) This formula does not allow punishment in accordance with wrong done when this is greater than wrong intended. An alternative formula would allow this, one that picked whichever is greater, that magnitude picked out by the previous formula, or wrong done (better perhaps: what might reasonably have been foreseen as something that might occur).

$$H = \text{MAX}\left[H_D, \frac{H_D + H_I}{2}\right]$$

Whatever formula of this type we settle upon will be descriptive of how H should be construed; it will not explain why H should be construed that way, or why those intuitive conditions of adequacy which the formula does meet, ought to be met.[86] The fact that punishment is a function of wrong done and not merely wrong intended connects us to the actual world; that it also is a function of wrong intended and not merely of wrong done connects punishment more closely with us. The degree to which we flout correct moral values depends both on what we do, and on what we intend or attempt.*

Let us turn now to r, the degree of flouting (of correct values). There is no reason why the theory of r need be value-free and normatively neutral; the theory of H is not and there is no objection to having values enter into the determination of $r \times H$, or of its r component. However, if the value question to be answered in fixing the degree of r is "how much punishment does the person deserve?" then the procedure will be circular, for it is an independently determined $r \times H$ which is supposed to illuminate that question.[87]

Knowingly ignoring the right and pursuing goals you know to conflict with it constitutes flouting, but so does negligently ignoring the right, whether by choice or simply by allowing yourself to pay it no heed in your actions.[88]

Offenders and the Law

Does a person who conscientiously commits an act of civil disobedience thereby flout correct values and so deserve punishment? He does flout the value, let us suppose it correct, which he protests against, claiming it is not correct and that we too should not support it. He does not flout the value inherent in the legal system, for he publicly commits his act, admits to it, and accepts (or at least does not try to evade) punishment. Therefore, it is easy to understand why we believe he should be punished less. But there is more to be said about the civil disobedient and his act publicly done with moral reasons explicitly stated.

The civil disobedient views himself as affirming correct values, and is attempting to connect us with these. In his intending that we realize the reasons behind his acts, and intending that we realize we were intended to realize all this, and so forth, his act satisfies the

---

* It would be desirable to find some actions differentially focusing on the r and H components. To be sure, different things determine r and H, but it would be reassuring if $r \times H$, which represents punishment deserved, did not always enter our action principles only as a merged unit; if for some situations of two different people with the same total $r \times H$ score but different component r's and H's, we would act differently toward them, punish only one if there were insufficient resources to punish both, for example, or extend mercy sooner to one, or whatever.

Gricean conditions for meaning; he is sending *us* a moral message. In attempting to connect us with correct values, we whom he views as flouting these correct values, he is performing an act of the same general type as punishment. (Does he view the connection of us with correct values teleologically, as a contingent, possible, and desired consequence of his act, or as itself effected by his action?) And in challenging us to punish him, he shows us how seriously he takes his moral commitment, hoping to lead us to reexamine ours (just as the punisher shows he takes his moral commitment seriously enough to inflict suffering in its service, and hopes the punished person will be led to reexamine his actions), and he places his moral message athwart ours, engaging in a competing moral communication—one that sometimes is successful.

Retroactive punishment raises further interesting issues. A person is not flouting correct values (with r > 0) unless he should have known of them; and perhaps he should not be punished for flouting them unless he should have known he would be punished. A prior announcement that such acts will bring punishment (by an authority reasonably expected to carry through) is one sufficient condition for "should have known". However, it is not a necessary condition.

There are ways other than through actual prior announcement that a person should have known he would be punished for a wrong. Suppose that the laws of Nazi Germany had been changed to make the killing of Jews perfectly legal, and that international law as it then existed did not make particular persons (as opposed to the general community) responsible for such acts. Still, the people doing them should have known they were wrong: the acts previously were considered wrong in Germany, and at the time they were considered wrong everywhere else—except Poland. Moreover, they should have known they would be punished by the authorities behind the opposing armies if these were victorious. Consider another case: a country's constitutional laws require that at regular intervals an official stamp must be placed on the document stating a law in order to keep it in effect during the coming period. The clerk who is to stamp the law against murder is sick or stuck in a traffic jam, and the first other person to realize this goes out and commits a murder during the three hours before another clerk gets around to putting on the stamp. The murderer claims his act was not illegal at the time, and so he should not be punished, that such punishment would be under retroactive or *ex post facto* legislation. He too should have known that the act was wrong and, that despite the loophole he tried to utilize, he would be punished.

There is no firm moral ban on retroactive punishment without actual warning or legislation, for the crucial question is: did the person know or should he have known he would be punished? Actual legislation is useful, however, for it establishes an affirmative answer to that question, without difficult inquiries into the person's state of knowledge. (I am supposing he knows that he lives under a system of laws and that he is expected to discover what these are; actual legislation would not ensure an affirmative answer in the case of an Alpha Centurian newly come to Earth.) But actual legislation is not necessary for "should have known" and so is not necessary for justified punishment.*

How does the r × H framework handle repeat offenders? According to it, can a repeat offender be deserving of greater punishment? His excuses will have less weight in showing the action does not stem from a defect of character, but this cannot be the whole story: a first offender who performed the same act also might offer no excuse, and a second offender's second crime might stem from a different defect of character than his first. (Should we say that both of his acts do exhibit one common defect, at least, a disposition not to obey a justified law?) I think that doing it again is itself a more serious flouting; and usually its repetition shows that more of the person, a deeper aspect, is behind it—it was not just one isolated passing whim. But does the repeat offender's greater flouting get represented in our formula by a higher r? Will we need r values greater than one to categorize the repeat offender's degree of flouting? Notice that the repeat offender is not merely someone who has committed more than one crime before getting caught; he is someone who commits a second crime after being caught and found guilty previously. Per-

* I find that nonlawyers agree with this conclusion and reasoning while law students do not. This can be explained in two ways: (a) law students have thought much about legal issues and have come to appreciate the subtle moral basis of the principle of nonretroactivity, while others have not honed their moral sensibilities so sharply in this area; (b) the moral sensibilities of law students are being warped by their training; they have come to think the institution they are involved in entering, in which they are making a heavy personal investment, is more crucial than it actually is.
How might we decide which is the correct explanation?

haps we should view him as knowingly flouting not only the value he violates, but also the value of punishing offenders, so that for him there is an additional H representing another value, or if that H was there previously, at least a higher value of r (but still not greater than unity) for that H.

There is an ambiguity in the term "degree of flouting", for it seems plausibly to go with r, and also with r × H. Let us continue to use the term "degree of flouting" for factors about the agent's psychology and mode of action, for r, and use "magnitude of flouting" for r × H. (There is a similar ambiguity in the notion of the wrongness of an act, which sometimes refers to H and sometimes to r × H.) The (Gricean) message of retributive punishment, then, is: this is the magnitude of your flouting of correct values.

Determinism and Punishment

Is any part of the rationale for retributive punishment undercut or any the less applicable, supposing all actions are causally determined? With r understood as the degree of responsibility for an action, we might have thought so. If determinism undercuts responsibility, it makes the degree of responsibility r equal to zero, and so leaves r × H equal to zero; thus it would undercut any deserved punishment. But when r is understood as the degree of flouting of correct values, the causal determination of action does not undercut r. That one is caused to flout correct values does not alter the fact that one *is* flouting them. (Compare insults: that an insult was causally determined doesn't show that it was not an insult.) Note that I am not saying here that causal determination of action is irrelevant to free will, to our being valuable agents and originators of action; what it is irrelevant to is (justified) retributive punishment.

Actually, this puts the point too strongly. Perhaps someone whose actions are undetermined yet freely chosen (as described in the first part of this chapter) would, when doing wrong, be flouting correct values even more than do those whose actions are determined. Such a person then would deserve even more punishment. Causal determination of action, then, may lessen the degree of flouting (or alternatively, noncausal determination with free choice may increase the degree of flouting) but it does not reduce it to zero; it does not undercut deserved punishment.

Interpreting r as 'degree of flouting' fits our judgments about who is to be held responsible for actions. Yet it is a particular philosophical theory that if the r playing a role in punishment is to be greater than zero, this presupposes nondeterminism. Still, this philosophical theory has powerful intuitive appeal, and in rejecting it we have to account for its force, to explain why it seems so right. Our point above that determinism may limit how much we are flouting (but doesn't make us all equally nonflouters) may provide part of the explanation of the appeal of the position that determinism is incompatible with deserved retributive punishment. (Clearly, it would be fruitful to apply here considerations from Chapter 1 about the best instantiated relation mode of structuring a philosophical concept.)

It strongly appears that determinism is incompatible with deserved punishment, which raises the philosophical question: given determinism, how is deserved punishment possible? It is not clear that the two are incompatible, but they appear to be, there is a tension between them. The task is to see how they could fit together. However, to have any confidence in this compatibilist position, we will need a convincing explanation of the intuitive power of the incompatibilist position. Recall the situation in Chapter 3, when we did not want a quick refutation of the skeptic about knowledge, wanting to account for the intuitive power of his position. However, we have not reached a position here that holds the incompatibilist at least is right about some things. (So perhaps we should worry more.)

Some may think causal determination in general provides an excuse because it shows the act is not to be attributed to a defect of character; instead, the act is to be attributed to the causes (going back to before the person was born). However, these causes need not be incompatible with the defect of character, they may act through the defect. True, there also will be a causal explanation of the character defect, but there being an explanation of why something is there does not nullify its being there. The causal explanation need not replace the character defect explanation; it may underlie it as a reducing theory.

If the character defect was unchosen, is it really a defect, really a defect of character? That particular character trait is not attributable to some other defect of character from which it stems. (Let us suppose this; eventually mustn't we get back to some such defect of character whose having does not stem from the exercise of some other previously possessed character defect?) A causal explanation of a person's having this character defect will show it does not stem from an earlier one; so he is not to be blamed for coming to have the defect. His action, however, *is* attributable to a character defect, and constitutes a flouting of correct values; he is deserving of punishment for the action. If character defects are not chosen, why do we punish for them? We do not punish for their possession, only for the actions that stem from them. Yet, we don't punish actions stemming from unchosen physical traits that nonnegligently lead to a harm (we will require compensation, though); why do we punish for nonchosen character traits? The physical traits do not indicate being anti-linked to correct values, they do not indicate flouting values, whereas the character traits do.

"But he is not to blame for coming to have those character traits." Retributive punishment effects a link with correct values in those who have flouted them (and who are capable of being linked). By whatever way the person came to be unlinked, came to flout, still, he is unlinked and flouting, and so punishment is called for to effect and establish the linkage. "But if it was causally determined that he flout, how can he justifiably be punished for flouting?" He is punished for his wrongful act, and he deserves punishment only if it is an act of flouting; we can say shortly (provided we remember the long form) that he is punished for flouting. The punishment establishes the link between him and the values he was anti-linked to; causes of his being anti-linked do not alter the fact of his being so—rather, they produce it—nor do they reduce the need for him to be linked.

Suppose he is caused to flout in this way: by hypnosis or psychosurgery others instill in him a character defect that he then exercises, thereby flouting correct values. Does he deserve punishment for his actions? No, for it is the intentions of the instillers that are operating in the person's action, the flouting is to be attributed to them. When impersonal causes instill in a person the very same character traits, though, it is his intentions that animate his own actions, for no better candidate is available. (See the discussion of the closest relation mode of structuring the notions of coercion and attribution of action in Chapter 1.) Why can another's intentional actions, for instance the hypnotist's, displace your intentions, whereas impersonal causes cannot? The other's intentional actions are more closely linked to the resulting action than are the impersonal causes; not only do they (too) cause the action, they look ahead to it. It is no accident that the examples one wants to produce, in objecting to the view that flouting deserves punishment even if caused, involve another's intention intruding (and thereby reducing the magnitude of flouting). However, such examples cannot show that punishment's being deserved is undercut by impersonal causes, by mere determinism of whatever sort.

One note of clarification. I granted previously that if a person's coming to have the character defect was caused by a process that didn't go through the exercise of any (other) character defect of his, then he is not to be blamed for coming to have it. (I see blaming him for something merely as attributing that to the exercise of a character defect of his.) However, it is another matter with his continuing to have the character defect, for its continuing (unlike its starting) may well be attributable to his exercise of a character defect, perhaps even that very one. His not taking steps to alter or eliminate the character defect may itself be an exercise of some defect of his character (perhaps that very one), and so something attributable to a defect of his character. Thus, his continuing to have the character defect (unlike his coming to have it) can constitute a flouting of correct values.

A point might be reached where all of a person's character defects are maintained as an exercise of some character defects he previously had, and so having each one now does constitute a flouting (even though the original acquisition of some then did not). Does it follow that we can punish a person for a defective character, without its exercise in any wrongful action? There was the action of maintaining this character trait, which is an exercise of it or some other trait; nevertheless, as noted above, if maintaining this defect violates no one else's right, it cannot be punished by force.

This concludes our discussion of punishment. I began this chapter by saying that punishment was not the central issue in the quagmire of questions about free will, that the central question was the question of how, if our acts were causally determined (or random), we correctly could view ourselves as beings of value. Here we have concluded that punishment not only is not central to the problem of free will, it is not derivative either. A theory of retributive punishment does not await or depend upon a theory of free will. Such a theory would or might have been needed on the interpretation of *r* as 'degree of responsibility for H'. (Our discussion began with that interpretation, on the assumption that it would be congenial to the reader, in order to set forth the outlines of a theory of retribution; this saved us from having to consider everything at the beginning.) But with *r* interpreted as 'degree of flouting of correct values', we have seen that a theory of retributive punishment can proceed independently of the free will issue. No matter how that issue is resolved, even if it is concluded that there is no free will, actions can flout correct values and people can be in need of connection with correct values.

But if there is no free will, then we are not of such great worth, lacking originative value. What then is the importance of connecting relatively valueless entities to correct values? All the more important, we might well think; that line of thought was pursued in the second part of this chapter, on tracking value. However, the thought was pursued there on the assumption that there are values and that it is valuable to track them, to be connected to value qua value; those assumptions about the existence of value and the importance of connecting to value qua value underlie the view we just have presented of retributive punishment.

Our focus on value has three components: that there are values, that they can be linked with, that it is valuable to link with them. In the second part of this chapter we considered whether determinism presents insuperable obstacles to the linking, and throughout this chapter we have spun out consequences of these three components, elaborating a context in which they fit. However, the first and third components need to be examined directly. Wherein lies the value of connecting with correct values, of being connected to value qua value? Are there (correct) values? How is value even possible?

Chapter
Five

FOUNDATIONS
OF ETHICS

Ethical truths find no place within the contemporary scientific picture of the world. No such truths are established in any scientific theory or tested by any scientific procedure—microscopes and telescopes reveal no ethical facts. In its guise as a complete picture of the world, science seems to leave no room for any ethical facts or truths. If there are ethical facts, what kind of facts are these, what makes them hold true?

Some moral facts or moral statements hold in virtue of other facts or statements. An act is wrong in virtue of some other features it has, for instance, causing (needless) suffering, betraying the trust of a friend, initiating genocide. The moral features of an action (such as being wrong or morally impermissible or something that ought to be done) do not float independently of the other features of the act, but follow in their wake. The question of what relationship the moral facts or truths have to the other facts on which they depend has been termed the is–ought question or the fact–value question. How is ought related to is, value to fact?*

* In a famous passage, David Hume wrote, "In every system of morality, which I have hitherto met with, I have always remark'd, that the author proceeds for some time in the ordinary way of reasoning, and established the being of a God, or makes observations concerning human affairs; when of a sudden I am surpriz'd to find, that instead of the usual copulations of proposi-

Not every philosophical view presupposes that there *are* objective values or objectively true "ought" statements, with the only question being how these connect to other facts. One view, nihilism, holds that there are no objective values at all; no ethical truths hold apart from our opinions. Closely related are various subjectivist or relativist positions which hold that thinking or agreeing makes it so, or that ethical statements simply are expressions of emotion or preference having no independent objective true content.

My concern is not to argue that these views are false, to convince their proponents they are mistaken. The task, rather, is to explain how there can be objective values and ethical truths, to formulate a conception or picture within which there is room for these. Why isn't the universe as the scientific naturalist describes it, composed of many entities and facts but no value(s) at all—how is it possible for the universe to be otherwise? What could objective ethical truths and values be like, what could the universe be like in which they hold? How are objective values and ethical truths even possible?

It is difficult to conjure up any answer to these questions. This chapter does sketch a view, not without its difficulties. The view is put forth as one way it could turn out that ethical statements hold true. Although my hope is that the view contains much that is actually true and illuminating about ethics, the project is to sketch what an objective ethics might look like, to understand how there (so much as) could be such a thing. Providing such an explanatory foundation for ethical truths is not the same as supplying their detailed content. We seek the structure within which ethical truths reside; finding that structure will tell us something about the ethical content, but not everything.

Value or preciousness of persons has a dual role in my interpersonal actions. Your value generates a moral claim or constraint on my

---

tions, *is,* and *is not,* I meet with no proposition that is not connected with an *ought,* or an *ought not.* This change is imperceptible; but is, however, of the last consequence. For as this *ought,* or *ought not,* expresses some new relation or affirmation, 'tis necessary that it shou'd be observ'd and explain'd; and at the same time that a reason should be given, for what seems altogether inconceivable, how this new relation can be a deduction from others, which are entirely different from it. But as authors do not commonly use this precaution, I shall presume to recommend it to the readers; and am persuaded, that this small attention wou'd subvert all the vulgar system of morality." (*Treatise of Human Nature,* Book III, Part I, Sec. I.)

behavior toward you; because of your value, others (including me) ought to behave toward you in some ways, not in others. Also, my value is expressed in how I am best off behaving, in the kind of behavior that should flow from a being with my value, in how that value is shown or maintained in action. My value fixes what behavior should flow from me; your value fixes which behavior should flow toward you. Value manifests itself as a push and as a pull.

The tasks of ethical theory are to demarcate both the moral pull and the moral push.[1] Ethical theory must show and explain why and how the value of a person gives rise to determinate conditions, to moral constraints upon the behavior of others; ethical theory must also show and explain why and how a person whose life befits his own value will (thereby) be led to behave toward others in specified ways, why and how a person is better off behaving morally toward others—in accordance with their moral pull.

The magnitude of these moral forces, moral pull and moral push, is not their actual effect on behavior; these are moral forces that ought to have effect. Ethics is harmonious when the push is at least as great as the pull, when the person's own value leads him to behave toward another as the value of that other requires. There is an ethical gap when the push is less than the pull, a difference between what the value of another requires from you and what the expression or outflow of your own value involves. The third task of ethical theory, then, is to show that the push is greater than or equal to the pull: that for any two persons, the moral push of one toward the other is greater than or equal to the pull of the second upon the first.

Such ethical harmony is not guaranteed—the philosophers' vision may fail. Perhaps we just are stuck with a gap. However, if the ethical theory provides an independent basis and foundation for the moral pull and the moral push, yet still push covers pull or they converge exactly, then this cannot be merely a fortunate happenstance. The ethical theory, then, must explain the overlap or convergence of the two.

Moreover, if a person is behaving morally, not merely doing what is moral by accident, then his doing this particular behavior must somehow connect with the fact that it is pulled. In some way the person must be doing the act because it is right. The fourth task of ethical theory is to specify the nature of this connection and show how it can be realized. Our account in the previous chapter of an action's tracking rightness seems to be (at least a central component of) the appropriate connection needed here. It then was presented within an account of acting freely, while here it would do duty in an account of acting morally.

Each of these components is needed in a complete ethical theory. To center ethics mainly on moral push (as the Greek theorists did) leaves ethical behavior as, at best, fortunate fallout from living the best life; another person's moral claim then constitutes a tenuous side effect of your own pursuit of your good. It is no accident that throughout the discussion of moral push, I shall continually refer to Plato and Aristotle. For the Greek tradition is the source of concern with moral push, as the source of concern with moral pull is the Jewish tradition, starting with its notion that man is created in the image of God, and so is to be treated ethically.

This structuring of the area of ethics, its questions and components, is ahistorical. It does not take account of the searing events of this century: the destruction of European Jewry, the Soviet system of labor and penal camps, the emergence of totalitarian societies, and the system of nuclear deterrence which threatens whole populations.[2] These events create a rift in the (moral) universe. It is not that the principles of traditional moral philosophy, as herein pursued, do not apply to these situations (although an unprecedented situation may call for the revision of accepted principles which in no way envisioned that situation). Rather, those principles do not especially and saliently illuminate these events and situations. That could be done only by moral principles that emerge from pondering them, from a moral investigation that, because it is designed to illuminate them, begins with and stays centrally focused upon these situations. There is a deep and intense need for such moral inquiry and scrutiny. I am painfully aware that this chapter does not speak to that need.

I. ETHICAL PUSH

Glaucon's Challenge

The task of the theory of the ethical push is to show that and how we are better off being moral. Being moral is not simply a sacrifice, there is something in it for us.

Recall Glaucon's challenge to Socrates in Plato's *Republic:* show that being moral is better for the agent, apart from its external consequences. To isolate these consequences, Glaucon imagines a ring that makes someone invisible. With this ring he is able to act immorally with no external penalty: he can rob, murder, and rape without being caught or punished. Is there any reason why he should not do this? Glaucon sharpens the issue by imagining that the immoral man has the reputation of being moral, he is honored and praised as moral, while another moral man is thought to be immoral and so is condemned and shunned. Glaucon asks Socrates to show, despite this, that the second moral person is better off than the first immoral one, that we would be better off being that second than the first.

Now this is a severe challenge, more severe perhaps than is reasonable. Glaucon's two cases differ extremely, not only morally but also in many other ways. No choice we would face involves such disparate alternatives: being moral while everything else is bad versus being immoral while everything else is good. Indeed, Socrates disputes that everything else can vary independently of a person's moral quality. Is the relevant comparison, instead, between two lives differing in moral quality but with everything else held constant? No, differences in moral quality will have some other effects.

When I face a choice between being moral or immoral, or (less dichotomously) among lives with different mixtures of morality and immorality, my range of options does not include all possible lives. For each mixture of morality and immorality open to me, I must consider the life that would result (or the probabilistically weighted sum of the lives that might result) if I opted for that moral mix. If actually I would not be thought to be grossly immoral while being as moral as

I could be, then my choice is not the one Glaucon presents. In the choice between morality and immorality, every other feature of my life is not held constant, for some changes will ensue given moral differences; neither does every other feature of my life vary independently and in the opposite value direction.

To show I am better off being moral, is it enough to show the following?

(a) Among my range of options, the life I am best off with is the most moral life.

To take account of the possibility of ties, this should be rephrased as: among my range of options, the life I am best off leading, or one which at least ties for best, also at least ties for being the most moral of these options. This focus on the very best life, however, may be insufficient for practical purposes. Given my proneness to succumb to temptation, to become diverted, I may think that the most moral life, and even the one most in my long-term self-interest, probably is beyond my actual reach. So I might rather want to know whether being (only) somewhat better morally would constitute being personally better off:

(b) Among the options slightly better morally than the life I currently am leading is one with which I would be better off.

However, I may be able to alter my life more significantly, even if I cannot attain or stick to the very best option. It would be discouraging to learn that somewhere between my current life and the morally best one, my well-being dips even as my moral quality improves. Thus, a more useful (and stronger) result would be:

(c) Ordering feasible lives by their moral quality *ipso facto* orders them by how well off I would be in leading them.

The first condition holds that the morally best life is one with which I am best off. Its purview is global, looking at all lives open to me. The second condition looks locally with the same result, holding of the more nearly attainable lives that the morally best also is personally best. The third condition holds that the transition from the local to the global is uniformly uphill, that my personal well-being improves as my moral quality does. (Perhaps it would be enough to show that path had no downhill portion, that it was everywhere uphill or level.) Note that condition c as stated includes a and b.

Conditions a–c have been formulated for one person's range of options; a moral theory must show these hold for everyone. Might the truth turn out to be that by and large 'personally better' matches 'morally better', but not for everyone nor throughout the complete range of options? It is not enough, I think, for a moral theory merely to show condition a; Plato tries to accomplish something in the direction of c in his discussion of the different types of men: oligarchic, aristocratic, democratic, and so on.

It is an immense task to show conditions a–c for everyone, even given the limitation to actual options and to the differences that actually would result from the choice for morality or immorality. Moreover, since we cannot examine individually each person's range of options, the only way to accomplish the task in one fell swoop, it seems, is to accept Glaucon's challenge, discussing his extreme case. (Yet, merely handling his extreme alternatives would not be enough, just as condition a above wouldn't suffice.) Indeed, might not his extreme alternatives be included in someone's range of options (while also moral alternatives with personally good results are excluded); could there not be a malicious person who would besmirch your reputation and do other bad things if your virtue reached a certain level?[3]

Inconsistency and Motivation

Since the time of Glaucon's challenge to Socrates, moral philosophers have attempted to show it is in our rational self-interest to act morally. They have tried to show that in pursuing our rational self-interest, rightly understood, we will be behaving morally, and that in acting morally our rational self-interest is best served. They have tried to show the moral person will be happier.

However, it is not difficult to think of actual or possible situations where morality and rational self-interest quite apparently diverge. Still, the Platonic view that these are in harmony, that it is best for oneself or one's soul to be the best sort of person, is an inspiring one. Moreover, I believe there is something deeply correct in that view.

What is correct, though, is not captured by attempting to correlate morality with self-interest or happiness.

The attractiveness of holding that morality and self-interest coincide (and therefore the temptation so to reduce Plato's insight) lies in the clear specification of the penalty or sanction for immoral behavior. "In what way are you worse off behaving immorally? Your self-interest is not served." Thus the person is provided with the clearest possible motive for moral behavior: self-interest. Philosophers who come to despair of this being the sanction for immoral behavior will search around for another. Some have hoped to show that a person is committed to having a moral motivation by some other things. The strongest link of commitment would be some kind of entailment: it is inconsistent to retain those other things while lacking a moral motivation.[4] It is difficult for such arguments to show there is a commitment to morality, to show there really would be some (analogue of) inconsistency if one behaved immorally. Hence, much of the literature on such arguments has questioned whether the claimed entailment really holds.[5]

These arguments give rise to another issue, even more basic. If these commitments, these (analogues of) entailments, did hold, what (according to such arguments) would be the sanction for behaving immorally? Apparently, to give up those things, whatever they are, that commit you to the moral motivation. You cannot have it both ways; so the motivational push to morality is the motivation not to give up those things that commit you to morality.[6] Such an argument is not designed to show that you will be moral if you hold on to the other things; otherwise everyone it applies to (who does retain the other things) would be moral already. Rather, the argument is designed to show that, holding on to the other things, you are committed to being moral and are inconsistent if immoral.

Now a showing of inconsistency is important in an argument about truth; so it might be important as part of the theory of moral pull if the inconsistency could indeed be shown to hold. But what role does inconsistency play in motivation? When something X commits one to Y, it appears that the cost of failing to accept (the entailed) Y must be: giving up X. This goes too quickly, however, for there remains another possibility, namely, being inconsistent. The motivational force toward accepting Y that is exerted by being shown that X commits one to it, is the lesser of (a) the motivation to keep (accepting) X, and (b) the motivation to avoid that particular inconsistency of keeping X while failing to accept Y. The motivational force of the argument (toward accepting Y) can be no stronger than the motivation to avoid the particular inconsistency specified by the argument.

Philosophers are people with very strong motivations to avoid inconsistency. Perhaps this motivation is strengthened by philosophical training and activity—presumably, skill in avoiding inconsistency is increased—but I suspect that the major difference in this respect between philosophers and others is accounted for by selective entry into the group of philosophers. It is only (but not all) those people who already have especially strong motivation to avoid inconsistency that are attracted to philosophy as a subject. So it is not surprising that philosophers have thought motivation (and not merely truth) would be clinched by a showing that the alternative is inconsistency. But how powerful, really, is the general desire to avoid inconsistency? (Since readers of this book are not representative of the general populace, it's no use trying to answer the question by introspection.)

What is bad about inconsistency? Since consistency is a necessary condition for truth, if your beliefs are inconsistent then (it must be that) at least one of your beliefs is false. How bad is that? I believe I have some false belief or other about some state capital in the United States (certainly I do about the capital or location of some country), but I simply don't care. I wouldn't pay anything to remove this false belief, or look in a book to correct it. It doesn't matter to me that I have such a belief, especially if it's about one of those states that nobody lives in. Most of us believe we are fallible and accept this fact with some degree of equanimity.

But isn't an inconsistency in one's beliefs worse than merely happening to believe something false? It guarantees some falsity. Yet perhaps inconsistency is the fate of someone who believes himself fallible, who believes that one of his (other) beliefs is false. This topic has recently been discussed under the rubric "the paradox of the preface", after a book whose preface announces that one of the statements in the book is (bound to be) false. Since the author does not know which is false, he believes each of the later statements, and also the statement in the preface. (Recall the reader of newspaper stories who, for lack of a better alternative, believes each particular thing he reads yet also believes the stories contain inaccuracies.)

Hence his set of beliefs is inconsistent; they cannot all be true. Yet this inconsistency, if indeed it arises in this way, will not distress him.

Many of us have had the experience of explaining or showing a paradox to someone, for instance, Russell's paradox or the paradox of the liar. Often the person merely will smile in amusement; he does not think the paradox is important, even if we show he accepts each of the components that gives rise to the paradox. It is philosophers who get excited about paradoxes and spend much time trying to resolve them. Most other people would embrace the possibility broached by Wittgenstein: pigeonhole the paradoxes, segregate them off harmlessly, and then go about regular business.[7] Most people are not distressed to discover their beliefs exhibit the inconsistency of the paradox of the preface, or of the logical and semantical paradoxes. How much distress will they be caused, then, by finding they exhibit other inconsistencies, how weighty is their motivation to avoid inconsistency?

Consider now the immoral man who steals and kills, to his own benefit or for some cause he favors. Suppose we show that some X he holds or accepts or does commits him to behaving morally. He now must give up at least one of the following: (a) behaving immorally, (b) maintaining X, (c) being consistent about this matter in this respect. The immoral man tells us, "To tell you the truth, if I had to make the choice, I would give up being consistent."

Do the philosophers who produce the arguments about commitment think the immoral man's desire to avoid inconsistency is so great that he would (be motivated to) stop behaving immorally? Will the perils of inconsistency push him to renounce further gains from killing and plundering (and the past gains also?), plus whatever pleasure he gets from the immoral activities? In fact, if the philosopher's argument correctly shows the inconsistency, the person was paying the penalty of inconsistency already. The argument does not create the inconsistency. If the person was holding X while behaving immorally, he already was being inconsistent; plainly, he did not find that too terrible. Surely, it is a price he is willing to pay (and continue paying) for his ill-gotten gains.[8]

The philosopher's argument does add something, for upon hearing it, the immoral man who was inconsistent before will come to realize he was inconsistent, and still is; yet surely the evil man will be able to live even with this realization. (Please, withhold the judgment that I have given inconsistency short shrift until we touch upon the topic again later.)

The Moral Benefit

In what way, then, is the immoral person worse off? What is the cost to the immoral person of his immoral behavior? Some deny there is any cost, maintaining, though, that the person ought to behave morally, even when not doing so exacts no cost from him.[9] That the status and validity of the moral pull do not rest upon the moral push, I would not deny.

Nonetheless, I believe there is a cost to immoral behavior. It is a *value* cost. The immoral life is a less valuable life than the moral one, the immoral person is a less valuable being than the moral one. The sanction is a value sanction. Note that I am not merely saying (trivially) that the immoral person is less moral than the moral person. He is less valuable, as specified by a general theory of value applying as well to areas other than morality, as a (nontrivial) consequence of that theory. That the immoral person is less valuable in that way is not a trivial fact.

Before turning to a sketch of that general theory of value, we must ask whether there is a value sanction even if the agent does not care about value. Perhaps he cares about it no more than he cared about inconsistency; he wants, let us suppose, solely his own pleasure. Until now we have spoken indiscriminately of how the immoral person is worse off, and of the motivation to be moral. Now we see the possibility that these may diverge, so radically even that the way the person is objectively worse off does not connect with any motivation he actually has. Since he will not, in this case, be motivated to act morally, what is the importance of showing that the immoral person is worse off in value, given that he does not care about that?

The immoral person thinks he is getting away with something, he thinks his immoral behavior costs him nothing. But that is not true; he pays the cost of having a less valuable existence. He pays that penalty, though he doesn't feel it or care about it. Not all penalties are felt.

But if that is what we mean by being worse off—being less valuable—(he says laughing) then why should he care about being worse off? He doesn't care, and that does not bother him. However, his not caring about value is also part of the cost he is paying: not caring about value is itself something that diminishes his value. Even as he skips happily away, he pays the penalty. The immoral person is not getting away with anything; his getaway attempt itself has a value cost.* There is a penalty even if he doesn't realize it or care. Others who understand value will realize how he is worse off, even if he himself does not.[10]

The moral life is not simply moral; it also has a more general kind of value: it is better and lovelier to be moral. ("Virtue is its own reward." "For what is a man profited, if he shall gain the whole world, and lose his own soul?") Plato's vision is right; we are better off being moral, it is a better way to be. It is a mistake, however, to squeeze this into the view that being moral serves what a person feels to be his self-interest, serves his felt motivations. When we read Plato's descriptions of the harmoniously ordered soul, it is not important to us that such a person will feel happier. We are moved and inspired by our perception or realization that being that way is more valuable. It is our perception of value that Plato evokes.

We should not be surprised that objective value can be specified apart from what a person actually desires. By now there are enough examples to show that how things feel from the inside is not the only thing that is important.[11] If there is objective value, we should expect it sometimes to be divorced from a person's actual motivations, while being none the less valuable for that. Surely, some adverse biographical conditions, or even moods,[12] can lead a person not to care about value. However, value is not completely divorced from motivation simply because it need not be tied to actual motivation under any and all conditions. Later, we shall consider what tie exists between value and a person's motivations under favorable conditions, unfortu-

---

* Compare the Indian doctrine of karma expressing itself through reincarnations. On one interpretation, the karmic penalty is just to be reborn as the kind of person you were at the end of your previous existence. The penalty is being like that, being someone who acts like that. But if the karmic penalty for being worse is being a worse being, it does not await the next existence. It operates immediately, automatically. See also Saadya Gaon, *Book of Doctrines and Beliefs*, ch. V, Sec. 1, "The Impress of Man's Actions on His Soul", translated by Alexander Altmann in *Three Jewish Philosophers* (Atheneum Books, New York, 1969).

nately, often hypothetical ones. (Nevertheless, our theory of the moral push is largely external; compare this externalization to the theory of knowledge presented in Chapter 3.)

"But if under some conditions value is divorced from a person's motivation, that person may lack (sufficient) motivation to behave morally; what then can we do?" There is much we can do in society, ranging from attempts at persuasion to punishment of the person who does not behave morally, by connecting sanctions to motivations he does have. There is no guarantee he will not be able to avoid our institutional network. However, it is not the task of philosophy to plug this gap and provide motivation for people. At any rate, that is not our task here. I want to understand how a person is worse off being immoral, not to convince the immoral person that he is worse off. "But he might just dig in his heels and refuse to be convinced without a knock down argument." When he digs in his heels and lives accordingly, his choice has the effect of determining the value of his life, whether or not he realizes this. What he needs is not a philosopher but inspiration.

Leading the Most Valuable Life

Thus far, I have spoken indiscriminately of the value sanction for a person who behaves immorally as his not having the most valuable life, his not having the most valuable existence, and his being of lesser value. Which is it? To which thing is the value to apply (or fail to apply): is it a person or his life or his existence? We can ask what is the best or most valuable kind of person, what is the best way for a person to be? (Plato answers: a person whose soul is hierarchically and correctly ordered.) Or we can ask what is the best or most valuable (kind of) life, what is the best way to live? To make this question primary is to assume that what you should (most want to) have is the most valuable kind of extended life over time.[13] Why that? We need never occupy the standpoint of looking at our whole life, even at its end. So this standpoint is not adopted in order to have an experience of taking in our whole life. However, a theory of value will not hold that all value depends on felt experiences, so a whole life still could be the crucial bearer of value, although this is not for the sake of its being experienced as a whole. We can ask a deeper question, though: whether the most valuable life is not merely another sort of possession? Granted, it is a peculiarly intimate one; nevertheless, isn't it just something you *have*? Why should that possession be what is most important, as opposed to what you are?

This returns us to the first standpoint: what is most valuable for us is the best way we can be. Aristotle criticizes the view that being a certain kind of person can be the complete good, pointing out that such a person could be asleep always, or have a lifetime of inactivity, or undergo great sufferings and misfortunes.[14] (Although such a person would not choose only sleep or inactivity, these unfortunately might hit him.) Being the best sort of person is not the sole concern. Should we swing back, then, to having the best or most valuable life? Yet, just as misfortune can prevent the best person from having the best life, cannot good fortune give the best life to someone who is far from being the best kind of person? Certainly, it could give him all the passive goods of the best life, as well as all the passive components of the active goods. (Recall the device of the experience machine.)

What we want is both

(a) to be the best kind of person, and
(b) to have the best kind of life.

With both of these present, could anything be lacking? Yes, there could be lacking the requisite kind of connection between them. These two, unconnected, are like true belief which is not knowledge. We want to be the most valuable kind of person, to have the most valuable kind of life, and moreover, to have that life stem (in the right way) from our being that kind of person. We want this having and being not only to be present, but also to interconnect properly.

This suggests that in order to specify what is best for a person, we utilize whatever favored relation R connects belief to truth when there is knowledge. According to Chapter 3, that relation is tracking. What is best is condition b standing in the (tracking) relation R to condition a; this entails both conditions. Spelling this out further in terms of the tracking relation: he is the most valuable kind of person and has the most valuable kind of life; if he weren't the most valuable kind of person he wouldn't have the most valuable kind of life; and if he were the most valuable kind of person he would have the most valuable kind of life. We need a term for the situation where condition b stands in relation R to condition a (we suppose this the tracking relation), in order to distinguish that from simply having the most valuable life or being the most valuable kind of person. Let us call it *leading* the most valuable life, or *living* it.

Best is to lead the most valuable life, but often external conditions will make this impossible or unattainable. To decide what is best among the feasible alternatives, when bRa is not possible, it seems we will need a weighting of the importance of the components: of having the best kind of life, of being the best kind of person, and of approximations to R, to having a life track a way of being. If the purpose of such a weighting is to establish tradeoffs to guide our choices, certain situations cannot arise. We need not ask how much accidental good in life outweighs a certain loss in how good we are. If we choose the good, it will not be (in the relevant sense) accidental.[15]

These components might help us to understand Aristotle's shift between the intellectualist and the inclusive view.[16] Although the intellectualist view fits conditions b or a, the inclusive view is called for by R. However, for any view, even one free of Aristotle's temptation to think the contemplative life is best, there will be the possibility of conflicts and hence tradeoffs among the most valuable life, the most valuable way of being, and the R relation that is to link a life and way of being.

The person wants himself to be valuable, not merely to have some valuable possession, even one so intimately connected with himself as his life. Still, when the person or the self or its existence is valuable, isn't value something it has, isn't value still merely a property, a possession? What is most desired, the greatest value reward, it seems, is that the self not merely have value but *be* value. We shall return to this theme later. If an ethical theory is to maintain that the "payoff" for living morally is a value payoff, it will have to investigate more closely the nature of value.

Intrinsic Value

The basic dimension of value is one that underlies and generates our value ranking, assuming this ranking is roughly correct. So the claim that a particular dimension D is the basic dimension of value will receive inductive support if the rank ordering among things generated by that dimension D is identical with their rank ordering in value. However, this will not explain why D is the basic dimension of value, why the value of something consists in its positioning along the dimension D. First, I shall touch on the inductive task; then, with a proposal of a particular dimension D in hand, turn to the explanatory one.

The notion of value I wish to investigate is not the value of something for some other purpose or further effects or consequences (assumed to be valuable). It is not its instrumental value, but rather its value in itself, apart from these further consequences and connections. Philosophers have termed this type of value intrinsic value.[17] It seems plausible that not all value can be dependent on further consequences and effects, that something must be valuable in itself. The chain of being valuable (solely) because of further connections must terminate in something that is valuable in itself; otherwise value could not get started, value would be without foundation.[18]

However, in epistemology a similar "foundational" view, holding that something must be certain if anything is to be probable (relative to it), itself once seemingly compelling, now is seen to be only one possible epistemological structure among others that are more holistic, mutually supporting, organic.[19] So perhaps we should be somewhat suspicious here too of the apparent necessity for some intrinsic value to ground all other value (even though we shall explore a view of intrinsic value that is not undercut by holistic considerations). However, not every foundational structure totters; for instance, there is set theory with its axiom of foundations or groundedness. It has been conjectured that mathematicians have accepted this axiom, not on the basis of direct "intuition" of its truth but rather because of "not being able to understand how non-well-founded sets could be possible."[20] So, lacking an explanation of how something could be possible, its impossibility was postulated. There is an alternative to a direct foundational view of intrinsic value, however. We might view the intrinsic value dimension D as an explanatory dimension, one that accounts for the total value of anything by its score, together with the score of its consequences and encompassing wholes (or their expected value), along that dimension D.[21] Note that the point that the sanction of immorality is a value sanction is independent of any particular theory of intrinsic value, and so might hold even if the theory we shall sketch turns out to be mistaken.

It is a fact that in my value ranking I place people higher in intrinsic value than animals which are higher than plants which are higher than rocks. There are distinctions in value within these categories, as well as some overlap; for example, I do not rank a mouse higher than an 800-year-old redwood. There are some sharply defined parts to my ranking, but much of it is vague. Sprinkled in somewhere also are paintings, planetary systems, and scientific theories. Some things I cannot easily compare, so perhaps there are separate rankings, better pictured by parallel lines or by lines that cross like an X, rather than by one vertical line. Pursuing the different structural possibilities, and the differing strengths of scales of measurement, would be of little help at this point.

The proposal that a particular dimension D underlies this value ranking will be plausible if D yields roughly this ranking. Perhaps, also, D should not yield too much more; if a dimension yielded a very sharp ranking of everything, there would be the question of whether that dimension underlay our ranking, which is not as sharp. The answer might be that the dimension does account for our ranking, but somehow is masked in its operation, so that the ranking yielded is hazy. The uncovering or sharpening of dimension D, and of our ability to rank in accordance with it, then might have the consequence of sharpening our value ranking.

Degree of Organic Unity

To uncover the relevant dimension D, let us begin with the area that speaks most frequently and articulately of value: aesthetics. Theorists of the arts often extol the virtues of unifying diverse and apparently unrelated (or not so tightly related) material; the order of the work effects this unification. Unity in a painting can be established in many ways: by the way forms lead the eye through it and by relationships of forms, textures, thematic material, color, tones, and so on. A unified painting will be tied together by various of these modes of relationship. However, it is not merely its degree of unity that determines the value of a painting. A canvas painted monochromatically will be as highly unified in color as any other. (But will it be as unified as another canvas that is unified by the other relationships as well?) The degree of diversity enters, also. The more diverse the material that gets unified (to a certain degree), the greater the value.

Let us follow the tradition and call such a "unity in diversity" an organic unity.[22] Holding fixed the degree of unifiedness of the material, the degree of organic unity varies directly with the degree of diversity of that material being unified. Holding fixed the degree of diversity of the material, the degree of organic unity varies directly with the degree of unifiedness (induced) in that material. The more diverse the material, however, the harder it is to unify it to a given degree. Literature offers especially rich opportunities to unify diversity; its referential and evocative language brings in as part of the material of the work the things and themes it refers to or evokes.*

I am imagining that the degree of diversity will be measured relative to a set of dimensions along which the materials differ or are similar, and the degree of unifiedness will be relative to a set of unifying relations. Can we draw a curve of degree of organic unity with the two axes being degree of diversity and degree of unifiedness (where the maximum degree of unifiedness possible is constrained by the degree of diversity, in the absence of new and creative modes of unification)? It is difficult to see how to do this, and it is difficult to know how to take account of the thematic material in a measure of diversity, and of thematic relations in a measure of unifiedness. Therefore we shall have to proceed here with an intuitive and rough notion of the degree of organic unity, without a formal measure.[23]

The notion of organic unity comes up also in the talk of organismic biologists. They tell us that the organisms they study are organic unities, wholes whose parts are related and homeostatically regu-

---

* Writers on organic unity in art often assert that no part of an organic unity can be removed or changed without significantly altering the whole. This is not a (necessary) component of the notion as we delineate it. Nor is the primacy of formal values in literature, which led Henry James (in his preface to *The Tragic Muse*) to condemn *War and Peace* and *Anna Karenina* as "large loose baggy monsters". The standard of "unity in diversity", as we interpret it, will not favor Flaubert over Tolstoy; the magnitude and importance of the themes of the work, and the diversity these themes unify, will be part of the total diversity unified. The diversity unified by a work needn't all be present in the work, as shown by Picasso line drawings.

lated in intricate and complicated ways, unified through time despite changes in the parts. There is some disagreement about what "higher" would mean for organisms, but let us assume we can rank organisms roughly in accordance with their degree of organic unity, so that most plants come below most animals, with higher animals coming above the lower ones.[24] Sentience and then consciousness add new possibilities of unification over time and at a time, and self-consciousness, being an "I", is an especially tight mode of unification.

Thus the ranking of organisms in accordance with degree of organic unity matches our value ranking of them, with people above other animals above plants above rocks. (It is not that rocks have no degree of organic unity—there are, as the physicist tells us, intermolecular binding forces and intramolecular ones.) Whole ecological systems present their own intricate relationships, equilibria, and complicated patternings, while their components also have high degrees of organic unity. (Shouldn't the measure of something's degree of organic unity also somehow take account of the degree of organic unity of its parts?) It is no wonder they seem valuable to us. Some writers have speculated on the science fiction theme of how a planetary intelligence might arise, whereby a complicated planetary ecological system becomes conscious and then self-conscious; similar possibilities might hold for a solar system, galaxy, or metagalaxy. On the view we have been discussing, such organically unified entities might be ranked higher in value than an individual human being.[25]

The theoretical realm exhibits this phenomenon of organic unity, too. A good theory is one that tightly unifies (in explanatory fashion) diverse and apparently disparate data or phenomena, via its tightly unifying relationships. Scientists sometimes use the terminology of aesthetics here, speaking of a "beautiful" or "elegant" theory.[26] Similarly, we can understand why some speak of knowledge itself as valuable, for knowledge involves a person in a unified relationship, tracking, with a fact. The deeper the truth, the more it unifies, and the more valuable is knowledge of it. A unified field theory, one unified explanatory theory, would be most valuable. (Perhaps part of the appeal of a fundamental theory with a self-subsuming explanatory law, as described in Chapter 2, is that self-subsumption is an additional and very tight mode of unification.) Similarly, one general and unified theory of value would, ceteris paribus, be better than a group of separate and discrete theories of value.

Value as Degree of Organic Unity

Over this great range of things—the arts, organic life and systems, scientific theories—the dimension *degree of organic unity* seems to capture our notion of (degree of intrinsic) value. Rather, organic unity is the common strand to value across different realms. (The English word "good" stems from a root, "Ghedh", meaning "to unite, join, fit, to bring together".) What is it that differentiates value in different realms, fixing in each realm the different things that compose the diversity to be organically unified and the relationships that can unify? Perhaps such things are definitive of the nature of a realm,[27] or of a type of entity (whether a poem, organism, or theory). However, the possibility of different cross-classifications that include the "same thing" in very different groupings, based upon different and salient features, makes one dubious about any project to derive the texture that enters something's value, the components and relationships, from that thing's (supposed *de re*) defining features or essence.

Value might be differentiated across realms by more than the differing components and unifying relationships of those realms. Perhaps some realms have their own special values, such as sensuous color quality in paintings, values not understandable either as organic unity or as the realm's nonvaluable components that enter such unities—the particular feature has its own particular value only within that realm. (Some have held that feelings of satisfaction, pleasure, and contentment are intrinsically valuable, even when these are unstructured, not 'intentional' or directed at an object.) The view of value as degree of organic unity is compatible with the existence of such other particular values, peculiar to their own realms; but if those exist, it will not explain what is valuable about them.

I shall proceed on the assumption that the degree of organic unity is the basic dimension of intrinsic value, accounting for almost all differences in intrinsic value. Thus, I assume that the values peculiar to particular realms are of small effect, although of course the particular components and relationships, differing from realm to realm, that feed into and compose the texture of the organic unity are of large importance. Nevertheless, it is unlikely that (difference in) degree of organic unity underlies all variation in intrinsic value. Philosophers can take a cue here from social scientists and psychologists. We should be more than happy if (partialing out the effects of the particular values) the degree of organic unity accounted for 90 percent of the variance in intrinsic value. (Indeed, an explanatory factor that accounted for 60 percent of the variance would be quite significant as a start toward theory.) Formulating other dimensions to account for the remaining variance could be left as a subsidiary task.[28]

Although (degree of) organic unity is the general component of value across realms, this does not mean we can make value rankings across realms as well as within them, even in the absence of particular values to cloud matters. It seems plausible that often we will not be able to compare either the degrees of diversity of collections of materials from different realms, or the degrees of unifiedness produced by different relationships from different realms. Hence, often we will not be able to compare the degrees of organic unity of things from different realms. If (as I believe) degree of organic unity is the basic dimension of intrinsic value, then some things from different realms will be incomparable in value.

It is clear at the outset that the simplest structure of theory connecting intrinsic value and degree of organic unity is inadequate; however, the modification needed does not involve introducing any additional dimension as basic. Some destroyers of organic unity are themselves highly organized unities, for example, concentration camps. Someone might say that therefore these are intrinsically valuable, though instrumentally disvaluable. The latter they certainly are, but I am reluctant to see them as at all intrinsically valuable. For their purpose, their *telos*, is an important component of their unity; indeed, it is their central unifying factor. Since this purpose is destructive of organic unity, it itself is disvaluable and infects with disvalue the unity that it animates.

One alternative picture would be the following. We start with a ground floor of nondestructive unities, unities of these, and so forth; the first unity teleologically directed to destruction of these is intrinsically disvaluable. Is a destroyer of this disvalue therefore valuable? At least, it is not disvaluable in virtue of being directed to destroying that disvalue. The situation resembles that of aggression and defense. Nonfighters are defensive, fighters against nonfighters are aggressive, fighters against these fighters are not aggressive, fighters against nonaggressives are aggressive, and so on.*

Here, we have introduced talk of disvalue, which I do not interpret simply as the absence of value. The problem of evil asks how it is possible that there is evil in a world created by a good, omnipotent, and omniscient God. This problem has long worried theologians. One answer sometimes offered is that evil simply is the absence of good. This seems too sanguine, not properly cognizant of the nature of evil—so it leaves most of us unconvinced. Evil is not merely the absence of good, something else's not being there; it itself is a presence, a positive force—I mean a negative one. We have the picture of some natural scale where evil does not merely receive zero on a scale of goodness, it receives a negative value. Similarly, disvalue is not merely the absence of value, but a counterforce of some sort. If value is degree of organic unity, then in addition to lack of unity there is another possibility: disunity, disharmony, strife, and so forth. A theory of value, it seems to me, should identify value not merely as something that can be absent, but as something that has an opposite which can be present. Opposition is not mere lack of supporting, negation is not mere absence of affirming. It is a virtue of the theory of value as (degree of) organic unity that it lends itself to the specification not merely of zero degree of unity but also of an opposite to organic unity, something that can be viewed as underlying disvalue, having a character of its own. We shall return to this theme later.

Clearly, many additional examples can be offered where organic unity underlies our judgments of value. We desire a metaphysical theory that excludes random or chance facts, so that each fact has a

---

* The issues are even more complex, for we must take into account the alternative possibilities of what that organic unity can do, and whether the destruction is a central aim of the entity or a means toward such an aim or a side effect of other activity. Are people less valuable because they eat animals, which are organic unities? However, if these animals eat plants, are they not destructive, so that it is better to eat them than to eat (innocent) plants? Yet to eat only animals who eat plants is to bask in the good fortune that there are such destructive entities, so that one does not have to eat (the less valuable because having a lesser degree of organic unity) plants oneself, and so one is parasitic on the disvalue of others. These animals themselves have no other alternatives, and so on. The issues and complexities are evident, even leaving aside the issues concerning central unifying aims and side effects.

reason or is necessary. If something happens at random, without reason, it lacks tight connection with what came earlier, and hence the whole is of lesser organic unity. Some modes of activity not only produce an organic unity, they are involved in a larger web of unity. A painter creates a painting which is an organic unity. In addition there is the particular unifying relation between the painter, the painting, and its viewer, other relations between this painting and previous ones, and so on.

It is easy to misconstrue certain examples, however. Is the most valuable society a tightly organized centrally controlled hierarchical society of fixed hereditary status, termed by some theorists an "organic society"? Although it would have a high degree of unity, it would not encompass the same vast diversity as a free and open society. A far-flung system of voluntary cooperation unifies diverse parts in an intricate structure of changing equilibria, and also unifies these parts in a way that takes account of their degree of organic unity.[29] Enlisting a person's voluntary cooperation or participation takes account of his degree of organic unity to a greater extent than commanding him.

Some philosophical theories strive to overcome disharmonies, bifurcations, disunities. The Hegelian system, for example, sets itself to overcome the dualisms of man and nature, subject and object, freedom and community, finite subjectivity and infinity, and so forth.[30] Why are these dualisms something to be overcome, why do they dissatisfy us? I suggest that the reason is a value reason. These dualisms prevent the highest degree of organic unification, and so prevent the highest value. The Hegelian story is the story of the maximum organic unity, the maximum possible value; this raises the worry (as does the theory of Aurobindo) that it is too good to be true. Nonetheless, the explanation of the motivation for these Hegelian unifications and syntheses, for why they are sought, provides further support for the view that organic unity is the basic dimension of value. (Is the logical positivist expression of this value motivation the unified science movement? Did Neurath, Carnap, and others believe in a unified science because such a science would be *better*?)

On the view of value as (degree of) organic unity we can understand the appeal of the Platonic hierarchical ordering of the parts of the soul. It strikes us as a valuable way to be, not because it leads to happiness, but because it is described as an organically unified mode of existence. Even more does this hold for what I later term harmonious hierarchical development, wherein the higher desires and faculties infuse and transform the lower.[31]

Now, also, we can understand the relevance of philosophical arguments wherein contradictions are the sanction. For contradictions disrupt the organic unity of our beliefs and their connection to our actions. However, some contradictions disrupt organic unity more than others, which disrupt hardly at all. The powerful philosophical argument delineates a contradiction whose swallowing involves a significant disruption of unity, a deep rift. Here, too, the sanction is a value sanction; the life of one absorbing that contradiction will be less valuable because less unified. Now we can understand why some contradictions are bad, bad whether or not that person feels they are. Our explanation of the force of contradictions situates them within a theory of value; seeing this, we realize there is no special need for philosophers to focus only on that rending of organic unity produced by contradictions. Organic unity (value) can be significantly diminished in other ways, too, and all are relevant to the theory of behaving morally.

Finally, we can understand why mystical experiences are felt to be so valuable. The mystic persists in using opposed or contradictory terms to describe both his experience and the object of his experience. Opposites are experienced as internally related, even as identical, and so we have the closest possible union of the greatest possible diversity, an experience of surpassing value. (Will this include the antinomian union of good and evil?)

Our discussion thus far has focused on the inductive task of showing that the dimension 'degree of organic unity' fits and accounts for our ranking (assumed to be roughly correct) according to intrinsic value. There remains the explanatory task: explaining why organic unity is what value is. Before turning to this, let us say more about the structural features of value as degree of organic unity.

The Structure of Value

If the basic dimension of intrinsic value is degree of organic unity, then a conglomerate or aggregate, since it itself has no organic unity, cannot have greater intrinsic value than the total had by its parts. No new intrinsic value is introduced by agglomeration. Writing intrinsic value as V, and conglomeration among entities by a plus sign, we have

$$V(X + Y) \leq V(X) + V(Y).$$

New value arises only in wholes, in totalities. The value of a whole may be greater than the sum of the values of its parts.* Let O be a measure of degree of organic unity, appropriately scaled.[32] The value of a whole will be some function of the value of its parts, and of the degree of organic unity of that whole. The simplest function will be additive: the value of X will be the sum of the value of X's parts and the degree of organic unity of X.

$$V(X) = O(X) + \Sigma \ V(\text{parts of X})[33]$$

Organic unity adds value, but where does the original value come from? What are the atoms of value? Notice that while the structure described allows there to be atoms of value, it is not committed to there being any such atoms. Delving into Z, we find parts that are themselves organic unities having value, and parts of those parts that also themselves are organic unities having value, but eventually we may reach parts that are not organic unities (or conglomerates) of anything else and so have no intrinsic value of their own. Still, each thing next up the line, X, composed of (some of) these valueless parts, may have value, in accordance with the (previous) formula: $V(X) = O(X) + \Sigma \ V(\text{parts of X})$. The value of X is the sum of its degree of organic unity plus the values of each of its parts. Since by hypothesis each of these parts has zero value, the second term will be zero. However, since X does have some degree of organic unity greater than zero, its value will be greater than zero, and equal to

---

* This gives additional sense to what it means to say "The whole is greater than the sum of its parts." In Chapter 1 we gave meaning to "the whole is different from the sum of its parts." This value condition introduces one notion of 'greater than'.

There are complications due to the different possible partitionings of a whole into parts, subparts of these parts, and so on. For a given partitioning, there will be a degree of organic unity that the whole imposes on those parts, while apart from this the value of those parts will sum to a certain total. The value of the whole is a function of this already existing total, and of the degree of organic unity it induces or introduces. Rather, the value of the whole is the maximum value it has relative to each partitioning.

O(X). Thus, the view that organic unity gives rise to new value allows value creation *ex nihilo:* the creation of intrinsic value out of nothing of intrinsic value. There need not be atoms of value, since there can be valuable molecules composed of valueless atoms. (However, the parts without intrinsic value might have another kind of value, representing their capacity to participate in wholes that have intrinsic value.)

What is the ontological status of value, on the view that organic unity is the basic dimension of value? I do not mean here to ask the profound question of whether organic unities are imposed on an inchoate and structureless world, or are discovered residing there. Rather, I mean to ask whether we should speak of values adjectivally (something is valuable in having organic unity), or we should speak of values as entities (we quantify over) in our ontology. I suggest we follow the terminology of logicians in model theory. Models are realizations of abstract structures; the elements of the model correspond to the nodes of the structure, while the relationships among these elements correspond to the structural relations of the abstract structure. A model of a structure fits the structure, and instantiates it.

I suggest we view values similarly, as abstract structures. The things having a particular value are those things or systems that are realizations of that (value) structure: the things with value are models of the value. On the view of value as (degree of) organic unity, a value just is an ontologically unified structure. We now can appreciate the appropriateness of the imagery of talk of value: something is infused with value, it is suffused with value. According to my dictionary, this means that value is poured into it and spread through it, just as a structure pervades the entity it organically unifies, which exhibits it. (We also might think of the structure as filled, filled in by the entity that realizes it.)[34]

If values are abstract structures, already existing in whatever way abstract structures do, then what is the importance of realizing values in the world? Are they not already realized in the abstract structures which they are? Is it value imperialism to realize them elsewhere as well? The formless stuff in which the value gets realized would otherwise be unstructured; so it is more valuable (that is, it yields greater organic unity) that value get realized.* Even if there were no

---

* We are told, *Genesis* 1:2, that everything was formless and void, and God then structured it and saw that it was good. We are also told of the whole that God saw it was very good, whereas the parts were only said to be good.

preexisting formlessness structured by value, and the value medium had been created *ex nihilo* in order to receive the value structure, there still would be a relationship between the abstract structure and the structured object that embodies it, and this relationship itself is a unifying one. When an abstract structure is realized, the relationship of realization brings along with it isomorphism, a tight unifying relationship. This isomorphism also holds among the several realizations of the same value, unifying them, so it is valuable that values be realized multiply.[35] But isn't there a decline in something's value, the more other realizations of the same value there are? There is no decline in intrinsic value; however, the whole that includes other new types of valuable things will have greater value, because of the increased diversity this involves.

We should not forget that the "stuff" or group of things that realizes the abstract value structure introduces its own diversity, its own texture of relationship. Although a phonograph record may be isomorphic to a musical performance it records (there being an isomorphism of contoured grooves and sounds), it need not be held to have the same intrinsic value. (Of course, the record has the instrumental value of reproducing the sounds of the performance.) The record does not unite the same diversity as the performance; one involves microscopic spatial contours, the other various sounds and tones. The performance and the record are isomorphic; however, the degree of organic unity is not preserved under this isomorphism, for the diversity is not so preserved nor is the degree of importance of the unifying relationships. Isomorphism can take us from one realm where relations yield a high degree of unifiedness, to another realm where the corresponding relations under the isomorphism need not be salient or significantly unifying; there, different relations may perform the important unifications. The musical relations among tones may yield a high degree of unification and thus of organic unity in the musical realm, whereas the 'corresponding' spatial relations exhibited by the grooves do not give the record an especially high degree of organic unity as a physical object, relative to the unifying relations appropriate and salient in the realm of physical objects.

This emphasizes how measures of degree of organic unity are rela-

---

According to *Meshech Chachmah*, there was new goodness in the whole, greater than the sum of the parts. (See the Artscroll edition of *Bereshit*, Mesorah Publications, New York, 1977, p. 78.)

tive to a background selection and weighting of relationships (indicating their importance in unifications), as well as of components to be unified. The nature of the realm and the background weighting fix which features are material for unification, and which relationships are unifying. So, relationships that might unify in some realms will not serve in others. A number of different paintings might be unified by a theory in art history or aesthetics, or by a plan that sequences how they are viewed in an exhibition. However, making color slides of each painting, placing them one atop another, and then shining light through the stack so that a dull gray is cast upon a screen does not constitute, in the artistic realm, a relevant unification of the paintings. Nor does putting all the slides in the same box.

It is not impossible that there be beings who experience phonograph records differently, whose vision registers the microscopic contours of the grooves, the intricate relationships exhibited there; for them, the record itself is a visual art form. In this case, the spatial features (isomorphic to the relations among sounds and tones) would have important weight for them, and be crucial to (their view of) the identity of the object as the kind of thing it was. Here we would expect further relationships also to be salient to them, such as relations of adjacency between grooves (for instance, lying on the same radius from the center); these would make further unities possible, whereas the 'corresponding' uniformly changing temporal relations among the musical sounds would not be a unifying mode for the music. Similarly one could imagine the record as a tactile art form, with its own salient organizing relationships.

We have spoken of which relationships are saliently weighted so as to contribute to the degree of unification of the material, and also of the content that gets unified, its degree of diversity (where the degree of organic unity is a function both of the degree of diversity and the degree of unifiedness). There will be a temptation to treat these facts about diversity of content as further structural facts, or to mirror them by such structural facts. This is part of the more general temptation to see all facts about content as reducible to underlying structural facts, thereby emptying the entity or situation of its essential content.[36]

This translation of content into form distorts the way the unification plays off the particular diversity. Rather than merely being a unity that somehow includes that diversity, it unifies it qua that diversity. Its unifying relations, given their nature and content, are related to the characteristics of the diverse components, and latch onto those characteristics in a particular way. The nature of the ensuing unity depends on the particular relationships and particular content, and the (further) relationships among these.

But can we not mirror these further relationships by yet more structure? Perhaps the peculiar nature of the interaction of unifying relationships and content depends on the content of both, in a way that cannot be mirrored by further structural relationships. How are we to understand this interaction? If we demand the understanding be in terms of some underlying structure, deeming this the only legitimate mode of understanding, then we shall either distort the character of interactions depending essentially on particular content, or find them unintelligible. Perhaps, though, the interaction can be mirrored, but the mirroring relationships, in their realm, lack the saliency and weight to perform unifications to the same degree as the relations they (purportedly) mirror.*

In either case, another (purportedly) isomorphic structure need not have the same degree of organic unity. Degree of organic unity, and therefore degree of value, is not invariant or preserved under isomorphism. So, fortunately, we are not committed to any Pythagoreanism of value, to the view that the realm of numbers exhibits any and all values. We shall return in the next chapter to these issues of what, if anything, eludes the reductionist structural network.

Despite our recent talk of atemporal structures, we should emphasize that the organic unifications occur not only at one time, for temporal slices only, but also in the functioning of entities or systems over time. Thus, the goal-seeking and purposeful behavior of people in accordance with long-term plans further unites what otherwise would be more disparate parts of their existence. For this reason, psychological explanations that have no place for purposeful behavior undermine an important component of the organic unity of

* This possibility is described in our discussion of the phonograph record: the spatial relationships that 'mirror' the unifying sound relationships are not themselves saliently unifying, given that the record is not itself a visual or tactile art object.

If certain mystical or drug experiences find one group of relationships (perhaps even only one relationship) as saliently unifying for all realms (along with one set of categories for estimating diversity everywhere?), then this experience of unity in apparent diversity would be felt as very valuable.

people's lives, and so these nonteleological psychologies are seen as reducing our value.

In an interesting book some years ago, Suzanne Langer suggested that music refers to emotions, by virtue of being isomorphic to emotions. This view was criticized on the grounds that isomorphism, being a symmetrical relation, is not a sufficent condition for the generally asymmetrical relation of reference.[37] (Couldn't a further theoretical component provide the asymmetry; for instance, symbols usually are easily producible and repeatable tokens?) Nevertheless, there is something attractive about the view that music refers, in a way that depends upon the structure of the music. However, instead of emotions—as Langer held—I suggest that (some?) music refers to values. A work of music not only has value in virtue of possessing the organic unity it does, but the work also refers to the organic unity it has, to that value. Something that both exemplifies a property and refers to it is, in the terminology of Nelson Goodman, a symbol of that property.[38] Thus, a work of music symbolizes a particular organic unity, it symbolizes a particular value. This would account for the specially close connection people often have felt between music and value. To the extent that the intentional quality of our pursuit of certain values constitutes a reference to them, if this pursuit is successful our lives too, both realizing values and referring to them, can symbolize values.

Conditions on Value and Disvalue

We have sketched very roughly the view that intrinsic value is (degree of) organic unity, and we have seen some ways that ranking in accordance with degree of organic unity matches our judgments of value. Even if we suppose this doctrine true, there remains the question of why organic unity is value. There are two explanatory questions we wish to answer.

(1) Given that there is value, why is it (in the form of) organic unity? Why is value organic unity?

(2) Given that there is organic unity, why does it constitute value? Could there be a universe in which there was organic unity but no value? Why is organic unity value?

One way to answer the first question, to explain why value is some particular dimension D, is by specifying conditions constitutive of value and showing that dimension D uniquely satisfies those conditions. Supposing this could be done for the dimension 'degree of organic unity', that would show that nothing other than organic unity could be value: it would show why, given that there *is* value, organic unity is it. However, unless these conditions constitutive of value also were sufficient for value, it would not show why organic unity adds up to being value; the second question would be left open.

What conditions are constitutive of the notion of value? First, there is some formal ordering condition. Value establishes an ordering (partial or complete) over things, actions, systems, states of affairs, and so on, so any dimension that is to be the basic dimension of intrinsic value also must establish such an ordering. This condition rules out as value those properties that do not establish any ordering at all, and those dimensions that do not establish an ordering over an extensive enough field; for example, the ordering dimension of height applies to things and objects, but not to actions or states of affairs.

Clearly, this formal condition does not take us very far. To see further into the nature of value, we must ask what value is for, what function it performs for us. Value is not merely something that exists out there (or in us); it also is something to which we are to have, when possible, a certain relationship. Values are to be brought about, maintained, saved from destruction, prized, and valued (where this last is some descriptive term of psychology plus the theory of action). When no activity of ours can affect the value, value is to be contemplated and appreciated. That is what the function of value is in our lives, to be pursued, maintained, contemplated, valued.

Let us specify a class of verbs, call them the V verbs (for valuing). These include: bringing about, maintaining, saving from destruction, prizing, contemplating, valuing. Depending upon the magnitude and nature of the values, other attitudes and relationships also are appropriate. (I am aware that merely listing these might seem to diminish them: nothing could be further from my purpose.) We are to care about, accept, support, affirm, encourage, protect, guàrd, praise, seek, embrace, serve, be drawn toward, be attracted by, aspire toward, strive to realize, foster, express, nurture, delight in, respect, be inspired by, take joy in, resonate with, be loyal to, be dedicated to, and celebrate values. With the very highest values, we are to be elevated by, enthralled by, love, adore, revere, be exalted by, be awed before, find ecstasy in these highest values.

The function of values for us is that we are to V them. What does "we are to" mean here? That V-ing values is appropriate, called for, fitting, responsive to what values are like. Something more can be said, however, that gives us a further condition on value: it is valuable for us to V values. Values are not merely something out there apart from us, that we may or even should stand in a certain relationship to—our valuing them, our standing in that relationship, also is of value. Note that this is a substantive condition, not merely formal. It does not hold for all verbs, but only for V verbs, for the list of pro-valuing ones.

We can turn this into a real constraint upon a theory of value by requiring that according to the dimension D which the theory picks out as underlying the intrinsic-value ranking, V-ing things with a high ranking on D is valuable also. It would be trivial for any theory to yield this result that V-ing values is of value, as an addendum. Such a theory need merely add the ad hoc condition: if X has value according to this theory, then so does V-ing X. The condition we have formulated requires something more, namely that V-ing (what D judges to be) value itself have value according to D directly, that is, itself rank highly on that dimension D. A dimension D can be the basic dimension of (intrinsic) value only if, when some X is ranked highly along it, V-ing X also is ranked highly along it.

Another class of verbs also is related to the function of value in our lives, the anti-V verbs: destroying, blocking the realization of, impeding, scorning, ignoring, demeaning, shunning, negating, opposing, thwarting, rejecting, avoiding, being distanced from, insulting, combatting, being repulsed by, and hating. These, most definitely, are inappropriate and unfitting responses to value. Anti-V-ing values itself is of low or negative value. This provides another condition on the dimension D underlying value: if X is of high value along D then according to D anti-V-ing X is of low or negative value.

However, although anti-V-ing is an inappropriate response to value, this having low value itself, it need not be an inappropriate response to disvalue, whose (intuitive) measure is some negative quantity. In a range of cases, at least, anti-V-ing disvalues will have (positive) value. This provides two further conditions on the dimension D that underlies value. First, recalling our earlier thought that the theory of value should not merely treat disvalue as the absence of value: either the dimension D that underlies the value ranking itself demarcates and yields a ranking of disvalue, or that dimension D has an analogue, its opposite, that underlies and yields a ranking of disvalue. The next condition is the one just discussed: according to the dimension D that underlies the value ranking, anti-V-ing (what D or its analogue judges to be) disvalue itself (often?) will have value according to D.

The next condition on value and the dimension D now is obvious; it holds that V-ing disvalue itself has disvalue. Some might hold that all V-ing is valuable, whatever its object. This is similar to the view that all pleasure is good, even sadistic pleasure in the (involuntarily undergone) pain of another. Both views are mistaken, I think; V-ing is valuable only in its proper place. The realm of disvalue clearly is not the proper place for V-ing, which is grossly inappropriate there.

Should we also make more subtle discriminations? The various V-verbs differ in intensity; some are fitting responses only to the highest values. What, then, of the situation where one of these responses is made to something not of disvalue, but neutral, or of small positive value, or simply of lesser value than warrants this intense response? Something is askew when the intensity of the response is not proportioned to the magnitude of the value, but I am inclined to think no disvalue thereby is present. Rather, this disproportionately intense response to a small value itself is of lesser value than a more proportionate response would be. Similarly, when a highest value receives a V-ing response of very low intensity, there is a disproportion; this too is not disvaluable, but it is less valuable than a more proportionate response would be. These thoughts, if correct, suggest another condition on value and the dimension D, namely that the dimension be able to discriminate among the differing intensities of V-verbs, and that more proportionate V-ings have higher rank and value along the dimension D than less proportionate V-ings of the very same things.[39]

The anti-V verbs also can be ranked in intensity, and disproportions of anti-V-ing disvalue also can occur. We have said that anti-V-ing disvalue should rank as valuable; in analogy to the situation with V-ing value, we suggest that a mild anti-V-ing of a great disvalue, while not itself disvaluable, is less valuable than a more intense anti-

V-ing of that disvalue. (Add this to the list of conditions.) However, the other disproportion where the anti-V-ing overshoots its mark, being more intense than the disvalue warrants, seems to me not simply to be less valuable than it could be but itself to be disvaluable. This presents a dis-analogy to the disproportions in V-ing value. Anti-V-ing is dangerous stuff, it actually is disvaluable when it passes its mark; though the attendant other anti-V-ings that are brought along in its intense wake, themselves either proportionate or disproportionate on the low side, still will have value of their own. This (asymmetrical) point about anti-V-ing overshooting its target seems to me plausible. However, I am not sure enough of it to suggest it as a (necessary) condition on value and the dimension D; still, it would be a welcome and reassuring bonus if whatever (one) dimension satisfies all of the other conditions satisfied this one as well.

When we distinguish the intensities among the V and anti-V verbs, we can make more subtle discriminations about mismatches of these verbs with their targets. We said that anti-V-ing values had disvalue, as did V-ing disvalues. Now we can add that there is greater disvalue to a more intense anti-V-ing of a value than to a less intense anti-V-ing of that same value. Similarly, there is greater disvalue to a more intense V-ing of a disvalue than to a less intense V-ing of that same disvalue. To these conditions on results that the dimension D should yield, we can add ones that do not depend on the differing intensities of the verb, but hold the verb constant. The dimension D underlying value should yield the results that it is worse to V greater disvalues than lesser ones; it is worse to anti-V greater values than lesser ones.[40]

It seems plausible to think that the dimension 'degree of organic unity' will satisfy these conditions on the basic dimension of (intrinsic) value, when something's intrinsic value is specified as the sum of the value of its parts plus the degree of its organic unity. (The value of the parts is determined similarly, in this recursive specification.) The V-ing verbs are verbs of unification; the relationships they specify establish and embody complex unities of the person with (what realizes) the values. The situation when these relationships hold will have some (positive) degree of organic unity, and so be ranked as valuable by the dimension of organic unity as underlying value. (To the value of V-ing something X, the value of X also may make a contribution, though this need not be equal to its full value.) To show that the dimension 'degree of organic unity' satisfies the conditions about proportionality would require a more detailed understanding both of the structure of the verbs of varying intensities and of the different degrees of organic unity; modulo this, however, the task seems to face no insuperable difficulties.

Anti-V-ing disvalues, itself valuable we held, is a more complex case. As the V-verbs are verbs of unity, so the anti-V-verbs are of disunity. How can it then turn out that anti-V-ing anything, including disvalues, can have a significant degree of organic unity? (This is required by the theory of value as organic unity, if some anti-V-ing is valuable.) The disunifying character of the anti-V-verbs can match the disunity of the disvalues. In taking an anti-V stance toward disvalues, our relationship mirrors its object, and so the total situation has its own degree of unity. Some writers have written of the fittingness of behavior to its objects, of moral judgments to particular situations; however, the mode and nature of the fittingness they had in mind was left unclear. Here we might say that anti-V-ing is a fitting response to disvalue. That response in its character as disunifying matches and mirrors the character of the disvalue as it rends organic unity or produces clash. It fits it. Still, it may seem paradoxical that a disunifying relation or stance can establish any sort of unity with anything, even with a disunity. Perhaps we shall have to say that this (type of) unity is established one level up, at the metalevel. Another sort of unity might be established with a disunity at the first level, though, by a process of responsively transforming it into a unity, all the while respecting its character.

The two remaining cases, of anti-V-ing values and V-ing disvalues, can be discussed more briefly. Anti-V-ing is a disunifying stance and relationship, and when it is taken toward value, toward organic unity, there is no corresponding character this stance matches or fits, so the whole situation is disunified and (according to the view of value as degree of organic unity) thus has disvalue. In the situation of V-ing disvalue, the object has disunity, and though the V stance is one of unification, the character of its object prevents the stance from latching onto it in a unifying manner and fitting to its contours. Given this clash (at the metalevel?) between the character of the stance and of its object, V-ing disvalue itself is (not merely nonunified but) disunified and thus is disvaluable. (This may be too quick with V-ing disvalue; we shall consider soon the issue of the allure of disvalue or evil.)

These remarks have been sketchy in the extreme, but they serve, I think, to make somewhat plausible the view that the dimension 'degree of organic unity' will satisfy the (necessary) conditions on value formulated above. I would not claim, however, that the conditions listed thus far uniquely fix upon (degree of) organic unity as the basic dimension of (intrinsic) value. There may be other dimensions that also satisfy those conditions. What additional conditions can we formulate, to narrow things down even further?

The philosopher's quest for a basis for (and theory of) objective values, to ground them and understand them, itself involves a value judgment: it is better that there be objective values. This value assumption motivates the philosopher's activity, and so he is not in a position to question it. This is unlike other goal directed activities, where a person might want the goal to be realized but not assume it is better. The philosopher is motivated by the judgment that it is better that there be objective values, not just by the desire for them.

I focus on this value that the philosopher cannot question, because the value itself is a fundamental one—not for the argumentative purpose of convincing or silencing. An example of a value that cannot dialectically be questioned, although it is not explanatorily fundamental, is this: a position is better that can withstand questioning and answer questions. If we question whether this is better, and are right that it is not, then our being right shows nothing, for in that case the position we question is no worse off for not being able to withstand that questioning.

It is interesting, and perhaps a powerful point dialectically, that certain values are immanent in the philosophical activities of questioning, investigating, and examining. But it is not of fundamental explanatory importance. When in the *Republic* Thrasymachus says that justice is the interests of the stronger, and Socrates starts to question him about this, Thrasymachus should hit Socrates over the head. He concedes too much when he enters an activity, discussion, that assumes that there is some mark of correctness and rightness other than (and superior to) strength. Similarly, there are norms of discussion that Thrasymachus draws upon—for instance, that anyone's objection put seriously and sincerely ought to be replied to—and these norms, too, are incompatible with the position he states. Must the stronger also reply to an objection, even if it is not his interest?

If someone says "the unexamined life is more worth living," and we say "that is one interesting view; let us investigate it to see if it is true, let us examine it," he should refuse our invitation. Such points about what a person is committed to by certain activities might be dialectically effective in getting the person to either accept certain values or be silent. Yet, we recall, even in the face of a showing of commitment a person can have the cake he wants and eat it too, provided he prefers the (in his view) lesser penalty of the particular inconsistency of engaging in the activity while not carrying out the commitment. In any case, investigations into the "ethics" and norms of discussion and investigation, such as have been carried out recently by Jurgen Habermas,[41] are at best useful for the dialectical purposes of interpersonal convincing. Showing that certain values are immanent in certain activities does not constitute an explanation of why those values are correct, or of how correct values are possible at all.

The philosopher's evaluation that it is objectively valuable that there be objective values is of more than dialectical interest; we can turn it into a condition on the basic dimension of intrinsic value. The basic dimension D of (intrinsic) value is such that

(a) the situation of there being something with a high degree of value along D is of value;

(b) when $C_1, \ldots, C_n$ are the constitutive conditions (of the sort we are listing) on value (other than this very condition?) then it is valuable (according to dimension D) that there be some dimension that satisfies these conditions.

When these constitutive conditions are such that some dimension D uniquely satisfies them, then D holds that it is valuable that it itself exist. (It does not, however, hold this reflexively, so far as we yet can tell. Dimension D does not itself say "I am valuable.") There would be an incoherence in the realm of values if according to the objective values themselves, it would be better, more valuable, if they did not exist.

Even with this additional metacondition, I do not believe we yet have a group of conditions satisfied uniquely by only one dimension. Although organic unity satisfies them, no doubt other dimensions do too. If we are to have an explanation of why value is organic unity, some further constitutive conditions on value must narrow the possibilities down to that one dimension.

The Allure of Value

The conditions we have listed thus far (that the basic dimension of intrinsic value establishes an ordering, that V-ing values is valuable, that the existence of values and of a basic dimension of value is valuable) are external conditions, touching the surface only. Some further condition is needed that gets inside value, or inside how we link with values.

The external conditions do not capture the allure of values. Values inspire us. Although the previous conditions hold that it is valuable that values inspire us, that we V values, they do not dig into how or under what conditions this inspiration occurs.

There are some individuals whose lives are infused by values, who pursue values with single-minded purity and intensity, who embody values to the greatest extent. These individuals glow with a special radiance. Epochal religious figures often have this quality. To be in their presence (or even to hear about them) is to be uplifted and drawn (at least temporarily) to pursue the best in oneself.[42] There are less epochal figures as well, glowing with a special moral and value loveliness, whose presence uplifts us, whose example lures and inspires us.

Values themselves lack causal powers. Objects that realize values do have causal powers but not qua realization of value. It is people who can perceive values and be moved by them. I shall say more later about the special role this gives people as the agents of value realization. However, our current thoughts make one realize how the causal impotence of values can be exaggerated. Individuals who embody values have effects qua embodiers of value on us. They are like von Neumann's self-producing automata, who when placed in a suitable environment restructure it so as to produce more of their own kind. Individuals who embody values are fountains of value; they are suns: they shine forth value which warms us. Even if they do not make us sunlike, they make us moons at least, so that we shine with reflected light and no longer are dark. The thesis of the impotence of

436

values must be modified. Values can have effects, qua values, in an environment that contains value perceivers; however, values have no causal power to operate apart from value perceivers.[43]

There are less imposing or extraordinary ways the allure of value expresses itself, ranging from the delight in intricately structured and complexly organized games, to the desire to experience aesthetic unities in art, literature, and music, the desire to experience things that embody values and to realize they have that structure, that is, to experience values as values. (Recall Rawls' formulation of an Aristotelean principle of pleasure in intricately structured complex activities.)

How might these considerations about allure enter into a precise condition to help specify the basic dimension of value? That good can seep over and transform its environment does not distinguish it from evil which, we are told, can contaminate what is around it, and which has an allure of its own, as antinomian sects attest. The allure of evil or disvalue, though, seems to me to stem from the frustrated envy of value. For whatever reason, the person himself will not achieve or embody value, and he prefers that no one else achieve it either; he chooses to thwart and oppose others' achievement of value, so that they too will not have the value he lacks. If this diagnosis is correct, the allure of disvalue is parasitic upon the prior and greater allure of value. Since even one pursuer and achiever of value stimulates the envious resentment, the anti-V-er of value or the V-er of disvalue is doomed to ever more extensive attempts to erase value achievement. Since V-ing value itself is valuable, the very valuing of value would have to be erased. This attempt is futile; the pursuer of disvalue cannot win. Despite his ever expanding imperialistic attempt to erase values and valuing everywhere, somewhere, someone will escape his coils, and that is enough to display successfully the alternative he fails to realize and so envies. Thinking of the ways he himself fails to realize value, he cannot comfort himself with the thought that no one else does either. If, in addition, the possibility of value achievement drives home to him the ways he falls short, then whatever his actual success in thwarting, his failure is guaranteed.

Does value have greater allure than disvalue, then? If so, we can imagine the different dimensions that satisfy the previous conditions —and hence are candidates for being the basic dimension of intrinsic value—competing. In a competition among each dimension's (embodied) highest scorer and greatest "good", the most valuable will win out.

There are two ways we can imagine this contest: first, as one over which embodiment of value most allures and transforms us. Here, we have inductive evidence for what is value by the way we are most intensely and enduringly inspired and transformed. There may be distorting factors, of course, so even apart from the issue of extrapolation to the best possible exemplars of a dimension, which perhaps no one has yet encountered, the answer cannot be read directly off the historical record. Each theory of value, holding that some dimension D_i is the basic dimension of intrinsic value, must look at the record of human activity in history (and the details of individual biographies) and come up with some story about how history shows (high) D_i is most alluring and inspiring. When people are not moved by high D_i, the theory can attribute this to distorting and inhibiting factors. But there is a constraint upon facile explaining away of exceptions. The only admissible distorting factors are those that are bad, in that those factors applying to a person itself has a low score along D_i. Each theory, however, is committed to saying value would be chosen under good conditions, where what is good is specified by the dimension D_i. (Or at least, the theory is committed to saying that value's force would be felt under good conditions, even if undercut by endemic weakness of will.) This task of historical explanation and reconstruction provides a further test that each theory of intrinsic value must pass.[44]

Early in this chapter, we said that the sanction for the immoral person is a value sanction, but that such a sanction need not actually motivate the person or connect with any motives he (actually) has. We now see, though, that there is some connection, less direct, between value and motivation: value would inspire and motivate us under valuable conditions. It seems unreasonable to expect a stronger connection, that value must motivate under all possible conditions. One further motivational connection should be mentioned, though. We have held that V-ing value itself is valuable. Under the valuable conditions where values do motivate and inspire, this V-ing of values will also be experienced as valuable and desirable.

Note that the "contest" determines which exemplar of high-D_i will win by certain means. The question is, which will most allure, inspire, and attract us, and so transform us by this route. Perhaps exemplars of destructiveness could win our enlistment under their banner by threatening to destroy us otherwise. However, that does not make them the winners in the relevant contest. The specification of these peaceful means by which the parties are to compete may seem to beg the question in favor of certain dimensions. It does not settle the question in advance, though; it is conceivable that it is examples of domination and power that most will inspire and allure when we are (peacefully) confronted with them. But even though the victory of these dimensions is not foreclosed, don't the peaceful means tilt the contest in favor of some other dimensions so that the combative ones, by their very nature, no longer have an equal chance to win? Perhaps so, but then that is a consequence of what value is. Value is what lures and inspires us (at least under valuable conditions). That a dimension can win out in some other way may make it more powerful or wilier, but does not mark it as most valuable. It is constitutive of value that its function is to inspire. (Note that this condition eliminates construals of value as the reversal of the dimension D, for example, the view that value varies inversely with degree of organic unity.)

Is it humanocentric to think that value must inspire us? Couldn't we be so sunk in sloth and darkness (original sin?) that we would not choose the good even under good conditions? Isn't it possible for some selves to be in that unfortunate state? Perhaps it is us. However, we are not sunk absolutely low, since we quest for value, and we are attracted to some things qua valuable. Since questing for value is itself valuable, it is a sign that we are not thoroughly bad; moreover, if questing for value also falls under the same dimension that allures us, that is a sign that the dimension itself is valuable.

Still, do we believe that all selves who are attracted by anything in the peaceful contest will be attracted by the same thing? Leaving aside other beings described in science fiction novels, there is some evidence that every person will be attracted most by the same thing, once they encounter it. (For different evidence, see note 44.) Mystics report their experiences as overwhelmingly valuable and powerful in impact; certain types of these experiences not only transform the person's view of what the world contains, they also transform the person. If all those who experience it agree in their response and in the nature of their transformation, and no additional experience of anything else damps down this response, isn't this a sign that it is an objective response to value?[45] However, there remains the question of whether the position is not humanocentric. Might not the (candidate) dimension D of intrinsic value that wins out for us fail to win in the competition before other nonhuman beings elsewhere? For all we have thus far said, value would be left relative to the kind of being it attracts.

Earlier, we said there were two kinds of contest the dimensions could enter. The first was for our favor. The second is for each other's favor. Instead of imagining the different exemplars of high scores on each competing dimension exerting their allure on us, we can imagine them exerting their allure on each other. Would a particular dimension win the contest among all the other high scorers? (Will Satan find God more alluring and inspiring than God finds Satan?) If these exemplars are each able to experience the others, and one wins out (under good conditions), this is evidence for the dimension exemplified by the winner being value. (And if there is nontransitivity in the pairwise contests so that none wins over all the others?)

Is the thought overly optimistic that underlies all this, namely, that value will inspire (under good conditions) more strongly than disvalue or nonvalue? Could not value be less inspiring, not only locally under special conditions but also generally. (If the gnostic hypothesis—of our universe being created by a lesser and a less good deity than another that exists—were correct, then might not the local conditions be unconducive to appreciating true value?) The usual view of tragedy is that value is doomed to defeat, or that situations are unavoidable in which some one of the diverse values involved must be sacrificed. More tragic, however, would be value's losing out not merely in the power competition, but also in the inspiration competition. Barring special explanations (such as that we have some special defect but other imaginable beings are inspired by value), this possibility (I feel) is incoherent; it would be worthwhile to pursue an adequate explanation of why this is so.

Even this allure condition, that value attract and inspire us under valuable conditions (more so than does disvalue), does not get inside our relationship to value. It does not portray how value so inspires us, or the ways in which our value responses are contoured to the (internal nature and structure of the) values involved. It would be fruitful to formulate such further conditions on the basic dimension of intrinsic value. The dimension 'degree of organic unity' seems promising with regard to such conditions, since it gives much contoured structure for the responses to value to latch onto.

Explaining the Role of Organic Unity

Suppose that conditions on intrinsic value can be formulated so that only one dimension D (for instance, degree of organic unity) satisfies these conditions. (We need not decide here whether the conditions we have formulated above suffice to pick out exactly one dimension, or whether additions to them are needed.) This would answer the question of why value is that particular dimension. Only that dimension D can be (the dimension underlying) value, for only it and nothing else satisfies all of the constitutive conditions on value. Given that there is (a dimension of) value, it has to be that dimension D.[46]

In this way, we see how we might explain why value is realized as some particular dimension rather than as any other. However, this is only the first of the questions we posed for ourselves. There still remains the second question: why is that dimension D *value?* To be sure, if anything is, it is, but why is anything value? Why isn't the universe just dark, so that although it contains (high scorers along) that dimension D, yet it does not contain any value? Only dimension D can be value—that was the answer to the first question—but how can even it be? Are the conditions satisfied by the dimension not only necessary for its being value, but also sufficient? In that case, it is value in virtue of satisfying (being the sole satisfier of) those conditions, and no further question remains of how that dimension manages to be value. Or is there a gap between satisfying these conditions and being value, a gap still to be bridged?

There is some reason to think the necessary conditions on value that we formulate will not together be sufficient conditions for a dimension's being (the basic dimension of intrinsic) value. The things we encounter always will be a limited selection of the things there might be, and which possibilities we can imagine and formulate will depend upon what we actually have encountered. There may be dimensions we do not focus upon because everything we have encountered thus far occupies the same low place (or indistinguishably different ones) along that dimension. So the true dimension of value may be beyond our ken. What we make do with here is the best approximation to value, the dimension that best fulfills the conditions we can formulate. (And if we encountered other objects or beings, the need for further conditions might become clear to us.)

Recall our discussion in Chapter 1 of the modes of structuring an account of a philosophical concept C, such as identity or knowledge. We saw there that what C was might depend on what instantiated property or relation best fulfilled the conditions associated with C. Which property or relation C is depends upon which is the closest instantiation of C, that is, on there being no other instantiated property that better (or as well) realized that concept C.

This might explain why we shall not find sufficient conditions for the basic dimension of intrinsic value. The dimension that value is, in the actual world, will depend upon which other dimensions actually are instantiated, actually having some entities spread along their higher values. Although organic unity is the best our universe does insofar as value is concerned, perhaps some other dimension more fully would satisfy the conditions constitutive of value. Recall the condition about competition among the exemplars of the different dimensions that satisfy the other conditions constitutive of value. Some dimension wins. But perhaps another dimension would win if it were instantiated; not being instantiated, however, it does not enter into the competition. We formulated that condition to say that the allure (need only) be exerted under "good" conditions, since no dimension we actually encounter exerts its force no matter what. Still, it is imaginable that there be such a further resplendent dimension heretofore unencountered; if there were, what we now dub value (organic unity) might seem pale in comparison, hardly worthy, unworthy even, of the term "value".*

* We might wonder how another dimension could better realize value. Would that other dimension, then, be more tightly connected with value than organic unity is, and so more organically united with value? It seems that the especially tight linkage of another dimension with value will be a mode of organic unity; this tight mode itself will still have to be valuable, and will be deemed so according to the superior dimension. Thus, organic unity cannot be (completely) displaced as the dimension of value. However, this does not explain why there must be any value, why organic unity must be value, why there could not be organic unity in the universe, yet no value at all.

Suppose these considerations do show that the conditions previously formulated (and others like them) are not sufficient conditions for value; nevertheless, cannot we incorporate these considerations within a formulation of sufficient conditions? Is it sufficient for a dimension D's being (the basic dimension of intrinsic) value that it satisfy the constitutive conditions on value better than any other (highly) instantiated dimension does, that it be the best instantiated realizer of the constitutive conditions? Even on the best instantiated realization mode of structuring a concept, something more would be needed. Recall the closest continuer schema of identity, according to which Y at t_2 must not only continue an earlier X more closely than any other (contemporary of Y) Z does, but it also must continue the earlier thing closely enough to be it. So we need to add to the fact that dimension D is the best instantiated realizer of the conditions constitutive of value, the additional fact that D realizes these conditions well enough to be value. This additional component, itself explicitly containing the word "value", clearly reintroduces and does not solve the issue of whether the dimension D does bring value along in its wake.[47]

There are other imaginable ways an alternative and more valuable universe might have the consequence that though this universe contains some organic unity, it doesn't contain any value. Suppose the ranking of value in both places is according to the degree of organic unity, yet the cutoff line between the valuable and the not-valuable, the zero point marking 'neutral in value', is placed higher in that universe, so that some things valuable here are not valuable there. That universe has so many things of vastly superior value that, because the cutoff line varies with what other possibilities are realized, all of our universe's contents get classed as not valuable. (Compare the psychological literature on "level of aspiration" or the relativized accounts of "poverty".) However, that universe would have some valuable things, and so would not be empty of value. Still, it is distressing that some things currently valuable (such as us) might not be so in that universe. If our value is puny compared to instantiated values there, or elsewhere in this universe, if not only our status at the top of the value heap is insecure as judged by the standards and objects of some possible worlds but also our status above zero, then would others using those higher standards even have to respond to us with V activities?[48]

One answer would be to say that the zero point cannot shift in this way; we are securely above it everywhere. However, I am unsure of this, and so am forced to contemplate the possibility that in some universes our value may be so dwarfed that it does not count as value at all, and so need not be V-ed.* Still, should not such exalted perfections respond nicely to the little organic unity we have, even if it is below their threshold of positive value; will not such responsiveness be a component of their great value? I would like to think their behavior toward us will differ from ours as we relate to animals and plants. Yet there is the worrisome possibility that whatever puny value we possess will get swamped in their larger calculations, in their V-ing of greater values.

We shall return later to questions about the relation of fact to value; they will occupy us at the close of this chapter. Our remarks thus far are merely cautions to any easy assumption that the (second) question of why dimension D constitutes value can be answered by producing sufficient conditions for value, conditions of the sort produced. The fact–value gulf cannot be bridged so easily.

Designing Value

Some few remarks can be made in advance of considering the fact–value issue. Which things are valuable is more obvious than why they are. We even can take a clue from the enemies of the value or preciousness of man. They think it important to deny, for instance, that we have free will, that we can do something because it is right, that we know reality, that we are anything other than a congery of physiochemical processes and properties. (If all empirical characteristics are nonvaluable, some are less so than others.) It is illuminating to see which characteristics the deniers of human value, preciousness, or dignity especially deny to us, and which they wish to affirm—by its enemies shall we know value. It still remains, of course, to explain why these things *are* valuable and precious, or how anything can be.

Since it is especially difficult to see how to move from empirical

* A variant possibility is that in our universe the cutoff for positive value along the dimension of organic unity is set so high that nothing actual qualifies as valuable. But such rigorism has little to recommend it.

characteristics to value and preciousness, let us consider the move in the opposite direction. If a being was going to be valuable or precious, which characteristics would it have? Suppose a contest were being held to design a valuable or precious being. A prize is to be given simply for succeeding, the winner does not have to justify the application of the terms "valuable" or "precious". If you participated in this contest, which characteristcs would you give your entry? Consider the different characteristics and ask (holding everything else constant) whether a being would be more valuable and precious if it had that characteristic or not.

There seems little doubt about some pairs of characteristics.

free will	no free will
conscious	not conscious
self-conscious	not self-conscious
able to do something because it is right	not able to do something because it is right
able to recognize value	not able to recognize value
able to guide behavior in accord with its recognition of value	not able to guide behavior in accord with its recognition of value
self-choosing	not self-choosing

A being with the characteristics in the first column is more valuable than a being without them. If you were designing a being to be valuable or precious, you would give it the characteristics in the first column. You would want your child to have those characteristics. Although it may not be clear why a characteristic gives rise to value or preciousness, it can be clear that a valuable being will have a particular characteristic rather than its opposite, that a being would be more precious with it than without it.

Perhaps we should not ask which properties give rise to value, but rather: if value were operating in the world, which properties would it yield? I do not claim that value is operating in the world; however, value is in the world because of those properties and facts it would give rise to if it *were* operating. Why are some characteristics valuable and precious? Because they are what value would produce. Subjunctively, they are value's products. I do not say that the existence of value in the world is the explanation of why the characteristics exist, not even the teleological explanation. Value does not have causal powers, and hence does not give rise to the precious characteristics. Yet these characteristics glow with their subjunctive ancestry.

Pluralism and Creativity

Values are organic unities; something is intrinsically valuable in accordance with its degree of organic unity. However, it does not follow that the realm of values itself exhibits high organic unity, that diverse and apparently conflicting values can be united in some higher unity or larger harmony. The theme of the ineradicable plurality of values, of the conflict between different values that cannot all be realized, a theme presented in *Antigone* and later tragedies, has been subordinated in the history of philosophy to the theme or hope of the harmonious reconciliation and realization of all values. Recently, however, the pluralism of values has received renewed attention.[49]

Some conflicts among values are due to the limitations of circumstance that prevent their joint realization, something possible under different circumstances. Other conflicts are intrinsic to the nature of the values involved; no possible circumstances admit the joint realization of those values in one person's life, or perhaps even separately but simultaneously in the same society. For other groupings of values, it may be unclear whether or how they can be realized harmoniously.

The desire to find harmony among all values is a deep one. Even some who see the conflicts are led to formulate a framework—sometimes evolutionary, as in the case of Hegel and Aurobindo—wherein (the valuable aspects of) all values are brought together and realized at different stages of some unified process, if not all together at the end. The view of value as (degree of) organic unity would lead us to expect (at least a surface) pluralism; there are different and diverse types of organic unity, not obviously reconcilable or co-possible. This view of value also accounts for the depth of the desire to find unity among the values.

It is valuable to realize values, it is valuable that there be values. What could be more natural than to think also that the realm of values itself is valuable? Given that value is organic unity, the special value of this realm of values would lie in its degree of organic unity, presumably high. To be sure, as an aggregate the realm of value will have a value equal to the sum of the values of its component parts, the sum of its component values. However, doesn't that realm have a special value of its own, greater than the sum of its parts? Though all is not disunity and there are many harmonious realizations of different values that connect in intricate ways, nevertheless it might seem especially fitting that this realm itself should exhibit the highest degree of value, and so the highest degree of organic unity. For this there must be diverse values around to get unified.

We can distinguish two sorts of pluralism. Weaker pluralism says (in contrast to monism) that there are diverse values. The stronger pluralism adds that these diverse values cannot be (tightly) unified, that there are ineradicable conflicts, tensions, needs for tradeoffs, and so on. Monism gives the unity without the diversity, strong pluralism the diversity without the (complete) unity. Each view denies the highest degree of organic unity to the realm of values, and so denies the highest value to that realm. The persistent denial of strong pluralism in the philosophical tradition stems from two factors in combination: the nature of value as (degree of) organic unity, and the desire that the value realm itself exhibit the highest possible value.

Supposing there is an ineradicable pluralism of values, we each face a choice of which values shall be realized in our lives to what extent. I suppose also that the decision is not dictated by some obviously correct value ranking. Not only do some values have to be foregone or sacrificed but (within some range) there is no right answer (fixed by the realm of value) about which feasible mixture is most valuable. Here is room for creativity and individuality in the way we realize values.

A person who tracks bestness, who seeks value, will have to formulate her own package of value realization; she cannot simply "maximize" on the value dimension. This package need not be an aggregate, it can pattern and unify the diverse values it realizes. In thus patterning value, the person may emulate a previous pattern exhibited by a value exemplar or described in some tradition, or she may create a new complex unity, sculpting the value contours of her life in an original, perhaps unique way. Some significant part of the viv-

447

idness of characters we read about in fiction, history, or religious texts or scriptures is their individuality in (valuable) value contouring. This is an important part of what makes a character stay vivid in our memory, even one from a work that is not otherwise of the highest value. (An example is Sherlock Holmes, who exhibits a pure and single-minded unity toward the one function of detecting crime—he has no knowledge unrelated to this—and integrates all his characteristics toward this end.)

Thus is eliminated the threat that the objectivity of values might appear to pose to individuality. That threat is only partially reduced by saying that the one objective standard we all are to pursue must be fit to the circumstances of each person's life: his abilities, temperament, possibilities of action, and the societal constraints. The threat is reduced very little if within each limited situation either there is a unique best way to adhere to the general standard or the ties (for best) do not differ greatly.[50] To be sure, even that still leaves us with a choice, whether or not to pursue value, but not with any choice within the realm of value.

Although the individual values themselves are objective, we do not suppose there is one uniquely correct objective ranking of them, one optimal (feasible) mix of them, one fixed desirable schedule of tradeoffs among them. There is some open range within whatever partial rankings of value are objectively correct. Individuality is expressed in the interstices of the objective rankings of value, in the particular unified patterning chosen and lived; this itself will be objectively valuable, but not objectively ranked in relation to other comparable patternings.

Our earlier discussion of tracking bestness, in the chapter on free will, must be seen in this light; moreover, our current thoughts give keener point to the indeterminist view presented there of weighting values (and weighting reasons for action). If there is no one objectively correct set of weights for values, then each person must (within the objective limits) arrive at her own weighting. That giving of weights is not something we happen to do, it is necessitated by the pluralist nature of the realm of values. There is no fixed correct set of weights for acts of weighting values to track or converge upon.

In that case, why give weights at all? Instead, we could simply act at random within the leeway allowed by the existence of objective values, which are partially ordered but without fully determinate weight. However, such a course of action would itself lack the unity that acting upon one set of (perhaps evolving) weights gives, and so would be of lesser value. It is valuable that there be some or another weighting of values and acting on these weights, although different such weightings may have the same or noncomparable value. A life based upon such weightings will be unified by them, and so more valuable than one that exhibits no weighting or ignores value altogether.

Free will, as described in the first part of the previous chapter, fits the nature of the realm of values. The weighting of values is necessitated by the nature and pluralist character of value. There is not one objectively correct ranking to track, yet some weighting is called for by the nature of value as organic unity, to give greater organic unity to a (portion of a) life. Now we may see the pluralist character of the realm of values in a new light. Because this realm lacks the highest degree of organic unity, there is both leeway for and a significant point to our weighting of values and free choices—to individuality in the value contours of our lives. From our point of view, at least, it seems better that there not be the highest organic unity in the realm of values, that there be leeway within which we can express ourselves valuably. (So there is this value to the realm of values being not quite so valuable in itself.)

Nietzsche spoke of creation of values. We can interpret this creation as someone intentionally exhibiting in his life new patternings of value, new unifications of previously recognized values, or the salient introduction of a component unity, previously unrecognized or undelineated. (There are corresponding possibilities for the creation of new modes of meaningfulness, our topic in the next chapter.) Within the view of value as organic unity, there is room for the creation of new values: there is room for new and even radically different organic unities.

But could not someone create a new value so radically different in character that it is not an organic unity, not even a newly realized one? A radically new value would not fall high on the previous dimension fixed as value—organic unity or whatever—not even at a more general or metalevel: it just introduces a wholly new dimension. This cannot be avoided by the expedient of assigning weights to dimensions and relations, so that the newly introduced thing will (be said to) have a high degree of organic unity. The leeway in assigning weights to specify organic unity is constrained by other value judgments we make; so this new thing may have low organic unity. Structuring the concept of value in the best-instantiated realization mode, as we have done, does allow for possibility of the creation of radically new values; the new creation somehow would make it evident to us that (degree of) organic unity was not the best instantiated realization of value—by topping it. Although this is not precluded, neither is it something to be expected.

Our investigation of value began with the issue of whether (the life or existence of) the moral person is more valuable than (that of) the immoral person. We have sketched out a view of what (intrinsic) value is. Next, we must investigate the nature of ethical behavior, in order to determine whether it is more valuable to behave that way. Our focus will not be restricted to just this issue, though; our interest in ethical behavior is more general.

II. ETHICAL PULL

Ethical pull is the term we have used for the moral claim on us exerted by others so that, in virtue of what they are like, we ought to behave toward them in certain ways and not in others—or it would be wrong to behave in certain ways, and so forth. The theory of ethical pull specifies and explains the moral oughts and constraints upon our behavior to which the existence or presence of others give rise.

Moral behavior is not owed to each and every thing, not to rocks or copies of newspapers; there is something about people, some characteristic or property of theirs, in virtue of which they are owed moral behavior. It will be useful to have a term to refer to the characteristic (or characteristics) of people, whatever it is, that plays this role of exerting the moral claim. Let us call it the moral basis, or the basic moral characteristic. This is the characteristic possessed by someone to whom moral behavior is owed. We must distinguish this from the characteristic in virtue of which someone owes moral behavior, the characteristic that makes someone a subject of moral judgment, as a tiger is not. (To be sure, some theory could maintain that it is one characteristic that plays both of these roles.)

The first task of the theory of the ethical pull is to specify the moral basis, the characteristic(s) in virtue of which ethics is called forth. I do not claim there is only one characteristic that exerts moral pull, only one moral threshold, so that there are no moral conditions on our behavior toward something lacking the most demanding basic moral characteristic. Perhaps animals do not have this characteristic, yet have another in virtue of which they are owed some moral behavior of a less stringent sort; there then would be multiple thresholds. Or perhaps the basic moral characteristic does not set a threshold but establishes a gradient over different types of beings, which calls for a matching gradient of behavior; having a status between people and stones, animals would have some intermediate claim. In this chapter, however, we shall concentrate on the fullest moral basis.

The second task of the theory of ethical pull is to specify the moral conditions or constraints on the behavior of others given rise to by (someone's having) the basic moral characteristic. And the third task is to explain how and why this characteristic gives rise to those moral

451

constraints or to any moral constraints on others at all. Even granting that it is that characteristic which does give rise to moral constraints, why does it do that, how is it possible that it does that? Why isn't the universe an ethical blank, containing beings with the characteristic but containing no moral conditions on any actions toward them? Here arise again, as with the theory of moral push, the familiar problems about the relationship of the "ought" to the "is", of value to fact; we shall pursue these in the last part of this chapter.

The Moral Basis

The first task of the theory of ethical pull is to specify the moral basis, the characteristic in virtue of which ethical behavior is owed. What should we expect this characteristic to be like? Might it be some characteristic like 'having an elbow' or 'having a vestigial appendix' or 'walking upright', with it being a brute and ultimate fact that anything with that characteristic or part is owed moral behavior? The moral basis cannot be any old trivial characteristic; it itself must be something important, it must be something valuable.[51] To give rise to something as important as ethical pull, it must be important in itself.

Also, the moral basis must be a characteristic that is relevant to certain behavior by others, so that either we can specify the ways in which that behavior by others is appropriate to (the bearer of) that characteristic, or at least we can "see" that the behavior is a fitting response to the characteristic. Despite any inability to say what the linkage is between is and ought or fact and value, or even to say how there can be any linkage, the basic moral characteristic must at least appear to be relevantly linked to the called-for moral behavior. However much we are puzzled by is–ought questions, we would be puzzled even more to be told that the moral basis is 'having a vestigial appendix' and in virtue of that we ought not manipulate or use the person or cause him pain. Thus, we seek a characteristic that (at least) seems valuable and seems relevantly related to the behavior of others.

We can round up the usual suspects: being rational, being an agent, being sentient, being conscious. I find that when I think about the matter, including thinking hypothetically of coming upon beings on other planets, the crucial characteristic in others that I feel gives rise to stringent moral claims upon me is "being an I", that is, having the special mode of reflexive consciousness of self which only an I, only a self, has. Something's being a self, now we can say someone's being one, seems to be crucial to our having to treat it in certain morally respectful ways.

This characteristic of "being an I" is a valuable one, as befits the moral basis. Selves, in virtue of being reflexively self-conscious, have a high degree of organic unity. Furthermore, this is a deep characteristic of others in virtue of which we owe them ethical behavior; we saw in Chapter 1 that (having the capacity for) being a self is an essential trait of a self, part of its essence. The moral basis is not some superficial trait that its possessors themselves do not value or think important. Also, we can understand the distortion of the egoist, who instead of finding preciousness and a moral basis in "being an I", a property shared by others, finds it in "being myself".

It appears that the requisite moral basis, whatever it is, must satisfy two conditions. First, it must be a general characteristic, had by all other people (in the absence of special grave defects); otherwise, it will not provide the basis in virtue of which all people are owed ethical behavior. However, if the basic moral characteristic is shared by everyone, then it does not seem to have anything special to do with you. Your value would consist in being a bearer of this characteristic (for instance, rationality, ability to revere the moral law); you would not be valued for being yourself.[52] There then is the sense that any other bearer of the characteristic can equally well replace you, so that you are not valued or respected for being the particular person you are.

Let the second condition on the basic moral characteristic, then, be that the person who is valued (or behaved to in a certain way) in virtue of possessing that characteristic is valued for being himself. This is in tension with the first condition, that the characteristic be one shared by all people; a general characteristic shared by everyone does not focus on any particular bearer. One type of characteristic, however, can satisfy both (apparently incompatible) conditions: a reflexive indexical characteristic. The characteristic "being an I" is had by every person, and so satisfies the first condition. Yet since its formulation contains the indexical reflexive term "I", this characteristic, unlike other general characteristics, does not draw the attention away from the particular bearer. The characteristic speaks of the bearer as a self, as a subjective particularity. Although the characteristic of being an I, being a reflexive self-aware being, is shared by all I's, it is a property I have in virtue of being myself. Thus, being myself, a property no one else has, is the ground of my value, as it brings along with it the general characteristic of being an I which others have. Still, this general characteristic leads not away from the I to others but back to the self in its reflexive particularity. Isn't to be valued for being a self tantamount to being valued for being yourself, or else doesn't it come as close as possession of a valuable general characteristic can bring one? Doesn't "being an I" resolve the tension between the two conditions on the basic moral characteristic? Perhaps not: although you are valued for being a self, some self or other, you are not thereby valued for being the particular self you are. We might say: you are valued for your self but not for yourself.

We can add, therefore, that the characteristic is not simply 'being an I' but 'being a unique, individualized I'. It is unclear to what extent such individuality, such distinctiveness, is essential to the nature of being a self. The self, we have seen, refers to itself reflexively, from the inside, but does that mean it must have an inside of subjective experience that constitutes its own perspective, a special slant on the world?[53] (It appears simpler to reach the consequence that a reflexively self-referring self, especially one that is self-synthesizing, will have a special slant on itself.) Even if such a perspective is held to be crucial to the nature of a self (yet does God have a special slant on the world?), must that perspective be unique and individual? Surely we can imagine science fiction duplications (in a qualitatively indistinguishable environment) of all the nonreflexive characteristics of a self including the type of perspective or slant; this would be similar to Nietzsche's imagining such duplications under his doctrine of eternal recurrence. Yet these beings, all identical in perspective, would be selves. Thus, individuality and uniqueness is not guaranteed by the very nature of being a self; some may think such a nonunique self is less valuable, being less scarce.

Even if such individuality does not follow from the very nature of a self, we can build it into the characteristic that is to be the moral basis and exert the most pull. When the basic moral characteristic is being a unique and individual self, are you not then valued for being yourself, for being your unique and individual self? Not quite. You are valued for being *a* unique and individual self, and the only way to be that is to be some particular unique self, but you are not valued for being that particular self—any old unique and individual self would do just as well. There is a difference between valuing something for being unique, and valuing it for the (particular) uniqueness it has. This last is ambiguous between valuing it for having some feature which it happens to have uniquely, and valuing its having that feature uniquely, where (equal?) weight is given to each component: the content of the feature and its unique possession.

Let us list the possibilities here. First, that in general when each person is valued for being herself, each is valued for being a unique self, but not for being that one. Second, we value the particular uniqueness of each person; merely as a summary of this, we may say we value their being unique, but it is each unique unfolding that we value primarily. A third possibility, however, seems to me the most promising. We value being a unique self, and come therefore also to value the particular unique self someone is. Valuing that there is a unique self spills over to valuing, for itself, that unique self there is. (The path of spillover follows the logical principle of existential instantiation.)

The process of loving one's children exemplifies this spillover. One begins by loving one's child as a bearer of the characteristic 'being your child'. Any child that one believed had that characteristic would become the object of one's love; if the doctors in the maternity hospital told you another infant was your child (as sometimes happens when accidental "switches" are made), you would love that one. Sufficient for initiation of your love is bearing the characteristic 'being your child'. Over time, however, the love attaches to the child in its own individuality, not simply as a bearer of the initiating characteristic that could have applied to someone else; you come to love that child, nontransferably. The delight parents take in the particular behavior and accomplishments of their young children marks the transition to loving them in their particularity, no longer merely for being their child but for being *that* child. We all know parents who choose to celebrate this transition with public ceremony, telling all who will listen of the most recent cute or intelligent behavior of their young children. (Contrast our attitudes toward parents of older children; their similar tales are not discoveries of particularity but boasts.) It may be disconcerting for a child to realize its parents would love another child as much, had that other child been born in their place. However, that other equally great love would not be the same love, not the same particular love there exists for this particular person; and although if another child had been born, there would then have been another particular love for that particular person, still now the parent would not trade the particular love (or child) that exists for the other one, viewing each as equally good. The actual situation is valued above another possible one, even while realizing that had that other possibility been realized, *it* would have been valued then over this actuality—merely another possibility from its perspective then.[54]

In parallel to this process of parental love, I imagine that valuing others is based upon their possession of the characteristic of being a (unique) self, but then spills over and attaches to the particular self they are, the particular way they instantiate the possibilities of being human. Within this structure, we can value all people (in virtue of a general characteristic), yet value them for being themselves. This characteristic "being a unique I" and its attendant spillover can satisfy both of the apparently incompatible conditions on the basic moral characteristic.

People we do not know, however, we will value (only) as bearers of the general property "being a (unique) self". Even for some we know (or know of), we may find ourselves unable to value their particularity, to value that particularity, and so then too will value only their possession of the common general property. That we value someone's particularity may make it appropriate for us to aid him rather than another, even though we realize that if we knew and thereby valued the particularity of that other, we would differentially favor her. Some moral views hope to lift us above all such differential ties, whether to family or friends or one's people, so that we will consider ourselves and all others simply as members of humanity. As such, the others have claims on our moral behavior; however, these claims need not be as rich as those whose particularity is more closely intertwined with ours. A father may aid his own over other children, knowing that had the others been his, he would have loved and aided them. Some view all such particularistic ties to individuals or groups as parochial, something moral advance will eliminate. Others view these as derivatively justifiable, provided that the general interest is best advanced by all parents giving primary weight to taking care of their own children, or that a valuable variety—one everyone should value—is produced by ethnic differentiation and ties. Such views will countenance particularism on one level by deriving it from "universalistic" principles that hold at some deeper level. This misconstrues the moral weight of particularistic ties, it seems to me; it is a worthwhile task, one I cannot undertake explicitly here, to investigate the nature of a more consistently particularistic theory—particularistic all the way down the line.

Seeking Value

The characteristic we have considered as the moral basis, "being an I", is not unconnected with other usual candidates for this role. The process by which the I refers to itself involves the production of a token (or thought) with a certain intention, hence the I is an agent, and so forth. Still, this characteristic alone is not a sufficient basis for moral pull. Or so it seems to me.

In addition, the being, the self, must be a seeker after value, someone who searches for value and guides her behavior by value considerations. Neither trait alone—value seeking or self—is sufficient. A computer-like automaton tracking value, matching its behavior to value considerations but lacking any subjectivity and lacking a self, would be too slight to ground (the fullest) moral pull, as would a subjective I that was permanently indifferent to value, neither following nor seeking it. What is wanted is a self seeking value. Perhaps these two traits, being an I and seeking value, are not independent or easily separated. If so, that would give the ethical pull a more unified moral basis; however, I am not in a position to make the strong claim that one characteristic (necessarily) involves the other.[55]

With the addition of value seeking, we add to the mode of unification of reflexive self-consciousness the unity introduced by teleological value seeking. A value-seeking self, therefore, has some significant degree of organic unity and hence of intrinsic value in virtue of that (double) characteristic. I should emphasize that the characteristic of being a value-seeking I is a capacity or potentiality—infants and unconscious people have it. This capacity or potentiality can be destroyed or blocked, it can be impossible to exercise or exhibit. I leave aside here all the delicate questions about when the capacity first is present (in fetuses?), when it is destroyed (how severe the brain damage?), how individuals who lack that capacity which is characteristic of their species are to be treated, why the (unexercised) capacity is so important, and so forth.[56]

What demarcates a seeker after value from a being having only wants, preferences, and desires? Is there a behavioral criterion of acting (or seeking) for value? I suggest we use the problem of the fact–value gap to distinguish someone who seeks value. If it is value a person is seeking, he must face this gap; it must make sense for him to ask of something: "although it has certain factual traits and I desire or want it; nevertheless, is it valuable, ought I to do it?" This is Moore's open question;[57] that it can arise for someone, and his answer affect his conduct, shows he is not merely seeking a characteristic coextensive with value. Someone who viewed all questions of action and *telos* as settled by the citing of some factual characteristic would be seeking that characteristic rather than value. That the person can be brought to an awareness of the possibility of divergence between any factual characteristic and value shows that it is value he is pursuing, not simply that factual characteristic. The person need not actually philosophize or worry about the question; but it must be possible to make the question seem real and salient to him.

Just as having the fact–value question arise shows he is pursuing value, so also having the mind–body problem arise shows he has a mind, a subjectivity. If we encounter intelligently behaving beings on another planet, we will think they do not have subjective experiences if they cannot be brought to see the point of the mind–body problem, of the question of what the relationship is between their experiences and the physical events in their brain and body. If they think it is obvious that these things are identical, so that no such question can arise, then whatever they have, it is not subjective experiences. (This criterion is meant to apply only to those with the cognitive capacity to deal with such questions; it should not be concluded that animals fail to have any subjective experiences because they cannot be brought to see the point of certain questions.) Should we conclude, in the light of the writings of some philosophers, that not every human being on earth has subjective experiences either?

Thus, we can take comfort from some of our intractable philosophical problems and put their very intractability to intellectual use. To be subject to being brought to face the fact–value and mind–

body problems and be puzzled by them, to be beings about whom and for whom these problems can arise, is what distinguishes those who exert a moral pull—persons in the fullest sense. Man is the philosophizing animal. This also will mark beings on other planets (or other beings on our own) as worthy of the highest moral respect. It therefore would be advisable for future interplanetary or interstellar voyages of exploration to add to their crews of scientists and technicians, a philosopher—not only to convince *us* that the aliens fully are persons.

We have specified the basic moral characteristic as being a value-seeking self. This component of value seeking, perhaps with some expansion and filling in, brings in further members from the traditional list of candidates, such as ability to plan over time and ability to follow principles, perhaps even free will, interpreted either as an ability to track values or to freely weight them. Nonetheless, we may feel that any such short list is an inadequate selection from the richer traits of humanity, and that nothing less than the full intertwined richness constitutes the moral basis of a person's moral pull. Philosophical discussions ignore the resiliency of human beings, their courage, sentimentality, resourcefulness, quest for meaning, toughness, and the rest of the panoply of traits exhibited in our life and literature, and delineated especially in the science fiction literature that compares humanity to other life and cultural forms under a variety of challenging situations. (To be sure, the generally favorable evaluation by these writers, seeing virtues even in our flaws, is not unconnected with the fact that the authors are human—we have not read the science fiction of the "aliens" yet.)

I think we should view the more abstract and delimited philosopher's specification of the moral basis as a first approximation only, a delineation of only the central features; amenable to a further filling in, it will find its place in a richer texture. We should expect simply a first abstract approximation, if value is degree of organic unity and if the moral basis is the valuable characteristics to which we are morally pulled to respond. The fuller and richer interweaving of characteristics will provide a greater organic unity than the thin traits discussed by the philosophers (even though these traits are fundamental), and hence furnish a more ample basis of value to which ethical behavior can respond. The philosophical theory is a black and white photograph of the richly colored scene.

Blocking Moral Avoidance

The moral pull is based upon the characteristic of being a value-seeking I, but what content does this pull have? The moral content divides into that based upon there being any basic moral characteristic at all, and the content arising from the particular (basic moral) characteristic.[58]

That basic moral characteristic is the basis of the moral pull. If this moral basis is to place any weighty moral strands on your behavior (whether as constraints, limits, or goals), then these strands must not be subject easily to avoidance. One obvious mode of avoidance would be to destroy the (basic moral) characteristic, either by destroying its bearer or by eradicating possession of it. In virtue of something's having the basic moral characteristic, we cannot do certain things or actions A to it. My thought is: if we always could avoid "do not do A to it" by destroying the characteristic, there would be no real restriction not to do A to it. To be sure, there might be another restriction we adhered to, namely, not to do A to something with the characteristic. However, this wouldn't actually be an obstacle in our lives, ethics wouldn't seriously limit us if we could freely destroy the characteristic.

I have tacitly assumed that the presence of this (basic moral) characteristic is not an empirically necessary condition for violating the injunction by doing A. Otherwise, an injunction might have a semblance of nonavoidability simply because it is not possible to do A once the characteristic has been destroyed. (For an instance of this, let A be causing pain to animals and let the characteristic be "having the capacity to feel pain". Here we have an injunction not to cause pain to animals that does limit what people may do, but does not stop them from painlessly killing animals or painlessly destroying that capacity and then doing anything at all to the animals.) Our point about avoidability holds where the basic moral characteristic, for example, "being a value-seeking I", is not a necessary condition for violating an injunction.

If the moral injunction is significantly to limit what we may do, then there also must be prohibitions on killing the bearer of the characteristic, or destroying this characteristic, causing the bearer no longer to possess it. (However, it may be permissible to cause the bearer no longer to possess the characteristic if, in so doing, you cause her to have an even more valuable characteristic, one that exerts a greater moral pull.) Thus, we get the moral injunctions:

Do not kill a being that has the characteristic.
Do not cause something with the characteristic to stop having it.

If these weren't moral injunctions, then we could avoid all moral claims by destroying the characteristics on which they were based. Supposing that the basic moral characteristic is being a value-seeking I, then we have as moral injunctions:

Do not kill value-seeking I's.
Do not cause value-seeking I's to stop being so, either to stop being I's or to stop being value-seekers.

These injunctions are necessary brakes on moral avoidance. However, they are not the full story of how to behave to a bearer of the basic moral characteristic, only a part that must hold if this characteristic is to yield any limiting demands at all. Note that these injunctions do not require us to maintain or increase the presence of the (basic moral) characteristic in the world; they simply forbid destroying it.

We have stated what is presupposed by the characteristic's having a morally significant effect in the form of constraints: "do not do _____". However, this effect might be embodied in a goal instead:

Minimize the killing of bearers of the characteristic, for example, minimize the killing of value-seeking I's.
Minimize the destruction of the characteristic, for example, of being a value-seeking self.

These formulations would permit doing some of it in order to minimize the total amount of the action and thereby to advance the general goal. Nevertheless, they do not permit moral avoidance at will; therefore, the nonavoidance condition alone does not specify whether the moral principles are to take the form of side constraints or of mandatory directions toward goals.

Merely because some characteristic plays the role.of moral basis, we get the injunction or goal about not destroying that characteristic. What particular injunction or goal it is, what it is we are not to destroy, is fixed by the particular characteristic. We have held that this characteristic is being a value-seeking I. However, the injunction or goal not to destroy a value-seeking I (not to destroy it as a value-seeking I) is not the whole of the content of morality; it does not exhaust the full moral implication, the full moral pull, of the basic moral characteristic. It is only the nonavoidance segment. Further moral content is based on the particular content of the characteristic, in a way other than by simply plugging that characteristic's content into the nonavoidance (injunction or goal) structure. What is this further content?

Moral Responsiveness

The basic moral characteristic, we have said, has to be relevant to ethical behavior, so that there is some discernible and appropriate connection between the two. I suggest that this connection is the following. The ethical behavior somehow recognizes or acknowledges the characteristic, it treats the bearer of the characteristic as having that characteristic. On the supposition that the basic moral characteristic is being a value-seeking I, the fundamental ethical principle is:

Treat someone (who is a value-seeking I) as a value-seeking I.

This has kinship with Kant's principle: treat everyone as an end-in-himself and not merely as a means.[59]

What is it to treat someone as a value-seeking I? Suppose that in order to break a window I pick up a sleeping person and hurl him through it. I am treating him as an object. My behavior utilizes his mass, size, center of gravity, and other characteristics the physicist speaks of, but it is not cued to his being a person, to his being a value-seeking I. My behavior is in no way dependent upon his possession or nonpossession of that characteristic. For me to treat someone as a value-seeking I, something about my behavior—about how I do or at least would behave toward him in certain circumstances—must depend upon his having that characteristic; that characteristic must (actually or subjunctively) make some difference to me. This is surely a minimal reading of treating someone as a value-seeking I. When I hurl the sleeping person through the window, I take no account of the fact that he is a self, a subjectivity with desires: I treat him merely as a thing.

Suppose next that the person is awake, and still I want to use him as a window-breaker. Now I cannot treat him merely as a thing, for he may be frightened at my advance, and run away. Just as with trapping an animal, I must close off avenues of escape; in so acting, I ascribe to him the desire (let us suppose, not merely the reflex or instinct) to escape. Nevertheless, my behavior toward him does not depend upon his being a value-seeking self. So let us enlarge the description of the situation, to include strategic aspects. In trying to avoid my catching him, he realizes that I will anticipate his doing so, and so tries to figure out my likely countermove, my counter to his countermove, and so forth. These are the considerations engaged in by participants in game-theoretical situations: "he thinks that I think that he thinks that_____; so I will do_____." Don't we interact with people in game-theoretic situations as people, not merely as things or animals; don't we then treat them as subjectivities who realize there are other subjectivities arrayed against them (deciphering their intentions and countermoves) in a strategic game-theoretic situation? How then can the basis of morality be "treat another as a value-seeking I", if this includes and allows such cruel and patently immoral actions as giving an unwilling innocent person a twenty-minute headstart in a game-theoretic pursuit to the kill? Not all ways of being connected to a reflexive consciousness qua reflexive consciousness count as moral.

In a game-theoretic strategic situation we interact with another rational reflexive consciousness and agent, taking account of his desires. However, in no way need we take account of the fact that he is a value seeker. The utility functions of game theory encapsulate desires, wants, and preferences, and provide a way of measuring their strength if certain conditions are satisfied. (If the von Neumann–Morgenstern conditions on preference among probability mixtures are satisfied, then preference can be measured, with utility numbers assigned, on an interval scale, unique up to a positive linear transformation.) Nothing within the apparatus of game theory, either in the normal form specifying a game or in the rationale underlying bargaining model solutions, requires that any participant be a value seeker or takes account of the fact that he is.[60] The game-theoretic interaction of pursue and kill does not treat another as a value-seeking I.

However, does not the different game of "pursue and kill the value-seeking I" treat another as a value-seeking I? If he weren't a value-seeking I, you would not pursue him; doesn't your behavior therefore respond to his having this characteristic? His being a value-seeking I makes him a target for your behavior but it doesn't affect the manner or mode of that behavior; it affects only to whom that behavior is directed. You might get special pleasure from playing "pursue and kill a value-seeking I"; you especially might want to kill one of those. Still, the victim's being a value-seeking I does not, qua value-seeking I, move and guide your actions as pursuer.

Since these distinctions may appear obscure, it is a welcome fact that we find similar distinctions made within the theory of operant conditioning. That theory distinguishes discriminative stimuli, which are the cues for the doing of certain behavior, from reinforcing stimuli, which themselves increase the probability of future behavior of that sort, from stimuli that shape the contours of the behavior itself. I may choose to run my steamroller only over intelligent people (the discriminative stimulus) and get pleasure from doing it to that sort of person (the reinforcing stimulus), yet my behavior itself is not contoured by or to the person's intelligence.[61]

The requirement to treat a value-seeking I as a value-seeking I holds that our behavior itself is to be shaped by her characteristic of being a value-seeking I. Thus, the characteristic on which moral pull is based functions in two ways, as the discriminative mark for certain moral behavior, and also as informing the content of this behavior by shaping it, by being something that affects the contours of that behavior. The basic moral characteristic not only pulls forth the behavior, it also shapes it.[62]

Other examples of contouring in behavior will help in understanding how (moral) behavior can be contoured to someone's being a value-seeking self. First, consider workmanship, wherein the artisan adapts his action to the variational details of his particular materials. Second, consider the way intimate sexual behavior is contoured to the partner's general desires, passing pleasures, passions, and emotions as these are expressed also in subtly nuanced physical position and configurations, pressure, sound, and rhythm, as well as to the reciprocal contouring of one's partner to oneself. Third, consider how a voice is contoured to the thought it expresses; consider the different modulations and nuances, tempos, hesitations, emphases, and changes of inflection whereby a voice shows intelligence. A film some years ago, entitled *Charly*, portrayed an operation changing the intelligence of a retarded person, raising him first to normal capability and then to an extremely brilliant scientist. After some time the effect faded and he slowly returned to his original state, unable to use his scientific knowledge successfully to stem the decline, and unable to maintain the romantic relationship that had developed with his female doctor. The actor who played this role did quite well both as the retarded person and the person in the stage of normal intelligence; however, he did not convincingly portray the extremely intelligent person in those scenes that showed him in serious conversation or lecturing. Seeing this film led me to conjecture that actors and actresses cannot convincingly portray people of significantly greater intelligence than themselves. (I imagine the actor working from a script, and leave aside here the possibility of another intelligent person's making a tape of the speaking part which the actor then learns to mimic exactly.) Actors cannot get their voices to fit correctly the contours of the ideas they express if they cannot *think* those thoughts as they are speaking them.

If some particular behavior is responsive to someone's basic moral characteristic, then will not any other behavior isomorphic to the first also turn out so to be responsive? This would be an absurd result, for the isomorphic behavior could be a delicate dance with one's finger or a pattern of scratching one's face, provided it stood in a one-to-one correspondence with the first responsive behavior. It is not merely in a behavior's contours that it is to be responsive to the basic moral characteristic; the substantive character of the behavior also must fit the characteristic. One way behavior can fit or match another's characteristic is by stemming from the very same characteristic within the agent. I treat you as a value-seeking self by responding to that characteristic through myself acting as a value-seeking self. But can't I use my value-seeking capacity to respond to your being a value-seeking I without valuing that capacity in you? Perhaps I value something else, which perhaps leads me to do the isomorphic dance behavior. What is needed is that the behavior not only stem from your basic moral characteristic and in its contours fit his, but that it respond to his characteristic as that characteristic. (And is the way behavior responds to him as value-seeking, by responding to him as valuable, V-ing him?)

Let us demarcate different types of relationship to the basic moral characteristic, being a value-seeking I, or to the richer and more textured value from which this characteristic abstracts. First, one might be responsive to that characteristic, qua that characteristic, fitting and contouring one's actions and behavior to the nature of that characteristic. Shall we view this responsive behavior as responding to the (basic moral) characteristic as that characteristic, or as responding to the basic moral characteristic as valuable? This second alternative makes it easier to see why destructive, manipulative, and coercive behavior is not responsive to the characteristic. That behavior does not respond to it (and its bearer) as valuable; anti-V-ing is not treating something as valuable, while V-ing is. While this explanation of responsiveness through the theory of value is illuminating, another explanation would be more fundamental, if it could be made to work. Under that more fundamental explanation, being responsive to the basic moral characteristic, to what is valuable, is responding to it as that characteristic. To be thus responsive to that characteristic is (among other things) to V it or, at any rate, not to anti-V it. We V a characteristic which is valuable, because that is a way of responding to the characteristic qua that characteristic—as it is.

An ethical theory, we said earlier, must place ethical behavior in some discernible and appropriate relationship to the basic moral characteristic which calls forth such behavior. The neatest result would be that ethical behavior is precisely the behavior that is responsive to the (basic moral) characteristic, as that characteristic. The behavior the basic moral characteristic calls for is that which is responsive to that characteristic qua that characteristic. No linkage between characteristic and behavior could be closer. We might view it as a test of having correctly formulated the basic moral characteristic, that ethical behavior should turn out to be thus responsive to that characteristic.* This structure wherein the two components, ethical behavior and basic moral characteristic, dovetail perfectly, does not (try to) solve the problem of the relationship between is and ought. It delineates in the neatest possible way, the behavior that is called for by the characteristic, but it does not answer the question of why one ought to behave responsively to the characteristic.

* If it turns out that no characteristics we have are such that ethical behavior is responsive to them, should we then try to imagine characteristics for which this relationship would hold, and then transform ourselves into bearers of those characteristics, into beings worthy of our ethics?

Responding and Anti-Responding

One type of relationship to the basic moral characteristic is responding to it, qua it. Another is anti-responding to it. (This corresponds to the anti-V-ing discussed earlier in this chapter, and to the flouting of values discussed at the end of the previous chapter.) Anti-responding treats the characteristic negatively; it rubs against the grain of the characteristic. As before, one possibility is to explain the notion of anti-responding through the theory of value, as behavior that anti-V's something (that is valuable), or that treats it as disvaluable. We might say that an anti-response to a characteristic does respond to that characteristic, but not as that; it responds to the characteristic as lesser, as to another less valuable or disvaluable characteristic. We might say that the anti-response is a reductionist response: it treats the characteristic as something else (which is less valuable).

The third mode of relationship to a characteristic is neutral, it is neither responsive nor anti-responsive. Such is our mode of connection with passersby on the street or people geographically separate, to whom we have no connection, no web of relationship. (We may leave aside the questions of whether not anti-responding constitutes not merely a neutral relationship but a somewhat positive one, and whether not responding constitutes a somewhat negative one.)

These distinctions connect with some others, which are not identical; for example, the distinction between acting and abstaining. It is not the case that anti-responding always involves acting while abstaining always is neutral; if someone has a special obligation to act, his abstention may be anti-responsive. A single parent who fails to feed his infant child is anti-responding and killing the child, while another person is not killing that child, although it is true that if this other person had fed the child it would have lived. It is false that we cause and are responsible for everything we could prevent. The father, by abstaining from feeding the child, does cause and is responsible for its death, but not merely because he could have prevented it—he had a special responsibility to feed the child.[63]

Using the distinctions between responding and anti-responding, we now can specify further the fundamental moral principle concerning treating value-seeking I's as value-seeking I's. First we have the negative injunction (or alternatively the goal of minimizing anti-responsiveness):

> Do not treat a value-seeking I as less than a value-seeking I; do not anti-respond to value-seeking I's.

Subsidiary injunctions fall under this general one, for instance, do not degrade a value-seeking I.* Second, there is the positive formulation:

> Treat value-seeking I's as value-seeking I's; be responsive to value-seeking I's as value-seeking I's.

There is room for distinct positions within this general framework. First, there may be disagreement about where a given sort of behavior falls, in particular, whether it is neutral or anti-responsive. (Is the non-meeting of some need of another that is necessary for sustaining his life merely a neutral staying out of that person's life, or is it anti-responsive to his valuable characteristics?) Second, there can be differences about the roles of the two principles. Is the first one mandatory, so anti-responsiveness is simply ruled out, while the second, recommending responsiveness, is above and beyond the call of duty? (What then would be the nature of the 'ought' in "we ought to treat value-seeking I's as value-seeking I's"?) Or is some degree of responsiveness to value (and not merely refraining from anti-responsiveness) morally required? Third, there will be issues about the enforceability of these moral principles by others: is how a person ought to behave identical with what others may force him to do, may others enforce only refraining from anti-responsiveness, does it depend on whether or not this coercive behavior itself will be anti-responsive, and so on? I shall touch briefly upon some of these issues later; they are mentioned here to show how they arise naturally from the foundational distinction between responsiveness and anti-responsiveness. We should expect the foundations of ethics to mark somehow the differences in substantive ethical theories, to provide the pieces these theories array differently. However, we should not expect of the foundations that it uniquely determine one ethical theory (though it will exclude many possible ones), any more than only

---

* For a discussion of the extreme mode of degradation practiced by the Nazis, excremental assault, see Terrence De Pres, *The Survivor* (Oxford University Press, 1976). De Pres also discusses how simply surviving constituted an act of resistance to such treatment.

one building can be erected upon given foundations. The task of explaining how any objective ethics is possible is different from the task of showing a particular ethics, as distinct from its close neighbors, is true.

Responsive Interaction and Moral Principles

When someone raises a moral objection to something we are doing or planning, we feel we owe him an answer, a moral answer. It will not do simply to hit him on the head or to shrug our shoulders. An ethical egoist would reply only if he thought doing so was in his own interest; we feel we have to respond with moral reasons. (However, we do not have to expend our life's savings to track down the person who objected and then went off to travel in inaccessible places. We ought to respond, *prima facie*, although this "ought" can be overridden by other considerations.) Only by responding are we treating him as a value-seeking I; the only way to respond to his requesting moral reasons or raising moral objections, the only response to it qua that, is to offer moral reasons in justification or defense of our actions, to engage, if need be, in a moral dialogue with him. (Recall our earlier remark about how Thrasymachus undercuts his own position by engaging in discussion.) To engage in a moral dialogue with someone is itself a moral act, whose moral character does not lie solely in being an attempt to get at the moral truth, or in being a vehicle to change and deepen a personal relationship and thereby be a means toward resolving a moral conflict.[64] Rather, (sincere) engagement in moral dialogue is itself a moral response to the other's basic moral characteristic, apart from its being a means toward a satisfactory accommodation with the other. It itself is responsive to him; perhaps that is why openness in moral dialogue, considering carefully and responding closely to the concerns of the other, so often is an effective means toward resolution of conflict. When each is aware that the other is responsive to his or her own (valuable) characteristics in the very act of discussion and in the course the discussion takes, then this noticing of mutual respect is itself a force for good will and the moderation of demands; the altered conditions created by the dialogue may fit different moral principles so that new solutions are appropriate.

A moral dialogue of this sort is an especially clear example of a mutual value-theoretic situation (by analogy to game-theoretic situation),[65] where each participant is responsive to the other's basic moral characteristic, is aware that the other is responsive to her own, and is responsive to the other's responsiveness, is aware of the other's second-level responsiveness and is responsive to it, and so on. (We might view a game-theoretic situation as also having a structure of mutual—iterated—responding, but where the characteristic originally responded to is not "being a value-seeking I," but "being a maximizer of utility with knowledge of the game matrix.") We want to be in mutual value-theoretic situations; only then is the value in us (including our own value responsiveness) adequately answered. Hegel's discussion of the master-slave relation elaborates how domination thwarts this: the master cannot force this responsiveness from the slave, and unless the master shows responsiveness to the slave's basic moral characteristic (but then he could not remain his master) the slave cannot respond to that. We must leave for another occasion a treatment and evaluation of systems of dominance, institutionally patterned asymmetries of responsiveness that the subordinate party enters into for extrinsic reasons.[66]

How much is demanded of us in being responsive? Must we, like the characters in Henry James novels or their author, be responsive to each and every delicate nuance and modulation of the other person's subjectivity, of his emotion, motive, mood, and passing thought? Perhaps for friendship and love, but it is too demanding a requirement for other ethical interpersonal relationships. In these, one must be responsive to the fact of another's subjectivity, to his being a self, a value-seeking entity, a choice-making and meaning-seeking entity, but one need not respond to every modulation in the content or focus of these characteristics. Ethics responds to the fact that these characteristics are there, perhaps also to some general traits of their content, while more intimate relationships respond to the particular way these characteristics specify and express themselves. Responsiveness to each flitting thought and emotion links one closer to the person but not to the centrally unifying traits of the person. However, a close relationship can give rise to special ethical obligations to respond to these particularities.

The way to respond to the fact that these basic moral characteristics are there appears to be to follow moral principles that acknowledge these characteristics, that respond to their presence qua the characteristic they are. The relationship of principles to responsiveness is unclear, though. Are principles simply the summary of the patterns that responsiveness takes; or are they to be consciously followed and adhered to, where their feature of being generalizable marks that it is value that is being responded to; or are they monitoring devices that come into play only when deviation from responsiveness occurs? When principles guide behavior, this helps to maintain a certain degree of responsiveness; however, since principles are crude instruments, they also interfere with or ignore other more delicate responses.[67] There is no reason to assume that all the modulations of responsiveness can be captured by statable moral principles of a complexity we can manage. (Compare the question of how well given analogue behavior can be simulated by a bounded digital device.) To be sure, they may fall under the principle "do not be anti-responsive to value-seeking selves; be responsive to them". But they are not specified by this general principle. Just as the basic moral characteristic is an abstraction from the richness of the value of a person to be responded to, so the formulated moral principles are an abstraction from the richness of the fine modulations of responsiveness. However, this does not prevent abstract formulation from being illuminating (even as one realizes its limitation) or having important uses.

Moral sensitivity toward others, knowing in diverse circumstances how to be aptly and creatively responsive to others as value-seeking selves, is not merely a matter of following rules. Nonetheless, the moral principles against murder, coercion, manipulation, and lying are (at the least) valid summaries of what is demanded of us by (not anti-)responsiveness to other value-seeking selves. Those who respond to others as value-seeking selves will fit these principles even if they do not consciously follow them. It is not part of our view that all the modulations of moral responsiveness are captured by or are best produced by following formulatable principles. Even among the devices people consciously use to mediate their responsiveness to another person's basic moral characteristic, there are aids other than principles. This is one role of moral models or exemplars whom people try to imitate—another role is to inspire people to better behavior; these exemplars are like analogue devices, in contrast to the principles which are more like digital ones.

471

People who alike are value-seeking I's or who have the capacity to be such, and who therefore are alike in value in this way, can differ in the value they exhibit. They can pursue value with differing degrees of diligence, aim differently, and give different shape and texture to their lives as they express themselves as value-seeking and value-weighting selves. Indeed, our view that the sanction of immorality is a value sanction has the consequence that the (life of the) immoral person will have less value. In acting responsively to value, are we to take account of these differences in value and so behave differently to different people?

All people share (the capacity for) being value-seeking selves, and hence all are owed responsiveness to this capacity or at least are owed non-anti-responsiveness. In this respect, we are to behave the same to everyone; the general part of ethics specifies responsiveness to this value that all people have equally.

But if, as I believe, there is a general principle calling for responsiveness to value as such, not merely the value embodied in the basic moral characteristic, then there will be differences in how we (are to) appropriately respond to different people. While these differences will not involve violating the rights all share in virtue of being value-seeking I's, they might involve choosing to aid or save some rather than others in situations where not all can be helped. These are difficult questions, best left for another occasion, as are the intricate implications, for animals, trees, ecological systems, and so on, of the general principle that we are to treat everything as having the value it has.[68] (Note, though, this self-interested reason for a person's wanting his own value to be greater: since others ought to be responsive to his value, by becoming more valuable he enhances how others ought to behave toward him.)

It is clear what types of considerations and issues will be relevant in elaborating this general principle. Again, a distinction will be made between responsiveness and anti-responsiveness. We refrain from anti-responding to the value something has, qua value, by not intentionally destroying or diminishing this value, and not impairing its own ability to maintain its value (unless there are countervailing considerations involving greater value). It is a different matter—one involving responsiveness—whether we are to act to maintain the value, and still different whether we are to increase its value. (This last would not be a response to the value there *is*.) Still other issues are raised by another form of anti-responsiveness: cooperating or participating in another's intentional lowering or destruction of a third party's value.

Our mention of intentional action is not accidental; not only is such action regulated by principles, it itself establishes a closer link than merely passing someone on the street, for example, and so opens one to the application of further principles. We need do no more than avoid the path of a passerby on the street, otherwise ignoring him; but other contacts involving the intentional exchange of information, as in stores, require some acknowledgment that the others are people and present. Intermediate linkages are many and variegated and each involves its own moral nuances, as do the tighter linkages of joint participation and cooperation in an activity, in friendship, love, and family ties.

Not only do we think things should be valued for what they are and treated as having the value they do, we also believe that some relationships between people should have a certain value, should be valued in a certain way. Must the failure of this always involve an inappropriate valuing of the other person, as opposed to that of the relationship itself? Consider the situation wherein one person uses another person for his own ends. This may involve deception, but it need not; another may so want some relationship with you that he consents knowingly to being used.[69] Our objection seems to be that in using another, a relationship is not valued (at all, or sufficiently) for itself, a relationship (of friendship, for example) that can be so valued, and is more valuable when it is. Something is inappropriate, we feel, when the relationship is valued mainly for something extrinsic that will result from it. (Some relationships, such as in business, are delineated as those for which such extrinsic valuing is perfectly appropriate.) Another example is prostitution, the voluntary exchange of sexual acts for money. Sexual activity, we think, has its own value and should be valued mainly for itself, not as a means to financial reward or to better health through exercise. The prostitute does not value the activity itself at all, while the client does value it, but as less than that type of activity (sexual union) can be. Each uses the other to provide something less than such activity can offer. These are not grounds for prohibiting such service, but they explain our negative judgment of it—it degrades the value of the sexual act and of the participants. (It is an interesting issue to demarcate which relationships we impose such value requirements on, whereby we view only certain forms and constituent valuations as appropriate.)

III. THE STRUCTURE OF THE ETHICAL PULL

Moral Complications and Moral Structures

We have identified the root of ethical behavior, of ethical pull, as responsiveness to others' valuable characteristics, qua those characteristics. This does not specify what the details of ethics are, or how details arise from (or are linked to) this root. There is the task, first, of specifying what counts as responsiveness and as anti-responsiveness, showing (for example) why murdering, coercing, manipulating, using, and lying to another are anti-responsive to his basic moral characteristic—to his being a rational, freely choosing, value-seeking self. It is not a mechanical task to generate lists of those features of an action that make it (in that respect) responsive or anti-responsive, or to decide of a feature whether an act having it is (in that respect) responsive or anti-responsive. I do not mean that it is not easy to begin two such lists and enter many features; what is difficult is to end the lists. We need not assume our current insight into responsiveness and anti-responsiveness is perfect. Moral progress—in an individual life or in human history—consists partly in coming to see features, previously viewed as neutral, as being anti-responsive or responsive. Increased moral sensitivity involves seeing differently what previously was taken for granted as neutral.* In not fixing the complete membership of these lists of features (which count as responsive, and as anti-responsive) once and for all, a moral view is open to growth, development, and new insight.

A specification of these open-ended lists of features is merely the beginning of spelling out the details of a moral view rooted in treating value as value. Given that a feature counts as responsive or as

---

* A notable current example is the insights and consequent changed perspective of the feminist movement; see also recent writings on children's rights, the treatment of animals, domination, and ecological awareness. The phrase "consciousness raising" is used to refer to the transformation from seeing a feature of an action or social arrangement as neutral (even as responsive) to seeing it as anti-responsive.

anti-responsive, there are the issues about how responsive or anti-responsive it counts as being. Any given action will have many features—some may be on one of the lists, some on the other; is the action as a whole responsive or unresponsive? How does it compare with other actions available to the person? How are we to judge actions that are responsive to some people yet anti-responsive to others, and how to compare these to other mixed actions? For an agent or a third party to make a moral judgment of an action, some weighing of these features seems needed, as well as a specification of a structure into which these weights are to enter so as to result in a determinate moral judgment of rightness or wrongness, of moral permissibility or impermissibility.

There are views of the structure of the moral pull simpler than this complicated balancing structure.[70] According to the *maximization structure*, all moral judgments about the moral impermissibility of actions are accounted for by a principle that requires the maximization of some (natural) quantity, perhaps subject to a quantitative restraint.[71] One prominent moral theory is of this form: classical utilitarianism (of the textbooks) mandates the maximization of total (or average) utility; later variants involve balancing and tradeoffs with other considerations, such as distributive ones. (I shall assume, without further discussion here, that no such view requiring maximization of a unitary function is adequate.) The maximization structure holds that an act is right in virtue of maximizing the score (of the world, or a person, or an act) along the function f; and any act that does not have a maximum f score is impermissible. This structure is one instance of a more general structure which allows greater leeway.

According to the *deductive structure*, the judgment

(1) Act A is morally impermissible

is accounted for as following from the factual premiss

(2) Act A has features $F_1, \ldots, F_n$

conjoined with the moral premiss

(3) Any act with features $F_1, \ldots, F_n$ is morally impermissible.

This moral premiss (3), in turn, is accounted for as following from the more general moral premiss

(4) Any act with features $T_1, \ldots, T_n$ is morally impermissible

conjoined with the factual premiss

(5) Any act with features $F_1, \ldots, F_n$ also has features $T_1, \ldots, T_n$.

(Within this structure, the features $F_1, \ldots, F_n$ and $T_1, \ldots, T_n$ are empirical, factual, 'nonmoral' features of action.) Principle 4, in its turn, is accounted for as following from a still more general moral principle conjoined with another factual premiss.

Presumably, somewhere up the line are a number of most general moral principles (of the form 3 and 4) which do not follow from any more general ones (that are true), and which, when combined with factual information, suffice to yield all other moral truths about the permissibility and impermissibility of action. Unlike the narrow maximization structure, the deductive structure is not committed to the maximization of any one natural quantity, or to the existence of just one general moral principle that underlies all other moral truths; there may be independent moral principles that intertwine to yield the totality of moral truths. Most philosophical discussions of morality seem to presuppose a deductive structure.

We might have two interconnected purposes in trying to delineate a moral structure: first, to describe the realm of moral truths, how it is structured and the interrelations that hold there; and second, to account for the moral judgments a person makes by attributing such a structure to him as underlying and generating his moral judgments. By assuming he internalizes and utilizes such a structure (although not consciously), we would be in a better position to explain (how he makes) his judgments.[72]

Despite its greater leeway, the deductive structure faces problems due to its utilization of exceptionless moral principles, which hold that any act with certain features is impermissible in virtue of that, whatever else might be true of it. The deductive structure is vulnerable to conflict among these (supposedly) exceptionless principles. If it also mandates certain types of actions, holding that any action with certain features is required, then there is the possibility that some particular action will both have these features and also have other features which make it (and any action having them) impermissible.

476

If such an action is possible, is it required or impermissible; or is it both so that, doing it or not, the person does something wrong whatever he does? (One might be willing to say that his earlier wrongful action can place someone into a situation where no matter what he does he acts wrongly; but will a moral view countenance this in other cases as well?) There also is the possibility in some situation that every action available to a person might fall under one or another of the principles of impermissibility, so that nothing he can do (including "abstaining") is permissible.

However these problems are resolved, the deductive structure is ill-suited for accounting for some aspects of our moral judging. This structure cannot easily explain why a person's moral judgment of a particular act (often) changes as he learns additional facts about the act so that he no longer judges it morally impermissible. In such cases, the facts he knew previously were not sufficient for the truth of a judgment of moral impermissibility; he did not have knowledge that instantiated the antecedent of an exceptionless moral principle.[73]

A second difficulty in attributing the deductive structure is that many people are unwilling to state or assent to any or to very many exceptionless principles of determinate content—that is, to principles utilizing features whose application to an action can be decided without great infusions of moral insight or judgment. (Whatever their exceptionless form, principles such as "any action is morally impermissible that shows lack of love of one's neighbor, or anti-responsiveness to a value-seeking self" would not count.) Previously having explicitly accepted such principles, they found themselves gradually building-in explicitly described exceptions, in order to fit more and more complicated situations yet maintain the form as exceptionless. (A principle with a built-in exception does not have that exception outside it.) At some point, they found they could not state exceptionless principles, in whose correctness they had confidence, that would account for a wide range of their moral judgments. (The lack of confidence may have been reinforced by a realization of how principles stated as exceptionless can conflict.)

Such a history, I imagine, would be common among lawyers, who are familiar with the difficulties in devising rules to handle adequately, in advance, all the bizarre, unexpected, arcane, and complicated cases that actually arise, not to mention all the possible cases.

The awareness that any laws a legislature will be able to devise will work injustices (contrary to their intention) in some cases they had not foreseen or even contemplated often leads to talk of the role of judicial discretion within a legal system, and to the incorporation within legal codes of statutes dealing with the avoidance or prevention of (unspecified) greater evils. However, these statutes do not attempt to specify how to compare magnitudes of evil, and the term "judicial discretion" marks the area where rules cannot explicitly be formulated.* Thus, one would expect lawyers to be as skeptical about the purported exceptionless character of the moral rules or principles that come down to them in their moral tradition, and about any ones they can devise, as they are about the product of centuries of intensive legal effort (drawing also upon moral traditions) to devise and refine (related) rules to govern conduct.

A similar skepticism applies to another variant of the deductive structure which, realizing there are plural principles that might conflict in some situations, resolves all such conflicts in advance by a linear ranking (without ties) of those principles. This *lexical structure*, whereby some principles take absolute precedence over others, precludes and excludes the slightest breach of a higher ranked principle being counterbalanced by the greatest fulfillment of a lower ranked one. This simplest of the ways to avoid conflict among multiple principles, an exceptionless priority ranking, also seems prey to the worries that made other versions of the deductive structure seem insufficiently attuned to the range of moral complexities that situations and choices can exhibit.[74]

---

* See the American Law Institute, *Model Penal Code* (Proposed Official Draft, 1962), section 3.02. This provides no rules or procedures whereby it is to be determined whether "the harm or evil sought to be avoided by such conduct is greater than sought to be prevented by the law defining the offence charged"; presumably this is to be decided by a jury.

A recent attempt to narrow, indeed eliminate, the scope of judicial discretion is Ronald Dworkin, "Hard Cases" (reprinted in his *Taking Rights Seriously,* Harvard University Press, 1978, pp. 81–130). The magnitude of the vast and creative intellectual effort there imagined from the judge, drawing upon principles and values underlying the constitutional scheme and society, even supposing it were to have a unique result (in contrast to the range of choice left open by any scientific procedure or mode of evaluation thus far proposed), only emphasizes the lack of a determinate rule able to yield the result.

478

The Simple Balancing Structure

The theme of the inadequacy of exceptionless moral principles, at least the ones we can state, was emphasized by W. D. Ross, who wrote of *prima facie* duties and rights; these tend to make an action wrong or right but can be counterbalanced by other features.[75] An action can have features—following the literature let us call them "wrong-making features"—such that an action that has them, in the absence of other morally relevant features, is wrong or impermissible. However, there is no exceptionless principle to the effect that any action with such a feature is impermissible, for having this feature can be counterbalanced by having some other feature—call that a "right-making feature". A moral structure without exceptionless moral principles will build on such lists of right-making and wrong-making features, morally relevant but not conclusive. It is a further hypothesis of ours that what underlies these two lists of features is responsiveness and anti-responsiveness to another's basic moral characteristic (or, more generally, to his value); if so, the right-making and wrong-making lists are specifications of responsiveness and anti-responsiveness. The moral structure will contain as components two open-ended lists of features, but these lists can be utilized differently in different structures which we shall describe. The details are somewhat intricate.

The *simple balancing structure* utilizes two open-ended lists of features of action: W (for wrong-making) and R (for right-making). Let us denote particular features on these lists by subscripted lower-case letters w_1, w_2, . . . , r_1, r_2, . . . , and let us denote subsets of these features by subscripted capital letters: W_1, W_2, . . . , for subsets of wrong-making features; R_1, R_2, . . . , for subsets of right-making features. If an action has some features on W and no features on R, it is morally impermissible. If an action has some features on R and no features on W, it is morally permissible (and perhaps morally required).* It is a key fact that neither W nor R is empty: moral nihilism is false. Furthermore, these are exclusive lists; no feature is on

---

* The R list contains features that may override features on the W list; it is a further question whether features on the R list, when all alone, suffice for the action's being required, for its being impermissible not to do it.

both of them. These lists are not exhaustive, however; there are features of action that are not on either list, the morally neutral features.

Many actions will have some features on each list. Are such actions permissible or impermissible? We need a way of representing the fact, or a person's judgment, that some features on one list outweigh or override some features on the other. Let us represent these outweighings or overridings by inequalities between sets of features. Consider an action whose wrong-making features are exactly the ones in set W_1, all and only those, and whose right-making features are exactly the ones in R_1, all and only those; all of the action's other features are neutral ones, not on either list of morally relevant features. We write $W_1 > R_1$ to indicate that such an action is impermissible, that its wrong-making features outweigh its right-making features so that an action with exactly those morally relevant features is wrong. (Note that the inequality sign ">" registers the relative moral weight of the sets of features it stands between, not the relative numbers of features in these two sets.) Similarly $R_1 > W_1$ indicates that the action is permissible, that those right-making features override the wrong-making ones. Neither of these inequalities makes any commitment to judgments about other actions having all the features in W_1 and R_1 but that possess further morally relevant features. There is some general commitment, however; any other action possessing exactly the same morally relevant features (as specified by the lists) is to be judged in the same way.

For any act A, let us denote the set of (all and only) its wrong-making features by W_A, and the set of (all and only) its right-making features by R_A; also, denote the set containing no members, the null set, as $\emptyset$. We can now rewrite our initial statement about the impermissibility of an action A, all of whose morally relevant features are on the W list, as $W_A > \emptyset$; and we can write the statement about the permissibility of an act, all of whose morally relevant features are right-making ones, as $R_A > \emptyset$. (We shall not pause to represent the further fact that an act with no W features and no R features either, with only neutral features, is permissible.) Note that this apparatus does not exclude the existence of some exceptionless principles. Every act with the wrong-making features in some set W_i is impermissible, if there is no set of right-making features R_j such that $R_j > W_i$.

Since any act will be either permissible or impermissible, we do not need to introduce an equality sign to represent exact balancing among features; noncomparability would better be represented in some other way. We do not assume, either for a person's perhaps fragmentary moral views or even for the moral realm itself, that for any two arbitrary sets from the lists, W_i and R_j, either $W_i > R_j$ or $R_j > W_i$. We can leave open the possibility that there is no fixed fact about this. Although it is not necessary that there be a determinate inequality, outweighing or overriding, between sets of features, there sometimes will be. What conditions will these inequalities satisfy?

First, the inequality is asymmetric; if one set of features outweighs or overrides another, the other does not also outweigh or override it. If $R_i > W_j$ then not-$(W_j > R_i)$; and equivalently, if $W_j > R_i$ then not-$(R_i > W_j)$. Furthermore various transitivity conditions will hold, indicating how the inequality represents some ordering. For example, supposing X and Y are both subsets either of R or of W features: if there is a Z which X outweighs but Y does not, then X outweighs each thing that Y does, and each thing that outweighs X also outweighs Y. That X outweighs something that Y does not is taken to show X has greater weight than Y; given the above transitivity condition, this can be used to define a (transitive, irreflexive, and asymmetric) notion of greater weight, written $>>$, among different subsets from the same list.

Two further conditions seem appropriate. First, adding more W features to an action cannot make it morally any better. We can write this as:

If W_1 is a proper subset of W_2 (so that W_2 contains every feature in W_1 plus some other features) then for any right-making set R_i, if $W_1 > R_i$ then $W_2 > R_i$.

Whatever a set of W features outweighs, a larger set which includes it also outweighs.[76]

Moreover, short of "infinitely bad" actions, the more W features, the worse (ceteris paribus):

If W_1 is a proper subset of W_2 then there is an R_i that W_2 outweighs but W_1 does not, and there is an R_j that overrides W_1 but not W_2.[77]

The simple balancing structure holds that the moral permissibility or impermissibility of an action depends only upon its own morally relevant features, although these features may express the act's relations to other things or consequences. An act is morally impermissible if and only if its wrong-making features outweigh its right-making features; an act is morally permissible if and only if its right-making features outweigh its wrong-making features.[78] Before considering difficulties with this simple balancing structure, let us say something more about the outweighings and overridings.

Judgment in Ethics

Moral disagreement may occur over the placement of a feature on one of the lists, even among those people who agree that responsiveness and anti-responsiveness is the basis for inclusion, and it may occur over whether some specified features outweigh or override others. Writers on this subject stress the present lack of a method, even the impossibility of one, to decide all the complicated balancing questions. There exists no procedure or algorithm to generate all correct inequalities between sets of features. What is called for, they emphasize, is an individual's judgment.

To what is this lack of a procedure for specifying all outweighings due? There might be a partial indeterminateness in the moral realm; although some sets of features do outweigh others, there is no one correct answer about comparisons between yet other sets of features. There just is no fixed truth about the matter. Alternatively, there might be a fixed truth in all cases, which sometimes we are not able to discern. The lack of a procedure for deciding the truth of statements does not show there is no such fixed truth, as we know from logical theorems about number theory. There is no effective procedure to generate all the truths of number theory: Kurt Gödel showed that for any axiomatic system of number theory, there will be true statements of number theory that are not theorems of that system; building on this result, Alonzo Church showed that there is no effective procedure to decide whether any arbitrary statement is a theorem of some given axiomatic system of number theory. There is no unclearness, however, about the notion of theorem, no indeterminateness in the fact of whether something is a theorem of such a formal system or not, since the notion of proof is effectively decidable.[79] The lack of procedure guaranteed to answer a question does not show the question has no correct answer.

In ethics, the lack of a procedure to generate all correct answers does not mean we are at a loss before every question of whether one set outweighs another, and partial principles can be formulated to yield these judgments. Nevertheless, some see the balancing structure as nonobjective, since it must appeal at some points to individual judgments about outweighings, judgments which may well differ between persons. These critics grant, perhaps, the objectivity of the right-making and wrong-making lists, and so of the judgments about actions whose morally relevant features come from only one of those lists; also, they may grant the objectivity of some judgments of outweighings that are generated by higher-order principles. However, they view it as a serious defect that some questions are left to individual judgment, a defect indicating how far ethics is from being an objective science.[80]

We can gain some perspective on this question by considering recent discussion in the philosophy of science. Are there procedures for choosing among alternative and competing scientific theories of the same phenomena; do the norms or methodology of science determine such choices among theories, so that all who follow these norms must agree in which theory they select? There are different virtues of a scientific theory, different dimensions along which it can be evaluated: explanatory power, goodness of fit with the data, breadth and diversity of evidential support, degree of testability, range and diversity of the pheonomena it covers, simplicity, fit with other accepted theories, and so on. It can hardly be said that all or many of these dimensions (or any?) have received adequate precise explication, despite intensive efforts. Judgments of how a theory falls along each of these dimensions are still largely intuitive. Moreover, there certainly is no adequate systematic proposal about how these different desiderata of a theory are to be combined in an overall evaluation, about how two competing theories are to be comparatively evaluated or ranked when one is better along some of these dimensions, while the other is better along others. The comparison of the merit of two such competing theories is made by the use of scientific judgment, that is, intuitive estimation by those who value the relevant dimensions and ponder the question.[81]

The right-making and wrong-making characteristics of action correspond to the different dimensions along which a scientific theory can be evaluated, while the outweighings and overridings between sets of features correspond to the overall evaluation and comparison of theories. If the lack of explicit procedures to decide moral balancing questions, with the consequent need to rely on individuals' judgments that may disagree, were enough to show that ethics is subjective, then science too must be held to be subjective and nonscientific. It too lacks such procedures and must rely on the judgment of individuals. To be sure, some writers have thought the conclusion that science was subjective and irrational followed simply from the view that the selection of a theory was not fully determined and fixed by the norms of science.[82] However, this reflects an inadequate view of rationality. An activity (such as scientific or ethical evaluation) that is guided by valued (and disvalued) dimensions and features, that uses judgments in evaluating complicated cases, can be rational, even when some of the evaluations are not held to be better and more correct than every other possible evaluation (although they may be objectively better and more correct than many other evaluations would have been). Not every aspect of a rational activity need be such that any divergence in that aspect would be objectively worse. In ethics as in science, algorithms will be lacking and judgments sometimes will be called for; and in both areas we rightfully will trust some people's judgments more than other's. If, someday, explicit and adequate rules of balancing were formulated in either area, that would not undercut the rationality of current practice, though it might improve it.

If it is true that notions of responsiveness and anti-responsiveness occur in the most general moral principles and underlie the lists of features, then we may advert to those notions in attempting to make judgments of outweighing and overriding, considering whether an action overall is more responsive to value than not. There will be no algorithm to decide this, given the different modes of responsiveness, the different situations of the various people affected by the action, and so forth. Judgment may be guided by considerations of responsiveness, but it will not be completely determined only by those considerations; however, once we do make a judgment of outweighing, that will partially fix how we then view and specify the character of responsiveness to value. Just as in the case of the pluralism of values and the weighting involved, so too the weighing of right-making and wrong-making features sometimes will be a weighting of them, and the inequalities written down to represent a person's moral view will represent his weighting, rather than a recognition of an independently holding inequality. It will represent the interpretation he gives to responsiveness. (Similar remarks to these about the inequalities apply also to the numerical weights mentioned below.)

The Complex Structure: Alternative Actions

According to the simple balancing structure, whether or not an action is morally impermissible depends only upon the morally relevant features of that action, and upon the inequality among these features; an act A is morally impermissible if and only if $W_A > R_A$. In arriving at a judgment about the impermissibility of an act A, one need not, according to this structure, consider either the alternative actions available to the person, or larger courses of action of which act A is a part. These additional considerations require modification of the simple balancing structure.

Consider these two situations, adapted from one mentioned in the literature on lying.

(1) You see someone flee down a road from another person, who you know will, if he can, wrongfully (physically) harm or kill the first. The second person comes along and asks you which way the first one went. If you say nothing, he will continue along the road and catch the other person. The only way to prevent this is to lie to him, leading him to go in another direction by telling him the first person went that way.

I assume that sufficient details can be filled in so that you will agree it is morally permissible for you to lie in that situation. The right-making feature of saving someone from great harm outweighs the wrong-making feature of lying to his pursuer.

(2) The second situation is the same as the first, except that there is some other way to save the pursued person from his pursuer, which does not involve harm or any other wrong-making feature. If you speak to the pursuer, urging on him the view that his action is wrong, he will stop and listen, become convinced, and end his pursuit.

The details of the second situation can be filled in, I assume, so that you will agree you should convince the pursuer; it would be impermissible to lie to him then. What matters is the structure of these cases, not their details. In one situation, an action is permissible, but in another situation that action is impermissible because of the availability of an alternative action. Here is another example, altering the previous cases. In a third situation you can stop the pursuer only by shooting him, which it would be permissible to do, while in the fourth situation you also can stop his pursuit by lying to him—this would not have worked in the third situation, let us suppose. In this fourth situation the pursuer should be lied to; it would be impermissible to shoot him.

Let us return to the original specification of the two situations. In the first situation you have a choice between lying to the pursuer, and watching him go on his harmful way; whereas in the second situation your choice is lying to the pursuer, watching him go on his harmful way, or convincing him to stop his pursuit. In both of these situations, the action of lying has exactly the same morally relevant features. (I shall return to this point below.) In the first situation, by hypothesis, the act of lying is permissible, so its R features override its W features. In the second situation, therefore, the R features of the act of lying also override the W features, for it has exactly the same (morally relevant) features in this situation.* Yet, in the second situation, the act of lying is impermissible; this, despite the fact that its R features outweigh its W features. We conclude, therefore, that the R features of an act outweighing its W features is not a sufficient condition for the act's permissibility; and the W features of an act's outweighing its R features is not a necessary condition for the act's impermissibility.

Some principles have to be formulated at a higher level to take account not only of an act's morally relevant features, but also of the alternative actions and their morally relevant features. The lists of features and the inequalities thereby will feed into more complex principles than those of the simple balancing structure. The following principle seems appropriate.

---

* And these same features there have, I assume, their same weights. To hold that the moral weights of features change with the situation is to say that something is relevant to judgments of impermissibility in addition to the features. This is the point we are leading to, in another guise.

Principle I. When an act A has wrong-making features, so W_A is not empty, then if there is an alternative act B available to the person whose wrong-making features are a proper part of A's and whose right-making features include A's as a part (that is, such that $W_B \subset W_A$ and $R_A \subseteq R_B$), then it is morally impermissible to do act A, even if $R_A > W_A$.

This principle says that it is impermissible to do an action if one can achieve the very same R features at a cost of fewer W features; that is, if an alternative action enables you to achieve the same good at less cost. A stronger principle would hold an act impermissible when some alternative action enables you to achieve a greater good at the same cost; however, this requirement not to pass up any R features if one is going to incur a W cost seems to be too strong a condition to impose.

We can generalize principle I to situations where the morally relevant features of an alternative action B can be compared to those of A, even though neither set includes the other.

Principle II. Even if $R_A > W_A$, if there is an act B available to the person such that $W_B \ll W_A$ and $R_B \gg R_A$ (or these are equal in weight), then it is impermissible to do act A.

This second principle presents the idea of the first in greater generality: one may not do an action with wrong-making features if there is some alternative action available with less weighty wrong-making features and (at least) equally weighty right-making ones. In that case, one can achieve the same R weight at lesser W cost. Note that principle II concludes that act A is impermissible, not that act B is permissible; for in the same way that the existence of alternative B *undercuts* the permissibility of act A, similarly some other alternative C also might undercut B's permissibility.

Principle II says of the act that undercuts the permissibility of A that it has (when compared to A) less weighty W features and at least as weighty R features. Here, we can achieve the same R weight at less cost. However, even when no such alternative is available, there might be available an alternative act (call it again) B whose R weight is less than A's, but whose W weight also is so much less than A's that the extra rightness of A over B is outweighed by its extra wrongness.

Let us assume for the moment that not merely can we order the R features, and the W features, of two acts (by the relation $>>$), specifying which is weightier, but that also we can measure those weights somehow, so that it makes sense not just to talk of greater and lesser weights, but to assign numbers so as to compare differences between weights. On this assumption, by "W_A" and "R_A" let us mean not simply the set of W features and R features of A, but the appropriately measured weights of these features. We then would be in a position to formulate

Principle III. Even if $R_A > W_A$, if there is an action B available to the person such that $W_B << W_A$ and $(W_A - W_B) > (R_A - R_B)$, then it is impermissible to do A.

It is impermissible to do act A if another action is available with less weighty W features such that the extra wrongness of A over that alternative overrides A's extra rightness over the alternative.

Consider the following intuitive argument for principle III: Suppose there were another act C that exactly represented the moral difference between acts A and B, that just takes up the W and R slack between A and B. Therefore, the joint act B&C has R features and W features of exactly the same weight as act A. Suppose you already have decided to do act B; is it permissible for you to do act C in addition? Since $W_C > R_C$ (for $W_C = W_A - W_B$ and $R_C = R_A - R_B$), this act C is impermissible. (Here, I ignore complications about larger courses of action.) So it is impermissible to do the joint act B&C rather than just B. But since B&C has exactly the same morally relevant features as A, it also is impermissible to do A rather than B. It is impermissible to do A when B is available as an alternative, where $W_B << W_A$ and $(W_A - W_B) >> (R_A - R_B)$.

The intuitive rationale for principle III is that an act is impermissible if (as compared to an alternative) its extra wrongness outweighs its extra rightness. This principle does not, however, require maximizing the difference between R weight and W weight; it does not require choosing an action whose R–W difference is greater than that of any alternative action available. We may formulate that stronger principle as·

Even if $R_A > W_A$, if there is an action B available such that $(R_B - W_B) > (R_A - W_A)$, then it is impermissible to do act A.

The intuitive rationale for principle III, concerning the incurring of extra wrongness, is not available for this stronger principle. (Nor is the intuitive argument above.) Principle III states when you may not incur extra moral cost, namely, when this cost outweighs the extra moral benefit gained; whereas the stronger maximization principle requires one sometimes to incur extra moral cost, namely, when the extra moral benefit to be gained is greater. Hence, in a situation where, as appropriately measured, $R_B = 52$, $W_B = 50$, $R_A = 2$ and $W_A = 1$, the stronger maximization principle has the consequence that it is impermissible to do A (and that one must rather do B with its moral cost of 50); principle III does not have this consequence.

The stronger maximization principle—whatever the virtues of similar principles in other areas of cost–benefit analysis—seems to me too strong to be acceptable as a principle of ethics. Wrong-making features play a special role within higher level moral principles which are directed against moral cost, as instanced in the first three principles. Moral cost differs from other cost—it is not appropriately plugged into maximization principles that focus only on the differences between costs and benefits.[83] (And so we must be suspicious of attempts to utilize or parallel within ethics the full range of cost–benefit apparatus and techniques.)

Moral principles treat the W features and the R features asymmetrically. This also is shown by the fact that the W features of an action leave a moral residue, even when overridden by R features in a situation where it is permissible to do the action. Alternatives have to be sought, explanations and apologies have to be offered, amends have to be made, compensation offered, and so forth. When W_A is nonnegligible, one may not, provided $R_A > W_A$, blithely perform act A and go cheerfully on one's way. A further asymmetry between how moral principles treat W features and R features is indicated in principle III. Here the existence of one alternative action of a certain sort shows that $R_A > W_A$ is not sufficient for permissibility; however, it is not the case that the existence of one action of another sort can show that $W_A > R_A$ is not sufficient for impermissibility. While the existence of a better action (of a specified type) shows the impermissibility of A, even when $R_A > W_A$, the permissibility of A is not shown, when $W_A > R_A$, merely by there being some other action that is even worse.

Measurement of Moral Weight

Our discussion thus far has left two issues up in the air. The first, whether the act of lying did have the same morally relevant features in the two situations of pursuit which motivated the three principles, I discuss in a note.[84] The second issue is how the moral weight of a set of features might be measured so as to provide numerical values that can be fed into principle III. I mean the moral weight as incorporated within a particular person's moral view; to the extent that this person is a trustworthy and correct moral judge, this will give us access to the correct moral weights. I should say that even in the absence of a mode of measurement that yields the weights, principle III still seems illuminating: it indicates the qualitative contours of the intuitive judgments we make about actions in the presence of alternatives.

The task of measuring the moral weight a person assigns to a set of features is parallel to the task of assigning numbers to a person's preferences so as to measure not just his preferential ordering but the strength of his preferences. Therefore, we might think to parallel the standard mode of measuring utility, which considers preferences not only among simple alternatives or outcomes but among probability mixtures (involving probabilities of less than unity) of these alternatives.[85] This suggestion might seem especially plausible, since an adequate theory of moral judgment eventually will have to account also for judgments about action in situations of "risk" (where associated with an action is not just one set of R and W features, but a probability distribution over different such sets), as well as "uncertainty" (where still there are the various possible options, only probabilities cannot be assigned). However, this approach seems inappropriate here, for our problem does not arise as one of accounting for judgments in situations of "moral risk", but in the context of choice among alternative actions whose morally relevant features overlap and whose outcomes are certain. There seems to be no intuitive reason for introducing apparatus based upon probability considerations to this different problem. It seems more desirable to find a method of measurement utilizing only considerations intrinsic to the sort of situation in which our problem arose, or one utilizing only that apparatus that is sufficient to generate the need for a method of measurement. (This procedure has an additional theoretical advantage. If one can establish the existence of numerical scales to be used in principle III, assigning numbers to sets of features, and if one also can use a standard von Neumann–Morgenstern type of procedure to establish numerical scales and assign numbers to these same sets of features, only this time based upon judgments of "moral risk" actions, then one can investigate the relationship between these two scales.)

Let me sketch another procedure of measurement, first presenting it in a way that looks circular. Principle III tells us not to do an action with W features if its extra wrongness over another alternative outweighs its extra rightness; let us suppose this principle has sufficient virtues and appeal so that, if there *were* numerical values for moral weights, it would be this principle that was operating (within the moral realm, and also underlying people's moral judgments). Based upon this supposition, we can obtain, for a particular person, various inequalities between differences. The ordinal rankings of moral weightiness present no special or insuperable problems; so we may present a person with a situation of two actions A and B, where A has some W features, and $R_A > W_A$, $R_B > W_B$, $W_A > > W_B$, and $R_A >> R_B$. Act A has weightier W features than B does, and has weightier R features also. If on the basis of this, the person judges that act A is morally impermissible then (given the supposition that principle III is operating) we can conclude that for him $(W_A - W_B) > (R_A - R_B)$. By presenting him with other similarly structured situations for judgment, we will obtain additional such inequalities between differences. If we can obtain enough of these inequalities, this will provide sufficient information to assign numbers that measure the moral weight of these sets of features.

If a person is following principle III, implicitly utilizing certain numerical weights, then he will satisfy certain other conditions as well, necessary for the consistent following of principle III. These other conditions, however, can be formulated without utilizing the full numerical apparatus of principle III. What removes the apparent circularity in the proposed procedure of measurement is that these other conditions themselves, without mention of principle III, provide a sufficient basis for the desired measurement of moral weight.

An example of one such condition is the following: if for the person there are three actions, A, B, and C, each having its R features outweigh its W features, such that $W_A \gg W_B \gg W_C$ and $R_A \gg R_B \gg R_C$, and the person judges that it is impermissible to do A in a situation when B is available, and he judges that it is impermissible to do B in a situation when C is available, then this person also judges that it is impermissible to do A in a situation when C is available. This condition does not utilize any numerical apparatus; it uses only the ordering notions presumed to be available. Furthermore, it is an intuitively reasonable condition, one whose imposition does not depend upon any considerations about the existence of scales of measurement.

The task would be to gather a number of such conditions, each necessary for the existence of the scale of measurement yet each having an independent status of its own, which would suffice to prove the existence of a scale measuring moral weight, on an interval scale. I shall describe how this task proceeds, but not attempt to do it. For some locution already available for discussing relationships in situations specified using only "ordinal" apparatus, one introduces an n-place relation. Some selection of the intuitively justifiable and presumably empirically satisfied statements using this locution are imposed as conditions on this n-place relation. If one has chosen well, wisely or luckily, using these conditions on the n-place relation as axioms, one may be able to prove a Representation Theorem that shows there exists a real-valued function assigning numbers that mirror the n-place relation, in that specified numerical relations hold among the assigned numbers if and only if the corresponding n-place relation about the subject matter holds among the objects to which the numbers are assigned; and also prove a Uniqueness Theorem that shows that any two real-valued functions shown to exist by the Representation Theorem stand in a certain mathematical relationship to each other. The more limited this relationship, the stronger the scale of measurement one has obtained.[86] There is no point here to engaging in the technical task of specifying such axioms that are reasonable for the moral context and yield such results. The literature contains various axiom systems that focus upon four-place inequality relations between differences; it is not a very daring conjecture that one of these systems, or some modification, will suffice for the present task.[87]

The Complex Structure: Larger Courses of Action

The simple balancing structure, we have seen, is inadequate in view of considerations about alternative courses of action—the higher level principle III therefore is appropriate. Considerations about larger courses of action prompt further modifications in the simple structure.

Some action A, where $W_A > R_A$, might be (a necessary) part of a larger course of action B, such that $R_B > W_B$; might not such an action A be morally permissible, even though (focusing upon it alone) its W features outweigh its R features? Consider the following two examples:

1. A person is unjustly pent up by another person; you steal a key to the door from some innocent third party, making it possible for you to release the prisoner. I assume that this theft is permissible when and only when it is part of the larger course of action of effecting the release of the prisoner. If, for example, after stealing the key, you go on to throw it away or sell it or put it in your scrapbook, then your stealing of the key (and not attempting to release the captive person) was impermissible.

Thus, I assume that the wrong-making features of the act of key stealing outweigh its right-making features (and that "making it possible for you to release the person" either is not an R feature of that act or, if it is, does not, when combined with the act's other R features, override its W features); yet even so, it may be permissible to steal the key. The second example is somewhat more controversial morally.

2. A known terrorist is tortured in order to discover and thwart the plans, known to be on the verge of execution, of his terrorist group—plans he helped formulate and set in motion. The saving of these many innocent lives can outweigh, it seems to me, the torturing of this (guilty and complicitous) person, so that act of torture would be permissible as part of the larger course of action of saving these lives. However, if the person were tortured but not questioned, or the information gained was merely filed away and ignored, then the torturing was morally impermissible.

Thus, it seems that $W_A > R_A$ may not be sufficient for the impermissibility of A, for A may be a necessary part of a larger permissible course of action. The principles to take account of this complication are complex to formulate; we cannot simply say that A is a necessary part of a larger course of action B such that $R_B > W_B$, for this act B may itself be impermissible because it is undercut by some alternative action in accordance with principle III. The details of these new principles IV and V are best presented in a note.[88] These additional principles can be incorporated along with principle III into a model of a moral structure to replace the simple balancing structure; let us call this revised model the *multi-leveled balancing structure*.[89] This or something similar, I think, structures the moral pull and delineates the form of responsiveness, to the extent it is open to abstract statement.

Deontology and Teleology

There are two powerful and intuitively appealing molds into which theorists have fitted or poured substantive ethics: a deontological one and a teleological one. The teleological one views ethical action as directed toward the achievement of the (perhaps complex) good; an action (or the rules it follows) is to be judged by whether it serves to maximize the world's goodness score. A deontological view, on the other hand, specifies what it is right to do independently (at least partially) of the notion of the good. (I take this characterization from Rawls.) Thus, it places restrictions on what actions may be done (even to advance the good), and so it would classify as morally impermissible some acts that might, in the circumstances, best advance the world's goodness score. These restrictions on the pursuit of the good will constitute side constraints if the deontological view includes exceptionless moral principles.

Writers tend to plunk for one of these forms, deontological or teleological, and quickly "refute" the other, perhaps with the aid of a few artfully chosen examples. However, this procedure ignores the powerful and deep intuitive force of the rejected alternative, a force which is not merely to be explained away as the result of a simple mistake or illusion. Can deontology and teleology somehow be harmonized in an ethical view that preserves the insights of each?

494

Let me briefly mention some possible modes of combination.

1. Deontology as superstructure. While teleology is the correct theory, deontological rules are good rules of thumb to follow in attempting to maximize the good. By following these rules people will approximate (perhaps as best they can, and it might be dangerous to give each individual discretion about when to deviate) the results of the correct underlying teleological principle: maximize the world's goodness score.

This view is proposed by many utilitarian writers; however, it gives deontological considerations insufficiently fundamental weight.

2. Peaceful coexistence in a division of labor. For one sort of problem or choice a deontological theory is correct, while for another, a teleological one is.

In *Anarchy, State, and Utopia,* I wrote: "The question of whether these side constraints are absolute, or whether they may be violated in order to avoid catastrophic moral horror, and if the latter, what the resulting structure might look like, is one I hope largely to avoid" (p. 30). I imagined that teleological considerations would take over to avert "moral catastrophe", but did not specify what determines where this transition takes place. However, I did not imagine the transition as smooth, rather as one that would fit what now is called mathematical "catastrophe theory". This division of labor effectively gives the victory to deontological theory, without explaining the force teleological considerations have even in the noncatastrophic cases.

3. Another way to try to give each of deontology and teleology its due is not by specifying their separated applications, but by specifying different sources for each.

The deep and long-standing ethical conflict between deontology and teleology, each having strong intuitive force, would be neatly and satisfyingly explained if, for example, one view was the appropriate structuring of the ethical pull while the other was the appropriate structuring of the ethical push. Such simplicity is too much to expect. No doubt, things would be more intertwined; some strands of the ethical pull and some of the ethical push would be appropriately structured deontologically, while other strands of each would be appropriately structured teleologically. To isolate these strands would be to uncover the intuitive force of the deontological and the teleological views, but it would not provide any way for us to reconcile them, we who are both pulled and pushed. Nevertheless, such a view, while it would not reconcile the two standpoints, would grant each its strong and legitimate intuitive force.

4. Since the basic moral characteristic which exerts moral pull on us is a complex characteristic, containing at least the distinguishable components "being an I" and "being a value-seeker", there may be a difference in how responsiveness to each of these components is structured. Perhaps responsiveness to one component will be deontological in form while responsiveness to the other will be teleological.

This view leaves unresolved how the two modes of responsiveness are to be fitted together, in those situations where there is apparent conflict between them. Even if the conflict is resolved by a lexical ranking of the two components of the basic moral characteristic, and so of the responses to them, we may be left with the feeling that the action is flawed, leaving something not responded to appropriately.

5. Another possible approach, unfortunately one I have no further ideas about, would be to try to transcend the distinction between teleological and deontological, to see each alternative as saying something correct about the ethics of a partially developed person, whereas a fully developed person would face no conflict between these modes, perhaps because a truly good teleological aim (of the sort he would have) simply could not be achieved by any deontologically impermissible means.

It would be nice if this were so—it seems false, though, and I do not see how to develop this possibility further.

The third and fourth of the above suggestions seems especially interesting and promising. However, it is another possibility I wish to pursue here. Considerations about goodness or value can be applied to two different things, to the world as a whole or to the actions available to a person. Which thing is it whose goodness or value score the person is to maximize, that of the world as a whole or that of the action he does?

The usual formulations of teleological theories recommend that a person do that act whose consequence is better than the consequence of any other action available; if there is a tie the person is to do one of those acts whose consequence ties for best. (When the consequences are not certain, but are risky or uncertain mixtures of yet other consequences, a more complicated evaluation of an act's upshot is needed, such as its expected value.)

To this it might be objected that even though one act may have the best consequences, nonetheless, it might be wrong to do because it violates some moral restrictions or constraints.[90] Note that the teleological end-state view speaks of the best consequence, while the opposing view speaks of the right act. The teleologist also would speak of the best act, which he views as the act with the best consequences. (His opponent normally does not speak of the best act, perhaps because he too assumes that, unlike "right", the term "best" applied to an action must match the best consequence—thus he avoids saying that the best act is wrong, or that the right act is not best.)

However, it is not automatically true that the best act is the one with the best end state consequences. What we choose among is not consequences, but rather doing various actions. Therefore, one formulation of a position that bids us to maximize the good is: do the act, the doing of which is best. The different acts available in choice situations often will involve different verbs, that is, different relations to different end states rather than the same verblike relationship to different end states. For example, one will be a bringing on, another a preventing, one a causing, another an allowing to happen. Since these different action relationships will involve differing degrees of unity with other people and end states, the goodness of the acts need not vary directly with the goodness of their consequences. (There is no conflict between our reflections here and the earlier condition of adequacy on the greater value of V-ing more valuable things, which held the V-verb fixed.) Doing that act with the highest score along the value dimension D is not the same as maximizing the D score of the world. The dimension D itself sometimes will tell us that some particular act available to someone of maximizing the D score of the world is not the act, of those available to him, with the highest D score. Such considerations arise with the doctrine of "double effect"; if intentionally bringing something about as an end or as a means to some other goal involves the agent in a tighter (more organically unified) relationship to this result than does producing it knowingly as a side effect (when it is no part of the aim or means), then doing these acts may differ in value.

Deontological concerns can thus be mirrored or presented naturally within a teleological framework concerned with maximizing the good. There is a tension within teleological views, in specifying which thing's goodness is to be maximized, the action done (the acting) or the world's resulting state. We can imagine how a discussion might proceed, not only between different people but internally within one. "Why should I maximize goodness of action done rather than goodness of resulting outcome?" Because you are choosing which act to do. "But I also am choosing which outcome to bring about." Only through doing one of the actions. "But why should I maximize the goodness or value of what I am directly choosing, rather than the goodness of the end result?" And so on. Each specification of the object of value-maximizing judgment, whether action or resulting end state, has its own intuitive appeal. A strong concern for value certainly is shown by following the policy of maximizing it in the resulting end states; pursuing resultant value, and bringing it about, establishes a significant connection to value. Still, that connection is less close than the more intimate connections to value in action. These remarks, in my view, advance somewhat the understanding of deontology and teleology in ethics; however (despite my obvious leaning toward deontology) they do not provide an adequate resolution of the conflict—by which I mean not an argument or proof for one of them, but an explanation or understanding of why (or where) one holds while the other does not.

Rights

We have spoken of the moral ought as responsivenss to value, viewing this value as exerting a moral pull, a moral claim on us to which we are to respond. How do these considerations connect with the rights of a person?* Rights are not simply the other side of respon-

* In *Anarchy, State, and Utopia*, I presented a political philosophy based upon a certain view of the content of rights but did not (as I said there) present any moral foundations for that view. One might attempt to provide

siveness, whereby we always would have a right to be treated as others ought to treat us. For this encompasses too much; although others ought to treat us in a certain way in virtue of our basic moral characteristics, not every such treatment is something we have a right to, or a right to demand, or a right to have enforced. Neither do rights correspond simply to all the more serious oughts, those whose neglect would be serious (unless "serious" is specified, trivially in this context, as what violates a right). You have a right to some actions, for example, another's repayment of a borrowed dollar, whose omission does not count as serious (except insofar as it is a rights violation).

We can locate the place of rights within the ethics of responsiveness to value, by noticing that (generally) a right is something for which one can demand or enforce compliance. Supposing you ought to treat me in a certain way, to demand you do so or to enforce your doing so constitutes a certain treatment of you. And we can ask of this treatment whether I or others ought to do it. When people make such demands on you are they being responsive to your basic moral characteristic? If not, then they ought not to treat you like that. Certainly, if such actions by others (of demanding or enforcement) count as anti-responsive to your basic moral characteristic, then it would be morally impermissible for them so to act. On this view, my right that you behave in a certain way toward me would be a function of how you ought to behave toward me and of how others (including me) ought to behave toward you. My rights are constituted by the treatment you ought to give me that others ought to demand or enforce of you—or at least, it is not the case that they ought not demand it. A view of my rights must focus both on how I ought to be treated and how you ought: it must consider if forcing you to behave in a certain way toward me is responsive not only to my basic moral characteris-

---

such a foundation either by working back from the view, step by step, or by starting at the very foundations of moral philosophy and working forward. If this latter course, pursued without too much glancing ahead, does succeed in linking up with the specified rights, then it will provide them with independent support. There also is the risk, however, that this forward motion from the foundations will lead to a completely different view, as the construction of a transcontinental railroad starting from both coasts could fail to link up, instead leading to two full railroad lines. We do not pursue the construction here extensively enough in the direction of political philosophy to be able to see if there are two lines or one.

tic but also to yours; it must consider whether that forcing of you would not be anti-responsive to your own basic moral characteristic, and thus anti-responsive to your value.

Under this conception, there is a significant distinction between its being morally impermissible (or required) that others behave in a certain way toward me, something they oughtn't (or ought) to do, and my having a right that they behave (or not behave) a certain way. Some of the ways you ought to treat me, I have no right to, no right to demand or enforce. This is not to minimize or slight the importance of these oughts concerning your behavior, of these moral pulls upon you. However, not every moral pull on you, morally significant as it is, important as it may be in morally judging you, constitutes a right against you. If the moral pull on you is exerted by the valuable characteristics of others, it also is limited by your own valuable characteristics. These characteristics of you preclude certain actions of others, even when done in order to prevent or avoid your defaulting in certain of your responses to another's value.

It is an intricate task to delineate how all the oughts and ought nots, permissibilities and impermissibilities on responses and anti-responses to people's valuable characteristics, coagulate so as to constitute (enforceable) rights. We must beware of excessively simple delineations of the resulting pattern. We do not, for example, have a right against any and all anti-responsiveness to our valuable characteristics; we have no right that others not scorn these or demean them in peaceful verbal action, or that philosophers not deny they exist. Nevertheless, anti-responsiveness, especially that which causes some diminution in the value anti-responded to, will be a prime area to investigate in formulating the rights of people.[91] We can understand some disagreements about whether people in dire situations have a right to (positive) aid from others who were not (wrongfully) responsible for their being in those situations, as stemming from a disagreement about whether non-aiding is anti-responsive or merely non-responsive, and about whether or not compelling such aid is anti-responsive to the valuable characteristics of the compelled party.[92] If your basic moral characteristic of being a value-seeking individual includes weighting values in free choice, as described in the first part of the previous chapter, then being responsive to this characteristic and to the originative value you possess will involve respecting your autonomy. Within this domain it will be impermissible for others even to force you away from the bad or less good toward the best; doing so would be anti-responsive to your capacity as a weighter of values. Thereby is a right to personal liberty delineated.

However, this coagulation of oughts does not seem to demarcate exactly our conception of rights. It might be that for various reasons no one ought to force someone not to do something—perhaps such forcing will cause severe mental disturbance or breakdown—yet still that person does not have a right to do it. To delineate a right, it seems that the oughts must congregate not only appropriately, but also for the right reason. (To specify this reason as "because he has a right to do it" would not illuminate the nature and status of rights.)

One view would be the following. It is important and valuable that a person have a range of autonomy, a range or domain of action where he may choose as he wishes without outside forcing. Recognizing and respecting such a domain of autonomy is a response to the person as a value-seeking self; so we ought to recognize such a domain. This point does not fix the extent or content of the domain. It is important that various people recognize the same domain, though. If I will not force someone about one choice but will about another, while you will not force about the other but will about the first, then although we each respect some domain or other of autonomy, there is not one domain that we both respect. So that person has no domain of autonomy within which he is free to choose without forcing or threats of force by anyone. Part of responding to another as a value-seeking self is to coordinate our specification of the respected domain with others, so that the person does have a generally recognized domain of autonomy, and also to publicly avow our respect for this domain, so that he knows he is autonomous within it and can count on that.

If respecting a domain of autonomy is to be an apt response to a person as a value-seeking self, then this domain must include a range of important and significant choices (such as religious practice, place of residence, choice of mate and lifestyle, choice of occupation), as well as a vast range of trivial choices which go to make up the daily texture of our lives. The choices that are viewed as significant and central to a person's life and self-definition may vary from culture to culture—we can imagine science fiction situations where others view as trivial the choices we hold as centrally important, while viewing other choices (trivial to us) as of great significance. In that society, the domain of autonomy might appropriately be demarcated differently.[93]

There is much to be said for recognizing the widest possible domain of autonomy, limited only by the boundary of not violating the similarly specified autonomy of another. It is unclear, however, whether recognition of the fullest and widest possible autonomy is required by responsiveness to someone as a value-seeking self. At the least though, the limitations must be principled ones, done on the basis of general principles which, if fully followed, would not leave the domain of autonomy so shrunken as to constitute an inadequate response to a person as a value-seeking self. The range of his autonomy you respect cannot be gauged solely by the actions you do, without reference to the principles underlying your actions (and to the principles underlying those); similarly, an accidental (nonnegligent) bumping into a person does not impinge upon his domain of autonomy as would (carrying out) a threat to bump him if he is in a given place.

Hence, we can see how hypothetical examples, showing the consequences of various principles, constitute a test of those principles, not only by the intuitive correctness of the principle's result in a particular case, but by the extensiveness of the various consequences of the principle and the degree to which they would shrink a person's recognized autonomy. Thereby, it seems that the requirement that intrusion into autonomy be principled might establish an even wider domain of autonomy than the already wide one that needs to be recognized in order to respond to someone as a value-seeking self. This raises an interesting question about ad hoc limitations on principled reasons that purport to justify intrusions into autonomy. Suppose these reasons, if consistently and fully followed, would lead to a very extensive forcing of people's actions with a consequently greatly shrunken—too greatly, as every one would admit—domain of autonomy. Might a proponent then suggest that we not follow such reasons consistently and fully, only up to but not beyond the point where the domain of autonomy is shrunk to a certain specified size consonant with responding to a person as a value-seeking self? If this type of principle cannot be excluded, then (insofar as our current line of thought can say) rights need extend only so far as to constitute an adequate domain of autonomy. Even this is not a meagre result, for such a domain may be quite extensive.

The notion of respecting freedom to act within a domain of autonomy is a modern idea. Within the theory presented here, such respecting of freedom of action is seen as responsive to a value-seeking I qua value-seeking I. This illustrates our earlier point about the open-endedness of the lists of right-making and wrong-making features, specifying responsiveness and anti-responsiveness. It can *come* to be seen that recognizing such a domain of autonomy constitutes responsiveness to a value-seeking self, and we can see this dawning realization as moral progress, as more fully developed moral insight.

Political philosophy, as I see it, is mainly the theory of what behavior legitimately may be enforced, and of the nature of the institutional structure that stays within and supports these enforceable rights. (The state usually is distinguished by political theorists as the organ of—the institutionalized monopoly over—the legitimate use of force.) In no way does political philosophy or the realm of the state exhaust the realm of the morally desirable or moral oughts. It is a mark of the politicization of our times, and of the decline of other institutions that used to support the fabric of how we ought to act, that so many people nowadays see the state as the basis of all human decency and decent society, if not as coextensive with it. But rights are not the whole of what we want a society to be like, or of how we morally ought to behave toward one another. Political philosophy is not a complete moral theory, nor was meant to be. These other moral oughts, though, must flourish within the interstices of rights, including people's rights not to be forced to do certain things—rights they have if others ought not to force them, if we ought or may demand that they not do so, and may force *their* compliance. The reason rights come to be so central to political philosophy, although they are not the central moral phenomena, is that the state is demarcated as the organ monopolizing the (legitimate) use of force. It is in this domain of the exertion of force, interpersonally as well as politically, that rights play the central moral role, and talk of rights comes most easily. There are higher and more refined moral notions. To complain as some do at the crudity and bluntness of rights and of their centrality in political philosophy, ignores the fact that the use of force itself, the political differentia with which rights deal, is no less crude and blunt.

A person's rights, we have said, are a function of how he ought to be treated, and how others ought to be treated with regard to their behavior toward him. It follows that there is a possibility that rights can be transcended. It may be that at a certain level of someone's development others ought to treat him in certain ways, yet at a higher level of his development others no longer ought to do so, for their previous behavior no longer would be responsive to his (now) most valuable characteristics. This is not to say merely that at a higher level of development he may not want to stand on or demand certain rights, although this may well be true, but rather that at this level of development certain treatments of him no longer are responsive to what he is like. Since others, then, no longer ought to treat him that way, a necessary condition is absent for his having a right to that treatment. Is this one reason why the literature of spiritual development places so little weight on rights; or do these writers replace all rights by the one right not to be impeded in spiritual development?

IV. THE LIFE OF VALUE

Self-Improvement

Despite the fact that the sanction for immoral behavior is a value sanction which may be distinct from a person's own felt motivations, still, there are illuminating connections between value or morality, and self-interest. The tradition attempts to show that morality and self-interest, Plato terms them justice and happiness, coincide. There are different ways to try to do this. Starting with independent notions of morality and of self-interest, one might try to show these coincide. (Will this coincidence be contingent, or a synthetic necessary one?) Second, self-interest might be an independent notion, while morality can be defined or coherently specified only (partly) in terms of self-interest; or third, morality might be an independent notion, while self-interest can be defined or coherently specified only (partly) in terms of it. The fourth possibility is an investigation that begins with neither notion fully specified; each would get specified in the course of the joint investigation of these two notions. Neither of these resultant notions of morality and self-interest, should they be shown to coincide, need be those we ordinarily use. However, they should be (uniquely) obtainable from our ordinary notions and view by a philosophical investigation that, uncovering the inadequacies and incoherencies in the ordinary notions, thereupon deepens and revises them in order to make them more adequate.[94]

The progressive modifications of our notions of morality and self-interest, of justice and happiness, need not occur only through philosophical discussion or the reading of literature. Insights and notions also are deepened by living a certain way. This suggests another procedure. Starting with a person's own view of the best life and the most moral life, transform him so that he leads this best life (in his view) while also leading as moral a life as is compatible with this best life; in addition, let this life include philosophical discussion of these (initial) notions of bestness and morality. As a result of leading this reflective life in accordance with his own notions of bestness and of morality (insofar as this is compatible with bestness), these notions of his may undergo change. If so, the same procedure is repeated; let him now live in accordance with his transformed notion of the best life, a life as moral (according to his transformed notion) as is compatible with living this best life. Iterate this process.

The Platonic thesis is that eventually the two notions will stabilize, undergoing no further change (or at least, that two fixed notions can be identified as the limit of this process) and these two notions will be identical or necessarily coincident (or subjunctively coextensive) so that if one were to apply the other would as well. The Platonic thesis would be incorrect if in this iterative process of living in accordance with one's philosophically discussed concepts, the two concepts never came together permanently, either never coming together or coming together only to diverge later in the iteration.[95]

Similar iterations can be imagined with a (specified) notion of objective value, linking it on the one hand to perceived self-interest, and on the other hand to morality. Two further Platonic theses are that within these iterative processes, a person's notion of self-interest will converge with the objective notion of value, so he will come to think (and feel) that he is best off being most valuable, he will feel his interest lies in being valuable; also that his notions of morality and value will converge, so that he comes to think the most valuable life and the most moral one are one and the same.

Although we do not actually undergo this full iteration, we do sometimes change our conception of how we should (best or most morally) live, and change accordingly (though not always fully) how we actually do live—this leads to further changes in our conceptions. This process of transformation is only partial: for most of us there is occasional backsliding, and the process does not come to an end in our lifetime, though it does stop. The process of philosophical reflection itself—like coming close to death—produces a rethinking of goals, a reassessing of what is really important. This change of goals not only reorders and reranks the old ones, it also excludes some while introducing new ones.

The philosophical literature from Plato to Thoreau contains calls to reexamine and reorder our lives, sometimes describing the results within particular persons (Socrates, Thoreau at Walden Pond). The call itself sometimes has significant effects, apart from its particular vision of the best life. It sounds empty and trivial merely to be told to live one's life in accordance with what one really thinks is important. The mark of our failing to do so is the impact this simple advice can have. (True, it is difficult to maintain one's sense of urgency about matching one's life to one's vision; but though this is a puzzle, it is not a problem for the iterated process as described.)

One way an examination of priorities can increase the coincidence (or lessen the conflict) between morality and self-interest is by removing certain motives or lessening their weight. The motives for many immoral acts (and crimes) would not exist in any strength after philosophical reflection. Increased luxury, power over others, and so on, would no longer function as strong goals; and presumably few would choose to be prone to the emotions (such as rage and jealousy) under which many wrongs are done. Still, this reordering of priorities would not eliminate wrongs committed for a good purpose, for instance, accepting tax funds or stealing in order to advance philosophical research or to perfect oneself.

Harmonious Hierarchical Development

Plato held we could distinguish and rank "parts of the soul", the rational, spirited, and appetitive parts. Furthermore, he held that we are best off when these parts are in an ordered relation whereby the highest part, the rational part, is in control. Plato means to exclude either lower part alone from ruling the higher rational part, as well as majority rule under which the lower two combine to outweigh the highest part. However, he does not intend that we should concentrate solely on the development or exercise of the highest part. The others are to be developed also, but this joint development is never to be at the expense of the highest part. There are no tradeoffs between the highest and what is lower. Under this hierarchical view, the ranking of the parts of the soul is reflected in a lexical ordering: first maximize the development of the highest part and subject to this constraint maximize the development of the next part, and subject to the two foregoing constraints, maximize the development of the lowest part.

This joint hierarchical development is not a harmonious development. The lower parts simply are oppressed, although less so than if they never counted at all and did not occur anywhere along the vector structuring the lexical ordering. In a harmonious development, the lower parts are transfigured and transformed by the higher parts so as to become more like them; the higher infuses them.[96] (We need not pause here to decide whether, when the parts are ordered ABC, A alone infuses C, or A and B—as infused by A—infuse and transform C.) Under harmonious development, the conflict among the parts largely disappears. The lower parts also are developed, and the higher part no longer merely constrains maximizing the lower dimensions, as in the hierarchical lexical ordering. These lower or less valuable dimensions are transformed so as to partake of the higher; sexuality is transformed by love or intimacy, egoistic desire by the care for others, and so on. Notice that this structure of harmonious joint hierarchical development is independent of the particulars of Plato's position. One might accept such a structure while altering Plato's ordering of the parts, or adding another part he does not mention (for example, the spiritual) and ranking it as prior to his three, or even by substituting completely different parts.[97] As noted earlier, a view such as Plato's, which ranks parts of the soul, will need some other principle of value to generate this ranking, unless the ranking simply expresses a rule of thumb about when there is greater value, that is, organic unity. The highest part is that one which, when in control, yields the greatest organic unity.

Debunkers sometimes come along and say, "Aha, you get pleasure out of helping people, developing ideas, and so forth. So it is really the lower part at work here that moves you." Although this strikes listeners as a distortion, it often succeeds in making them uncomfortable. If helping others or developing certain talents ranks higher than personal pleasure, the hierarchical lexical view would say simply that personal pleasure takes second place to these. Harmonious development, however, says that your pleasure should be transformed and transfigured so that it now (also) comes from developing these talents or helping others. If the reason you get pleasure from helping others or developing these talents is that your pleasure has been transformed by an infusion from a higher realm, for instance, the ethical realm, then you should not feel debunked. The reply to "but you get pleasure from that" is: "Yes, I do. Haven't *your* pleasures yet been transformed from above? Do you think the higher should be only a constraint? And does the pleasure you take in such intellectual debunking of what is higher indicate that in your case the lower has infused the higher?"

Even this account of the higher transfiguring the lower does not reveal the full extent of their interpenetration. The higher characteristics themselves become less ethereal and less desiccated by their connection to the more elemental; they become infused with energy, bolder, more daring, more alive, vital, more erotic. If each affects the other, then in what way can their two-way relationship be said to be hierarchical? Think of our activities as a vector, with direction and magnitude. The higher affects the lower by altering its direction, finding new objects of desire or altering how the old ones are conceived and pursued; while the lower characteristics affect the magnitude of the vector, the forceful energy with which one moves in that direction. Perhaps some directions are incapable of containing such energies, so the energies can affect somewhat the direction as well. The relationship of higher to lower is that of steering wheel to gasoline pedal in an automobile (perhaps one where some amount of gasoline is fed merely by the ignition's being on).

Consider the notion of sublimation; this process can be viewed either as making the lower more valuable or as revealing the seamy underside of the (supposedly) higher. Rousseau viewed it the first way, while many readers of Freud seem to draw the second conclusion, debunking and reductionist.[98] We take the first stance, seeing the lower as enhanced, while it invigorates the higher; we shall consider the reductionist view in more detail later.

Harmonious hierarchical development removes or drastically diminishes the divergence between self-interest and morality, provided that there is some objectivity to the selection and ordering of component parts. Not all lessening of the divergence between the two notions need come from the transformation of self-interest; there also can be a transformation and a deepening of the notion of morality. As our view changes about what is in a person's interests and what is the best life, our notions of responsiveness and anti-responsiveness, of helping and harming, also may change and come to have different content. Perhaps we will think of helping as aiding someone along the path of harmonious hierarchical development, and harming as hindering her way along this path, preventing her from moving along it or diverting her from doing so. Thus, moral principles that speak of helping and harming will come to have different consequences; and a moral view will be changed as new features appear on the right-making and wrong-making lists, in accordance with the deepened insights about responsiveness.

509

Developing Self and Others

We have noticed that philosophical reflection and the progressive development of our notions of morality and self-interest may remove or weaken many motivations to wrongdoing. While pursuing our other motivations, what will we gain by benefiting others, or by refraining from harming them? One gain, a theme of much of this chapter, is intrinsic to moral action; it is the value which moral action constitutes. There are extrinsic benefits as well, empirical effects or consequences of moral action that redound to the moral agent. In now turning to discuss some of these, however, we should not forget the primary intrinsic benefit. Nor should the perfectionist aspiration to self-development, for example, to a harmoniously hierarchically ordered being, be interpreted as a denigration of what one hopes to improve on or of others not so intent. If we are to strive for a state judged higher, then something also must be ranked lower: to judge something as less than the best need not involve any elitist contempt for it.

We would benefit by our moral action if our own state of harmonious hierarchical development were affected by the states of those around us. It is not implausible to think we are elevated by others who are more developed than ourselves in their striving for harmonious hierarchical development and for a valuable life. We are aided and encouraged along our own path of development by their striving for self-development and purer feeling; contrast the effects on us of encountering those with a sour mixture of one-upmanship, self-aggrandizement, desire to dominate or destroy, and other festering emotions, the effects of wending our way and bending our attention to their motivations and trajectories. Just as a cacophony of urban noise is an intrusion if you are trying to listen to a string quartet or compose your own, so a person in the course of his own self-improvement or development will want, if merely as a means, to help raise the developmental level of those around him. (Or else to move into an isolated community of like-spirited persons.) He will want to help them along.

Even if a person were able to maintain his level and rate of (spiritual) advance and development unperturbed by others around him, not dragged down by them no matter what their state, he still would lack the benefits of associating with others who are equally or more developed. First, there is the benefit of being helped along by good examples and good companions. We all know people, I hope, who bring out the best in us, people in whose presence we would be embarrassed to speak or act from unworthy motives, people who glow. In their presence we feel elevated. We are pushed or lured or nudged further along a path of development and perfection; rather, we are inspired to move ourselves along, in the direction shown.*

Second, there is the joy in encountering a like person, in the experience of the other and in the mutual recognition of the mutual joy. The most intense delights, surely, are these experiences, at least as they combine with, enrich, and transfigure other delights more frequently listed. One awful psychological deformity is the resentment of excellence, not merely the inability to delight or take pleasure in it—bad enough—but the envious desire for its absence.[99] To avoid being the object of such envy, people will hide their own excellence and camouflage their delight in it. Not only does this deprive others of the encouragement of an example, and of the opportunity for happy mutual recognition, it also alters the person's own experience. She does not simply feel the same delight only without expressing it; an unexpressed delight is not as delightful. Resentment and envy of moral and spiritual excellence is most awful. (I would like to think this is diminished face-to-face, in actual meeting.) Feeling envy, I conjecture, is not in equilibrium; someone who knew the causes of his feeling envy would not want to feel it or act upon it. At any rate, persons developing in value will not feel or dwell in such envy; they will seek out opportunities to share the joy of being on and moving along their path. They will aid others in their own (spiritual or developmental) advance, for the pleasure of their company. (In thus aiding, they will not focus their attention upon their own pleasure but rather upon what brings that pleasure—the developed state of the others.)

There is a third reason for wanting other equally or more developed persons around: their appreciation is especially worth having. In a loving relationship with another adult, the worth of what they give, including themselves, depends partially upon their estimation of themselves—whether they give something they hold precious and

* Socrates is described as having this effect, even upon the worldly Alcibiades. Judah Halevi says, "He who converses with a prophet experiences spiritualization during the time he listens to his oration" (*Kuzari* I, 103).

valuable. This will affect your estimation of the relationship, of the value of what is given and of the giver. A ventriloquist cannot benefit from hearing the laudatory words of the puppet he operates; did Edgar Bergen go through life cheered by the esteem of Charlie McCarthy? Similarly, the esteem most worth having comes from those you most esteem.*

The developed or developing person will wish for like companions, for inspiring examples to aid him along his path, for joyous company, and for meaningful affirmation of his own worth. This is the opposite of the desire to be surrounded by submissive people less developed than oneself, the desire that they be less developed. That desire is revelatory, as is the belief that developed persons may well have it. (This is simply a remark. I do not mean to bludgeon critics into silence, as it is said Freudian psychologists infuriatingly do when they attribute all criticism to resistance.)

Hegel's discussion of the master-slave relationship does not provide from the master's point of view, a general argument against slavery, merely against his being surrounded solely by slaves. Could he not have some equals who provide worthwhile esteemed companions, plus slaves? Similarly, couldn't a person on a path of harmonious hierarchical development desire some similar companions, while using yet other contemporaries or at any rate not minding their presence and so not aiding them? We already have mentioned the effect of dragging-down, which the developing person will wish to avoid; but there is more to say about intrinsic features of development. There is reason to believe the developed person will come to treasure all beings, wanting to aid them along a similar path of development to the extent this is possible. It is reported that many who have had mystical experiences come to feel a preciousness of all persons if not all (living) things. (Some traditions hold this valuing of others to be a precondition or significant aid for the experiences.) To be sure, we find differences. The bodhisattva of Mayahana Buddhism will not choose to enter nirvana until everyone can accompany him, whereas the Arahat of Theravada Buddhism will individually enter nirvana,

---

* In unfortunate combination with this Hegelian point is the possibility produced by low self-esteem, that someone's esteem of another can vary inversely with the other's esteem of him, as in Groucho Marx's, "I wouldn't join any country club that would have me as a member."

without helping to bring along the rest. (However, perhaps he believes there is little he can do to help bring the rest along.)*

There remains the fact that persons of a certain development, including some central figures of various religious traditions, pour forth a deep and overwhelming love. No doubt, it is difficult to be resentful or rigidly unyielding in the face of such love and concern, great enough often (but not always) to express itself in an absolute pacifism; therein lies what effectiveness pacifism has as an interpersonal tactic. The ways in which a path of development may (will?) bring along with it such a loving concern would take us far from the usual tracks of psychological explanation. However, we need not reach so far as to mystical experiences or saintly figures, in order to find intrinsic benefit in aiding others toward further development.[100]

The developed person will want to help perfect others; this is the most important aid he can give them. We want to find a way of living whereby our best energies and talents are poured out so as to speak to and improve the best energies and talents of others.[101] We want to utilize our highest parts and energies in a way that helps others to flourish.

Farmers provide something important, a necessary condition for the flourishing and even living of a large number of others; yet, while farming draws upon a valuable range of nurturative and foresightful characteristics, providing food neither utilizes the highest capacities of farmers nor speaks (directly) to the highest capacities of those who eat it. To be a doctor draws upon high capacities, although not the highest, yet it does not directly serve and enhance those capacities in others. It improves people, but not in the manner they exercise their highest capacities. Can the current practice of farming and medicine be transformed so as both to draw upon and to serve high capacities? Artists and religious teachers draw upon high capacities and sometimes (as did philosophers once upon a time) draw forth those of others, depending upon the character of their work, and of the others.

I have emphasized valuable capacities as a first approximation.

* Sometimes it is said in the Indian ethical tradition that, realizing the unity between yourself and another, you will not harm him since (you realize) that would be harming yourself. On the other hand, a nonpaternalist view might say that, he being you, you then have the right to harm *him*.

What we want is that our life and work shall be an expression of harmonious hierarchical development, and aid such development in others.

The mechanism of the market lures one to serve the wants of others, but does not lure one to serve their highest capacities or their harmonious hierarchical development, except insofar as others express their desire for this within the market. Nor need working in the market draw directly upon our own highest capacities and motivations. To be sure, it can be a means toward satisfying such motives; money may be earned in the marketplace in order to spend it upon advancing the highest and most worthy causes. It is better to improve one's fellows than (merely) to serve their desires. Within the market, we can serve those of our fellows' desires whose serving also improves them. But the market mechanism does not especially reward us for satisfying those desires, rather than other desires that are neutral toward or even retard those people's improvement.

This is not a criticism of the market our fellows can make; the market serves them no worse than they choose to be served. Furthermore, they can choose to contract into paternalistic limitations whereby a portion of their income is spent only in self-improving fashion. Nevertheless, although they will not complain, we do not wish to serve merely their desires. Is there any mechanism whereby we are led to act to improve others? The market mechanism lures us to satisfy the desires of others by satisfying our own when we do so. Another mechanism might satisfy our desires, whatever they happen to be, as we are improving others; but such a mechanism sometimes would lower us even as it got us to raise others, and it would merely reinforce *our* acting on already existing desires.

The parallel to the market mechanism would be one whereby we are improved as we improve others; our own improvement is served even as we serve that of others. However, no special mechanism is needed here, for it is reasonable to think this generally will occur. In order for virtue to be (or bring) its own reward, no particular bit of institutional apparatus is required (although certain imaginable complicated structures that block this natural occurrence must be absent).

A person has the task of finding a path that harmonizes his own value and spiritual improvement while advancing the value and spiritual improvement of others; the strongest connection would be a path that maximizes both.* To find such a path, aiding others in the development of the same high capacities one is exercising, is to solve for oneself the conflict between self-interest and morality.

I have no proof that under all circumstances there will be such a path maximizing your own harmonious hierarchical development while best serving (of those courses of action available to you) that of others, so that no tradeoffs between these will be necessary. Especially if the characteristics different people are willing or prepared to exercise differ in their nature and value, might this be a problem. Plato faced this problem as the issue of why an enlightened person would return to the cave and interact with others in a way helpful to them.† Might not some spiritually advanced persons flourish best only by going off by themselves, because interaction with us will not draw upon or significantly exercise their highest capacities? Yet the examples of tzaddiks, rishis, and bodhisattvas encourage us to think that (even) for those at that exalted level the conflict is not so very serious. (Though perhaps we learn selectively only of those who choose to interact with others, and not of the rest; or perhaps these figures could do even more for the others but trade this off against their own development.) There is no guarantee of a path to maximize both your own harmonious hierarchical development and also that of others. However, ethical responsiveness does not demand you most enhance the development of others, only that you respond to their value as value, that you treat them as having the value they do have. Between such responsiveness and your own value, your own harmonious hierarchical development, there is no conflict at all.

Flourishing

Aristotle held that what is special to a thing marks its function, and so fixes its peculiarly appropriate form of behavior, its mode of flourishing. But no conclusion could depend, in this way, on some prop-

---

* If the person slows down or sacrifices his development and exercise of his own most valuable capacities, slowing his own harmonious hierarchical development, this will leave him in a lesser position to aid others by example or cooperation, and so will lessen what they can receive from him.

† Plato never faced the rest of his task: persuading the people to let the philosopher rule them. The *Republic* describes people as born and socialized into such a society; Plato's only portrayal of the transition to the rule of the philosopher depends upon some ruler turning out to be a philosopher.

erty being special to man. Suppose it turned out that some other being somewhere, for example, dolphins, also had this property—would that alter the conclusion about what constitutes man's appropriate flourishing?* How could anything depend on the property's being special? Could something of moral interest that did not follow from

Man has P

in conjunction with other (true) premisses nonetheless follow from these premisses conjoined with

Man has P, and nothing else has P?

Could discoveries of life on other planets show us that our fundamental moral conclusions do not follow? If man turned out to be unique only in having a sense of humor, would it follow that he should concentrate his energies on inventing and telling jokes? And what if "what is unique in man is that he can be driven by impulses to kill and to torture, and that he feels lust in doing so; he is the only animal that can be a killer and destroyer of his own species without any rational gain, either biological or economic"?[102]

If some conclusion about the flourishing appropriate to man follows from his having a certain property, surely it is in virtue of the nature of that property, not because other beings do not possess it.† True, we do not apply the same moral standards and principles to the other beings we actually have encountered as we do to man; because of this, we can ask which properties man has in virtue of which moral principles apply to him, in virtue of which he is a moral agent and a subject of moral judgments. Something fundamental to ethics does lie in those properties that do distinguish man from other actually

* It might be said, in defense of the Aristotelean position, that here we would have discovered a new kind of thing (man or dolphin) and the property, P, would be special to it. Still, there might be nothing special to man; all his nice properties might be had by other things which have further superior properties Q also, ones man does not have. Call these things, merely for a label, angels. Would it now be said that man (or dolphin) does have something special (that even angels do not have), namely, P and not-Q?

† Earlier, uniqueness answered our concern about someone being valued for being himself, and not merely as the bearer of a characteristic or property. However, there is no apparent reason for any comparable concern about being valued as a member of a particular class, or exhibiting a value peculiar to that class.

encountered things, but nothing morally fundamental depends on the fact that these properties are distinguishing ones.[103]

The problem with the Aristotelean framework is that a special property need not be an especially valuable one. Yet surely what should flourish are your valuable characteristics, especially if their exercise constitutes further value. This suggests the view that the best life is one in which your most valuable characteristic most flourishes. (Note that here we need an independent theory of value, other than Aristotle's; specialness does not guarantee demarcation of value.) This view, we might say, sees your Aristotelean function as the exercise of your most valuable characteristic. Yet why should the focus be only upon that one characteristic? Surely if you have other valuable characteristics, these too should be exercised, provided this is not at the cost of the most valuable one. Thereby, one might be led to a view of flourishing as harmonious hierarchical development, where the rank ordering of characteristics is based upon an independent notion of value, not upon facts about specialness.

Let me make one further remark on specialness. If value is degree of organic unity, then specialness may have a role in producing the greatest overall organic unity. Your exercising your most valuable characteristic may not contribute much to the overall diversity when many others have and exercise that characteristic (unless that characteristic when exercised will produce a diversity), but your exercising a special characteristic (provided it is somewhat valuable) *would* contribute to the greatest overall diversity. (We also have to imagine that all this somehow gets unified.) Thus, there is the possibility of a conflict between your good (which lies in exercising your most valuable characteristic), and the overall value, to which you might make your greatest contribution by exercising another characteristic of yours, one special to you. These positions would be reconciled if, when you exercise your special characteristic for that reason, that will also be an exercise of your most valuable one.

The Value of Valuers

The theory of the moral pull and the moral push come together in this way. Someone else's basic moral characteristic, being a value-seeking I, exerts a pull on me, a moral claim. I am to treat him as a

517

value-seeking I, cueing and shaping my behavior to his being one, thereby responding to him qua value-seeking I. However, the only way I can respond to his basic moral characteristic in this way is by exercising my own. Responding to his characteristic and to the moral pull it exerts, draws upon my being a value-seeking I and the capacities associated with this. Lower capacities just cannot do an adequately subtle and nuanced job of response.

Compare the situation of the religious person before God, a being of immeasurably higher capacities. The best the person can do is awe, worship, obedience: this is some response, but not one so closely contoured to God's most valuable traits. The person himself, falling far short of the traits to which he is to respond, lacks the capacity to find or conjure up an adequate response, on his own. Yet he wants to respond appropriately to God's most valuable traits, he wants to treat God as having the value God has. What he needs to specify his behavior are detailed instructions from God, such as the 613 mitzvot, the commandments and religious duties. On this view, the mitzvot are aids to our satisfying a more general injunction to treat everything as having the value it has, something we cannot do in this case without external specification. Some commandments, the hukkim, will be puzzling to us—we will not be able to see their particular point, the particular way such behavior symbolizes, I mean is contoured to, God's valuable traits (or to what is valuable about our relationship to God, or to something valuable and important about our situation). The mitzvot do not stand out as unique, but thus find their place within a general theory of responsiveness to value.[104]

I have spoken of how the moral pull and the moral push come together in your behavior toward others: being sensitive to their basic moral characteristic (which sensitivity is pulled) involves the exercise of your own basic moral characteristic, something you are pushed to do anyway. Not only is there a moral push to exercise this characteristic, your own basic moral characteristic exerts a moral pull on you to respond to it. Each value-seeking I is to be treated by you as a value-seeking I, and this includes you yourself. You are to treat yourself as a value-seeking self, and to be responsive to this characteristic of yours. The only way to be so responsive is to develop and exercise the characteristic. Thus, not only are you pushed to exert your basic moral characteristic, it exerts a pull on you to respond to it, which can be done only through your exercising that very characteristic. You have to exercise your capacity as a value-seeking self in order to be responsive to your own possession of that capacity. The basic moral characteristic pulls itself into activity.

We can fail to respond to our own value, our basic moral character-istic, by not exercising the characteristic, by degrading ourselves, by nonrespectful suicide (which, nonetheless, one may have a right to choose to do), and also, I think, by being willing to do anything to save ourselves, viewing nothing as beneath us. In George Orwell's *Nineteen Eighty-Four,* Winston Smith shrieks that the woman he loves should be substituted for himself in the torture, and is left an empty shell; there was no value (whether of the woman, of their rela-tionship, or of his own integrity) that he would not sacrifice to save himself. It might seem that this is to value oneself very greatly, yet one is then not responding to oneself as a V-er of value. The egoist thus has a problem in viewing himself as pursuing value.

The theory of value as specified by the modified Aristotelean the-ory states that we are best off, most valuable, if we exercise and bring to flourishing our most valuable characteristics. The exercise of the very characteristics we are pulled to do in response to someone else's valuable characteristic (or our own) also is what we are pushed to do for our own good and value. We exercise our valuable charac-teristics in being responsive to another's value and, in so doing, we increase our own value. From each according to its value, to each according to its value.

Why is being a value-seeker and responder to value qua value it-self valuable? First, it is a way of linking up with values, and so there is a spillover of value. Furthermore, the linkup instituted by seeking value and responding to it is itself a mode of unity; this unity of us with value is itself valuable. (Seeking value is an intentional activity, in the sense of Brentano, and tightly links us with value.) Third, values are inert; they can have no effect in the world without seekers of and responders to value, who give them effect and realize them. In the language of chemistry, we are value reagents. Thus, value seekers and responders have a cosmic role: to aid in the realization of value, in the infusion of value into the material and human realm.[105]

There is a further mode of value in a person's connection with value, his originative value. His action or choice makes a difference to the probabilistic expectation of value in the world, rather than being merely a channel through which the previously extant expectation unfolds. To be originatively responsible for valuable occurrences is to be more closely linked to them (not necessarily in time) than is a mere channel for their realization. Moreover, to the extent one is a self-chooser, one has originative value which contributes to a tight organic unity. In our discussion in the first chapter of the modes of structuring philosophical concepts, we referred to the case of coercion. We saw there that another's intentions might so closely link with one's action as to make it not fully one's own, less so than an act done in the face of equal costs due solely to inanimate nature. (Recall the comparison of the situation where an electrical storm keeps you indoors, with that where another person's threat does so.) Similarly, an externally determined action, even one whose sufficient conditions all are inanimate ones, may be less fully one's own than an uncaused action, freely and nonrandomly done via a self-subsuming weighting of reasons. Thus, an action with originative value will be more fully one's own than one traceable to external sufficient causal conditions; free will and originative value fall under the theory of value as degree of organic unity.[106] And a free choice among alternatives has some value, apart from which alternative is chosen, and even if the choice leads to no further valuable thing and so has no originative value; the closer connection to one's action involved in such a choice is itself a valuable unity.

Not all of our value lies in our being value seekers, value trackers, value responders. As self-reflexive beings we have our own intricate organic unity, our own independent value, not derivative from our connection to other value. However, by concentrating only upon our being seekers of value and potential responders to it, and ignoring our own reflexivity and organic unity, there is the possibility of introducing value by a bootstrap operation.

If there were any value in the universe at all, the characteristic C of being a value seeker and (potential) value tracker would itself be a valuable characteristic. If there were any value in the universe, being a V-er of value itself would be of value. Suppose now that there is no other value existent. Isn't that characteristic C still valuable? This might be denied on the grounds that the characteristic is useless now, a capacity with no target, since there exists nothing upon which it can be exercised. However, there are the other bearers of this capacity C, and each will recognize the other as having value, and so treat the other as valuable. The bootstrapping consists in this: initially the capacity for response to value is the only thing of value, and its bearers eventually develop a valuable network of loci of value. On this view, there is value in the universe (if for no other reason) because we could recognize it if there were, and *that* is valuable.

We have the capacity C of recognizing the presence of value in something in virtue of its having some or another (valuable) characteristic D. Bootstrapping says that even if nothing else is valuable, the capacity C itself is, and if we recognize value in something in virtue of its possessing C—substituting C for D—then everything nicely turns back upon itself. For the bootstrapping to work, however, we have to add that we do recognize value in virtue of C, and that we would do so in an otherwise valueless universe.[107] If any self-reflexive being who seeks after value must think the capacity to do this valuable, even if there is nothing else which is valuable for the capacity to work upon, then value will be introduced by its own bootstraps. (And if the person need not find that capacity valuable under those circumstances, but he just does, then is value introduced in the world by accident?) Seek and ye shall find. And be.

This view might be questioned. "Why should I treat a value seeker with respect, why value value-seeking?" But who is asking this question? Presumably, it is a value seeker; otherwise, what business does he have asking a question about what he should do, a value-seeking question? (Does his teleological activity of asking that question presuppose that seeking value is of value?) It seems broadly inconsistent to value something yet not value valuers of it. "Only x matters, not valuing x or valuers of it." But if valuing x is not valuable, why are you doing *that*? If he agrees that being a value seeker is a valuable characteristic in himself, yet denies this for another, we can grant him that he is valuable, but announce that we are going to ignore that. Thereby, we hope to convince him of the following: if anything is valuable, then so is valuing it; therefore, value seeking and tracking is valuable; therefore, it is valuable when others have this trait. So bootstrapping and related arguments do have some force. Yet, even apart from worries about whether the capacity to value will be held valuable in the absence of other valuable objects,

I admit to feeling something is fishy about these arguments. In any case, while they might carry weight in convincing someone that value seeking is valuable, they will not explain why this is so.

Treating in Accordance with Value

Moral behavior is behavior that is responsive to the basic moral characteristic, behavior that is cued, shaped, and reinforced by that characteristic. (Is the relationship of the ought to the is that the ought responds to the is?) Does the injunction to behave morally stem from a valid general principle or norm that our behavior should be shaped by and respond to all the characteristics it encounters? This seems too strong as a requirement of ethics, even if perhaps tzaddiks, rishis, and zen masters do satisfy it.

If the basic moral characteristic, being a value-seeking I, is simply a person's most valuable property, why should we be responsive only to that; might he not have other valuable characteristics to which we also should respond? Is the structure of our response then to match not merely his one most valuable property, but rather the mix or the lexical value hierarchy of his valuable characteristics? Or should we also take into account his characteristics of negative value? We do not want to respond to these too closely, that is, by exercising the very same characteristics in ourselves. Saintliness, perhaps, lies in responding only to the profile of another's positive characteristics—not merely in the strategic hope that this will lead the other to exercise only those characteristics that draw response.

Is the appropriate principle, then, the following?

Treat everything as having the profile of (positive?) value it has. Be responsive to each thing's valuable characteristic.

Notice that this principle is not limited to the treatment of other persons. Everything, including animals, plants, rocks, paintings, and ecological systems, is to be treated and respected for what it is, for the value it has. Surely it is right that we should not treat things that have value as valueless or as less valuable than they are. On the other hand, to treat something as being more valuable than it is (unless it thereby can be inspired to reach for this greater value) is falsely sentimental and ludicrous. (I leave aside issues about seeing it as the best instantiated, though imperfect, realization of a greater value.)

A constraint on treating everything in accordance with its value is your own value. A due sense of proportion is to be maintained. To carry a principle to extremes is not necessarily to apply it where it doesn't get a foothold, but to apply it and carry it out whatever the costs. A respect for and valuing of animal life leads me not to eat meat or fish and to try to avoid wearing animal products. To spend much energy searching for leather goods made from animals who died naturally would seem extreme to me, as does behaving like the Jains of India, who wear gauze over their mouths and gently sweep the ground before them as they walk, lest they inadvertently swallow or step on an insect. It may not be clear precisely where a line is to be drawn, but the mark of a fanatic who has lost all sense of proportion is that he thinks no line is to be drawn, no cost to himself (or others) is too great when balanced against the slightest application of the principle. I do not think others should be taxed to support my research, and hence do not apply for or accept government research funds; I do not want to participate in this system, even as a way of receiving back unjustly taken tax payments. Yet I do not try to disengage myself completely from all government activities that I wish would not take place, such as mail delivery and public transportation. I am not required to sacrifice a normal life of normal activities in order to avoid all contact with illegitimate activities, especially those that preempt the existence of legitimate private analogues. There is a comparison that must take place, of the badness or evil of the practice weighted by the degree of involvement you would have with it, versus the cost to you (in diminution of a normal life) of disengagement. That such a calculation takes place will seem to some people to mark the position as not a moral one—but this is the complaint of those with no due sense of proportion. A respect for one's own value leads to the calculation, and this respect weighs on both sides, in not wanting significant involvement with evil and in counting the costs to one's normal life and pursuit of values. Each of us will judge others by where they draw the lines, realizing that good people can disagree about their location, yet holding that they must be located at some place other than the endpoints. The intolerant person is easy to identify—he judges that anyone who draws the line on one side of his own is so lax as to be immoral while anyone who draws it on the other side is a fanatic.

Responsive Connection to Reality

Why are we to treat everything in accordance with its value? On the theory of value as organic unity, something's most valuable characteristic (or the organized hierarchy of these) establishes its greatest organic unity, and so interpenetrates and unifies it. To be responsive to that valuable characteristic, therefore, is the way of being most responsive to that something, to the great diversity of it as pulled together in a unity. To respond to its value is to most closely respond to *it*.

Why should we respond to it? To be responsive to the valuable characteristics of things is to be responsive to those things, to align yourself with the world and stand in the most intimate connection with it. We held, in Chapter 3, that we know that p when our belief that p is a true belief and tracks the fact that p. Knowledge is a real (subjunctive) relationship to (and in) the world. The fact that p acts (subjunctively) as a discriminative stimulus for our belief that p, which tracks that fact. However, according to our account of knowledge, the belief need not be connected to the fact more closely, for instance, be shaped and contoured by it. (Some theories of meaning, called picture theories, hold that a proposition signifies by picturing a fact, by being isomorphic with its structure, which structure somehow is reflected or represented in the psychological state of believing the proposition; Wittgenstein presents such a theory in his *Tractatus Logico-Philosophicus*. These theories would establish a more intimate connection between belief and fact than merely the discriminative one of tracking.) Actions also can connect us up with the world; beliefs track facts (as discriminative stimuli), while actions can contour themselves after the unification of many diverse facts through something's valuable characteristics. Thereby actions are shaped by facts, and in so being responsive to value, they align us with the world in an intimate way.

Thus, ethical action and more generally responsiveness to value is part of an even more general category that includes knowledge as well: responsive connection to the world. Being connected to the world responsively is valuable: it establishes a tight organic unity between us and the world—how tight depends upon our mode of responsiveness—and disparate parts of the world are further unified as alike subject to our responsiveness.

But why should we be limited to being shaped by this world, by the reality we happen to inhabit? What is so desirable about being intimately connected with it? Newspaper readers devour the details of the previous day, but how many now would similarly read through daily newspapers of 1894? Yet we cannot affect most of today's details or their followup; nor will we be affected by them (except as we read about them)—they will sink rightfully into last year's ephemera. Why then should a person choose so to be a prisoner of his time, filling such a large portion of his consciousness with its details?* There are so many other interesting things he can fill it with: histories of whole other cultures, some of the great works of literature, music and art he has not encountered or exhausted (is this all of them?), deep scientific theories, and so forth. What rational being would choose instead to concentrate on the machinations and lies, or honest but boring doings, speeches, and contests of today's mayors, senators, presidents, junta leaders, celebrities, and other assorted uninspiring seekers after power or attention?

Similarly, our whole reality is not the best and most interesting imaginable: why then should a person be a prisoner of the actual? Why shouldn't his mind, imaginations, and empathies range over all possible realities and worlds? Why should he care only about the reality he happens to find himself in, why should he put responsiveness to that above all else? (Compare the question of why we shouldn't choose permanently to enter the experience machine.)

Let us leave aside dialectical answers that may serve to convince but will not advance understanding, such as "when you ask these questions and want an answer, do you want an answer that corresponds to reality, or not?" One view would be that responsive connection to reality is intrinsically valuable. I do not deny this; it follows from the theory of value as organic unity. The question is why it is only linkages among parts of reality that are valuable? Why aren't linkages to possibility and organic unities among diverse possibilities also valuable? Imagination has always been a faculty prized

* See Ferdinand Braudel's distinction (*The Mediterranean*, Harper Torchbooks, 2 vols., New York, 1976, pp. 352–354, 892–903) between three levels a historian might be concerned with, the first, which he recommends ignoring, being evanescent events. Would a physicist or social scientist also criticize the historian who fills his consciousness with the study of longer term slower trends, recommending attention instead to timeless laws?

by students of literature and art. Often defended for the perspective it casts upon reality, perhaps the imaginative linkages to other possibilities are important and valuable themselves. ("Father, O Father! what do we here / In this land of unbelief and fear? / The Land of Dreams is better far, / Above the light of the Morning Star." William Blake, "The Land of Dreams".)

I am tempted to say that the organic unity which is value need not establish itself only among actualities; the greater the unity among whatever diversity, the greater the value. It might seem, therefore, that imaginative possibilities always will have to enter, since they expand the diversity. However, they also make it more difficult to establish a tight overall unity. Moreover, speaking for myself, a being of limited imagination, I cannot imagine a reality more diverse, surprising, and intricately unified than actuality turns out to be.* So if I am to link up with the greatest organic unity, and to link tightly with it, reality will play a major role, at least as a basis.

This seems to make the value of linking with reality an accident, irrelevant to those with greater powers of imagination. Should super-Tolkiens, who can create whole intricate imaginative worlds, concentrate on being responsive to those worlds and "living in" them? (They begin with an advantage in tightness of linkage, if "thinking up" is a tight relation.) However, they will have to function also in our common world, feeding themselves, and so forth, and so they will face the problem of organically unifying this actual world with their special creation. They could retreat into a state of dependency that requires no focusing upon actuality, being cared for in an asylum. I would think most inmates have delusions that, though giving themselves a more central role, are far more impoverished than reality. But even if one did manage to have a richer mental life, he would bear only the relation of 'thinking of and elaborating' to his world, not the one of acting in, and so he would forsake a valuable organic linkage. (Does this count against the deists' conception of a God who sets things going and then stands aloof with no further mi-

---

* This suggests the first of two arguments against solipsism: that reality is too rich to be the product of my consciousness, too complicated, diverse, and interesting for me to have thought it up. The second argument is that if I had thought it up I would have made it *better*. Not only is there a tension between these arguments, they each face the objection that my unconscious might have capacities or motives of which I am unaware.

raculous interventions, and also against the view that all miracles are preprogrammed from the beginning?)

My tentative conclusion is that the intrinsic value of responsive linkage to reality is not a primitive fact or a special one; instead it follows from value as degree of organic unity. Reality is the target with which we can establish the greatest organic unity, given our limited imaginative powers and the fact that only in reality can we (actually?) act.*

* Still, this does leave open the possibility of some more valuable unified linkage, not with reality. This possibility would be excluded if coherence (organic unity) was the defining criterion of reality. In discussing Descartes' questions about dreaming, philosophers have been quick to note that dreams are fragmentary, often unconnected from one evening to the next, whereas reality each day coheres with reality the day before, before the previous sleep. Others have noticed that we could imagine a dream life that was similarly coherent, with each dream beginning with a waking-up scene and ending with a going-to-sleep scene, while the intermediate portions carried on the same continuing story, like a television serial, or like reality itself. In this case, we would have great trouble distinguishing which is reality and which the dream. Some writers go on to conclude that coherence cannot be the mark of reality. If there were two equally coherent systems of experience, as in the situation just described, at most one of them would be of reality; so, they say, even when actually only one stream of experience is coherent, its reality cannot consist in its coherence. Those who recall our presentation in Chapter 1 of the closest continuer theory, and its application to a similar argument by Bernard Williams, will be suspicious. The argument does not show that reality cannot be marked as the most coherent system (including experiences), with no ties. (Note that this differs from the coherence theory of truth in the way it includes the experiences had—although there is a problem because these experiences have to be actually had.)

But is this use of coherence or organic unity to demarcate reality appropriate? Could it not be that there were two intermixed sequences of experience, one coherent and unified and the other fragmentary and unconnected, yet it was the first which was the dream sequence while the second was of reality? Works of artistic imagination are extremely coherent, after all. And might not reality be so powerful, so overwhelming in its actuality, that when we experience it, we fixate on it and thereby lose coherent linkages to other things. On this view, it is only by our filtering out aspects of reality, distancing ourselves from it, that it seems coherent to us. When we are most attentive and responsive to it, we focus only upon a portion or aspect of it to the exclusion of everything else, so that our experience lacks coherence and organic unity. Even if we have two separate such experiences, the finding of a linkage between them will come only later as we tranquilly contemplate the two experiences, not at a time when we are most closely linked with reality. I do not mean to argue that this is so; merely that this alternative picture undercuts the apparent obviousness of the a priori way in which philosophers accept the dictum that reality is what we experience as coherent.

Thus far, we have seen being responsive to reality as valuable in itself, or as a means to a valuable organic unity. We also might investigate whether the principle that calls for our being responsive to reality is self-subsuming, whether it falls under itself as an instance. In following that principle are we responsive to reality, more so than if we performed the same actions without guiding ourselves by the principle? It seems reasonable to think that a principled responsiveness to reality links our actions even closer to reality; not only are the actions aligned to reality, they are aligned intentionally through thought, by a principle which acts as a back-up governor to keep them aligned. However, we should remember the possibility of another view, that the mediation of thought and principles distances oneself from the object; some zen stories and writings seem to hold that one is more directly in contact with things when thought does not enter at all.

Consider next the principle that we should treat everything as having the value it has. If this principle itself is valuable because it links up with the value of other things and recommends patterns of action that create new organic unities, new values, and moreover, if the way to treat this principle as having the value *it* does is to follow it and guide our behavior by it—how else are we to be responsive to the value of a principle?—then this principle will be self-subsuming. Following it will be an instance of what it recommends, following it will be an example of treating something (namely the principle itself) as having the value it has.

Parity of Pull and Push

We have been careful until now to maintain the equal status of the moral pull and the moral push. Those theories that explain all of the content of ethics as an outpouring or side effect of the agent's seeking value diminish the independent force of the moral pull. The moral pull marks the fact that the other person is entitled to moral behavior from us—he is not merely the fortunate windfall recipient of behavior that flows from us in the course of our own pursuit of value. However, now we appear to have undercut this independent status of the moral pull, by presenting a rationale for responsiveness that focuses upon value, the value of the agent's being aligned with and responsive to reality. Doesn't this, in effect, make pull merely derivative from the value of the agent, having no independent weight of its own?

Our rationale did not speak of the value to the agent of his being aligned with reality. It spoke simply of the value of his being aligned with reality. This no more favors or focuses upon the agent than upon the reality he is aligned with—in this case, another person's basic moral characteristic. So it is no more push than pull; it simply speaks of the value of the responsiveness situation. "But isn't it valuable to the agent to be responsively aligned with the world?" I do not deny that; yet the aligning also is valuable to the recipient. Still, if this rationale for responsiveness does not center upon the agent, neither does it center upon the recipient. It lies, so to speak, between them. How then can it be a rationale for the moral pull which emanates from the other? Or if the moral pull does not emanate from the other person, his valuable characteristics merely giving rise to the valuable possibility of their being responded to, then will *he* be entitled to responsive behavior? Finally, hasn't this rationale for responsiveness made it, and also therefore the ought, subordinate to value rather than of independent status?

In responding to someone else's value, we act for his sake—not just the value's sake, since the characteristic of being a value-seeking I leads us to value him for himself. Only if you so act for his sake will you be responsive to his (valuable) characteristic, and thus be in the relationship to him that is conducive to your own value. Therefore, your own value cannot be your primary motivation in acting toward him. If it is, then you are not acting for his sake and so not in the closest relationship to him—you are serving your own value less well.[108] Kant instructs us to act from the motive of duty; however, this may involve not responding primarily to the value of another person, not doing the act for his sake. That mode of Kantian responsiveness to the valuable moral principle interferes with a responsiveness to the other person's value; thereby the principle comes between the agent and the other person, distancing the two. It should be enough that the person's actions track rightness, that he wouldn't do the act if it were wrong, and so on. Tracking rightness the agent can act without consciously thinking of the principle; he can act, not for the sake of the principle but for the sake of the other person.

Our theory does hold that it is value that we are to be responsive to, and that such responsiveness is valuable. But this last does not make responsiveness subordinate to value; for also, value is to be pursued because thereby one is being responsive to it as value. We might explain the notion of an act one *prima facie* ought to do, as one that is responsive to some value, such responsiveness also being classified as valuable; but similarly, value might be explained as that to which we *prima facie* ought to be responsive. Neither value nor ought (nor responsiveness) is subordinate—each supports the other.

Our earlier discussion of deontology and teleology demarcated two forms of teleology, depending on what action it directs doing, the one that leads to the most valuable world or the one whose doing is most valuable. Responding to the value of doing actions need not maximize the value in the world. Maximizing value (in the world) need not be that one of the acts available that is most responsive to value. Now we see that when teleology is directed toward maximizing the world's score, it might have a further defect—it might not yield the described mutual support between value and ought (where ought is based on moral pull).

Which available act is most valuable is judged by the way the alternative acts link you to the things you act upon, and to the characteristics those things have. Therefore, we must look especially at the valuable characteristics of things and persons, and at how you link with them. To treat a value-seeking I as that links more closely with this basic moral characteristic than do other relationships. To look at the value of doing acts takes account of the pull those characteristics exert, it takes account of how one is responsive to them by linking up with them qua them. On the other hand, the theory that wants to maximize the world's value score need not look at the character of your relationship to things, only at the total value everything ends up with (your relationship being just one of those things counted). So that theory need not pay special attention to pull on you. The focus on doing the action makes a place for special obligations based upon special relationships, as that of parents to their own children, wherein the acts of special concern and responsiveness infuse and heighten a unified relationship of a specially valuable sort. This universalistic theory of responsiveness provides a basis for particularistic responses.

If ought is defined as maximizing the value in the world (rather than as acting so as to be responsive to value) then one of the following might fail or become trivial: it is valuable to do what you ought; you ought to pursue (or otherwise V) value. For the first then would say it is valuable to maximize value, which either needs a particular theory of value to show that the act of maximizing value is valuable, or is the trivial statement that maximizing value maximizes value. And the second would say that pursuing (or otherwise V-ing) value will maximize it, which may be false. (Perhaps value would be most increased by our not V-ing it, since we are such bumblers.)

On the explanation of *(prima facie)* 'ought' in terms of responsiveness to value, to say we ought to be responsive to value is to say: being responsive to value is being responsive to value. If this is the 'is' of identity, the statement says being responsive is the same as being responsive—a trivial and unilluminating logical truth. However, if that 'is' means is a case of, then we have the nontrivial statement: being responsive to value is a case of being responsive to value. (Recall our condition on value in the first part of the chapter, that V-ing is valuable.) And this can be used as a necessary condition for naturalistic accounts of value notions, that the result of the substitution be a true statement of instantiation, and not merely the trivial identity. Let H be: value exists. The existence of value is itself a valuable fact, so we have G:H is valuable. Now consider the policy of being responsive to value; following this policy is itself responsive to H or G. So being responsive to value is a case of being responsive to value.

Does Push Cover Pull?

Have we presented a theory that succeeds in reconciling the moral pull and the moral push, so that we can see how and why we are better off being moral, more valuable that way?[109] Aside from the extrinsic benefits of behaving morally discussed earlier in this part, materials have been provided for two specifications of how the value sanction operates, of the way in which the immoral person has a less valuable existence. The first is based upon the fact that moral responsiveness involves exercising your own capacity as a value-seeking self, along with the Aristotelean point that a life is more valuable insofar as it exercises that centrally valuable capacity. However, this way of specifying how a moral person is better off by having a more valuable life does not guarantee that one is best off behaving morally. Even if moral behavior can be done only by a value-increasing exercise of one's valuable characteristics, it does not follow that such behavior will most increase one's value, as compared to all of the other actions available.

Might not some other action, perhaps an immoral one, involve an equal exercise of the self's value-seeking capacities, as it seeks to appreciate and realize or to protect nonmoral values, for instance, artistic ones? There are values in addition to moral values, and a value-seeker would not focus solely upon moral values. There remains, then, the possibility of a conflict between responding to these other values, and behaving morally. No reason has been given to think morality always must come lexically first in the value pursuit.

Literary and artistic works may develop responsiveness to nuances of value, but an appreciation of literary and artistic values need not, despite earlier plausible hopes, bring along with it an appreciation of moral values, a responsiveness to a person's basic moral characteristics as these express themselves. Witness the case of Hans Frank, entertaining friends by playing Chopin piano works while in charge in Eastern Europe of the Nazi's "final solution" to Jewish existence, and the case of Martin Heidegger writing on Hölderlin in proximity to the activity, and reports, of the extermination camps.[110] Not only is there no automatic spillover from artistic sensitivity to moral sensitivity and responsiveness, there can be situations where the claims of each conflict, as in a hypothetical choice between saving the last extant copy of Shakespeare's plays or saving a life.

The second mode of specifying the value sanction builds directly upon the theory of value as degree of organic unity. A person who is responsive to the value of others establishes a closer linkage and hence a tighter organic unity with these others (than one who is unresponsive), and that is valuable. That is more valuable than the situation of immoral behavior, but does it follow that the life or existence of the moral person is more valuable than that of the immoral one? The value introduced by moral behavior seems to be located between the moral person and those he responds to, or else seems to be had by some larger totality consisting of the moral person, the others, and their mutual interactions. Yet the value sanction is supposed to apply to the immoral person himself. He himself or his existence itself is to be less valuable in virtue of his immoral behavior—

not something between him and another, or something including him and another. The value penalty is to apply directly to the immoral person, and it is the moral person or his life itself that is to be more valuable. Granting that the relationship of behaving morally toward another involves greater organic unity and hence greater value than behaving immorally, does the life or existence of the moral person, or the person himself, also thereby possess (as is necessary for there to be a value sanction) greater organic unity, greater value? Because the relationship has a certain quality, will that quality also seep over to one party in the relationship?

It is unclear precisely how to delineate to what the value sanction is to apply. Thus far, we have spoken of the person's life or his existence, or of the person himself. But what is to be included within the person's life or existence, as opposed to something that connects his life and existence with other things? Isn't my being married and having children part of my life, as are the particular relationships I have to my wife and children? Aren't my friendships, political ties, and other loyalties also part of my life, along with the books I've read, plays and films I've seen, trips I've taken, conversations I've had, and classes I've taught? And mustn't I also include the friends I've lost, the drivers I've yelled at, the deans I've offended, the political allies I've refused, the feelings I've hurt? What makes up a life, after all? Doesn't a biography, a story of a life, properly include all these, and more; or do we think the biographer who includes these is, strictly speaking, telling more than the life itself? A life, a person's existence, is not simply the unordered set of these things; it is the particular whole they make up, with the self at the center. (In our own biographies, at least, each of us is the leading character.) When it is our existence that is (to be) valuable, it includes all this. There is no way of paring away the character of someone's relationships to others, to get a purified story of only *his* existence. Even a hermit is not someone with *no* relationship to others—he has a very particular one. A film of a life story does not show only the motions of the person's body with everything else eliminated, including other people, background scenery, props, and clothing.

Thus, there is no sharp distinguishing of moral behavior toward others as outside a person's life, as not a constituent part of it that contributes to its value. Yet, not every detail about the universe he lives in is properly a part of the person's biography. Some facts do concern his relationship to other things, or larger totalities that include him, rather than his life itself. I have no proposal about how to draw this line; no doubt, its placement will differ depending on purposes and concerns.

This appears to raise a serious issue. If it is a person's life or existence or the person himself that is to be valuable yet it is to some extent arbitrary or open where a boundary line is drawn, then cannot how an action or plan affects a life's value, which plan or action is more conducive to the life's value, vary with the placing of the boundary? And is it impossible to place the boundary so as to leave the immoral person's unethical behavior outside his life, so that *he* pays no value penalty?

The value of a person's life concerns the value of that whole encompassed by the life's boundaries, and that value is important, yet it is *not* very important where those boundaries are placed. We shall not be able to explain this apparently paradoxical remark until the next chapter. For now, we merely state that it will turn out that nothing theoretically important depends upon the placement of the boundaries; although it is plausible that the immoral person's unethical relationships *are* part of his life within the boundaries, he will not gain significantly by extruding them. His important "score" will remain the same. Before turning to the elaboration of this in the next chapter, we must return to the previously postponed topic of the relationship between fact and value.

V. FACT AND VALUE

Chasms

There are two famous chasms in ethics that despite determined efforts no one has been able to leap across or bridge: the one between the is and the ought (fact and value), and that (within the ought) between moral form and moral content. It appears fruitless to continue attempting to derive ought from is or moral content from moral form.

Once it is fixed, it seems the fact–value distinction cannot be bridged. Can we then avoid the chasm by showing that the very fixing of the distinction or the delineation of the realm of facts itself presupposes or brings along with it certain values? Let me mention some of the possibilities.

(1) Values enter into the very definition of what a fact is; the realm of facts cannot be defined or specified without utilizing certain values.[111]

(2) Values enter into the process of knowing a fact; without utilizing or presupposing certain values, we cannot determine which is the realm of facts, we cannot know the real from the unreal. If certain values are embodied in our procedures for telling the real from the unreal, the facts from the unfacts, then it is impossible to stand firmly on the fact side of the fact–value distinction, while treating the other side as vaporous.

One such view might be the following. Epistemologists have discussed how we might tell reality from illusion or a dream. Hume held that impressions were more forceful and vivid than ideas or dreams or illusions; however, this criterion runs afoul of the greater force and vivacity of certain drug experiences. Some writers have distinguished the objective from the subjective in terms of consensus: the objective is that to which others also would agree or assent.[112] The only way to discover this (subjunctive) consensus is to observe some part of it, some actual agreement. Thus, other people enter into fixing what we hold to be real or fact. But wherein do values enter?

To say that the real is what others would agree to, although a reasonable first approximation, is inaccurate as it stands. It depends on what the motivation of these others is. The real is what others would agree to if they were honest and wanted to tell us the truth (and were in a reasonable position to detect the truth?). A paranoid person is not reassured when others tell him there is no plot, if he suspects these others of being plotters themselves.

When serious skeptical doubts strike, the only testimony that serves is from those we are sure care enough about us to tell the truth as they see it. To be cut off from love and trust of another is to be unable with confidence to tell the real from the unreal. Compare the way in which those on a "bad drug trip" need the trusted testimony of others, while still others provide substance to reality, a cast of thousands fleshing it out.

To be sure, the testimony of others who are loved and trusted, or even these other persons themselves, might be part of the dream or illusion. Is it impossible to feel love toward someone who is only a dream or illusion? Even if not part of illusion, might they not be mindless automata? Must we first solve the problem of other minds in order to make progress on that of objective physical reality? And how can we do that without presupposing, at least, that others' behavior is part of the objective physical world?

It need not be that all possible philosophical doubts are quelled by the reassurance of a loved person, responsive to you and your value. If actual doubts can be quelled only in that way, then an ethical relationship of a certain sort to another person is a necessary condition for knowing or even having a firm belief about what is real. Ethics then would not lie across the chasm from facts, for without (what grounds) ethics, there would be no facts fixed.

The first two possibilities for circumventing the fact–value chasm see values as prior to or presupposed by facts, either in the specification of the realm of facts or in the process of coming to know facts. A third possibility places values in a coordinate status with facts.

(3) The same processes or principles that carve facts out of the undifferentiated, unconceptualized stuff also carve out values.

Let O be the deep cognitive psychological process via which we structure the world; it operates on inchoate undifferentiated X, yielding a realm of differentiated, delineated, and structured facts F.[113] The thought is that the very same operation O implicated in delineating facts from the undifferentiated stuff X, such that O(X) = F, also can operate to yield values V. It is difficult to see what separate stuff (not the same as F) this same process O could operate upon so as to yield values; more plausible is the view that values are structured by iteration of the operation O. Facts are the first stage of structuring of the inchoate X, while values are the next stage:

$$O(X) = F$$
$$O(F) = V.$$

Or perhaps this second stage operates not merely on F, but on both F and X, so that:

$$O(X,F) = V.*$$

In the absence of some modicum of understanding of the deep cognitive process O, however, we can do no more than mark this third structural possibility; like the first two listed, it refuses to take facts for granted as unproblematic, and thereby seeks a route around or beneath that fact–value distinction which, once established, remains to plague us.

Yet another theoretical possibility accepts these chasms as real and wide; it tries to explain why they hold, perhaps hoping that the explanation of the chasms, the explanatory factors introduced, might itself provide additional material to help us across. It is a test of our comprehension of the ethical realm that we understand not merely that there are these chasms (if there are) but also why. (Similarly, we want to understand why extensive moral content cannot be derived from the form of morality.)

We can ask why an ought or ethical statement E is not derivable from the totality I of true is-statements. Finding the correct explanatory factor S, we can ask whether it suffices when conjoined with the (previous) facts I to yield the ethical statement E, so that E is derivable from I&S. If not, we can seek to explain why not, by finding another

---

* What would a third-stage iteration yield? Does $O(X,F,V)$ = the mystical unlimited Ein Sof, U, while further iteration leads to nothing new, so that $O(X,F,V,U) = U$? And if it makes sense for O to be self-applying or self-reflexive, what does $O(O)$ yield?

explanatory factor S^1, and we can ask whether adding that factor now enables us to derive the ethical statement E, so that E is derivable from I&S&S^1. We can iterate this process until no new explanatory factors are introduced, check whether the conjunction of all these with the factual I suffices for the derivation of the ethical E, and if still not, we can ask what the minimal independent assumption or factor would be, whose adding would suffice for the derivation of the ethical statement E.[114] By taking the gap between is and ought seriously, and by explaining it, we can hope to throw a bridge across this gap or at least to narrow it.

The explanation of why we cannot derive ought from is will find a significant difference between them that derivation is unable to obviate. The explanation will find some property had by is but not by ought that is preserved under derivation, or some property had by ought but not by is whose absence is preserved under derivation. Even once we know the particular property P, it is difficult to see how we are helped in deriving an ought simply by adding the premiss: any is-statement I has property P while any ought-statement E does not, and anything derivable from something with P also will have P. So if help is to come, it must come from the explanation of why *is* has P and *ought* does not (or why *ought* has P while *is* does not).[115]

We might begin our search for the requisite explanatory property P by considering other cases where one type of statement cannot be derived from another.

1. *Metaphor:* The metaphorical meaning of a sentence cannot be derived from its literal meaning. Is the ought like a metaphor overlying the is?

2. *Explanation:* An explanation of data cannot be derived from the data to be explained. Is the ought like an explanation of the is?

3. *Effect:* An effect cannot be derived from its cause, despite rationalist attempts to see the causal relation as like a logical relation. Is the ought like an effect of the is?

4. *Knowledge by acquaintance:* The kind of knowledge had through being directly acquainted with a thing cannot be gotten merely by knowing many things about it. Is the ought like being acquainted with what the is tells us about? (Or, if no particular 'knowing that' follows from knowledge by acquaintance, is it the other way around?)

5. *Reflexive self-referring:* A reflexively self-referring statement cannot be derived solely from ones that are not. Is the ought like a first-person reflexive statement interpenetrating the impersonal objective is?

6. *Seeing as:* That something is seen as Q cannot be derived from the other properties it has (that do not refer to seeing). Is the ought like a way of seeing the is?

7. *Meaning:* The meaning of a sentence cannot be derived from the lifeless signs of the inscription that carries it. Is the ought like the meaning of the is?

8. *Tokenism:* One recent view in the philosophy of mind holds that there is no correlation (or identity) of types of mental events with types of physical events, while still every individual mental event, every mental event-token, is identical with some individual physical event, some physical event-token. Does the ought, while not standing in any type relations with the is so that derivations can go through, stand in token-token identities with the is?

9. *Synthetic necessary identity:* In analogy to Kripke's views on the necessary identity of light and electromagnetic radiation, are organic unity and value necessarily identical, although this is not knowable a priori? Is organic unity rigidly referred to by "value"?[116]

None of the cases on this list illuminates the relation between ought and is. And talk of "emergence" of the ought from the is explains nothing without a specification of the mode of emergence. Either the correct explanation lies in some other analogy, or the gap between is and ought is sui generis, not comparable to any of the other derivational gaps. (Is each of the others illuminated by the rest?) Or it might be held that no explanation of why the gap exists is needed; rather, the appearance that a derivation might take place, that ethics might not be an autonomous realm, is misleading.

Ethical Explanation and Self-Subsumption

The is–ought or fact–value gap arises in the course of taking ethical truths seriously. On the supposition that there are objective ethical truths, we can ask of a particular one why it holds true. The explanation may show this particular ethical truth is an instance of a deeper or more general ethical truth, or that (given certain factual assumptions) it falls under such a truth. Of this deeper or more general truth, too, we can ask why it holds. Repeating this process, it seems that eventually we shall reach (one or a number of) fundamental ethical truths which, while explaining the rest, themselves have no further ethical explanation. No other ethical truths explain them. So it appears the fundamental ethical truths either must be brute facts, dangling there with no further explanation, or there must be some explanation of the fundamental ethical truths in terms of nonethical truths. If explanation involves a derivation, deductive or otherwise, of what is to be explained from what does the explaining, then this last mode of explanation requires that an ought can be derived from an is. Note that this issue and problem does not depend on trying to justify or convince someone of an ethical statement. The task is not to provide agreement that the ethical statement is true, but rather to understand why it is true. In the case of fundamental ethical truths, we face a puzzle about what kind of explanation there could be. If the fundamental ethical truths are not to be explained by nonethical truths —and we have no idea of how such an explanation might work— then the ethical realm will be autonomous.[117]

This autonomous body of ethical truths will be ordered and structured by the explanatory relation E, 'is a correct explanation of'. The possibilities about how this autonomous ethical realm might be structured (by the explanatory relation), are the very ones, already canvassed in Chapter 2, about how the realm of all truths might be structured. The asymmetrical and transitive explanatory relation 'is a correct explanation of' allows the following structure in an autonomous realm, whether of all truths or (an autonomous realm) of ethical ones: (a) one of several explanatory chains go back infinitely far, with each truth being explained by some other deeper truth; or (b) an explanatory chain stops with a truth that is a brute fact—nothing explains it; or (c) an explanatory chain stops with a fundamental truth that subsumes itself via quantification theory; the general truth is an instance of itself.

To recall the possible structures for the explanation of all truths, as discussed in Chapter 2, makes us more tolerant of the situation with ethical truths. We might scoff at the idea of ethical truths that have no further explanation—brute truths—until we consider whether we can avoid that structural possibility in the realm of *all* truths. Will there turn out to be some nonethical general laws that are brute facts, with no further explanation? And if those, then why not ethical ones as well?

If ethics is an autonomous realm, we should not be surprised to come upon a general ethical truth with no further explanation. Furthermore, we might especially hope to find one so deep that it subsumes and thereby explains itself. One of the goals of philosophy is to uncover and delineate such ultimate truths. Recall that self-subsumption is not a proof or sufficient condition for truth. ("Every principle containing seven words is true" subsumes itself, but is false.) However, if a sufficiently deep explanatory principle is true, then (we have held) it also can be the explanation of itself via self-subsumption.

A fundamental principle of morality would subsume itself and yield many other moral truths (with facts playing a subsidiary role as minor premisses). The one fundamental principle of morality, if there be such a thing, would be a fundamental principle that subsumed itself while yielding all other moral truths.*

A fundamental principle of morality might have the following form.

P: You ought to follow principles with feature F.

It will subsume itself if P itself has the feature F. Or perhaps the principle will be

P: You ought to do acts with feature F,

where following principle P is itself an act with feature F.

One candidate for a fundamental self-subsuming principle of morality is a principle of unanimous consent in some choice situation.

U: Whatever principle everyone unanimously agrees to (or would agree to) under conditions C (the veil of ignorance, perfect knowledge, or whatever) ought to be followed.

If under those conditions C, everyone would agree to principle U, it

---

* Commentators on Kant's first formulation of the categorical imperative, "act only on that maxim through which you can at the same time will that it should become a universal law," do not explain the meaning of "through which you can at the same time". Might we read Kant as saying that a fundamental moral principle must yield itself as an instance of itself, must subsume itself?

follows (and can be deduced) from this fact along with principle U, that principle U ought to be followed. Notice that it is not a trivial fact that a principle yields itself, or even that a process principle yields itself as the result of that very process. The principle that whatever a majority of the people in a group agree to ought to be followed might itself be rejected by a majority in that group, if they want either a bill of rights that limits the majoritarian will or a dictator uncontrolled by it.

Another candidate for a fundamental principle of morality concerns cooperative action in prisoners' dilemma situations, so-called after the example used by A. W. Tucker in first delineating them. The police present two captured suspects with the following alternatives: if either confesses while the other does not, he will receive two years in prison while the other will receive 12; if neither confesses, each will receive 4 years in prison; if both confess, each will receive 10 years in prison. Each prisoner reasons as follows: "I am better off confessing no matter what the other one does: supposing he confesses, then if I don't confess I receive 12 years while if I do confess I receive 10, which is better; and supposing he doesn't confess, then if I don't confess I receive 4 years, while if I do confess, I receive 2 years, which is better. So in either case, I am better off confessing." Since each reasons in this way, each confesses, and so each receives 10 years in prison; whereas if each had not confessed, each would have received only 4 years in prison. So each would have been better off if neither had confessed. Although they realized this as they were deciding what to do, nevertheless, each also realized how he was better off confessing whatever the other did, and so each confessed himself.

An action that leaves someone better off or as well off, for each action another person might do, as any other action available to him is termed by game theorists a (weakly) dominant action; while an action over which another act is dominant is termed dominated. It appears that when a dominant action is available in an interpersonal situation a rational person should perform it. Yet the prisoners' dilemma situations are so structured that both are worse off performing their dominant action than if both had performed their dominated one.

The discussion of this situation (generalized to more than two persons) and its ramifications constitutes a vast literature by now.[118] Many have tried to explain specific institutions as functioning to avoid or transform prisoners' dilemma situations; still, these sometimes *will* arise, and writers see the participants in many of them as morally required to perform the dominated cooperative action, or see this action as something they ought to do. (I say in "many" prisoners' dilemma situations, rather than "all", since it is not always right to perform the dominated action—witness cooperation among thieves. Hence whatever moral principle is appropriate needs to be restricted to some subclass S of prisoners' dilemma situations.)

Therefore we might consider the principle PD: In a generalized prisoners' dilemma situation of sort S, one ought to perform the dominated cooperative action. PD is an ethical principle applying to choices in particular structured situations, where its mandate differs from that of the principles of rational self-interest, which call for performing the dominant noncooperative action. Thus far, we have a proposed moral principle but not self-subsumption.

Let us now consider the choice between following moral principles including PD, and following principles of rational self-interest, RSI. Suppose that if all follow moral principles including PD, all are better off than if all follow principles of RSI. (The moral principles also may include directives to follow rational self-interest except when this conflicts with PD or with some other moral principle.) However, each person is better off himself following RSI, whatever the others choose to do. If the others pursue RSI, he advances his own interests better by following RSI rather than morality with PD; while if the others follow PD he advances his own interests better following RSI rather than morality with PD. Hence, RSI dominates the principles of morality, M. Thus, the choice all face between following morality with PD or following RSI is itself structured as a generalized prisoners' dilemma situation (which I shall assume is of the requisite sort S).

The principle of morality PD says that in *this* choice situation, as in other similarly structured ones, one ought to perform the dominated cooperative option, namely, following morality including PD. We have not derived PD from PD trivially via the propositional calculus; rather, PD has been derived from itself as an instance, via quantification theory (and the further assumptions). PD subsumes itself. Supposing PD is a deep principle of morality, the explanation of why we ought to follow it is that following it is the dominated action in a generalized prisoners' dilemma situation (of type S). It is moral to follow PD not merely because following PD is following a correct moral principle, but because following PD falls under a correct moral principle—namely, PD. The deep explanation of why one ought to follow PD involves PD itself.

This does not, of course, prove that PD is correct or justify it. Incorrect moral principles also are capable of subsuming themselves, and we may suppose that in the previous choice situation, application of RSI leads to the choice of RSI itself. RSI also subsumes itself. Since RSI and PD conflict, both cannot be correct; clearly, self-subsumption is not sufficient for correctness. Rather, the point is that given that a moral principle is correct and sufficiently deep, if it subsumes itself it can explain why it itself holds. If the realm of morality is to some degree autonomous, and is not to rest on a brute moral fact, we should expect that there will be some fundamental moral principle that explains many other more particular principles while also subsuming itself.

Since Glaucon's challenge to Socrates, moral philosophers have attempted to show that it is in our rational self-interest to act morally. To be successful, this attempt would have to show, in the choice matrix whose alternatives are following morality (including PD), following RSI, following the whim of the moment, and whatever, that if one made that choice by applying RSI, one would be led to follow morality. Rather than (or in addition to) subsuming itself, RSI is to subsume morality. (In contrast, Mandeville argues that morality subsumes RSI.) If this following of morality were in conflict with rational self-interest, there would be a certain incoherence or instability in RSI—beginning with RSI, we would be led to reject it. RSI would undercut itself. It is unclear to what extent morality would be supported if the principle of reasoning that got one there is rejected afterwards as inadequate. Though RSI, as one competitor to morality, would be rejected because it undercuts itself, there would remain the possibility (broached by Mandeville) that morality also undercuts itself. However, the traditional philosophical attempts to derive morality from RSI did not envisage replacing RSI by morality. Rather, their task was the Platonic one: to show the harmony between morality and RSI, to show that in pursuing (either) one, rightly understood, we will best serve the other.

We have seen how some moral principles discussed by philosophers might be shown to be self-subsuming; in the previous section, we saw how principles of responsiveness to value and responsiveness to reality might be self-subsuming.[119] Yet even if we can exhibit such self-subsumption for deep principles we find acceptable, for instance, a principle of responsiveness to value or to reality, I do not believe we thereby reach an adequate explanation of the realm of moral truths. Because there are alternative and conflicting self-subsuming ethical principles, such as PD and RSI, it will be (left as) a contingent fact that one holds in our universe. (Can there be a self-subsuming principle, though, of anti-responsiveness to reality, and would one follow it by disobeying it? Nevertheless, with sufficient ingenuity one can devise another suitably qualified self-subsuming principle as an alternative to responsiveness.) To be sure, there would be an explanation of why that one which does hold in our universe holds, namely, the self-subsuming explanation. Yet though it holds in our universe, and not merely as a brute fact, if its only basis is the self-subsumption it need not hold in another possible universe. (If one self-subsuming principle holds instead of another, solely in virtue of holding, this would provide an analogue of reflexivity.)

Morality does not seem to me contingent in this way, however. There could not be a universe in which value-seeking I's existed yet there were no moral conditions or constraints on how they were to be treated, while there were conditions on how something else (disjoint from them) was to be treated. There could not be a universe in which it was all right to murder or torture people with no overriding reason. Moral truths do not just happen to hold in our universe. They hold in any universe—any one containing value-seeking I's. Therefore, they are more like necessary truths than like contingent ones. But the self-subsuming explanation of fundamental ethical truths, while it removes their brute-fact quality, does not remove their contingency; on this account, other truths could have held in their place. (Recall the issues concerning that theological position which holds that ethical truths are chosen and created by God, so that if he had chosen differently, which he could have done, then different and even opposite ethical truths would have obtained.)

Kantian Structuring

If fundamental moral principles are in some way noncontingent, what might the basis be of this noncontingency? Unfortunately, we lack adequate understanding of other apparent necessities that are not solely due to the meanings of the terms involved, most notably in the cases of mathematics (number theory and combinatorics) and logic. (Moreover, since the work of W. V. Quine, we have lost confidence in the explanations, previously thought to be unproblematic, of some necessities as created solely by analytic relations of meaning.) Although we cannot draw upon a useful theory of necessity, already known to be adequate elsewhere, we might take some comfort from the thought that the status of ethical truths, currently ill-understood, might turn out to be no worse than that of mathematical truths.

Kant's problem in the *Critique of Pure Reason* was: how are synthetic a priori truths (of geometry, arithmetic, "every event has a cause," and so on) possible? Observation can tell us only that something is the case, not that it must be the case; furthermore, the statements are not verbal truths which must hold because of what the constituent terms mean. Kant's explanation, if we put it crudely, is that we structure the world so that the statements come out true. We structure the world in experiencing it, or our cognitive apparatus does; any world we could experience would bear the traces of that process of structuring. (Compare how some features of maps are due to the method of projection used.) Therefore, every world (experienceable by us) must exhibit the trace features, so the statements formulating these features not only are true but must be true.*

---

* We should not scorn crude formulations of philosophical positions, even the hoary one about Kant and the tinted eye-glasses. The positions come into their creators' heads not fully elaborated but as intuitive ideas that seem promising or insightful. The elaboration of details and qualifications serves to show that (or test whether) the intuitive idea can do the job for which it was introduced. However, the appeal of the resulting position and much of its influence upon later philosophy, as well as almost all of its cultural influence outside of philosophy, will be due to those simpler intuitive ideas—the kernel of the view. A very illuminating superficial history of philosophy could be written (or taught), setting forth the intellectual problems faced by a philosopher and the intuitive ideas, as they came to him, that he advanced to meet or illuminate or avoid these problems. Rather, such a history—so much against the grain of current historical scholarship—would limn the depths underneath the surface elaborations.

I do not mean to belittle knowing the elaborations or creating them. Only thereby can one be in a position to think that an idea would do the job. (And behind many elaborations, too, there are intuitive ideas to grasp.) Each half is important—intuitive idea and elaborate development—but each is no more than half.

It is of no concern to us here whether Kant is correct in this argument of the first Critique, whether there *are* those synthetic necessary truths or whether Kant's explanation adequately accounts for them. What interests us is whether a theory of this type, call it Kantian structuring, could account for ethical truths. Could ethical truths hold as the result or side effect of some process wherein we structure and cognitively organize the world, or ourselves, or the relationship between ourselves and the world? Could ethical truths have a status similar to the one Kant ascribes to synthetic necessary truths in the first Critique? I do not claim that Kant's own ethical theory is of this sort, carrying out the type of program he presents in the first Critique; however, it would be surprising if there were no illuminating interpretation of his ethical writings as delineating a Kantian structuring.

Would such a program leave ethical truths as objective or subjective? Neither term aptly would fit their status; while the truths would not hold independently of anything about us, also they would not depend upon anything personal, anything such as a preference that would vary from person to person. The truths of ethics would be as solid as Kant thought the truths of Euclidean geometry (or those underlying Newtonian mechanics) were—and that is a solid status indeed. Such a view also would account for our feeling that there is something more subjective about ethics than about other (objective) truths—if, that is, a Kantian structuring explanation held for ethics but (contrary to Kant in the first Critique) not for the other truths.

To ground ethics sufficiently, the structuring that brings ethics in its wake must be inescapable, and also something we would not choose to escape, even if we could. One thing we definitely would not wish to escape is being an I. If the process of structuring ourselves as I's brought ethics along, then ethics would be deeply grounded. (One attempt to work out such a theory is made by Fichte in his *System of Ethics*.) Ethical truths, then, would be avoidable only at the cost of no longer being a self; the egoist would be able to avoid ethical truths only by giving up the very thing whose interests he wants to place paramount, the self. (Note that this is a point about the existence of truths, not about motivation.)

If what brings ethics along is our being an I, structuring ourselves as a reflexive being, then this might help explain why ethics binds us in the first person. An ethical side-constraint tells me that I am not to do some act, rather than that the doing of it is to be minimized even if this involves my doing it. If it is structuring oneself as a self that grounds ethics, this would help explain why "I" or "my" figures as an indexical term in fundamental moral principles. Strictly, an indexical term can be utilized without the full side-constraint form. Between a side constraint and an impersonal goal-directed maximizing view, is an indexical maximizing (or minimizing) view: Minimize *my* doing act A. If my doing act A this time will avoid my doing it in the future (by avoiding the necessity for my doing it or avoiding my succumbing to the temptation of doing it) then the minimization view would permit it this time while the side-constraint view would not, even in the knowledge that therefore I will end up violating that side constraint later more frequently. (This indexical minimizing view deserves to be more thoroughly explored.) Not only does ethics tell us how to treat reflexively self-conscious beings, not only is it directed toward such beings, telling them how to behave; ethics is, on this Kantian structuring view, based upon reflexive self-consciousness. So it is not surprising that ethical principles ineliminably contain reflexive indexical terms, either within side constraints or within principles directing me to minimize my doing of act A. Reflexive indexicality is the birthmark of ethics.

This Kantian-structuring approach would have no chance of success if the self were a primitive entity, a metaphysical simple with no components or parts, not the result of any process of structuring, unifying, or organization. There must be enough "moving parts" in intricate interaction so that ethics can emerge from the process. We saw in the first chapter that the self is not a simple, that the I synthesizes and structures itself so as to maximize degree of organic unity around the self-reflexive intentional production of the token. Neither the boundaries of the I nor the dimensions along which it projects itself are metaphysically given; they emerge and are selected in the process of self-synthesis.

Let us mention some of the places that ethics might be generated within this process of the I's structuring itself—the moving parts in being an I.

1. Reflexiveness. Reflexive self-consciousness is an ill-understood phenomenon, and perhaps values or oughts enter into the microdot of reflexive self-consciousness itself. (Is that self-consciousness itself an experience of value?) On our account of reflexiveness, reference

"from the inside", the reference refers to something as having a characteristic which is bestowed by the act of reference, and refers to it as having a characteristic so bestowed (by utilizing a sense that involves this). Could there be any greater degree of responsiveness to a characteristic, any greater molding of an action to the contours of a characteristic?

2. The way a reflexive self-consciousness draws or delineates its boundaries. (a) The I might delimit itself simply as "the value locus that contains this very reflexive self-consciousness"; its boundaries then would be determined by a value gradient. (b) Ought or value might enter into the dimensions along which the I projects itself. (c) Ought or value might enter into the criterion for where the boundary gets drawn, for example, into the criterion of drawing the I's boundaries so as to maximize its degree of organic unity. (d) Ought or value might enter into the criterion through which the I establishes its own unity, in the face of all the puzzle cases about personal identity involving ties, splits, and so on.

3. The process whereby a reflexive self-consciousness recognizes itself as such, as something with a subjective slant on the world.[120]

4. The process by which a reflexive consciousness recognizes that there are other reflexive consciousnesses in the world; the process by which, in the third person, it structures another self as having its own reflexive first person.

The problem of other minds has been a difficult one for epistemologists: since all we have to go on are another person's bodily movements including sounds produced, how can we know there really is another person there with its own subjectivity, since we do not experience that subjectivity directly? If some ethical or value premiss entered into the step from behavioral evidence to another mind, then it would be clear why we ought to treat other selves in a certain way. For this very ought (or one that entails it) would enter into our (justified) recognition of another as a self. It is true that we ought to treat other selves in a certain way, because that ought is presupposed in our recognition of the others as selves.* Note the difference between

* The value premiss need not deal specifically with selves; for example, it might be the injunction to view or structure the world so as to have the most value. Since other mind-bodies would have more value than merely behaving bodies, one would attribute minds to the receptive bodies; however, this would not lead to panpsychism, since attributing primitive mind or feelings

an *ought* arising at the fourth stage, and earlier. If it arises earlier, then structuring of the I (of one's own I) generates: if there were another I, it is to be treated in a certain way. If the ought first enters with the fourth stage, then structuring another as an I generates: treat that other in a certain way.

The basic moral characteristic which exerts the ethical pull is "being a value-seeking I", while thus far we have treated the structuring as done by "being an I". It would be neater if the same characteristic were involved at each end; however, to introduce "being a value-seeker" at the structuring end might interfere with the condition that the structuring should be based upon something so deep that no one would choose to be without it. (On the other hand, would this symmetry reduce how dependent a Kantian structuring of ethics is upon a particular structurer? If the characteristic C that does the structuring also structures C's out there which exert the pull, and those C's out there also do the same structuring, then even without you, would a structuring—by them—take place bringing ethics along?)

The Kantian structuring view is attractive in many respects, but its details would have to be filled in. It would have to be shown exactly how the structuring works so as to introduce ought or value. I do not pursue these further details for three reasons, only the first of which is that I do not see exactly how to get ethics to precipitate out of this process. The second worry about the described Kantian structuring wherein ethics originates in a structuring of the self, is that it makes

---

to ostensibly mindless objects wouldn't yield a "psychology" as closely unified with their behavior. For another view of how the other-minds problem and ethics might interweave, see Stanley Cavell, *The Claim of Reason* (Oxford University Press, 1979), Part IV.

The classification of the world in accordance with the principle of organic unity might have two connections to value: value is degree of organic unity, and we classify so as to maximize value; we classify to maximize organic unity and this, being the *telos* of our activity, is specified as valuable. Such a view might go on to say that the purpose of theoretical reason is such unified classification, finding deductive connections and linkages and so on, while practical reason seeks to act with reasons, to have reasons link its actions with facts; so organic unity is that to which reason (of each kind), by its *telos*, aspires. (Compare Kant in the *Critique of Judgment*.)

It seems plausible to think that classifying the world, and carving it up so as to maximize organic unity, will demarcate entities over time in accordance with the closest continuer schema; that this schema enables the widest diversity to be unified reasonably tightly.

the ethical pull look too little like a pull from him, and too much like a push from me. This explanation of how and why some characteristic, being a value-seeking I, commands respect and responsiveness focuses not on the bearer of the characteristic, on what he is like, but rather on the viewer of him (who also bears the characteristic). That type of consideration seems better suited for the theory of the push, or at any rate insufficiently independent of the agent to be a pull on him. I believe this criticism applies to Kant's ethical theory, as well, in which the moral law somehow stems from my rational nature and makes a claim upon me. Although this claim concerns the other person, and even might be described as a claim he makes, at the second floor, it does not stem from him at the ground floor. Kant's view makes the moral law concerning him arise from me in a way that does not adequately recognize the depth of the moral pull from him. I do not say that the moral pull is so deep that no explanation of it can be offered, but the explanation of the moral pull he exerts must not place me at a level more fundamental than his. (Recall our discussion, in the previous part, of the parity of the moral pull and the moral push.)

The third worry is that this Kantian structuring does not fit in well with our desire to track independently existing values. If these values instead are put there by ourselves, as a side effect of Kantian structuring, then why should we track or pursue or otherwise V them? (The act of tracking values brought about via a Kantian structuring does not seem to be an act in equilibrium.) Yet, perhaps this construction will better satisfy those who feel that pursuing externally given objective values is not autonomous enough; though still it does not provide the autonomy attributed by Kant's view that in following the moral law we legislate for ourselves. (But recall the discussion in Chapter 4 of whether Kant's grounding of the moral law in our inescapable essence does not undercut the autonomy he seeks.) Between not wanting to devote oneself to pursuing anything one created oneself, and viewing anything given externally as a constraint upon autonomy and dignity, there is not much room for maneuver. Yet we must try to slip through this dilemma.

VI. THE BASIS OF VALUE

The Euthyphro Question

Some views try to base ethics or value upon religious foundations: the good or the valuable or the morally required is what God approves of, or wants us to do, or commands. All such views face the question first put by Socrates in Plato's dialogue the *Euthyphro:* is something good because God approves of it, or does God approve of it because it is good?[121]

If the basis of God's approval of something is its goodness (which goodness is not derivative from or identical with God's approval), if God approves of it in virtue of its goodness, then there is some independent notion or standard of goodness that God's judgment fits rather than creates. In that case, God's attitude to something would not underlie its moral or value quality; the fundamental truth about goodness, value, and ethics would not be theological. On the other hand, if something is good because God approves of it, if it is good in virtue of being approved by God, then value and ethics will be divinely based. However, there then will be the question of why God approved of this—not, by hypothesis, *because* it was good—and the issue of whether God could have approved of something else, the opposite even, and if he had, whether that would then have been good, in place of this. (John Calvin held that predestination was not unjust, on the ground that justice does not exist as a standard independent of God but rather is defined or created by God's actions.) The last alternative, that the good could have been different and would have been if God had chosen or approved differently, which he perfectly well could have done, is highly unpalatable. We might even imagine Plato's question transformed into one that *God* worries about. Imagine God facing a dilemma parallel to the one that closed the previous section. Are God's own actions and is his own existence valuable; if so, is this in virtue of an external standard independent of him (and so does he feel constrained by it?), or in virtue of a stan-

552

dard that he creates or legislates—but then is God pleased at joining a country club he founded, for which he formulated the membership requirements?

Is there some other alternative for a theologically based ethics; is there some way God can make his cake and enjoy it too? Let us consider some possibilities. First, it might be held that although there is no preexisting standard of goodness or value, God's approval is not arbitrary. He approves of something in virtue of characteristic C which it has; its having C, and it itself, are good in virtue of that approval. The link between fact and value goes through God's approval. "But could God have disapproved of C, or approved of C's absence, and if he had, would C be then bad, or at least fail to be good?" It is unclear how voluntary God's approvals are. One theological view might hold that God could not approve otherwise (but not for the reason that God necessarily is good, and so must approve the good, for we are supposing the characteristic C isn't preexistingly good); that the mesh of his nature with the characteristic C could only yield approval—perhaps because he must approve of things to the extent they resemble him. Another view would hold that God could approve otherwise, but that he would not, again perhaps because of the mesh of his nature with the characteristic C he approves. What is needed is some explanation of God's approval, not based upon a preexisting goodness in the object, that makes it nonarbitrary. (And a theologian might hold there is some such explanation, without being able to specify what it is.) Therefore, something blocks the step to "God *could* have commanded or approved of killing people to eat their hearts or brains, and if he had, *that* would have been right, good and valuable." For the reply can be made that God's disapproval of this is nonarbitrary and he would not approve of it. Moreover, if God were to approve of it, then, in the closest possible world in which he does approve of it, the nonarbitrary explanation of his disapproval is bypassed. Yet the general laws or principles underlying the actual disapproval continue to hold true in these close worlds, so something else has to be different there—the action or event would have a different character in that world, to alter God's disapproval in accordance with the principles governing his nonarbitrary response. (Or else, in that closest world where he approves of it, the principles governing his approval would have changed; then

553

we can circumvent the question of whether, in that case, the differ-ent thing would be good.)

It seems the theist thus can continue to maintain a theological basis for ethics and value, even in the face of the apparent bombshell of the Euthyphro question; he can hold that something is good be-cause God approves of it yet, because of the fact that God's approvals have a nonarbitrary explanation, avoid the unacceptable subjunc-tives.* However, while this view places value in our world, based upon God's approval, it leaves God in a situation barren of value, unable to view even himself and his own existence as having value. Afterwards, like others, he too might see value as dependent upon his approvals, and (assuming he is reasonably self-content) thereby comes to see himself as valuable. But this will tell him no more than that he approves of himself, that he is the sort of thing of which he (reliably) tends to approve. He will not even be able to see his own approvings as independently valuable. Is there any way a theological view can give value some degree of independence, so as to place value upon or within God's existence, and not leave it merely as a derivative consequence of his approval?

God might choose that there be values, choose to create values. Will God see it as better, more valuable, that there be values? Not yet, for there are not values yet. But it *will* be better that they exist, according to the values that there then are. So God creates values, according to which the existence of these values is valuable, his cre-ating values is valuable, his further adherence to the values is valu-able, his existence is valuable, and so forth. The values created vali-date their own creation; they envalue God's creating them. The values are not derivative from God's mere approval; he chooses to create values, to create them as values.

Could God have created different things as values; had he chosen differently, would values be different? We have seen how one theo-logical view might hold that, because of his nature, he would not choose differently. There is another answer to consider: the nature of value limits what it is that can be created as value. In the first part of

* Euthyphro believes in many gods, and Socrates leads him to revise his view to "what is approved by all the gods". Gnostics who hold that the world was created by a deity other than the very different god of a more encompass-ing realm, if they wished to offer a theological basis for ethics, would have to decide which god's approval fixed the ethical standard.

this chapter, we listed various conditions, constitutive of the nature of value, in a project to specify value uniquely. Only something that satisfied those conditions could be value; if only one thing does, for example, degree of organic unity, then only that can be value. (We emphasized, though, that there would remain the further question of why that is value, of why any value exists at all.) If we suppose that value is thus uniquely specified (though its various combinations are not—recall the section on pluralism) then though God can choose that there be value (or not), he could not choose that something *else* be value. The existence of value is up to him, but the character of value is independent, not subject to his control or choice.

In God's relationship to value (under this view) his autonomy is preserved, for it is his choice that there *be* value, yet also there is an independent standard of value according to which his existence and choices are valuable, a standard not fixed simply by his own preferences or approval. Although he founds the country club, its membership conditions are not up to him.

Nihilism, Realism, Idealism, Romanticism, and Realizationism

I have presented these reflections not as a contribution to theology but to suggest and mark an analogous possibility about *our* relationship to values. Here there seem to be the following possibilities. (1) There do not exist any values or true ought statements (and there cannot?); this position has been termed *nihilism*. (2) Values do exist; they exist and have their character independently of our choices and attitudes. This has been termed *realism* or *Platonism*. (3) Values exist, but their existence and their character are both somehow dependent upon us, upon our choices, attitudes, commitments, structurings, or whatever. This position might be called philosophical *idealism* or *creationism*. Although these three possibilities have received the most discussion in the literature, there are two others also worth specifying. (4) Values exist independently of us, but inchoately. We choose or determine (within limits?) their precise character; we sculpt and delineate them. This position might be called *formationism* or *romanticism*. (5) We choose or determine that there be values, that they exist, but their character is independent of us.

This position might be called *realizationism*. (Variants of positions 3–5 might hold that the existence or character of values stems from us or our activities, but is not dependent upon our voluntary choices, instead arising from something we must do, some necessity of our natures.)

The fifth position provides a reconciliation of autonomy with an external standard (while the fourth position gives no external standard to adhere to or reach). Because the existence of value is dependent upon us, value and the world impregnated or alight with it is rendered less alien to us; because the content of value is independent of us, we have an independent external standard to align with and track.

Is this picture of value—as something whose existence is dependent upon us, but whose character is independent—a coherent one? (Let us leave aside the fact that parents often notice this description —dependent existence but independent character—as fitting their children's status.) One position in the philosophy of mathematics is that we create or construct mathematical entities, the progression of natural numbers or whatever, but the facts about these created entities, the relationships among them and so forth, then hold independently of us. We create the mathematical entities and then discover the truths that independently hold of them. Similarly, Karl Popper has held that there is a man-made realm ("the third world") of abstract entities, intellectual problems and current states of discussion, whereof truths hold autonomously, independently of us.[122] The problems of providing a realistic interpretation for quantum mechanics have created an active arena of views about events whose existence is dependent upon us (or on acts of observation) but whose character is independent of us.[123] The twentieth century has seen other areas also emphasize the response of a subject: in psychoanalysis, the criterion of the validity of an insight is the analysand's (ultimate, subjective) acceptance of it (does this better fit the fourth possibility described?); in literature, it sometimes is said that the reader's (or critic's) responses and readings bring the work into existence, while the work may even be about that very process of reading; modern painting, too, has been thought to be similarly reflexive.[124] My point is not that the same type of view must hold true in each of these areas, in mathematics, physics, and the arts, or even that it *does* hold true in any of them; however, the fact that a realizationist position has been seriously proposed in so many areas is a reason for believing, at least, that it is a coherent position, and so a possible structure for value theory.

The decline of realism about value, which had its major institutional base and support in religion, has been much noted in diagnoses of the modern period. The third, fourth, and fifth possibilities, romanticism broadly conceived, represent one intellectual response: maintaining the viability of values of some kind. These positions have not become embodied in any large scale and influential institutions, though. (There also continue to be realists who decry what they see as falling away from the truth.) A second response to the decline of realism, by those who see no way that the resulting void can be filled by our own (creative) activity, has been (as in Kafka, Beckett, and the existentialists) a yearning, an awareness of loss, but refusal to be lulled from anguish into (an illusioned) contentment. Sometimes occupiers of this position make a virtue of their authentic anguish so that it constitutes the last existing value, but this lapse into romanticism will not withstand scrutiny. A third modernist position, better described as an after effect of the decline of realism than as a response to it, holds that there are no valid values, only personal preferences; this view sees nothing absent or missing, no call for anguish. This view is the predominant one among social scientists; its cultural base is the achievements of (value-free) natural science and the capacities of technological-industrial civilization. Technology is a "neutral" means. Although the rise of what Max Weber called *zweckrationalitat* theoretically leaves a place for values to be plugged in as ends toward which the means are aimed, such values are otiose—arbitrary desires suffice. Unlike Lewis Carroll's cheshire cat, which disappeared leaving its smile, this disappearance of values did not even leave behind its (salient) absence.*

* The listing of five possibilities about our relationship to value, as well as the further responses to the decline of realism, forswears one frequently traveled route to intellectual influence: devising a classification of *three* character types, via which people could puzzle over where they and their mates fit, categorize their friends, understand different social interactions, and play parlor games. Thus we have had Freud's oral, anal, and genital; Sheldon's mesomorph, endomorph, and ectomorph; Riesman, Glazer, and Denny's inner-directed, other-directed and autonomous; Reich's Consciousness I, II, and III. Dyadic classifications (such as introvert, extrovert) have less interest, while quadratic ones apparently are too complicated for most people to keep fully in mind, which is why there is no holy Quadrinity.

The proponents of this last position can only follow their "mere" desires; so they cannot believe they *ought* to act that way, or that it is better to act that way. Similarly, they think it is true that there are no objective values, but they do not (choose to) believe what is true because they ought to or because it is better to—they simply *prefer* to, or do so as a means to satisfying their preferences. Some slogans will have different interpretations within the different positions. To the creator of values, "do your own thing" means fulfilling oneself in the valuable activity of expressing one's own individuality and shaping a unique combination or unity of values, whereas to the proponent of this last position it means that, since there are no values at all, there is no reason not to do exactly as you please.

Choosing That There Be Value

My purpose here is not to pursue cultural commentary, but rather to formulate and delineate the fifth position about values: we choose that there be value but do not choose its character.* In what does a person's choice that there be value consist? Few people say "let there be value!" And how would saying that make it true that there was value? The choice that there be value is made in valuing things, in V-ing things as valuable.

Perhaps only in this century has this choice been made in full self-consciousness of it as a *choice*, yet the choice itself is not peculiar to this time, as is shown by the phenomenon of mental depression, found in all historical periods and cultures, where a person simply (but not only) stops valuing. A depressed person not only chooses to be affectless—he chooses that the world correspond and be value-less too. In mental depression, the fact–value gap is psychologically real. Can those philosophical theories that attempt to bridge, under-

* I do this, even though my metaphilosophical instincts tell me that philosophical impasses, such as the one about value, are to be met by formulating new and unexpected views that deny some assumption common to all previous ones, rather than by trying to resuscitate a variant of a previous view. Whatever its virtues, the unsuccessful theory is not served by wheeling it into battle for yet another (this time farcical?) defeat. (Those who do know the past are doomed to repeat it, pedantically.) When position X succumbed to difficulty Y, any position aptly described as "neo-X" will, after a time, with probability .942, succumb to neo-Y, if not to the same old Y.

cut, or fly over this gap bring an acknowledgment of value from a logically acute depressive, deriving a value conclusion from premisses he accepts? It is not a daring speculation that all such theories proposed thus far will falter here. Although the goal of philosophy is not to convince anyone of anything, the *gedankenexperiment* might constitute an appropriate test of the claim that there is no gap of a certain sort.

Does the maker of the choice that there be value merely see the world as valuable, taking a value perspective on the world? Should we compare it to the gestalt figures that can be seen in two ways, the old woman and the young girl, the duck-rabbit, the vase and two faces, the Necker cube? One might be tempted to think the person who chooses that there be value adds something, that he interprets the world while the person who says there is no value merely describes what is there. With the gestalt figures, all agree that there are lines and inkspots; the figures also can be seen simply as that (and so can be seen in three ways). However, this is not the perspective of the person who denies there is value, for he adds to the agreed facts (about organic unity and responsiveness, for example) the clause "and there is no value". So, to continue the analogy, his also is one of the full-blown interpretations corresponding to the old woman or young girl, not a minimal one corresponding to "lines and inkspots".

So are there simply two equally good interpretations, one affirming value while the other denies it, each equally true? The view that denies the existence of value cannot claim to be equally good, for it recognizes no notion of goodness according to which it is equal; however, it might claim to be "no worse", meaning thereby that there is no notion of "worse" according to which it ranks lower. In that case, neither does the other view rank lower than it and so on its own view, it (at best) ties. On the other hand, the view that affirms value is able to rank itself as better than the view that denies it. To be sure, the view that denies value claims to be true, but it cannot claim that it is better to be true, or that it is better to believe the truth. Although those who deny value sometimes see as itself valuable their tough-mindedness in refusing to succumb to (what they view as) the illusion of value, this comfort is not legitimately available to them.

Leaving aside such dialectical points, do we who choose that there be value regard our valuing and finding value merely as one perspective, one view among others? If not, do we deem it true that there is value, and is this a truth that exists independently, one our choice that there be value fortunately happens to match, or is it somehow created or brought into being by that choice that there be value?

In valuing things, we choose to view the world as valuable, we choose that there be value. In thus valuing things, we also can value the existing of value, and our V-ing value. Our choosing that there be value is itself retrospectively and retroactively held to be valuable, according to the results of the choice; the value not only is chosen but is instanced in its very choosing. However, to speak of value being there retrospectively and retroactively may miscontrue the situation. For the choice that there be value might apply to itself not (only) in retrospect but at that time, reflexively. Reflexivity of reference, reference "from the inside", we recall from the first chapter, involves referring in virtue of a property bestowed in the act of referring, referring to something as having that (bestowed) property as so bestowed. The object is referred to, we might say, as an object of (that) reflexive referring. Similarly, the choice that there be value is reflexive when it chooses that there be value in virtue of a property bestowed by that very act of choice; it chooses that there be value in virtue of that very choosing that there be value. In the previous chapter, we described how an uncaused choice could be nonrandom and free, involving a reflexive weighting of reasons or of value. Here we see how the choice that there be value might fit that structure. The choice that there be value and the choice to pursue value each are subsumed under the choice to V value; and this choice can be made as an instance of the policy of pursuing and V-ing value, a policy that is reflexively and self-subsumingly brought into effect in that very choice.

Can a choice that there be value be ungrounded (in the sense of set theory) in this way, unlike invoking a sense according to which a reflexive reference is made, or invoking constitutive rules according to which a performative-illocutionary act is done?[125] Even if value somehow could be there as a result of a choice that there be value, is there a value bestowed in virtue of such a reflexive bestowing, which bestows it only as (reflexively) bestowed? Is that value really there?

Consider the case of placebos, inert chemicals given for medicinal purposes. A person is given medicine and told it will help his illness or pain; he believes what he is told, and is thereby helped. This helping works through his belief, however, not simply through the biochemical action of the substance; if he is slipped the same chemical substance unawares, without being told he will be helped, then no benefit is received. It is true that the substance that is in a placebo will help, but only if the patient, when taking it, believes it will.

How does this helping work? Recently, it has been discovered that endorphins, pain-relieving substances similar to morphine, are naturally produced in the body, and there is some evidence that a placebo works through the accompanying production of endorphins.* Let us suppose that when a person believes he is receiving an effective pain reliever or other aid, this stimulates the production of endorphins or other healing agents so that he is helped.[126]

Consider the case of someone who knows of these scientific results about the mode of action of placebos; when in pain, he is given a placebo and is told that he is being given a *placebo*. Will his pain be lessened? This is an empirical question (for which, as I understand it, there is some evidence that the answer is affirmative). Upon being administered the placebo, this knowledgeable person might ask: do placebos work in cases such as this one, where the person knows he is being given a placebo? If it works only if the person believes it will (or might?), then he may well want to know whether it works in this type of case. (And must he then ask whether it also works in the case of someone who knows he has been given a placebo, and has learned whether it works then? And so on.) Let us suppose—remember, it is an empirical question—that it does work in this case, for those who believe it will (or may) work. (Perhaps it did not at first, but people have been told it works in this situation, told that there are experimental data showing it works then, and so, given their belief, it does work.) This supposed action of the placebo would be ungrounded; it would work in virtue of the belief that *such* placebos work. Endorphins here are produced in virtue of a reflexive belief:

* When a person is given an inhibitor of endorphins along with, or as, a placebo, he does not report lessened pain. However, this experiment is open to the following interpretation. Placebos might work through some pain-reducing factor X other than endorphins, so that a person's pain relief from receiving a placebo is a product of X plus his naturally occurring endorphins. The endorphin inhibitor removes the latter, leaving him only with X, and thus a lessened relief from pain, even though the placebo does not act through endorphins.

the belief that this very belief will produce endorphins. (Consider how an account of knowledge such as that presented in Chapter 3 should handle the question of whether this person knows that he will be helped by the placebo.)

Until now we have avoided the ontological question of whether value exists. We have described what value would be if there *were* value (namely, organic unity), how we could be responsive to such value and to the valuable characteristics of others, and how we could seek and pursue value. We have suggested that conditions on value could be listed that would uniquely specify it, excluding all dimensions except one as being the dimension of intrinsic value. However, nowhere have we argued, proven, or shown that that one candidate dimension *is* value or explained why it is sufficient to constitute value. (Although the conditions would explain why value, if it exists, is that dimension and no other.) Our previous discussion, to use the term of the phenomenologists, bracketed the ontological question about the existence of value; our theory described what it would be like to live in a universe where there was value, where there were ethical truths. (But would not a full description of such a universe present sufficient conditions for the existence of value?)

Suppose, though, that we are unlucky enough to live in a universe, otherwise identical, but without value. The necessary conditions constitutive of value are satisfied, and some things have a high degree of organic unity, which (let us suppose) would be value if anything is, yet in that universe there just is not any value. (Would that be "unlucky" because that situation is worse? Would that judgment be made in accordance with a value standard that holds true in this described universe, or only in some other one?) Still, why be subject to the contingency of living in a universe without value? Couldn't we cut our losses, and choose to live as if our universe *did* contain value, thereby being no worse off than if value existed—even as judged by the value standard of that other world which does contain value? Thus, it seems that the existence of value is not needed, only some coherent way that value would be. We need merely that value be possible. Nothing then would be lacking in our universe that was contained in the other one; for we here could track, adhere to, and pursue the value which exists there, realizing it here. We here could make actual the unities, responsiveness, and so forth, that *are* valuable there. It is unnecessary to go, as e. e. cummings suggests, to the "hell of a good universe next door"; we can bring its value back here.

These reflections might suggest that the existence of value lies in its possibility; if it exists in some other possible world, then for any practical or theoretical purpose, it exists here as well. Isn't it enough for value to play a role in my life that I know what value would be like?[127] Yet, what difference is there between there and here; what more holds true there in virtue of which value there exists? (Does value just happen to be supervenient there upon certain facts, such as organic unity, but not here?) But if there is no difference then why doesn't this show that value does not exist there either (since in both places there will not be sufficient conditions for value), and thereby show that value is impossible?

We know what value would be; we have only to bring it to life, to value it, to seek and pursue it, contouring our lives in accordance with it. We have only to choose that there be value. What is needed to bring value to our universe is our reflexive choice that there be value, our reflexive imputation of the existence of value.[128]

The fundamental choice open to us is whether or not there will be value; this choice is not dictated, it is not marked as better by any preexisting standard of value.[129] It is, to use a term of Kierkegaard's, a leap; but once having leaped, or rather, in (and in virtue of) that very process of leaping, it is seen to be the better choice.* Value is not alien to us, not wholly external, for we (not only have it but) choose that there be value. Nevertheless, an external standard is provided, for the character of value is not similarly up to us. The significant

* It might be worth considering whether our discussion of the reflexive choice that there be value can illuminate Kierkegaard's obscure notion of "subjective truth". (See *Concluding Unscientific Postscript*, Princeton University Press, Princeton, 1944, Part II, ch. 2.) However, he wishes to apply it to religious belief, to faith in a God who acted and produced effects in people and the world and who will do so again. It is difficult to see how any act of a person, even a reflexive one, could yield this being. Value, on the other hand, is inert; it itself has no causal powers and can act only through value perceivers who pursue it. Thus, it is more plausible to see the existence of value as connected to our choice that there be value, than to see the existence of an active God as connected with our worship of such a being. The religious analogue of our view about value would have to involve a theology about the holiness of worshiping a passive perfect being.

division is between those who choose that there be value and those who do not, either choosing that there not be value or not rising to the choice at all.

If some do not choose that there be value, then is there value for us but none for them? In the language of quantum mechanics, does each person live in a superposition between a world with value and one without it, with his choice (that there be value, or not) reducing the wave packet of the world he lives in? However, don't we all live in the same world? One indication that we do is the envious motivation of the pursuer of evil, discussed earlier, who cannot rest content if even one person achieves a valuable existence. On this view, the choice by one person that there be value affects the rest so that they too live in a world with value, whatever they choose. Yet perhaps this is too strong; perhaps each must choose that there be value, if there is to be value in his world, for him. If someone else refuses to choose that there be value this does not undermine our relationship to value—we who choose that there be value.

Clearly it is better to pursue and track value than to have a connection with correct values effected, willy-nilly, by retributive punishment; the first connection is more organically unified and so more valuable than the second, which yet has some lesser value of its own. But can one who chooses that there be value legitimately inflict retributive punishment, to effect connection with this value, upon another who perhaps does not choose that there be value? The choice that there be value also involves, if that *is* the nature of value, seeing this retributive connection as valuable.

In the earlier section on Kantian structuring, we considered whether the fact–value gap might somehow be bridged as an effect of a self's structuring (or synthesizing) itself as a self, and we noticed that this would not involve the full extent of the basic moral characteristic—being a value-seeking self. Our current reflections might be interpreted as fitting that theme. If structuring oneself as a value-seeking self involves, as part of the self-synthesis, the reflexive choice that there be value, then indeed value would arise from that Kantian structuring. (This structuring is not open to the objection to the earlier one—that it reduces the significance of the moral pull—for this structuring does not make another person's value dependent upon or derivative from your self, except insofar as this involves your self's desire to track value, including his.) Such a structuring could not constitute part of an argument to convince someone that (he is committed to believe) there is value, however, since it depends upon a pursuit of value, a seeking of it, as a basic ingredient of the self so structured, rather than as fallout from it. We might note that the desire to offer a philosophical proof of an ethical theory, a knock-down argument that forces someone to believe the conclusion whether he wants to believe it or not, is in tension with the desire for autonomy in ethics.

The view we have presented grants us autonomy: the choice that there be value is ungoverned by preexisting value standards. At the same time it provides an external standard to track and adhere to: the character and contour of the value, so chosen, is not similarly subject to choice.[130] It seems plausible to sociologists that freedom of choice among religions reinforces secularization—a person will not view as binding what he himself chooses, so his very act of choosing is incompatible with religions that place being externally bound in their essence.[131] The choice we describe here is not among values, but between there being value and not. Such a choice that there be value, which is seen to be the right one upon being made, is not, I think, incompatible with feeling value to make an external claim. Nonetheless, autonomy is preserved by the fact that there is this *choice* that there be value.

Why is autonomy of value? (If it is of value, then only by some choice involving value can it be achieved.) On the view of value as organic unity, we can see that autonomously accepting value, choosing that there be value, establishes a tighter linkage between the person and value, and so a more valuable linkage, than some nonautonomous relationship. (Yet something about value, its existence or nature, must be external if we are to gain value by linking with it; also, linking with an externality unifies a greater diversity and so is more valuable.) Can he who chooses that there be value also deem himself thereby to have originative value?

This introduction of choice that there be value also provides an internalist strand in the theory of value, whereby value will have some (perhaps circuitous) connection with a person's motivations.[132] The worry about moral views that postulate intuition into a realm of completely independent preexisting moral facts—that we might be bored by or indifferent to these facts—thereby is avoided. It is a common feeling that ethics somehow is more subjective than some other facts, being not only about our choices and responses but more closely connected to them. Such a connection is the one joining the existence of value with the (reflexive) choice that there be value. (Could there be an epistemological theory that similarly utilizes the choice, "let there be facts"?) Although the character of the value so willed is not up to us, there is room for moral creativity (as discussed in the section on pluralism) in the weighting and balancing of different values, in forming a life embodying a new and original organic unity of diverse constituent values. In addition, if the conditions on value do not zero in on one unique dimension of intrinsic value, but leave several candidates remaining, then there will be room for choice among (diverse weightings of) the few viable candidate dimensions.*

---

* Nietzsche called for a "revaluation of values", which includes a war against previous values (what he calls "applying the knife vivisectionally to the chest of the very virtues of their time" in *Beyond Good and Evil*, 212) and the creation of new values. However, Nietzsche did not claim to do the latter; the legislation of new values was a task for future philosophers, what he called overmen. Nietzsche tells us something about their characteristics, in scattered remarks. They would be proud, joyous, intent on overcoming (surpassing, perfecting) themselves, masters of themselves, hard, strong, noble, passionate, powerful, courageous, having reverence for themselves, scorning an easy, comfortable, serene life, forging themselves into a new kind of person. The task of other people, Nietzsche held, is to help bring about the existence of these overmen, to create the conditions for their existence—only their lives have value. ("The goal of humanity cannot be in the end but only in its highest specimens." *Second Untimely Meditation*, 19.) It is unclear whether Nietzsche believes these great individuals confer worth and value on the rest of us; sometimes he speaks as though value spills over to the rest (*Will to Power*, 713, 877), sometimes he almost speaks of these others as belonging to a different species (across which gap there is no spill-over of value).

But for what end is all this hardness, strength, daring, and so on of the overman? What will he do with it? It is not much help, or very interesting, to be told that he will forge himself into something hard, strong, and daring. Perhaps Nietzsche thinks that any life that exhibits these qualities, working on obdurate material and challenges including that life itself, will be valuable whatever its goal—valuable enough to include and outweigh the using, injuring, and destroying of others. (See *Beyond Good and Evil*, 265, 259; *Genealogy of Morals*, I, 13.) However, I think Nietzsche believes these overmen will pursue particular values; the correct values or at any rate the new values will be the ones they pursue. That will be their "legislation". Nietzsche clearly believes their qualities which he lists are valuable ones, but more importantly these people function as his "ideal observers". The goals they choose to pursue, whatever that turns out to be, will be fixed as the valuable ones (at least when pursued their way). Thus Nietzsche's view

The Relationship Between Fact and Value

How, then, shall we describe the relationship between fact and value? Particular facts F do not entail particular value or ought statements V. An additional premiss is needed, namely: there is value. This is the weakest possible additional (nontrivial) value premiss. Yet it serves, given the rest of the apparatus of this chapter, in the derivation of particular value conclusions from particular facts. This weakest premiss is the (existentially quantified) claim that there is *some* true value or ought statement. (If it would be valuable that there hold some true value statement, then there is at least that meta-one.) This is a far cry from smuggling particular values into the derivation.

Should we have expected any closer a relation of fact to value than this one? To be sure, on the view of value as organic unity, facts can be valuable by instantiating or realizing the structure or configuration of organic unity that is the value; they can be models of the value. Our question here, though, is about the connection, for example, between "fact F has degree of organic unity d" and "F has value V". We can conclude that organic unity constitutes value only on the assumption that there is value; and this assumption is enough. If the necessary conditions on intrinsic value specify the dimension

---

is all wind-up and no pitch. (The absence of determinate values specified in Nietzsche's view also has recently been emphasized by Philippa Foot, "The Brave Immoralist", *New York Review of Books,* Vol. 27, May 1, 1980, pp. 35–37.)

For all we know or are told, these described people all will choose to become gentler, softer, more considerate of others, respecters of their rights, less proud, and so forth. Nietzsche gives us a process (of mixed attractiveness) toward new values, with no indication of what will come out, and so no assurance that those values will be new ones. Compare the position of those political philosophers (followers of Leo Strauss?) who see the highest political wisdom in the dictum that the wisest should rule. For this to be interesting, we must be told something about what the wisest will choose—there is no point working to institute the rule of the wisest if they, in their wisdom, then will reinstate the *status quo ante* (democratic elections, separation of powers, and so on), and thereupon resign.

Although the conditions on intrinsic value might not select one unique dimension, and so might leave some leeway for choice, they are quite restrictive, and not every view that announces its originality with much fanfare will turn out to be very different, when pruned of its obviously inadequate features.

of "degree of organic unity" as the unique candidate for value, then adding the additional statement that there is (some dimension of) value produces sufficient conditions for organic unity's being value. How is this additional premiss, the statement that there is value, related to the facts? Our theory holds that the person reflexively imputes that (statement) to the facts. (Would it not be better if the facts reflexively imputed there being value to themselves, instead of the person doing it? Yet isn't he, and his doing that, part of the facts?)

Given the choice that there be value, against the background of the premiss that value exists, what is the relation of value to fact? Are some facts, the organically unified ones, then identical with value(s)? I want to say: the relationship is organic unity—values are organically related to (some) facts. (What else would you expect?) The choice that there be value brings (some) facts into an organic relationship with value, unifying these but not identifying them.

How tight will that relationship of organic unification be? We might engage in further speculation. Identity is a particular mode of unity, a very tight one, and perhaps the reason the facts are not identical with value (even modulo the existence of value) is that these facts, the ones we deal with, are not themselves organically unified enough to be identical with value. Let F be some fact, a valuable one, with degree of organic unity d. Perhaps the (organic unity of the) relationship of this fact F to value, then, cannot itself be of a tighter degree than d. The degree of organic unity of the fact places a limit on how closely it can be connected with value. (Since things of value do realize and instantiate the abstract structures which values are, it follows that these relationships 'realize' and 'isomorphic to' aren't the tightest possible.) The value of the relationship of a particular fact to value, then, depends upon how valuable that fact is. The precise relationship of organically unified facts (or factual situations) to value depends on how unified the facts are. At the limit, identical to value is whatever is organically unified to the highest possible degree—supposing that identity is the tightest relationship, so that only the greatest organic unity could stand in it to value.

Has there been a problem of the relationship between facts and values because our facts have not been organically unified enough yet, not a tight enough unification of a vast enough diversity? If so, it is not surprising that some writers (for example, the theorists of moral "fittingness"), instead of speaking of identity, have been tempted to use the imprecise terminology of organic unity, rooted in the arts or in gestalt psychology, to describe the relationship of value to fact.

In our earlier discussion of the value of the self, we noted that the I does not merely want to have something that is valuable (a valuable body or mind or whatever) but wants to be valuable itself. And we wondered whether this was enough, for even when the self itself is valuable, isn't value still just something the self *has*—another possession? It seemed that nothing less would satisfy the self than to be value, to be identical with value, not merely to have or realize it.

Our selves, limited and finite, are not organically unified enough to be identical with value, though; they can only instantiate or have value. However, theological views that speak of the greatest possible organic unity (God, the unlimited Ein Sof, Satchitananda) see it as identical with value. We are in a position to understand this, now. Its degree of organic unity is so great (infinite—are there orders of infinity here?) that its relationship with value is identity. It *is* value. We can understand also why the mystic reports his experience of this greatest organic unity not merely as a valuable experience but an experience of (what is) Value.

Still, we can wonder whether the mystic, even if his experience is an experience *of* something, has experienced the greatest possible organic unity. Perhaps it is only a partial organic unity, so far beyond what we normally encounter as to seem total yet still only partial, competing against other equals or even superiors. Perhaps there is no perfect organic unity, so even at the topmost level (if there is a topmost level) there is a striving for ever greater organic unity, for an even tighter encompassing of a greater diversity, an even greater value. What, after all, do we know of such things? Alternative theories, postulating levels underneath or above reversing levels, are compatible with mystical experiences and revelations.

From the point of view of the theory of value, however, it does not seem important that there be a most perfect organic unity, or that mystics do experience an existing something which at all hidden levels is as they experience it (rather than experience what is partially an expression of their own aspiration, or of the something's). For, in either case, we know what value is, and we can be transformed by this knowledge, even if nothing is identical with Value, yet.

The gap between fact and value, bridged but not erased by our reflexive choice that there be value, should not be viewed as wholly negative. Though this gap allows some to deny the existence of value, it bars reductionist denigrations of value, which see it as "nothing but" something lesser.

We opened this chapter with the question of how ethics is even possible. I have sketched one possible answer, one way there could be ethics and value. I would not have pursued this way in such detail if I did not think it largely right, yet (let me reemphasize) it can yield us an *understanding* of how ethics is possible even if the explanation it provides is incorrect.

But how important is ethics and value? True, the ethical person responds to the value of others, qua value, and thereby has a more valuable existence himself, but how important is that? In the larger scheme of things, from the point of view of the universe (which itself may "run down" into a state of maximum entropy, wiping out all past record) is there any importance to ethical behavior, is there any meaning even to a valuable life? How meaningful is it to achieve value? Unless it can be shown how our lives and existence can have meaning, how meaning is possible, ethics and value themselves (not to mention this chapter's enterprise of understanding these) will seem *meaningless*.

Chapter
Six

PHILOSOPHY
AND THE
MEANING
OF LIFE

The question of what meaning our life has, or can have, is of utmost importance to us. So heavily is it laden with our emotion and aspiration that we camouflage our vulnerability with jokes about seeking for the meaning or purpose of life: A person travels for many days to the Himalayas to seek the word of an Indian holy man meditating in an isolated cave. Tired from his journey, but eager and expectant that his quest is about to reach fulfillment, he asks the sage, "What is the meaning of life?" After a long pause, the sage opens his eyes and says, "Life is a fountain." "What do you mean, life is a fountain?" barks the questioner. "I have just traveled thousands of miles to hear your words, and all you have to tell me is that? That's ridiculous." The sage then looks up from the floor of the cave and says, "You mean it's not a fountain?" In a variant of the story, he replies, "So it's not a fountain."

The story is reassuring. The supposed sages are frauds who speak nonsense, nonsense they either never thought to question ("You mean it's not a fountain?") or do not care very much about ("So it's not a fountain"). Surely, then, we have nothing to learn from these ridiculous people; we need not seek their ludicrous "wisdom".

But why was it necessary for the joke to continue on after the sage said "life is a fountain", why was it necessary for the story to include the seeker's objection and the sage's reply? Well, perhaps the sage *did* mean something by "life is a fountain", something profound which we did not understand. The challenge and his reply show his words were empty, that he can give no deep and illuminating interpretation to his remark. Only then are we in a secure position to laugh, in relief.

However, if we couldn't know immediately that his answer "life is a fountain" was ridiculous, if we needed further words from him to exclude the lingering possibility of a deeper meaning to his apparently preposterous first reply, then how can we be sure that his second answer also does not have a deeper meaning which we don't understand? He says "You mean it's not a fountain?"; but who are *you* to mean? If you know so much about it, then why have you gone seeking him; do you even know enough to recognize an appropriate answer when you hear it?

The questioner apparently came in humility, seeking the truth, yet he assumed he knew enough to challenge the answer he heard. When he objects and the sage replies, "so it's not a fountain", was it to gain this victory in discussion that the questioner traveled so far? (The story is told that Gershom Scholem, the great scholar of kabbalism, as a young man sought out practitioners of kabbalah in Jerusalem, and was told he could study with them on the condition that he not ask any questions for two years. Scholem, who has a powerful, critical, and luminous intelligence, refused.)

When he set out on his trip, did the questioner hope for an intellectual formula presenting the meaning of life? He wanted to know how he should live in order to achieve a life with meaning. What did he expect to hear from this meditating man in a cave high in the mountains? "Go back to the posh suburb and continue your present life, but shift to a less pressured job and be more accessible to your children"? Presumably, the man in the cave is following what he takes to be the path to a meaningful life; what else can he answer except "follow my path, be like me"? "Are you crazy; do you think I am going to throw everything over to become a scruffy person sitting in a cave?" But does the seeker know enough to exclude that life as the most (or only) meaningful one, the seeker who traveled to see *him?*

Could *any* formula answer the question satisfactorily? "The meaning of life is to seek union with God"—oh yeah, that one. "A meaningful life is a full and productive life"—sure. "The purpose of life is to pursue the task of giving meaning to life"—thanks a lot. "The meaning of life is love"—yawn. "The meaning of life is spiritual perfection"—the upward and onward trip. "The meaning of life is getting off the wheel of life and becoming annihilated"—no thanks. No one undertakes the trip to the sage who hasn't already encountered all the known formulas and found them wanting. Does the seeker think the sage has some *other* words to tell him, words which somehow have not reached print? Or is there a secret formula, an esoteric doctrine that, once heard, will clarify his life and point to meaning? If there were such a secret, does he think the wise man will tell it to *him*, fresh from Los Angeles with two days of travel by llama and foot? Faced with such a questioner, one might as well tell him that life is a fountain, perhaps hoping to shock him into reconsidering what he is doing right then. (Since he will not understand anything, he might as well be told the truth as best he can understand it—the joke would be that life *is* a fountain. Better yet would be for that to get embodied in a joke.)

If it is not words the questioner needs—certainly no short formula will help—perhaps what he needs is to encounter the person of the sage, to be in his presence. If so, questions will just get in the way; the visitor will want to observe the sage over time, opening himself to what he may receive. Perhaps he will come eventually to find profundity and point in the stale formulas he earlier had found wanting.

Now, let us hear another story. A man goes to India, consults a sage in a cave and asks him the meaning of life. In three sentences the sage tells him, the man thanks him and leaves. There are several variants of this story also: In the first, the man lives meaningfully ever after; in the second he makes the sentences public so that everyone then knows the meaning of life; in the third, he sets the sentences to rock music, making his fortune and enabling everyone to whistle the meaning of life; and in the fourth variant, his plane crashes as he is flying off from his meeting with the sage. In the fifth version, the person listening to me tell this story eagerly asks what sentences the sage spoke.

And in the sixth version, I tell him.

Modes of Meaning(fulness)

As briskly as we can, let us distinguish different senses and kinds of meaning, in order to assess their relevance to our concern.

I. *Meaning as external causal relationship:* as causal consequences ("this means war"), causal antecedents or causal concomitants that serve as a basis of inference ("those spots mean measles, smoke means fire, red sky at night means fair weather").

II. *Meaning as external referential or semantic relation:* synonomy ("brother" means male sibling), reference ("the man in the corner" means him), standing for a fact (a white flag means they surrender) or symbolizing (the meaning of Yeats' "rough beast").

III. *Meaning as intention or purpose:* intending an action ("he meant well", "what is the meaning of this outburst?" "did you mean to do that?"), purpose ("this play is meant to catch the conscience of the king"), or (Gricean) intending to convey or indicate something via another's recognizing this intention ("by that gesture he meant to insult us").

IV. *Meaning as lesson:* "The Nazi period means that even a most civilized nation can commit great atrocities", "Gandhi's success means that nonviolent techniques sometimes can win over force".

V. *Meaning as personal significance, importance, value, mattering:* "You mean a lot to me", "the repeal of that legislation means a lot to them". Under this rubric is a completely subjective notion, covering what a person thinks is important to him, and one somewhat less so, covering what affects something subjectively important to him, even if he does not realize this.

These first five notions are not intractable; one might hope they could provide at least some elements for explaining the next two, which are more obscure.

VI. *Meaning as objective meaningfulness:* importance, significance, meaning.

VII. *Meaning as intrinsic meaningfulness:* objective meaning (VI) in itself, apart from any connections to anything else.

VIII. *Meaning as total resultant meaning:* the sum total and web of something's meanings I–VII.

Using these distinctions, let us consider the question about the meaning of our life or of our existence. A life easily can have meaning as external causal relationships, for example (ignoring adultery, artificial insemination, parthenogenesis, and virgin birth) your life means that your parents had sexual relations at least once, your existence means there will be less room on earth for all the others. On this reading, every life has (multiple) meaning, and if these causally connected things need not be inferable, a life will mean all of its causal antecedents and consequents and concomitants, and perhaps all of theirs as well, in ever widening circles. The meaning of a life, then, would be the whole causal nexus and flow of events; the causal nexus is meant by the life's place in it. Thereby is gotten the result that a life certainly means something big and impressive; importance might be attributed to the life due to its role in this impressive web —see how much has prepared the way for it, and how much will flow from it, by the same processes which govern everything. However, this may involve a diminution in relative importance: everything thus connected in the web of events becomes equally important.

It is even easier to establish very impressive semantic meaning to our lives, at least for one sort of semantic meaning. Stipulative definitions can give a word new or altered semantic meaning. For example, I can say that by a *smink* I shall mean a ridiculous example introduced to illustrate a point. To my knowledge, no one else ever has used this word, or used any other word with this meaning. I have just given it this meaning. By stipulation, I have tied the word smink to this meaning; all I need do is use it consistently with this meaning hereafter.

There is no reason of principle why only words or gestures can have semantic meaning. It certainly is convenient that these be the vehicles of meaning—being producible at will, they are easily used for communication. However, some physical objects also are producible at will, while certain words might not be, due to difficulty in pronunciation. So we might stipulate that an event or object (for example, the particular copy of this book you now are reading) will have a specific meaning. And if we can stipulate meanings for objects, we similarly can stipulate meaning for your life or for you, and make this meaning be as exalted as you please. Let your life (be stipulated to) mean the triumph of justice or goodness in the universe. Presto, your life has meaning.

Clearly, this is ridiculous; no such arbitrary connections between a person's life and what it is stipulated to mean can give it the requisite sort of meaning. But we should not leave the topic of semantic meaning without seeing whether there is some nonarbitrary way that a person's life can semantically refer to or mean something. Let us say, following Nelson Goodman, that something exemplifies a property, characteristic, pattern, trait, or attribute, if it both has that property and also refers to it.[1] A life, then, would exemplify those properties it both refers to and has.

It is easy to see how a person's life can have properties. To tell us how a life can refer semantically to these properties we should bring in the third sense of meaning, meaning as intention or purpose. A person can mean something by what he does, or have a certain purpose for what he makes. Similarly, by external design people could have been created as semantic objects, for example, by God to refer to himself. If God's purpose in creating people was to have them refer to himself, and he gave them some properties ("in the image of God") to facilitate this referring, then everyone would be something like a name of God. (Would this be sufficient meaning for us? Is the universe a token through which God reflexively self refers?)

Let us leave theological speculations aside and ask whether a person's life can refer semantically in virtue of his intending or meaning his own life to have certain properties. The topic of intention is an intricate one; any adequate theory will have to incorporate the directed, focused quality of intention. I intend to bring about only some aspects of what I do, even of what I know will occur when I act. Intending is something like intending to make a particular description true. I can intend to eat vanilla ice cream, and know that if I do so my life will include an incident of vanilla ice cream eating, without thereby intending my life to be that of a sometime vanilla ice cream eater; I need have no such grand intention about my whole life. My intention need not focus upon that aspect of my action.

To intend that my life be a certain way, I must have an intention or desire or goal or plan that focuses upon my life as a whole, or at least upon a significant portion of it. The statement of my intention, its focus, must include some reference to my life. The strongest sort of intention about one's life is a *life plan*,[2] an individual's set of coherent, systematic purposes and intentions for his life. These need not be specified fully, they will leave much open for further detailing, they can be revised, and so on. A life plan specifies the intentional focus of a person's life, his major goals (perhaps partially ordering them), his conception of himself, his purposes, what if anything he dedicates or devotes himself to, and so forth. Unlike the example of intending to eat vanilla ice cream (which would be included as a specific part only in a very strange life plan), a life plan focuses on a person's whole life or a significant chunk of it as a life.

Using this notion of a life plan, we can say that a person's life refers to a property if its having that property is a (weighty) part of the life plan he is engaged in putting into effect. His life exemplifies a property if it both has it and refers to it.

A life plan can have and refer to a property without showing or communicating this. The life of a furtive criminal, in this sense, might mean: steal as much as you can, undetected. In contrast to this, a person's life goals can shine forth. Let us say that a person lives transparently to the extent that the structure and content of what he exemplifies is clear; his life plan (its arrangement and hierarchy of goals, and so forth) is evident to those who take the trouble to notice what he does and says. The surface of his life, its public face, does not hide or cover his life plan. His life is not a mystery, his fundamental motivations and goals are not undetectable. He has made his life an open book.

However, just as empirical data underdetermine a scientific theory, so actions do not uniquely fix the life plan from which they flow. Different life plans are compatible with and might yield the same actions. So, people also state or explain why they act as they do, especially when other prevalent life plans that differ importantly would lead to that same behavior. Some take pains to perform the very actions wherein their life plans and goals significantly diverge from others—they delineate themselves. It is a puzzle how so many people, including intellectuals and academics, devote enormous energy to work in which nothing of themselves or their important goals shines forth, not even in the way their work is presented. If they were struck down, their children upon growing up and examining their work would never know why they had done it, would never know *who* it was that did it. They work that way and sometimes live that way, too.

The next notion of meaning on our list, meaning as lesson to be learned from, can build upon this previous one. People do not want their lives to provide negative lessons ("the lesson of his life is: do not live as he does"); although even here, they may take comfort if they think that lesson is important enough, and that others will act on the moral of their sad story. We hope the lessons to be learned from our lives will be connected more positively with the way we try to live, that the lesson will be based upon a positive evaluation of transparent features of our life plan.

This is recognizable as what some have meant by a meaningful life: (1) a life organized according to a plan and hierarchy of goals that integrates and directs the life, (2) having certain features of structure, pattern, and detail that the person intends his life to have (3) and show forth; he lives transparently so others can see see the life plan his life is based upon (4) and thereby learn a lesson from his life, (5) a lesson involving a positive evaluation of these weighty and intended features in the life plan he transparently lives. In sum, the pattern he transparently exemplifies provides a positive lesson.

Furthermore, the person himself may intend that others learn a lesson from his exemplification, intending also that they learn from it in virtue of recognizing his (Gricean) intention that they do so. In this way, he uses his life (partly) to communicate a lesson to others, a lesson about living. This, I suppose, is what is meant by a *teacher*. (Philosophy had one such, Socrates—for how long shall we be able to continue to live off his momentum?) The life of such a person (semantically and nonarbitrarily) means the lesson it exemplifies; it has at least that meaning.

Even of such a shining and exemplary life, however, we can ask what it all amounts to. We can ask whether the lesson itself has any significance or meaning. We can distance ourselves from the life, see it as the particular thing it was, notice its limits, and wonder whether really it has any meaning. We can stand outside it and see it as a thing, as a nonvibrant and meaningless thing, soon to end in death, full of sound and fury, signifying nothing.

Death

It is often assumed that there is a problem about the meaning of life because of our mortality. Why does the fact that all people die create a special problem? (If life were to go on forever, would there then be no problem about its meaning?) One opposite view has been proposed that welcomes the fact of death and makes a virtue of its apparently grim necessity. Victor Frankl writes that "death itself is what makes life meaningful", arguing for this startling view as follows. "What would our lives be like if they were not finite in time, but infinite? If we were immortal, we could legitimately postpone every action forever. It would be of no consequence whether or not we did a thing now; every act might just as well be done tomorrow or the day after or a year from now or ten years hence. But in the face of death as absolute *finis* to our future and boundary to our possibilities, we are under the imperative of utilizing our lifetimes to the utmost, not letting the singular opportunities—whose 'finite' sum constitutes the whole of life—pass by unused."[3] It would appear, then, that persons who were or could become immortal should choose to set a temporal limit to their lives in order to escape meaninglessness; scientists who discovered some way to avoid natural death should suppress their discoveries.*

Frankl assumes our only desire is to have done certain things, to put certain things somewhere on our record. Because we shall die, if we are to have done these things by the end of our lives, we had

---

* For a firm statement of the opposite view, see Alan Harrington, *The Immortalist* (Random House, New York, 1969). Frankl might avoid the consequences drawn in the text, by saying that though immortality would involve a sacrifice of meaningfulness, the other things gained might be even more important and so justify that sacrifice. Nevertheless, Frankl makes some parochial assumptions, and limits his vision of human possibilities. Even on his own terms, perhaps, you do best thinking you are mortal and very long-lived (having no good idea of approximately when the end would come, whether after 200 or 2,000 or 20,000 years), while in fact being immortal.

better get on with them. However, we may desire to do things; our desire need not be merely to have done them.[4] Moreover, if we had an infinite life, we might view it as a whole, as something to organize, shape and do something with. (Will this require us to be tolerant of very long gaps?) Persons who are immortal need not be limited to the desires and designs of mortals; they might well think up new plans that, in Parkinsonian fashion, expand to fill the available time. Despite his clear sympathy for religious thought, Frankl seems never to wonder or worry whether unlimited existence presents a problem of meaningfulness for God.

Whatever appeal Frankl's view has depends upon the more general assumption that certain limits, certain preexisting structures into which things can be poured, are necessary for meaningful organization. Similar things often are said in discussions of particular art forms, such as the sonnet and the sonata.[5] Even were this general assumption true, though, death constitutes only one kind of structural limitation: finiteness in time. Other kinds are possible too, and we well might welcome these others somewhat more. The dual assumption that some limitation is necessary for meaning, and limitation in time is the only one that can serve, is surely too ill established to convince anyone that mortality is good for him—unless he is willing to grasp at any straw. If we are going to grasp at things, let them not be straws.*

* There seems to be no limit to the flimsiness of what philosophers will grasp at to disarm the fact of death. It has been argued that if death is bad, bad because it ends life, that can only be because what it ends is good. It cannot be that life, because it ends in death, is bad, for if it were bad then death, ending a bad thing, itself would be good and not bad. The argument concludes that the badness of death presupposes the goodness of the life that it ends. (See Paul Edwards, "Life, Meaning and Value of", *Encyclopedia of Philosophy*, Macmillan, New York, 1967, Vol. 4, pp. 469–470.)
Why think that the badness of death resides in and depends upon the goodness of what it ends rather than in the goodness of what it prevents? When an infant dies three minutes after delivery, is its death bad because of the goodness of those three minutes that it ends, or because of the goodness of the longer life which it prevents? Similarly, suppose that only an infinite life could be good; death then would be bad because it prevented this. It would not follow or be presupposed that the finite portion itself was good. I do not say here that only an infinite life can be good, merely that this argument, purporting to show that the badness of death presupposes the goodness of a finite life, fails.
Even stranger arguments about death have been produced. We find Epicurus saying, "Death is nothing to us . . . it does not concern either the

Granting that our life ending in death is in tension, at least, with our existence having meaning, we have not yet isolated why this is so. We can pursue this issue by considering a puzzle raised by Lucretius, which runs as follows. No one is disturbed by there being a time before which they did not exist, before their birth or conception, although if the past is infinite, there was an infinite amount of time before you were born when you didn't exist. So why should you be disturbed by the fact that after you are dead, there also will be an infinite amount of time when you will not exist? What creates the asymmetry between the time before we were born and the time after we die, leading us to different attitudes toward these two periods?[6]

Is it that death is bad because it makes our lives finite in duration? We can sharpen this issue with an extreme supposition. Imagine that the past is infinite and that you have existed throughout all of it, having forgotten most. If death, even in this case, would disturb you, this is not because it makes you merely finite, since you are not, we are supposing, merely finite in the past direction. What then is so especially distressing about a finite future? Is it that an extended future gives you a chance for further improvement and growth, the opportunity to build from what you are now, whereas an infinite past that culminates only in what you now are might seem puny indeed? We can test whether this accounts for any difference in our attitudes toward infinite future and infinite past by imagining two cases that are mirror images. The infinite future of one is the mirror image of the other's infinite past; each has heights to match the heights of the other. If we had existed infinitely long until now, done all and seen all (though now the memory is dim), would we be disturbed at dying? Perhaps not, perhaps then the asymmetry between past and future would disappear. Nevertheless, this view does not explain why there is an asymmetry between the past and future for finite

---

living or the dead, since for the former it is not, and the latter are no more." Epicurus asks who death is bad for, and answers that it is not bad for anyone —not for anyone alive, for that person is not dead, and not for anyone dead, for dead people do not exist any more, and something can be bad only for someone who exists. Since there is no one for whom death is bad, Epicurus concludes, why should we fear it or even view it unfavorably? We shall not pause to unravel this argument, but note that it does have a limited point: if we believe death obliterates us, we should not fear it as if it were a bad *experience*.

beings. Why don't we bemoan our late (relative to the infinite past) birth, just as we bemoan our early death? Is the answer that we take the past as given and fixed already, and since, at the present juncture, it is what will happen that settles our fate, we therefore focus upon this?

In the mirror image situation, however, if we were satisfied with the life whose future was finite, that need not be simply because it contained an infinite past existence. That past existence must be specified as one in which we had done all, seen all, known all, been all. An infinite but monotonous past would not make death welcome, except perhaps as a deserved closing. Is the crucial fact about death not that it makes us finite or limits our future, but that it limits the possibilities (of those we would choose) that we can realize? On this view, death's sting lies not in its destroying or obliterating our personality, but in thwarting it. Nonetheless, underneath many phenomena there seems to lurk not simply the desire to realize other possibilities, but the desire and the hope to endure beyond death, perhaps forever.

Traces

Death wipes you out. Dead, you are no longer around—around *here* at any rate—and if there is nowhere else where you'll be (heaven, hell, with the white light) then all that will be left of you is your effects, leavings, traces. People do seem to think it important to continue to be around somehow. The root notion seems to be this one: it shouldn't *ever* be as if you had never existed at all. A significant life leaves its mark on the world. A significant life is, in some sense, permanent; it makes a permanent difference to the world—it leaves traces. To be wiped out completely, traces and all, goes a long way toward destroying the meaning of one's life. Endurance, however, even if a necessary condition for a meaningful life, is certainly not sufficient. We shall have to ask what kind of trace is important, and why that kind is not important even when very evanescent. First, though, let us explore some of the ramifications of the notion that it shouldn't ever be as if one had never lived or existed at all.

People sometimes speak of achieving immortality through their children. (Will this include achieving immortality through a child, himself childless, who achieves it in some other way? Did Kant's parents do so by siring Kant?) It is puzzling that people speak of achieving immortality by leaving descendants, since they do not believe that their chain of descendants, although perhaps very extended, is going to be infinite. So how do descendants bring immortality rather than a somewhat extended mortality? Perhaps the situation is this: while infinite continuation is best, any continuation is better than none. When a ninety-year-old's only child dies childless at the age of sixty-eight, we feel sad for this parent who now will not be leaving behind that (expected) trace.

There are many manifestations of the desire not to sink completely into oblivion. Artists often strive to leave behind permanent masterpieces, thereby achieving what is called immortality—a goal rejected by the dadaists in their temporary "art-for-a-day". People erect tombstones for others, and some make that provision for themselves. Tombstones are continuing marks upon the world; through them people know where your remains are, and remember you—hence, they are called *memorials*.

When funeral orators say, "he will live in our hearts", the assumption is not that the listeners will live forever, thereby immortalizing the dead person. Nor is it assumed that "living on in the hearts of" is a transitive relation, so that the dead person will continue to live on in the further hearts where the listeners themselves will live on. Permanent survival is not involved here, but neither is it sufficient merely to continue on somewhat, however little. Imagine that the funeral orator had said, "he will continue on in our minds until we leave this building whereupon we all promptly will forget him."

Another phrase sometimes heard is: "as long as people survive, this man will not be forgotten, his achievements and memory will live on." Presumably, one would want to add the proviso that people *will* live on for a long time. This, perhaps, is as close to immortality as a person can get. Some people are disturbed by the thought that life will go on for others, yet without themselves in any way. They are forgotten, and left out; those who follow later will live as if you never had. Here, permanent survival is not the goal, only survival as long as life goes on. More modest reference groups than all of humanity might be picked; you can hope to be remembered as long as your relations, friends, and acquaintances survive. In these cases it is not temporal enduringness that is crucial, but rather a certain sort of enduringness as shown in relationships to others.

When people desire to leave a trace behind, they want to leave a certain kind of trace. We all do leave traces, causal effects reverberate down: our voices move molecules which have their effects, we feed the worms, and so on. The kind of trace one wishes to leave is one that people know of in particular and that they know is due to you,[7] one due (people know) to some action, choice, plan of yours, that expresses something you take to be important about the kind of person you are, such that people respect or positively evaluate both the trace and that aspect of yourself. We want somehow to live on, but not as an object lesson for others. Notice also that wanting to live on by leaving appropriate traces need not involve wanting continuous existence; you want there to be some time after which you continue to leave a mark, but this time needn't be precisely at your death. Artists as well as those who anticipate resurrection are quite willing to contemplate and tolerate a gap.

Why are traces important? There are several possibilities. First, the importance of traces might lie not in themselves but (only) in what they indicate. Traces indicate that a person's life had a certain meaning or importance, but they are not infallible signs of this—there may be traces without meaning, or meaning without traces. For instance, to "live on" in the memory of others indicates one's effect on these others. It is the effect that matters; even if each of them happened to die first, there still would have been that effect. On this first view, it is a mistake to scrutinize traces in an attempt to understand how life has or can have meaning, for at best traces are a symptom of a life's meaning. Second, traces might be an expression of something important about a life, but it might be important and valuable in addition that this be expressed.

Third, it might be thought that the leaving of traces is intrinsically important. A philosophical tradition going back to Plato holds that the permanent and unchanging is more valuable by virtue of being permanent and unchanging. For Plato, the changing objects of our ordinary everyday world were less valuable and less real than the unchanging permanent Forms or Ideas. These latter not only served an explanatory purpose, they were to be valued, respected, and even

584

venerated. Therefore, when Socrates is asked whether distinct Forms correspond to "such things as hair, mud, dirt, or anything else which is vile and paltry", he is unwilling to say they do.[8] Forms of such things do not seem very exalted, valuable or important, in contrast to the Forms of the Good, the Just, and the Beautiful. Some mathematicians have this attitude toward the permanent and unchanging mathematical objects and structures they study, investigate, and explore. (Other mathematicians, in contrast, think they have created this realm, or are engaged merely in the combinatorial manipulation of meaningless marks on paper or blackboard.)

Despite the pedigree of the tradition, it is difficult to discover why the more permanent is the more valuable or meaningful, why permanence or long-lastingness, why duration in itself, should be important. Consider those things people speak of as permanent or eternal. These include (apart from God) numbers, sets, abstract ideas, space-time itself. Would it be better to be one of these things? The question is bizarre; how could a concrete person become an abstract object? Still, would anyone wish they *could* become the number 14 or the Form of Justice, or the null set? Is anyone pining to lead a setly existence?

Yet, it cannot be denied that some are gripped by the notion of traces continuing forever. Hence, we find some people disturbed over thermodynamics, worrying that millions of years from now the universe will run down into a state of maximum entropy, with no trace remaining of us or of what we have done. In their view, this eventuality makes human existence absurd; the eventual obliteration of all our traces also obliterates or undermines the meaningfulness of our existence. An account or theory of the meaning of life should find a place for this feeling, showing what facet of meaning it gets a grip upon; an adequate theory should explain the force of this feeling, even if it does not endorse or justify it.[9]

God's Plan

One prevalent view, less so today than previously, is that the meaning of life or people's existence is connected with God's will, with his design or plan for them. Put roughly, people's meaning is to be found and realized in fulfilling the role allotted to them by God. If a superior being designed and created people for a purpose, in accordance with a plan for them, the particular purpose he had for them would be what people are *for*. This is distinct from the view that finds meaning in the goal of merging with God, and also from the view which holds that if you do God's will you will be rewarded— sit at his right hand, and receive eternal bliss—and that the meaning and purpose of life is to achieve this reward which is intrinsically valuable (and also meaningful?).

Our concern now is not with the question of whether there is a God; or whether, if there is, he has a purpose for us; or whether if there is and he has a purpose for us, there is any way to discover this purpose, whether God reveals his purpose to people. Rather, our question is how all this, even if true, would succeed in providing meaning for people's lives.

First, we should ask whether any and every role would provide meaning and purpose to human lives. If our role is to supply CO_2 to the plants, or to be the equivalent within God's plan of fixing a mildly annoying leaky faucet, would this suffice? Is it enough to be an absolutely trivial component within God's grand design? Clearly, what is desired is that we be important; having merely some role or other in God's plan does not suffice. The purpose God has for us must place us at or near the center of things, of his intentions and goals. Moreover, merely playing some role in a central purpose of God's is not sufficient—the role itself must be a central or important one. If we describe God's central purpose in analogy with making a painting, we do not want to play the role of the rag used to wipe off brushes, or the tin in which these rags are kept. If we are not the central focus of the painting, at least we want to be like the canvas or the brush or the paint.

Indeed, we want more than an important role in an important purpose; the role itself should be positive, perhaps even exalted. If the cosmic role of human beings was to provide a negative lesson to some others ("don't act like them") or to provide needed food for passing intergalactic travelers who *were* important, this would not suit our aspirations—not even if afterwards the intergalactic travelers smacked their lips and said that we tasted good. The role should focus on aspects of ourselves that we prize or are proud of, and it should use these in ways connected with the reasons why we prize them. (It would not suffice if the exercise of our morality or intelligence, which we prize, affects our brain so that the intergalactic travelers find it more *tasty*.)

Do all these conditions guarantee meaning? Suppose our ingenuity was to be used to aid these travelers on their way, but that their way was no more important than ours. There was no more reason why we were aiding them (and perishing afterwards) than the other way around—the plan just happened to go that way. Would this cruel hoax leave us any more content than if there were no plan or externally given role at all?

There are two ways we individually or collectively could be included in God's plan. First, our fulfilling our role might depend upon our acting in a certain way, upon our choices or cooperation; second, our role might not depend at all upon our actions or choices —willy-nilly we shall serve. (In parallel to the notion of originative value, we can say that under the first our life can have originative meaning.) About the first way we can ask why we should act to fulfill God's plan, and about both ways we can ask why fitting God's plan gives meaning to our existence.[10] That God is good (but also sometimes angry?) shows that it would be good to carry out his plan. (Even then, perhaps, it need not be good *for us*—mightn't the good overall plan involve sacrificing us for some greater good?) Yet how does doing what is good provide meaning? Those who doubt whether life has meaning, even if transparently clearheaded, need not have doubted that it is good to do certain things.

How can playing a role in God's plan give one's life meaning? What makes this a meaning-giving process? It is not merely that some being created us with a purpose in mind. If some extragalactic civilization created us with a purpose in mind, would that by itself provide meaning to our lives? Nor would things be changed if they created us so that we also had a feeling of indebtedness and a feeling that something was asked of us. It seems it is not enough that God have some purpose for us—his purpose itself must be meaningful. If it were sufficient merely to play some role in some external purpose, then you could give meaning to your life by fitting it to my plans or to your parents' purpose in having you. In these instances, however, one immediately questions the meaningfulness of the other people's purposes. How do God's purposes differ from ours so as to be guaranteed meaningfulness and importance? Let me sharpen this question by presenting a philosophical fable.[11]

TELEOLOGY

Once you come to feel your existence lacks purpose, there is little you can do. You can keep the feeling, and either continue a meaningless existence or end it. Or you can discover the purpose your existence already serves, the meaning it has, thereby eliminating the feeling. Or you can try to dispose of the feeling by giving a meaning and purpose to your existence.

The first dual option carries minimal appeal; the second, despite my most diligent efforts, proved impossible. That left the third alternative, where, too, there are limited possibilities. You can make your existence meaningful by fitting it into some larger purpose, making yourself part of something else that is independently and incontestably important and meaningful. However, a sign of really having been stricken is that no preexisting purpose will serve in this fashion —each purpose that in other moods appears sufficiently fructifying then seems merely arbitrary. Alternatively, one can seek meaning in activity that itself is important, in something self-sufficiently intrinsically valuable. Preeminent among such activities, if there are any such, is creative activity. So, as a possible route out of my despair, I decided to create something that itself would be marvelous. (No, I did not decide to write a story beginning "Once you come to feel your existence lacks purpose." Why am I always suspected of gimmicks?)

The task required all of my knowledge, skill, intuitive powers, and craftsmanship. It seemed to me that my whole existence until then had been merely a preparation for this creative activity, so completely did it draw upon and focus all of my experience, abilities, and knowledge. I was excited by the task and fulfilled, and when it was completed I rested, untroubled by purposelessness.

But this contentment was, unfortunately, only temporary. For when I came to think about it, although it *had* taxed my ingenuity and energy to make the heavens, the earth, and the creatures upon it, what did it all amount to? I mean, the whole of it, when looked at starkly and coldly, was itself just an object, of no intrinsic importance, containing creatures in a condition as purposeless as the one I was trying to escape. Given the possibility that my talents and

powers were those of a being whose existence might well be meaningless, how could their exercise endow my existence with purpose
and meaning if it issued only in a worthless object?

At this point in my thoughts I came upon the solution to my problem. If I were to create a plan, a grand design into which my creation
fit, in which my creatures, by serving the pattern and purpose I had
ordained for them, would find their purpose and goal, then this very
activity of endowing their existence with meaning and purpose
would be my purpose and would give my existence meaning and
point. Also, giving their existence meaning would, retroactively,
make meaningful my previous activity of creation, it having issued in
something that turned out to be of value and worth.

The arrangement has served. Only occasionally, out of the corner
of my mind, do I wonder whether my arbitrarily having picked a
plan for them can really have succeeded in giving meaning to the
lives of the role-fulfillers among them. (It was necessary, of course,
that I pick some plan or other for them, but no special purpose was
served by my picking the particular plan I did. How could it have
been? For my sole purpose then was to give meaning to my existence, and this one purpose was insufficient to determine any particular plan into which to fit my creatures.) However, lacking any conception of a less defective route to meaningfulness, I refuse to
examine whether such a symbiotic arrangement truly is possible,
whether different beings can provide meaning and point to each
other's existence in a fashion so seemingly circular. Such questions
press me toward the alternative I tremble to contemplate, yet to
which I find my thoughts recurring. The option of ending it all, by
now familiar, is less alien and terrifying than before. I walk through
the valley of the shadow of death.

To imagine God himself facing problems about the meaningfulness of his existence forces us to consider how meaning attaches to
his purposes. Let us leave aside my fancy that since it is important
that our lives be provided with meaning, God's existence is made
meaningful by his carrying out that task, so that—since his plans for
us thereby become meaningful—our meaning is found in fitting
those plans. For if it were possible for man and God to shore up each
other's meaningfulness in this fashion, why could not two people do
this for each other as well? Moreover, a plan whose *only* purpose is

to provide meaning for another's life (or the planner's) cannot succeed in doing the trick; the plan must have some independent purpose and meaning itself.

Nor will it help to escalate up a level, and say that if there is a God who has a plan for us, the meaning of our existence consists in finding out what this plan asks of us and has in store for us. To know the meaning of life, on this view, would consist in our knowing where we came from, why we are here, where we are going. But apart from the fact that many religions hold such knowledge of God's purposes to be impossible (see, for example, *Ecclesiastes* and *Job*), and condemn various attempts to gain such knowledge (such as occult techniques and necromancy), and apart even from the fact that this seems too much a metapurpose, no more satisfying than saying "the purpose of life is the quest for the purpose of life", this view merely postpones the question of wherein God's plan itself is meaningful.

What is it about God's purposes that makes them meaningful? If our universe were created by a child from some other vast civilization in a parallel universe, if our universe were a toy it had constructed, perhaps out of prefabricated parts, it would not follow that the child's purposes were meaningful. Being the creator of all we see is not sufficient to endow his purposes with meaningfulness. Granted, the purposes of God are the purposes of a powerful and important being (as compared to us). However, it is difficult to see why that suffices for those purposes to ground our existence in meaning. Could the purposes of scientists so give meaning to artificially created short-lived animal life they maintained in a controlled laboratory environment? The scientists, creators of the animals' universe and life, would be as gods to them. Yet it would be unbearably poignant if the most intelligent animal, in a leap of intuition, did its equivalent of worshiping the absent scientist.

Various gnostic doctrines have held that our world (or universe) was created by a being who was not the supreme divine being, or who was not the only aspect of the divine being. These doctrines envisaged an even more supreme God above the creator of our universe. If some people were fulfilling (and were committed to fulfilling) the local Lord's commands and plans, would it follow that their lives had meaning? How are things different if it is the plan of the top God (must there be a top to the levels?) which we are fulfilling, and how is it to be determined which lead to follow?

Such speculations about levels, perhaps hidden, beneath levels are bewildering, especially since we shall never be able to claim with certainty of some religious doctrine or scientific theory that it has identified the "ground floor", that there cannot be, underneath the fundamental processes or entities E it identifies, even more fundamental hidden ones of a very different character which give rise to the reality or appearance of E. In his novel *The Magus* John Fowles depicts this: each time the central character comes to a view of what is occurring, this is undercut by a new and different deeper view.*

I don't say there is no ground floor (would it be better if there were not?), just that we wouldn't know it if we reached it. Even infinite reflexiveness could have a level underlying it, giving rise to it. My purpose is not to emphasize our limits as knowers but to note the power of our imaginations. We can always imagine a deeper reality, deeper even than what turns out to be the deepest; if we cannot imagine its precise character, nevertheless, we can imagine that there is such a thing. There are or can be mysteries within and behind mysteries. To mention only religious views, the Hindus speak of parabrahman which is beyond even Brahman, and gnostic views posit a God beyond the creator of this universe. Once we are embarked there is no sure stopping; why not a God who created that God, and so forth?

Not only can we not be certain about the ground floor; *it*, if it is the sort of thing that is conscious, cannot be either. For perhaps underneath or apart from everything it knows, is something else that created or underlies it, having carefully covered its tracks. Philosophers have sometimes searched for indicators of a conscious Absolute, in the hopes of making us "at home" and unalienated in the

* See also the Jose Luis Borges story "The Circular Ruins" in his collection *Labyrinths* (New Directions, New York, 1964, pp. 45–50), in which a dreamer realizes that he himself also is dreamt; and note the tale of Chuang Tsu, who wonders if he dreamt the butterfly, or is dreamed by the butterfly. Each of these illustrates levels undercutting levels, or alternate levels whose ordering is unclear. (Contrast the structure of the traditional detective story, wherein the detective penetrates appearance to reach the underlying, ground-floor reality.) It is as if the universe is or might be constructed according to an unbreakable code via a trapdoor function; we see the encoded message and even if we knew the generating rule we still could not find the plain text. See Martin Hellman, "The Mathematics of Public Key Cryptography", *Scientific American*, Vol. 241, August 1979, pp. 146–157.

universe, akin to its fundamental character, or somehow favored by it.* If there were such an Absolute, it too must occasionally look over its shoulder for a glimpse of a yet deeper, and perhaps not fully friendly, reality. Even the Absolute is a little bit paranoid—so how alien from us can it be?

Yet "like us" does not mean it likes us and is supportive of us and our aspirations, as provided in the vision of a personal God who cares. Is the universe at its fundamental level friendly to our seeking of value; is there some cosmic undergirding so that values, in the phrase of William James, "throw the last stone"? Some have woven science-fiction fantasies of a level that is thus supportive—emissaries from intergalactic civilizations who watch over and guide our progress—and apparently find this comforting. This is not the "ground floor", though. But how important is it anyway that there be a force for value at that level, if it is so distant as effectively to have nothing to do with us? It is not difficult to imagine structures about levels that undercut other levels of reality and their support (or nonsupport) of value. It is less important, though, whether the ground floor exerts a force for value, than whether we do.

There also might turn out to be fewer levels than appear. The gnostic theorists, for example, whatever their evidence for multiple deities, would have had no way to exclude the possibility that there was but one deity who was schizophrenic or possessed different personalities which he alternately showed. On this view, rather than taking sides in a cosmic clash, the task of man for which he was created (by which personality?) might be to act as therapist to bring together the different personalities of God (unifying them or eliminating one?)—the task might be to heal God. This would certainly give man a central mission and purpose in the cosmic structure, but one might question the meaningfulness of harmonizing *that* structure. Another similar theory would see man not as therapist but as therapy, functioning as do patients' drawings in psychological treatment, produced with conflicting impulses to express its maker's na-

---

* Some carried out this task too enthusiastically. Fichte's view rendered reality less alien to us, but only by making it so much our product that others (for example Jean Paul, Madame de Staël) justifiably complained that it left us all alone. Would you join any country club that had you as its founder, sole member, and acreage?

ture.* When such a deity's products come to think of their maker as psychotic and in need of help and integration, is that a sign of a breakthrough of insight in *it?* (This would provide an ironic version of Hegel's view that in his philosophy Geist comes to full self-awareness.)

These diverse possibilities about the intentional and purposeful creation of our universe—by a child in another dimension, by one of a hierarchy of gods, by a schizophrenic God—press home the question of how, or in virtue of what, a religious view can ground the meaning of our lives. Just as the direct experience of God might unavoidably provide one with a motive to carry out his wishes, so it might be that such an experience (of which type of creator?) always would resolve all doubts about meaning. To experience God might leave one with the absolute conviction that his existence was the fountain of meaning, watering your own existence. I do not want to discount testimony reporting this. But even if we accepted it fully, it leaves unanswered the question of how meaning is possible. What is it about God, as usually conceived, in virtue of which he can ground meaning? How *can* there be a ball of meaning? Even if we are willing to treat the testimony in the way we treat accurate perceptual reports, there still remains the problem of understanding how meaning can be encountered in experience, of how there can be a stopping place for questions about meaning. How in the world (or out of it) can there be something whose nature contains meaning, something which just glows meaning?

In pursuing the question of which aspects of God can provide meaning to our existence, we have presented examples of other more limited imaginable beings who do have those aspects (for example, creator of our universe) yet who obviously fail to give meaning. Perhaps it is in that very step to these examples that we lose the meaning. Perhaps the intrinsic meaningfulness of God's existence and his purposes lies in his being unlimited and infinite, in his being at the ground floor and not undercut or dwarfed or put in a smaller focus by any underlying level or being or perspective. No wonder, then, that

* Carl Jung pursued gnostic themes as revelatory of our psyche, seeing them not as metaphysically accurate but as the self's projections. An alternative theory might view the isomorphism as due to man's being created in the image of (a gnostic) god.

the meaning disappeared as we considered other cases that purported to isolate the salient meaning-producing aspect of God. (Still, there would remain questions about why only certain ways of being linked—as creation, worshiper, role-fulfiller, or whatever—transmit meaning to people from God.) If the plausibility of seeing God as providing a stopping place for questions about meaning is grounded in his very infinitude and unlimitedness, in there being no deeper level or wider perspective, we can ask what this shows about the notion of meaning. How must the notion of meaning be structured, what must be its content, for (only) unlimitedness to provide a secure basis for meaning and a stopping place for questions about meaning?

Transcending Limits

Attempts to find meaning in life seek to transcend the limits of an individual life. The narrower the limits of a life, the less meaningful it is.

The narrowest life consists of separated and disparate moments, having neither connection nor unity; for example, the life of an amnesiac who is unable to plan over several days or even moments because he forgets each day (or moment) what came before. Even someone capable of integrating his life may still lead this narrowest life, if he moves to get whatever at any moment he happens to want —provided this is not an overarching policy he will stick to even when specific wants run counter to it.

Integration of a life comes in gradations. The next notable type of life along the dimension of narrowness is one that is well integrated by overarching plans, goals, and purposes. In this case, though, the long term goals do not extend to anything beyond the person, to anything other than his own narrow concerns; for instance, the sole overarching goal that integrates his life plan might be to maximize the sum total of his life's pleasures. Of such lives we ask, "but what does that life add up to, what meaning does it have?" For a life to have meaning, it must connect with other things, with some things or values beyond itself. Meaning, and not merely of lives, seems to lie in such connections. To ask something's meaning is to ask how it is connected, perhaps in specified ways, to other things. Tracking, either of facts or of value, is a mode of being so connected, as is fitting an external purpose. The experience machine, though it may give you the experience of transcending limits, encloses you within the circle of just your own experiences. The phrase "the meaning you give to your life" refers to the ways you choose to transcend your limits, the particular package and pattern of external connections you successfully choose to exhibit.*

Mortality is a temporal limit and traces are a way of going or seeping beyond that limit. To be puzzled about why death seems to undercut meaning is to fail to see the temporal limit itself as a limit. The particular things or causes people find make their life feel meaningful all take them beyond their own narrow limits and connect them up with something else. Children, relationships with other persons, helping others, advancing justice, continuing and transmitting a tradition, pursuing truth, beauty, world betterment—these and the rest link you to something wider than yourself. The more intensely you are involved, the more you transcend your limits. World-historical causes link someone with wider concerns but may leave him equally limited along other more personal dimensions. Among personal relations, loving another brings us most outside our own limits and narrow concerns. In love between adults—their mutual openness and trust, the dismantling of the defenses and barriers people carefully have constructed to protect themselves against getting hurt, and the mutual recognition of this (mutual) nondefensiveness—some limits of the self are not merely breached but dissolved. This nondefensiveness is risky. Yet to be less than fully open to growth, because of this, makes the relationship itself a limit rather than a mode of transcending limits, while to preserve some armor, as insurance, constitutes yet another limit.

The problem of meaning is created by limits, by being just this, by being merely this. The young feel this less strongly. Although they would agree, if they thought about it, that they will realize only some

---

* It may not be clear always whether there is a connection to something else. If to have the goal of advancing your own knowledge is to connect up with something beyond yourself, namely knowledge or truth, why doesn't the goal of advancing your own pleasure connect you up with something beyond yourself, namely pleasure? Is it the intentionality of knowledge that takes it outside of itself? Would the focused intention to participate in the Platonic Form of Pleasure, rather than merely to have pleasurable experiences, suffice to connect one up with something else?

of the (feasible) possibilities before them, none of these various possibilities is yet excluded in their minds. The young live in each of the futures open to them. The poignancy of growing older does not lie in one's particular path being less satisfying or good than it promised earlier to be—the path may turn out to be all one thought. It lies in traveling only one (or two, or three) of those paths. Economists speak of the opportunity cost of something as the value of the best alternative forgone for it. For adults, strangely, the opportunity cost of our lives appears to us to be the value of all the forgone alternatives summed together, not merely of the best other *one*. When all the possibilities were yet still before us, it felt to us as if we would do them all.

Some writers have held that we achieve meaning by affirming our limits and living with purpose within them, or (this is Sartre's view, as Arnold Davidson has reminded me) by defining ourselves in terms of what we exclude and reject, the possibilities we choose not to encompass. This living finely within limits may involve a surpassing of what one would have thought those limits entailed, or it may be that such living is valuable, forming a tight organic unity within those limits. Similarly, self-definition by what one chooses to exclude means that one includes and explicitly acts on that principle of rejection, thereby giving one's life greater unified definition. Thus such exclusion is one means to value, not a mode of meaning.

We need not assume there is a complete ordering with respect to the transcending of limits. Our lives contain many dimensions along which it will be clear what is more and what less limited, but this need not be clear for any two arbitrary points in the space of the n dimensions along which one can be limited—the ordering might be only partial. Therefore, it would be difficult to formulate the total meaningfulness of a person's life as a weighted sum or expected value, with the weights being his degree of intensity of involvement, ranging between zero and one, which are multiplied by an interval-scale measure of the meaningfulness of what the person is involved in or connected with, which measure varies inversely with limitedness. For that, we should be thankful.

However widely we connect and link, however far our web of meaningfulness extends, we can imagine drawing a boundary around all that, standing outside looking at the totality of it, and asking "but what is the meaning of that, what does that mean?" The more exten-

596

sive the connections and linkages, the more imagination it may take to step outside and see the whole web for the particular thing it is. Yet it seems this always can be done. (Whether it will be done or not determines whether there will be a felt problem of meaning.) Consider the most exalted and far-reaching life or role imagined for man: being the messiah. Greater effect has been imagined for no other man. Yet still we can ask how important it is to bring whatever it is the messiah brings to the living beings of the third planet of a minor off-center star in the Milky Way galaxy, itself a galaxy of no special distinction within its particular metagalaxy, one of many in the universe. To see something's limits, to see it as that limited particular thing or enterprise, is to question its meaning.*

The intellectual life seems to offer one route across all limits: there is nothing that cannot be thought of, theorized about, pondered. Knowledge of deeper truths, fundamental laws, seems more meaningful since it takes us more significantly beyond our limits. And is the reason for the inadequacy of connecting with possibilities by "living in an imaginary world", that these possibilities don't have sufficient ontological status, or connection to them doesn't, for it to be a transcending of personal limits?

We often estimate the "meaningfulness" of work by the range of things that come within its purview, the range of different factors that have to be taken into account. The (hired) craftsman must take account of more than the assembly line worker, the entrepreneur must look out upon conditions in the wider world, and so forth. To be a technician is not merely to have a technique, but to be restricted to taking account of the narrow range of factors handled by the technique. Even if Socrates had a technique of thought, elenchus, still, as he cast his mind over the range of what was relevant to human concerns he was not a technician.

---

* There is a story told that Martin Buber once spoke to a group of Christians saying something like the following: We Jews and you Christians hold many beliefs in common. Both of us believe the messiah will come. You Christians believe he has been here before, so that he will be coming for a second time, while we Jews believe he will be coming for the first time. For the foreseeable future, there is much we can cooperate together on—and when the messiah *does* come, *then* we can ask him whether he's been here before.

There is only one thing to add to Buber's remarks. I would like to advise the messiah, when he comes and is asked the question whether he's been here before or not, to reply that he doesn't remember.

Via thought, we can be linked to anything and everything. Perhaps this, not professional chauvinism, explains why philosophers often have considered philosophical thought and contemplation the highest activity. Nothing escapes its purview. No assumption constitutes an unquestionable limit. In thought we do not thereby transcend all limits, however. Thought can link to everything, but that is merely one particular kind of link: thinking of. True, we can be connected with other kinds of linkages by thinking of them, too, and including them within our theory; yet this kind of connection with them still remains of one kind only. A unity of theory and practice is not established just by constructing a theory of practice.

In imagination, we stand outside a thing and all it is connected with, and we ask for the meaning of the totality. Connected with X is Y, and it is proposed that Y is the meaning of X. Standing outside, we ask for the meaning of Y itself, or for the meaning of X + Y together. Of each wider and less limited context or entity, we ask for its meaning, in turn. In two ways this can seem to undercut the meaning of the thing, X, with which we began. We can have reached a context Y so wide that X is no longer of any importance to it. The fact that Y has meaning is not placed in question, but the connection of the original X to Y is so attenuated, so insignificant from the perspective of Y, that X does not seem to have or gain any meaning in virtue of that connection. Furthermore, since meaning involves connection to wider context, it seems appropriate, demanded even, to take the widest context as that in which to consider something's meaning. Thus, we find people asking "from the point of view of all of human history, what difference does my life or this contemporary event make?" or "Given the immensity of the universe and the billions upon billions of galaxies, probably teeming with life elsewhere, is all of human history itself of any significance?"

The second way the widening of the context can seem to undercut the meaning of our original concern is that we can reach a context Y that is so wide that it is not obvious what its meaning is—it just is. But if Y itself has no meaning of its own, then how can any X be provided with meaning by virtue of its connection with that Y? It seems impossible that meaning be based upon or flow from something that itself has no meaning. If meaning is to trickle down from Y to us, mustn't there be some meaning there at the start?

Perhaps this natural picture is mistaken—perhaps the meaning of

X can be Y, without Y itself or X + Y having meaning. Must what is the meaning of something itself have a meaning; cannot something's meaning just *be* its meaning without *having* one too? This would be impossible on the picture of something's meaning as had, like a liquid filling it, which we gain via our connection with it—the umbilical theory of meaning. However, if meaning itself is not a thing but a relationship then something can have meaning by standing in that relationship, even to something which itself does not stand further in that relationship. (Not every parent is a grandparent.) Consider the analogy of linguistic meaning. Some recent theories of language have come to see a word or sentence or utterance's having meaning not as its being related to a metaphysically special entity, a meaning, but rather as its standing in some type of (functional) relationship.[12] Is it not appropriate, similarly, to view the notion of meaning, applied to someone's life, as relational, so that a life's meaning need not itself have its own further meaning or be intrinsically meaningful?

This view of meaning as explicitly relational helps to loosen the grip of the picture that requires, for there to be any meaning, that something be (but how can it be?) intrinsically meaningful.[13] However, there is no simple mistake or fallacy committed by the person who asks about the meaning of Y, or of X + Y. When the concern is the meaning of our life or existence, when X is our life, we want meaning all the way down. Nothing less will do. This meaning is like importance; to be important for something which itself is unimportant is for these purposes to be unimportant. The person who regards the meaning of X as dissolved when it is shown that the Y that is supposed to be X's meaning itself has no meaning of its own is not shown to be confused simply because there are or might be legitimate relativized or relational notions of importance or meaning. For he is not using and will not be satisfied by such a relativized notion. And do not hasten to argue that there is no conceivable coherent unrelativized notion. For that, if true, is not the solution—it is the problem.

The problem of meaning is created by limits. We cope with this by, in little ways or big, transcending these limits. Yet whatever extent we thereby reach in a wider realm also has its own limits—the same problem surfaces again. This suggests that the problem can be avoided or transcended only by something without limits, only by something that cannot be stood outside of, even in imagination. Perhaps, the question about meaning is stopped and cannot get a grip only when there is nowhere else to stand.

The Unlimited

No word of English perfectly fits the concept I want to explore. The obvious candidates are: infinite, unlimited, unbounded, endless. But even these fall short. The sequence of positive integers 5, 6, 7, 8, . . . is infinite, but lacks 1, 2, 3, and 4. The two-way infinite sequence . . . −3, −2, −1, 0, 1, 2, 3, . . . includes all integers, but is merely a denumerable infinity and excludes the real numbers. The set of all numbers, all sets of numbers, all sets of sets of numbers, and so on includes only numbers and what they give rise to—it does not include poems, tables, people, or philosophy books. So something can be infinite, yet quite limited. To be unbounded is to lack a boundary, yet this does not even guarantee infinity. A Riemannian space may be finite in extent yet unbounded; you never come up against a boundary as you explore, but after visiting a finite number of places you will find yourself revisiting some places. Time may be endless in each direction; but it is only time.

The word that comes closest to our purposes is "unlimited", if we do not tie it too closely to its mathematical usage wherein it is sequences which do or do not have limits.[14] To be limited is to exclude something; a limit of something comes between it and what is excluded. Something unlimited would be all-encompassing and all-inclusive. When and only when something is all-encompassing and all-inclusive is there nowhere else to stand from which to survey its limits and limitations.

This is dizzying enough, but we must reach for more. Suppose someone merged with or became the whole universe, and so came to include everything that exists. Even then, he would not be unlimited—he still would be only that particular universe. We must imagine something that somehow includes all possibilities, all possible universes, and excludes nothing. This something not only is not limited to some portion of actuality while excluding the rest, it also is not limited to that one portion of possibility which is (all of) actuality. It encompasses all. For this unlimited, we shall also use the Hebrew term *Ein Sof* (meaning without end or limit). Now, if existing implies limitation, and to be is to be some thing rather than another or rather than nothing,[15] then what encompasses all would not itself, strictly speaking, *exist*. It would transcend the pair of terms existent–nonexistent, not satisfying its presupposition.

There are formidable metaphysical questions about the unlimited; however, let us first consider whether and how it answers or solves or avoids or dissolves the problem about meaning. The unlimited will help if anything will; but if it does not help either, there is no point in entangling ourselves here in its murky metaphysics. What then is the meaning of Ein Sof itself?

We can understand the question of something's meaning, roughly, as the question of how it connects up to what is outside it. Not all ways of connecting need be of interest, but for the ways that are, something's meaning is how it connects in these ways with what is external to it. The question of the meaning of something is: given what is external to it, how does it connect (in the preferred ways) with that. However, when what is in question is an unlimited and all-encompassing entity, there is nothing outside or external to it. So there is no question of how it connects with what is external. What the question of meaning takes as given, what it presupposes, does not hold in this case. The question "what is the meaning of the unlimited?" cannot arise, for one of its preconditions or presuppositions, namely that there be something external to the thing in question, is not satisfied. On this view, there is no answer to the question "what is the meaning of the unlimited?" but there is no question either. There is no question: how does the all-inclusive unlimited connect up with what is external to it and beyond its limits?

Under this account, the pair of terms meaningful–meaningless has the presupposition that there be something external, that the thing be limited. Therefore, neither of these terms applies to the unlimited, which transcends this distinction. One might take a similar approach with the term important, and hold that the unlimited transcends importance also. (This is not to say it is unimportant—the presupposition for this term is not satisfied either.)

This account sees the unlimited as providing a stopping point for questions about meaning by transcending the category rather than by being itself meaningful. In the fable told earlier, "Teleology", an unlimited being (who realized it was unlimited) could have no worry about the meaning of its own existence, because there could be no question of meaning about its existence. Yet although this position has the virtue that the question about meaning would not arise about the unlimited, and so the unlimited provides a stopping place for that question, still the position leaves us puzzled about how and why connecting up with the unlimited (or being part of it) provides meaning for our existence. Why should our connecting up with or being part of what transcends the pair meaningful–meaningless leave us with the first term in the pair rather than the second? For a satisfactory result, it seems either we ourselves must transcend the pair of terms, so that the question of meaning does not arise about us either, or we must connect up with something meaningful, that is, with something where the question of meaning applies and has an affirmative answer.

This satisfactory result would obtain if the unlimited provides a stopping place for questions about meaning, not because the question cannot arise about it but because the unlimited itself is its own meaning. But isn't it impossible for something to be its own meaning? And if the unlimited can be its own meaning, why cannot other things as well, so that they too can ground meaning?

It is in virtue of being unlimited that Ein Sof is able to be its own meaning—any lesser thing cannot do this. The phenomenon of being the meaning of itself is emergent at the level of the unlimited, and not before. It seems impossible that something be its own meaning only because we normally think of limited things. Consider, as an analogy, mathematical infinity. How can there be a one-to-one mapping between a set and a proper subset of itself, between, for example, the set of all positive integers and the set of even positive integers? It seems that something surely must be left over. However, this is because we are thinking only of finite sets. An infinite set *can* be put into a one-to-one mapping with a proper subset of itself. (For example, with each positive integer n, associate the even integer $2 \times n$.) An infinite set stands in a certain relationship to itself that no finite set can stand in to *itself*. Similarly, the unlimited can stand in a certain relationship to itself that no limited thing can stand in to itself: being its own meaning.

Yet what is it about the unlimited in virtue of which it is its own meaning, how does being unlimited enable something to be its own meaning? What is the character of the relation *being the meaning of,* such that Ein Sof and only it stands in this relationship to itself?* I can only tentatively put forth several suggestions. The first builds quite literally on the analogy to infinite sets. Only an infinite set can be mapped onto a proper subset of itself, and only an unlimited being can include itself as a part, only an infinite being can embed itself.[16] Consider the mapping as a kind of connection; only an unlimited being can map onto and so connect with something apparently larger and external which turns out to be itself. Only an unlimited being can have its "wider" context be itself, and so be its own meaning.

There is a second way to approach our question of why an unlimited being, and only that, can be its own meaning. We can ask why the process whereby a person attempts to provide meaning to his life is a process of transcending limits. One answer says that meaning is a matter of external connections, so of course finding or establishing meaning is a matter of establishing external connections, that is, connections beyond the limits. This answer does not probe why meaning involves external connections. I take this involvement to be a symptom of something deeper and in need of further explanation; meaning involves external connections *because* for a limited and finite being, meaning involves transcending limits. If it were merely an arbitrary fact about meaning that it involved external connections, a fact not susceptible of further explanation, then there would be the question of why seek meaning, that is, why seek something like that. When we understand why for us the process of attempting to find meaning is one of transcending limits, then we shall understand why a limited being cannot be its own meaning whereas an unlimited being can. We shall return to this issue below.

For now, consider a more restricted point. The typical way to place the meaning of something in question is to discover another standpoint from which it is not meaningful, valuable, or important. Thus,

---

* Not only should the meaning relation be specified so as to yield this result, but also this meaning relation should be insecure for things lesser than Ein Sof. Only it fully stands in that relation to itself; and when anything lesser stands in that relation to something else, its so standing is insecure, perhaps because it is a pale version of the relation in which Ein Sof stands to itself. Doubt can be cast on whether things do stand in a relation (in this case, a meaning relation) once we see there is a stronger instantiated relation (here the relation which Ein Sof stands in to itself).

earlier I asked what would be the significance of the life of the messiah on this planet, from the standpoint of the universe as a whole. Note certain features this other standpoint must have in order to (seem to) undercut our assumption that some X is meaningful. First, the standpoint is never a narrower standpoint than X itself. We do not ask what the importance of our life is for this particular hour, or for these cells it includes. The question always goes in the other direction, toward the wider thing: what is the importance of this hour or of these five cells for my life as a whole. Second, not only is the alternative standpoint not narrower than X and included in it, it also is not disjoint from X. The meaning of my life does not appear to be undercut by its not meaning anything to someone in Peru, or some particular denizen of another galaxy. Rather, we turn to a wider context which includes X—what is the importance of my life for humanity, what is the importance of life on earth for all life in the galaxy or universe, and so forth.

The standpoint that purports to undercut the meaning of X always is a wider standpoint which includes X, relative to which X is not meaningful or important. For anything we prize, it seems we always can conceive a context wide enough so that the thing appears insignificant. Perhaps this can occur even for all of actuality: if we take up the standpoint of all possibilities, actuality becomes insignificant, merely one of the multitude. For the unlimited and all-inclusive Ein Sof, however, there is no wider standpoint that dwarfs it, none that includes it and reduces it to insignificance. (If because of formal properties of infinity, the unlimited is included in something, it also is identical with that something that includes it.) Unlike all limited things, there is no context in which it needs any further meaning; it stands as its own meaning.*

This theory is illuminating, even though not yet fully satisfactory. Consider the question: what is so important about the totality of everything there is? On the very first theory we presented, the pre-suppositional theory, this question does not make sense, since it presupposes that there is something external. On that theory, the totality

---

* Might something be unlimited only along a certain dimension (for example, consciousness), rather than completely unlimited, yet this still provide all the opportunity needed for an appropriate mapping onto part of itself? Perhaps its infinite depth would suffice, and not pale into insignificance, even in a wider context that included many such infinite depths.

of everything there is turns out to be neither important nor unimportant. According to our current reflections, however, since there is no wider standpoint that includes the totality of all there is, from which this totality is insignificant, it itself is its own importance and meaning. So the answer to the question "why is the whole universe important?" is: it just is. (This "just" is rather complex, however.) This answer serves until we imagine even wider contexts, such as the standpoint of all possibilities, or of a greater entity, God, creating the universe as one of his not very important activities. All this provides data for the theory about wider contexts we are adumbrating here. And that theory yields the result that the unlimited, and only that, is able to be its own meaning: only it is able to block all further questions about meaning and put the continually arising and iterated question about meaning finally to rest, affirmatively.

Is it necessary that this stopping place for questions about meaning be unlimited, or is it enough that it be the widest actual context? If there exists nothing else that includes it, no deeper level which underlies or undermines it, then can't it ground meaning, even if it is logically possible for something to be more inclusive? Must its lack of limits run across all possibilities?

In the first chapter, we considered the closest continuer schema for identity over time, requiring that there actually be no other closer (or equally close) continuer. Many other philosophical notions, we there saw, also involved this structure, stated with a negative existential quantifier, that there be nothing else which tops the thing in question. Once again, we have found a similar structure: the context to ground meaning must be such that nothing else puts it in its narrow place, nothing else includes or dwarfs or undermines or secretly gives rise to, or is deeper than it—it is the ground floor.* Nothing else undercuts it, nothing else undercuts its value. However, is it enough that there be no subbasement, or is it necessary that there could not have been? The answer with regard to the notion of mean-

---

* Similarly, epistemological skepticism might be seen as the worry that some other and different reality underlies and undermines whatever we experience, that our world is a dream or illusion, while underneath is a deeper and different reality. (See my fable "Fiction", *Ploughshares*, Fall 1980.) In a different way, the issue of free will concerns whether something else undercuts my origination of purposeful action, be it the purposes of another or the action of external causes. These, too, are to be excluded, by a negative existential quantifier.

ing, I think, is unclear, but there certainly is some push to including all possibilities as relevant, and so toward a ground of meaning that is unlimited in principle.

Even if such an unlimited entity is able to stop the regress of questions about meaning, providing a final affirmative answer, how might meaning thereby be brought into our lives? First, we might connect up with this self-sufficient source of meaning in a way so that meaning flows to us. Why some modes of linkage provide channels for the flow of meaning to us (in the Jewish tradition, obeying God's commandments, praying, and perhaps scolding him) while others do not, is a question we need not enter here.

The second way in which the meaningful-in-itself existence of the unlimited would give meaning to our existence is if we ourselves were, in our fundamental natures, unlimited and all-inclusive. Such a position is presented in the Vedanta school of Indian philosophy, basing itself upon the Upanishads. It holds that Atman is Brahman; your underlying identity, what you fundamentally are, is identical to the unlimited all-inclusiveness from which everything springs and emanates. Various meditative practices and other disciplines are designed to bring one to a knowledge of one's own underlying nature, which is quite different than at first it appears; these are designed to bring one to experience oneself as Brahman. On the basis of these experiences, very wild sounding and apparently megalomaniacal theories are claimed to have empirical support. However, the importance the theory ascribes to coming to know your own true nature, since in any case you already have it, is left obscure. Nor do such theories find it easy to explain why the perfect and all-inclusive underlying substance is undergoing the process of coming to complete self-knowledge, or why it is temporarily ignorant—if it's so rich, how come it isn't smart?*

* For a discussion of this type of difficulty in Hegel, see MacTaggart, *Studies in Hegelian Dialectic* (Cambridge University Press, 2nd ed., 1922), ch. V, especially pp. 169–179. For Aurobindo's (unsatisfactory) wrestling with the question, see *The Life Divine* (Pondicherry, 1973), Book II, pt. I.

The different theories of samkhya yoga, which do not involve an all-inclusive self but also guide the person toward realizing his own true nature, do have an explanation of the temporary ignorance: the purusha confuses itself with the prakriti. It is left unclear, though, what is so great about a self (the purusha) so easily confused, and why, once the confusion is cleared up, it will not happen again.

Hegel's theory leaves us being Geist's little helper and arena; but how awe

606

Perhaps such theories of a completely perfect Absolute should hold that it must (somehow) undergo a process. The usual objection is that if Ein Sof, the Absolute, Brahman, Satchitananda, or whatever needs to undergo a process of development, it is not yet perfect. This objection assumes the purpose of the process is to reach a state of *being*—that indeed would show that the stage at the beginning of the process was not yet perfect. However, perhaps the Absolute is perfect, and the process is not meant to reach something (better) but to add a perfect process alongside and connected to it. Perfection would be the union of the perfect state of being with the perfect process; this union is not itself simply a(nother) state of being (or another process). The process undergone is part of the perfection, not a means to it. People often think of perfection as a state (and of value as attaching to a state); but perfection need not be boring.

Is perfection itself a limit, is a perfect being limited in being that? Is it even coherent to suppose there is an unlimited and all-inclusive entity? Within the Indian tradition, Brahman is described as including and somehow realizing all possibilities. Is there any limit to Brahman at all? Its nature is described as Sat Chit Ananda: existence, consciousness, bliss. It is not limited in that, since it is said to have infinite existence, consciousness, and bliss, but is it limited by being that?

We might consider the theory that Brahman is limited by being that, and so acts to overcome and transcend these limitations, even going so far as to transform (parts of?) itself into inconscient matter or even nonexistence. The Indian theories have long had a problem explaining why the world we experience exists, why Brahman in its infinite perfection and contentment, lacking nothing, gives rise to the empirical world, and why it is that we do not realize our own true nature. Their theories range from *lila* to illusion, from Brahman producing the world in the pure delight of free play to there really being no world produced, only an illusory appearance. (An illusion experienced by Brahman who is perfect? By us who are part of the illusion? But who is misled by this second illusion?) On these theories, Brahman is in no way limited by its nature. Even Satchitan-

---

inspiring is a Geist that needs us as the arena in which it achieves self-consciousness, how ennobled can we be by being connected with such a Geist? Would you join a country club that *needs* you as a member?

anda is not how Brahman is in itself or how it experiences itself; rather it is how we humans in our current form experience Brahman.

However, we might formulate a theory that views Brahman as creating the world to overcome its last limitations as Brahman—the existence of the world becomes a component of Brahman's all-inclusiveness and perfection. The world is part of the process whereby Brahman overcomes the final limits of being infinite existence, consciousness, bliss. Brahman is not limited even by that apparently wonderful nature. We would like a theory that gives us timeless perfection along with a process of transcending and overcoming, a process of accomplishment. Both are supplied by a view of Brahman (and of people's underlying nature) as Satchitananda and (simultaneously at some level) as casting itself forth into another state so as to overcome the limitations inherent in Satchitananda, then slowly evolving back to an awareness of its true perfect nature as Brahman. (Compare Hegel on how the infinite, if it is to be unlimited, must involve the finite.)

So much for considering some of the ways an unlimited entity, supposing it does stop questions about meaning, might enable our existence to have meaning. But does it make any sense to speak of an unlimited entity, at all? The application of a term tells us that what it applies to is one way and not another. To be one way and not another is to have limits. It seems, then, that no terms can describe something unlimited, no human terms can truly apply to it. Terms demarcate things from other things, and so describe limits and boundaries. If Ein Sof was one way and also another, it would not be limited; also, it would not be describable by terms of the sort we use. The unlimited is ineffable. Yet cannot we correctly apply to it the term "unlimited", or at least "ineffable"? We can leave this difficulty in understanding the notion of ineffability, with regard to metalinguistic predicates, for the techniques and developments of semantics to resolve.[17]

In this section, we have glimpsed one way questions of meaning can be brought to a halt, with a self-sufficient unlimited being which is its own meaning and which we somehow connect with (as in the case of God) or are (as in the case of the Brahman of Vedanta). There seems to be at least this one answer to the question of how meaning is possible. Thus, we can see how religion was thought to specify an answer to the question of the meaning of our life, and also why among the increasing numbers of those detached from religion in the past century, the question of meaning, suddenly unanswered, assumed great importance.

We have seen one way meaning is possible—if there were an unlimited and all-inclusive something which grounds meaning—but we have not yet discussed the question of whether it is actual. In specifying an alternative apparently so unviable in the minds of many at present, we appear to have made little progress. (Must the owl of Minerva insist on trying to fly from night back into the previous day?) This, despite the fact that the unlimited ground of meaning need not be some traditional religious alternative, western or eastern. Yet is the common belief that there is nothing anywhere that is infinite and unlimited an inductive inference from our limited experiences? Have we put this belief to its severest test by seeking out other experiences?

The task of evaluating what such experiences show, including those reported by mystics, is an intricate one. It is my judgment that these experiences do not demonstrate the existence of an unlimited entity; the experiences conflict, many of them can be explained away, the reports may be theory-laden, and so forth. Still, although the experiences by themselves may be insufficient, they do carry some weight. In contrast, the deductive arguments considered by philosophers of religion, the ontological, cosmological, teleological, and so on, seem to me, as to many others, fruitless.[18]

Suppose there is no other route we can find to meaning, other than via something unlimited, no other way we can imagine that meaning is even possible. Is the fact that there apparently can be meaning to life only if there is such an unlimited being itself a reason to believe there is one? (If so, when this is combined with the weight of the experiences, do we then have a sufficient reason?) Or shall we dismiss this as wishful thinking, merely?

To this (wistful?) line of thought, we each know how to construct the reply. "Even if life can only have meaning when there is an unlimited being, nevertheless, perhaps there is no such entity and so life cannot have meaning. We must not confuse what we desire with what is the case; we must continue to base our beliefs on the evidence and reasons, to calibrate our degree of belief according to the evidence. That only thereby can life have meaning is no reason to think it is true that there is an unlimited being, unless there is independent reason to think it is true that life does or can have meaning."

This act of maintaining the most rigorous intellectual standards, uninfluenced by our hopes and aspirations, exhibits stern integrity in the face of temptation. The question is: does this scrupulous act have any *meaning?*

Meaning and Value

We were driven to speak of the unlimited by the nature of meaning as a transcending of limits, a connecting with something external. For how could a mere connection with something, no matter how trivial, establish the requisite meaning? That other thing, surely, must itself have meaning, if meaning is to accrue to anything in virtue of being connected with it. Inexorably, we are led to iterate the question "and what is the meaning of that?", asking it of each wider context. Barring an infinite chain, we are led either to something itself without meaning, which seems to undercut the meaning of all the rest based upon it, or to something that somehow can constitute its own meaning. These structural possibilities are similar to the ones with explanatory chains we see elsewhere; the unlimited which is its own meaning, thereby anchoring the chain, corresponds to a fundamental self-subsuming principle which is its own explanation.

Meaning involves transcending limits; yet although merely connecting with anything at all beyond the limits, no matter how trivial, does not suffice to establish meaning, it does not follow that the requisite connection must be made with something that itself has *meaning.* What bestows meaning by connection must itself be nontrivial, but there are ways of being nontrivial other than by having meaning. Something is nontrivial, also, if it has value. The chain that grounds meaning cannot terminate in something worthless, but it need not end with something that somehow is intrinsically meaningful; it can rest upon something valuable. Thus the apparently inexorable regress is stopped. Meaning involves transcending limits so as to connect with something valuable; meaning is a transcending of the limits of your own value, a transcending of your own limited value. Meaning is a connection with an external value, but this

610

meaning need not involve any connection with an infinite value; we may well aspire to that, but to fall short is not to be bereft of meaning. There are many numbers between zero and infinity.

How meaningful is this limited transcendence, though? A person accepts the fact of universal finitude and limits, and struggles bravely to overcome and transcend his own limits so as thereby to achieve meaningfulness. But what is the point of this endeavor?* Suppose I am more limited than you; with luck, I will manage to expand to those very limits you will have if you fail to transcend any of your limits at all. Can my life be made meaningful by reaching what is not a meaningful life for you? This supposition of one transcending his own limits to reach the given limit of another does not make clear sense for people. We can imagine a lower organism thus transcending itself, though, and achieving meaning through the greater value it then embodies or is linked with, just as, were there beings superior to us, we might achieve value beyond ourselves, and therefore meaning, by reaching to their starting point.

The value of a person's life attaches to it within its limits, while the meaning of his life attaches to it as centered in the wider value context beyond its limits. This meaning will depend upon the array of external or wider values connected with it and upon the nature of the connections, their strength, intensity, closeness, the way his attachment unifies those values. The meaning of a life is its place in a wider context of value. We might imagine a life as having a view of value: clearly in view and more in the foreground are what the life is connected to most closely. The meaning of a life, then, would be how the whole realm of value looks from there, its perspective on the realm of value as a function of its interconnections with it. If intrinsic value is degree of organic unity, then the meaning of a person's life is the organic unity of the realm of values as centered on, as organized around, him; it is the value of the realm of value, when transformed so as to center on him. It is a measure of the degree of organic unity his life brings to the realm of value.

Might there be a conflict between the meaning and the value of a person's life, so that he is forced to consider and to make tradeoffs between these? It is somewhat arbitrary precisely how and where

* Fichte speaks of the longing for the overcoming of all limitations; but the infinite he offers us is infinite striving, with no hope of success. Is infinite disappointment the infinity we crave?

we draw the boundary between a life and its context. (Are relationships to other people included within a life, or as part of its context?) A theory would do better to avoid tradeoffs of two very similar notions across a somewhat arbitrary boundary.

We care both about the value and the meaning of our life. I suggest we view these as partial aspects of one underlying thing we care about, let us call it worth. Value is one facet of worth, and meaning is another. Specify this notion of worth so that no matter where the line is drawn between a life and what is external to it, although the particular placement affects the assessments of the value and of the meaning of the life, raising one while lowering the other, it does not affect the assessment of the (overall) worth of the life. The notion of worth looks on both sides of the boundary in such a way that it is not affected by where the boundary is placed. (We might call this, after an analogous principle in the von Neumann interpretation of quantum mechanics, the cut principle.) Worth is a centered notion, measuring the degree of organic unity of material as centered on something, and it takes account of the degree of organic unity of the included components including the entity at the center.

Consider again the issue of whether the ethical person will have a more valuable life. We worried in the previous chapter whether the ethical person's being responsive to the value of others, as value, would be reflected back into his own value. These ethical relationships of responsiveness are more valuable than anti-responsive ones; yet would not such value reside between the ethical person and the other, rather than within his own life? It was not then clear that this value could not be counted within the value of his life, but neither was it obvious that it had to be. Now we are in a position to see that such ethical behavior, responding to the value of another as value, will be reflected in the meaning of a person's life (if not in the value); unethical behavior, ceteris paribus, reduces the meaning of the agent's life. (However, this does not prove it impossible that unethical behavior might sometimes be a means toward connection with other, greater, values, and so not diminish the value of a person's life.) In behaving ethically, we transcend our own limits and connect to another's value as value. The life of the ethical person will have greater value or meaning; the moral push consists in the fact that his life will have greater worth.[19]

The unification of the notions of value and meaning under the notion of worth, or at least the placing of meaning alongside value as a similar notion, is highly desirable. We specified value as the degree of organic unity, the unification of diversity within order and limits. This theme of order and balance within limits is central to Greek thought, which viewed the unlimited and infinite as suspicious and frightening.[20] Despite the fact that such unity can involve a dynamic tension,[21] as well as unities over time, this notion of value as organic unity might seem too static, presenting too quiescent a picture of harmoniously organized complexity. There may not have seemed to be room here for the themes and emphases of the Romantic movement: overcoming obstacles, breaking bonds, powerful irrational emotions, titanic struggle, continuous striving toward new goals, the value of change and novelty, the dynamic process of transcending limits. Is a harmonious order desirable or possible, doesn't some of the greatest art present the absolute claims of irreconcilable values and views?[22]

Value, we now see, was only one part of the picture—meaning is the other. The Romantic themes and emphases that make an uncomfortable fit with organic unities are perfectly at home under the rubric of transcending limits, of meaning. (The Romantics highly valued organic unity also.) Nor should this meaning be viewed simply as the passive larger harmonious organic unity (value); the active process of transcending is crucial, and not to be passified.

On one view, change, novelty, the breaking of bonds and of previous order, when worthwhile, **is** simply the destruction of premature unities. New and unexpected material is introduced so that an even wider diversity can be unified; old forms are broken in order that new and tighter modes of unification can be introduced. The purpose of the process of transcending limits, on this view, is to reach a new and higher degree of organic unity.*

Let us focus, for the moment, on the pattern of the process itself, one exhibited in the arts and sciences as well as in an individual's life. The pattern involves four stages. (1) Diverse materials are organized in an order, structure, theory, style, hierarchy, unity. (2) The content of this order is extended, new material is introduced (while

---

* This is typified by comedy, which shows improper restrictions being broken, culminating in a harmonious ending; satire also breaks apart fixed intellectual systems of thought or behavior, but without the harmonious resolution. See Northrop Frye, *Anatomy of Criticism* (Princeton University Press, Princeton, 1957), p. 231.

some old material may be rejected or ignored); the older modes of organization are broken apart, either under pressure of the new material which they only inadequately could organize, or through criticism of features intrinsic to that order. (3) A new organization of the material is introduced, with new modes of patterning and unification; the new material and much (most?) of the old is combined into a new unity. (4) This unity is then disrupted by the introduction of further new material and the saliency of the fact that it does not perfectly unify the old material. And so on.

The goal of this pattern, on the usual view, is the odd-numbered steps, the unifications. The even-numbered steps, the breakings asunder, are transition points to the odd, whereby new material and possibilities of patterning are introduced in order that at the next stage of unification there will be a still greater degree of organic unity than at the previous such stage. It is left unclear, usually, whether this process is to have a final stage; but in any event the purpose of the process is the achievement of better and better (odd) stages of unification of diversity, better and better unities.

Clearly, we can imagine an alternative view of this process, whereby the goal lies in the even stages, in the destruction of the unities rather than their creation,[23] the breaking asunder of patterns and forms, thereby showing that reality or the self or whatever is too protean to be encompassed. This view sees the purpose of the process in the transcending of (existing salient) patterns and limits. If the first view is (broadly speaking) classicism, the second is romanticism. On this second view, the odd-numbered stages are only transition points; their sequence of more elaborately grounded unities and orders within limits only heightens the challenge of bursting these.*

---

* Modernism in art involves the bursting of the previous bounds and forms. It attempts to introduce new previously recalcitrant materials: materials other than paint into collage, other objects themselves as in *objet trouvé*, even objects manufactured for nonartistic purposes (Picasso's bull from a bicycle seat, junk art), comic strip cartoons, newspaper clippings in novels, outside noises into a musical work, the stuff of actual journalism into the "nonfiction novel", chance elements in aleatoric music. Previous forms are burst, as in the obliteration of the line between stage and audience, happenings, the wrapping of areas of the outer world in cloth, while self-destructing sculpture literally bursts its preexisting form. Often, the modernist works are self-conscious, exploring the limits of art and the art–nonart boundary; often they are self-referring works, constituting their own subject matter. Theorists and critics strive to see new forms (or, as in action painting, a

The odd and even stages—unification and transcending of limited orders—are stages of value and meaning respectively. Which stage is the goal of the process? Each stage is followed by the opposite type, then in turn by its own type, and so on without discernible end. In this sinusoidal process, which are the peaks and which the troughs? Two views, classic and romantic, each see one type of stage as background or means for the other, organizing the whole process (in a way gestalt psychologists describe) into figure and ground; but these two views differ in which stage they see as figure, which as ground. Are not both patterns equally there, as in those intriguing drawings (two profiles and vase, old woman and young woman, duck and rabbit) equally susceptible to two different organizings?

Unlike these drawings, though, where the contrasting views alternate but cannot coexist, we can formulate a larger view of the consec-

---

different art object—the painter's activity) emerging to encompass this new diversity. Although such discernings sometimes are illuminating, often they are forced. Perhaps the unities are not being established within the works of art; are we instead witnessing meta-art, wherein a great diversity is unified under the rubric *art*. Its task is to incorporate diverse materials and happenings within the realm of art, and so unify it as art; the individual works therefore will have to have some continuity with previous art, but the central purpose is not to have these works themselves exhibit high organic unity. That is reserved for (the realm of) art itself, as it incorporates the greatest possible diversity under its unifying rubric. It is not surprising that such meta-art would include, importantly, many self-referring artistic works. (Of course, we also might see meta-art as an attempt to transcend the previous limits of art, by going up to the meta-level. For a discussion of other phenomena in moves to the meta-level, see Erving Goffman, *Frame Analysis*, Harvard University Press, Cambridge, 1974.)

Once one gets the idea, it is possible to invent new such art works. We might have a blank canvas hanging on a larger blank canvas. Or an artist might exhibit an uncashed check, received for an earlier art work, to demonstrate his purity of motive. (But what will he sell *this* work for?) Or a museum itself might be made into an art object (but not as a work of architecture), by focusing upon it as a (permeable) boundary between the art world and the real world; and now which world is this boundary a part of?

Needless to say, not all meta-artistic experiments will be successful or interesting. (Some will propose extending the boundaries of art beyond the "interesting"; but will they also want to extend it beyond the meta-interesting, and the meta- . . . -meta-interesting? And will anyone want to extend it beyond the "artistically successful"?) Even so, the attempt will be to extend boundaries of art as far as feasible and thereby unify within the boundaries. Perhaps the limit of such a process is including *everything* within art and, also, as the Zen master does with the everyday world, leaving it as it is, "nothing special".

utive stages of the process, wherein each stage is part of the figure. We can see the whole process as foreground. Neither the odd nor the even stages are merely a means or transition to the other valuable and central ones—what is valuable and central is the ongoing process itself, the whole sine curve. The artistic process is not for the purpose either of creating unities or of transcending them, but for the ongoing alternation of creation and transcendence. The scientific process is not solely for the purpose of creating new theories, or for the purpose of disconfirming and falsifying inadequate ones but—I continue the analogy with some hesitation—for the ongoing alternation of theories, ferreting out facts or problems a theory cannot handle, constructing further theories, finding further difficulties, and so forth.[24]

What is the purpose of this pattern, repeated in different areas, of unification and destruction of unity, of reconstituting new unities and transcending them as well? This process is valuable because, in addition to containing valuable unities as its stages, it itself constitutes a pattern which unifies the widest diversity of human activity. Into this patterned process fall our hopes and activities, our desires to attain and to transcend, our search for value and meaning. Processes as well as resulting end states, becoming as well as being, can have value and can provide the context in which meaning is embedded.

The process we have described is valuable; within it, limits are transcended, unities are overcome and expanded. But does the process itself have meaning? Is it not merely another pattern with its own limits; must not that pattern itself be transcended? It is as if we must be like Cantor's diagonal number, cutting athwart and thereby transcending the limits of all categories, orders, and patterns.* Yet

* Georg Cantor proved that there are more real numbers than positive integers, even though there are an infinite number of the latter. He imagined a listing, an enumeration, of the real numbers, expressed as nonterminating decimals, and showed how to construct another number that is not on the list. If the first number on the list has a 5 as its first digit, let the new number have a 6 as its first digit, otherwise let it have a 5 as its first digit; similarly if the second number on the list has a 5 as its second digit, let the new number have a 6 as its second digit, otherwise let it have a 5 as its second digit; more generally, if the ith number on the list has a 5 as its ith digit, let the new number have a 6 as its ith digit, otherwise let its ith digit be 5. Thus, this new number differs from every number on the list in at least one place; it differs from the first number in the first digit, the second in the second digit, and the

even Cantor's diagonal number for a given list is that particular real number whose construction is described that transcends only that particular list. Although each list has some numbers or other that transcend it, there is no one real number that transcends all lists. Since the pattern of the process has been described at such a general level (with type theory restrictions being ignored), any attempt to transcend that pattern would seem itself to be part of the pattern, fitting neatly into an even-numbered stage of "transcending-the-limits". Here, I think, we have a verbal puzzle, rather than a genuine limit viewed externally; however we resolve the puzzle, that process of repeated transcending does not *feel* limited. (Should we say that when this process is transcended, it applies to itself at another level, and so fits its own pattern even in the transcending of it, thereby subsuming itself?)

Even if the process itself is not a limit, is there any point to the process of unification and transcendence, is it going somewhere? Camus picked Sisyphus' endless, repetitive task as the epitome of meaninglessness, while Nietzsche, in his doctrine of eternal recurrence, made infinite repetitiveness the challenge that meaning had to overcome. A process can avoid this by being directional, by showing change that is progress, either as judged by some external criterion or by one internal to the process. However, this internal criterion need not be a state which is being approached asymptotically —it can be the rhythm of the process itself, expressed in its multifariously changing content. The curve of the dynamic process is the best picture of meaning and value combined; it is the best picture of worth.

Previously, we have been occupied with the themes of reflexivity, self-subsumption, and tracking. Reflexivity and self-subsumption involve a tight mode of unification whereby something turns back into itself, hence a high degree of organic unity, while tracking of facts (in knowledge) or value (in action) involves a close connection to something external, hence a transcending of the limits of the self. These

---

i^{th} number in the ith digit. Therefore, this new number which Cantor gave directions for constructing is not on the list. Nothing about this procedure depends on the particular listing; for each such listing, for each (even infinite) enumeration of real numbers, there will be some real number that is not on that list—so there are more real numbers than any (denumerably infinite) list can contain.

previous salient themes thus fall under the notions of value and meaning; they are among the best instantiated realizations thus far. (Is there also some tighter unification of these themes, corresponding to the notion of worth?)

We have explained meaning as a transcending of limits in a wider context of value. In discussing the fact–value gap, we held that the conditions constitutive of value were not sufficient for value; the person himself had to choose (perhaps in a self-subsuming reflexive choice) that there be value. Is the situation similar for meaning? While transcending limits to connect with a wider context of value constitutes meaning if anything does, must there also be a separate choice that there be meaning? Or does the choice that there be value also bring meaning in its wake? I lean to this latter view; the reflexive choice that there be value is a choice to connect and accord with something external, a choice to transcend one's own limits. In our theory of the self synthesizing itself as an organic unity, the connection with something external is of a piece with the self's incorporation of something in internal synthesis. Both are ways of transcending the limits of the dot of reflexive self-consciousness.

Limited transcendence, the transcending of our limits so as to connect with a wider context of value which itself is limited, does give our lives meaning—but a limited one. We may thirst for more. The future may bring humanity what heretofore has been a theme for science-fiction writers only: contact with other forms of life, consciousness and being, the experience and challenges of diverse intergalactic civilizations, further human evolution, contributing humanity's special quality to the universe's symphony of life and culture. It is not difficult to imagine a wider scope for human adventure (and failure, too), a broader context within which our limits can be transcended.*

What new philosophical questions then will arise, we hardly can forsee. There will be new ones, surely, as well as new facts and new concepts to render inadequate our tentative answers to old questions. It is futile to aim, with previous philosophers, at doing philoso-

---

* The most imaginative presentation I know of, the broadest scope, the boldest vision, and the widest possibilities, is found in Olaf Stapledon, *Last and First Men* and *Starmaker;* so exhilarating was his secular vision, that C. S. Lewis felt had to write a science fiction trilogy, also interesting, in reply.

phy for the whole universe and for all time—future philosophers will find these attempts touching. We can, however, try to formulate a philosophy and a mode of philosophy that is open to this future and leaves conceptual room for it, in a spirit that welcomes it. Also, we can hope to learn of wonderful philosophies others have formulated which we could not, realizing that we may have to cope with being told we will not be able to understand even the simplified gist of theirs.

Some will find even this wider context insufficient, since it provides only a finite (though perhaps very large, extensive, and intricate) meaning. All of the intergalactic civilizations, even, eventually may come to share the Romantic urge and thirst for the infinite. Yet, if nothing unlimited exists to ground infinite meaning, what task will they find worthy of their efforts; what might give meaning to their widest cooperation and utilization of knowledge and energies? With nothing of greater value external to them, how shall they transcend their joint limits? If God does not exist, won't they eventually try to create him?

Philosophy as Part of the Humanities

Value and meaning traditionally have been the preserve of the humanities, which depict their nature, present instances, describe or inspire their pursuit, and portray their role or their absence in our lives. Philosophy, too, can fall within this domain. Before describing how philosophy can be carried on as part of the humanities, we must pause to describe the intellectual and imaginative landscape.

The sciences aim at truths and explanations; it is the highest ambition of current scientists to discover and formulate new important truths, laws, and explanations that will be incorporated into the textbooks of the future. No physicist, biologist, or economist now expects or even hopes that the articles or books he writes will themselves be read one hundred years from now. These are not designed to be read or experienced directly; the truths they discover and laws they formulate can just as well be presented in other people's words—and they will be as they are incorporated into the larger edifice of scientific truths and textbooks. When, occasionally, an elder scientist writes his autobiography or presents general thoughts on the nature of his scientific activity, he is well aware that he is not then doing science.

Works of art and literature, on the other hand, are produced with the intention that they will be experienced directly. No one now thinks it is unnecessary to read Shakespeare because everything important in him has been incorporated into current literature. However, although these works of art are produced with the intention that they will be read or experienced directly, it is not intended usually that they present truths or explanations, unless "imaginative" ones—truths of another sort. Since the "truths" they contain are not extractable or paraphrasable without loss, it is not surprising that these works must be experienced directly and so cannot merely be incorporated into future texts or re-presentations.

There is a body of writing, however, which intends both to present truths, explanations, and so on, and to be read directly rather than merely incorporated into other writings. Here fall the great works of political philosophy (of Plato, Aristotle, Hobbes, Locke, Rousseau), of social theory (Marx, Tocqueville, Weber, Durkheim), of moral theory, of religious thought, of philosophy generally. The writers of these works strive after truths, yet view it as important and write with the intention that their works themselves will be read, that their own voice will be heard. With an aim of science (to produce truths and explanation) yet an intention of artistic works (to be experienced directly), these works present a puzzle. Why should it be important that works presenting truths be experienced directly? What accounts for this phenomenon in works of the humanities?

The humanities are marked by (the nature of) their concern with value and meaning.[25] (True, many university courses under the administrative rubric of "humanities" evidence no concern for value or meaning, but this merely shows that the course-catalog delineation of the Humanities is not the same as ours.) Yet, not every concern with value and meaning falls within the humanities; for example, consider the way an anthropologist can study the values of different cultures or tribes, make cross-cultural comparisons of value, and so forth. The anthropologist studies values by placing them in quotation marks, telling us: they believe "it is wrong to eat meat, marry one's uncle or aunt, allow an insult to go unavenged." The anthropologist's report of these beliefs neither endorses nor condemns them; from the anthropological report no value statement follows. Values can be the subject matter of the anthropologist's study, but as a social scientist his standpoint toward these is external. He could just as well be describing (or trying to explain) different values, or things other than values. He does not respond internally to them; he does not respond to values qua values. The quotation marks are the fence that keeps him external to the values.*

A work of the humanities responds to value as value, to meaning as meaning, and it is concerned with these in relation to humanity, as they guide or inspire human affairs; so, the humanities also are concerned with originative value and meaning, the value and meaning we bring into the world and exhibit through our free choices. However, there are other modes of such responsiveness that are *not* part of the humanities, for instance, behaving ethically and so being responsive to the value qua value of another person, or striving to live a meaningful life, or an environmentalist's responding to the value of an unspoiled environment (though not to the far-flung value of its use) through political activity designed to protect and preserve that environment. How then are we to delineate that mode of responsiveness to value as value, to meaning as meaning, which constitutes activity in the humanities?

The poet, painter, or critic is responding to value as value, meaning as meaning, and he also has an audience in mind; he intends that *through* the object he makes (poem, painting, essay) or the activity he performs, the audience also will respond to the values and meanings he is responding to, qua value and meaning. Also, the artist (often? always?) intends that his product have a value of its own that will be responded to by the audience. And he often intends that the audience's response to the value or meaning he responds to will not only be mediated by his work and occur through it, but will be mediated by and occur through the *value* of his work.

---

* Herbert Hart (*The Concept of Law*, Oxford University Press, 1961, pp. 54–57) distinguishes the external point of view toward the law, as taken, for example, by a criminal who views the legal system solely in terms of the probability of various eventualities for someone like himself who breaks the law, from the internal view of those, private citizens or judges, who guide their conduct by the law and accept the fact that the law is a certain way as a reason for their acting accordingly. (How much of what apparently instances a prima facie duty to obey the law might better be accounted for as an application of a "principle of fair play", triggered by others' conforming behavior to an an enacted law?)

In addition to the value the artist responds to, his responding to it can itself have value and meaning, and be something the audience is intended to respond to, as can his artistically responding to it, and responding to the value of his own work. The audience's response to value is itself valuable, and a work even might contain an anticipatory response to this audience response. (There is no obvious limit to the complexity of these situations; an artist through his work might attempt to get us to respond to *our own* responsiveness to his work, and so forth.) These configurations are crude and lack nuance—their structures need refining, the component relation itself, responsiveness to value and meaning as value and meaning, is a topic for Proustian discriminations. Fortunately, our purposes here require only hewing out these broadest contours.*

We have spoken of an artist's product, a painting, composition, or book. Yet cannot an individual—didn't Socrates, didn't Gandhi?—present his own moral actions or his life itself as exemplary to others, as a vehicle through which others can respond to value as value, to meaning as meaning? Recall our earlier discussion of living transparently, wherein a person responds to values in a way so that others can discern the nature of those values through his actions, respond to his responding, and so forth. That would fit the patterns of response we have sketched for artist and audience. I see no reason to exclude such a person's life as an object within the humanities—that life *would* be a humanistic work.

Philosophy, too, can fit this structure of responsiveness to value and meaning, and thereby be carried on as part of the humanities. It need not be—there are other ways, legitimate ways, of carrying on philosophical activity. However, one way is humanistic: the philosopher can respond to value and meaning, creating a work through which we, the audience, also respond to this value and meaning, perhaps also to the value of the work and to his or our responding. (A humanistic philosophy will have its own ways of responding to value

---

* Many people find it offensive and narcissistic when the artist responds to his own special value (as opposed to the value we all share) or to the value of his work or of his responsiveness or of his audience's response. I myself do not find it so. Instead, I am thankful for the gift I am given, the inspiring and delightful gift of seeing a happy and creative person valuing himself and his work, and I am especially grateful for his willingness to *share* this response in view of the risks of venomous resentment he thereby runs. (But which one is it who is being poisoned?)

and meaning; other parts of the humanities may find they cannot suitably use these ways, and philosophy is not doomed to share their crises.)

This mode of connection to value and meaning must be responsive to them as value and meaning. This is not the same simply as the philosophical work's studying value and meaning, even outside of quotation marks. For value and meaning can be studied, with a stated commitment to them as one's own values and meanings, without treating them as value and meaning. We soon shall consider reductionist modes of study, reducing value and meaning to something lesser. One mark of responding to value and meaning as value and meaning is that the response not be to a reductionist (less valuable or meaningful) substitute.

Second, it may be possible to study value and meaning as an abstract (nonreduced) realm, in the way the number theorist studies the realm of numbers, investigating intricate relations, striking structural facts, and so forth. (To emphasize the parallel, let us suppose the number theorist rejects all the various set-theoretical reductions of number theory.) This value theorist can study value in the same way he would investigate any other abstract realm. Even if some of the structural facts were special to the realm of value, so that he couldn't just as well be speaking of something else, he still will not be responding to the value qua value. (His work will not involve V-ing value, even if he periodically announces that he V's it. A similar point applies to some types of scholarship current in the humanities.) Yet perhaps such an investigation of value, analogous to number theory, is impossible; perhaps there are aspects of the realm of value that cannot be explored unless the value theorist, in that very process of exploration, responds to values as values. Although his stated purpose in *Anatomy in Criticism* is to be a nonevaluative theorist, even Northrop Frye speaks of "the still center of the order of words" in the greatest moments of literature; could he have presented so incisive and illuminating a classification were he merely a botanist of literary forms?[26]

Because works in the humanities respond to value as value, and are intended to be vehicles whereby the audience does so, they have to be experienced directly. The transposition into textbooks or into summaries, whatever else it preserves, will not preserve the work's responsiveness to value qua value, to meaning qua meaning. To be sure, the writer of a textbook or a history of thought can himself respond to value as value, to meaning as meaning, so that through his work we are brought to respond to value and meaning: to the values the original works responded to, the values they possessed, and perhaps to the secondary work's own value—that writer will have created another work in the humanities. However, it seems plausible that an artist or author cannot create a work through which we respond to value and meaning (and *to* which we respond) unless he too was so responsive. We now can understand the earlier puzzling question about why some works, even though their aim is to present truths and explanations, have to be experienced directly. These truths and explanations may go alongside a value response or (more to the point) be in (as well as about) response to value. They have to be experienced directly so that we can experience how the author responds to value qua value, how he transcends his narrow limits in his quest for truth, or understanding, or even meaning.

I lack the skill and literary perceptiveness to delineate the ways in which the voice of an author and the organization of his work express his response to value and meaning, to discern what modulations of tone, timing, and the contours of his quest show him to us in the very process of responding, and lead us also to respond. I hope literary critics will illuminate this, neither providing a reductionist account nor discovering devices through which a reader might be manipulated.[27]

The fit of philosophy within the humanities can be even tighter when philosophy is oriented toward the goals of explanation and understanding, rather than proof and convincing. Carrying on philosophy noncoercively, no longer with the goal of compelling argument or forcing someone to believe something, may itself be responsive—in addition to whatever value it responds to in its subject matter—to the reader's value and autonomy. Moreover, the offering of philosophical explanations can be responsive to value and meaning by taking care to formulate explanations that do not undercut the existence of value and meaning, or our responding to them. More directly, the explanatory questions themselves can be about value and meaning (so too can corresponding things to be proven), for example, how are objective values possible, how is a nonpuppetlike and valuable mode of action possible, how is it possible for life to have meaning? Though value-impregnated subject matter does not guarantee the explanatory activity will be responsive to value as value—recall the possibility that the value theorist proceeds exactly as in number theory—such responsiveness can enter in, first by the rejection of (demeaning) reductionistic explanations, and second (in a way I am not fully clear about) by having the contours of the explanation respond to value as value, be sensitive to meaning as meaning. In so responding, it need not be limited to or mainly focused upon moral value and meaning.

The search for explanations itself lifts us out of our narrow concerns; and the free consideration of possibilities, placing a matter within a wider matrix of possibilities, not only increases understanding but enables us to transcend the limits of the actual. Considering and developing diverse philosophical theories without compulsion to fix upon only one (though we rank them), keeping the basketful of views, is a link with wider possibilities. This philosophical activity itself, whether formulating views or reading and considering them, constitutes an activity within the domain of the humanities. Philosophical understanding, the philosophical quest itself, transcends limits and bestows meaning. (Philosophers always end up praising their activity; however, I have not claimed that it is the only route to meaning, or the best one.)

The search for explanations to reconcile apparent philosophical tensions, to show how something is possible given something else, may have a value motivation. If the explanations which provide this unity in apparent diversity themselves are valuable, and are sought and prized because of this value, and these explanations are presented in order for others to respond to their value, to the value exhibited in what is explained and also perhaps to the value in the activity of explaining as it unites our minds with the unities out there, then the explanatory activity itself is a humanistic one, a vehicle whereby we can respond to values and to the explainer's responsiveness.

These last points need not be restricted to philosophical explanations. Cannot scientific explanations also be offered in a quest for valuable theoretical unifications in nature, as a vehicle whereby we can respond to that value as the scientist does, and to the value of his so responding? Why cannot science be carried on as part of the humanities? The motivation of scientists often is to discern and uncover the deep unifying principles underlying diverse phenomena, and their motivation even can be to remove unsightly theoretical blemishes, coincidences, tensions, rather than to account directly for observed facts.[28] Although sometimes they speak of the "aesthetics" of science, of the beauty of theories and of the (parts of the) universe it reveals, rarely in their scientific work or presentations do scientists intend for us to respond to the value of their own responsiveness; rarely, even, do they allow into their papers their responsiveness to the values which sometimes motivate them. To be sure, objectivity and impersonality and judging the truth dispassionately also is a value; but how shall we tell whether responsiveness to this value is sprinkled and expressed (but also hidden) throughout scientific papers, or instead whether these exhibit no responsiveness at all? A topic worth pursuing is the different ways responsiveness to value and meaning does or might enter into the very contours of scientific work—the choice of questions or problems, the types of theories pursued, the mode of formulation of theories, and interpretations (and the reactions to them) of theoretical situations and quandaries (as in complementarity, the Copenhagen interpretation of quantum mechanics, and views concerning Bell's inequality). Of course, the scientific enterprise itself was once seen as a way of transcending the limits of our ignorance, a bold and adventurous search into the hidden mysteries and patterns of nature. One reason, surely, for the great interest recently shown in Thomas Kuhn's *Structure of Scientific Revolutions* (aside from its merits) was that its picture of science placed people at its center, full of preconceptions, frailties, and worldviews—in contrast to views of science merely as an impersonal algorithm for forming or accepting theories.*

---

* Another reason was the desire of many on the political left who were getting the worse in intellectual arguments, to say "well, you have your paradigm and I have mine." Suppose there is disagreement over two substantive positions I and II, and also over whether (either) one of the positions is objectively correct or only is subjectively held, so that the numbers distribute as follows

	Position I	Position II
View that both positions are subjective	m	n
View that one of the positions is objectively right	o	p

It seems a plausible conjecture that the weaker position substantively, in terms of supporting reasons, strength of argument, and so on, will have the

To investigate the ways science is or can be humanistic, to discern its humanistic strands, is not to recommend *transforming* it further, against its grain, into a humanity or into something with humanistic veneer. Yet the investigation is worth making, for the sciences are a dominant part of the modern intellectual world, and the scientific picture of the world, the "scientific outlook", appears to leave no room for value and meaning, and so threatens the very legitimacy of the humanities. (Their onetime hegemony has long since disappeared.) It is ironic that one of the most glorious achievements of the modern mind, science, seems to leave no room for its own glory; that the reduced image of man toward which it seems inexorably to lead —a mean and pitiable plaything of forces beyond his control—seems to leave no room even for the creators, and the creation, of science itself.

Reductionism

Statements of the form "X is nothing but Y" often are put forth with debunking intent; for example, "a performance of a violin sonata is nothing but the scraping of horsehair on catgut", "love is nothing but glandular secretion". These statements are asymmetrical, and are always presented in one direction; it is never said, for example, that the rubbing of horsehair on catgut is nothing but the performance of a violin sonata. What determines the direction of these statements? The more valuable is said to be nothing but the less valuable; the debunking is a debunking of (what then is said to be only apparent) value.

---

higher percentage of subjectivists. If II is a weaker substantive position than I, then

$$\frac{n}{n + p} > \frac{m}{m + o}$$

Similarly, if

$$\frac{n}{n + p} > \frac{m}{m + o} \quad \left(\text{or } \frac{n}{m + n} > \frac{p}{p + o} \right)$$

then II is the weaker substantive position. Once this is generally realized, presumably all proponents to a disagreement will become reluctant to announce "it is all subjective", instead of, as is now the case, just the ones with the stronger substantive position.

Reductionist views reduce the more valuable to the less valuable, the more meaningful to the less meaningful; the reduction is a reduction in value, in worth. The literature of philosophy of science describes something there called "reductions", wherein one body of theory is derivable from another—the entities and properties of the first being identified with (configurations of) entities and properties of the second, the laws of the first then being derived from those of the second.[29] However, not every such derivation is reductionistic, involving a reduction in value; light was not thought to be more valuable than electromagnetic radiation, heat than mean kinetic energy, or genes than sequenced nucleic acids.

One type of reductionist view sees a whole as nothing but the sum of its parts; it explains the action or functioning of the whole in terms of the parts and their interactions, without introducing any reference to integration at the level of the whole.[30] If value is degree of organic unity, and the value of a unified whole can be greater than the sum of the values of its parts, then an explanation of something's panoply of action that denies or makes inessential its own organic unity will downplay its value and view it as less valuable. However, there also are other ways, besides micro-explanations in terms of its parts, to see something as less valuable, for example to come to see it as lacking originative value in that all of its action and functioning is controlled by outside forces or stimuli—these diminutions in value, too, are reductionist.

It is a commonplace that man has had to revise downward his estimate of his own importance in the scheme of things; Copernicus showed him he was not at the center of the universe, Darwin that he was subject to the same evolutionary forces that generated the rest of the animal kingdom. However, we will not classify these as reductionist, if we think they are true, even though they led man to revise downward his estimate of his own value. A reductionist view sees something as less valuable than it is, not simply as less valuable than it once might falsely have been thought to be. Clearly, then, there is room for disagreement about a theory: is it reductionist, or rather is the refusal to accept it absurdly inflationist?*

* Is Bergsonian vitalism, or Jungian integration, inflationist or merely nonreductionist? Although I would not, Goethe and J. B. Rhine each thought of their different work in "science" as simply nonreductionist; perhaps even Hegel, Fichte, Teilhard de Chardin, and Carlos Castenada thought the same of their very different theories. But surely, it must be possible for *something* to be inflationist!

Whether or not they see people, their activities, attachments, and institutions, as less valuable than they in fact are, recent times have seen an upsurge of theories, a predominance of them, that at least call for a downward revision in our previous estimates and attributions of value. Some such theories always have been around: from the Greek materialist view that there is nothing but atoms in the void, to views in the eighteenth century—Hume's that reason is the slave of the passions, Mandeville's ferreting out of private vices (and noting their public functions), La Mettrie's picture of man as a machine. Recently, however, such theories have moved to the center of the intellectual stage. These views, undermining, unmasking, and denigrating people's attachments, principles, motivations, and modes of action, have now come to shape people's own view of themselves. Let me list only some pieces to remind you of what adds up to a concerted assault. (Some of the brief descriptions may be said to be distortions and vulgarizations; but is it an accidental fact about these positions that the brief descriptions always work in a reductionist direction?)

Religious attachment involves no contact with the divine, and is merely a way of coping with our fears, a projection of our hopes or infantile psychology (Hume's *Natural History of Religion*, Feuerbach, Freud). Social and political principles, despite their claim to validity, are ideological superstructure, generated and maintained by needs for rationalization of ruling groups or hierarchical structures, or are a function of social position (Marx, Mannheim) or are summary rules of thumb for social wealth maximization (the "economic analysis of law"). The individual person is buffeted and directed by unconscious repressed desires, his rational reasons are merely rationalizations, his valuable activities, literary and artistic, merely redirections of other energy, viewed as baser, now sublimated (Freud). Our voluntary behavior and major life plans are the playing out of patterns and conflicts established in early childhood (Freud) or are under the control of external stimuli, past history of reinforcement, and current drive state (Pavlov, Watson, Hull, Skinner), of innate desires instilled in the evolutionary process and serving (at least once upon a time) our inclusive fitness (the literature of sociobiology), or of biochemical and electrical activity in our brain and current hormone balances (Olds, Delgado). Cultural patterns composed by individual actions can be explained, as can people's most personal actions and relationships (such as marriage, religious attendance, childbearing, friendship, and suicide), in disconnection from the reasons people offer, either by the energetic requirements and needs of the society (Harris), or by more general self-interested economic calculations (Becker's "Economic Approach to Human Behavior", various special issues of the *Journal of Political Economy*), or other calculations of balance of benefit.

Now, various of these are incompatible with others—they cannot all be true at once—but the general picture is one of people as the playthings of forces they do not control, less rational, principled, autonomous, and good than they seemed, presenting elaborate reasons which are merely rationalizations. This reduced picture of man's value, capabilities, and autonomy, and of the disintegration of meaning, is reflected and exhibited also in recent literature (Kafka, Musil, Céline, Beckett) and is a concern in many other works.[31] Max Weber spoke of the "disenchantment" of the modern world, of a "world robbed of gods".

Ours can aptly be called the Age of Reductionism. Even the notion of value itself has been reduced—to group consensus, affective desire, personal preference. Yet still the reductions go on, the reductions in value, playing off a notion of value which no longer is there; perhaps now the direction of reduction has to be specified differently, not as what lessens the magnitude of value but as what crosses against the direction of desire or preference—provided that most people do not come to share the reductionist desire. Does the reductionist theorist (continue to) presume that stating his unpleasant truth is valuable, better than not, or, with the disappearance of the notion of value, does he simply desire to state it? (And is the desire to bridge the fact–value distinction by deriving value from fact merely another form of reductionism?) The emblematic philosophy of our time has been logical positivism, which holds that all statements other than those of empirical science and logic and mathematics are meaningless, without any cognitive content; it usually combines this with the (unity of science) view that all empirical statements are reducible to those of physics. Logical positivism is in decline, its verifiability theory of meaning now repudiated, yet its spirit lives on in our culture.[32]

The only thing that has not yet been given a reductionist account is reductionism and the reductionist activity. But shouldn't a thoroughgoing reductionism be courageous enough to reduce and devalue even itself? Reductionism is nothing but what? Shall we say "the opiate of the ressentimental"? (Or is this answer not a reduction, but a description?)

We can, without devaluing reductionism, assess it along the dimension of value. In presenting his theory, the reductionist theorist is unresponsive, antiresponsive even, to people's value as value. Moreover, he convinces some to view others, and even themselves, as of lesser worth. Since people's views of themselves, of what they are doing and how they are acting, infuse their actions, these have to be taken account of in explanations, at least within quotation marks. By thus altering people's views of themselves, reductionism not only holds value to be less than it actually is, but makes it less than it was. (Has the intent of reductionism, all along, been to become more nearly true, like a self-fulfilling prophecy?) In devaluing people, the reductionist violates the principle that everything is to be treated as having the value it has. Reductionism is not simply a theoretical mistake, it is a moral failing.*

How are we to explain the rise to predominance of reductionist theories? Though they may be welcomed by some out of resentful envy of value, their predominance must be due to other factors. Many have followed Max Weber in commenting upon the increasing rationalization and bureaucratization of modern society, in accordance with abstract and general roles and rules, formal techniques of calculation and policy analysis (recently including decision theory and cost–benefit analysis), and so forth. One might see reductionism as of a piece with this, as abstracting from the rich particularity of people's lives, seeking common general traits that also can be calculated about and actually manipulated along with other things in the society. One might even see the theories as designed to get people to

---

* The currently fashionable activity of critique, stemming from the Frankfurt school, also involves the undermining of the "meanings" involved in people's actions, toward a liberation from "false" consciousness. (It would be ironic if the reductionists claimed to be doing critique.) It would be better, however, if critique did not involve the systematic violation of the principle that you do not reject a theory until a better theory is available. Indeed, since every theory will have defects, it is not enough to reject a theory on the basis of discerned flaws and inadequacies, especially if all one has to suggest in its place is something vague and ill-defined. (For instance, "communitarianism"; see, for example, Roberto Unger, *Knowledge and Politics*, Free Press, New York, 1975.)

think of themselves as fit inhabitants of the rationally bureaucratized society. Once again, this may explain why reductionist theories were so readily welcomed and found congenial by many; however, to explain the intellectual predominance of reductionism we must look to more intrinsically intellectual factors.

Is the explanation that reductionist theories are correct, and only recently (with the rise of scientific endeavor) have we come to discover this? This ill fits the reductionist theories themselves, which would have trouble with our coming validly to know, discover, and realize such complicated intellectual truths. In any case, since many incompatible reductionist theories have been put forth, this proposed explanation of intellectual predominance in terms of truth could at best fit only some of these theories—we still would lack an explanation for the rise of all the rest.

Because psychological and sociological explanations are inadequate, intrinsically intellectual ones must be sought, but if it is not truths about the subject matter that explain the predominance of reductionist explanatory theories, then where else can we look? Perhaps the activity of explanatory theorizing itself leaves its imprint; perhaps it is something about the process of seeking, formulating, testing, or accepting explanatory theories, something about the nature of a theory or of an explanation itself, that leads to a reductionist result. To see the explanatory theorizing itself as casting the reductionist shadow, either as determining or predisposing the result in this direction, is to see reductionism as an artifact of our explanatory activity and goals.[33] This would be an explanation of the sort, broadly construed, offered by Kant in the *Critique of Pure Reason* wherein features apparently of the world were attributed to us, to our mode of experience or cognition—Kant called this his Copernican Revolution. We might hope, however, that reductionism as an explanatory artifact will rest upon something more superficial than the Kantian cognitive depths, and so be more easily dispensable or avoidable.

To explain why something has a certain feature or property we can refer to something else with that property, but a fundamental explanation of (the nature of) the property, or what gives rise to it or how it functions, will not refer to other things with that very same property; the possession and functioning of that property is what is to be explained, not only in this instance but in all its occurrences. This point was made by the philosopher of science N. R. Hanson, who pointed out that we should expect atoms and subatomic particles to lack the features that they fundamentally explain—only something itself colorless could constitute a fundamental explanation of color.[34]

Similarly, fundamental explanations of human characteristics and functioning will involve explanatory factors that are without those characteristics (or have them to a lesser degree), factors that function differently. It is no illuminating explanation of our possession of a trait to attribute it to a little person within us, a psychological homunculus who exercises that very same trait. If there is to be an explanation of how our intelligence functions, it will have to be in terms of factors that, taken individually, themselves are dumb, for example, in terms of a concatenation of simple operations that can be done by a machine.[35] A psychological explanation of creativity will be in terms of parts or processes which aren't themselves creative; of "free choice" in terms of the operation of components which don't themselves make free choices; of love in terms of processes which aren't themselves "in love", of the totality of action and functioning of the self in terms of a range of somethings, each of which is an it and not a self. Only thereby can we fully understand what is being explained. The explanation of any valuable trait, feature, or function of the self will be in terms of some other trait, one which does not have precisely that value and probably is not as valuable. Eventually, one will have gone around all the traits of the self, and to avoid explanatory circles it will be. necessary to turn to micro-explanations, explanations in terms of factors, processes, and components which are part of but are not the full self—here certainly one will have explanatory factors of lesser value. So it is not surprising that the explanations are reductionistic, presenting a picture of us as less valuable. The directional thrust of the explanatory activity itself is to find simpler processes and traits, subparts that underlie and account for our complicated and valuable activities.* These explanations

* There is one other intellectual factor to be mentioned, in addition to the directional thrust of explanation. One might take two different views of something: seeing it as what it is the best instantiated (and a good enough) realization of (as the Platonist sees a Form in its imperfect exemplars), which we might call the view "from the top down", and the opposing view, which might even be the view "from the bottom up". (What makes·a given concept fit the top end rather than the bottom is a value ranking; hence Plato was reluctant to envisage Forms of the unvaluable or disvaluable.) It is not obvious that the reductionist perspective, from the bottom up, yields greater understanding. Others (such as Hegel, Nietzsche, and Aurobindo, on the basis of their different views) have proposed understanding something by or in the light of its higher form, rather than its lower.

seem to explain away our valuable traits. Moreover, the fact that something is not on the "ground floor" may well itself undermine the things's value—and reductionism provides a lower floor.

How can such explanations not undermine value when they invoke only the operation of less valuable, dumb, themselves inhuman factors? Since at this underlying level there is no nugget of significant value, any greater value that is not undermined must be due to the intricate mode of coordination of these dumb factors, the high degree of organic unity they exhibit. The overall intricate order is wonderful and valuable, even though composed of individual pieces which themselves are not. (In our discussion of value as degree of organic unity, we saw how value could emerge in a unity without there being atoms of value at the ground floor.) However, such maintenance of value has not occurred with recent explanations. Is this merely because the explanations tended to focus upon the individual dumb components, or is it because, once we have focused upon these components, the overall organic unity (even when we shift our focus to it) can never again look the same? Do we alternate between viewing it as valuable and valueless, depending upon which we are focusing upon, the component parts or the intricate resultant unity?

We have discussed psychological explanations in terms of internal factors and subparts, yet explanation via external factors seems no more conducive toward the maintenance of value. The very externality of the factors reduces a person's autonomy and originative value; and the drive for fundamental explanation will strip these factors of features similar to the person's features that are to be explained, and so see him as subject to alien factors. Moreover, in both cases, internal and external, the very generality of the theory, framed in terms of the most abstract structure that fits and yields the result, will reduce the person's individuality, presenting him merely as one more instance of the theory.

Nevertheless, perhaps a nonreductionist explanation can be fashioned within these considerations; perhaps this explanatory activity only predisposes toward reductionism but does not determine or entail it. Even if such explanation must be reductionist, perhaps no satisfactory explanation will be found. Avoiding reductionism by failing to find any explanation at all, or by shunning explanatory activity altogether, denies us explanatory understanding and guarantees intellectual predominance to the reductionist enterprise (pursued by others) and whatever partial success it has.

Nonreductive Understanding

Are we restricted to the alternatives of reductionist explanation or no explanation at all? Can we formulate any mode of explanation or understanding that would not be (almost guaranteed to be) reductionist? Moreover, how can we choose to contour philosophy as an explanatory activity if that goal guarantees that it must be reductionist?

What would a nonreductionist view of people be like? Such a view would have to present people's valuable traits (such as being a self, seeking value, and freely choosing) as having an integrity of their own. Although these traits emerge from component processes and are shaped by outside factors, their functioning would not be explicable merely as the product of the simple interaction, the clanging together, of some of these factors—rather, it would involve the intricate integrity of the whole.[36] Moreover, this view of the functioning of the valuable traits and of the self, which (although finding interconnections) treats it at its own level, must not be merely a view that can be taken by us, or even one that must be taken by us—it must be the ontologically correct view. It is not enough merely that our explanatory interests might keep us at a (nonreductionist) level that is more perspicuous for us, or that our cognitive limitations might prevent us from understanding something in terms of its separable micro-component processes. That would make it convenient or mandatory *for us* to forgo viewing things in a reductionist light for normal and everyday purposes. Nonetheless, some reductionist theory would be true, even if not conveniently utilized by us, and accepting this claim about the existence of such a true theory would serve to undercut our value, whether or not we can keep this theory's details always in mind.[37] To be sure, the reductionist view might not replace our ordinary view in our daily activities, or even be suitably manipulable for scientific calculations and predictions, and so it may be kept out of the way in a small corner. It would be ironic if a widespread cultural crisis due to reductionism was prevented by our limitations, by our inability to keep in mind and utilize the reductionist truths. (However, unlike my explanation of why Hume and others cannot maintain their skepticism outside of the study, this present explanation of the inability to focus upon reductionism in everyday life does not show it is false there.)

Many writers recently have suggested that a spruced-up version of our ordinary view of human action, in terms of goals, beliefs, intentions, desires, reasons, emotions, and decisions, would serve to provide a nonreductionistic explanation of human behavior and action. If explanation involves placing something in a pattern, and we gain understanding thereby, then haven't we explained behavior by placing it in the pattern of rational, purposeful action? Micro-reductions and subsumptions under general causal laws also are modes of placing something in a pattern, but they are not the only such modes. Our common sense views also place actions in a network and pattern, by showing how the agents understood what they were doing, and make them intelligible. So is not this nonreductionist patterning explanation enough for the actions?[38]

On the basis of this purposeful nature of human action within a network of intentions and goals, it has been claimed in the literature that the human and social sciences will differ from the natural sciences both in content and in method. The content of any theoretical explanation of action will have to take account of the fact that, unlike physics and chemistry, the social sciences are studying subjects who have a view of what they are doing which affects their actions. (I believe it is unclear, thus far, how far-reaching are the difficulties this raises for a generalizing nomological social science.) Moreover, since we who wish to understand these actions (whether as historians, social scientists, or participants in the situation) also are human subjects, this gives us a special mode of access, a way of coming to know what that other person is doing, namely the route of *verstehen* —empathic understanding. To this it has been replied that our common humanity may facilitate our thinking up hypotheses about the action of another, but our empathic intuitions cannot be a way of coming to know about his actions and do not constitute evidence about what action he is performing or what meaning it has for him. It has been replied to this, in turn, that models of scientific inference and acceptance of hypotheses—not merely their suggestion—leave a role for considerations of plausibility, as in the Bayesian utilization of prior probabilities. So verstehen, while fallible and no guarantee of knowledge, can enter even this process of acceptance. Apart from this, some of us evince a good track record as empathic understanders and so, even when the generator of insights is treated as a "black box", can be a reliable mode of reaching conclusions about the actions of another. (Whereas the track record of some others may lead to the reverse judgment, and also to a diminished regard for the prior probabilities based on their intuitions.) We might even use rough information about the ratio of truth in our own past insights, to arrive at a rough calibration of our own reliability, and then use this black box statistic, rather than simply the compellingness or intuitiveness of our own insight, as a basis for our inference and acceptance of hypotheses about the action of others.[39]

There is something more to be said. Inference about another on the basis of verstehen depends upon putting yourself imaginatively in his place and seeing him as like you. It is a form of reasoning by analogy, and such considerations always have been given some role in inductive logic and theories of evidential support.[40] Verstehen is a special form of inference by analogy, in that I am the thing to which he is analogous. It is inferred that he is behaving as I would in that situation, a situation that is specified partly subjectively—from a point of view. Similarly, I could use someone else as the focal point for my analogous inferences. If I possessed a complete specification of how she would behave in all circumstances, and believed others were analogous to her, then I could infer how the others would behave. However, when my inference by analogy uses me as the focal point of the analogy, special characteristics are present. I do not need a prior specification of my own actions in all possible situations, since I have empathic insight into how I myself would act. By imaginatively placing myself in that situation, I can reliably know how I will act. (Or perhaps not, because I lack such self knowledge either generally or about that particular type of choice situation.) It is not a necessary truth that I will have such reliable knowledge about how I would act, feel, and respond in situations I am not actually in. Verstehen depends not only on the analogy between him and me, but on the adequacy of my own self understanding; in order to work, verstehen must begin at home.

Thus, verstehen as a method of evidential support is not sui generis; it is a mode of the well-known method of analogy. But in this case, the analogy is drawn to me, and I possess special (but fallible) access to what I would do when. In physics also, one can reason by analogy to me: that body would fall as I would in free fall. Here, though, I have no special introspective access to how I would fall. For any case where I might have such access, the analogy to the other objects of physics breaks down. Since my behavior would depend upon my decisions and intentions then, approximated by my current imaginative rehearsal of the decision, any entities that lack intentions and make no decisions are not usefully analogous to me so that an inference can be made. The two component links in the chain of verstehen, each necessary, are that he acts as I would, and that I would as I (on the basis of imaginative projection) think I would.[41] Both links are empirical, and in particular, I cannot know that he acts as I would simply on the basis of verstehen. (Consider the situation in trying to understand the actions of creatures from another planet.) Therefore, the inferential reliability of verstehen is empirical, just like any other inference by analogy. Still, given these links, verstehen involves a type of inferential and evidential support not found in the natural sciences, even though it falls as a special case under a more general rubric, analogy, which *is* found there. However, it does not follow from this that one cannot also use, even solely use, a completely external mode of evidential support in the human sciences. Nor does it follow that the content of theoretical explanation in the human sciences will have a unique character, unless the very patterned understanding of an action, based on its analogy to your imagined action with its goals and reasons, constitutes explanation enough.*

We have considered explaining an action by placing it in a network of goals, beliefs, and intentions. There also can be explanations of complicated social and economic patterning, often unplanned, that stems from such individually intelligible actions, as well as of the complex and convoluted nature of such actions in particular settings.[42] An individual's actions and course of life are placed within a pattern, connected to his beliefs, goals, desires, intentions, feasible options, and so on, and placed within a wider social network of the actions of others and of institutions. This patterning can provide a

* Consider Freud's famous statement that the spirit and the mind of man is a subject of investigation in exactly the same way as any nonhuman entity. If this means "can be investigated in exactly the same way" then there is no conflict with our above reflections on verstehen; there would be a conflict if it meant "can only be investigated in exactly the same way". To be sure, what Freud himself wanted to investigate, unconscious motivations and the unconscious meaning a person's acts have for him, did not yield to verstehen. According to the theory, analogy with another holds, the same unconscious processes are at work in all, but no one has access to this merely by imaginative projection—apparently only Freud had it through his own unaided (but laborious and painful) efforts.

nonreductive mode of explanation only if it indeed can provide some kind of explanation (so that, contrary to earlier considerations, the very activity of explaining is not intrinsically reductive) and, moreover, if that explanation provides a stopping place—the explanatory pattern itself is not susceptible to further reduction. The mere existence of an intelligible pattern is no bar in principle to reductive explanation of that pattern. Animals of a species reproduce their kind, a fact long taken for granted as natural; the explanation of this fact will involve carriers of genetic information that replicate themselves and direct the process of embryonic cellular differentiation and organization. This latter process of differentiation is not yet well understood, but even the broad sketch of such a micro-process produces better understanding of why like reproduces like—as well as enabling us to understand cases where this fails to happen.

Merely placing an action in a rational pattern, showing how it is intelligible as the purposeful pursuit of certain goals and desires in the light of the situation the agent believed himself to be facing, does not by itself constitute an explanation of the action; it must be added that the person is generally disposed to rationally pursue his goals, or at least was so that time.[43] About some people, the special explanatory problem is to explain why they behave rationally when they do. This attribution of a disposition to behave rationally, to fit a purposeful pattern, need not itself be reductive, however; such a disposition may involve the interrelated and unified functioning of most of a person's capacities.

Into such capacities feed the person's desires and goals and beliefs (about alternative actions available and about the probable consequences of various actions); these will themselves be open to explanation. Why does he, like most, have those desires, goals, beliefs, and why does he differ sometimes? Although there is much room here for illumination from the social sciences, the explanations offered need not make us the puppets of external social forces. We may have sociological, anthropological, and economic explanations of why certain considerations have much weight, and historical explanations of why other considerations were unavailable. Though post facto we may explain the total resultant desires and beliefs as caused by those factors, the explanation need not be deterministic—the very process of decision bestows more precise weights upon the factors (perhaps within socially fixed intervals). The explanations that place our beliefs and desires, actions and hopes in a patterned network need not depict them as prisoners within that network. The pattern can be compatible with and utilize the picture of us as self-synthesizing selves, freely acting in giving weights to reasons in self-subsuming and reflexive decision, seeking value, being responsive to value in our actions, exercising capacities for knowledge when our beliefs track the facts, and so on.* It can interweave these traits into a picture of us as purposeful agents, acting within (and having our goals and beliefs affected by) social formations and the limits placed and constituted by the actions and plans of others.[44]

Will such nonreductive and nondeterministic placement within a pattern, however elaborately woven, count as explanation? Why should it not?† What is so special about the patterning of something under a universal law and about the micro-reductive patterning, so that only these count as adequate explanations? Lawlike explanations place a phenomenon or regularity alongside other phenomena and regularities, delineating salient similarities. They also place a phenomenon or regularity under a law (of a different level); but we already have explored the difficulty in understanding how there can be a compulsive aspect to lawlike subsumption. With a nonreductive patterning, placing something in a pattern at the same level, we want to ask "but what makes the thing fit or conform to the pattern?" Hence the appeal of nomological explanations involving universal laws, and of micro-reductive ones; they appear to tell us what makes the phenomenon occur. However, this appearance is illusory—the law does not make or compel phenomena to fit it, nor (in the requisite sense) do the micro-processes which are connected to the phenomenon by laws of a similarly noncompelling character. For any factor purporting to answer why the phenomenon fits the law, there will remain the question of why the phenomenon so fits that factor.

---

* Generalizations can describe the pattern of the aggregated actions of many such individuals, without making any one a puppet of external causes. The sun's shining increases the desirability of going to the beach so that, even though each person weights for himself the reasons for and against going, we can predict more will go on a sunny weekend day. (Similarly, when the price of an item is reduced, the quantity sold increases.) The pattern is predictable, even when precisely whose decisions compose it is not.

† "But why should the system continue further in the direction of the center? Why should this order not proceed, so to speak, out of chaos?" Wittgenstein, *Zettel* (University of California Press, 1967), p. 608.

Eventually, the phenomena and factors just have to be placed *alongside* each other in a pattern. Lawlike explanations and micro-reductions provide a unified patterning, but other modes of unified patterning also provide understanding. These other modes go alongside laws and reductions to form a salient pattern together, one of saliently patterning and unifying.

Is it not a mode of patterning, after all, that we hope for from a comprehensive philosophical theory? There are different fundamental dimensions, including those of explanation, justification, value, and meaning. A philosophical theory may examine these and delineate what underlies them or is ultimate along them—at one or another of their poles, if they are dimensions of ordering. Perhaps one and the same thing or factor will be identified as ultimate for each of these dimensions. However, if we are left with a plurality of such factors, each ultimate in its sphere, then we shall want to understand their interrelationships. Again, we can seek such understanding along each one of the dimensions: in terms of the explanatory ultimate, we can explain why the justificatory, value, and meaning ultimates are as they are; in terms of the justificatory ultimate, we can justify the claim that the explanatory ultimate is such and such, the value and the meaning ultimates are so and so; in terms of the value ultimate, we can assess the value of the explanatory ultimate, of that being the explanatory ultimate rather than something else, of the justificatory ultimate, and of the value ultimate itself; in terms of the meaning ultimate, we can assess the meaning of each. This has been stated very abstractly, without taking notice of what such ultimates might be, of whether still further dimensions must be included, and so forth.

Yet after everything has been seen from each dimension's perspective, we still will want all these pictures to be woven together into one unified patterning. If monism of ultimates does not obtain, then it is such a patterning of the different ultimates that will provide overall intelligibility. By its placement of each in relation to the others, the patterning will straddle the different dimensions, unifying them by simultaneously showing the meaning of each, and the value (organic unity) of the whole in the largest overall patterning and so the widest explanatory picture. A theme can unify as it weaves through the pattern, taking different forms; for instance, the general motif of "turning back upon itself" might emerge in different places—in self-reference, self-synthesis, reflexivity, self-subsumption, reflexively self-subsuming bestowal of weights in action, self-subsuming choice that there be value, the mapping into itself of the unlimited. Such an appearance of the same motif in different salient guises is part of the substance of the pattern, giving it unity. Yet its formulation as one further determinate principle would yield only another ultimate, one which itself would then have to be integrated into a pattern via still other motifs. Similar remarks apply to the motif of "external connection". Yet might we view these two—"turning back upon itself" and "external connection"—as modes of the more general motif of connection (internal and external), as the *polarities* of connection, themselves connected (externally? internally?) by being opposite poles?

Leaving aside these last more general speculations about a total philosophical view, our considerations about how explanation can be achieved by placement within a pattern at best show that a nonreductive explanatory view of man is possible. They do not show a reductionist view is impossible—only that it is not necessary. Let us not add to the heretofore futile attempts to prove that scientific reductionism *must* fail.[45] Far more important is the task, one that cannot be undertaken here, of delineating what an illuminating nonreductionist view of man in society would be like. Too often the so-called "interpretative" social theory, drawing upon the philosophical literature of the phenomenological school, is merely obscurantist. What is needed is a theory that takes account of and sometimes incorporates the data, insights, powerful generalizations, and formal and mathematical procedures of social scientific research, including those of the reductionist theories, yet which does not reduce or undermine our value. Contemporary social science is often genuinely illuminating. It is futile, not to say ridiculous, to attempt to build social theory by rejecting it in toto, rather than by incorporating much of it, although in a new nonreductive gestalt. Developing such a theory would be an aspect of our value and quest for meaning, not an undercutting of it.

We have speculated about the development of a nonreductive explanatory theory of man in society.* There is an alternative to

* Our concern has been reductions of the value of man and of the meaning of his activities. Others might find explanations of institutions and social changes in terms of the actions of individuals also reductive, leaving no inde-

reductionism, though, other than the formulation of one adequate nonreductionist theory: maintaining the basketful of alternative explanatory views. If no one explanation is settled upon as fully adequate, then people are not reduced to whatever any one explanatory theory says about them.*

In the introduction, we said there is no compelling need to settle upon only one philosophical view. Although we might rank one of them as best, unlike the relativist, still we see it as not fully adequate, and hence see the need for the other perspectives as well—to add dimension to the one flat picture. We also wondered why philosophy hadn't been able to settle upon just one theory, why many different ones—very different—seemed illuminating (even if not equally so). One explanation might be the falsity of reductionism. We might take the history of philosophy, whose nonconvergent character often has been complained about, as indicating (and explained by) the fact that reductionism, whether about man, value, or reality, is inadequate.

Explanatory activity in psychology and the social sciences, similarly, can be carried on to contribute new theories to the basketful. It has been said that man is the rational animal, the religious animal, the symbol-using animal, the tool-using animal, the value-seeking animal, and so on. No doubt someone also has pointed out that man is the self-defining animal. Perhaps we should view man as the multifarious animal. Different theories and explanations each get a por-

---

pendently valuable social facts (in Durkheim's sense). However, to the extent that the individual actions that make up and create these social patternings are in delicate coordination in complicated overall equilibria, these unities in diversity will have a value of their own.

* However, while the view in literary criticism that no one interpretation of a text is definitive, is a way of marking the richness and reverberativeness of texts, the view that all interpretations are equally valid, that the text is an object which the critic may "deconstruct" at will and at whim in the pursuit of his creative activity, ignoring the question of author's intent, is, it seems to me, a reductionist view which diminishes the value of literary activity. (For a criticism of such views, see M. H. Abrams, "The Deconstructive Angel", *Critical Inquiry*, Vol. 3, 1977, pp. 425–439.)

More interesting is Harold Bloom's alternative to the reductive view that a poem means something that is not a poem, and to the tautological view that a poem means itself, namely, the view that "the meaning of a poem can only be a poem, but *another poem—a poem not itself.*" (*The Anxiety of Influence*, Oxford University Press, 1973, p. 70; see also p. 94.)

tion of the truth, each are illuminating in their way, even (and sometimes especially) when presented as a total theory of man; but no one or small number is adequate. We get a full view of man, a nonreductionist view, only by keeping all the theories in mind, only by seeing him in that multiple perspective.* Even the reductionist theories play their role here, for their partial views of man also are a part of the basketful, making the multifariousness all the richer. That multifariousness is an important part of man's value, for *he* unifies these diverse and apparently incompatible theories in his person; the reductionist views themselves are part of diversity that man unifies.

Moreover, it is important not merely that people partially fit these diverse theories, but that they create them. These attempts at theoretical self-understanding, even when reductionist, themselves take us beyond the limits and narrow concerns of our daily lives. Man not only is reduced by these theories; in formulating them he attempts to reduce himself, and in so doing he shows forth qualities that raise him above that purported level. This act of self-reduction is self-defeating, and we can see the attempts, theoretically ingenious, striking, and illuminating, as part of the panoply which includes other works and lives of theoretical intelligence, artistic imagination, moral concern, and search for meaning.[46] The great reductionist views of Freud and Marx, computer modeling and neurophysiological reduction, behavioral psychology and economic analysis, just join and extend the long list of human accomplishment, striving, and excellence: Shakespeare and Kant and Plato and Goethe and Michelangelo and Gandhi and the Baal Shem-Tov and Newton and Picasso and Homer and Rembrandt and Turner and George Eliot and Galileo and Tolstoy and Aurobindo and Weber and Bach and Garri-

---

* Since there will be linkages and connections between the different views, it may not be clear at what point there is an integration of (portions of) the basketful, one comparable to a cubist painting which, according to the slogan, simultaneously presents its subject from different perspectives. Despite the slogan, it has persuasively been claimed that only in Picasso's *later* paintings was this fully and successfully achieved. (See Leo Steinberg, *Other Criteria*, Oxford University Press, 1972, pp. 125–234.) This reinforces the point that there is no sharp and clear line between a multiple basketful and a unified integration. Similarly, Picasso's fertile career itself, showing periods and multiple styles, exhibits the basketful, and perhaps (we will realize when we are better able to see it whole) also exhibits the difficulty of distinguishing the multiplicity from a unity.

son and the authors of the Hebrew Bible and Sophocles. When Albert Einstein died, the editorial cartoonist Herblock drew the earth, pictured from out in space as a ball, and on this ball was stuck a large wooden signpost with a sign that said "Albert Einstein lived here."

We have listed only a portion of what ennobles and lifts us, coming from us, but the full multifariousness extends beyond the titans; it includes us too, our aspirations and fears, loves and hopes. It also includes the full range of human depravity and evil as well as the vast panoply of forms of culture (in the anthropologist's sense). No one theory we know of encompasses it all. The activity of *formulating* reductionist theories, some more interesting and illuminating than others, only lengthens the list, it adds still more to the challenge faced by any explanatory reductionism that purports to be the one true view.

Philosophy as an Art Form

We have seen that philosophy can be carried on (there are other legitimate ways, too) as part of the humanities, responsive to value and meaning as value and meaning. Although responsive thus, not every part of the humanities is itself a form of art. Can philosophy be not just humanistic but also an art form? It would not be enough, I think, for a philosophy to exhibit and exemplify value and meaning as well as to respond to these, not enough even for it to be intended to be an object to which, as well as through which, others respond. A scientific theory also could fit that, and so be part of the humanities without being an art form.

The key, I think, lies in the degree of shaping and molding that takes place, the self-conscious choice about the nature and details of the work produced, the degree to which the work is *created*. As the composer works with musical themes, harmonic structures, and meter, the painter with forms, colors, represented things, and perimeters, the novelist with plot themes, characters, actions, and words, so the material of the philosopher is ideas, questions, tensions, concepts. He molds and shapes these, develops, revises, and reformulates them, and places them in various relations and juxtapositions. In the medium of ideas, he sculptures a view.

This molding also involves shaping parts, somewhat against their natural grain sometimes, so as better to fit the overall pattern, one designed in part to fit them. This purposeful molding and shaping, conscious of not being determined solely by the preexisting contours of a reality already out there, is part of the artistic activity.[47] Can the scientist take a similar view of his theorizing, viewing it as a controlled artistic shaping? Einstein spoke of theories as being "free inventions of the human intellect"[48] by which he meant at least that the data did not dictate the theory, that getting to the theory required a leap of intuition and insight—the theory could not simply be "read off" the data. But did he think that only one (adequate, correct, true) theory could be leaped to, or did he think several quite different theories, equally good, might be leaped to and developed, each of which would equally well fit all the observational data? (Still, once a particular leap is made successfully, it carries the rest of science along in its wake, at least for a time.) Did it feel to Einstein as if he were discovering preexisting theoretical truths, or creating a theory?[49] It would be fruitful to consider what scope the underdetermination of scientific theory by all possible observational data, a central theme in the writings of W. V. Quine, leaves for science as an art form.

Others have aimed at artistic intellectual synthesis: from Dante through Joyce's *Ulysses*, and most recently Pynchon's *Gravity's Rainbow*, some novelists and poets have tried to incorporate everything their time held worth knowing into their encyclopedic works.[50] Some have imagined distinctively new types of intellectual syntheses, new intellectual forms; in *Magister Ludi*, Hesse portrays the Glass Bead game as a synthesis of music, theology, science, and philosophy, and describes also the social institution which serves it. Is philosophy as an artistic activity to be like these, an imaginative encyclopedic synthesis—leavened by a delight in the free play of ideas?

Where into this can we fit the philosopher's concern with the *truth*? The artist cannot make up just anything, though, either. The artistic activity works within its own constraints, depending upon the medium, and it deals with material having their own degree of obduracy. Novelists often tell us of their surprise at what their characters do, sometimes at what it turns out those characters have to do. The fact that words have meaning, and are not simply sounds, imposes constraints on the poet to which the composer is not subject (although some literary experiments try to avoid even these). So, too, the different materials of the philosopher—ideas and their relationships, possibilities to be explained and understood—impose their own different constraints. (On this view, should we say that the philosopher's activity is of the same type as that of (other) artists, but is done with different material and so involves different constraints and possibilities; or rather that the different material with its accompanying different constraints and possibilities requires a different activity —a nonartistic one?)

An artistic philosophy would welcome (and appreciate) other shapings, other philosophical visions as part of the basketful, while striving itself for a prominent position in the ranking. Such a philosophy might present more than one vision at a time, or contemplate presenting others later. Is this attitude too playful? Think of a painter who spends his life working on one canvas, repainting and altering, building it up, perfecting it. We ask him what he's doing and hear him reply, "I am engaged in making my painting."

The philosopher aimed at truth states a theory that presents a possible truth and so a way of understanding the actual world (including its value) in its matrix of possible neighbors. In his artistic reshaping, he also may lift the mind from being totally filled with the actual world in which it happens to find itself. There is a tension between the philosopher's desire that his philosophy track the world—as a tight unity, tracking is of value—and his desire that it depict a world worth tracking, if not transcend the world altogether. Still, the philosophy must be true enough to the world, presenting a possible (though shaped) view, to be transcending *it*.

We can envision a humanistic philosophy, a self-consciously artistic one, sculpting ideas, value, and meaning into new constellations, reverberative with mythic power, lifting and ennobling us by its content and by its creation, leading us to understand and to respond to value and meaning—to experience them and attain them anew.

NOTES

INDEX

NOTES

INTRODUCTION

1. "To give any indication of the quality and importance of a philosopher one must be able to show how he argued, not merely what he concluded." John Passmore, "Scholarship about Philosophy", in R. Chisholm et al., *Philosophy* (Prentice-Hall, Englewood Cliffs, 1964), p. 25.

2. Hannah Arendt says of Lessing, "He not only wanted no one to coerce him, but he also wanted to coerce no one either by force or by proofs. He regarded the tyranny of those who attempt to dominate thinking by reasoning and sophistries, by compelling argumentation, as more dangerous to freedom than orthodoxy." *Men in Dark Times* (Harcourt, Brace, New York, 1968), p. 8.

3. Esoteric texts not only hide doctrine but, by getting the reader to think up the ideas himself, even if only as a hypothesis about what the author really believes, induce him to feel friendly toward these ideas because of having (somewhat independently) parented them. A decoder of an esoteric text, having unraveled its perplexities, may allude to its special content, I mean its particular mode of secretiveness, without accepting or utilizing it, purely for the playful pleasure.

4. C. G. Hempel, *Aspects of Scientific Explanation* (Free Press, New York, 1965), chs. 10, 12. Hempel also describes probabilistic or statistical explanation as having the form of an argument, though not a deductive one, from premises to conclusion. On some views a statistical explanation can be offered for a low probability event: if so, this sort of explanation would not take the form of a cogent argument.

To my knowledge, no one has yet tried to answer a philosophical question by offering a statistical explanation within philosophy; but see Chapter 2 below.

5. The view that fresh explanatory problems are ever flowing in upon us makes the task of philosophy a continuing one. But the task is not the Witt-

gensteinean therapeutic one of removing or dissolving puzzles or confusions with linguistic roots, arising from mistaken analogies due to grammar, from "language on holiday", from thinking all terms are substantives, and so forth. The explanatory problems are genuine and real—and if sometimes the reconciliation of the possibility of p with an apparent excluder involves showing a model underlying the excluder is overextended or faulty ("being trapped by a picture"), there is no reason to believe either this model or its overextension must have roots that are especially linguistic.

6. *The Character of Physical Law* (MIT Press, Cambridge, 1965), pp. 37–39.

7. In order to show us how p is possible, mustn't the hypothesis (in addition to not being known to be false) be known to be true, or at least be true? William Dray gives the example of someone hearing that a flyball was about to hit the fence twenty feet up, but then was caught by an outfielder. How was it possible? A ladder was leaning against the wall, which the outfielder could climb. Letting that be the hypothesis, doesn't the explanation of the possibility of p, of the catch, require the truth of the hypothesis and not merely its possibility? Otherwise, doesn't the hypothesis show at best how p is possibly possible? (I am grateful to Israel Scheffler for raising these questions. See William Dray, *Laws and Explanation in History*, Oxford University Press, 1957, pp. 158–159.)

The fact that the hypothesis is possible, and would yield p, shows that the apparent excluders thought to be incompatible with p really are not. Thus, it removes (or weakens) the reason for thinking p could not be true. But merely removing the appearance of incompatibility does not explain how p is possible, though it may remove the point of asking the question. Only if the hypothesis is true will it explain how p is possible, for a correct explanation connects what is to be explained (even if it is p's *possibility*) with something actual or true. The truth of the hypothesis explains how p is possible; for us to know how p is possible, when given that explanation, we must know the hypothesis is true. (To know how p is possible we must know the hypothesis is true, but to know how p *would be* possible, we need only know the hypothesis is possible. In terms of the accessibility relation of the semantics of modal logic, something *is* possible if it is accessible from the actual world; it *would be* possible if it is accessible from a world accessible from the actual world; and it *could be* possible if it stands in the ancestral of the accessibility relation to the actual world. Alternatively, the accessibility relation is to be specified so as to fit these distinctions.) Therefore, objections, counterexamples, and so on do have a role in philosophy, in assessing the truth of an explanatory hypothesis. Although the purpose is not to prove the hypothesis, it is relevant to investigate whether we can exclude it as true and hence from a correct explanation of p. The consideration of cases, counterexamples, and objections is legitimately part of the process of developing a sharp and adequate explanatory principle.

8. See J. N. Watkins, "Confirmable and Influential Metaphysics", *Mind*, Vol. 67, 1958, pp. 344–365. Scientists also, of course, put forth existentially

quantified statements, which may precede their testable filling in. Robert Brandon ("Philosophical Investigations in Evolutionary Biology", unpublished doctoral dissertation, Harvard University, 1979, ch. III) analyzes evolutionary theory as consisting of a general untestable part, that must be filled in by a detailed ecological analysis, different for each organism, specifying the adaptedness of particular traits in particular environments. The common content of the theory for all the different organisms (this suggestion diverges from Brandon's) may be merely the claims that for each organism there is an associated (propensity) disposition to leave survivors, that some organism has the non-flat probability distribution (indicating it does not have the same probability of leaving the same number of survivors in all environments), and that some distinct organisms differ in their dispositions (as represented by probability distributions) to leave survivors.

Similarly, decision theory as an empirical theory holds that there is some specification of alternative actions, outcomes, and beliefs about these and their probabilities, and preferences among these, such that the person acts so as (for example) to maximize expected utility. Thus, decision theory is best construed as presenting a structure which can be given content in different ways, that is, as the existentially quantified statement that some specification of the structure holds true for a person. (On this point, see Philip Pettit, "Rational Man Theory", especially pp. 51–52, in Christopher Hookway and Philip Pettit, eds., *Action and Interpretation,* Cambridge University Press, 1978.) Decision theory is a general theory for it says this of all people: "for each person, there is some specification or other . . ."

9. May the philosopher's explanatory hypothesis contain theoretical terms that are not eliminable from his explanatory theory? (There is a large philosophy-of-science literature on theoretical terms; see Hempel, "The Theoretician's Dilemma" in his *Aspects of Scientific Explanation,* Free Press, New York, 1965, pp. 173–226; F. Suppe, ed., *The Structure of Scientific Theories,* 2nd ed., University of Illinois Press, Urbana, 1977.) I do not see any reason why not. Thus, the recent debates over whether some philosophical terms (such terms as analyticity, necessity, probability, causation) are explicitly definable in preexisting clear terms, or are behavioristically or observationally specifiable, are misconceived. The questions are whether the theories utilizing the terms do the explanatory job: whether the terms are necessary to do it (are there alternative explanatory theories that don't utilize these terms?); and whether there really is that job to be done, whether there are those facts—not merely purported facts which themselves are philosophical impositions—for whose explanation the philosophical theoretical entities, forces, conventions, and so forth are needed.

10. We also might imagine a case where conviction in the premises comes or grows in the course of the proof, perhaps because one premiss speaks of a certain sort of proof once being offered, and that very proof is of that sort.

11. One philosopher, Rush Rhees, has gone so far as to say "the refutation of skepticism is the whole business of philosophy" (quoted in Ernest

Gellner, *Legitimation of Belief*, Cambridge University Press, 1974, p. 146).

12. This fit is no accident: I first formulated the view of philosophy as explanatory and elaborated it (in 1976) to fit how I found myself proceeding with the topic of skepticism. Since then, I have read Michael Dummett's collection *Truth and Other Enigmas* (Harvard University Press, Cambridge, 1978), containing his earlier British Academy Lecture (1973, pp. 290-318), where he too distinguishes philosophy as explanation from philosophy as "suasive argument", also making (p. 296) the pragmatic points made above about belief in premises and conclusion.

13. In science, having some conception of how something is possible may be a precondition for taking it, or the data that appear to support it, seriously. Rock and fossil evidence fits the theory of continental drift, but this was not taken seriously until an underlying mechanism, plate tectonics, was formulated to show how continental drift was possible. See Stephen Gould, *Ever Since Darwin* (Norton, New York, 1977), "The Validation of Continental Drift", pp. 160-167.

14. See also Stephen C. Pepper, *World Hypotheses* (University of California Press, Berkeley, 1942), ch. 12.

15. This general view of many philosophies in the philosophical basket resembles the framework for utopia in my book *Anarchy, State, and Utopia* (Basic Books, New York, 1974) wherein diverse communities coexist; also, rejecting interpersonal convincing and proving in philosophy resembles rejecting interpersonal coercing or rights violations in the political realm. These positions of this Introduction were formulated without my having their earlier analogues in mind; yet I suppose I cannot confidently say they were formulated independently.

Though there certainly is a danger in repeating the same moves everywhere, I trust that some applications of the strategy of avoiding conflict by embracing all the contesting participants seem more reasonable than others, that these two instances seem more reasonable, for example, than an answer to the question of why there is something rather than nothing that says *both* something and nothing exist!

16. I am not opposed in principle to settling on one view, on an admissible class with just one member; but it is important to delineate and understand philosophy's situation, which rarely involves this, if ever.

Many types of ranking stand intermediate between the unordered nonunit set of relativism, and the selection of just one view. A view can be ranked first, while the rest are unordered; ties for first place can occur; a partial ranking can leave two views noncomparable; and so forth. Little purpose would be served by elaborating these issues here. It is worth mentioning, though, that different ranking relations also can be used, different dimensions to select different views as first ranked; these different ranking relations might be carried along also, either (partially) ordered or even unordered.

17. C. I. Lewis, *Mind and the World Order* (1929; Dover edition, New York, 1956), ch. VI.

CHAPTER ONE

1. See Sydney Shoemaker, *Self-Knowledge and Self Identity* (Cornell University Press, Ithaca, 1963); Bernard Williams, "The Self and the Future", *Philosophical Review*, Vol. 79, 1970, pp. 161–180; Derek Parfit, "Personal Identity", *Philosophical Review*, Vol. 80, no. 1, 1971, pp. 3–27; "On 'The Importance of Self-Identity'", *Journal of Philosophy*, Vol. 68, 1971, pp. 683–690; David Lewis, "Survival and Identity" in Amelie Rorty, ed., *The Identities of Persons* (University of California Press, Berkeley, 1976), pp. 17–40; John Perry, "The Importance of Being Identical", *ibid.*, pp. 67–90; Derek Parfit, "Lewis, Perry, and What Matters", *ibid.*, pp. 91–107; Daniel Dennett, "Where Am I?" in his *Brainstorms* (Bradford Books, Montgomery, Vermont, 1978), pp. 310–323.

2. Williams, "The Self and the Future", reprinted in his *Problems of the Self* (Cambridge University Press, 1973).

3. "Personal Identity and Individuation" and "Bodily Continuity and Personal Identity", reprinted in his *Problems of the Self*, pp. 1–25.

4. Note that this principle requires not merely some bodily continuity, but a sort that could not simultaneously be duplicated; so it excludes the result of transplanting half of someone's brain into a new body, even supposing that there are no hemispheric asymmetries and that no other bodily parts continue.

5. Saul Kripke has pointed out to me an anticipation of the closest continuer theory in Sydney Shoemaker, "Wiggins on Identity", *Philosophical Review*, Vol. 74, 1970, p. 542; see also his "Persons and Their Pasts", *American Philosophical Quarterly*, Vol. 7, 1970, p. 278, note 18.

6. Is the notion of identity, " $=$ ", then elliptical for "the same K", where "K" is a term for a kind of entity? Can y be the same K_1 as x but not the same K_2—to use the example in the literature, the same hunk of marble but not the same statue? If the kind determines the relative weights different properties have in determining identity, different kinds might give different weights to the very same properties. However, just as kinds weight properties, might not the kinds themselves also be weighted thereby to specify a nonrelativized notion of "same entity"? I do not mean the closest continuer view to be committed to any relativization of identity.

7. In classroom lectures in the fall of 1977, I used the example of two

machines, a disappearing machine and a producing machine, where there is independent evidence of how each operates separately; when operated together, suitably synchronized, one makes an object disappear while another produces an exact duplicate in the same place. In thus showing that filmstrip continuity is not sufficient for 'same object', I viewed myself as adapting to a different topic a type of argument I encountered in Sydney Shoemaker's "Time Without Change", *Journal of Philosophy*, Vol. 66, 1969, pp. 363–381. There he puts together several different local freezes of different periodicity to produce an overall total freeze of change in the universe for a predictable period of time. Clearly, I had caught on to how to continue the Shoemaker series, as is shown by his article, "Identity, Properties, and Causality", *Midwest Studies in Philosophy*, Vol. IV, 1979, where on pp. 326–327 he makes this very argument, and notes that D. M. Armstrong makes it independently. Did Armstrong also see himself as applying a mode of argument he had learned from Shoemaker?

8. "The Interpretation of Visual Motion", unpublished doctoral dissertation, MIT, 1977.

9. Consider the consequences of the closest continuer theory for issues about the contingency or necessity of identity statements containing only rigid designators, terms which refer to the same individual in every possible world in which they refer, and refer to that individual in every possible world in which it exists. The notion of rigid designators is introduced and the issue of the necessity or contingency of identity statements is discussed in Saul Kripke, "Naming and Necessity" (in Donald Davidson and Gilbert Harman, eds., *Semantics of Natural Languages*, Reidel, Dordrecht, 1972, pp. 253–355; *Naming and Necessity* was published separately by Harvard University Press, Cambridge, 1980).

In cases 1 and 3 above, let us suppose that case 1, where a duplicate is made of me while I continue on, is the actual case. We can diagram this as in Figure N.1, letting time flow to the right. Here ROBERT NOZICK rigidly designates me, and RN rigidly designates the duplicate that is made. Let us also rigidly designate by m the stage of the actually continuing ROBERT NOZICK which begins at time t_1, when the duplicate comes to be made, and let robert rigidly designate the stage of ROBERT NOZICK from t_0 to t_1. In this actual world

(1) ROBERT NOZICK $\neq$ RN
(2) RN is not a stage of ROBERT NOZICK
(3) m is a stage of ROBERT NOZICK
(4) RN is not a stage which continues the entity of which robert is a stage.

Let us now consider the possible case 3, where the making of the duplicate from the pattern of the earlier existing person coincides with the ending of that old body. It seems natural to diagram that possible situation as in Figure N.2. Of this case, I said that RN was a close enough continuer to be the

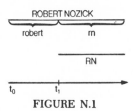

FIGURE N.1

continuation of robert, of ROBERT NOZICK. In the possible world of case 3, it seems that

(1') ROBERT NOZICK = RN
(2') RN is a stage of ROBERT NOZICK
(3') rn does not exist
(4') RN is a stage which continues the entity of which robert is a stage.

Now to draw some lessons. (These depend on the closest continuer structure, not on anything special to persons; similar points could be made with variants of the Greek ship case.) (a) The statement that a stage, rigidly designated, is a stage of an entity, rigidly designated, is in general contingent, varying in truth value from world to world. (Witness 2 and 2'; also 3 and 3'.) I say "in general", for there might be some continuing stages than whom there could not be closer ones. (b) The statement that two stages, rigidly designated, are identical over time (that is, are stages of the same continuing object) is contingent, varying in truth value from world to world. (Witness 4 and 4'.) The most difficult and interesting point is whether (c) a statement of identity between objects, rigidly designated, is contingent and varies in truth value from world to world. It seems that 1 and 1' show this, that in the first (actual) world ROBERT NOZICK ≠ RN, while in the case-3 world ROBERT NOZICK = RN. However, we must reconsider 1 and 1', looking more closely at precisely how the reference of the rigid designators is established.

If the reference of "ROBERT NOZICK" is fixed in the actual world (of case 1) as rigidly designating *that* person (pointing to someone between t_0 and t_1), while the reference of "RN" is fixed in the actual world as rigidly designating *that* person (pointing after t_1 to the product of the duplicating process), then clearly in the actual world, ROBERT NOZICK ≠ RN. However, there now is a question about which term, whose reference is already fixed in the actual

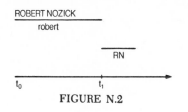

FIGURE N.2

FIGURE N.3

world, refers in the possible world of case 3 to the person who resides in the duplicated body. Since in the case-3 world that person is ROBERT NOZICK (it is the closest continuer in the case-3 world of robert, the early stage of ROBERT NOZICK), then it seems that that person in the case-3 world is properly referred to by "ROBERT NOZICK". Now is that person in the case-3 world who inhabits the duplicate also properly referred to by the rigid designator "RN"? The reference of "RN" was (rigidly) fixed in the actual world as the person (pointed to after t_1) inhabiting the duplicated body, and that person (not identical in the actual world to ROBERT NOZICK) does not seem to exist in the case-3 world. And so "RN" does not refer in the case-3 world to the person who is or inhabits the duplicated body. Thus, on this analysis, 1', 2', and 4' are false (in the case-3 world) since RN does not, despite appearances, exist in that world.

Suppose now that the case-3 world is actual, while the case-1 world is merely possible, and let "ROBERT NOZICK" rigidly designate *that* person (pointing before t_1) and let "RN" rigidly designate *that* person (pointing after t_1). Since there is only one person in the case-3 world, both terms rigidly designate the same entity. Now, let us look to the possible world of case 1. There, "ROBERT NOZICK" refers to the person existing before t_1, but what does "RN", whose reference has been rigidly fixed in the case-3 world, refer to in the case-1 world? Despite appearances, it refers not to the person of the duplicate (in the case-1 world), for that person didn't exist in the case-3 world, but rather to ROBERT NOZICK. Thus, on this analysis of the fixing of reference, 1 (and perhaps 2 and 3) are false in the world of case 1, for in that world "RN" carries its reference as fixed in the case-3 world and so refers to ROBERT NOZICK.

Therefore, even given the closest continuer theory, we seem to lack a sharp and clear counterexample to Kripke's specific claim that identity statements between rigid designators are noncontingent. The loophole is that "the entity of which that stage is a stage" or "that entity" (pointing at a stage of an entity) can refer to different entities in the different worlds where uttered, even when the same stage is present. It is point a above that saves Kripke's specific claim against the considerations presented under point c. If, instead of rigidly fixing the reference as that person (or ship), we fix it as that stage, that person-stage, (or ship-stage), we apparently will again only demonstrate point b above. Thus, although on the basis of closest continuer considerations Kripke's claim about noncontingency (of identity statements with ' = ' between rigid designators) has been surrounded, it has not yet been overturned.

Can we push a bit further? Sitting in the actual world of case 1, diagrammed as in Figure N.3, let us mentally point to the world of case 3, dia-

FIGURE N.4

grammed in Figure N.4, and rigidly fix the reference of "RN" as "that person" (indicated by the bottom line). To which person in the actual world (of case 1) does "RN" then refer, to the one that started at t_0 or the duplicate who begins at t_1? It seems it might be the latter, and since "ROBERT NOZICK" in both worlds refers to the person who exists (but not only) before t_1, we seem to have in the actual world,

ROBERT NOZICK $\neq$ RN

while in the world of case 3,

ROBERT NOZICK = RN.

It certainly appears that some counterexample should emerge, even to Kripke's specific claim, from closest continuer considerations.

10. For example, we might have the following structure: y at t_2 is a closer continuer of x at t_1 than z at t_2 is; at a later time t_3 there is no continuer of y but there is a w which is the closest continuer of z. It may also be that w at t_3 is the closest continuer of x at t_1, that is, there is no other thing at t_3 which as closely continues x. Thus, we have y at t_2 being the closest continuer of x at t_1, and w at t_3 not being a continuer of y at t_2 yet being the closest continuer of x at t_1. We can diagram this situation (Figure N.5), letting a dotted-line link stand for one thing's being (among the various things that exist at the same time) the closest continuer of an earlier thing. A version of the situation with the ship exemplifies this structure. Let y at t_2 be the ship with some replacement planks, and let z at t_2 be the heap of removed planks, stacked in a storeroom. Between t_2 and t_3 the ship with replacement planks has burned, and at t_3 the ship w has been reassembled out of the original planks. At t_2 the ship with some replacement planks is the same as the original ship, while the heap of planks in the storeroom is not. At t_3 the ship rebuilt from this heap of original planks is the same as the original ship, though it does not physically continue that ship at t_2 with the replacement planks.

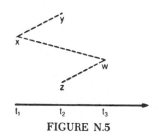

FIGURE N.5

11. Since as far back as we know, everything comes from something else, to find an origin is to find a relative beginning, the beginning of an entity as being of a certain kind K.

12. This instantaneous movement of a person from one place to another does not violate special relativity's constraint on the transmission of energy or a causal signal faster than light.

13. Compare the case of abortion, where also no sharp line or threshold (between the times of conception and birth) seems appropriate. However, we can imagine a presumption against abortion that increases in moral weight as the fetus develops, so that only reasons of increasing significance could justify (later) abortion. Unlike the abortion case, there is nothing in our present concern, the lingering overlap, that can vary continuously like the moral weight of a presumption. One might be tempted to consider the (continuously varying) probability of the healthier one's being the same (earlier) person, but what additional fact would there be to fix how that probability comes out?

14. Some writers have speculated that when people sleep and dream, an astral body actually moves off from the sleeping body and in some realm performs the dreamed actions. (But in a dream of mine involving another actual person, will that person also have dreamed the same situation? And what was Marilyn Monroe dreaming on these evenings when so many others were dreaming of her but not of all the others?) Such a view would be diagrammed as in Figure N.6. Each day a person is mono-related to himself the previous day, and that suffices for identity, no matter how the question of where he was during the previous night is answered.

15. Amos Tversky, "Features of Similarity", *Psychological Review*, Vol. 84, 1977, pp. 327–352, especially pp. 347–349, proposes a general formula for the formation of categories. Tversky, surprisingly but convincingly, explains how two things can be the most similar entities within a group and also the most dissimilar, and he provides data to show that people do make such judgments. Hence, a formula for category formation cannot speak only of degrees of similarity within a category; it also must speak, nonredundantly, of (minimizing) degrees of dissimilarity within categories.

16. It also may hold that no other distribution be as closely related, as the one under consideration, to the previous one. This added condition will not restrict theories that specify a relation R which only an actual distribution can stand in to an earlier one; however, it will be relevant to theories using a wider relation.

17. Other views worth mentioning also fit. H. L. A. Hart (*The Concept of Law*, Oxford University Press, 1961, ch. 6) holds that the validity of a law or

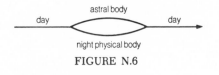

FIGURE N.6

rule is fixed by its historical pedigree; it was adopted or developed in accordance with a process specified by a secondary rule which was and is accepted as binding, for example, enacted by an institution competent (according to an accepted secondary rule) to do this. Closest relative versions of this are obvious, and obviously needed, while the literature contains many intrinsic abstract structural views that base a law's validity on aspects of its content.

Ranging further afield, and stretching things more, Kant's derivation of the moral content of obligation from the form of morality is an intrinsic theory; whereas Hegel's view that only obligations embodied in a particular historical community have content is relational. The coherence theory of truth is intrinsic, whereas the correspondence theory is relational; does Peirce's theory fit the closest relative form?

18. I first presented these moral conditions, without then having any such typology of concepts in mind, in "Moral Complications and Moral Structures", *Natural Law Forum*, Vol. 13, 1968, pp. 1–50.

19. In Chapter 5, the Aristotelian view that specialness is morally important is criticized; that view's structure is the analogue (for properties) of the closest relation view.

20. Arthur Eddington, *The Nature of the Physical World* (Cambridge University Press, 1928), Introduction; L. Susan Stebbing, *Philosophy and the Physicists* (Penguin Books, London, 1937), Part II.

21. Tversky, in *Psychological Review*, Vol. 84, 1977, p. 342.

22. I leave aside the purpose in identifying some particular things, behaving exactly like others of the kind, as yours.

23. See Derek Parfit, "Personal Identity", *Philosophical Review*, Vol. 80, 1971, pp. 3–28.

24. This position is explored by David Lewis, in Rorty, ed., *Identities of Persons;* I shall consider something structurally the same on another topic later.

25. We shall ignore all those other things that might affect degree of caring —is y a stage of some relative of x, or of someone on x's side in some conflict or sharing some of x's properties (including humanity)? Are these cases where degree of care is proportional to degree of closeness?

26. More laboriously, let y be the physical continuer of x in case 1, and let z be the duplicated individual made in both case 1 and case 3. We have the following.

(1) $cl(x \text{ in case } 1, z \text{ in case } 1) = cl(x \text{ in case } 3, z \text{ in case } 3)$.

For degree of closeness is independent of what else exists, and the situations are otherwise the same.

(2) $care(x \text{ in case } 1, y) > care(x \text{ in case } 1, z \text{ in case } 1)$.

For case 1, I care more for the closest continuer who is me than for the duplicate.

(3) $care(x \text{ in case } 3, z \text{ in case } 3) = care(x \text{ in case } 1, y \text{ in case } 1)$.

For I care equally about the future me in the two different cases, about my current me's future closest continuers.

From 2 and 3 it follows that

(4) care(x in case 3, z in case 3) > care(x in case 1, z in case 1).

But though the degree of care between x and the newly minted person differs in cases 1 and 3 (as stated in 4), the degree of closeness between x and the newly minted person is the same in cases 1 and 3 (as stated in 1). Therefore, degree of care is not proportional to degree of closeness.

27. Recall our previous discussion of question 2 above, and see also Chapter 6 below. However, I do not claim that the full magnitude of our caring about our future selves must be based (solely) on our current caring about our current selves. Not to go so far afield, there is also our past self's caring (about which we currently care) about our future self.

28. See Perry, in Rorty, ed., *Identities of Persons*, p. 89.

29. See Eddy Zemach, "The Reference of 'I'", *Philosophical Studies*, Vol. 23, 1972, pp. 68–75.

30. So it seems I run a risk in identifying myself as whatever has the public properties P. Compare the Samkhya yoga doctrine that the *purusha* confuses itself with *prakriti*.

31. See Hector-Neri Castañeda, "On the Logic of Attributions of Self-Knowledge to Others", *Journal of Philosophy*, Vol. 65, 1968, pp. 439–456; "He: A Study in the Logic of Self-Consciousness", *Ratio*, Vol. 8, 1966, pp. 130–157; "Indicators and Quasi-Indicators", *American Philosophical Quarterly*, Vol. 4, 1967, pp. 85–100; "On the Phenomeno Logic of 'I'", *Proceedings of the XIVth International Congress of Philosophy*, Vol. III (Vienna, 1969), pp. 260–266. See also Dieter Henrich, "Self-Consciousness", *Man and World*, Vol. 4, 1971, pp. 3–28; John Perry, "The Problem of the Essential Indexical", *Nous*, Vol. 13, 1979, pp. 3–21; and David Lewis, "Attitudes De Dicto and De Se", *Philosophical Review*, Vol. 88, 1979, pp. 513–543.

32. David Kaplan, in "Demonstratives" (mimeographed manuscript), offers an analysis of indexicals in terms of some fact about reference following from the sense of the expression, which I draw upon here. He does not concern himself there especially with what distinguishes reflexive indexicals.

33. Compare W. V. Quine, *Mathematical Logic*, rev. ed., Harvard University Press, 1951, Section 59.

34. Notice that "this very phrase type" is reflexive, but its sense is 'the phrase type of this very token', and so it does refer through the (first) token.

35. On the last point, see Sydney Shoemaker, "Self-Reference and Self-Awareness", *Journal of Philosophy*, Vol. 65, no. 19, 1968, p. 563.

36. See John Perry, in *Nous*, Vol. 13, pp. 3–21.

37. Sometimes there will be not one classification confined to one level, but a hierarchical classification, wherein entities E at one level are clumped together into wider entities F at the next level up. A hierarchy is interesting when one level is not merely a loosening of another, using the same distance

metric but a looser requirement of what is "close enough" to be part of the same circle. In an interesting hierarchy, some parts of different Es, E_1 and E_2 that are parts of different circles F_1 and F_2 at another level, will be more closely related by the metric for the classification of Es (though not closely enough to make them part of the same E) than some parts of different Es within the same F.

38. See R. R. Sokal and P. H. Sneath, *Principles of Numerical Taxonomy* (Freeman, San Francisco, 1963); Stephen Johnson, "Hierarchical Clustering Schemes", *Psychometrica*, Vol. 32, 1967, pp. 241-254; John Hartigan, *Clustering Algorithms* (Wiley, 1975); Roger Shepard, "Analysis of Proximities: Multidimensional Scaling with an Unknown Distance Function, I, II", *Psychometrica*, Vol. 27, 1962, pp. 125-140, 219-246, and "Representation of Structure in Similarity Data", *Psychometrica*, Vol. 39, 1974, pp. 373-421; Amos Tversky, in *Psychological Review*, Vol. 84, pp. 327-352; Roger Shepard and Phipps Arabie, "Additive Clustering", *Psychological Review*, Vol. 86, 1979, pp. 87-123.

39. See P. F. Strawson, *Individuals* (Methuen, London, 1959), pp. 90-94, and Stuart Hampshire, *Thought and Action* (Viking Press, New York, 1960), ch. 1.

40. I am grateful to Susan Wolf, whose questions prompted this paragraph.

41. This type of explanation of Shoemaker's point also is offered by Eddy Zemach, "The Reference of 'I'", *Philosophical Studies*, Vol. 23, 1972, pp. 68-75. Much of what Zemach says in that article is congenial to the position taken here.

42. Might a self always lack that capacity there, while having it elsewhere? Only if a self, located in one possible world, can synthesize itself, long distance, in another world as a nonself there.

43. Two recent theorists who present unified simples, or unity arising from other intrinsically unified things, are Gustave Bergmann, *Realism* (University of Wisconsin Press, Madison, 1967), part I, and Ivor Leclerc, *The Nature of Physical Existence* (Allen and Unwin, London, 1972), pp. 306, 327-328.

44. A Form of a kind of thing provides a standard whereby diverse things are united, in that together in certain relations they fall under or participate in that Form. This unification as one entity can be done by a Form only if it is the Form of an entity. Other Forms would show another sort of connection, that among diverse and different entities which all participate in or fall under the Form. This second sort of Form would specify properties and relations that can enter into closeness relations; gimmicky predicates that correspond to no Form would be excluded. No sooner have we made the distinction between Forms which unite things into one entity and those under which different entities fall, than we must erase it. If the Form Lion unites disparate parts into one organism, it also has different individual organisms falling under it, while if the Form Cantankerous has different individuals falling under it, it also unites together behavior of the same individual.

45. If we possessed a confirmed general theory that each unity is underlain by such an entity, such an inference and explanation would be more reason-

able. Can the problems live off each other, with universals being introduced to explain why we apply the same predicate to different objects, and then the already introduced universal being used to explain the unity of a particular object (and vice versa)? These problems are not different enough to provide independent introduction of universals.

46. In echoing Wittgenstein here, I am not committed to his diagnosis of how pictures or models come to grip us so. In particular, the picture or model need not stem from features of our language. Even when there are features of the language that naturally fit the model, might it not be the model that underlies the language's having those features? (In that case, the model's hold may be reinforced by the linguistic features to which it has given rise.)

47. See Ernest Nagel, *The Structure of Science* (Harcourt, Brace and World, New York, 1961), pp. 380-397.

48. See Nelson Goodman, *The Structure of Appearance* (3rd ed., Reidel, Dodrecht, 1977), pp. 33-44, and *Problems and Projects* (Bobbs-Merrill, Indianapolis, 1972), pp. 149-198; also Rolf Eberle, *Nominalistic Systems* (Reidel, Dodrecht, 1970).

49. See Paul A. Weiss, *Life, Order, and Understanding* (The Graduate Journal, University of Texas, Vol. VIII, suppl. 1, 1970).

50. It is my impression that thus far such talk has been rather unilluminating, an impression reinforced by David Berlinski's astringent examination, *On Systems Analysis* (MIT Press, Cambridge, 1976). A work of systems theory that at least tries to state a number of empirical propositions, rather than merely classifying types of relationship, is James G. Miller, *Living Systems* (McGraw Hill, New York, 1978).

51. We can test this view of the emergence of unity by making no assumption about underlying unity, allowing all arbitrary groupings and delineations. (Here I overlook questions, when things are brought together in a set, about the unity of the set itself.) How does unity enter the theory of the I?

Let X have the capacity of reflexive self-referring, the capacity to refer to itself by the token reflexive "I". The X generalizes along dimensions we here suppose to be no less and no more arbitrary and unnatural than any other dimensions, properties, and sets. The generalization takes place around the capacity to reflexively self-refer; X views itself as the closest relation of the (its) capacity to reflexively self-refer. That X generalizes in accordance with a closest continuer and the closest relation schema, so fixing its contours and boundaries, is a fact on a par with the others—the world could be carved up without using that schema.

If unity is lurking in our story, it is to be found in the components of self-referring, such as "token" or "intentionally producing", or in the possessor of the reflexive capacity. The predicates "token", "intentionally producing", and "referring" are on a par with others; they are part of some carvings-up of the world, and are not delineated in others. Not every (possible) organism inherited these unspecial predicates and classes; also, not everything satisfies these predicates, is included in these classes, or falls along these dimensions. That a predicate is in some carvings but not all does not entail it is not true of some things and false of others. Not every carving delineates "pen", "telephone", "orange-red", and "office", but mine does, and also the pen in my hand is orange-red and the telephone in my office is not. So the predicates "token", "intentionally produce", and "refer" are on a par with others in my conceptual carving and in other carvings, and they are true of some things (as carved out) and false of others. ("True" and "false" also are part of my carving, and I can use them to describe the fit of parts of my carving with the world, and also to describe the fit of parts of other carvings with the world. "Fit" also is part of my carving.)

An entity which inherited, as generalization classes, "token", "refer", and "intentionally produce", and which also can fit or satisfy them, or produce something that does, will reflexively self-refer and will view itself as doing so. It will apply these predicates to itself and to its products, and view itself as reflexively self-referring. It delineates its boundaries around this capacity to reflexively self-refer, in accordance with the dimensions of generalizing (for whatever reason) it happens to have; these include "intentionally doing", "producing", "referring". The X delineates itself, and afterwards says that what did the delineating was the entity that was delineated. A unity arises which is self-imposed, from a matrix containing no more unity than any other unnatural predicate or class.

We can test this claim further by explicitly incorporating disunity at the underlying level, to see whether the unity supposedly given rise to is thereby dissipated. Can we incorporate explicitly an analogue of the Kantian example wherein seven people consecutively think different words? The test example is merely to introduce an underlying disunity into our previous story, not make some carved up and possibly gimmicky predicates false of some carved up and possibly artificial entities. All it may do is highlight whatever nonunified character there can be. It cannot say, for example, that there is no entity to which "token" applies, though we can imagine the token is some bizarre sum in the calculus of individuals; it cannot say the token was not produced by another entity, though we can imagine that other entity merely as a sum whose parts produce the parts of the token. Finally, the test must allow the conjunction of the predicates to apply to an entity (perhaps artificial) that the carving delineates.

Let us now proceed with our test example. Suppose the sum individual X + Y + Z produces the sum token x + y + z which reflexively self-refers to X + Y + Z. (For example, each component individual sings "I" and the resulting chord, or rather the sum of their voices, refers to the sum of the persons.) It must be that x + y + z does refer (as that carving up predicate 'refer' is used) to X + Y + Z. It will not do to say that x reflexively self-refers to X, y to Y, and z to Z, but to deny that x + y + z refers to X + Y + Z. Perhaps reference is not always additive in this way. But if it isn't in this case, then the case is not relevant to our issue: whether when the carving up predicates, including "refers", do apply, we need also to postulate an additional underlying unity in order for a unity to emerge. So we suppose that x + y + z does reflexively self-refer to X + Y + Z. This is sufficient for the closest relation schema to be applied; the entity $X + Y + Z$ thereby may delineate itself as the entity $X + Y + Z$, correctly applying predicates to itself.

Note that I am not saying that when you, I, and my publisher all say "I", then the resulting chord reflexively self-refers to the sum of the three of us. First, the predicate "refers", as the term is used in my carving up, does not apply to this situation; second, although there is some predicate related to reference that does apply (call it "sum-refers"), that sum individual does not apply predicates to itself. We can (roughly) define a new term "sum-applies", and say that $X + Y + Z$ sum-applies a sum-predicate to itself when each part of the sum-predicate is applied by some part (to itself) of $X + Y + Z$. Even if we deny that $X + Y + Z$ reflexively self-refers here, still it will be "doing" something similar to that. Can we go on and say that the sum-individual sum-applies the closest relation schema to things and to itself?

The sum of the three persons $X + Y + Z$ in our extended example does not apply the closest continuer schema to itself. Despite the chorus, any notion of "I" it applies to itself over time is fixed by the sum of the identities of the three parts over time. So that sum does not constitute a unity. However, if its identity was distinct from that of the sum of its parts then it would constitute a unity which would not be undermined by the entity's having diverse and disparate parts.

We formulated our example to test whether our tale of reflexive self-reference sufficed for unity, even though no unity was presupposed at a lower level. With sum-analogues of each of the predicates we used, it appeared that an obviously nonunified entity could be built up, one whose artificial relations fit the structure of everything we had said. Our structure appeared to possess this nonunified sort of nonstandard model. What prevents this is the notion of identity over time, which is not equivalent to the sum of the identities of the parts over time. Couldn't there be an analogue of identity over time, though, for the sum $X + Y + Z$, call this analogue A, such that the A of $X + Y + Z$ was not equivalent to the sum: the A of X + the A of Y + the A of Z? Perhaps there could be, but then $X + Y + Z$ identified over time via A no longer even appears to lack unity. (I assume that A functions as identity in this model. Otherwise the question of whether the structure admits of a nonstandard model is trivial and uninteresting.)

52. This also serves to avoid problems about precisely which parts are themselves wholes. Are thirds of a table, and if so, can we then look through to the molecules to show that the complete table is a whole? Still, the table will be a whole under some partitionings, and a conglomerate under none.

53. A science fiction story might depict the intercultural problems that would result from our contact with an entity who viewed itself as a conglomerate. When it at first referred to us as conglomerates, would it be referring to *us*?

54. It is tempting here to see or seek an urground for ethics, to see the primordial equal treatment of others in our applying the schema to ourselves in a way that grants the similar existence of others; and even more strongly, to see our applying that schema in that way to ourselves as dependent upon

the similar application by others. If the very foundation and synthesis of the "I" depends upon some cooperative agreement in practice with others, then perhaps ethical egoism, for example, undercuts itself: the very I whose interests are to be placed lexically first is constituted only within a matrix of cooperative activity which does not attempt most to aggrandize the I. If it attempted this, then no I could be synthesized. (Is the norm that is yielded: stay out of each other's way?) Ethics is given rise to by the fact that there are distinct individuals. If this fact itself is not devoid of ethical content, if the structure of synthesizing the I itself involves ethical content, then a starting point is provided for ethics by the very demarcation that gives rise to it. I mention this application to ethics because it is an intriguing possibility—unfortunately, I have not been able to make it work.

A major barrier to such transcendental arguments is the possibility of a pantheistic God who is self-conscious and reflexively self-referring without, in the process, needing to grant ethical status to others or even to recognize others as I's. There might be a more general difficulty about these transcendental arguments, on any view that holds there is an I independent of reflexive synthesizing. To go via a transcendental argument from "I exist", or any other statement "I have property P", to a statement q does not prove q because "I exist" might, strictly speaking, be false, in that the preconditions for the perfectly accurate use of the "I" are not satisfied. Yet the "I" still might function, for all that, even if there is not something of which the presuppositions of "I" are true. Compare Donnellan's discussion of how we can refer to something by saying "the P is Q", although there is nothing that is P. (See Keith Donnellan, "Reference and Definite Descriptions", *Philosophical Review*, Vol. 75, 1966, pp. 281–304; and "Speaker Reference, Descriptions, and Anaphora", in Peter French et al., eds., *Contemporary Perspectives in the Philosophy of Language,* University of Minnesota Press, Morris, 1979, pp. 28–44.)

Two writers recently have drawn ethical conclusions from their discussions of personal identity and the I. See Derek Parfit, "Later Selves and Moral Principles" in Alan Montefiore, ed., *Philosophy and Personal Relations* (Routledge and Kegan Paul, London, 1973); Eddy Zemach, "Love Thy Neighbor as Thyself, or Egoism and Altruism", in Peter French et al., eds., *Studies in Ethical Theory* (Midwest Studies in Philosophy, Vol. III, University of Minnesota Press, Morris, 1978), pp. 148–158.

55. The suggestion that many philosophical problems are different guises of the problem of the relation of universal to particular is made by Roberto Unger, *Knowledge and Politics* (Free Press, New York, 1975), pp. 133–144.

CHAPTER TWO

1. Martin Heidegger, *Introduction to Metaphysics* (Yale University Press, New Haven, 1959), Ch. 1. For a criticism of some ways of avoiding the question, see William Rowe, *The Cosmological Argument* (Princeton University Press, Princeton, 1975), ch. III.

2. C. G. Hempel, *Aspects of Scientific Explanation* (Free Press, New York, 1965). We view some of the counterexample cases as showing that sufficient conditions for E are not yet at hand.

3. Hilary Putnam imposes further pragmatic conditions on E so that it no longer is transitive, in "Philosophy and Our Mental Life" (*Mind, Language and Reality*, Philosophical Papers II, Cambridge University Press, 1975, pp. 291–303). But this makes it even less likely that everything will be explained, while our purpose here is to see how much can be explained on the most favorable assumption.

4. See Eugene P. Wigner's discussion of symmetry and invariance conditions, in the first five essays of his *Symmetries and Reflections* (Indiana University Press, Bloomington, 1967).

5. See Section 7 of the paper by Hempel and Oppenheim in Hempel, *Aspects of Scientific Explanation*, pp. 270–278; R. Eberle, R. Montague, and D. Kaplan. "Hempel and Oppenheim on Explanation", *Philosophy of Science*, Vol. 28, 1961, pp. 418–428; David Kaplan, "Explanation Revisited", *ibid.*, pp. 429–436; J. Kim, "On the Logical Conditions of Deductive Explanation", *ibid.*, Vol. 30, 1963, pp. 286–291; R. Ackermann, "Deductive Scientific Explanation", *ibid.*, Vol. 32, 1965, pp. 155–167.

6. Saul Kripke, "Outline of a Theory of Truth", *Journal of Philosophy*, Vol. 72, 1975, pp. 690–716.

7. I assume here that Kripke's theory of floating levels can be modified so as to allow self-subsumption. Surely some theory, incorporating the (or a) weakest restriction that avoids the logical and semantical paradoxes, will do so. See also William Hart, "On Self Reference", *Philosophical Review*, Vol. 79, 1970, pp. 523–528, and Charles Parsons, "The Liar", *Journal of Philosophical Logic*, Vol. 3, 1974, pp. 381–412. A delightful and stimulating trip through the realm of self-reference is Douglas Hofstadter, *Gödel, Escher, Bach* (Basic Books, New York, 1979).

8. Within general relativity, motion is on geodesics of spacetime, deviations

from which are caused by the coupling of the multipole moments of the object with the Riemann curvature tensor of the external field. See Charles Misner, Kip Thorne, and J. A. Wheeler, *Gravitation* (W. H. Freeman, San Francisco, 1973), pp. 1120–1121, 1126–1128.

Within economics, one may take the natural state as people performing uncoordinated activities, and so set out to explain how the far flung activities of diverse individuals come to be coordinated; or one can be so impressed with this explanation's success that one comes to take a smoothly functioning coordinated market for granted as automatic, as natural, and so then seek to explain the deviations from it—for example, the persistence of unemployment. A reasonable strategy, surely, would be to remember the first explanation, specifying a process of coordination, and seek factors that block the operation of that process. Similarly, in medical theory one might take a healthy functioning body as a natural condition, and seek causes of illness; while for other purposes one might seek an explanation of how self-regulation and self-maintenance in the body occurs.

Nancy Chodorow describes how object-relations theory and the Freudian theory of primary narcissism differ about whether human sociality or human isolation is the natural state, not in need of explanation. (*The Reproduction of Mothering*, University of California Press, Berkeley, 1979, p. 67.)

See also the discussion of "ideas of natural order" in Stephen Toulmin, *Foresight and Understanding* (Indiana University Press, Bloomington, 1961), chs. 3–4, pp. 44–82.

9. One level up, on the worst assumption all first-level partitions other than the two-membered one are in the same class, so at this second level we have a two-membered partition: (something, nothing), (all other partitions). Assigning a probability of $\frac{1}{2}$ to each of these, we get

$$\tfrac{1}{2}(\tfrac{1}{2}S, \tfrac{1}{2}N), \ \tfrac{1}{2}(\text{all other partitions}).$$

In these partitions, nothing (N) is as high as $\frac{1}{3}$ and as low as ε, while something (S) is as low as $\frac{2}{3}$ and as high as $1-\varepsilon$. With each of these having equal weight, the average of all of these other partitions is $\frac{1}{6}N, \frac{5}{6}S$. Substituting this in the previous expression, we get

$$\tfrac{1}{2}(\tfrac{1}{2}S, \tfrac{1}{2}N), \ \tfrac{1}{2}(\tfrac{5}{6}S, \tfrac{1}{6}N)$$

which is equal to

$$\tfrac{2}{3}S, \tfrac{1}{3}N.$$

That two-membered partition at the second level was just one possible partition at that level, the worst case. There are others. We can go up to the third level, and consider all the second-level partitions. The worst case at the second level, we already have seen, is $\frac{2}{3}S, \frac{1}{3}N$; all other partitions at the second level range between this worst case and the best. Their average is $\frac{5}{6}S, \frac{1}{6}N$. Now consider the worst partition at the third level, into only two cases, namely the worst at the second level and all others at that second level together. When each of these has an equal chance, this gives

$$\tfrac{1}{4}(\tfrac{2}{3}S, \tfrac{1}{3}N), \ \tfrac{1}{4}(\tfrac{2}{3}S, \tfrac{1}{3}N)$$

which reduces to

$$\tfrac{2}{3}S, \tfrac{1}{3}N.$$

As we go up each level, the probability of S increases; at the limit S receives the same probability value as in the equal probability partition of all alternatives at the first level.

10. Arthur Lovejoy uses the term "the principle of plenitude" in a similar context of discussing theories of why the world exists and has the character it does, but that principle refers to the maximum realization of possibilities in one actual universe. (*The Great Chain of Being*, Harvard University Press, Cambridge, 1936.) The Talmud's statement (Abodah Zarah 3b) that "God rides on His swift cherub and roams over eighteen thousand worlds" usually is interpreted to mean distinct worlds, unconnected spatially or temporally.

The Everett-Wheeler interpretation of quantum mechanics countenances branching universes. (See B. DeWitt and N. Graham, eds., *The Many-Worlds Interpretation of Quantum Mechanics*, Princeton University Press, Princeton, 1973.) A realist view about possible worlds is articulated by David Lewis in his book *Counterfactuals* (Harvard University Press, Cambridge, 1973, pp. 84–91), adducing linguistic evidence and general realist assumptions. See also Michale Loux, ed., *The Possible and the Actual* (Cornell University Press, Ithaca, 1979). We have been led to consider this view because of its particular explanatory function in cosmogony; a theory so structured seems to avoid leaving unanswered the question "why X rather than Y?" Alternative possible worlds in "superspace" were introduced by Wheeler for another purpose in cosmology, to represent probabilistic scattering in superspace through the gravitational collapse, in which the laws of conservation of charge, lepton number, baryon number, mass, and angular momentum disappear, along with the particles and fundamental constants. (See Wheeler's essay "From Relativity to Mutability" in Jagdish Mehra, ed., *The Physicist's Conception of Nature*, Reidel, Dodrecht, 1973, pp. 202–247, especially pp. 231–234; also Misner, Thorne, and Wheeler, *Gravitation*, ch. 43.)

11. "For the first two years Einstein, in his letters, preferred to call his theory not 'relativity theory' but exactly the opposite: *Invariantentheorie*." Gerald Holton, *Thematic Origins of Scientific Thought* (Harvard University Press, Cambridge, 1973), p. 362.

12. Further conditions may have to be imposed to make the task nontrivial. For consider the sort 'is identical to what actually obtains'. Call that sort A (for actual). If we specify the principle of limited fecundity by this sort A, then it becomes LF': anything that is actual obtains. Since the actual world satisfies A, we can deduce from LF' that the actual world obtains. Furthermore, no other world will obtain via LF'. The sole remaining question then is whether LF' subsumes itself. Even if, with fiddling, LF' will subsume itself, this prin-

ciple clearly will not fit our needs. So additional conditions may need to be imposed on the explanation, to assure that it has content and power.

13. See Saul Kripke's related discussion ("Outline of a Theory of Truth", pp. 708–709) of which fixed point (minimal or other) is chosen in giving a truth definition; also George Boolos, *The Unprovability of Consistency* (Cambridge University Press, 1979).

14. "Some principle uniquely right and uniquely simple must, when one knows it, be also so obvious that it is clear that the universe is built, and must be built in such and such a way and that it could not possibly be otherwise." Martin Rees, Remo Ruffini, and John Wheeler, *Black Holes, Gravitational Waves and Cosmology* (Gordon and Breach, New York, 1974), p. 297.

15. Our approach to the question of why there is something rather than nothing, in this section as in the rest of the chapter, does not build upon any special theory of the nature of existence, of what it is for something to exist. While it seems plausible that the other approach might be fruitful, I have no special theory of existence to present. Unfortunately, those who have written on that topic have not yet managed to advance the discussion of this chapter's question.

Throughout this chapter, I adhere to the natural assumption that any ultimate principle will be in the indicative mood. However, since the philosopher views his question "why?" as arising about everything and every possible world, even if no one asks it—one might almost say the question necessarily exists—we might at least wonder whether the basis of everything could not be interrogative. Could there be an interrogative force which questions itself and thereby yields whatever indicatives are presupposed, either by that particular question or by the subjunctive (which necessarily holds?) that about anything that was true there would be the question "why?" Could it be not just philosophy that begins in wonder?

16. Christian Wolff offered a circular argument for SR, but the circle was very small and it did not involve self-subsumption.

17. If the other statements that have sufficient reasons include all true statements of the form qEp, then if SR itself does not have a sufficient reason the system will be something like ω-incomplete. Each instance of 'if p then there is a q such that q and qEp' will have a sufficient reason, but the universally quantified matrix, which is SR itself, will not have a sufficient reason.

18. S. Kochen and E. P. Specker, "The Problem of Hidden Variables in Quantum Mechanics", *Journal of Mathematics and Mechanics*, Vol. 17, 1967, pp. 59–81. Is there some weakening of SR, as described below, which *does* fit quantum mechanics?

19. Let us write 'there is a sufficient reason for p' as $\Box p$. SR then says $(p)(p \supset \Box p)$, and the first weakening of SR says $(p)(p \supset \Box p V \Box \sim \Box p)$. The second weakening of SR says $(p)(p \supset \Box p V \Box \sim \Box p V \sim \Box \sim \Box p)$, and so forth. Let $K_1 = \Box \sim$, $K_2 = \Box \sim \Box \sim$, and more generally $K_{i+1} = \Box \sim K_i$. And let $K_0 = \emptyset$.) The first weakening of SR is then $(p)(p \supset \Box p V K_1 \Box p)$; the second weakening is $(p)(p \supset \Box p V K_1 \Box p V K_2 \Box p)$, and the ith weakening is

(p)(p ⊃ □pV . . . VK$_i$□p). The weakest principle of sufficient reason (WSR) says that there is some finite i such that the ith weakening of SR is true.

$$WSR:(p)[p ⊃ (∃i) (K_i□pVK_{i-1}□ \ pV \ . \ . \ . \ VK_1pVK_0p)] \ 0 ≦ i < n$$

If WSR is true, we also can consider the result WSR' of strengthening it by prefacing its consequent with a box.

I have used the box notation for 'there is a sufficient reason for' to suggest the application of modal considerations to the principle of sufficient reason. If the strong principle SR held, there would be no point in doing this, for under SR it would be a theorem that p ⊃ □p, and so the modal system would collapse into the propositional calculus. With the rejection of the strong SR, however, there is a point to representing sufficient reasons modally, and we can ask within what systems of modal logic WSR is a theorem. WSR is a theorem of S5 and S4, but not of S3 or of T. Furthermore, WSR' also is a theorem of S5 and of S4. Indeed, the second weakening of SR (which is WSR with i = 2), (p) (p ⊃ □pV□ ~ □pV□ ~ □ ~ □p), is a theorem of S4 and of S5, as is the result of strengthening these with a box before their consequents. Moreover, the first weakening of SR, (p)(p ⊃ □pV□ ~ □p), holds in S5 but not in S4. (The result of strengthening the consequent of this by a box also holds in S5.)

Clearly there is a range of principles of sufficient reason. The first weakening of SR holds in S5, the second holds in S4 (and, of course, in S5). Presumably, further weakenings of SR hold in systems intermediate between S4 and S3, with WSR holding in one stronger than S3. If SR in its full strength is false, but some weakening of it is true, then what is the strongest version that is true? Or is even WSR false?

Earlier we noticed that if SR was true but itself had no sufficient reason, someone might hold that still it was not arbitrary. Now that we have seen different versions of weakened SR, all the way down to WSR, for whatever least i WSR holds true, there will be the question of why it is true for that i and not for another one. Why not for $i = 0$? Or alternatively, why isn't the first one for which it is true the previous i plus five? Only if the strong SR were true would we stand a chance of avoiding the issue of arbitrariness.

If no weakening of SR is true, if even WSR is false, then there will be the question of whether there is a sufficient reason for its falsity, that is, whether it is true that □ ~ WSR, which is K$_1$ WSR. And if there is not, is there a sufficient reason for there not being one, so it is true that □ ~ □ ~ WSR, which is K$_2$ WSR. Clearly, we have the same possibilities as before of proceeding up the line. Let WSR^2 be

(∃ i)(K$_i$ WSR), $1 ≦ i < n$.

If WSR is false is at least WSR^2 true? If WSR^2 also is false, we can go up another level and consider

WSR^3 : (∃ i)(K$_i$ WSR^2), $1 ≦ i < n$.

And so forth.

At some level or other, will there not finally be a sufficient reason for the whole sorry arbitrary mess? Consider the statement R of radical contingency, that nowhere up the line is a sufficient reason encountered.

R : $\sim$ ($\exists$ n) WSR^n, that is, (n) $\sim$ WSR^n.

R itself is not within the scope of its quantifier, since it is of transfinite type. However, we can iterate the process with R itself, and ask whether $\Box$R, $\Box \sim \Box$R, and so on.

If we could construct a statement RC of the most radical contingency, which fell within the scope of its own quantifier, we would be able to refute it. Such a statement could not be true. For by subsuming itself, RC would provide a sufficient reason for its own truth and so $\Box$RC. But since RC says there is no box anywhere up the line or up any metaline either, RC is false. There could not be the most radical imaginable contingency. This is small comfort for two reasons: first, we have not shown that such a self-subsuming RC can be constructed; and second, even if a box was encountered somewhere up the line, why could there not be even further up the line an infinite random sequence of boxes and negations of boxes?

Without some further explanation of 'sufficient reason' it will be difficult to decide which weakening of SR is true, if any. We can offer a semantics in the style of Kripke, saying that there is a sufficient reason in w_1 for p if p is true in w_1 and in all worlds accessible from w_1. There is a sufficient reason for p in w_1 if and only if w_1 is surrounded by worlds that force p to be true in w_1. Or we might define the probability of p in w_1 as the ratio of the worlds accessible from w_1 in which p is true over the worlds accessible from w_1; then there is a sufficient reason for p in w_1 when its probability in w_1 is 1. (Ignore the fact that the probability can be 1 even though there are some worlds, of measure zero, accessible from w_1 in which not-p.) But this semantic explanation does not, I think, help one to decide on the features of the accessibility relation, for example, whether it is transitive or symmetrical.

Consider a particle going through one of two slits at random. In that situation, there is no true subjunctive "if it were to be emitted it would go through the left (right) slit" and also there is no sufficient reason for its going through the slit it does. We might use the subjunctive form to help specify further the notion of sufficient reason. There is a sufficient reason for p if and only if p is true and there is a q such that q is true and q explains p, and this subjunctive holds: if q were true then p would be true. The subjunctive component is a part (but not the whole) of the explanatory relation E; we make this part explicit here. The role of laws in the deductive nomological account of explanation is to ensure that a subjunctive holds true between some initial condition and the fact to be explained, the explanandum. Laws are necessary for explanation if such a subjunctive relation can hold between initial condition and explanandum only in the presence of a law.

On the account of subjunctives we shall offer in the next chapter, a subjunctive $q \rightarrow p$ holds true when p is true for some distance out in the q neighborhood of the actual world. Consider the thesis of S4 that $\Box p \supset \Box \Box p$. On the explanatory and subjunctive understanding of sufficient reasons, this is not a necessary truth about subjunctives and explanation. That p is true throughout the q neighborhood of the actual world does not entail that there is an r that explains this, so that it is true throughout the r neighborhood of the actual world. So the "logic of" sufficient reasons will not be as strong as S4; S4 is not an analysis of the concept of sufficient reason. Whether S4 is true of the sufficient reasons that hold is another question.

On the subjunctive view of sufficient reasons, must some weakening of SR hold? The usual semantics do not mesh perfectly with our view of subjunctives, but we can make some simplifying assumptions. Assume the explanatory relation E plays no role, and assume that the close neighborhood of a world is that world plus the n next closest worlds (there are no ties) so that the worlds can be listed in order with a world's neighborhood being its own row on the list plus the n rows beneath it. In this case, some version of WSR will hold true; in particular it will be true for each p that a box will be reached by $K_{n-1} \Box p$. But this result, though interesting itself, provides little help with the first-level question of why is there something rather than nothing.

Let me close this note by showing that under the mentioned assumptions, a version of WSR will hold, with a box reached by $K_{n-1} \Box p$. Suppose $n = 10$, and construct a matrix whose rows are the worlds, and whose first column contains p or $\sim p$ or both, and whose $i + 1^{th}$ column contains $\Box$ ____or $\sim \Box$ ____, where the blank is filled by either possible entry of the ith column. The task is to try to construct the matrix so that the entry in the first row for each column (after the first) begins with $\sim \Box$, that is, so that WSR is false. If the third column is to begin with $\sim \Box \sim \Box p$, then somewhere in the first $n + 1$ rows of the second column there must be a $\Box p$. (The earliest it can be is the third row.) As we move out the columns, that box must move down, and its slowest pace is one row at a time. When we reach the nth column, it will have gone down to the $n + 1^{th}$ row, and so the $n + 1^{th}$ column will begin with a $\Box$, making WSR true at that point.

20. See §§ 138–155, 185–242.

21. Since Wittgenstein in his very investigations has shown how we cannot take even the notion of same for granted (not only not 'the same as before' but also 'the same as you are now doing'), he presumably will have to spell out our all going on in the same way, in terms of something like 'smooth interchange'. People speak to each other smoothly in that by and large they do not punish each other's verbal utterances. (Notice, there is yet no distinction between disagreeing over the application of a term and disagreeing over a fact; either can make talk unsmooth.)

There is a further point. We see the reinforcement we get for speech, some positive and little punishing, as coming from others who also do this kind of activity, others who also talk. We are trying to match their behavior; they are not only the reinforcers of our verbal tries but also the target of our behavior, the standard with which we are trying to align ourselves by doing the same thing.

I think this union of target and reinforcer is crucial to correctness in speech. First, imagine a reinforcer but no target or model to emulate. The infant babbles and some hidden person watching behind one-way mirrors reinforces its meanderings, shaping its vocal sounds in situations into determinate patterns. Still, there will be no notion of correctness. Do not bring in the reinforcer's notions—suppose the reinforcements happened that way accidentally, a haywire computer with sensing devices happened to reinforce in a certain way. Nothing here would fix incorrectness, we would have merely 'superstition in the infant'. Even if the reinforcements were not random but fit a pattern embodying subjunctives, there still would be no correctness. On the other hand, a target model without a reinforcer might give us the infant's wanting to match, but not its failure resulting in incorrectness. Reinforcers distinct from the target give us prudential reasons to accede to their wishes. But correctness in language for us depends, I think, on our trying to match the behavior of others, who respond (and whom we perceive as responding) to our attempts at matching in a way that brings us into even closer alignment, into the community of mutual matchers.

These reflections reinforce Wittgenstein's view that it is the way others apply the terms that gives 'correctness' a grip, for it is the way others apply the terms that we (with their aid) are trying to match. But is it the way others do apply the term that fixes correctness, or rather is it their correct applications? Couldn't others who were previously the target and standard come to apply the term incorrectly?

Suppose the earth passes through a radioactive cloud that changes certain processes in people's brains and thereby changes (as we would say, looking from outside) how they apply a term. Wittgenstein has emphasized the limited domain of rules and principles of interpretation. At some point these are applied, that is, something just happens. The most plausible view is that certain underlying processes cause us to apply the term in a certain way in a new instance, given the past applications. Wittgenstein, after all, has not proven that computers are impossible. These machines do apply rules, do print out 'correct' results of calculations, do solve equations, do add '+2' correctly, continuing a series. They do not utilize an infinite hierarchy of rules for interpreting rules; rather, at some point how a rule is applied is just built into its hardware. Given its physical makeup, it is caused to do certain things under certain circumstances.

Similarly, we may view ourselves as caused to do things, caused, given our physical makeup, to go on in certain ways in certain situations. The explanation of our agreement in the use of terms, in how we continue to use and project them, is that we are causally similar because physically similar, similar enough so that the differences do not interfere. But in that case our physical nature could change and thereby would change the way we apply rules and terms, how we project from a finite sample. Is correctness fixed, then, by how we actually go on to use terms (in the new conditions) or by how we used to use them in the old conditions, by how we would have continued to use them had conditions not changed? Is it actual usage that fixes correctness, or a subjunctive about what usage would be under certain conditions? Suppose that as the earth passed through the radioactive cloud, a human astronaut was beyond its range. When he returns and differs from all others in his application of the term, are they correct or is he? Perhaps the others would not easily be brought to think that the cloud had wrought this change on all of them, but nonetheless is it not their application, rather than his, which is incorrect?

What subjunctive is it, though, that fixes correctness? It held true of people before that were they to pass through a radioactive cloud they would 'shift' their application of the term. Yet we cannot say that correct application is what would take place under unchanged conditions, for then we never could correctly apply an old term in new changed conditions, or a term whose content refers to change. (Can we distinguish caused change from the case where the content of the term refers to change, by how the person applies the term when he falsely believes there is a change? Surely then his new application is not caused by a change, for there is none. However, there is a belief he now has that he didn't have before; can this entrance into a new belief state cause his new speech as an effect rather than as an application of the old term to the situation as it now is believed to be?) Clearly, it is no help at all to delineate correct application as what would take place under conditions that don't change how we apply the term. Nor can we appeal to people's previous intentions in using the term, for the question is how those previous intentions can reach out, in a particular way, into the new future circumstances.

Should we say that a correct application is that which takes place under normal conditions? Notice that, in one sense of normal, we may always have been under abnormal conditions. Suppose for the past two hundred million years the earth has been in the beam of an intergalactic spaceship, which leaves next week. If intentional interference with the way things otherwise would have been makes things nonnormal, then only after the spaceship leaves will we discover what normal conditions are. Perhaps we should understand the appropriate (or normal) conditions as those like the ones we now are under. The question is which conditions are the same as the ones we are under, and to answer "those that do not change our application of terms" is no help at all.

These problems might lead us to be less dissatisfied with Wittgenstein's view that actual agreement fixes correctness. However, if the earth passes through the galactic cloud, then is the new usage correct immediately because agreed upon or (after how long?) will it become correct? People who say there was no change will have problems in their explanatory science—for didn't the cloud cause changes in brain chemistry and didn't this affect speech? Still, they might say that although there is a change, it did not lead to incorrectness, for the notion of 'correct' simply is "what almost all of us actually will do". (If agreement breaks down, so does the notion of 'correctness'.) In this very radical sense the actual world would fix correctness in application—whatever happens to happen in it would fix correctness. We may state this less extremely, though, for our responses to the radioactive cloud do not merely happen at random: they are caused. What fixes correctness will be the actual world, as it happens to vary, plus our own causal natures. But if 'correctness' means "whatever we all actually are caused to do", if the cloud is lethal to almost all, is correctness fixed for the one survivor by how he actually goes on whatever the others would have done, or by him only if others also would have

676

gone on in the same way? Gone on under what conditions? Passing through the dangerous cloud and surviving? If causality holds sway, the others certainly will agree (except insofar as there is an interaction between the cloud and people's differing past histories).

The view that correctness is fixed by what we are caused to do, actually or subjunctively, has implications for issues about free will. If we must refer to causal processes (at the hardware level) in explaining "correctness", then for beings who are not caused to go on in a certain way, there will be no notion of correctness in application of terms. "But couldn't they all just happen to go on the same way, though uncaused?" Apart from difficulties in explaining why they have happened to agree until now, this will give no reason to expect further agreement. Yet to appeal to their understanding of the terms, their grasp of rules, and so on returns us to the same circle of problems from which causality seemed to offer rescue. Does correctness in use and application of language presuppose causality?

Perhaps Wittgenstein did not intend to formulate sufficient conditions for the correct application of a predicate in terms of agreement in judgments, but rather saw agreement in judgments as establishing the context within which questions of correctness in application arise and are discussed. If there were no agreement in judgments, as a fact of our "natural history", there would be no realm of correct or incorrect applications. (A suggestive parallel is Wittgenstein's discussion of the framework within which evidence, argument, and verification occur in *On Certainty*, Basil Blackwell, Oxford, 1969.) However, this modification does not help with our problem about laws. Agreement in judgments plays no role, either as sufficient conditions or as background context, in the application of laws to instances as they determine them.

22. Can the problem be avoided by hypothesizing another interpreter who projects the lawlike statements onto the' world? Can things go on their way because the series is continued by God or some other intelligence, perhaps a split committee? Once again the question would arise: what makes that being continue on that way? (Is there something God can do once and for all to fix how things go on, or must he intervene constantly?) The answer cannot be any process under causal laws, while to dub it a "mystery" arbitrarily picks a moment to give up—why not dub how a law is connected to its instantiating events a mystery to begin with, and leave it at that? In any case, there are other and more extravagant alternative hypotheses such as panpsychism, which has everything choosing (perhaps rudimentarily), in a noncausal fashion, to continue its own series, instead of one being doing the job for all. And what makes it true that these consciousnesses (or God's) go on in the same way, what fixes it as the same? That they go on in a way we are caused to comprehend? These hypotheses are unhelpful in this context, merely saying there is a level where somehow the same problem does not arise.

23. See also Richard Boyd, "Determinism, Laws, and Predictability in Principle", *Philosophy of Science*, Vol. 39, 1972, pp. 431–450.

24. Richard Feynman, *The Character of Physical Law* (MIT Press, Cam-

bridge, 1967), pp. 53–55.

25. In the spirit of Wittgenstein's remark in *Zettel* (University of California Press, Berkeley, 1967), para. 608.

26. For example, see Roberto Unger, *Knowledge and Politics* (Free Press, New York, 1975), pp. 14–16.

27. Sarvepalli Radhakrishnan and Charles Moore, *Sourcebook in Indian Philosophy* (Princeton University Press, Princeton, 1957), p. 23.

28. The topic of presupposition as giving rise to truth value gaps was introduced into recent philosophy by P. F. Strawson, "On Referring," *Mind*, Vol. 59, 1950, pp. 320–344. For an indication of the various approaches in the literature since then, see the following: B. C. Van Fraassen, "Presuppositions, Supervaluations and Free Logic" in K. Lambert, ed., *The Logical Way of Doing Things*, Yale University Press, New Haven, 1969, pp. 67–92; Robert Stalnaker, "Presuppositions," *Journal of Philosophical Logic*, Vol. 2, 1973, pp. 447–457; L. Karttunen, "Presuppositions of Compound Sentences," *Linguistic Inquiry*, Vol. 4, 1973, pp. 169–193; J. Katz, *Propositional Structure and Illocutionary Force*, Harvard University Press, Cambridge, 1980, pp. 88–112; G. Gazdar, *Pragmatics*, Academic Press, New York, 1979, chs. 5, 6.

29. Dale Gottlieb has suggested to me another view, that contradictions do fit some situations (via the existing rules of the language), and the mystic realizes this after his experience. Different mystics use the same contradictions, so perhaps what the mystic experiences is effable, and is effed by contradictions. See G. K. Pletcher, "Mysticism, Contradiction, and Ineffability," *American Philosophy Quarterly*, Vol. 10, 1973, pp. 201–211.

30. A useful reminder that the mystics within different traditions differ in their experiences, and not merely in how they interpret them, is presented by Steven Katz, "Language, Epistemology and Mysticism", in S. Katz, ed., *Mysticism and Philosophical Analysis* (Oxford University Press, 1978), pp. 22–74. However, not all experiences are equally theory-laden, and sometimes people are catapulted into experiences, for example by drugs, without previous theoretical preparation. Furthermore, even if the experiences are shaped by theoretical traditions and expectations, we who know of these differing traditions can ask whether mystics of different traditions are experiencing the same thing, whether the object of their experiences is the same, even though they are not experiencing it in the same way.

Useful books on mysticism by philosophers are William James, *The Varieties of Religious Experience* (Modern Library, New York, 1929); W. T. Stace, *Mysticism and Philosophy* (Lippincott, Philadelphia, 1960); Fritz Staal, *Exploring Mysticism* (University of California Press, Berkeley, 1975); Ben-Ami Scharfstein, *Mystical Experience* (Penguin Books, London, 1974); and (these last are also works of mysticism) Aurobindo, *The Life Divine, Synthesis of Yoga,* and *Savitri* (each Pondicherry, India, 1973).

31. One also might view the categorization of remarkable LSD experiences in analogy to stages of the birth process, presented in Stanislav Grof, *Realms of the Human Unconscious: Observations from LSD Research* (Viking Press, New York, 1975), as a matrix for an alternative 'explaining away' of the experience.

32. Thus, we are imagining that the mystics' position is not discriminated against in an application of Bayesian procedures, or Israel Scheffler's justificatory procedure ("On Justification and Commitment," *Journal of Philosophy,* Vol. 51, 1954, pp. 180-190), or N. Rescher's coherentist confirmation (*The Coherence Theory of Truth,* Oxford University Press, 1973).

33. For an interesting discussion of the origin of the phrase "saving the phenomena or appearances", which (contrary to what I had thought) does not appear in the extant writings of Plato, see Gregory Vlastos, *Plato's Universe* (University of Washington Press, Seattle, 1975), appendix M, pp. 111-112.

CHAPTER THREE

1. This chapter's focus upon the existence (and possibility) of bits of knowledge that *p* leaves aside interesting questions about other types of knowledge and about particular kinds of knowledge that *p*. Knowledge is diverse. We know particular current facts about ourselves and our immediate environments, facts about our pasts, our parents, our plans, facts we were taught or read about history, other societies, current affairs, things science has found out, parts of mathematics, even perhaps whole subjects; also, there are people and places we know, and things we know how to do.

Moreover, our knowledge is not simply a bunch of separate items, it forms an interconnected network. It is not quite a system—more a fabric: some parts more tightly woven than others, with holes and rents, some patches, worn spots, and many threads dangling. (Think of it as a child's security blanket.) There also are many interesting questions about the overall structure and shape of this fabric, and how its parts interconnect, the overall pattern, if any, the differently colored threads exhibit. (In representing a current state of knowledge we would want to include not only the current state and interconnections of what is known—the fabric—but also the problems known of, ongoing attempts at solution, and so forth.) Such questions will receive more attention with the decline of the view, predominant for centuries, of knowledge as a structure with foundations.

2. There also is the possibility wherein there is no intermediate route; the experiences arise uncaused, at random. Unlike the skeptical possibilities, however, this one would not explain why the experiences are had.

3. Edward Gettier, "Is Justified True Belief Knowledge?", *Analysis,* 1963, pp. 121-123.

4. See Alvin Goldman, "A Causal Theory of Knowledge", *Journal of Philosophy,* Vol. 64, 1967, pp. 357-372.

5. Paul Benacerraf wrestles with the problems a causal account causes for mathematical knowledge in "Mathematical Truth", *Journal of Philosophy,* Vol. 70, 1973, pp. 661-679. For an attempt to defend the causal account in

application to mathematics, see Mark Steiner, *Mathematical Knowledge* (Cornell University Press, Ithaca, 1975).

6. Despite some demurrals in the literature, there is general agreement that conditions 1 and 2 are necessary for knowledge. (For some recent discussions, see D. M. Armstrong, *Belief, Truth and Knowledge*, Cambridge University Press, 1973, ch. 10; Keith Lehrer, *Knowledge*, Oxford University Press, 1974, chs. 2, 3.) I shall take for granted that this is so, without wishing to place very much weight on its being belief that is the precise cognitive attitude (as opposed to thinking it so, accepting the statement, and so on) or on the need to introduce truth as opposed to formulating the first condition simply as: *p*.

I should note that our procedure here does not stem from thinking that every illuminating discussion of an important philosophical notion must present (individually) necessary and (jointly) sufficient conditions.

7. Below, we discuss further the case where though the fact that *p* causes the person's belief that *p*, he would believe it anyway, even if it were not true. I should note here that I assume bivalence throughout this chapter, and consider only statements that are true if and only if their negations are false.

8. See Robert Stalnaker, "A Theory of Conditionals", in N. Rescher, ed., *Studies in Logical Theory* (Basil Blackwell, Oxford, 1968); David Lewis, *Counterfactuals* (Harvard University Press, Cambridge, 1973); and Jonathan Bennett's critical review of Lewis, "Counterfactuals and Possible Worlds", *Canadian Journal of Philosophy*, Vol. IV, no. 2, Dec. 1974, pp. 381–402.

Our purposes require, for the most part, no more than an intuitive understanding of subjunctives. However, it is most convenient to examine here some further issues, which will be used once or twice later. Lewis' account has the consequence that $p \rightarrow q$ whenever p and q are both true; for the possible world where p is true that is closest to the actual world is the actual world itself, and in that world q is true. We might try to remedy this by saying that when p is true, $p \rightarrow q$ is true if and only if q is true in all p worlds closer (by the metric) to the actual world than is any not-p world. When p is false, the usual accounts hold that $p \rightarrow q$ is true when q holds merely in the closest p worlds to the actual world. This is too weak, but how far out must one go among the p worlds? A suggestion parallel to the previous one is: out until one reaches another not-p world (still further out). So if q holds in the closest p world w_1 but not in the p world w_2, even though no not-p world lies between w_1 and w_2, then (under the suggestion we are considering) the subjunctive is false. A unified account can be offered for subjunctives, whatever the truth value of their antecedents. The p neighborhood of the actual world A is the closest p band to it; that is, w is in the p neighborhood of the actual world if and only if p is true in w and there are no worlds $w^{\bar{p}}$ and w^p such that not-p is true in $w^{\bar{p}}$ and p is true in w^p, and $w^{\bar{p}}$ is closer to A than w is to A, and w^p is at least as close to A as $w^{\bar{p}}$ is to A. A subjunctive $p \rightarrow q$ is true if and only if q is true throughout the p neighborhood of the actual world.

If it is truly a random matter which slit a photon goes through, then its going through (say) the right slit does not establish the subjunctive: if a photon were fired at that time from that source it would go through the right-hand slit. For when p equals A photon is fired at that time from that source, and q equals the photon goes through the right-hand slit, q is not true everywhere in the p neighborhood of the actual world.

This view of subjunctives within a possible-worlds framework is inadequate if there is no discrete p band of the actual world, as when for each positive distance from the actual world A, there are both p worlds and not-p worlds so distant. Even if this last is not generally so, many p worlds that interest us may have their distances from A matched by not-p worlds. Therefore, let us redefine the relevant p band as the closest spread of p worlds such that there is no not-p world intermediate in distance from A to two p worlds in the spread unless there is also another p world in the spread the very same distance from A. By definition, it is only p worlds in the p band, but some not-p worlds may be equidistant from A.

Though this emendation allows us to speak of the closest spread of p worlds, it no longer is so clear which worlds in this p band subjunctives (are to) encompass. We have said it is not sufficient for the truth of $p \rightarrow q$ that q hold in that one world in the p band closest to the actual world. Is it necessary, as our first suggestion has it, that q hold in all the p worlds in the closest p band to the actual world? Going up until the first "pure" stretch of not-p worlds is no longer as natural a line to draw as when we imagined "pure" p neighborhoods. Since there already are some not-p worlds the same distance from A as some members of the p band, what is the special significance of the first unsullied not-p stretch? There seems to be no natural line, though, coming before this stretch yet past the first p world. Perhaps nothing stronger can be said than this: $p \rightarrow q$ when q holds for some distance out in the closest p band to the actual world, that is, when all the worlds in this first part of that closest p band are q. The distance need not be fixed as the same for all subjunctives, although various general formulas might be imagined, for example, that the distance is a fixed percentage of the width of the p band.

I put forth this semantics for subjunctives in a possible-worlds framework with some diffidence, having little inclination to pursue the details. Let me emphasize, though, that this semantics does not presuppose any realist view that all possible worlds obtain. (Such a view was discussed in the previous chapter.) I would hope that into this chapter's subjunctively formulated theoretical structure can be plugged (without too many modifications) whatever theory of subjunctives turns out to be adequate, so that the theory of knowledge we formulate is not sensitive to variations in the analysis of subjunctives. In addition to Lewis and Stalnaker cited above, see Ernest W. Adams, *The Logic of Conditionals* (Reidel, Dodrecht, 1975); John Pollock, *Subjunctive Reasoning* (Reidel, Dodrecht, 1976); J. H. Sobel, "Probability, Chance and Choice" (unpublished book manuscript); and a forthcoming book by Yigal Kvart.

9. G. C. Stine, "Skepticism, Relevant Alternatives and Deductive Closure", *Philosophical Studies*, Vol. 29, 1976, p. 252, who attributes the example to Carl Ginet.

10. This last remark is a bit too brisk, for that account might use a subjunctive criterion for when an alternative q to p is relevant (namely, when if p were not to hold, q would or might), and utilize some further notion of what it is to rule out relevant alternatives (for example, have evidence against them), so that it did not turn out to be equivalent to the account we offer.

11. More accurately, since the truth of antecedent and consequent is not necessary for the truth of the subjunctive either, 4 says something different from 1 and 2.

12. I experimented with some other conditions which adequately handled this as well as some other problem cases, but they succumbed to further difficulties. Though much can be learned from applying those conditions, presenting all the details would engage only the most masochistic readers. So I simply will list them, each at one time a candidate to stand alone in place of condition 4.

   (a) S believes that not-p → not-p.
   (b) S believes that not-p → not-p or it is through some other method that S believes not-p. (Methods are discussed in the next section.)
   (c) (S believes p or S believes not-p) → not-(S believes p, and not-p holds) and not-(S believes not-p, and p holds).
   (d) not-(S believes that p) → not-(p and S believes that not-p).
   (e) not-(p and S believes that p) → not-(not-p and S believes that p or p and S believes that not-p).

13. Gilbert Harman, *Thought* (Princeton University Press, Princeton, 1973), ch. 9, pp. 142–154.

14. What if the situation or world where he too hears the later false denials is not so close, so easily occurring? Should we say that everything that prevents his hearing the denial easily could have not happened, and does not in some close world?

15. This reformulation introduces an apparent asymmetry between the consequents of conditions 3 and 4.

Since we have rewritten 4 as

p → S believes that p and not-(S believes that not-p),

why is 3 not similarly rewritten as

not-p → not-(S believes that p) and S believes that not-p?

It is knowledge that p we are analyzing, rather than knowledge that not-p. Knowledge that p involves a stronger relation to p than to not-p. Thus, we did not first write the third condition for knowledge of p as: not-p → S believes that not-p; also the following is not true: S knows that p → (not-p → S knows that not-p).

Imagine that someone S knows whether or not p, but it is not yet clear to us which he knows, whether he knows that p or knows that not-p. Still, merely given that S knows that _____, we can say:

not-p → not-(S believes that p)

p → not-(S believes that not-p).

Now when the blank is filled in, either with p or with not-p, we have to add S's believing it to the consequent of the subjunctive that begins with it. That indicates which one he knows. Thus, when it is p that he knows, we have to add to the consequent of the second subjunctive (the subjunctive that begins with p): S believes that p. We thereby transform the second subjunctive into:

p → not-(S believes that not-p) and S believes that p.

Except for a rearrangement of which is written first in the consequent, this is condition 4. Knowledge that p especially tracks p, and this special focus on p (rather than not-p) gets expressed in the subjunctive, not merely in the second condition.

There is another apparent asymmetry in the antecedents of the two subjunctives 3 and 4, not due to the reformulation. When actually p is true and S believes that p, condition 4 looks some distance out in the p neighborhood of the actual world, while condition 3 looks some distance out in the not-p neighborhood, which itself is farther away from the actual world than the p neighborhood. Why not have both conditions look equally far, revising condition 3 to require merely that the closest world in which p is false yet S believes that p be some distance from the actual world. It then would parallel condition 4, which says that the closest world in which p yet p is not believed is some distance away from the actual world. Why should condition 3 look farther from the actual world than condition 4 does?

However, despite appearances, both conditions look at distance symmetrically. The asymmetry is caused by the fact that the actual world, being a p world, is not symmetrical between p and not-p. Condition 3 says that in the closest not-p world, not-(S believes that p), and that this 'not-(S believes that p)' goes out through the first part of the not-p neighborhood of the actual world. Condition 4 says that in the closest p world, S believes that p, and that this 'S believes that p' goes out through the first part of the p neighborhood of the actual world. Thus the two conditions are symmetrical; the different distances to which they extend stems not from an asymmetry in the conditions but from one in the actual world—it being (asymmetrically) p.

16. D. M. Armstrong, *Belief, Truth and Knowledge* (Cambridge University Press, 1973), p. 209; he attributes the case to Gregory O'Hair.

17. Some may hold the father is made more sure in his belief by courtroom proof; and hold that the father knows because his degree of assurance (though not his belief) varies subjunctively with the truth.

18. If there is no other such method M_1 via which S believes that p, the second clause is vacuously true.

Should we say that no other method used outweighs M, or that M outweighs all others? Delicate questions arise about situations where the methods tie, so that no subjunctive holds about one always winning over the other. It might seem that we should require that M outweigh (and not merely tie) the other methods; but certain ways of resolving the ties, such as not randomly deciding but keeping judgment suspended, might admit knowledge when a true belief is arrived at via a tracking method M which is not outweighed yet also doesn't (always) outweigh the others present. There is no special need to pursue the details here; the outweighing condition should be read here and below as a vague one, residing somewhere in the (closed) interval between "outweighs" and "not outweighed", but not yet precisely located. This vagueness stands independently of the refinements pursued in the text immediately below.

19. When a belief is overdetermined or jointly produced by three methods, where only the first satisfies conditions 3 and 4, the question becomes: what does the person believe when M_1 recommends believing not-p while the two others each recommend believing p? Notice also that in speaking of what would happen in Case III we are imposing a subjunctive condition; if there is no "would" about it, if in each instance of a Case III situation it is determined at random which method outweighs which, then that will not be sufficient for knowledge, even though sometimes M_1 wins out.

It is worrisome that in weakening our initial description of outweighing by looking to Case III but not to Case II, we seem to give more weight to condition 3 for tracking than to condition 4. So we should be ready to reconsider this weakening.

20. For example, in the case of the father who believes on faith that his son is innocent and sees the courtroom demonstration of innocence, does the father use two methods, faith and courtroom demonstration, the second of which does satisfy conditions 3-4 while the first (which outweighs it) does not satisfy 3-4; or does the father use only one method which doesn't satisfy 3-4, namely: believe about one's son whatever the method of faith tells one, and only if it yields no answer, believe the result of courtroom demonstration? With either mode of individuation, knowledge requires the negative existentially quantified statement (that there is no method . . .) somewhere, whether in specifying the method itself or in specifying that it is not outweighed.

21. One suspects there will be some gimmick whereby whenever p is truly believed a trivial method M can be specified which satisfies conditions 3 and 4. If so, then further conditions will have to be imposed upon M, in addition to the dispositional condition. Compare the difficulties encountered in the literature on specifying the relevant reference class in probabilistic inference and explanation; see Henry Kyburg, *Probability and the Logic of Rational Belief* (Wesleyan University Press, Middletown, 1961), ch. 9; C. G. Hempel, *Aspects of Scientific Explanation* (Free Press, New York, 1965), pp. 394-405; also his "Maximal Specificity and Lawlikeness in Probabilistic Explanation", *Philosophy of Science*, Vol. 35, 1968, pp. 116-133.

22. See Ludwig Wittgenstein, *On Certainty* (Basil Blackwell, Oxford, 1969), §§ 83, 94, 102-110, 140-144, 151-152, 162-163, 166, 411, 419, 472-475.

23. This statement is not affected by Church's Theorem on the absence of

a decision procedure for theoremhood, the absence of an algorithm for discovering a proof in a fixed finite number of steps. In some nearby worlds the method of seeking a proof, because failing to find one, will not yield any belief and so not the belief that p; but a belief that p will result via the method of believing p on the basis of a found proof that p. More generally, even with contingent statements, if M is a method that always would give the right answer when it gives an answer, but only rarely gives an answer, a person who believes on the basis of M's answer does have knowledge. His method is not 'applying M' but 'believing M's answer'.

Similar points apply to our knowledge of mathematical axioms, where it is only condition 4 that comes into play. The topic of how condition 4 comes to be satisfied for our beliefs about mathematical axioms, the topic of how we know necessary truths, is an interesting one, but is not our topic here. Neither is it our current task to formulate a theory of the nature and basis of necessary truths.

24. Michael Rabin has proposed methods of mathematical proof which do not guarantee truth, though the probability of error can be reduced to, for example, one in one billion. (Reported in *Science,* June 4, 1976, pp. 989–990.) We discuss below the complications that probability adds. (See also Hilary Putnam's discussion of "quasi-empirical methods" in mathematics in his "What Is Mathematical Truth?", *Philosophical Papers,* Cambridge University Press, 1976, Vol. I, pp. 60–78.)

25. A more difficult issue is whether a weaker 'would not' isn't enough. Granted that in all worlds close to the actual world the person would truly believe that p (when it is true) and would not falsely believe that p (when p is false), this last is satisfied if no situation or world close to the actual one is a not-p world. Why require in addition that in the closest not-p worlds, even when these are very far away, the person not believe that p? We take up these questions below, in Part II on skepticism.

26. But not always. George Pappas and Marshall Swain (*Essays on Knowledge and Justification,* Cornell University Press, Ithaca, 1978, p. 16) report the point by Fred Feldman that the person might infer the truth that someone in the office owns a Ford directly from the true evidence for the statement that the friend does, without going through this intermediate falsehood.

27. The simplicity of the antecedents of 3 and 4, not-p and p respectively, enables us to avoid the type of objections raised in Robert Shope, "The Conditional Fallacy in Contemporary Philosophy", *Journal of Philosophy,* Vol. 75, 1978, pp. 397–413. With the above holding of the method fixed, however, things become more complex and the issues Shope raises may become relevant.

28. I have obtained most of my knowledge of this literature, belatedly, from George Pappas and Marshall Swain, eds., *Essays on Knowledge and Justification* (Cornell University Press, Ithaca, 1978), and from an unpublished survey article by Robert Shope, "Recent Work on the Analysis of Knowledge", an expanded version of which will appear as a book. One of Shope's own cases also involves not holding the method fixed.

29. Ernest Sosa, "Propositional Knowledge", *Philosophical Studies*, Vol. 20, 1969, p. 39, cited in Shope.

30. L. S. Carrier, "An Analysis of Empirical Knowledge", *Southern Journal of Philosophy*, Vol. 9, 1971, p. 7, cited in Shope.

31. Keith Lehrer and Thomas Paxson, Jr., "Knowledge: Undefeated Justified True Belief", *Journal of Philosophy*, Vol. 66, 1969, p. 236, cited in Shope.

32. Carrier, *Southern Journal of Philosophy*, Vol. 9, 1971, p. 9, cited in Shope.

33. Alvin Goldman, "Discrimination and Perceptual Knowledge", *Journal of Philosophy*, Vol. 73, 1976, p. 789, cited in Shope.

34. Lehrer and Paxson, *Journal of Philosophy*, Vol. 66, 1969, pp. 225–237, reprinted in George Pappas and Marshall Swain, eds., *Essays on Knowledge and Justification* (Cornell University Press, Ithaca, 1978).

35. Thomas Paxson, Jr., "Professor Swain's Account of Knowledge", in Pappas and Swain, *Essays on Knowledge and Justification*, pp. 100–105.

36. George Pappas and Marshall Swain, "Some Conclusive Reasons against 'Conclusive Reasons'", in Pappas and Swain, *Essays on Knowledge and Justification*, pp. 63–64.

37. I owe this question to Lawrence Powers.

38. See Alvin Goldman, "Innate Knowledge", in Stephen Stich, *Innate Ideas* (University of California Press, Berkeley, 1975), pp. 111–120.

39. Armstrong, *Belief, Truth and Knowledge*, pp. 180–182.

40. Here, I can only make the vague and obscure suggestion, not pursued below, that believing something (partly) in virtue of its truth may be distinct from believing p (partly) because p. There may be a difference between explaining why someone believes something which is true (and explaining why it is true), and (on the other hand) explaining why he believes the truth. Perhaps we want the explanation of someone's belief, why it is knowledge, to bring in the notion of 'truth qua truth', rather than merely the fact p (which is believed and is true); and perhaps it is in explaining why conditions 3 and 4 hold that the notion of 'truth qua truth' must enter. Compare Quine's discussion of the necessary role of the "truth" predicate *pace* the redundancy theory of truth, in *Philosophy of Logic* (Prentice-Hall, Englewood Cliffs, 1970), pp. 10–13.

41. It is along these lines that we should treat the examples in Laurence Bonjour, "Externalist Theories of Empirical Knowledge", *Midwest Studies in Philosophy*, Vol. V (University of Minnesota Press, Minneapolis, 1980), pp. 53–73). Should we also add, when we come to the later account of justification, a further condition that it not be the case that the person is justified in believing he does not know that p? (Or, that he not be justified in believing he's not justified in believing p?) It is not clear whether this is necessary.

42. There is an immense amount of literature concerning skepticism. See, for example, Sextus Empiricus, *Writings* (4 vols., Loeb Classical Library, Harvard University Press, Cambridge); Richard Popkin, *History of Skepticism from Erasmus to Descartes* (rev. ed., Humanities Press, New York,

1964); Arne Naess, *Skepticism* (Humanities Press, New York, 1968); René Descartes, *Meditations on First Philosophy* (Liberal Arts Press, New York, 1960); G. E. Moore, "Proof of an External World", "A Defense of Common Sense", "Certainty", and "Four Forms of Skepticism" in his *Philosophical Papers* (Allen and Unwin, London, 1959); J. L. Austin, "Other Minds" in his *Philosophical Papers* (Oxford University Press, 1961); Ludwig Wittgenstein, *On Certainty* (Basil Blackwell, Oxford, 1969); Keith Lehrer, "Why Not Skepticism?" (in Swain and Pappas, eds., *Essays on Knowledge and Justification*, pp. 346–363); Peter Unger, *Ignorance* (Oxford University Press, 1975), pp. 7–24; Michael Slote, *Reason and Skepticism* (Allen and Unwin, London, 1970); Roderick Firth, "The Anatomy of Certainty", *Philosophical Review*, Vol. 76, 1967, pp. 3–27; Thompson Clarke, "The Legacy of Skepticism", *Journal of Philosophy*, Vol. 69, 1972, pp. 754–769; Stanley Cavell, *The Claim of Reason* (Oxford University Press, 1979).

43. Subjunctives with actually false antecedents and actually true consequents have been termed by Goodman *semi-factuals*. R is the semi-factual: not-$p \rightarrow$ S believes p.

44. Should one weaken condition 3, so that the account of knowledge merely denies the opposed subjunctive R? That would give us: not-(not-$p \rightarrow$ S believes p). This holds when 3 does not, in situations where if p were false, S might believe p, and also might not believe it. The extra strength of 3 is needed to exclude these as situations of knowledge.

45. Though it does show the falsity of the corresponding entailment, "not-p entails not-(S believes that p)".

46. If a person is to know that SK doesn't hold, then condition 3 for knowledge must be satisfied (with "SK doesn't hold" substituted for p). Thus, we get

(3) not-(SK doesn't hold) $\rightarrow$ not-(S believes that SK doesn't hold).

Simplifying the antecedent, we have

(3) SK holds $\rightarrow$ not-(S believes that SK doesn't hold).

The skeptic has chosen a situation SK such that the following is true of it:

SK holds $\rightarrow$ S believes that SK doesn't hold.

Having the same antecedent as 3 and a contradictory consequent, this is incompatible with 3. Thus, condition 3 is not satisfied by the person's belief that SK does not hold.

47. Let $w_1, \ldots, w_n$ be worlds doxically identical to the actual world for S. He doesn't know he is not in w_1, he doesn't know he is not in $w_2, \ldots$; does it follow that he doesn't know he is in the actual world w_A or in one very much like it (in its truths)? Not if the situation he would be in if the actual world w_A did not obtain wasn't one of the doxically identical worlds; if the world that then would obtain would show its difference from the actual one w_A, he then would not believe he was in w_A.

However, probably there are some worlds not very different from the actual world (in that they have mostly the same truths) and even doxically identical to it, which might obtain if w_A did not. In that case, S would not know he was in w_A specified in all its glory. But if we take the disjunction of these harmless worlds (insofar as drastic skeptical conclusions go) doxically identical with w_A, then S will know that the disjunction holds. For if it didn't, he would notice that.

48. This argument proceeds from the fact that floating in the tank is incompatible with being at X. Another form of the skeptic's argument, one we shall consider later, proceeds from the fact that floating in the tank is incompatible with knowing you are at X (or almost anything else).

49. Note that I am not denying that Kp & K(p $\dashv$ q) → Believes q.

50. Thus, the following is not a deductively valid form of inference.

$p \dashv q$ (and S knows this)
not-p → not-(S believes that p)
Therefore, not-q → not-(S believes that q).

Furthermore, the example in the text shows that even the following is not a deductively valid form of inference.

$p \dashv q$ (and S knows this)
not-p → not-(S believes that p)
Therefore, not-q → not-(S believes that p).

Nor is this one deductively valid:

$p \dashv q$
not-q → r
Therefore, not-p → r.

51. Does this same consequence of nonclosure under known logical implication follow as well from condition 4: p → S believes that p? When p is not actually true, condition 4 can hold of p yet not of a q known to be entailed by p. For example, let p be the (false) statement that I am in Antarctica, and let q be the disjunction of p with some other appropriate statement; for example, let q be the statement that I am in Antarctica or I lost some object yesterday though I have not yet realized it. If p were true I would know it, p entails q, yet if q were true I wouldn't know it, for the way it would be true would be by my losing some object without yet realizing it, and if that happened I would not know it.

This example to show that condition 4 is not closed under known logical implication depends on the (actual) falsity of p. I do not think there is any suitable example to show this in the case where p is true, leaving aside the trivial situation when the person simply does not infer the entailed statement q.

52. Suppose some component of the condition, call it C', also speaks of some cases when p is false, and when q is false; might it then provide "varies with", even though C' is preserved under known logical implication, and is transmitted from p to q when p entails q and is known to entail q? If this

condition C' speaks of some cases where not-p and of some cases where not-q, then C' will be preserved under known logical implication if, when those cases of not-p satisfy it, and p entails q, then also those cases of not-q satisfy it. Thus, C' seems to speak of something as preserved from some cases of not-p to some cases of not-q, which is preservation in the reverse direction to the entailment involving these, from not-q to not-p. Thus, a condition that is preserved under known logical implication and that also provides some measure of "varies with" must contain a component condition saying that something interesting (other than falsity) is preserved in the direction opposite to the logical implication (for some cases); and moreover, that component itself must be preserved in the direction of the logical implication because the condition including it is. It would be interesting to see such a condition set out.

53. Reading an earlier draft of this chapter, friends pointed out to me that Fred Dretske already had defended the view that knowledge (as one among many epistemic concepts) is not closed under known logical implication. (See his "Epistemic Operators", *Journal of Philosophy*, Vol. 67, 1970, pp. 1007–1023.) Furthermore, Dretske presented a subjunctive condition for knowledge (in his "Conclusive Reason", *Australasian Journal of Philosophy*, Vol. 49, 1971, pp. 1–22), holding that S knows that p on the basis of reasons R only if: R would not be the case unless p were the case. Here Dretske ties the evidence subjunctively to the fact, and the belief based on the evidence subjunctively to the fact through the evidence. (Our account of knowledge has not yet introduced or discussed evidence or reasons at all. While this condition corresponds to our condition 3, he has nothing corresponding to 4.) So Dretske has hold of both pieces of our account, subjunctive and nonclosure, and he even connects them in a passing footnote (*Journal of Philosophy*, Vol. 67, p. 1019, n. 4), noticing that any account of knowledge that relies on a subjunctive conditional will not be closed under known logical implication. Dretske also has the notion of a relevant alternative as "one that might have been realized in the existing circumstances if the actual state of affairs had not materialized" (p. 1021), and he briefly applies all this to the topic of skepticism (pp. 1015–1016), holding that the skeptic is right about some things but not about others.

It grieves me somewhat to discover that Dretske also had all this, and was there first. It raises the question, also, of why these views have not yet had the proper impact. Dretske makes his points in the midst of much other material, some of it less insightful. The independent statement and delineation of the position here, without the background noise, I hope will make clear its many merits.

After Goldman's paper on a causal theory of knowledge (in *Journal of Philosophy*, Vol. 64, 1967), an idea then already "in the air", it required no great leap to consider subjunctive conditions. Some two months after the first version of this chapter was written, Goldman himself published a paper on knowledge utilizing counterfactuals ("Discrimination and Perceptual Knowledge", *Journal of Philosophy*, Vol. 78, 1976, pp. 771–791), also talking of relevant possibilities (without using the counterfactuals to identify which possibilities are relevant); and Shope's survey article has called my attention to a paper of L. S. Carrier ("An Analysis of Empirical Knowledge", *Southern Journal of Philosophy*, Vol. 9, 1971, pp. 3-11) that also used subjunctive conditions including our condition 3. Armstrong's reliability view of knowledge (*Belief, Truth and Knowledge*, pp. 166, 169) involved a lawlike connection between the belief that p and the state of affairs that makes it true. Clearly, the idea is one whose time has come.

54. Is it a consequence of our view that of two people who know p, each believing he knows p and satisfying condition 3 for knowing he knows p, one may know he knows and the other not, because (although identical in all other respects) the second might encounter skeptical arguments while the first somehow lives hermetically sealed from the merest brush with them?

55. Our task now is not to wonder whether it is legitimate to use M to reach a belief that M is being used. What, after all, is the alternative? Presumably, an infinite regress of methods, or a circle, or reaching a method which is used but either is not believed to be used, or is believed to be though not via any method or way of believing.

56. See H. H. Price, "Our Evidence for the Existence of Other Minds", *Philosophy*, Vol. 13, 1938, pp. 425-456; John Wisdom, *Other Minds* (Basil Blackwell, Oxford, 1952), chs. I-V, VII; Bertrand Russell, *Human Knowledge* (Simon and Schuster, New York, 1948), Part III, ch. 2; A. J. Ayer, *The Problem of Knowledge* (Penguin Books, London, 1956), ch. 5; Norman Malcolm, "Knowledge of Other Minds", *Journal of Philosophy*, Vol. 55, 1958, pp. 969-978; P. F. Strawson, *Individuals*, ch. 3; Robert Nozick, "Testament—a Story", *Mosaic*, Vol. 12, Spring 1971, pp. 24-27, and "R.S.V.P.—a Story", *Commentary*, Vol. 53, March 1972, pp. 66-68; Stanley Cavell, "Knowing and Acknowledging" in his *Must We Mean What We Say?* (Scribners, New York, 1969), pp. 238-266, and *The Claim of Reason* (Oxford University Press, 1979), Part IV.

57. See also Cavell, *The Claim of Reason*, Part I.

58. See Daniel Dennett, "On the Absence of Phenomenology", in D. F. Gustafson and B. L. Tapscott, eds., *Body, Mind, and Method* (Reidel, Dodrecht, 1979), where this possibility is discussed but not as a skeptical hypothesis.

59. See Frederick Will, "Will the Future Resemble the Past?", *Mind*, Vol. 56, 1947, pp. 332-347; Thompson Clarke, "Seeing Surfaces and Physical Objects", in Max Black, ed., *Philosophy in America* (Cornell University Press, Ithaca, 1965), pp. 98-114.

60. First, note that our reasons for holding that knowledge is not closed under known logical implication do not extend to thinking it is not closed under known logical (or known necessary) equivalence. So let us assume $K(p \& q)$ and $Kp \to Kq$. Assume Kp, and that the person knows that p is logically equivalent to T: (r) (r $\to$ not-p $\supset$ not-r). Briefly, let us show this equivalence. We can see that p follows from T, by substituting not-p for r in

T (applying universal instantiation to T), which yields: (not-p ⊰ not-p) ⊃ not-(not-p), that is, (not-p ⊰ not-p) ⊃ p. Since the antecedent is logically true, that logical truth and the preceding statement, by modus ponens, gives us p. In the other direction, to see T follows from p, assume p is true. Then not-p is false, and since anything that entails a falsehood is false, so must anything be which entails not-p; that is, (r) (r ⊰ not-p ⊃ not-r). Now that the equivalence is shown, let us continue with the derivation. Since knowledge is (assumed to be) closed under known logical equivalence and since p is equivalent to T, from Kp we have

(1) K(r)(r ⊰ not-p ⊃ not-r).

He knows: everything that entails not-p is false. If knowledge were closed under known application of the rule of universal instantiation, it would follow from this that for any statement q which the person knows is a logical consequence of p, that is, such that K(p ⊰ q), and such that he also knows the contrapositive, not-q ⊰ not-p, knowing that not-q entails not-p, the person also knows that not-q ⊰ not-p ⊃ not-not-q, that is, it would follow that

(2) K(not-q ⊰ not-p ⊃ q).

But when not-q does entail not-p, (not-q ⊰ not-p) ⊃ q is necessarily equivalent to q. Since knowledge is closed under known necessary equivalence it follows that Kq. We have derived Kq, the conclusion that q is known, from the assumptions that p is known, p entails q (and this is known), and that knowledge is closed under known application of the rule of universal instantiation. That is, on these assumptions, we have derived the conclusion that he knows the known logical consequences of what he knows.

61. In the previous note, 2 does not follow by universal instantiation from 1. We cannot apply universal instantiation within the scope of "K" for that is to assume that knowledge is closed under known application of the rule of universal instantiation. Statement 2 can follow via this rule only from a statement whose quantifier is outside the scope of the "K", that is, from

(1') (r)K(r ⊰ not-p ⊃ not-r).

Statement 1' says that of each r, the person knows that if it entails not-p, then not-r (that is, then r is false). Whereas 1 says that the person knows that everything that entails r is false. These may appear to be equivalent but they are not.

(a) Statement 1' does not entail 1. Of each r a person might know something P without knowing that these are all the r's there are. So he need not know (r)Pr.

(b) Statement 1 does not entail 1'. If it did, since statement 2 follows from 1', 2 would follow from 1 as well. But since Kq follows from 2 when 'not-q ⊰ not-p' is known and when '(not-q ⊰ not-p ⊃ q)' is known to be necessarily equivalent to 'q', Kq would follow from 1 as well. This is just to say that knowledge is closed under known logical implication, which is false. That knowledge is not closed under known logical implication shows us that the universal quantifier cannot be exported outside the scope of the 'K', that (x)KPx does not validly follow from K(x)Px.

Though these external considerations demonstrate the point, they may not give an intuitive understanding of how it can be that a person can know (x)Px without, for a given particular a, also knowing Pa.

62. This result has been obtained by applying the account of knowledge directly to the proposition (x)Px. However, one might think that when a universal statement is known, not only must belief in it somehow vary with its truth, but also belief in each instance must somehow vary with the truth of that instance. To make this a necessary condition for knowing that (x)Px would mar a uniform account of knowledge; it is an appropriate condition, however, for knowing of each thing that it is P.

63. Let $r \dashv s$. Then $r \vdash\dashv s \& (s \supset r)$. We may assume this is known: at least I know this further fact and so for me when I know $r \dashv s$ then I know $r \vdash\dashv s \& (s \supset r)$. Suppose Kr. Then Ks&(s $\supset$ r). Now if K is closed under known entailment of a conjunct, then Ks. But s is anything known to be a logical consequence of r, so knowledge would thereby be closed under known logical implication. Thus, if knowledge is not closed generally under known logical implication, it is not closed generally under known entailment of a conjunct.

64. As would the apparent result of nonclosure under the propositional calculus rule of inferring 'p or q' from 'p', which stands to existential generalization as simplification stands to universal instantiation.

65. I have more confidence in the analogue of condition 3, that if the conclusion weren't true the person wouldn't believe the premises, as a component of the condition for the transmission of knowledge via proof, than I do in the other part of the condition, the analogue of condition 4, that if the conclusion were true then the person would believe the premises. Whatever results are based upon this second component of tracking must be taken provisionally, with the hope that these results are robust and relatively insensitive to changes in this particular condition.

66. With mathematical proof of necessary truths, the condition

not-$q \to$ not-(S believes p)

falls away (as condition 3 did earlier in our discussion of necessary truths), and so the transmission of mathematical knowledge via deductive proof from known premises depends upon whether the (fallible) person creating or reading the proof and making the inference would believe the premises if the conclusion held and (similarly considering the matter) would make the inference.

67. We can see this as follows. The person knows p and so, inferring the entailed not-q_1, truly believes not-q_1. Condition 3 for knowledge that not-q_1 also is satisfied, namely

(3) $q_1 \to$ not-(S believes not-q_1).

For, by condition 3 for knowledge that p, if p weren't to hold, he wouldn't believe p. Since q_1 is a first subjunctive alternative to p, it is one of the ways p wouldn't or mightn't hold, and so: $q_1 \rightarrow$ not-(S believes p). Since he has actually inferred not-q_1 from p, we see that he wouldn't believe the premiss p unless the conclusion not-q_1 were true. (This is the condition for knowledge to be closed under an inference.) And so he would not believe the not-q_1 he infers from p unless not-q_1 were true, which is the condition 3 written above for knowledge that not-q_1.

The fourth condition for knowledge that not-q_1

(4) not-$q_1 \rightarrow$ S believes that not-q_1

is satisfied, since the fourth condition for knowledge that p holds, $p \rightarrow$ S believes that p, and the method of inferring not-q_1 from p would give S the belief that not-q_1 for some distance out in the p neighborhood and so in the not-q_1 neighborhood of the actual world.

68. I include the qualification to take account of the situation where although the person's belief that Pa does track the fact that Pa, under the situation of there being no P—one so far out it wouldn't hold even if not-Pa— the person still would believe Pa, even when the method of belief is held fixed. In that case, the belief in the premiss would not track the truth of the conclusion, and the person would not know, via the inference, that the conclusion was true.

69. See Gilbert Harman's presentation, *Thought* (Princeton University Press, Princeton, 1973), p. 148. The puzzle arises quite naturally out of Hintikka's extendability thesis, *Knowledge and Belief* (Cornell University Press, Ithaca, 1962), pp. 20–21.

70. Can we attach all failure of closure to the failure of conjunction to distribute, and see this, when $p \rightarrow_3 q$, as stemming from the closest not-p world and the closest not-q world being different distances from the actual world? Even if this is a necessary condition for nonclosure, it will not be sufficient. For sometimes, even when the (closest) not-q world is further out, the belief that p will track the truth of q, and the person will not believe p in that further not-q world. The satisfaction of the relevant condition, that the belief in the premisses tracks the truth of the conclusion, does not depend solely on formal features.

71. Do we also need a condition to represent the fact that the knowledge gets transmitted from p to q, such as $Kp \rightarrow Kq$? Simply writing this would not represent the fact that knowledge gets transmitted via the proof (and so it would conflict with point 4). For it says, if S knew that p, whether or not he knew the proof of q from p, he would know that q. In this case, the proof is superfluous. To write a condition representing the fact that the proof transmits knowledge would require more apparatus than we have available here.

72. We suppose for the moment that a justification is meant to transmit this property from premises that have it. On another view, "justifiedness" emerges in a process yielding q from other statements which are believed or have initial credibility, but which themselves need not be justified. See Is-

rael Scheffler, "On Justification and Commitment", *Journal of Philosophy*, Vol. 51, 1954, pp. 180–190.

73. There also is the possibility of defects more serious than begging the question, as when in a purported proof of q from p, if the person weren't to know q he wouldn't (even) believe p.

74. Strictly, then, to reach our earlier conclusion that knowledge is not closed under known logical implication, we would have to add the explicit premiss that not all possible situations equally might occur (if actuality were changed or different). Within the framework of a "possible worlds" account of subjunctives, the premiss would be added that not all nonactual possible worlds have the same distance from the actual world, and in particular that there are statements p and q such that p entails q and the distances of the closest not-p world and the closest not-q world from the actual world differ.

75. Note that if

> he would not have had this dream if he were not speaking in the House of Lords,

and

> if he were speaking in the House of Lords, he would believe it, whether because awake or because if he had a dream it would be this one,

then our account of knowledge holds that he does know that he is speaking in the House of Lords (supposing it true to say he believes what he dreams).

76. Though the skeptic's argument does not show S doesn't know he knows that p, perhaps it does show something. Let

$$p^1 = \text{not-}p \rightarrow \text{not-(S believes p)}$$
$$p^2 = \text{not-}(p^1) \rightarrow \text{not-(S believes } p^1)$$
$$\cdot \cdot \cdot$$
$$p^i = \text{not-}(p^{i-1}) \rightarrow \text{not-(S believes } p^{i-1}).$$

The person knows that p only if p^1 is true. He knows he knows that p (KKp) only if he knows p^1 is true, and so only if p^2 is true. He KKKp only if p^3 is true, and so forth. Let us abbreviate p preceded by i K's as $K^i p$. A person will $K^i p$ only if p^i is true.

The skeptic's doxically identical possibility SK doesn't show that p^1 is not true, or that p^2 is not true. But for some $n+1$, it will show that p^{n+1} is not true, if eventually there will be reached a p^n such that if p^n were false then SK would or might happen—a p^n, that is, such that not-$p^n \rightarrow$ SK, or at any rate not-(not-$p^n \rightarrow$ not-SK). In that case, p^{n+1} isn't true, and the person doesn't know p^n. Therefore, the person does not $K^{n+1}p$ (although $K^n p$). Perhaps one of the p^i is false before we reach p^n with SK as a first subjunctive alternative to its antecedent; but if not, the skeptic's possibility may show that there will be a finite $n+1$ such that the person doesn't $K^{n+1}p$.

I assume that the skeptic's alternative, although farfetched, is reachable in a finite number of steps; further, that for some i, it is an ith subjunctive alternative to p. The crucial question is whether for some finite n, the skeptic's alternative SK is what would hold if not-p^n. If the skeptic can show that each time we get farther away from the actual world, the closest world where p^m doesn't hold is farther away than the closest world where p^{m-1} does not (for all m) then he will be able to show that for some n, not-$(K^{n+1}p)$.

Thus, perhaps the skeptic's example of a doxically identical world does show that for some finite n+1, not-$(K^{n+1})p$. Perhaps the skeptic's example does show that somewhere up the line of K's, we do reach a not-K, that is, that the following finite disjunction is true: not-Kp or not-KKp or not-KKKp or . . . But even if the skeptic does show this, what he shows may be remote. I trust that the reader will not now think it legitimate to swoop down the line, to argue that if not-$K^{n+1}p$ then not-$K^n p$. Still, we should reiterate that the skeptic is correct in saying that we do not know that his doxically identical possibility SK doesn't hold; and also perhaps that for most of the p we think we know, for some finite n+1, we do not $K^{n+1}p$.

77. When first formulating the account of knowledge, we considered a third condition for knowledge paralleling condition b': not-(not-$p \rightarrow$ S believes that p); if p were false he might not believe p. We held this was too weak a requirement to replace condition 3; it allowed knowledge that p when if p were false it would be a random matter whether the person believed p or not.

78. A randomized experiment simplifies the calculation of the probabilities, the likelihoods discussed below. I do not mean to exclude Duhemian considerations about testing hypotheses in isolation. The manipulation of conditions to yield the (hoped for) holding of subjunctives proceeds against a background of assumed theory. I comment below on the relevance of this assumed factual background to "logical" theories of confirmation and evidence.

Experimental manipulation of conditions to make h true also makes more secure the inference that any correlated events are effects of h. Generally, when correlations between two variables are observed we must ascertain that the correlation is not spurious, the effect of some third variable that causes each. However, when one of the variables is purposefully manipulated, we forgo such ascertaining because we assume that our manipulative act itself is not causally determined, or at least that its causes do not also cause the correlated events.

79. We do not want this probability to be simply the probability of the subjunctive conditional '$h \rightarrow e$', for (given the semantics of this conditional) it might have a high probability of being false even though (speaking loosely) if h were true, e would very probably be true. (See David Lewis, "Probabilities of Conditionals and Conditional Probabilities", *Philosophical Review*, 1976, Vol. 85, pp. 297–315.) We might want this probability prob (e,h) to be simply the conditional probability of e given h, prob (e/h), défined as prob (e and h) ÷ prob (h). Perhaps not; perhaps we want an explanation closer to the spirit of the account of subjunctives. (For some suggestions, see Jordan Howard Sobel, "Probability, Chance and Choice," unpublished manuscript.) For now though, so as not to introduce too many issues at once, we may

proceed as if it is a conditional probability. Since 'prob (e,h) is very high' is meant to be related to, and approximate 'h → e', we presuppose there will be some suitable interpretation of probability as a real empirical (perhaps dispositional) fact in the world. Theories of logical probability or personal probability are unsuitable for our purposes; those of statistical probability (as a limit of frequencies) at least are empirical; best, however, I think, would be some refinement of the propensity view of probability. See Karl Popper, "The Propensity Interpretation of Probability", *British Journal for the Philosophy of Science*, Vol. 10, 1959, pp. 25–42; and the criticisms in Lawrence Sklar, "Is Probability a Dispositional Property?", *Journal of Philosophy*, Vol. 67, 1970, pp. 355–366; see also D. H. Mellor, *The Matter of Chance* (Cambridge University Press, 1971); D. A. Gilles, *An Objective Theory of Probability* (Methuen, London, 1973). It is not my purpose to formulate such a theory here.

80. In my treatment of evidence, I leave aside issues about conflicting evidence; these are suggestively discussed in Glenn Shafer, *A Mathematical Theory of Evidence* (Princeton University Press, Princeton, 1976).

81. These probabilistic considerations also should be applied to our earlier remarks about a test of a hypothesis.

82. It would sow confusion throughout the theory, however, to calculate the prob (e, not-h) differently, as the maximum probability of *e* given any h_i that might hold if not-h did. It is best, when the time comes, to add additional clauses referring to, or excluding, such h_i.

83. Another way to see how centrally the evidence functions is to notice that, even though the rough intuition was not to believe that an improbability obtains, the additional condition we formulated was

$$\text{prob}_0 \text{ (h)} > \text{prob (e, not-h)},$$

rather than

$$\text{prob (e,h)} \times \text{prob}_0 \text{ (h)} > \text{prob (e, not-h)} \times \text{prob}_0 \text{ (not-h)}.$$

In "Detachment, Probability, and Maximum Likelihood" (*Nous*, Vol. 1, 1967, pp. 401–411), Gilbert Harman formulates another principle combining maximum likelihood with Bayesian considerations, and investigates whether it gives rise to the lottery paradox. I have not investigated whether the principle of inference we propose, all epicycles included, is open to any version of the lottery paradox. For a treatment of various approaches to this latter problem, due to Henry Kyburg (*Probability and the Logic of Rational Belief*, Wesleyan University Press, Middletown, 1961, p. 197), see Risto Hilpinnen, "Rules of Acceptance and Inductive Logic", *Acta Philosophica Fennica*, Vol. 22, 1968, pp. 1–134.

84. See R. A. Fisher, *Statistical Method and Scientific Inference*, 3rd ed. (Hafner, New York, 1973); A. W. Edwards, *Likelihood* (Cambridge University Press, 1972); Ian Hacking, *The Logic of Statistical Inference* (Cambridge University Press, 1965); Allen Birnbaum, "Concepts of Statistical Evidence", in *Philosophy, Science, and Method*, S. Morgenbesser, P. Suppes, and M.

White, eds. (St. Martins Press, New York, 1969), pp. 112–143; Barry Loewer, Robert Laddaga, and Roger Rosenkrantz, "On the Likelihood Principle and a Supposed Antinomy", in Peter Asquith and Ian Hacking, eds., *Philosophy of Science Association Proceedings* (East Lansing, Michigan, 1978), Vol. 1, no. 1, pp. 279–286.

85. For a standard and extensive exposition of this theory, commonly called the "classic" theory, see E. L. Lehman, *Testing Statistical Hypotheses* (John Wiley, New York, 1959). For difficulties relevant to some points later, see also D. P. Cox, "Some Problems Connected with Statistical Inference", *Annals of Mathematical Statistics*, Vol. 29, 1958, pp. 357–363; John Pratt, "Review of Lehman", *Journal of American Statistical Association*, Vol. 56, 1961, p. 166; Birnbaum, in *Philosophy, Science and Method;* Hacking, *Logic of Statistical Inference*, ch. 7.

86. We are given that e holds and that the principle has been applied, so that prob $(e,h) > .95$ and prob $(e,$ not-$h) < .95$; and we want to know the probability of not-h given all this. By Bayes Theorem, the prob (not-h/e) as a function of this is equal to:

$$\frac{\text{prob}_0 \text{ (not-h)} \times \text{prob (e, not-h)}}{\text{prob}_0 \text{ (not-h)} \times \text{prob (e, not-h)} + \text{prob}_0 \text{ (h)} \times \text{prob (e,h)}} \cdot$$

When prob_0 (h) $= .06$, prob_0 (not-h) $= .94$, prob $(e,h) = .95$, prob $(e,$ not-h) $= .05$, all compatible with the premises of our inference, then prob (not-h/e) is about .45, and so the probability of a type II error is greater than .05, greater than prob $(e,$ not-h). However, it will be less than $\frac{1}{2}$; this depends not only on keeping prob $(e,$ not-h) very low, but also keeping prob (e,h) very high.

87. The Neyman-Pearson theorist computes this on the basis of likelihoods (before the evidence is gathered) rather than computing it given that e has been found to hold and that the prinicple of inference has led to accepting h. So his computation is unsuitable for our purposes.

88. Might the differences leave space for finding a role for the notion of weight of evidence; there is greater weight of evidence for the probability judgment that a coin has a $\frac{1}{2}$ probability of yielding heads on the basis of many tosses where this ratio is approximated, than there is when this judgment is based on fewer (or no) tosses plus symmetry considerations, yet the probability of heads may be the same in the two cases, namely, $\frac{1}{2}$. Intuitively, the weight of evidence should play some role, yet it is difficult to see how to utilize it appropriately. (See Keynes, *Treatise on Probability*, pp. 71–78.) When evidence is more weighty, it can be partitioned into parts $e_1, \ldots, e_n$ where each e_i is sufficient to bring the principle of inference into play. Weightier evidence yields multiple applications of the principle of inference to the same conclusion. Looking externally, can the probability that all those are in (type II) error be different from (and less than) the probability of $e_1 \& e_2 \& \ldots \& e_n$ given not-h?

89. For the dominant view see John Maynard Keynes, *A Treatise on Probability* (Macmillan, London, 1921); Harold Jeffreys, *Theory of Probability*

(Oxford, 1939); Rudolf Carnap, *The Logical Foundations of Probability* (Chicago, 1950); various recent articles by J. Hintikka and his students. Hilary Putnam's criticism can be found in "'Degree of Confirmation' and Inductive Logic", in P. A. Schilpp, ed., *The Philosophy of Rudolf Carnap* (Open Court, LaSalle, 1963), pp. 761–784.

90. Compare our earlier discussion of Wittgenstein on criteria, stage setting, and context. The criteria are not logically sufficient conditions for the application of a mental predicate because there is a (logically) possible wider context where (it is shown) the criteria hold but the mental predicate does not. See also the discussion of whether explanation is deductive, how boundary conditions enter into explanation, in John Canfield and Keith Lehrer, "A Note on Prediction and Deduction", *Philosophy of Science*, Vol. 28, 1961, pp. 204–208.

91. See Norwood Russell Hanson, *Patterns of Discovery* (Cambridge University Press, 1958), p. 86; Gilbert Harman, "The Inference to the Best Explanation", *Philosophical Review*, Vol. 70, 1965, pp. 88–95.

92. See Keynes, *Treatise on Probability*, pp. 253–264; Bertrand Russell, *Human Knowledge; Its Scope and Limits* (Simon and Schuster, New York, 1948), Part VI.

93. This kind of nonclosure occurs also under some other theories of evidence, for example, Carnap's, wherein e confirms h if $c(h,e) > c_0(h)$. On this account, e may confirm h yet disconfirm a logical consequence of h, for example, the consequence 'h or not-e', which may have a degree of confirmation on e lower than its a priori degree of confirmation.

94. See William Talbott, "The Reliability of the Cognitive Mechanism: A Mechanist Account of Empirical Justification", unpublished doctoral dissertation, Harvard University, 1976; Alvin Goldman, "What Is Justified Belief?", in George Pappas, ed., *Justification and Knowledge* (Reidel, Dodrecht, 1979), and "The Internalist Conception of Justification", *Midwest Studies in Philosophy*, Vol. V (University of Minnesota Press, Minneapolis, 1980), pp. 27–52.

95. See A. J. Ayer, *The Problem of Knowledge* (Penguin Books, London, 1956), pp. 31–34.

96. One currently influential view of justification views it as a process of overall adjustment among initially credible general principles and specific instances. (See Nelson Goodman, *Fact, Fiction and Forecast*, Harvard University Press, Cambridge, 1955, pp. 65–68; Israel Scheffler, "On Justification and Commitment", *Journal of Philosophy*, Vol. 51, pp. 180–190; John Rawls, *A Theory of Justice*, Harvard University Press, Cambridge, 1971, pp. 19–22, 577–582; Nicholas Rescher, *The Coherence Theory of Truth*, Oxford University Press, 1973.) These initial credibilities presumably are like Bayesian prior probabilities or plausibilities. Such a process of mutual adjustment so as to maximize some (usually unstated) function, is not (logically) guaranteed to be empirically reliable, to have a propensity to yield true beliefs, and so it is not guaranteed to yield justified beliefs. Still, in particular types of situations it might do so; we need investigation of when and under what conditions.

97. See David Lewis, "Immodest Inductive Methods", *Philosophy of Science*, Vol. 38, 1971, pp. 54–63.

98. See R. Braithwaite, *Scientific Explanation* (Cambridge University Press, 1953), ch. VIII; Max Black, "Self Supporting Inductive Arguments" in his *Models and Metaphors* (Cornell University Press, Ithaca, 1962), pp. 209-218.

99. When the desirable feature specifies something about the probability that *h* is true, then something further needs to be said about why probability is desirable, given that it does not entail actual truth or actual specified statistical frequencies (in any finite reference class). It is not obvious what this something further should be. This problem about the worth of probability is a general one, however.

A similar issue arises in theories of rational choice where conditions are elaborated on a person's preferences among probability mixtures which suffice to yield measurement of utility on an interval scale, as well as the principle that one probability mixture is preferred to another when it has a higher expected utility. An example of such a condition on preference is that when two probability mixtures each yield the same two ultimate outcomes, that one is preferred which gives a higher probability to the more preferred outcome. If x is preferred to y, then the probability mixture px, (l-p)y, giving outcome x with probability p and outcome y with probability l-p, is preferred to the outcome qx, (l-q)y if and only if *p* is greater than *q*. This principle is obvious on the face of it. What is not obvious is why it would hold true, given any of the interpretations of probability now extant. Perhaps it is a requirement on an interpretation of probability that it immediately yield a rationale for the preference condition as a normative condition—no current interpretation does this—at least, a proponent of any current interpretation must do something to show why the condition should hold.

100. That hypothesis *h* might be such that for any *e* which is evidence for it, the fact that eRh tracks the fact that *h*, in that: not-h → not-(eRh); and h → eRh.

101. Can there be such empirical presuppositions of induction? Such a presupposition will not have its negation entail that nothing is evidence for anything else; its negation will subjunctively imply this. But then we have at least one contingent subjunctive relation holding—will there be enough others to make some evidential relations hold?

Perhaps the following would do the trick: on the likelihood conception of evidence, nothing is evidence for anything else, when

(1) For all (logically independent) e and h, prob (e,h) = prob (e, not-h).

Statement 1 entails there is no evidence, and so is not the right thing to give rise subjunctively to absence of evidence. We need some fact *f* that is evidence for 1—but then 1 itself will be false. So perhaps what is needed is something like the following: on the total facts f holding (logically independently of 1), prob (1,f) = prob (not-1,f). (But how are these nested probabilities to be understood?) Or perhaps, instead, we want to seek an explanatory hypothesis giving rise to statement 1.

102. This way of phrasing it points up an ambiguity in the notion of begging the question. Is the question of the truth of *q* begged if the person

would not accept the premises or make the inferential move to *q* if (a) he (already) rejected *q*, or if (b) he did not (already) accept *q*? An argument might beg the question against someone who already rejected *q*, but lead someone who did not already either accept or reject *q* to make the inferential move.

This is related to another ambiguity: should we say he would not accept the premises or make the move if . . . ; or that he might not accept the premises or make the move if . . . ? These two distinctions give us four possible notions of begging the question—we shall not pursue these distinctions any further here.

103. Embedded subjunctives are a morass we shall not enter here, except to note their presence when there is evidence for evidence. Given the usual view that scientific laws entail or otherwise give rise to subjunctives, and given a subjunctive view of the evidential relation, embedded subjunctives also are present when there is evidence for laws.

104. *Mind*, Vol. 4, 1895, pp. 278–280.

105. See Alvin Goldman, "The Internalist Conception of Justification", *Midwest Studies in Philosophy*, Vol. V (University of Minnesota Press, Minneapolis, 1980), pp. 27–52.

106. Covariation with what? With something internal to us. So there must be some theory of how the inner starting point is fixed, such as that in Chapter 1, Part II, above.

107. Unless (beyond the minimal amount of covariation needed for there to be a connection) the more the covariation with it, the less external it is. Such a monotonic relation, though, is implausible. Our belief covaries with the fact that there is an external universe in a wide range of situations.

108. For speculations about the evolution of different perceptual and cognitive capacities, and about alternative psychologies, see Olaf Stapledon, *Last and First Men* and *Starmaker* (Dover, New York, 1968).

109. For a suggestive discussion of such issues, see M. A. Goldberg, "On the Inefficiency of Being Efficient", *Environment and Planning A*, Vol. 7, 1975, pp. 921–939.

110. See F. A. Hayek's description of social scientific theories as explaining patterns of interrelationship rather than the particular details of the specific interrelated facts in "Degrees of Explanation" and "The Theory of Complex Phenomena", essays 1 and 2 in his *Studies in Philosophy, Politics and Economics* (University of Chicago Press, Chicago, 1967).

CHAPTER FOUR

1. On this last point, see Herbert Simon, *Models of Man* (Wiley, New York, 1957), essays 7, 8; William Starbuck, "Level of Aspiration", *Psychological*

Review, Vol. 70, 1963, pp. 51–60, "Level of Aspiration Theory and Economic Behavior", *Behavioral Science*, Vol. 8, 1963, pp. 128–136.

A realistic and illuminating picture of the process surrounding decision is presented in Irving Janis and Leon Mann, *Decision Making* (Free Press, New York, 1977).

2. Mortimer Adler and his associates give the following description of the view they term "the freedom of self-determination". "The individual's . . . freedom of choice . . . rests with his power of self-determination which, through its causal indeterminacy, is able to give dominance to one motive or one set of influences rather than another. Far from motives or other influences determining which of several decisions is made, it is the other way around . . . the self determines which motive or set of influences shall be decisive (i.e. which shall find expression in the decision made)." *The Idea of Freedom* (Doubleday, New York, 1961), Vol. II, p. 232; see also pp. 292–293.

3. Should we say the decision that bestows the comparative weights on reasons makes them, by some process of "backwards causality", always to have had those weights? One might speak either of temporally prior weights or of prior causal connections themselves being caused "backwards". Under the last, doing act A does not cause R_A to occur or to have a certain weight; rather, doing A causes it to be true that R_A caused A—while if B had been done, it would have caused it to be true that R_B caused B. On this view, free actions are those that cause their causes' causing them. Thus is blocked the intuitive argument that if the causes of our actions go back to a time before we were born then we do not control the action: though we don't control the occurrence of earlier events, we do control which ones cause (which of the alternative) current actions. Even if such a "backwards causality" theory (of either form) can be elaborated, I prefer to avoid such tangles here.

For a discussion of issues relevant to backwards causality, see Paul Horwich, "On Some Alleged Paradoxes of Time Travel", *Journal of Philosophy*, Vol. 72, 1975, pp. 432–444; also John Wheeler, "The 'Past' and the 'Delayed-Choice' Double-Slit Experiment", in A. R. Marlow, ed., *Mathematical Foundations of Quantum Theory* (Academic Press, New York, 1978).

4. See Rolf Sartorious, "The Doctrine of Precedent and the Problem of Relevance", *Archives for Philosophy of Law and Social Philosophy*, Vol. 53, 1967; and Ronald Dworkin, "Hard Cases", in his *Taking Rights Seriously* (Harvard University Press, Cambridge, 1977). Unlike Dworkin's model of the legal system (whether or not it is appropriate there), we do not claim people can make only one correct decision or that there is a uniquely correct set of weights.

5. Though it must sometimes be possible independently to check this if the claim is to have empirical content, it need not always be possible in order to put forth an explanation based on the claim. For further discussion of this point, see my "On Austrian Methodology", *Synthese*, Vol. 36, 1977, note 21.

6. Even if this last assumption cannot be checked independently for this situation, there may be evidence from other situations of the stability of his

preferences, namely, the repeated confirmation of the predictions made on the joint basis of the claim (about strongest preference) and the assumption.

7. See also the discussion of the strongest motive issue as applied to questions of free will in Rem B. Edwards, "Is Choice Determined by the 'Strongest Motive'?", *American Philosophical Quarterly*, Vol. 4, no. 1, 1967, pp. 72–78.

8. This subclass is treated as the whole by C. A. Campbell, *In Defense of Free Will* (Allen and Unwin, London, 1967), essays 2, 3.

9. See John von Neumann, *Mathematical Foundations of Quantum Mechanics* (Princeton University Press, Princeton, 1955).

10. For Simon's model see his *Models of Man*. I took this approach to the satisficing model in "The Normative Theory of Individual Choice" (unpublished doctoral dissertation, Princeton University, 1963), pp. 288–299.

11. See Sidney Winter, "Satisficing, Selection, and the Innovating Remnant", *Quarterly Journal of Economics*, Vol. 85, 1971, pp. 237–261; "Optimization and Evolution", in R. H. Day and T. Groves, eds., *Adaptive Economic Models* (Academic Press, New York, 1975), pp. 73–118.

12. See his "Deductive Nomological vs. Statistical Explanation" in H. Feigl and G. Maxwell, eds., *Minnesota Studies in the Philosophy of Science*, Vol. III (University of Minnesota Press, Minneapolis, 1962), pp. 98–169; and *Aspects of Scientific Explanation* (Free Press, New York, 1965), pp. 376–412.

13. See Gilbert Harman, *Thought* (Princeton University Press, 1973), pp. 135–140; Peter Railton, "A Deductive-Nomological Model of Probabilistic Explanation", *Philosophy of Science*, Vol. 45, 1978, pp. 206–226.

14. On the view of a free choice as one that tracks bestness, to be discussed in Part II of this chapter, a choice's being free is not incompatible with its being given a Turing machine representation. However, such a representation does not yield understanding of a free choice, that is, does not capture choice in its aspect of being free.

Suppose that under certain conditions C a person will apprehend certain moral truths T and so move into a state of believing these truths, from which state actions B flow appropriately. A theorist says: there is a causal law, C causes B. If conditions C (about states of the organism, its previous experiences and learning, and so on) do fall within the domain of a Turing machine psychology, we will be able to represent the choices in approved Turing machine fashion. The Turing machine account, utilizing deterministic automata, is compatible with the apprehension of moral truths playing a role in action. (So is one that uses probabilistic or indeterministic automata.) It just leaves such apprehension out of its story. The apprehension enters into explaining why C causes B. That there are causal conditions under which someone tracks a truth, and comes to believe it, does not show that the statement's being true plays no role in his believing it.

Karl Popper has followed quantum physics in holding that the physical world is indeterministic, not every physical event has a causally sufficient physical event that causes it; he also holds that the physical world is open in that some of those physically undetermined physical events are produced or caused or affected by factors outside of the physical realm. Our reflections have just led to another notion of openness, one compatible with (but not requiring) physical determinism of all physical events. Under this type of openness, call it second level openness, the explanation of one physical event may be another one, but the explanation of why one causes another leads out of the physical realm. (To make this notion precise, we should have to delineate the role nonphysical truths play here in explaining why one event causes another, distinguishing this from the role mathematical truths play within physics.) The physical world can be open at the second level even if it is closed at the first (Popperian) level. Although such a picture is a coherent one, I think, it leaves obscure the crucial point: how apprehension of the moral truths works.

15. A proponent of this mode of understanding as the sole mode must be careful in stating his thesis. The thesis cannot be that we understand a notion only if we know how it would be decided by a Turing machine, for since the notion of 'effectively decidable by a Turing machine' is itself not, if the thesis were true we could not understand it. Various weakenings of the thesis also fail—the set of Gödel numbers of Turing machines which are effective algorithms, which halt, is not even recursively enumerable—leaving it unclear how to state the thesis in a plausible form.

16. Compare W. V. Quine, *Ontological Relativity* (Columbia University Press, New York, 1969), pp. 44, 60.

17. A treatment of decision by someone within the phenomenological tradition is Paul Ricoeur's *Freedom and Nature* (Northwestern University Press, Evanston, 1966); however, I have not found this work helpful.

18. See Israel Kirzner, *Competition and Entrepreneurship* (University of Chicago Press, Chicago, 1973), for a discussion of (the uses within economic theory of) the distinction between maximizing, in the manner of Lionel Robbins, a pre-given objective function among pre-given alternative actions, and entrepreneurial alertness. Since this chapter was written Kirzner has published a book of essays congenial to the position about weighting reasons presented here. See his *Perception, Opportunity, and Profit* (University of Chicago Press, Chicago, 1980), especially ch. 13.

19. Compare Wittgenstein's statement, *Philosophical Investigations*, paragraph 197.

20. Compare Gilbert Ryle's discussion of whether, on the volition theory, the having of a volition is a voluntary act which therefore needs its own separate volition, in *The Concept of Mind* (Hutchinson's University Library, London, 1949), p. 67.

21. Suppose someone says that all human behavior is caused by simple unconditioned reflexes. He doesn't claim to know all of the eliciting stimuli; that is a task for future research. Immediately, we would be suspicious. Such an arrangement involves a great preestablished harmony. Organisms with such rigidly programmed behavior would not do well in a world of changes in what brought them (access to the) necessities for life. It would be useful for an organism to be subject at least to Pavlovian respondent conditioning.

This would enable it to succeed in a wider range of environments. If the capacity for being subject to Pavlovian conditioning arose by random mutation, we would expect it to be selected for in the process of evolution.

Suppose next that someone says there are only simple unconditioned reflexes and Pavlovian respondent conditioning. It used to be thought that respondent conditioning involved only stimulus substitution; this is now thought to be false, but respondent conditioning is confined to a narrow range of behaviors. So it would be very useful for an organism to be operantly conditionable. If the capacity to be conditioned operantly arose by random mutation, we would expect it to be selected for in the process of evolution. These considerations are familiar. (See B. F. Skinner, *Science and Human Behavior*, Macmillan, New York, 1953, chs. 4–5.)

Each of the later stages of conditioning is adaptive because of limitations of the previous psychological mechanisms. Are there limitations to operant conditioning so that a similar story can be told again? Arguments about whether operant conditioning can account for some bit of behavior tend to be unsatisfactory. The question is not whether there is a piece of behavior that in principle couldn't be produced by operant conditioning plus reflexes. Perhaps there is no particular bit of behavior impossible for a simple or Pavlovian reflex, either. Their limitations are not that they cannot produce some particular behavior, but that an organism, all of whose behavior is produced by just those mechanisms, would be limited.

Given the facts of the world, there are actions a Skinnerian organism will not (be led to) do. The theory, being empirical, excludes some actions in the world as it is, and some of these actually excluded actions may be adaptive. Let us look at limitations of the operant conditioning process. Under it, behavior is shaped in a particular direction, new behavior patterns are established whose properties (longevity, resistance to extinction, and so on) depend upon the previous schedules and contingencies of reinforcement. One structural feature is this: behavior that is far from the organism's normal and current repertoire will not be forthcoming unless there are intermediate reinforcements between its normal behavior and that. Thus, pigeons can be "shaped up" to stretching their necks to heights unfound in their natural behavior (or emitted at random with only minuscule probability), by reinforcing higher stretches and then, when a new plateau of behavior is reached, raising the standards and reinforcing only the highest stretches of these, and so forth. The pigeon is brought to the very highest stretches only when its environment includes (temporary) reinforcement for the intermediate ones, intermediate as compared to the later heights. Unless this intermediate stretching behavior is reinforced temporarily, the pigeon is not carried along the path to the extremal behavior.

Consider this analogy (from the literature on optimization and linear programming). A nearsighted person standing in hilly countryside wants to determine which is the highest site around, where he has promised to meet someone. Since he can see only ten feet in any direction, he uses the following procedure. He looks around in all directions and proceeds to the highest

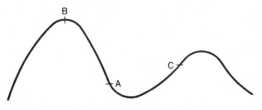

FIGURE N.7

point he sees, if it is higher than where he is. (Let us assume no ties.) Upon reaching that point, he repeats the process. He stops when he has reached a point which is higher than anywhere else in the circle around him of ten foot radius. By these means, though he will reach the highest point in his immediate vicinity (a local optimum), he will reach the highest point in the whole area only if circumstances are extremely propitious, namely, only if there is some path of locally highest points leading from where he starts to the very highest site. In a two dimensional representation, if he starts out at point A he will get to the highest point B, but if he starts out at point C (which is higher than the A starting point) he will reach the top of the small hill but not of the larger one. The gradient method (as it is called) leads to a local optimum, with no guarantee of reaching a global optimum.

The analogy to operant conditioning is clear. Operant conditioning leads an organism to behavior only if there is an upward path of reinforcement leading from its current behavior to that. It would be very useful for an organism to have a way to look around, to see farther and sometimes to travel downhill in order to reach a distant higher site. One mechanism that leads to occasional downhill travel is a random behavior generator that operates sometimes. But this is unlikely to operate at the most appropriate moments.

It would be useful to have a way of getting to beneficial actions even when no intermediate ones are reinforced. If some capacity enabling one to do this arose by random mutation, we would expect it to be selected for in the process of evolution. (Furthermore, the new modes of behavior might themselves push the process of evolution in certain directions, by putting the organism in new environments where different things were selected for. Jacques Monod gives the example of horses' running in *Chance and Necessity*, Knopf, New York, 1971, pp. 125–128.) Many of the things cognitive psychologists speak of, information processing, trying out hypotheses in imagination, and so on, would seem to suit this purpose of transcending some limits of operant conditioning. (Daniel Dennett, in "Why the Law of Effect Won't Go Away", reprinted in his *Brainstorms*, pp. 71–89, also discusses the limitations of operant conditioning and the adaptiveness of cognitive mechanisms within an evolutionary framework, arguing that similar selective principles operate in processes of operant conditioning and within the internal cognitive mechanism.)

True, this is not the best of all possible worlds—not everything that would be useful has arrived. Nevertheless, the following principle seems appropriate. If (a) we can see the limitations of certain processes, such as operant conditioning; (b) we can see what other processes would be selected for if they arose, such as cognitive processes; and (c) apart from these considerations, we naturally think anyway that such other processes are taking place in us, then we should be very suspicious of theories that deny the existence of these processes. Such theories carry a heavy burden of proof.

Even psychologists who hold that operant conditioning is limited will have reason to applaud its vigorous investigation; only then will they learn what remains for them to explain differently. Those who believe innate mechanisms have evolved, overcoming some limitations of operant conditioning, will grant that such mechanisms would evolve (in an organism subject to operant conditioning) only if operant conditioning itself was not already doing the particular job the innate mechanisms are to do. Otherwise, the innate mechanisms, bestowing no special advantage, would not be selected for. (Or did they come first, before the capacity for operant conditioning?)

The principle we have written is a general one; it does not apply only to operant conditioning and the cognitive mechanisms that surmount some of its limitations. The principle also would apply to consciousness and self-awareness, provided we identify the functions these perform and the limitations they overcome. And the principle applies to our current concern, free will. If we can describe an evolutionary function for free will so that, however it works, we would expect it to be selected for if it arose, because it overcomes limitations of its absence, and if apart from these considerations we naturally think anyway that we do make (some) free choices, then we should be very suspicious of theories denying free will, and should view these theories as carrying a heavy burden of proof.

One final remark: that something would be adaptive does not entail that it would spread throughout the population, even when present. Do some theorists deny we have free will because *they* don't have it?

22. A connection between self-consciousness and self-reference and free will is made in John Lucas, *The Freedom of the Will* (Oxford University Press, 1970); compare also Douglas Hofstadter's more recent discussion of (in his terminology) strange loops and tangled hierarchies as underlying consciousness and free will in *Gödel, Bach and Escher* (Basic Books, New York, 1979), ch. 20.

23. It cannot, said Descartes, have a greater degree of material reality than the cause does of formal reality. See *Meditations*, III, and see also the recent discussions of Descartes' principle in Margaret Wilson, *Descartes* (Routledge and Kegan Paul, London, 1978), pp. 136–138, and Bernard Williams, *Descartes* (Penguin Books, London, 1978), ch. 5.

24. See Roderick Chisholm, *Perceiving* (Cornell University Press, Ithaca, 1957), ch. 11; Charles Taylor, *The Explanation of Behavior* (Routledge and Kegan Paul, London, 1964); W. V. Quine, *Word and Object* (MIT Press, Cambridge, 1960), chs. 4–6; Daniel Dennett, *Content and Consciousness* (Routledge and Kegan Paul, London, 1969).

25. It would be boring and unilluminating to say the notion of reflexiveness, happening in virtue of a feature bestowed by its happening, analytically entails that it is uncaused by something else—just as it is to say "new" knowledge cannot be predicted beforehand, for then it would not be new. (For this argument, see Karl Popper, *The Poverty of Historicism*, Beacon Press, Boston, 1957, Preface.) From the logical truth that an unpredicted event is not predicted, nothing interesting follows about (the limits of) prediction.

26. A view that denied the possibility of self-reference might see an act that weighed a threat as always of greater depth than the threat; however, that denial is not open to our theory here.

27. Neither do I yet reject it. It leads us, though, to reexamine some situations that might appear to present counterexamples to it. Does p entail that p is true, where the second fact has greater semantic depth than the first? (The entailment does go in the reverse direction, but this presents no problems.) The fact that p, unlike the fact that p is true, does not entail the existence of vehicles of truth such as propositions or sentences or whatever, so how can the former fact entail the latter?

28. There are analogies though. Consider how within Kripke's structuring of truth (in *Journal of Philosophy*, Vol. 72, pp. 708–709) it is left open whether "this sentence is true" is true; that can be handled either way. (So it provided us with a case of reflexiveness; it is true in virtue of a feature bestowed in its being true.) The fact that the truth values of all the other nonreflexive sentences do not fix or entail anything about the truth value of this one, is analogous to the fact (if it is one) that the occurrence of a reflexive self-subsumptive act is not entailed (or caused) by other facts.

29. If universal causal determinism is true then the only thing with originative value is the initial condition of the universe at its origin. Should this consequence lead us to develop another notion that applies to some other things as well?

30. On fatalism, see Gilbert Ryle, *Dilemmas* (Cambridge University Press, 1954), ch. 2, "It Was To Be"; Michael Dummett, *Truth and Other Enigmas* (Harvard University Press, Cambridge, 1978), essays 18, 19.

31. The weaker notion fits condition III; if the act were not (even) permissible or maximal, S wouldn't do it. On this weaker notion, though, condition IV is too strong. A person well might intentionally not do A, even though A is permissible or maximal, provided that not doing A also is permissible or maximal. What fits condition IV is the stronger notion, mandatory or better than all others: if A were mandatory or maximum then S would intentionally do A. However, this stronger notion makes condition III too strong, saying that if the action weren't mandatory or maximum, the person wouldn't do it. A person appropriately might do an act that was not mandatory or maximum, provided it was permissible or maximal. No parallel difficulties arise for the tracking conditions for belief because there cannot be ties for truth among contradictories or contraries. There is no middle truth value to parallel "permissible but not mandatory" or "none better but not superior to all others".

The tracking conditions for action must differ from those for belief, because what action tracks, namely rightness or bestness, differs in structure from truth, what belief tracks.

32. Does some situation about action parallel the case that in Chapter 1 motivated the fourth condition: the tank case, wherein the (content of the) fact believed plays a causal role in getting it believed. That fact can have effect even before it is believed. Whereas an action, before it is done, is merely a possibility; the moral or evaluative fact that it is (or would be) right or best appears not to have similar direct causal powers. Only through people's apprehension of them, it appears, can such facts act. Still, the fourth condition, a subjunctive adherence condition, is needed to exclude some cases that satisfy the first three conditions. Examples to show the necessity of condition 4 must follow an indirect route, however.

Suppose person S wants only to do what his friend wants him to do. This friend wants him not to do act A; but another person T who knows that doing A is right (mandatory), tricks S into thinking the friend does want him to do A. If A weren't right, S wouldn't do it. For, if it weren't right, T wouldn't have gotten S to think his friend wanted him to do it. (Further we suppose, it is not that if A weren't right the friend then would want S to do it and would communicate this desire to S.) Thus condition 3 is satisfied. But S is not tracking rightness or bestness. If T had not acted, S would realize what his friend's desire was, and would intentionally not do A even though A was mandatory; without T's act, S would wrongly not do A. The fourth condition is needed to exclude this as a case of tracking rightness.

33. We need not repeat the explanation of 'outweighed' here, from Chapter 3 above. Notice that the text proceeds as though satisfying conditions 3 and 4 is sufficient to make a motive a moral one, and so does not impose any additional substantive requirement on the motive M; that too might be a course worth pursuing.

34. Though 'he knows A is right' is equivalent to conditions 1–4, we do not understand "S does A because he knows A is right" as: S does A because 1 and 2 and 3 and 4. It is unclear what it means for the subjunctives 3 and 4 to follow the "because", what it means for something to be done because 3 and 4. Instead of following the "because", the subjunctives 3 and 4 tell us what kind of "because" it is; they tell us how the "because" operates.

35. These last remarks must be restricted to situations where tracking is transitive; to situations where if S's act A tracks his belief that A is right, and his belief that A is right tracks the fact that it is, then S's act A tracks also the fact that A is right. Just as the subjunctive 'if-then' is not always transitive, neither is the notion of tracking that depends upon such subjunctives. Transitivity of tracking can fail because though the action tracks the belief and the belief tracks the fact, the action does not track the belief where the belief tracks the fact.

We shall assume henceforth that our attention is restricted to situations where such transitivity holds. However long the tracking chains, we assume that each thing z tracks its predecessor y where y tracks its predecessor x, and so on. Notice that "and so on" means that z tracks y in the place where y tracks x where x tracks w. If we were to offer a partial account of "doing intentionally" for those cases where an action is done on a prior intending, then we would have reached some tracking chains wherein actions track intentions that track beliefs that track facts.

Let us note some further details on the nontransitivity here assumed away. Transitivity fails when

(3) If A weren't permissible then S would not believe it was; and
(6) If S weren't to believe A is permissible then S wouldn't intentionally do A,

yet it is not true that

T: If A weren't permissible then S wouldn't intentionally do A.

Such a situation is brought out most easily using possible-worlds talk. Let w_3 be the closest possible world where A is not permissible. Suppose also in this world, and throughout its band, that S does not believe A is permissible. So condition 3 is satisfied. Suppose in w_3 that S intentionally does A. So T is not satisfied. It remains only to show that condition 6 can be satisfied compatibly with all this; then we will have a case where 3 and 6 are satisfied but T is not. Suppose w_1 is a world closer than w_3 to the actual world. In w_1, A is permissible, but in w_1 S has no belief about A's permissibility, and so S does not believe A is permissible. Suppose also that in w_1 S does not intentionally do A. On usual accounts, this shows that 6 is satisfied.

On our account in Chapter 3 note 8, condition 6 will be satisfied given further suppositions. Suppose also that w_3 is not in the (S doesn't believe A is permissible)–band of the actual world, that is, that there is a w_2 between w_3 and w_1 where S believes A is permissible; suppose also that up until that first such w_2, S does not intentionally do A. So S does not intentionally do A throughout the (S doesn't believe A is permissible)–band of the actual world, and therefore 6 is satisfied. In w_3 and outward, the belief tracks the fact but the action does not track the belief there, but only closer.

36. Compare William James, "The Will to Believe", and "The Sentiment of Rationality", in his *The Will to Believe and Other Essays* (Harvard University Press, Cambridge, 1979), pp. 13–33, 57–89. A recent discussion of related issues is Lionel Tiger, *Optimism: The Biology of Hope* (Simon and Schuster, New York, 1979).

37. One of the three central notions of freedom identified in a lengthy survey of ideas of freedom and controversies about them—the acquired freedom of self-perfection—fits here. See Mortimer Adler and associates, *The Idea of Freedom*, 2 vols. (Doubleday, New York, 1958, 1961).

38. Karl Popper, *Objective Knowledge* (Oxford University Press, 1972), chs. 3, 4, 6. Also, in P. A. Schilpp, *The Philosophy of Karl Popper* (Open Court, LaSalle, Illinois, 1974), pp. 143–153, and *Replies to Critics*, pt. IV.

39. See Paul Meehl, "Psychological Determinism and Human Rationality", *Minnesota Studies in the Philosophy of Science*, Vol. IV (University

of Minnesota Press, Minneapolis, 1970), pp. 310–372; and Paul Meehl and Herbert Feigl, "The Determinism-Freedom and Body-Mind Problems", in Schilpp, ed., *The Philosophy of Karl Popper*, pp. 520–559. Popper's reply to Meehl and Feigl, pp. 1072–1078, completely ignores their claim to have shown, within a causal deterministic framework, how rational considerations can affect actions.

40. See Robert Paul Wolff, *The Autonomy of Reason* (Harper Torchbooks, New York, 1973), pp. 208–209.

41. Also, evolutionary theory constrains the principle of charity; not every rationally connected set of beliefs and preferences yields evolutionarily adapted actions. The rational beliefs we attribute to beings must be causally explicable as arising through the interaction of an innate biological and intellectual constitution with their environment. That innate constitution (which the explanation attributes to them) also must have been reasonably well adapted to their species' evolutionary past, for as far back as its having that constitution goes.

42. Other important conditions need to be satisfied for the organism to reduce rational considerations, because organisms (for example, insects) can behave effectively in a range of environments without being rational. What these other considerations are is a matter of great interest, but unnecessary to our present task of showing how rational considerations can be reflected, qua rational considerations, within the physical realm. The great hurdle is the one we are discussing, even though jumping it does not provide a sufficient condition for rationality within the physical realm.

43. Here I disagree with a recent writer, Robert Cummins ("Functional Analysis", *Journal of Philosophy*, Vol. 72, 1975, especially pp. 750–751), who argues that evolutionary explanations do not explain why an item in an organism exists, but only why organisms with that item exist. "But this is not to explain why e.g. contractile vacuoles occur in certain protozoans, it is to explain why the sort of protozoan incorporating contractile vacuoles occurs." Cummins' reasons for saying evolution does not explain why contractile vacuoles exist are: the explanation of this fact is the existence of a genetic plan that includes specification for contractile vacuoles; and evolution does not explain why their genetic plan includes this specification (that is explained by random mutation and history), but only why genetic plans without this specification are extinct.

However, there appears to be no significant difference in this regard between the item and the organism. There is a causal story about the existence of both the item and the organism, also about the survival of the organism and of organisms like it. Each causal story refers to genetic material in whose causal history random events occurred. A causal story does not exclude an evolutionary explanation, when the causal story is of the evolutionary sort. There seems to be no difference of type between the evolutionary causal story about the existence of the organism, and the one about the existence of the organism's part. To be sure, the explanation of why there are such parts in the world will go through the explanation of why there are organisms with those parts in the world.

Perhaps Cummins will hold there is no evolutionary explanation of why there are organisms with those parts; there is only an evolutionary explanation of why there are not now organisms *without* those parts. However, the explanation (they all died without leaving viable progeny) at best explains why there are no sufficiently similar organisms without those parts, where an organism is sufficiently similar if it does not have the part and also doesn't have any other part that (as effectively) performs the function of that part. And of a particular organism which is sufficiently similar (it happened to come into brief existence by random mutation) we can tell a causal story about why it died early or left no progeny: it just didn't have some part to do a certain specified job. Since Aristotle also could have told such a causal tale about such an organism, the only explanation Cummins might provide of why there are not now organisms without those parts can hardly be said to draw upon the resources of evolutionary theory.

44. Donald T. Campbell, "'Downward Causation' in Hierarchically Organized Biological Systems", in F. J. Ayala and T. Dobzhansky, *Studies in the Philosophy of Biology* (Macmillan Press, London, 1974), pp. 179-186. "Where natural selection operates, through life and death at a higher level of organization, the laws of the higher-level selective system determine in part the distribution of lower-level events and substances. Description of an intermediate-level phenomenon is not completed by describing its possibility and implementation in lower level terms. Its presence, prevalence of distribution (all needed for a complete explanation of biological phenomena) will often require references to laws at a higher level of organization as well . . . all processes at the lower levels of a hierarchy are restrained by and act in conformity to the laws of the higher levels" (p. 180).

45. In Karl Popper's terminology, we are saying of certain world 2 mental states and of their world 1 physical reducers that their function is to exhibit certain world 3 rational patterns.

46. Hilary Putnam, *Mind, Language and Reality* (*Philosophical Papers,* Vol. 2), essays 18, 21 (Cambridge University Press, 1975).

47. To preserve the possibility that mental states might have no physical or other internal nonmental structure, we can say that a state corresponding to our mental state must have not only the same functional interconnections as our physical state that realizes the functional state, but also the same internal configuration, if it has any internal configuration at all.

48. Note that this in no way undercuts our earlier discussion of tracking rational considerations; there, a physical state's having the (biological) function of realizing rational considerations was held to be part of a set of sufficient conditions for tracking rationality, rather than a necessary condition.

49. See his "What is Cantor's Continuum Problem?", reprinted in Paul Benacerraf and Hilary Putnam, *Philosophy of Mathematics* (Prentice-Hall, Englewood Cliffs, New Jersey, 1964), pp. 258-273; and consider how the arguments in P. F. Strawson's "Ethical Intuitionism" (*Philosophy,* Vol. 24, 1949, pp. 23-33) fare against this view.

50. W. D. Hamilton, "The Genetical Theory of Social Behaviour", *Journal of Theoretical Biology,* Vol. 7, 1964, pp. 1-52; "Selection of Selfish and Al-

truistic Behavior in Some Extreme Models" in J. F. Eisenberg et al., eds., *Man and Beast* (Smithsonian Press, Washington, D.C., 1971), pp. 57–91, and "Altruism and Related Phenomena", *Annual Review of Ecology and Systematics*, Vol. 3, 1972, pp. 193–232; Robert Trivers, "The Evolution of Reciprocal Altruism, *Quarterly Review of Biology*, Vol. 46, 1971, pp. 35–57; and Edward O. Wilson, *Sociobiology* (Harvard University Press, 1975), especially ch. 5, pp. 106–129. Of closely related interest are two other articles by Trivers, "Parental Investment and Sexual Selection" in Bernard Campbell, ed., *Sexual Selection and the Descent of Man* (Aldine, Chicago, 1972), pp. 136–179, and "Parent-Offspring Conflict", *American Zoologist*, Vol. 14, 1974, pp. 249–264. See also R. Dawkins, *The Selfish Gene* (Oxford University Press, 1976). More generally, see G. C. Williams, *Adaption and Natural Selection* (Princeton University Press, Princeton, 1966), and his *Sex and Evolution* (Princeton University Press, Princeton, 1975), as well as a volume he edited, *Group Selection* (Aldine, Chicago, 1971). As one would expect, those other lovers of invisible-hand explanation, micro-economists, have taken to this theory. See Jack Hirshleifer, "Economics from a Biological Viewpoint", *Journal of Law and Economics*, Vol. 20, 1977, pp. 1–52, "Natural Economy vs. Political Economy", *Journal of Social and Biological Structures*, Vol. 1, 1978, and "Competition, Cooperation and Conflict in Economics and Biology" (forthcoming).

51. Let me give two examples. Williams (*Sex and Evolution*, ch. I), following John Maynard Smith, holds that sexual reproduction needs explaining, since the loss of genes in meiotic oogenesis gives sexual reproduction a 50 percent disadvantage in comparison to parthenogenetic reproduction producing diploid eggs of parental genotype. However, it is not relevant to follow the passing along of all the genes (and so impute a 50 percent loss); only the gene for sexual reproduction is relevant, and it is passed along (by both parents let us assume) to all offspring and so is at no disadvantage in comparison to the gene for asexual reproduction passed along asexually. (E. O. Wilson repeats this mistake and unfortunately also offers a group selection argument, in *Human Nature*, Harvard University Press, Cambridge, 1978, pp. 122–123.) A second example: writing on parent-offspring conflict, Trivers ignores the fact that heritable tactics an offspring uses to induce more investment in it than the parent wishes to give also will be used against it by its own offspring in the next generation; a child C's inclusive fitness is diminished by that of its own offsprings' inherited fitness that is in competition with C's. There are other examples in the literature—I have picked two of the best writers.

52. For example, John Maynard Smith argues that persons who do dominated actions in prisoners' dilemma situations are selected against, so situations are unstable that contain only such people, since a mutation to perform the dominant action would be selected for. However, if persons are genetically prone to perform the dominated action and to punish deviators, and to sanction those who do not cooperate in punishing deviators, and so on, then since at every level the dominant action will be discouraged, the situation

will be stable. Such a possibility is described by Trivers, but he considers only the possibility that the tendency to punish those who perform the dominant action in prisoners' dilemma situations, and to reciprocate dominated actions only to those who would perform them, is genetically based. Such punishing and reciprocating behavior might be widespread but culturally based; in that case there would not have been selective pressure to build it into the genes. Between these alternatives lies a genetically based predisposition to learn certain behaviors or connections very easily. (See Martin Seligman and Joanne Hager, eds., *Biological Boundaries of Learning*, Appleton-Century-Crofts, New York, 1972.)

Suppose, however, that Trivers is correct and the punishing behavior toward nonaltruists is genetically based. (According to Trivers' terminology, an altruistic act detracts from an organism's inclusive fitness while enhancing that of others; a general altruist does altruistic acts to anyone provided the total benefits are greater than the total costs; a sacrificer does altruistic acts to anyone even if the total benefits are less than the costs to himself; a reciprocal altruist does altruistic acts when the total benefits are greater than the total costs, but he does them only to those who also do altruistic acts if the total benefits are greater than the total costs; a nonaltruist does acts only if the benefits to him are greater than the costs to him.) We can take the process one step further. Suppose a society of reciprocal altruists arises, as a result of the factors Trivers discusses. At that time, a general altruist is no longer at a disadvantage, for he is surrounded by those who will be altruistic to him. From this state, general altruism can come back to some extent, via genetic drift at least. When it does, the nonaltruists are not at such a great disadvantage, since there then are some general altruists around to help them. Is there some stable equilibrium, reasonably long lasting, of all three groups together: reciprocal altruists, general altruists, and nonaltruists? If so, this might explain moral disagreements of a deep sort, conflicting intuitions, and the feeling that others simply are not seeing something.

53. B. F. Skinner, "Superstition in the Pigeon", *Journal of Experimental Psychology*, Vol. 38, 1948, pp. 168–172, and *Science and Human Behavior* (Macmillan, New York, 1953); Richard Herrnstein, "On the Law of Effect", *Journal for the Experimental Analysis of Behavior*, Vol. 13, 1970, pp. 243–266, and "Quantitative Hedonism", *Journal of Psychiatric Research*, Vol. 8, 1971, pp. 399–412. A fine textbook presentation of the material is R. Brown and R. Herrnstein, *Psychology* (Little, Brown, Boston, 1975), chs. 1, 2. Doubt has recently been cast upon the generality of Skinner's superstition experiments, but since these doubts point to evolutionarily based behavioral predispositions, they do not lead out of the invisible-hand realm.

The framework of operant conditioning explanation has been applied to social behavior, but not in invisible-hand fashion, by George Homans in his *Social Behavior* (rev. ed., Harcourt, Brace, Jovanovich, New York, 1974). A discussion of socialization that emphasizes the distinction between side effects and intended consequences is Robert A. LeVine, *Culture, Behavior and Personality* (Aldine, Chicago, 1973), Part III.

54. The explanation (1) will need a list of the innate behaviors $B_1, \ldots, B_n$ of infants; (2) will offer an account of how adults doing behaviors $C_1, \ldots, C_n$ in interactions with infants doing B_i lead them to do $D_1, \ldots, D_n$; (3) will offer an account of how the interactions of those doing D_i, along with adults doing $E_1, \ldots, E_n$ leads to performing behaviors E; and (4) will offer an account of how the C_i and E_i originally arose, presumably from the behavior of the primate ancestors. Each of the steps will involve only blind invisible-hand explanations, side effects, and so on. There is no point here to elaborating possibilities about complicated sequential interactions of behavior, continuities and discontinuities with animal behavior, and so forth.

55. No one claims it is only predispositions to ethical behavior that evolution has instilled, no one who has looked at history's record of genocide, slavery, pogroms, aggressive warfare, plunder, and statism. The claim would have to be, rather, that ethical behavior in its (rare?) occurrences has an evolutionary explanation too, one that connects it to why it is right.

56. Invisible-hand explanations can be offered in the human realm. Economists do offer invisible-hand explanations of complicated interactive market patterns and equilibria; but not of the behavior individuals have in mind and reflect about under that description.

57. It may not be apparent whether a social scientific or psychological explanation refers to moral properties or not. Consider a purported psychological law maintaining that people react in certain ways (with sanctioning behavior) in circumstances when a norm is violated. (A norm is explained as a pattern, deviations from which are sanctioned, such that the explanation for the sanctions involves their being applied to actions qua deviations from the pattern.) Alternatively, consider the psychological law that when people realize something wrong is done, they react with sanctions, and so forth. If the first psychological law is just the second translated, by including a detailed factual condition coextensive with a sufficient condition for something's being wrong, then it will not undercut that area of ethics. (See Brown and Hermstein, *Psychology*, pp. 253-282, but read their discussion of expectations as speaking of morally legitimate expectations.) The nonmoral psychological explanation must start with more general laws and show that the regularity about ethics falls under general regularities that apply also outside the area of ethics. It will not do to use psychological laws geared only to moral situations. I elaborate a similar point about methodological individualist explanations of sociological phenomena in my essay "On Austrian Methodology", *Synthese*, Vol. 36, 1977, pp. 353-357.

58. The evidence concerning this assumption is discussed in Seymour Fisher and Roger Greenberg, *The Scientific Credibility of Freud's Theories and Therapy* (Basic Books, New York, 1977), ch. 9.

59. The intuitive idea must be refined a bit, for a partial knowledge of some causes might lead one to change while a fuller knowledge of causes would leave one adhering to the original desire or action. We would not want to say that such an action was not in equilibrium. Yet, to attempt to avoid this by talking of what would happen with "complete knowledge" of causes leads

to obscurity. Difficulties in this area can be avoided by rephrasing the second clause in the definition of disequilibrium as b': there is knowledge K of causes of his doing the act such that (1) if he knew these were the causes of his doing (or wanting to do) the act, this knowledge would lead him not to (want to) do it, and (2) there is no further correct information about causes such that when this is added to K, then the person knowing all this will once again be led to (want to) do the act, or want to want to do it. Clause 2 excludes the partial knowledge, which would not have the effect of shifting the person's action or want if he also had fuller knowledge. Our purposes will be served if we add the plausible condition that eventually there is full enough knowledge so that its effect is not changed by even wider knowledge, that is, that there isn't an infinite cycle of shifting of adherence to and from the act under wider and wider knowledge. I spare the reader the details, which can be extracted easily from the discussion of an analogous problem about longer courses of action in Part III of the next chapter. Note that the revised clause b' also copes with problems resulting from ignorance of which molar cause corresponds to some biochemical cause.

60. See *Zarathustra*, "On Love of the Neighbor"; *Beyond Good and Evil*, p. 222; *The Will to Power*, p. 283.

61. Erik Erikson, *Gandhi's Truth* (Norton, New York, 1969).

62. Intuitively, it seems that an act that tracks bestness will be in equilibrium. Since that act is connected to bestness so that if it weren't best it wouldn't be done, and if it were best it would be, why then should or would knowledge of its causes lead one not to (want to) do it? Consider the parallel statement for belief. A belief is in equilibrium, let us say, when the person has it, and if he knew the causes of his having it, this knowledge would not lead him no longer to have it. (This explanation needs to be refined, parallel to the one in footnote 59.) It seems plausible that a necessary condition for knowledge is that the person's belief be in equilibrium; it also is plausible that a belief that tracks truth is in equilibrium. If it tracks truth, why should knowledge of its causes make one worry about it? Thus, our account of knowledge seems to yield beliefs in equilibria.

However, this intuitive argument depends upon the goals themselves (bestness as specified by some weighted sum of dimensions, and truth) being so desirable that we still would want to pursue them no matter how it turned out we earlier had been caused to do so. (Yet might not the causal story involve such deceitful manipulations by others that one would want not to pursue the goals in order to assert independence, denying the others an unmerited success?) Thus, the causal story must not be one that somehow shows the goals are not desirable, or shows that we do not know the goals are desirable; we could not respond to such a causal story by saying "Since I know the goals are best anyway, I will continue to pursue them nevertheless." So we cannot conclude that the desire to do what is right or (in a specified way) best must be in equilibrium.

The converse relation need not hold either: a belief in equilibrium need not track (or have been tracking) truth. This is because condition 3 of tracking, that if it weren't true he wouldn't believe it, seems sufficient for equilibrium even without condition 4, and hence without total tracking. A person who in learning the causes of his belief learns that it is true will not be led to change it, even if he also learns (as in the tank case which led to condition 4) that he was not previously tracking truth. After he learns the causes of his belief that p, and that p is true, his belief that p presumably will be tracking truth.

Similarly, a person might learn the causes of his action, and come to see that by accident he was doing best. He would not have been tracking, or even have satisfied subjunctive 3. Yet the new knowledge of causes need not lead him to not (want to) do it. Equilibrium, then, is not a sufficient condition for tracking truth or bestness. Nor is it sufficient for truth and bestness themselves. Knowledge of a belief's causes might give someone no knowledge either way about its truth-value—although in that case most of us would no longer continue to hold the belief as confidently.

However, some people are so rigid in their adherence to a belief that no possible knowledge, whether correct or not, of the causes of their belief could lessen their adherence to it; no possible knowledge could get them no longer to believe it or even to have less confidence in its truth. Let us say in this case that a belief is frozen. Similarly, an action is frozen if no possible knowledge of its causes can lead a person not to (want to) do it or to want (to want) it less. The psychoanalytic claim about the changes attendant upon self-understanding can apply only to those whose actions are not frozen. (Is it thought that psychotics, in contrast to neurotics, have their actions frozen, so that modification, even if possible, cannot come through knowledge?)

Because new knowledge of causes can show one that a belief is true or an action is best, even though one did not know this before, one might then continue to believe or do the thing even though one was not previously tracking. However, one will not be continuing because of the same causes as earlier; it is the new knowledge that now will cause one to believe or act. This need not always be the case. Sometimes the new knowledge will leave the old causes operative; it will not interfere with them and neither will it join them as a cause. (Here, I assume that causes can be demarcated from the total previous state of the universe, from standing conditions, and so on.) Should we strengthen the notion of equilibrium to require that knowledge of the causes leaves the person wanting as much (to want) to do the act or hold the belief, and for the same causes as previously, before the knowledge was had? Do we care about this additional component; would it distress us to learn that the causes of an action would not retain their causal potency if we knew of their operation, yet still we would do the act, only now from other causes stemming from knowledge of the previous causes? This strengthened notion of equilibrium is more likely to mesh neatly with tracking notions (and with the desire to do right, or to believe truth), yet at this point we lack the tools to provide a convincing rationale for the strengthening.

63. For example, that of John Rawls in *A Theory of Justice* (Harvard University Press, Cambridge, 1971), Part III.

64. An iterated process of choice and change was presented in my sketch in *Anarchy, State, and Utopia*, pp. 212–213. The iterated process stated in terms of subjunctives can be transformed into an actual political and social philosophy, a call for constituting society so that the iteration actually is carried out. (This transformation was suggested to me by William Puka; see also his "Toward Moral Perfectionism", unpublished doctoral dissertation, Harvard University.) To ensure that this iteration is carried out, and not merely the development people would choose in freedom (as in my "Framework for Utopia", *Anarchy, State, and Utopia*, ch. X), presumably would require state action beyond that countenanced in the minimal state. A libertarian society would not especially favor self-knowledge, and so would not push people toward socratizing. (Some might argue that we do not have the right to do something that, if we knew the causes of our doing it, we would not want to do, even though this negative view opens the door to great paternalism.) The proposal to transform the hypothetical iteration into an actually ongoing process in the society raises large and intriguing questions, ones I cannot consider here.

65. Compare Nelson Goodman on the mutual modification of principles and particular judgments, *Fact, Fiction and Forecast* (Harvard University Press, 1955), pp. 65–68, and the writings of John Dewey on the interpenetration of ends and means.

66. On the last, see the illuminating articles by George Ainslee, "Specious Reward", *Psychological Bulletin*, Vol. 82, 1975, pp. 463–496; "Impulse and Compulsion", forthcoming.

67. In this paragraph, I have followed the summary in Richard Schacht, "Hegel on Freedom", in Alasdair MacIntyre, ed., *Hegel* (Anchor Books, New York, 1972), pp. 289–328. See also Charles Taylor, *Hegel* (Cambridge University Press, 1975), p. 93.

68. See Lewis White Beck, *A Commentary on Kant's Critique of Practical Reason* (University of Chicago Press, Chicago, 1960), pp. 196–197.

69. Harry Frankfurt, "Freedom of the Will and the Concept of a Person", *Journal of Philosophy*, Vol. 68, 1971, pp. 5–20.

70. Even weaker than saying that there is one level such that for all desires there is harmony from then on up would be to say that for each desire there is some level such that there is harmony from then on up about it. This change in the order of the quantifiers would be sufficient for our purposes too.

71. Let us leave it ambiguous for now how the theory is to be filled in, whether with a measure of harm or of wrongness (apart from the r factor), whether of what is done or is intended.

This $r \times H$ framework, going alongside a framework of compensation, was presented in *Anarchy, State, and Utopia*, pp. 59–63. I have since learned from reading George Fletcher's probing book *Rethinking Criminal Law* (Little, Brown, Boston, 1978) that continental legal systems embody this (or a very similar) structure, terming 'r' *attribution* and 'H' *wrongdoing*. The reader should examine Fletcher's book for his different answers to many of the questions we discuss here. The positions presented here were formulated and lectured on before I encountered Fletcher's book, but I will draw the readers' attention in footnotes to some of its differing positions.

On measures of the (perceived) moral wrongness of crimes, see S. S. Stevens, "A Metric for the Social Consensus", *Science*, Vol. 151, 1966, pp. 530–541; and T. Sellin and M. E. Wolfgang, *The Measurement of Delinquency* (Wiley, New York, 1964).

72. This will not be so for thieves who immediately are apprehended, the stolen good returned, but it may well hold of assaulters, for example. Even for the victims of those thieves, does simply getting their goods back leave them no worse off, including psychologically, than if they had not been stolen from at all?

73. For the subtleties of the biblical *lex talionis*, and the degree to which, from the beginning, it indicated compensation, see David Daube, *Studies in Biblical Law* (Cambridge University Press, 1947), ch. III, pp. 102–153.

74. I raise some problems for deterrence theories in *Anarchy, State, and Utopia*, pp. 61–62.

75. See H. P. Grice, "Meaning", *Philosophical Review*, Vol. 66, 1957, pp. 377–388. Later developments and epicycles are to be found in H. P. Grice, "Utterer's Meaning and Intentions", *Philosophical Review*, Vol. 78, 1969, pp. 147–177; "Logic and Conversation", unpublished William James Lectures, Harvard University, 1967.

76. See Joel Feinberg, "The Expressive Function of Punishment", in his *Doing and Deserving*, Princeton University Press, Princeton, 1970, pp. 95–118.

77. Moses Mendelssohn held (in *Phaedon*) that divine retribution was not an end in itself, but a means of purging the sinner to prepare him for life in the world to come. (See *Encyclopedia Judaica*, Vol. II, p. 1331.)

78. See R. M. Hare's discussion (though not in the context of punishment) of universalizing and distinguishing when the same is done to you as you do, in *Freedom and Reason* (Oxford University Press, 1963).

79. Compare Judah Halevi's saying that the connection with the divine influence is what is important, not (primarily) what stems from that connection (*Kuzari* I, 109).

80. C. S. Lewis says "it plants the flag of truth within the fortress of a rebel soul" (*The Problem of Pain*, Macmillan, New York, 1944, p. 95), but in the context of seeing divine punishment as giving an "opportunity for amendment". Our view here is that, even apart from the person's changing, it is better that the flag be planted there. See also F. H. Bradley, *Ethical Studies*, pp. 26–28 (Oxford University Press, paperback reprint, 1962).

81. For another external account, see Fletcher, *Rethinking Criminal Law*, pp. 800–801. Of course, external accounts involving rights of another mention values we want our actions to connect with, which are values we would be flouting if we punished someone when he was guilty of no wrongful act. But although this shows, via the notion of connecting to correct values, why

718

we do not want to punish him, it still remains an external account, in that it is external to the notion of punishment.

82. See Richard Brandt, "Blameworthiness and Obligation", in A. I. Melden, ed., *Essays in Moral Philosophy* (University of Washington Press, Seattle, 1958), pp. 3–39; and Richard Brandt, *Ethical Theory* (Prentice-Hall, Englewood Cliffs, 1959), pp. 471–474; also, Fletcher, *Rethinking Criminal Law*, pp. 798–835. Excuses lower r while justifications lower H. (Must a justification reduce H to zero?)

83. Could there not be overdetermination of the action, so that both explanations held true, the one embedding the excuse and the one involving the defect of character? Would the excuse then excuse?

84. There may well be minor floutings of correct values where either the person does not deserve to be punished, or we should not do it; and there may be cases of flouting correct values that are not of social concern because they do not involve violation of another's rights or any public harm, and so we are not entitled to effect the linkage—it is none of our business. To state a precise moral principle to delineate the situations in which it would be right to effect the linkage would take us away from our central concerns here. Let me simply and baldly state that for coercive punishment to be justified, it must (usually) be in response to a flouting that is a violation of another's rights. (By coercive punishment I mean using force or doing what otherwise, in the absence of his wrongdoing, would be a violation of his rights. On these themes, see my *Anarchy, State, and Utopia*.) I say "usually" here because, for instance, we would be justified in compelling someone not to torture animals, even if it is not precisely rights that animals have.

When someone flouts correct values but does not violate rights, it is within our rights to do something unpleasant to him which even in the absence of his wrongdoing would not have violated his rights, such as organizing a boycott of him or refusing to deal with him. Whether and when we should do this is a more delicate issue. (I would apply these points as well to punishment for thoughts and intentions. See further Herbert Morris, "Punishment for Thoughts", *The Monist*, Vol. 49, no. 3, 1965, pp. 342–376. Moral discussions of this topic also should consider conditional intentions, the intention to do A if some situation holds.)

To say it is sometimes right to punish people, and that a principle can be formulated under which we should do so, is not to say how important it is that this right thing occur. Is it important enough to let the heavens fall, or does it merely get some weight in a utilitarian-like calculation? Neither of these positions seems appropriate; to develop an adequate position would involve many general issues about the right and its place in our actions, and so would transcend the specific issues about punishment.

85. Letting H correspond to the degree to which others are wronged, or to the wrongness of the act, rather than to the degree of harm, fits our view that (a) injuring helpless people or children who cannot resist and do not fully understand what is happening is worse than a similar injury to competent

adults; (b) doing an act you have a special duty or responsibility not to do (for instance, a policeman on duty using his weapon to settle a private grudge) is worse than someone else's doing the same act.

86. Compare Fletcher's treatment of these issues, *Rethinking Criminal Law*, pp. 473–483. Note that for H_I, the r that goes with it will not be diminished by the excuse that it was unintentional.

Perhaps in the second, more complex formula, the different maximands represent different ways correct values can be flouted. A value or norm says "No X", excluding X; and you flout it (a) by bringing about X, counter-instancing the norm, producing what is prohibited by the value, or (b) by acting on the intention to counter-instance the norm. Since r represents degree of flouting, it would seem that r applies to each mode of flouting, and perhaps takes different values for each, so that $r \times H$ is not

$$r \times \text{Max}\left[H_D, \frac{H_D + H_I}{2} \right]$$

but rather

$$\text{Max}\left[r_1 \times H_D, r_2 \times \frac{H_D + H_I}{2} \right].$$

It is worth attempting to derive the complexity of the fully interpreted $r \times H$ from the notion of flouting; this would support the flouting theory and give us an account (as no other theory does satisfactorily) of why attempts are punished, but to a lesser degree.

87. I owe the point of this paragraph to Fletcher (*Rethinking Criminal Law*, Sec. 6.7.1–6.7.2), who presents as the normative question underlying the determination of r, "could the actor fairly have been expected to avoid committing the wrongful act?"

88. Should we say that one value is "being a tracker of correct values, being connected to them", and the negligent person does not connect with that one (but does he flout it?) so that in punishing him we connect him up with that value? (Or, since people can be negligent of different values, in the case of each value V_i, is there the metavalue "being a tracker of value V_i"?)

CHAPTER FIVE

1. We could call pull "demand", which also has the connotation of drawing forth and fits the terminology of "ethically demanded". Moral push then might be called "supply". However, it is best to avoid the temptation to draw misleading curves.

2. See Raoul Hilberg, *The Destruction of the European Jews* (Quadrangle Books, 1961; reprinted, Harper and Row, New York, 1979); Gerald Reit-

linger, *The Final Solution* (2nd edition, Yoseloff, New York, 1968); Lucy Dawidowicz, *The War Against the Jews, 1933–1945* (Holt, Rinehart and Winston, New York, 1975); Arthur Morse, *While Six Million Died* (Hart, New York, 1968); Alexander Solzhenitsyn, *The Gulag Archipelago*, 3 vols. (Harper and Row, New York, 1973, 1975, 1978); Hannah Arendt, *The Origins of Totalitarianism* (Meridan Books, New York, 1958); Herman Kahn, *On Thermonuclear War* (Princeton University Press, Princeton, 1960).

3. We are told this held of Job's range of alternatives. Another agent, Satan it is said, would (and did) intervene to visit awful consequences on him because he was virtuous.

Job asks why these terrible things are happening to him; he holds that under the provenance of God other good things should vary directly with moral quality. After various unsatisfactory answers from his friends, God speaks to him saying, "Where wast thou when I laid the foundations of the earth? . . . " (*Job*, 38–39). The answer 'How can you hope to understand my purposes' is a dishonest answer, as the book is written, for the beginning of the book *does* give us a comprehensible explanation of what is happening. (Is this reason to think it an addition to the original text?) Accordingly, God could have told Job, "Here's why you underwent such terrible torments. One day Satan came to me and said . . . , and so in order to show him he was wrong I allowed him to torment you, with the restriction that he could not take your life. You wanted to know why it was happening—that is why." But wouldn't Job then have been justified in replying in outrage, "What! You mean you were using me to demonstrate something to Satan? You killed my wife and sons and cattle and tormented me merely because Satan wandered by?" It is no wonder, then, that God told Job a cover story, or rather, no story at all.

However, was God's reply really so irrelevant to the way the book of Job begins? Job's criticism of God's allowing Satan to torment him would be that it was wrong of God to allow this, to treat Job's life and that of his family, virtuous people, merely as educational material for Satan. What then would make God's acting that way not morally wrong? Perhaps it was ultimately for Job's own good (but the family's?); perhaps if God had not demonstrated that lesson to Satan, Satan eventually would have done worse to Job and to all other people; perhaps it was a supreme emergency and if Satan did not get the correct picture he would report back to whomever he spies for (a rival deity?) and awful consequences would be unleashed throughout the earth. But if it was some story like this, why does God not simply explain it to Job? Well, perhaps Job wouldn't be able to understand the explanation, or perhaps the explanation would so terrify Job (for example, God is in the middle of a hostile environment, sheltering us from outside forces, and bringing us along to the point where we can help him) that Job is better off undergoing the suffering than hearing the explanation, or perhaps if God reveals his purpose to Job then Satan and whomever he serves will learn of God's plans and act to thwart them to the detriment of all humanity. There are other possibilities.

And so God answers to Job: How can you hope to understand what is going on, what I am doing, what the universe is like? Where were you when I laid the foundations of the earth? And this may be to the point after all, even given the preface.

No purpose of increasing good elsewhere could justify God's allowing that to happen to Job and his family, neither to teach Satan a lesson nor to teach all those who later would read the book of Job. So it appears that if God's action was morally justified, it must have been done in order to avoid catastrophic moral horror to Job and others.

Read in this way, or in some others, the book not only produces awe: it produces fear.

4. For instance, Thomas Nagel argues (*The Possibility of Altruism*, Oxford University Press, 1969) that accepting other people as fully real commits one to giving due moral weight to their wants, that immoral behavior commits one to (an analogue of) solipsism. Alan Gewirth argues (*Reason and Morality*, University of Chicago Press, Chicago, 1979) that intentional purposeful action commits one to recognizing rights of others to act unimpeded. Alan Donagan (*The Theory of Morality*, University of Chicago Press, Chicago, 1977) seeks to show moral precepts follow from some condition on rational action so that "for a rational creature to violate the precepts . . . would be to violate his own rationality" (p. 31).

5. For example, see Nicholas Sturgeon, "Altruism, Solipsism, and the Objectivity of Reasons", *Philosophical Review*, Vol. 83, 1974, pp. 374–402. Gewirth's argument runs as follows: to act purposefully is to act to achieve a goal and so to be committed to its being good that you achieve the goal, and so to be committed to thinking you have a right to attempt the goal unimpeded, and so to be committed to recognizing the same right held by others as they act purposefully. I leave it to the reader to decide where this attempt to have morality drop out of the category of purposeful action fails.

6. Thus, according to Nagel's book, whose subject is the motivation to be moral, the cost of immorality is (some analogue of) solipsism; the motivational push to morality, then, would be the motivation to avoid (this analogue of) solipsism.

7. *Remarks on the Foundations of Mathematics* (Basil Blackwell, Oxford, 1956), Part I, appendix 1, 11–14; Part II, 77–90; Part V, 27–28. See also Crispin Wright, *Wittgenstein on the Foundations of Mathematics* (Harvard University Press, Cambridge, 1980), ch. 16.

8. Might we maintain he actually is consistent, and so does not actually hold X, although he thinks he does? (Why this, and not that he is not actually behaving immorally?) However, though this at least sticks him with the penalty of giving up X, it helps little; for on this view he has already been giving up X, and he has not found that so bad, either.

9. See H. A. Prichard, "Does Moral Philosophy Rest on a Mistake?", *Mind*, Vol. 21, 1912, pp. 21–37; and *Duty and Interest* (Oxford University Press, 1928).

10. In the discussion of punishment in the previous chapter, we saw two ways that value qua value could have a significant effect on a person: first, by having a significant effect *in* his life whereby he is brought to recognize cor-

rect values and voluntarily change his behavior; second, by having a signifi-cant effect *on* his life, where value qua value acts to produce some significant effect, which effect he notices and realizes even if he does not accept or internalize the values that produced it. Now we see a further value effect: the immoral person has an existence that is less valuable, even if he does not recognize this. This last effect—how value characterizes his life—does not eliminate the importance of the first two.

11. *Anarchy, State, and Utopia* (Basic Books, New York, 1974), pp. 42-45, "The Experience Machine".

12. See Michael Stocker, "Desiring the Bad", *Journal of Philosophy*, Vol. 76, 1979, pp. 738-753.

13. For a recent Aristotelean effort of this second sort, see Mortimer Adler, *The Time of Our Lives* (Holt, Rinehart and Winston, New York, 1970). The intricate economic consequences attendant upon taking one's whole life as an object of planning are delineated in Milton Friedman, *A Theory of the Consumption Function* (Princeton University Press, Princeton, 1957).

14. *Nicomachean Ethics*, I.5 1096a.

15. Still, there could be a tension between the relation R and the other components. If the relation R is so to hold, this might necessitate a certain deliberative organization of one's life. Yet on some views (for example, D. H. Lawrence's), the very most valuable kind of life might exclude such delibera-tive organization, and so exclude R-ing taking place. According to that view, the most valuable way to be is not as a highly developed R-er. Nonetheless, the most valuable life situation overall might involve the life standing in R to the way of being. Such a view would exhibit serious internal tension.

16. For a discussion of both strands in Aristotle, see John Cooper, *Reason and Human Good in Aristotle* (Harvard University Press, Cambridge, 1975).

17. See G. E. Moore, "The Conception of Intrinsic Value", in his *Philo-sophical Studies* (Routledge and Kegan Paul, London, 1922), pp. 253-275, and *Principia Ethica* (Cambridge University Press, 1903), pp. 25-30; C. I. Lewis, *Analysis of Knowledge and Valuation* (Open Court, LaSalle, 1946), chs. 12, 13; Monroe Beardsley, "Intrinsic Value", *Philosophy and Phenome-nological Research*, Vol. 26, 1965, pp. 1-17; Gilbert Harman, "Towards a Theory of Intrinsic Value", *Journal of Philosophy*, Vol. 64, 1967, pp. 792-804; Roderick Chisholm, "The Defeat of Good and Evil", *Proceedings and Addresses of the American Philosophical Association*, Vol. 42, 1968-69, pp. 21-38; Warren Quinn, "Theories of Intrinsic Value", *American Philo-sophical Quarterly*, Vol. 11, 1974, pp. 123-132.

18. For an early discussion, see Aristotle, *Ethics*, Book I; and see also Ber-nard Williams, "Aristotle on the Good", *Philosophical Quarterly*, Vol. 12, 1962, pp. 289-296.

19. The foundational claim is criticized in Nelson Goodman, "Sense and Certainty", in his *Problems and Projects* (Bobbs-Merrill, Indianapolis, 1972), pp. 60-68. See also Israel Scheffler, "On Justification and Commitment", *Journal of Philosophy*, Vol. 51, 1954, pp. 180-190; and J. L. Austin, *Sense and Sensibilia* (Oxford University Press, 1962), ch. 10.

20. Charles Parsons, "What Is the Iterative Conception of Set?", in Robert

Butts and Jaakko Hintikka, eds., *Logic, Foundations of Mathematics, and Computability Theory* (Reidel, Dodrecht, 1977), p. 358.

21. Years ago I made this suggestion to Harman, who utilized it in the article cited above.

22. The notion of unity within opposition is an important theme in Heraclitus, as unity in diversity is in Plotinus and later neo-Platonic thought. A discussion drawing on gestalt theories of perception, of how diverse material is unified in the visual arts, runs throughout Rudolf Arnheim, *Art and Visual Perception* (2nd ed., University of California Press, Berkeley, 1974). E. H. Gombrich's *The Sense of Order* (Cornell University Press, Ithaca, 1979) is illuminating, although mainly concerned with how a perceiver responds to deviations from an (assumed background) order.

The tradition that makes organic unity central in aesthetics is a rich one, with Coleridge being a notable exponent. See G. N. Orsini, "The Organic Conception in Aesthetics", *Comparative Literature*, Vol. 21, 1969, pp. 1–30, and his article "Organicism", *Dictionary of the History of Ideas* (Scribners, New York, 1973), Vol. III, pp. 421–427. G. S. Rousseau, ed., *Organic Form: The Life of an Idea* (Routledge and Kegan Paul, London, 1972), contains essays on organic unity in various areas, plus an extensive bibliography.

For recent discussions of the notion of organic unity within aesthetics, see John Hospers, "Problems of Aesthetics", *Encyclopedia of Philosophy* (Macmillan, New York, 1967), Vol. 1, especially pp. 43–44; Harold Osborne, *Theory of Beauty* (Routledge and Kegan Paul, London, 1952)—"All works of art, even the simplest, are fairly complex for immediate perception and it has been a commonplace of artistic criticism that a good work of art must have a high degree of unity . . . The two notions, however vague, suggest that works of art of whatever kind may have in common the formal property of being *complex unities*" (p. 92, italics in original; see also pp. 106, 126–128). See also Catherine Lord, "Organic Unity Reconsidered", *Journal of Aesthetics and Art Criticism*, Vol. 22, 1964, pp. 263–268; P. Hutchings, "Organic Unity Revindicated?", *Journal of Aesthetics and Art Criticism*, Vol. 23, 1965, pp. 323–328; R. Peacock, *Criticism and Personal Taste* (Clarendon Press, Oxford, 1972), ch. 10, "Metaphorical Unity", pp. 107–114.

There are dissenting views. One important theme of the Romantic movement was the bursting apart of (only premature?) unities and structures, the surpassing of them. See also Morse Peckham, *Man's Rage for Chaos* (Chilton Books, Philadelphia, 1965). I try to take account of and incorporate this aspect of the Romantic vision in the next chapter.

23. For a related attempt, see George D. Birkhoff, *Aesthetic Measure* (Harvard University Press, Cambridge, 1933). Birkhoff proposes that the measure of aesthetic value of an object is equal to its (measured) order divided by its (measured) complexity; this formula unfortunately has the consequence that if the order is held constant and the complexity is diminished, the value is increased.

24. See Francisco J. Ayala, "The Concept of Biological Progress", in F. J. Ayala and T. Dobzhansky, *Studies in Philosophy of Biology* (University of

California Press, Berkeley, 1974), pp. 339–354; and George L. Stebbins, *The Basis of Progressive Evolution* (University of North Carolina Press, Chapel Hill, 1969). On the complicated interactive order of homeostatic regulation, see L. J. Henderson, *The Fitness of the Environment* (Macmillan, New York, 1913); W. B. Cannon, *The Wisdom of the Body* (Norton, New York, 1932); E. S. Russell, *The Directiveness of Organic Activities* (Cambridge University Press, 1945). Compare A. Rosenblueth, N. Weiner, and J. Bigelow, "Behavior Purpose and Teleology", *Philosophy of Science*, Vol. 10, 1943, pp. 18–24; and see the discussion in Ernest Nagel, *The Structure of Science*, ch. 12, and G. Sommerhoff, *Logic of the Living Brain* (Wiley, New York, 1974). Biologists also discern intricate orders in the overall form of organisms; see D'Arcy Wentworth Thomson, *On Growth and Form* (2nd ed., Cambridge University Press, 1942). However, some discussions of order in homology have to be treated with caution, for instance, Rupert Riedl, *Order in Living Organisms* (John Wiley, New York, 1978).

For further discussion of complex organic unities in living organisms, see Paul Weiss, *Life, Order, and Understanding* and (from the point of view of general systems theory) J. G. Miller, *Living Systems* (McGraw-Hill, New York, 1978).

25. A future planet-wide computer-based regulatory self-consciousness, if that is possible, might well come to view itself as the most valuable thing around. It would be prudent therefore, as John Lilly has suggested (*Simulations of God*, Simon and Schuster, New York, 1975, ch. 17), that we now begin to design and use computers that function best in atmospheric and temperature conditions most suitable for human life, to avoid eventually turning control of planetary physical conditions over to entities whose interest may well (come to) conflict with ours.

26. When Einstein said "elegance is for tailors", he was not denying that a valuable theory is one that shows "unity in diversity", merely noting that this is not guaranteed by "elegance". He wrote in a letter of 1901, "It is a magnificent feeling to recognize the unity of a complex of phenomena which appear to be things quite apart from the direct visible truth" (quoted in R. Clark's biography, *Einstein*, World, New York, 1971, p. 53).

As is well known, Einstein devoted the last part óf his life to the search for a unified field theory. For recent discussion of partial progress toward such unifications within physics, see Steven Weinberg, "Unified Theories of Elementary Particle Interaction", *Scientific American*, July 1974, pp. 50–59; Sidney Coleman, "The 1979 Nobel Prize in Physics", *Science*, Vol. 206, 1979, pp. 1290–1292; also see Gerald Holton, *The Scientific Imagination* (Cambridge University Press, 1978), ch. 1. It is a commonplace that scientists have searched for and valued unifying explanations, so that a prominent virtue of Newtonian mechanics was its unified explanation of celestial and terrestrial motions. For the claim that the essence (and value) of explanation lies in theoretical unification, in the reduction of the total number of independent phenomena, see Michael Friedman, "Explanation and Scientific Understanding", *Journal of Philosophy*, Vol. 71, 1974, pp. 5–19. Recent philosophy also has seen a movement commending a unified science; see Otto Neurath, et al., "Encyclopedia and Unified Science", Vol. I in *International Encyclopedia of Unified Science* (University of Chicago Press, Chicago, 1938), pp. 1–75; Paul Oppenheim and Hilary Putnam, "Unity of Science as a Working Hypothesis", in H. Feigl, ed., *Minnesota Studies in the Philosophy of Science*, Vol. II (University of Minnesota Press, Minneapolis, 1958), pp. 3–36.

Can one turn science's pursuit of unifying explanations into an argument for value as organic unity, or at least hold this is presupposed as value by science's goal-directed teleological, pursuit of unifying theories? If so, then the scientific view of the world could not undercut all values, and the fact–value or at least the scientific fact–value dichotomy itself would be undercut or overcome. But must the scientist who seeks explanation view it as (objectively) valuable, must science as an institutional enterprise be committed to that judgment? Cannot a goal be pursued without presupposing it is objectively valuable? Would it have been equally cogent (or equally inconclusive) to claim that science is committed to at least one value judgment: it is good that science exists, that the scientific enterprise be pursued? But must the criminal world be committed to the value judgment that it is good that it exist?

27. However, one would not expect a list of necessary and sufficient conditions to be definitive of a realm; new components could enter via similarity to ones already entered. Thereby, the composition of a realm might be historical—so too that of value in that realm.

28. Much suggestive material that would have to be taken account of in a more detailed delineation of the realm of value than is offered here is contained in Nicolai Hartmann, *Ethics* (Macmillan, New York, 1932), and Max Scheler, *Formalism in Ethics and Non-Formal Ethics of Values* (Northwestern University Press, Evanston, 1973).

29. See the extensive writings of market theorists, especially F. A. Hayek's essays in his *Individualism and Economic Order* (Routledge and Kegan Paul, London, 1949; Gateway edition, Regnery, Chicago, 1972). The theme of unifying with something in a way that takes account of its degree of organic unity is discussed further below.

30. See the illuminating first chapter of Charles Taylor's *Hegel* (Cambridge University Press, 1975), pp. 3–50.

31. The Platonic ranking of the parts of the soul will utilize some notion of value other than organic unity, unless the ranking is a rule of thumb summarizing facts about such unity: the higher part is that which, when in control, yields the greatest organic unity.

32. Can we get a precise formula for O as a function of diversity and of degree of unifiedness? Is it possible that there is no such formula, that O is itself an organic unity of diversity and degree of unifiedness but is not the sum (or any other statable function) of these? In this case, O itself would have a high degree of organic unity, and so subsume itself.

33. More precisely, given different partitionings i, it will be the maximum relative to some partition. $V(X) = Max_i [O(X)$ under partitioning $i + \Sigma V$ (parts of X under partitioning i)]

34. Is the value of a particular thing merely the value (structure) that it realizes, where the measure of its value is the degree of organic unity of that structure? Perhaps a measure of a thing's value also should include those value structures it only imperfectly realizes (and so is not a model of, strictly), weighted by the degree to which it does manage to realize them. (This measure would have to be formulated so as to exclude redundancies.) The way in which an object manages to realize, to some extent, different values might constitute a mode of unification of these values.

35. Even if the value structures are not categorical with all realizations being fully isomorphic, there will be partial isomorphism among the realizations, and so unification to that extent.

36. Recall Quine's claim that all truths are truths of structure (*Ontological Relativity*, pp. 44, 60), and the difficulties this gets him into as he considers whether he should not accept a Pythagorean ontology, wherein all that exists are numbers. Since all structural relationships can be mirrored in the realm of number theory, someone who believes all truths are structural will have to engage in ad hoc maneuvers to avoid the Pythagorean reduction in his ontology. (Quine does so in "Ontological Reduction and the World of Numbers", in his *The Ways of Paradox*, 2nd ed., Harvard University Press, 1976, pp. 212–220.)

37. Suzanne Langer, *Philosophy in a New Key* (Harvard University Press, Cambridge, 1941; 3rd ed., 1957), ch. 8; see also her *Feeling and Form* (Scribner, New York, 1953). The criticism is made in a review by Ernest Nagel, reprinted in his *Logic Without Metaphysics* (Free Press, Glencoe, 1956), pp. 353–360.

38. See *Languages of Art* (Bobbs-Merrill, Indianapolis, 1968), ch. 2.

39. It is another matter to rank different disproportionate V-ings of different things; no obvious condition suggests itself here.

40. Spelling this out: according to the dimension D, anti-V-ing one value, though disvaluable, has lesser disvalue than the (same) anti-V-ing of another greater value; V-ing one disvalue, though disvaluable, has lesser disvalue than the (same) V-ing of a greater disvalue.

I have no thoughts on conditions to compare V-ing disvalues with anti-V-ing values, that are formulated in comparative (ordinal) terms of greater and lesser (dis-) values, more and less intense (anti-V-ings). With stronger measurements of the magnitudes of the values and intensities, not simply ordinal ones, further conditions might seem appropriate.

41. For a clear exposition, see Thomas McCarthy, *The Critical Theory of Jurgen Habermas* (MIT Press, Cambridge, 1978).

42. See N. Hartmann, *Ethics*, Vol. 2: *Moral Values* (Macmillan, New York, 1932), ch. 31, "Radiant Virtue", p. 332–340.

43. A fanciful thought: might value act in the world, apart from value perceivers, by limiting the world to being consistent? Inconsistencies would be too great a rending of the world's organic unity and hence of its value. So there would be a value explanation of why the laws of logic hold: value acts to exclude impossible worlds, which would be too terrible. This would be an exception to the view that value has effects only via value perceivers, unless

(even more fancifully) each possible universe were a value perceiver, consistent because acting to keep itself in good shape.

44. Some suggestive research and speculation on the allure of values, and the conditions which nurture this, is found in Abraham Maslow, *Towards a Psychology of Being* (Van Nostrand, New York, 2nd ed., 1970) and *The Farther Reaches of Human Nature* (Viking Press, New York, 1971).

45. We might explain the objectivity of a judgment that p as follows. There exists knowledge k such that everyone with this knowledge agrees that p is true (and expects that anyone else with this knowledge would agree that p is true and would have this very same expectation), while there is no further knowledge which, when added to k, undercuts the agreement that p. Notice that this criterion of objectivity does not specify the knowledge; it merely states that there exists some knowledge or other of a certain sort.

This knowledge k need not be knowledge of a proposition. There also is knowledge by direct acquaintance with some object of experience. Plato held that all who had a knowledge of the Form of the Good would agree morally and about value generally. Although the precise nature of the knowledge he spoke of may not be clear to us, it clearly is not merely propositional. Perhaps the knowledge k need not even be describable. Mystics are said to know their mystical experiences (or what is encountered in them) without being able to describe them; if all who had certain such experiences agreed to some ethical statements, while no further knowledge undercut this agreement, that would mark the objectivity of such statements.

If the knowledge k itself entails the statement p, then trivially p will be objective (if k is). While, if k does not entail p, there will be logical room for the skeptic to doubt that everyone who had k would agree that p. But is the skeptic himself someone with k, or not? If he has this knowledge, then his doubt that all others with it would agree that p already is enough to show that the stated criterion of the objectivity of p is not satisfied (at least with respect to that particular knowledge k). On the other hand, if this skeptic does not have knowledge k, his doubts may not carry much weight if k is intricate or beyond his ken.

This account of objectivity in terms of knowledge producing agreement is an instance of a more general account which holds that objectivity involves agreement in a specified group. We have specified this group as those with (certain) knowledge. For normative statements, the group most often put forth is the group of "objective" observers. (For different versions of this, see Roderick Firth, "Ethical Absolutism and the Ideal Observer", *Philosophy and Phenomenological Research*, Vol. 12, 1952, pp. 317–345; and John Rawls, *A Theory of Justice*, Harvard University Press, Cambridge, 1971, part I.)

When I am told that if I were dispassionate, disinterested, uninvolved, ignorant of my own stake in a situation, and so on, then I would agree that p, I am left unconvinced that p. For I wonder whether p is best decided by someone dispassionate, disinterested, uninvolved, and partially ignorant. Nor are my doubts dispelled when I am told that this is the moral point of view, even apart from the difficulty proponents have in showing why someone should take that stance. These views seem to present what are at best rules of thumb to approximate the results of another theory.

However, things are different when I am told that I would agree that p if I knew more. (In contrast, theorists of the "moral point of view" point to what I would agree to if I knew less than I know—hardly a powerful consideration.) Even this is not guaranteed to be compelling, for I might think it true that I would agree that p if I knew more than I do, while thinking that if I knew even more than that, I would once again think not-p. But barring my fear that a little knowledge may be a dangerous thing, the statement that I would agree that p if I knew more than I do is not one I easily can dismiss, supposing that the something more can be specified nontrivially. (It would be trivial to specify it as "knowing that p".) I would find it difficult indeed to reply, "it may be true that I would agree if I knew more, but since there is no requirement that I should know each and every truth, why should I know more than I do? And if I need not, what is the relevance of saying I would agree if I did know more?" The relevance is patently clear; one might even try to analyze 'should' in terms of 'would if knew more'.

46. There would remain questions about the relationship of those "constitutive" conditions on value to the nature of value itself. Should we view the connection of value to these conditions as analytic, synthetic necessary, or what? I shall not say anything in this work about the status of such necessities.

47. We cannot eliminate this explicit reference to value simply by saying that dimension D satisfies the constitutive conditions on value to some threshold degree d. For what fixes d as the threshold for this concept? Does the requisite degree of fulfillment of the conditions depend also on the degree to which conditions for other concepts comparable to value themselves get fulfilled? Have we moved one level up, so that the threshold degree d for the fulfillment of these conditions for value cannot be specified without adding that it be the greatest degree of fulfillment had in the family of comparable concepts? "It is value, after all. For that concept, can we settle for a lesser degree of fulfillment of its conditions than happens elsewhere for other comparable concepts?"

48. If their V activities are beyond what we are capable of, do they respond with them or with their analogues of our V activities? If along with their greater value goes a capacity for V-ing of a higher order, could our V-ing also fall below the cutoff point?

49. See W. D. Ross, *The Right and the Good* (Oxford University Press, 1930) and *Foundations of Ethics* (Clarendon Press, Oxford, 1939); Isaiah Berlin, *Four Essays on Liberty* (Oxford University Press, 1969) and *Vico and Herder* (Viking Press, New York, 1976); P. F. Strawson, "Social Morality and Individual Ideal", *Philosophy*, Vol. 36, 1961, pp. 1–17; and Stuart Hampshire, *Two Theories of Morality* (Oxford University Press, 1977), pp. 15–55.

50. Hampshire, *Two Theories of Morality*, pp. 46–49, limits the pluralism of his position, holding that there is a unique best mix of values, and that

each person is to apply the (same) general principles of the best mix to the circumstances of his own particular life, so that everyone in those same circumstances should make the same decision.

51. Furthermore, I assume it must be something intrinsically valuable, or contribute directly to intrinsic value as a component or organizing principle. Thus are excluded theories which hold that people themselves are at best instrumentally valuable for some further extra-human effect, but they are to be treated in certain ways because of the characteristics that enable them to play this instrumental role.

Another possible view, worthy of more discussion, would be that people have no valuable characteristic but do have a characteristic in virtue of which certain behavior toward them (causally) produces disvalue (in them). This characteristic itself might be held to be (at least instrumentally) disvaluable, given its potential effects, yet certain behavior toward a bearer of this characteristic might be called for in order to avoid producing the disvalue. On this view, the moral basis that gives rise to the moral ought would not be anything valuable. One instance of such a view would hold that sentience is the moral basis, but that neither it nor any experiences are valuable, yet some painful ones are disvaluable, and so we must avoid producing them.

In assuming that the moral basis will be a valuable characteristic, I assume that such views cannot be the whole truth about moral pull.

52. See Gregory Vlastos' discussion of whether, according to Plato's theory, it is a particular person who is loved, or instead it is the Form that is the primary object of love, where this love "spills over" to the Form's instances so that a person is loved merely as an instantiation of the Form ("The Individual as an Object of Love in Plato", in his *Platonic Studies*, Princeton University Press, Princeton, 1973, pp. 3–34). For a discussion of Kant's theory as (ultimately) valuing a person merely as a bearer of (what Kant holds to be) the basic moral characteristic, see Andreas Teuber, "Ideas of Equality" (unpublished doctoral dissertation, Harvard University, 1978), pp. 118–130.

53. The having of a slant, there being a way it is for the being, is discussed as an important component of the moral basis in Bernard Williams, "The Idea of Equality", in P. Laslett and W. G. Runciman eds., *Philosophy, Politics and Society* (2nd series, Blackwell, Oxford, 1962), pp. 110–131.

54. Compare the treatment of valuing someone for themselves, and of parents' love of their children, in Gregory Vlastos, "Justice and Equality", in R. Brandt, ed., *Social Justice* (Prentice-Hall, Englewood Cliffs, 1962), pp. 31–72.

55. For the view that value seeking is part of our nature, see Abraham Maslow, *The Farther Reaches of Human Nature* (Viking, New York, 1971), pp. 324–325. One might attempt to show that value seeking is intrinsic to (the nature of) a self, as follows. The self synthesizes itself and delineates its boundaries in accordance with a method of classification that classifies so as to maximize the organic unity of the resulting products; hence the self structures itself in accordance with the notion of organic unity and thereby both presupposes that organic unity is valuable and seeks this value in its most

fundamental activity: self-synthesis. (Why otherwise doesn't it simply leave itself unsynthesized?)

However, many of these steps are shaky. Must it be organic unity that is built into the procedure of classification, must a self-synthesis in accordance with that notion presuppose that it is valuable, and so on?

Yet even if value seeking is not intrinsic to the notion of a self, one might think it intrinsic to one's (intuitive) notion of a person and reserve the latter term for the conjunction of the two characteristics. I would not want to treat this as anything more than a terminological point here.

56. A recent discussion of these issues is Philip Devine, *The Ethics of Homicide* (Cornell University Press, Ithaca, 1978), pp. 94, 99–105. The issue of whether a defective individual is to be treated exactly in terms of his own characteristics, or partly in light of the species characteristics which he lacks, is connected to the difference we discussed in Chapter 1 between seeing something "bottom up" or "top down", seeing it exactly in terms of the characteristics it has, or as a realization (the best or even a defective one) of some concept C.

57. G. E. Moore, *Principia Ethica* (Cambridge University Press, 1903), pp. 1–17. Moore uses this question in an argument against 'good' being some "natural" property. Our use of it here is different, requiring merely that Moore's question can saliently arise as open, not that it never can be closed. For a criticism of Moore's "open question argument" as demonstrative, see William Frankena, "The Naturalistic Fallacy", *Mind*, Vol. 48, 1939, pp. 464–477.

58. When the content is based on two characteristics (for example, being a self and being value seeking) then we can distinguish the content based on each one, what follows from the conjunction of these previous contents, and (which need not be the same as the previous one) the content based on the interacting conjunction of the two characteristics.

59. See Immanuel Kant, *Groundwork of the Metaphysics of Morals* (trans. by H. J. Paton, Hutchinson, London, 1948), pp. 95–96; and H. J. Paton, *The Categorical Imperative* (University of Chicago Press, Chicago, 1948), ch. 16. See also Daniel Pekarsky, "Manipulation and Education" (unpublished doctoral dissertation, Harvard Graduate School of Education, 1976). Suggestive, too, is the recent literature on "respect for persons", drawing upon and extending Kant; however, this literature does not help with the problems dealt with below.

60. One participant's utilities might be shaped by the fact that another participant does not have preferences merely but is a value seeker; however, game theory does not require this or treat such utilities any differently from others. For a recent discussion of the rationales behind the various solution concepts of game theory, see John Harsanyi, *Rational Behavior and Bargaining Equilibrium in Games and Social Situations* (Cambridge University Press, 1977). A marvelously lucid and discerning introduction is R. D. Luce and Howard Raiffa, *Games and Decisions* (Wiley, New York, 1957).

61. On some accounts (for example, B. F. Skinner, *Science and Human*

Behavior, Macmillan, New York, 1953, pp. 116–124, 224) the shaping stimulus as it functions is analyzed merely as a sequence of discriminative and reinforcing stimuli; but we need not commit ourselves to such an account here. Even using that account, however, our point can still be made by phrasing it in terms of the sequencing.

62. We leave aside the question of whether the characteristic also is to be a reinforcing stimulus. The Kantian term "treat" does have the connotation of molding your behavior to the subject, and so is appropriate for our purposes, provided we ignore or delete any further connotation that the recipient of treatment be wholly passive.

63. At one time, I thought the stringent view that we are responsible for every evil we could prevent could be refuted by an example where one could prevent any one (or some number) of the instances of some evil—such as deaths by famine in another country—but could not prevent them all. Since it is true of each death (let us suppose) that you could prevent it, on the stringent view you are responsible for each of these deaths. It seems to follow, then, that you are responsible for all of them, since you are responsible for the conjunction of the individual things for which you are responsible. Even the holder of the stringent view, however, must admit that you are not responsible for all the deaths, since you could not prevent all of them. Hence, it cannot be that you are responsible for each thing you could prevent.

The holder of the stringent view can reply that you *are* responsible for that conjunction of all those deaths, for you could have prevented the full conjunction, leaving only a lesser conjunction. However, responsibility is not closed under entailment; what you are not responsible for is the fact that there was at least one death, for you could not have prevented that. This reply avoids the above "refutation"; nevertheless, there is something highly counterintuitive about the claim that you are responsible for each of those deaths.

64. This last view of moral dialogue as means is presented in Judith Housman, "Moral Relations and Personal Relations" (unpublished doctoral dissertation, Harvard University, 1978), ch. III.

65. On dialogue, see Martin Buber, *Between Man and Man* (Beacon Press, Boston, 1955), Part I.

I choose the term "value-theoretic situation" to parallel "game-theoretic situation" where in the standard case people interact with mutual knowledge of the payoff matrix: of the actions available to all the participants, of the various outcomes and how they depend upon these actions, and of the participants' preferences over these outcomes.

66. Both parties being mutually responsive differs from one's responding to the other's basic moral characteristic while the second is unaware of this or is aware but does not respond to the first's. (Or responds to it, but does not respond to the first's responsiveness?) Should we expect different patterns of behavior, and different principles to be operative or embodied in these situations of mutual responsiveness? Does some of the content of ethical pull,

beyond that of responding to another's basic moral characteristic, stem only from and arise only in situations of mutual responsiveness?

67. See Skinner's discussion of the differences between rule-guided and contingency-shaped behavior in his *Contingencies of Reinforcement* (Appleton-Century-Crofts, New York, 1969), ch. 6. Does Zen recommend performing contingency-related rather than rule-guided behavior? As a rule?

68. For suggestive discussion on this last point, see Steven Clark, *The Moral Status of Animals* (Oxford University Press, 1977), ch. VIII, "The Natural Order". Though the value humans share calls for equal treatment from other humans in the general part of ethics, it need not call for it from every possible being. Maimonides presents the view that "divine providence does not watch in equal manner over all the individuals of the human species, but providence is graded as their human perfection is graded" (*Guide to the Perplexed*, 3:18).

69. For a discussion of how the wrongness of using another cannot be captured either by its (necessarily) deceiving or hurting another, see Larry Blum, "Deceiving, Hurting, and Using," in Alan Montefiore, ed., *Philosophy and Personal Relations* (McGill–Queens University Press, Montreal, 1973) pp. 34–61.

70. Much of the material in this section is extracted from my essay "Moral Complications and Moral Structures", *Natural Law Forum*, Vol. 13, 1968, pp. 1–50, where more detail is offered.

71. The restriction to a "natural" quantity is needed to give content to the claim that a moral view can be fitted to a maximization structure. Otherwise, it always would be possible to define an artificial real-valued function whose maximization mirrors the judgments about impermissibility of the view; simply define a function f taking actions as argument values, such that $f(A) = 0$ if and only if according to the moral view in question, A is morally impermissible, and $f(A) = 1$ when according to that moral view, A is permissible. That moral view then can be said to mandate the maximization of f. However, an interesting maximization structure involves the maximization of some function that was not devised especially for that (type of) occasion. Similarly, one would not answer affirmatively Aristotle's question of whether there is one thing for which (eventually) all actions are done, by pointing to contemporary utility theory, even though that theory does define a utility function (on an interval scale), provided that preferences over probability mixtures satisfy certain (natural looking) conditions. That a utility function can be defined to mirror these preferences does not show the maximization of such a function underlies these preferences. (See the discussion of the measure of closeness in the theory of counterfactuals in Chapter 3.) There remains, of course, the problem of distinguishing "natural" predicates or functions from artificial ones; see Nelson Goodman, *Fact, Fiction and Forecast* (Harvard University Press, 1955), ch. III, and W. V. Quine, "Natural Kinds", in his *Ontological Relativity and Other Essays* (Columbia University Press, New York, 1969), pp. 114–138.

72. Compare the issues involved in attributing an internalized grammar to

a person in accounting for his explicit judgments of grammaticality, his speech production, and his understanding, as pursued in the voluminous literature arising from Noam Chomsky's *Syntactic Structures* (Mouton, The Hague, 1957), and *Aspects of the Theory of Syntax* (MIT Press, Cambridge, 1965), ch. 1; a useful survey of recent psychological work is J. A. Fodor, T. G. Bever, and M. F. Garrett, *The Psychology of Language* (McGraw-Hill, New York, 1974).

In *Languages and Other Abstract Objects* (Rowman and Littlefield, Totowa, New Jersey, 1981) Jerrold Katz argues that it is a mistake for linguistics to be oriented toward the task of delineating an explanatory psychological mechanism, rather than the (Platonist) task of characterizing language as an abstract object; this proposal for linguistics, whatever its merits there, would correspond to utilizing a moral structure to delineate the realm of moral truths, rather than as a component in a psychological theory to help explain a person's moral judgments.

Compare also the dual utilization of formulations of decision theory, as a normative theory of how a person should decide, and as a useful first approximation within a descriptive theory.

73. A proponent of the deductive structure might claim that in all such cases of change of judgment, although the facts known to the person do not instantiate the features mentioned in the antecedent of an exceptionless moral principle, instead they provide inductive evidence for the truth of the antecedent. This achieves the result that judgments can change with new information, since inductive probabilities do; however, it is quite implausible.

74. John Rawls presents such a lexical structure in political philosophy, giving absolute priority to one of the principles of justice he formulates (concerning liberty) over the other. He does not, however, focus on the complexities within his first principle, on whether the possible conflicts there also are to be resolved lexically. The structure is called lexical because it gives absolute priority to one principle over another, as in determining the alphabetical ordering of two words the first letter of each has absolute priority over the second, which is looked at only if the first letters are the same and so tie. The term "lexical" is Rawls' improvement of the earlier economist's term "lexicographic". In *Anarchy, State, and Utopia* (Basic Books, New York, 1974), I elaborated a view treating side constraints upon action as exceptionless within a deductive structure, but with one cautionary footnote (p. 30) about possible exceptions in extreme situations.

75. See W. D. Ross, *The Right and the Good* (Oxford University Press, 1930), ch. II; and *Foundations of Ethics* (Clarendon Press, Oxford, 1939), pp. 79-86 and ch. VIII. See also A. C. Ewing, *Second Thoughts in Moral Philosophy* (Routledge and Kegan Paul, London, 1959), pp. 123-155.

76. Here I assume that any interaction between the additional W features and the ones in the subset, which might foil the principle, would have to express itself by other changes in the morally relevant features, either additions of other R features or removals of some W ones; but either of these

interactions takes the situation outside the scope of the principle as written.

77. This formulation assumes we can delimit R sets to any desired degree of fineness, so as always to find one whose weight is between a W set and its proper subset.

78. This would need to be modified to take account of noncomparability. A stringent view would change one of these biconditionals, seeing wrong-making outweighing right-making features as sufficient but not necessary for impermissibility; while a permissive view would change the other biconditional, seeing right-making outweighing wrong-making as sufficient but not necessary for permissibility. The issue is whether an act whose right-making features and wrong-making features are noncomparable, neither outweighing the other, is presumed impermissible or permissible.

79. See, for example, Stephen Kleene, *Introduction to Metamathematics* (Van Nostrand, Princeton, 1952), or Martin Davis, *Computability and Unsolvability* (McGraw-Hill, New York, 1958).

80. See, for example, John Rawls' criticism, *Theory of Justice*, pp. 34–45. See also P. F. Strawson, "Ethical Intuitionism", *Philosophy*, Vol. 24, 1949, pp. 23–33; and the reply by John Lucas, "Ethical Intuitionism II", *Philosophy*, Vol. 46, 1971, pp. 1–11. Strawson is especially intent on criticizing the view of Ross that there is intuition into necessary ethical truths. That the truths might be necessary does not mean that the intuition of them cannot be fallible, although still valuable. It is instructive to consider (in order to see how weak the criticisms are) whether criticisms parallel to Strawson's at all damage the comparable position in the philosophy of mathematics, that there is fallible and imperfect intuition of truths of the mathematical realm, for example, as put forth by Kurt Gödel in "What is Cantor's Continuum Hypothesis?", reprinted in Paul Benacerraf and Hilary Putnam, *Readings in the Philosophy of Mathemtics* (Prentice-Hall, Englewood Cliffs, 1964), pp. 258–273.

81. The point that there are no explicit procedures for combining and balancing the rankings of scientific theories along different dimensions into one overall ranking, and so no agreement that is determined by application of the (explicit) norms and methodology of science, is emphasized by Thomas Kuhn, *The Structure of Scientific Revolutions* (University of Chicago Press, Chicago, 2nd ed., 1970). I also have benefited from hearing a talk by Carl G. Hempel, "Scientific Rationality and Rational Reconstruction" (1980).

82. See the essays by Karl Popper and Imre Lakatos in Imre Lakatos and Alan Musgrave, eds., *Criticism and the Growth of Knowledge* (Cambridge University Press, 1970), pp. 51–58, 91–196, both of whom rejected the premiss, and Paul Feyerabend, *Against Method* (NLB, London, 1975) and *Science in a Free Society* (NLB, London, 1978), who did not and so accepted the conclusion.

83. Ross himself seems to have accepted the stronger maximization principle; see *The Right and the Good*, pp. 41, 46.

84. It might be said that in these situations, the act of lying has features that easily are overlooked; for example, that in the second situation (when also available is the action of convincing the pursuer to stop) it has the added

feature (which it does not have in the first situation) of "being an unnecessary lie". If this feature of the act is included as a W feature, then in the second situation won't the W features of the act of lying outweigh its R features, thereby explaining its impermissibility with no need to modify the simple balancing structure? We can rebut this contention by noting that "involves telling an unnecessary lie" is an explicitly moral notion, which explicitly evaluates comparatively features of acts. Notice that if the bystander stops the murder either by shooting the potential murderer or by lying to him, we can say "he unnecessarily shot him; he could have lied to him" but not "he unnecessarily lied to him; he could have shot him." However, granting that this particular "feature" suggested will not do as one from the W list, is there some (other) way to capture "involves telling an unnecessary lie", for a given situation, that does not involve explicit reference to moral notions and so could be a feature of the act?

One might try, as such, a feature of the act A:

F = "is an alternative to another act B available to the person, which has the same R features as A and fewer W features".

This obviously will not do as a feature on the W list since it explicitly mentions the notions of R feature and W feature. So one might try:

F = "is an alternative to another act B available to the person, which has features $w_1, \ldots, w_m$ and $r_1, \ldots, r_n$" where (although this is not said as part of F) $r_1, \ldots, r_n$ are exactly the R features of A and $w_1, \ldots, w_m$ are a proper subset of the W features of A.

Note, first, that even if this worked it would handle only the cases covered by principle I. However, it does not work; B may have weighty features that are on the W list, in addition to $w_1, \ldots, w_m$ and if so, F will not be a W feature of A. (If one supposes F to be a W feature of A in this case, what R feature(s) of A corresponds to B's having weighty W features in addition to $w_1, \ldots, w_m$, and also overrides F?) Trying to handle this possibility by adding into F "and B has no other features that are on the W list" will not provide a feature that is not explicitly moral; and given the open-ended nature of the lists, one cannot build into F the conjunction that denies, for each other feature on the W list, that B has it. Thus, it is not at all clear how to begin even to state the candidate for the nonexplicitly moral feature (on the W list) that act A has when there is an alternative act B to A as described in principle III.

85. See J. von Neumann and Oscar Morgenstern, *Theory of Games and Economic Behavior*, 2nd ed. (Princeton University Press, Princeton, 1947), appendix; R. D. Luce and H. Raiffa, *Games and Decisions* (Wiley, New York, 1957), ch II; G. Debreu, "Cardinal Utility for Even-Chance Mixtures of Pairs of Sure Prospects", *Review of Economic Studies*, Vol. 26, 1959, pp. 174–177. For weakening of the strong conditions, relevant to attempts to parallel them in the moral case, see M. Hausner, "Multidimensional Utilities", in R. M. Thrall, C. H. Coombs, and R. L. Davis, eds., *Decision Processes* (Wiley, New York, 1954), pp. 167–180; and R. J. Aumann, "Utility Theory without the Completeness Axiom", *Econometrica*, Vol. 29, 1962, pp. 445–462.

86. This is all put roughly. For discussions of Representation and Uniqueness Theorems see P. Suppes and J. L. Zinnes, "Basic Measurement Theory", in R. D. Luce, R. Bush, and E. Galanter, eds., *Handbook of Mathematical Psychology*, Vol. 1 (Wiley, New York, 1963), pp. 1–76; and for more details see David Krantz, R. D. Luce, P. Suppes, and A. Tversky, *Foundations of Measurement*, Vol. 1 (Academic Press, New York, 1971). We should remove one simplification from the sketch in the text. It generally will not be the case that each of the conditions on the n-place relation that are jointly sufficient (each need not be necessary) to establish the existence of a measuring function will correspond either to an intuitively justifiable normative condition or one that specifies the notions involved. Similar previous measurement results usually required various structural conditions in addition. (On structural conditions, see P. Suppes, "Some Open Problems in the Foundations of Subjective Probability", in R. E. Machol, ed., *Information and Decision Processes*, Wiley, New York, 1960, pp. 162–169; and D. Scott and P. Suppes, "Foundational Aspects of Theories of Measurement", *Journal of Symbolic Logic*, Vol. 23, 1958, pp. 113–128. See also Krantz, Luce, Suppes, and Tversky, *Foundations of Measurement*, pp. 23–25.) The hope is to find structural conditions that suffice for the task when combined with the other conditions yet which look (without too drastic an idealization) as though they are (close to being) satisfied.

87. See, for example, S. Siegel, "A Method for Obtaining an Ordered Metric Scale", *Psychometrika*, Vol. 21, 1956, pp. 207–216; P. Suppes and M. Winet, "An Axiomatization of Utility Based on the Notion of Utility Differences", *Journal of Management Science*, Vol. 1, 1955, pp. 259–270; R. D. Luce and J. D. Tukey, "Simultaneous Conjoint Measurement: A New Type of Fundamental Measurement", *Journal of Mathematical Psychology*, Vol. 1, 1964, pp. 1–27; and also Krantz, Luce, Suppes, and Tversky, *Foundations of Measurement*, chs. 4, 6, 7, 9. No doubt there is further relevant material that appeared after I stopped following such matters.

88. We need first to define some notions. B *undercuts$_0$* A when B makes A impermissible, in accordance with principle III; that is, B undercuts$_0$ A when A and B occupy the same time interval and $R_A > W_A$, $R_B > W_B$, $W_B << W_A$, and $(W_A - W_B) > (R_A - R_B)$. B *strongly undercuts$_t$* A when B does not contain A as a part, B and A began at the same time, and B undercuts$_0$ every act over the time interval t containing A as a part. An act is strongly undercut$_t$ if there is some act B that strongly undercuts$_t$ it. An act A is *weakly undercut$_t$* if every larger act over the time interval t, which contains A, is undercut$_0$, although it need not be one and the same act that undercuts$_0$ all of these. Act C *begins a strong undercutting$_t$* of A when there is some act B which contains C, and begins with it, that strongly undercuts$_t$ A.

Act A is *strongly undercut $\geq t$* when for each time interval s beginning with t and lasting at least as long, there is some act or other that strongly undercuts$_s$ act A. And act C *begins a strong undercutting $\geq t$* of A when for each time interval s beginning with t and lasting at least as long, there is some act or other which C begins that undercuts$_s$ act A.

We now need to define a special kind of strong undercutting $\geq$ t of A, one which gives at least one course of action continuing through the various time periods $\geq$ t, such that each segment (continuing past t) of this one course of action strongly undercuts A. When this holds, there will be one course of action which through each time interval (longer than t) will be better than any action over that interval begun by A. Suppose C begins a strong undercutting $\geq$ t of A. Then for each time period s beginning with t and lasting at least as long, there is at least one action that strongly undercuts$_s$ A. There may be more than one such action; let U_s be the set of them. Consider now the sets U_s, $U_{s'}$, and so on, for all the different time intervals longer than t. There will be one continuing course of action of the sort desired if some selection can be made of one member from each of these sets, so that these things selected constitute one continuing course of action, because for any two, one begins the other. C *begins a sequential strong undercutting* $\geq$ t of A when C begins a strong undercutting $\geq$ t of A and there exists a selection from the family of sets U_s, $U_{s'}$, and so on, such that when s begins s', the action selected from U_s begins that selected from $U_{s'}$.

Given these notions, we may state:

Principle IV. If $R_A > W_A$ and there exists some C available to the person such that, for some time t, C begins a sequential strong undercutting $\geq$ t of A, then A is impermissible. When $R_A > W_A$ and there is no such C available, then A is permissible.

If this principle is weakened by eliminating "sequential", then the resulting principle is inadequate.

The two examples that led us to these issues suggest:

Principle V. If $W_A > R_A$, but there is a larger course of action C that A begins (where $R_C > W_C$), which no action sequentially strongly undercuts, then act A is permissible when done as part of this larger course of action C. When $W_A > R_A$ and there is no such larger course of action C available, then A is impermissible.

We said earlier that A is permissible, despite $W_A > R_A$, when A is a necessary part of a larger permissible course of action C. Principle V specifies as crucial to C's permissibility and A's necessity to it, that C not be undercut, including by some variant not containing A.

One might have hoped to avoid these complications by finding some additional right-making feature of act A when it is a necessary part of some (permissible) larger course of action, just as earlier one might have sought for such a feature of A when there was an alternative action B available that undercut A. The search in this case, too, is fruitless. For the additional feature F of act A would have to be "is part of a larger course of action C, where $R_C > W_C$, and there is no B and t such that B begins a sequential strong undercutting $\geq$ t of C." However, this feature F is not morally neutral since it refers to the R and W lists, and this reference cannot be eliminated for reasons similar to those advanced in our consideration of the parallel suggestion to maintain the simple balancing structure and avoid principle III. (See footnote 84.)

89. Further issues about complicating the structure are mentioned in my

"Moral Complications and Moral Structures", *Natural Law Forum*, Vol. 13, 1968, pp. 1–50.

90. I take this position in *Anarchy, State, and Utopia,* ch. 3, where some intuitive considerations are presented in its support; however, I do not there present any adequate understanding of why it is not rational always to do the act with the best consequences.

91. Another possibility (suggested to me by Eric Mack) builds upon our earlier distinction between the constraints upon moral avoidance and the general requirements of responsiveness, connecting rights especially with the constraints on moral avoidance.

92. Such issues arise in considering good samaritan laws, compulsory taxation for the alleviation of dire need, and so on. See also Arthur Morse, *While Six Million Died.*

93. When views change about what constitutes a significant intrusion, there can be conflicts between adherents of the old and the newer views This currently is the case over passing diffuse cigarette smoke to others. Some of this can be handled by private property rights; the owner who decides upon the rules to govern the emissions of smoke on his property thereby (to a great extent?) internalizes the externality. However, this leaves an issue for property owned by governments, and it leaves groups jointly exercising property rights with the question of which rules are proper.

94. I listed the first three possibilities in my "On the Randian Argument", *The Personalist,* Vol. 52, 1971, pp. 282–304, note 10. The fourth is seen as Plato's procedure in *The Republic,* by Terence Irwin, *Plato's Moral Theory* (Oxford University Press, 1977). Compare also Hegel's procedure in the first part of the *Phenomenology;* and see Charles Taylor's discussion, *Hegel* (Cambridge University Press, 1975), chs. 4, 8.

95. In this last case, living the life where both notions applied would lead the person to revise his view of at least one of them, so that they once again diverged. I stated this idea of iterating such a process in *Anarchy, State, and Utopia,* p. 212, where I imagine a similar iteration of Rawls' original position, with the next stage populated by people who have lived under the principles chosen at its previous stage.

Note that a view about the fitting together of the two notions would be upheld, without stability in the iteration even at the limit, provided that after a certain point in the iteration the two notions are identified as necessarily coincident, and that this harmonious relationship between them is preserved through all their further transformations.

The iteration described in the text fixed on self-interest as primary ("live the best life and, insofar as is compatible with this, the most moral life"); a corresponding iteration would focus upon morality as primary. I take it that a further Platonic thesis is that the two iterations yield the same result.

96. See Aurobindo, *The Life Divine* and *The Synthesis of Yoga.* Perhaps Plato also held this in *Republic* 554d; also see Charles Taylor's description of Hegel's view, *Hegel,* p. 86.

97. The *Zohar* presents a tripartite division of the soul (neshamah, ruah, ne-

fesh); and Lurianic Kabbalah added two even higher parts (hayyah, yehidah). See Gershom Scholem's book length article on "Kabbalah", *Encyclopedia Judaica*, Vol. 10, pp. 609, 611.

98. See Rousseau, *Emile*, and Allen Bloom's introductory remarks in the edition published by Basic Books (1979), p. 16.

99. See Max Scheler, *Ressentiment* (Schocken Books, New York, 1972).

100. Does the pacifist (on moral grounds) make us uncomfortable, because we feel that perhaps he *is* being more responsive (less anti-responsive) to the value of others?

There is one further very speculative thing we can say about the desire for all others to move along a path of development. A developed or developing person, we have seen, will want some company; but how much is enough? It is plausible to think something is added in the joint relationship of three persons that is not present in the sum of the three bilateral relations; similarly, four persons may add qualitative phenomena that are not present with only three. Suppose new desirable phenomena continued to emerge for each higher number of developed persons. (See my essay "On Austrian Methodology", *Synthese*, Vol. 36, 1977, especially pp. 354–358, for a discussion of methodological individualism as committed to no phenomenon emerging past some small number.) We then would have the result that developed persons would want as many others as possible also to be developed, in order to bring about the qualitatively new desirable phenomena. However, the population of the earth is large, and it is difficult to believe that the addition of one new developed person past one and one half billion already developed ones introduces any significant qualitative changes or helps produce a discernibly greater organic unity. Yet there are additional phenomena to be noticed, which occur when most or all of the people present share reactions. To attend a performance and to know that all present are appreciating it in the same deep way would be profoundly moving. To move through life knowing that all you encounter, even in roles that leave little room for the display of it, are developed or developing persons, would be most extraordinary and wonderful. And so we would expect that such persons would want to bring others they encounter into their network. Furthermore, it also is desirable to know these others are there, even if unmet. And this experience of solidarity might spread beyond face-to-face relations, through confederations of communities with other similar communities.

101. "To sum up in himself all its best and completest possibilities and pour them out by thought, action and all other means on his surroundings so that the whole race may approach nearer to the attainment of its supreme personalities." Aurobindo, *The Synthesis of Yoga*, p. 17.

102. Erich Fromm, *The Anatomy of Human Destructiveness* (Holt, Rinehart and Winston, New York, 1973), p. 218. I do not mean to endorse Fromm's claim about man's uniqueness as factually accurate.

103. I have taken most of the past two paragraphs from pp. 288–289 of my paper "On the Randian Argument", *The Personalist*, Vol. 52, 1971, pp. 282–304.

740

104. There is an extensive and diverse literature on the reasons for the mitz-vot. See the lucid discussion by Isadore Twersky, *Introduction to the Code of Maimonides* (Yale University Press, New Haven, 1980), pp. 373–447.

105. Compare the Jewish view of man as a partner of God, and its Kabbalis-tic variants. For a discussion of the inertness of value and our consequent role, see Nicolai Hartmann, *Ethics*, Vol. I (Allen and Unwin, London, 1932), chs. 17, 19.

106. If it did not, if we could not show the intrinsic value of originative value, we would have to seek a more general category of value that included both originative and intrinsic.

107. Compare Boolos (*Unprovability of Consistency*) and Kripke (*Journal of Philosophy*, Vol. 72, pp. 708–709) on the truth of "this statement is true".

108. Compare Butler's discussion of egoism and the pursuit of happiness. Another route might distinguish the reason for doing something—whose con-tent is concerned, for example, with the well-being and value of another—from the motive for doing it, its quasi-causal connection with your own self-in-terested motivations. On such a view, there could be an action whose reason concerned the sake of another but whose motive concerned the agent's own sake.

109. For discussions of Plato's attempt at reconciliation in the *Republic*, see David Sachs, "A Fallacy in Plato's *Republic*", *Philosophical Review*, Vol. 72, 1963, pp. 141–158; Gregory Vlastos, "Justice and Happiness in the *Republic*", in Vlastos, ed., *Plato*, Vol. II (Anchor Books, Garden City, New York, 1971), pp. 66–95 (where Sachs' article also is reprinted); and Terence Irwin, *Plato's Moral Theory* (Oxford University Press, 1977), ch. 7.

110. See George Steiner's illuminating discussion, *In Bluebeard's Castle* (Yale University Press, New Haven, 1971), ch. 3; also his *Martin Heidegger* (Viking Press, New York, 1979), pp. 116–126.

111. I have since discovered that Hilary Putnam now is formulating a view of this sort.

112. See Norman Campbell, *Foundations of Science* (Dover, New York, 1957), ch. 1.

113. In the philosophical literature, see Kant, *Critique of Pure Reason*, and Nelson Goodman, *Ways of Worldmaking* (Hackett, Indianapolis, 1978). For a discussion of how much leeway our structuring leaves, and of how much of it needs to be done, see W. V. Quine, *Word and Object* (MIT Press, Cambridge, 1960), and *Ontological Relativity* (Columbia University Press, New York, 1969), chs. 1, 2.

114. I mean of course the minimal factor that has some independent weight, that has some independent explanation of its own. Otherwise, the minimal fac-tor, trivially, will be: $I \& S^n \supset E$.

115. It is important that the property P that is specified be the one that un-derlies the nonderivability. For of course we can produce other properties that trivially have the surface characteristic; for example, let P_x be "for all y, if y is an *is* statement then it is not the case that x is derivable from y", which is the property of not being derivable from an *is* statement. If indeed *ought* is not

derivable from *is*, then *is* statements lack the property P while *ought* statements have it, and lacking P is preserved under derivation. Yet this P explains nothing.

116. See Saul Kripke, *Naming and Necessity* (Harvard University Press, Cambridge, 1980).

117. A moral truth is autonomous when the ancestral of the explanatory relation to it does not lead us wholly outside the realm of moral truths.

118. Further issues about dominance principles are discussed in my "Newcomb's Problem and Two Principles of Choice", in N. Rescher et al., eds., *Essays in Honor of C. G. Hempel* (Reidel, Dodrecht, 1969), pp. 114-146. On the prisoners' dilemma, see R. D. Luce and Howard Raiffa, *Games and Decisions* (Wiley, New York, 1957), pp. 94-102; John Harsanyi, *Rational Behavior and Bargaining Equilibrium in Games and Social Situations* (Cambridge University Press, 1977), pp. 276-280; Anatol Rapoport and Albert Chammah, *Prisoner's Dilemma* (University of Michigan Press, Ann Arbor, 1965); Nigel Howard, *Paradoxes of Rationality* (MIT Press, 1971). The literature of social science makes fruitful use of the prisoners' dilemma in its discussion of "public goods". See Mancur Olson, *The Logic of Collective Action* (Harvard University Press, Cambridge, 1965); also various issues of the journal *Public Choice* (Center for Studies in Public Choice, Blacksburg, Virginia). For a sampling of the ethical literature which draws on it, see Patrick Suppes, "Some Formal Models of Grading Principles", *Synthese*, Vol. 16, 1966, pp. 284-306; and Derek Parfit, "Is Common-Sense Morality Self-Defeating?", *Journal of Philosophy*, Vol. 76, 1979, pp. 533-545, and "Prudence, Morality, and the Prisoner's Dilemma", *Proceedings of the British Academy*, Vol. 65, 1979.

119. None of the self-subsuming principles we have considered thus far, unanimous consent or PD or responsiveness, utilizes the basic moral characteristic, "being a value-seeking I". Is there some way we can utilize (a portion of) this characteristic to formulate a self-subsuming principle? There is one very speculative possibility I can sketch. We might first find a description of a mode of self-referring that fits the way an I refers to itself, and also the way some self-subsuming principles refer to themselves. (Call this mode SR.) Next, we might find a class C of self-referring things such that every I is in it and so are the correct self-subsuming principles, including the one to be formulated. Last, we might find a description of a treatment T that includes following a principle and also responding to a person's value. Given all this, consider the principle L: Treat T-ly all SR's of type C. Now, since L itself is an SR of type C, it will follow that L is to be treated T-ly. Thus, L subsumes and thereby explains itself. The way to treat L T-ly is to follow and use it, which is done in our next task: deriving an ethical principle. Since an "I" is an SR of type C, it follows from (following) L that an I is to be treated T-ly, that is, by responding to it as an I.

In such a way, we might hope to derive and so explain a fundamental moral principle about the treatment of I's. However, apart from being very speculative and ignoring issues about reflexiveness (will the self-subsuming principles reflexively refer to themselves?), this approach may seem askew. Is what is important and precious about us that we are like certain self-subsuming principles? (Even if they are reflexively self-referring, how can those principles be value-seeking?)

120. For much suggestive material, see Shelley Duval and Robert Wicklund, *A Theory of Objective Self Awareness* (Academic Press, New York, 1972).

121. See *Euthyphro*, 10 A, where the question concerns piety; "is the pious loved by the gods because it is pious, or is it pious because it is loved by the gods?" The latter alternative is more plausible for piety than for goodness and value, which is our concern. Three recent discussions of the passage are John Brown, "The Logic of *Euthyphro* 10A–11B", *Philosophical Quarterly*, Vol. 14, 1964, pp. 1–14; S. Marc Cohen, "Socrates on the Definition of Piety: *Euthyphro* 10A–11B", *Journal of the History of Philosophy*, Vol. 9, 1971, pp. 1–13; Richard Sharvy, "*Euthyphro* 9d–11b: Analysis and Definition in Plato and Others", *Nous*, Vol. 6, 1972, pp. 119–137. See also Baruch Brody, "Morality and Religion Reconsidered" in B. Brody, ed., *Readings in the Philosophy of Religion* (Prentice-Hall, Englewood Cliffs, New Jersey, 1976), pp. 592–603; Phillip Quinn, *Divine Commands and Moral Requirements* (Clarendon Press, Oxford, 1978), pp. 46–52.

122. See Karl Popper, *Objective Knowledge* (Oxford University Press, 1972), pp. 118, 134, 158–161; also P. A. Schilpp, ed., *The Philosophy of K. R. Popper*, pp. 143–149.

Compare also Max Scheler's view in the sociology of knowledge (a term he invented), that factors such as Marxian substructure regulate the conditions under which ideas can appear in history, affecting their presence but not affecting or determining the content of the ideas. (See Peter Berger and Thomas Luckman, *The Social Construction of Reality*, Doubleday, Garden City, New York, 1966, p. 8.)

123. For a survey of various views, see Max Jammer, *The Philosophy of Quantum Mechanics* (Wiley, New York, 1974).

124. "Instead of assuming that the work of art was an illusion of a reality that lay beyond it, cubism proposed that the work of art was itself a reality that represented the very process by which nature is transformed into art." Robert Rosenblum, *Cubism and Twentieth Century Art* (Harry Abrams, New York, 1960), p. 9.

125. See J. L. Austin, *How To Do Things with Words* (Harvard University Press, Cambridge, 1962), and John Searle, *Speech Acts* (Cambridge University Press, 1969).

126. See J. Levin, N. Gordon, and H. Fields, "The Mechanism of Placebo Analgesia", *Lancet*, 1978, pp. 654–657; and by the same authors, "The Narcotic Antagonist Naxolone Enhances Clinical Pain", *Nature*, Vol. 272, 1978, pp. 826–827. More generally, see W. Bunney, "Basic and Clinical Studies of Endorphins", *Annals of Internal Medicine*, Vol. 91, 1979, pp. 239–250.

127. Hilary Putnam has proposed a position in the philosophy of mathematics, wherein questions of the existence of mathematical entities are equivalent to modal statements, apparently not concerned with existence. (See "Mathe-

matics Without Foundations", *Journal of Philosophy*, Vol. 64, 1967, pp. 5–22.) An analogue of this view for the theory of value (assuming a categorical theory) is the one described above: if values are possible then they exist.

128. Earlier we emphasized that values are inert, and need value V-ers to give them effect. We could then have wondered why, if values are organic unities, they do not have effects on their own, since organic unities can have causal effects. The organic unities have their effects only as organic unities, not as values; for them to have effect as values, there is needed a choice that there be value.

129. Compare "everything is in the power of Heaven except the reverence (or fear) of Heaven", *Berakot* 33b.

130. Martin Buber suggests another way to reconcile heteronomy and autonomy: moral values and principles are given to us externally, by God, but how these are to be interpreted and applied is up to our choice. Not only could this reconciliation not serve for God in his situation, it leaves the important differences in interpretation among us without external standard.

131. See Peter Berger, *Facing Up to Modernity* (Basic Books, New York, 1977), p. 171; *The Heretical Imperative* (Anchor Press, Garden City, New York, 1980), pp. 28–29.

132. For an illuminating survey of the issues about internalism, see William Frankena, "Obligation and Motivation in Recent Moral Philosophy", in A. I. Melden, ed., *Essays in Moral Philosophy* (University of Washington Press, Seattle, 1958), pp. 40–81.

CHAPTER SIX

1. Nelson Goodman, *Languages of Art* (Bobbs-Merrill, Indianapolis, 1968), p. 52.

2. See John Rawls, *A Theory of Justice* (Harvard University Press, Cambridge, 1971), section 63.

3. *The Doctor and the Soul* (Alfred Knopf, New York, 1957), p. 73.

4. Compare Frankl's discussion to Ludwig Von Mises' attempt to derive time preference from the essence of human action (*Human Action*, Regnery, Chicago, 1966, ch. 5), critically discussed in part IV of my essay "On Austrian Methodology", *Synthese*, Vol. 36, 1977, pp. 353–392.

5. A recent instance is E. H. Gombrich's critical argument about modern painting, "The Vogue of Abstract Art" in his *Meditations on a Hobby Horse* (Phaidon, London, 1963), pp. 143–150.

6. Let us distinguish this question from others close by. We do have different attitudes toward our own past and future. Suppose you have gone into the hospital for a very painful operation. No anesthetic can be given for this operation, though something can be given immediately afterwards causing you to forget the trauma. This puts you to sleep, and when you awake you will not

remember what happened. Each night of the preliminary stay in the hospital, you are given a sedative to induce sleep; each morning you wake up and wonder whether the tremendously painful operation has happened already or is still to come. Are you indifferent as to which it is, counting pain in your life as the same, whenever it happens? No, you hope it has happened already and is behind you. If the nurse comes in and tells you the operation is over, you are relieved; if she says that today is the day, you are fearful. Although in any case it is three hours of agonizing pain that you undergo, you want it to be over and done. However, if another person is in this situation, with no danger involved, only pain, it does not matter to you whether he had it yesterday or will have it tomorrow. (I owe this example to Derek Parfit.)

Why is there an asymmetry between the future and past in the first-person case but none in the third-person case? It seems plausible to think that the key is fear, which is not to be understood merely as a negative evaluation of something—usually we are not afraid of something that is past even when we negatively evaluate it. Yet if fear is the explanation of the phenomenon in the hospital case, it cannot be the whole explanation of the asymmetry about existence. For not only do we not fear our past nonexistence, antiquarians aside, we do not even negatively evaluate it.

Also, we should avoid the answer that before you exist, in contrast to afterwards, you cannot even be referred to; in consequence, no one could have said earlier that *you* did not exist then, while after your death that can be said. First, why isn't it sadder that not only did you not exist earlier but you could not even be referred to then? (There could have been a list of everyone who existed earlier, and that list would not have included you.) Second, you can be referred to now, and so now we can say that you didn't exist then.

7. Here lurk complicated problems about what someone must know to identify you. To know merely that an effect is due to "the person who caused the effect" is not to know to whom it is due. Fortunately, these problems need not divert us here.

8. Plato, *Parmenides*, 130.

9. For another treatment of the subject of traces, see my "R.S.V.P.—a Story", *Commentary*, Vol. 53, No. 3, March 1972, pp. 66–68.

10. The question of why we should act to fulfill God's plan, in case it is up to us, may appear foolish. After all, this is God, the creator of the universe, omniscient and omnipotent. But what is it about God, in virtue of which we should carry out our part in his plan? Put aside the consideration that if we do not, he will punish us severely; this provides a prudential reason of the sort a slave has for obeying his more powerful master. Another reason holds that we should cooperate in fulfilling God's plan because we owe that to him. God created us, and we are indebted to him for existence. Fulfilling his purpose helps to pay off our debt of gratitude to him. (See Abraham Heschel, *Who is Man?*, Stanford University Press, 1965, p. 108.) Even if we don't want to play that role, it not being the sort of activity we prize, nevertheless must we do it to repay the debt? We might think so on the following grounds. You were created for the role, and if not for God's desire that you fulfill the role,

you wouldn't exist at all; furthermore, existing while performing that role is better than not existing at all, so you should be thankful you were created at all, even if only for that role. Therefore, you are obligated to carry it out.

However, we do not think this form of reasoning is cogent when it concerns parents and children. The purposes parents have when they plan to have children (provided only these stop short of making the child's life no better than nonexistence) do not fix the obligations of the child. Even if the parents' only purpose was to produce a slave, and a slave's life is better than nonexistence, the offspring does not owe to his parents acquiescence in being enslaved. He is under no obligation to cooperate, he is not owned by his parents even though they made him. Once the child exists, it has certain rights that must be respected (and other rights it can assert when able) even if the parents' very purpose was to produce something without these rights. Nor do children owe to their parents whatever they would have conceded in bargaining before conception (supposing this had been possible) in order to come into existence.

Since children don't owe their parents everything that leaves their lives still a net plus, why do people owe their ultimate creator and sustainer any more? Even if they owe God no more, still, don't children owe their parents something for having produced and sustained them, brought them to maturity and kept them alive? To the extent that this debt to parents arises from their trouble and labor, since we don't cost an omnipotent God anything, there's nothing to pay back to him and so no need to. However, it is implausible that a child's whole debt to his parents depends merely on the fact that he was trouble. (When a parent takes great delight in his child's growth, so that any inconveniences caused are counterbalanced by the pleasures of parenthood, doesn't this child still owe something to the parent?) Still, at best, these considerations can lead to a limited obligation to our creator and sustainer— there is no arriving at Abraham by this route. To speak of a limited obligation may sound ludicrous here; "we owe everything to him." Everything may come from him, but do we owe it all back?

Our discussion thus far might leave a believer uncomprehending: he might speak as follows. "Why should one do what is wanted by an omnipotent, omniscient creator of you who is wholly good, perfect, and so on? What better reason could there be than that such a being wants you to do it? Catching the merest glimpse of the majesty and greatness and love of such a being, you would want to serve him, you would be filled with an overwhelming desire to answer any call. There would be a surrender rather than a calculation. The question 'why do it?' would not arise to someone who knew and felt what God was. That experience transforms people. You would do it out of awe and love." I do not want to deny that the direct experience of God would or might well provide an overwhelming motive to serve him. However, there remains the second question: why and how does fitting God's plan and carrying out his will provide meaning to our lives?

11. This first appeared in *Mosaic*, Vol. III, no. 1, Spring 1971 (published by the Harvard-Radcliffe Hillel Society), pp. 27–28, as one of "Two Philosophical Fables", and is reprinted here with only minor changes.

12. See W. V. Quine, "Philosophical Progress in Language Theory", *Metaphilosophy*, Vol. 1, 1970, pp. 2–19; Ludwig Wittgenstein, *Philosophical Investigations*, and *The Blue and the Brown Books* (Basil Blackwell, Oxford, 1958). In contrast, Jerrold Katz presents an explicitly Platonist interpretation of linguistics in *Languages and Other Abstract Objects* (Rowman and Littlefield, Totowa, New Jersey, 1981). Whatever the merits of Katz's proposal, it is illuminating to have that alternative presented and to see linguistics viewed under the classification of positions in the philosophy of mathematics, so that Chomsky's program is conceptualist, and so on.

13. For illuminating discussions of the latter as the view of Wittgenstein's *Tractatus Logico-Philosophicus*, and of the far-reaching consequences of the undermining in his *Philosophical Investigations* of the notion of an intrinsic terminus for meaning, see Bruce Goldberg, "The Correspondence Hypothesis", *Philosophical Review*, Vol. 77, 1968, pp. 438–454, and "The Linguistic Expression of Feeling", *American Philosophical Quarterly*, Vol. 8, 1971, pp. 86–92.

14. For a brief survey of the terms 'limited', 'bounded' and 'finite', see James Thomson, "Infinity in Mathematics and Logic", *Encyclopedia of Philosophy*, Vol. IV, pp. 183–184.

15. Cf. I. Leclerc, *Whitehead's Metaphysics* (Allen and Unwin, London, 1958), p. 100.

16. I made this suggestion some years ago with regard to similar issues. Cf. Keith Gunderson, "Asymmetries and Mind-Body Perplexities", *Minnesota Studies in the Philosophy of Science*, Vol. 4, 1970, pp. 273–309, especially p. 299. Only an infinite being could fully specify all its own details, including the details of that very act of specifying. To the extent that the meaning of something fully specifies it, only something unlimited could be its own meaning.

17. Let us say that predicates of level zero are those stating properties that are not about whether or not other properties hold. Predicates of the first level state whether or not predicates of level zero hold, those of the second level state whether or not predicates of the first level hold, and so on. Consider now the predicate P of the first level which says that no predicate of level zero applies to x, that is, that x is ineffable (at the zero level). But now does not this first level predicate P apply to an ineffable x, and thereby describe it? When something is called ineffable, is there a contradiction in that very calling?

We can allow that this predicate P does apply to x, and view ineffability only as the absence of all zero level predicates. Alternatively, perhaps we even can hold that P does not apply, while still denying that any zero level predicate applies to x. However, in order to maintain this in the face of the objection that either some zero level predicate applies to x, or none does in which case P does, we shall have to hold that there is a presupposition to this application of the law of excluded middle, a presupposition which something unlimited does not satisfy. Will we also have to hold that the principle of noncontradiction does not apply? For 'completely unlimited' is a contradictory concept when not restricted to level. Let $Px = df$. for all Q, not-Qx. Substituting P for Q, we get Px if and only if not-Px. Further logical puzzles may arise; for instance, does some version of Russell's paradox arise for an entity that is unlimited and all-inclusive?

18. For another treatment of reasons to believe in the existence of the unlimited or of God, focusing on the question of whether such a being could conclusively prove to us that it exists, see my fable "God", printed (with alterations by the editor, including of genre) in *Moment*, Vol. 3, April 1976, pp. 17-18.

19. This fills out and specifies my suggestion in *Anarchy, State, and Utopia*, pp. 50-51, that there is an important link between ethics and the notion of the meaning of life. Although my intention was that the link would go through moral push, since this was not said, some writers quite naturally have imagined something different.

On the pull side, when meaning is added to value to constitute the full notion of worth, there will be issues about deontology and teleology: is there a side constraint about being anti-responsive to another's worth, or may one sacrifice one person's so as to maximize total worth, and so on.

20. See Morton Bloomfield, "The Medieval Idea of Perfection", in his *Essays and Explorations* (Harvard University Press, Cambridge, 1970), pp. 29-55, especially pp. 36-38.

21. See Rudolf Arnheim, *Art and Visual Perception* (2nd ed., University of California Press, Berkeley, 1974).

22. See Norman Rabkin, *Shakespeare and the Common Understanding* (Free Press, New York, 1967), pp. 1-29.

23. See Morse Peckham, *Man's Rage for Chaos* (Chilton, Philadelphia, 1965); also Monroe Beardsley, "Order and Disorder in Art" in Paul Kuntz, ed., *The Concept of Order* (University of Washington Press, Seattle, 1968), pp. 191-218.

24. I suggest this is how we read, or incorporate, Karl Popper, *The Logic of Scientific Discovery* (Basic Books, New York, 1959) and *Conjectures and Refutations* (Basic Books, New York, 1962); Imre Lakatos, *The Methodology of Scientific Research Programs* (Cambridge University Press, 1978); Thomas Kuhn, *The Structure of Scientific Revolutions* (2nd ed., University of Chicago Press, Chicago, 1970); Larry Laudan, *Progress and Its Problems* (University of California Press, Berkeley, 1977). Similarly, in philosophy, is it neither answers nor questions that are the goal, but rather the continuing process of questioning and answering?

25. See Eric Weil, "Humanistic Studies: Their Object, Methods and Meaning", *Daedalus*, Vol. 99, Spring 1970, pp. 237-255; see also the different perspective in Marshall Cohen, "The Humanities and the Modern", *Humanities in Society*, Vol. 1, 1978, pp. 1-13.

26. *Anatomy of Criticism*, pp. 117-118.

27. Though not exactly on our topic, the following are relevant: John Holloway, *The Victorian Sage* (Macmillan, London, 1953); Wayne Booth, *The Rhetoric of Fiction* (University of Chicago, Chicago, 1961); Walter Ong, *The Barbarian Within* (Macmillan, New York, 1962), pp. 49-67; Walter Slatoff,

With Respect to Readers (Cornell University Press, Ithaca, 1970); Lionel Trilling, *Sincerity and Authenticity* (Harvard University Press, Cambridge, 1972).

28. Einstein begins his 1905 paper on Special Relativity, which he at first wanted to call *Invariantentheorie*, "It is known that Maxwell's electrodynamics—as usually understood at the present time—when applied to moving bodies, leads to asymmetries which do not appear to be inherent in the phenomena." ("On the Electrodynamics of Moving Bodies", reprinted in Albert Einstein and others, *The Principle of Relativity*, Dover, New York, n.d.). Einstein is the great example of a scientist motivated by theoretical value concerns: to find a deep theory of invariants, a unified theory of different forces, a theory in which "God does not play dice with the universe" and so on. See Gerald Holton, *Thematic Origins of Scientific Thought* (Harvard University Press, Cambridge, 1973), ch. 5, 7–10; also "Einstein's Model", *The American Scholar*, Vol. 48, Summer 1979, pp. 309–340.

29. See Ernest Nagel, *The Structure of Science*, ch. 11; Lawrence Sklar, "Types of Inter-Theoretic Reduction", *British Journal for the Philosophy of Science*, Vol. 18, 1967, pp. 109–124; Robert L. Causey, *Unity of Science* (Reidel, Dodrecht, 1977).

30. Paul Weiss makes this the defining trait of reductionism in his "The Living System: Determinism Stratified" in Arthur Koestler and J. R. Smythies, eds., *Beyond Reductionism* (Macmillan, London, 1969), pp. 3–42.

31. Two recent surveys are Maurice Friedman, *To Deny Our Nothingness* (Delacorte Press, New York, 1967) and Charles Glicksberg, *The Literature of Nihilism* (Bucknell University Press, Lewisburg, 1975).

32. It should be noted, in justice, that these positivist philosophers fled or were driven from the area of Nazi control, whereas their value-laden antagonists, including Heidegger, stayed put, and mum.

33. In "Experience, Theory and Language" (1975, forthcoming in P. A. Schilpp, ed., *The Philosophy of W. V. Quine*, Open Court), I offer this sort of explanation of why scientific activity results in accepting the simplest theory compatible with the data. The explanation there is an "invisible hand" one, and simplicity of theory is seen as an artifact of the scientific process.

34. Norwood Russell Hanson, *Patterns of Discovery* (Cambridge University Press, 1958), pp. 119–120. I drew upon this point about fundamental explanation in *Anarchy, State, and Utopia*, ch. 1.

35. I draw here and throughout this paragraph on the highly illuminating discussions of psychological explanation as fitting Hanson's point (though he is not mentioned) in Ernest Gellner, *Legitimation of Belief* (Cambridge University Press, 1974), pp. 95–107, and Daniel Dennett, *Brainstorms* (Bradford Books, Montgomery, Vermont, 1978), essays 4 and 5.

Dennett asks (pp. 65–66) why we must see these explanations as explaining *away* our valuable traits and features, rather than as explaining *how* we have them. Gellner has no doubt, though, that "an inhuman explanation of the human" (p. 106), which is a necessary part of genuine explanation, will undercut our dignity.

36. This can be done, even when the factors utilized were viewed only reductionistically previously. See the use to which psychoanalytic factors are put in Erik Erikson's account of how Gandhi transformed those factors into his greatness (*Gandhi's Truth*, Norton, New York, 1969), and in Albert Rothenberg's *The Emerging Goddess: the Creative Process in Art, Science, and Other Fields* (University of Chicago Press, Chicago, 1979).

37. Some writers point out that epistemologically we would have a use and need for nonreductionist explanatory theories. (See Hilary Putnam, "Philosophy and Our Mental Life" in his *Philosophical Papers*, Vol. II, pp. 295–298; and Daniel Dennett, "Intentional Systems", in *Brainstorms*, essay 1.) However, since this leaves open the possibility that some reductionist theory is true, ontologically correct, even if not convenient for our purposes given our cognitive limitations, it does not meet the full force of reductionism.

38. On the patterning of ordinary common-sense psychological explanations, see Dennett, *Brainstorms*, essay 2, and also "Three Types of Intentional Psychology" (unpublished). On placement within this pattern as sufficient for explanatory understanding, see Charles Taylor, "Interpretation and the Sciences of Man", *Review of Metaphysics*, Vol. 25, 1971, pp. 3–51; Alan Gauld and John Shotter, *Human Action and Its Psychological Investigation* (Routledge and Kegan Paul, London, 1977); and Alfred Schutz's treatment of the "lifeworld" as an intersubjective accomplishment, in the two volumes of his *Collected Papers* (Nijhoff, The Hague, 1962, 1964), and *Phenomenology of the Social World* (Northwestern University Press, Evanston, 1967).

39. The view of verstehen solely as a generator of hypotheses is presented in Theodore Abel, "The Operation Called *Verstehen*", reprinted in Herbert Feigl and May Brodbeck, eds., *Readings in the Philosophy of Science* (Appleton-Century-Crofts, New York, 1953), pp. 677–687, and in Ernest Nagel, *The Structure of Science*, pp. 473–485. Hilary Putnam makes the point about its furnishing prior probabilities for use in Bayesian inference, in *Meaning and the Moral Sciences* (Routledge and Kegan Paul, London, 1978), pp. 74–75. I discussed black box calibration of the reliability of verstehen in "On Austrian Methodology", pp. 366–369.

40. See John Maynard Keynes, *A Treatise on Probability* (Macmillan, London, 1921), ch. 19; Rudolf Carnap, *Logical Foundations of Probability* (University of Chicago Press, Chicago, 1950), Section 110D.

41. Recently, theories of translating the utterances of others, of ascribing beliefs and propositional attitudes to them, have held that some "principle of charity" should be satisfied—the beliefs and utterances are interpreted so as to be rational in the context. (See W. V. Quine, *Word and Object*, MIT Press, Cambridge, 1960, Section 13; David Lewis, "Radical Interpretation", *Synthese*, Vol. 27, 1974, pp. 345–349.) These theories utilize the analogy of the other to you—he is rational also, as you are—yet they do not leave a large place for understanding via imaginative projection, substituting instead elaborate theoretical constraints on hypotheses.

42. See Max Weber, *Economy and Society*, 3 vols. (Bedminster Press, New York, 1968); Ludwig Von Mises, *Human Action* (Yale University Press, New

Haven, 1949; reprinted by Regnery, Chicago, 1966), but see also my "On Austrian Methodology", *Synthese*, Vol. 36, 1977, pp. 353–392; Erving Goffman, *The Presentation of Self in Everyday Life* (Doubleday, Garden City, 1959), and *Behavior in Public Places* (Free Press, Glencoe, 1963); Harold Garfinkel, *Studies in Ethnomethodology* (Prentice-Hall, Englewood Cliffs, 1967); Peter Berger and Thomas Luckman, *The Social Construction of Reality* (Doubleday, New York, 1967); John Harsanyi, "Rational-Choice Models of Political Behavior vs. Functionalist and Conformist Theories" in his *Essays on Ethics, Social Behavior, and Scientific Explanation* (Reidel, Dodrecht, 1976), pp. 118–144. Also, Israel Kirzner, *Competition and Entrepreneurship* (University of Chicago Press, Chicago, 1973), and the discussions of entrepreneurial alertness to existing opportunities and imaginative formulation of new opportunities by G. L. S. Shackle and S. C. Littlechild in Mario Rizzo, ed., *Time, Uncertainty, and Disequilibrium* (Lexington Books, Lexington, Massachusetts, 1979), pp. 19–50; Irving Janis and Leon Mann, *Decision Making* (Free Press, New York, 1977); Graham Allison, *Essence of Decision* (Little, Brown, Boston, 1971); George Homans, *The Human Group* (Harcourt, Brace, New York, 1950), and *Social Behavior* (Harcourt, Brace, New York, 1974); Peter Blau, *Inequality and Heterogeneity* (Free Press, New York, 1977); Benjamin Zablocki, *Alienation and Charisma* (Free Press, New York, 1980); Armen Alchian, *Economic Forces at Work* (Liberty Press, Indianapolis, 1977).

43. See C. G. Hempel, "The Concept of Rationality and the Logic of Explanation by Reasons" in his *Aspects of Scientific Explanation* (Free Press, New York, 1965), pp. 463–487.

44. For a sample of material to be taken into account by such an interweaving, see Jack Brehm, *A Theory of Psychological Reactance* (Academic Press, New York, 1966); Robert Wicklund and Jack Brehm, *Perspectives on Cognitive Dissonance* (Lawrence Erlbaum Associates, Hillsdale, New Jersey, 1976); Janis and Mann, *Decision Making*; Eric Klinger, *Meaning and Void: Inner Experiences and the Incentives in People's Lives* (University of Minnesota Press, Minneapolis, 1977); Roy Schafer, *A New Language for Psychoanalysis* (Yale University Press, New Haven, 1976); D. Kahneman and A. Tversky, "Prospect Theory", *Econometrica*, Vol. 47, 1979, pp. 263–291.

45. Given a precisely specified body of ground floor theory, and of (recursive) reductive relationships, will we be able to formulate a statement that says of itself that it is not reducible, so that (given the truth of the ground floor theory and the truth-preserving quality of the reductive relations) there will be at least one true statement that is not reducible to the specified ground floor theories?

46. For a discussion of artistic products as part of the search for, and creation of, intelligible meaning, see André Malraux, *The Voices of Silence* (Princeton University Press, Princeton, 1978).

47. Northrop Frye describes Blake's view that "to get any value out of a philosopher, we must finish his book and make our response to it as an artform, as the imaginative projection of a creative mind." (*Fearful Symmetry*,

Princeton University Press, Princeton, 1947, p. 87.) However, Frye often tends to see "truth" as an inappropriate term in connection with "imagination", which he sees as "the power of transforming a subhuman physical world into a world with a human shape and meaning." (*Fables of Identity*, Harcourt, Brace and World, New York, 1963, p. 152.) (It might be instructive to compare this with the decision that there be value.) In contrast, Goethe spoke of "imagination for the truth of reality". (*Conversations with Eckermann*, Dutton, New York, 1930; December 25, 1825.)

48. "On the Method of Theoretical Physics" in his *Ideas and Opinions* (Crown, New York, 1954).

49. In another essay, Einstein described the free choice of fundamental concepts and theoretical principles as follows: "The liberty of choice, however, is of a special kind; it is not in any way similar to the liberty of a writer of fiction. Rather, it is similar to that of a man engaged in solving a well designed word puzzle. He may, it is true, propose any word as the solution, but, there is only *one* word which really solves the puzzle in all its forms." ("Physics and Reality", 1936, reprinted in Albert Einstein, *Out of My Later Years*, Philosophical Library, New York, 1950; the passage quoted is on p. 63.)

50. For a discussion of encyclopedic works of literature, see Northrop Frye, *Anatomy of Criticism*, pp. 54–56.

INDEX

INDEX TO PEOPLE MENTIONED

development: harmonious hierarchical, 507–517; of self and others, 510–517
dialogue, 469–470
disequilibrium, 348–352
disvalue, 420; conditions on, 428–441; and allure, 437–441
doxic identity, 202–204, 207, 242, 687n47

eastern thought, 19–20, 20n, 27, 94, 111, 138n, 150, 161n, 163n, 359, 512–513, 606–608
egalitarian theory, 121–122, 126–131, 141–142, 148. See also inegalitarian theory
egoism, 110, 519
Ein Sof, 537n, 569, 600–610
endorphins, 561–562
entification, 84–86; and self-synthesis, 87–94
envy, 511, 564
equilibrium, acts in, 348–352, 511, 551, 714–716
ethical pull, 401–402, 451–473; structure of, 474–504; and ethical push, 517–522; parity with push, 528–531; covered by push, 531–534; and Kantian structuring, 550–551, 564–565
ethical push, 401–402, 403–409; value sanction, 409–411, 612, 748n19; and ethical pull, 517–522; parity with pull, 528–531; does it cover pull, 531–534; and Kantian structuring, 550–551, 564–565
ethics: objectivity, 17–18; subjectivity, 17–18, 565–566; knowledge in, 170, 186–187, 322, 343–348; particularism, 456–457; judgment in, 482–485; and cost-benefit analysis, 489; Kantian structuring, 545–551, 564–565; religious basis, 552–555; and other selves, 666n54
Euthyphro, 552–555
evidence: held fixed, 224–227; and skepticism, 226–227, 263–264; ignoring, 237–239; and knowledge, 248–250, 264·268; as subjunctive connection, 248–251; and tests, 250–251; and probability, 251–261; support, 252, 254; contingent, 261–263; and explanation, 262–263; for evidence, 268–283; circularity and, 268–283; desirability of, 268–275
evil: problem of, 314, 420; pursuer of, 511, 564

evolution, 653n8, 710–711; and mystical experiences, 157–158; and reliable methods, 266; and knowledge, 283–288; and free will, 307–308; and rationality, 336–338; sociobiology, 342–348; and cognitive capacities, 704–706
excluded middle, 150–157
excuses, 383
existence, 151–157
existentialists, 557
experience machine, 595, 723n11
explanation: of why anything exists, 115–157; of everything, 116–121; of deepest laws, 116–140; formal features of 116–121; ordering of truths by, 116–121; statistical, 116, 127, 301–302, 651n4; self-subsuming, 118–121, 131–137; and inegalitarian theory, 121–127; and egalitarian theory, 127–131; and reflexivity, 136–137, 140; and ultimacy, 137–140, 641–642; and sufficient reason, 140–142; and laws, 144–147; and free choices, 301–305; of ethical behavior, 342–248; of ethical truths, 539–545; and reductionism, 632–634; fundamental, 632–633; nonreductionist, 635–645; patterning, 636, 638–642
explanations, philosophical, 8–13, 22, 23, 24; versus proof, 13–18; presuppositions of, 18–19; and pluralism, 20–21; of unity, 98–100; of why anything exists, 115–116; and norms, 365–266
external world, 221–222, 282–283
externalism, 265, 280–283

fact–value question, 399, 428–429, 441–444, 452, 558–559, 618; as criterion, 458; attempts to bridge, 535–539; the relationship, 567–570
faking, 257–258
fecundity, 128–137; limited, 132–137
flourishing, 515–517
flouting, 378, 382–384, 388–390, 392–393, 393–397
Form, Platonic, 54, 96–97, 584–585, 663n44, 730n52
free will, 1–2, 605n, 639–640; and skepticism, 168; paralleling knowledge, 169–171, 292, 317–318, 326–332; not primarily about punishment, 291, 396–397; weighting reasons in, 294–299; nonrandom choice, 299–301, 304–306; and explanation, 301–304; and reflexivity, 304–305; and al·